MW00618255

THE ECONOMY OF THE COVENANTS

BETWEEN GOD AND MAN

VOLUME 1

Herman Witsius

with Introductions by
Joel R. Beeke
and
J. I. Packer

Reformation Heritage Books
Grand Rapids, Michigan

The Economy of the Covenants
Reprinted 2021

Published by
Reformation Heritage Books
2965 Leonard St., NE
Grand Rapids, MI 49525
616-977-0889 / Fax: 616-285-3246
e-mail: orders@heritagebooks.org
website: www.heritagebooks.org

The facsimile in this volume is of *The Economy of the Covenants between God and Man* (London, 1822). The publisher is deeply grateful to the den Dulk Foundation for making this reprint possible.

ISBN 978-1-60178-095-9

THE LIFE AND THEOLOGY OF HERMAN WITSIUS (1636–1708)

by

Joel R. Beeke

Herman Wits (Latinized as Witsius) was born on February 12, 1636, at Enkhuizen, The Netherlands, to God-fearing parents who dedicated their first child to the Lord even before he was born. His father, Nicholas Wits (1599–1669), was a man of some renown, having been an elder for more than twenty years, a member of Enkhuizen's city council, and an author of devotional poetry.[1] Witsius's mother, Johanna, was a daughter of Herman Gerard, pastor for thirty years of the Reformed church in Enkhuizen. Herman was named after his grandfather with the prayer that he might emulate his godly example.[2]

Education

Witsius was an avid learner. He began Latin studies at age five. Three years later his uncle, Peter Gerard, noticing the boy's gifts, began to tutor him. By the time Witsius took up theological studies in Utrecht at age fifteen, he could speak Latin fluently. He could read Greek and Hebrew and had memorized numerous scriptures in their original languages. At

---

1. B. Glasius, ed., *Godgeleerd Nederland: Biographisch Woordenboek van Nederlandsche Godgeleerden*, 3 vols. (Leiden: E. J. Brill, 1861), 3:611.

2. For biographical detail on Witsius, see especially the standard work on his life and thought, J. van Genderen, *Herman Witsius: Bijdrage tot de kennis der gereformeerde theologie* ('s-Gravenhage: Guido de Bres, 1953), 5–107, and its extended bibliography, 243–59. Also, J. van Genderen, "Herman Witsius (1636–1708)," in *De Nadere Reformatie: Beschrijving van haar voornaamste vertegenwoordigers*, ed. T. Brienen, et al. ('s-Gravenhage: Boekencentrum, 1986). This introduction aims to summarize much of van Genderen's research and is an updated revision of D. Patrick Ramsey and Joel R. Beeke, *An Analysis of Herman Witsius's The Economy of the Covenants* (Grand Rapids: Reformation Heritage Books and Ross-shire: Christian Focus, 2002), iii–xxiv, which is reprinted in Joel R. Beeke, *Puritan Reformed Spirituality* (Darlington, England: Evangelical Press, 2006), 331–52.

Utrecht, he studied Syriac and Arabic under Johannes Leusden (1624–1699) and theology under Johannes Hoornbeeck (1617–1666), whom he called "my teacher of undying memory." He also studied under Andreas Essenius (1618–1677), whom he honored as "my father in the Lord," and Gisbertus Voetius (1589–1676), whom he called "the great Voetius."[3] From Voetius he learned how to wed precise Reformed orthodoxy to heartfelt, experiential piety.[4] Though he never fully embraced Voetius's high scholastic method, he did fully embrace Voetius's commitment to the practice of piety (*praxis pietatis*)[5].

After studying theology and homiletics with Samuel Maresius (1599–1673) at Groningen, Witsius returned to Utrecht in 1653, where he was profoundly influenced by the local devout pastor Justus van den Bogaard, who was a close friend of Jodocus van Lodenstein (1620–1677). According to Witsius's later testimony, van den Bogaard's preaching and fellowship brought him to understand the difference between theological knowledge gleaned from study and the heavenly wisdom taught by the Holy Spirit through communion with God, love, prayer, and meditation. Witsius wrote that he was born again in "the bosom of the Utrecht church by the living and eternal Word of God." Through this godly pastor's influence, Witsius said, he was preserved "from the pride of science, taught to receive the kingdom of heaven as a little child, led beyond the outer court in which he had previously been inclined to linger, and conducted to the sacred recesses of vital Christianity."[6]

As a teenager, Witsius had already demonstrated his gifts in public debate. In 1655 he defeated some of the leading debaters at the University of Utrecht by showing that the doctrine of the Trinity could be proven from the writings of ancient Jews. When Witsius thanked the

---

3. Van Genderen, "Herman Witsius," 193.

4. Joel R. Beeke, *Gisbertus Voetius: Toward a Reformed Marriage of Knowledge and Piety* (Grand Rapids: Reformation Heritage Books, 1999).

5 Arie de Reuver, *Sweet Communion: Trajectories of Spirituality from the Middle Ages through the Further Reformation*, trans. James A. DeJong (Grand Rapids: Baker Academic, 2007), 263.

6. Donald Fraser, "Memoir of Witsius," in *Sacred Dissertations, On What Is Commonly Called the Apostles' Creed*, by Herman Witsius, trans. Donald Fraser (1823; repr., Grand Rapids: Reformation Heritage Books, 2010), 1:xiv.

moderator for his assistance, the moderator replied, "You neither had, nor stood in need of, any assistance from me."[7]

In 1656, Witsius passed his final examinations and was declared a candidate for the ministry. Due to the abundance of ministers, he had to wait a year before receiving a pastoral call. During that time he applied to the authorities of the French church in Dort for a license to preach in French-speaking Reformed churches. Witsius often preached in French at Utrecht, Amsterdam, and elsewhere.

Pastorates

On July 8, 1657, Witsius was ordained into the ministry at Westwoud, where his catechizing of young people bore special fruit. But he also encountered opposition because of the congregation's ignorance of their Reformed heritage. Medieval customs such as praying for the dead were still evident. These problems convinced Witsius early in his ministry of the need for further reformation among the people. It also prompted him to publish his first book, 't Bedroefde Nederlant (The Sad State of the Netherlands).[8] In this book, as in all his writings, Witsius demonstrates the convictions of the Nadere Reformatie (Dutch Further Reformation). The Dutch Further Reformation was largely a seventeenth-century movement within the Dutch Reformed churches that zealously strove for the inner experience of Reformed doctrine and personal sanctification as well as the purification of all spheres of life.[9] This movement was heavily influenced by and, for the most part, paralleled English Puritanism.

In 1660, Witsius married Aletta van Borchorn, daughter of a merchant who was an elder in Witsius's church. They were blessed with twenty-four years of marriage. Aletta said she could not tell what was greater—her love or her respect for her husband. The couple had five children—two sons, who died young, and three daughters: Martina, Johanna, and Petronella.

---

7. Erasmus Middleton, Biographica Evangelica (London: R. Denham, 1786), 4:158.

8. The full title is 't Bedroefde Nederlant, ofte Betooninge van den elendigen toestant onses Vaderlants (Utrecht, 1659). For a study of this scarce work, see K. Slik, "Het oudste geschrift van Herman Witsius, in NAKG, Nieuwe serie, deel 41 (1956): 222–41.

9. For a summary of the Nadere Reformatie, see Joel R. Beeke, The Quest for Full Assurance: The Legacy of Calvin and His Successors (Edinburgh: Banner of Truth Trust, 1999), 286–309.

In 1661, Witsius was installed in the church at Wormer—one of Holland's largest churches—where he succeeded in uniting warring factions and training the people in Reformed theology. He and his colleague, Petrus Goddaeus, took turns teaching a doctrinal class on weekday evenings to "defend the truth of our teachings against false doctrines" and to inculcate "the sanctity of our teachings in terms of God-fearing conduct." The class began in private homes, then outgrew that space and moved to the church. Eventually people had to stand outside the church due to lack of room.[10]

These class lectures were eventually published in 1665 as *Practycke des Christendoms* (The Practice of Christianity), to which Witsius appended *Geestelycke Printen van een Onwedergeborenen op syn beste en een Wedergeborenen op syn slechste* (Spiritual Portraits: Of an Unregenerate Person at His Best and of a Regenerate Person at His Worst).

Practycke des Christendoms explains the primary grounds of godliness by developing practical themes like faith, sanctification, and prayer, while the appended work applies those grounds by teaching what is laudable in the unregenerate and what is culpable in the regenerate. John Owen said he hoped he could be as consistent as Witsius's unregenerate man at his best and that he would never fall so deeply as Witsius's regenerate man at his worst!

Witsius accepted a call to Goes, in Zeeland, in 1666, where he labored for the two most peaceful years of his life. In the preface to *Twist des Heeren met zynen Wijngaert* (The Lord's Controversy with His Vineyard), published in Leeuwarden in 1669, he said he had labored with much peace in this congregation together with three colleagues, "two of whom were venerated as fathers, and the third was loved as a brother." Of these four ministers working together in one congregation, Witsius noted, "We walked together in fellowship to God's house. We did not only attend each other's services, but also each other's catechism classes and other public services, so that what one servant of God might have taught yesterday, the others confirmed and recommended to the congregation the next day." Under the influence of these four ministers,

---

10. J. van der Haar, "Hermannus Witsius," in *Het blijvende Woord*, ed. J. van der Haar, A. Bergsma, L. M. P. Scholten (Dordrecht: Gereformeerde Bijbelstichting, 1985), 243.

"all sorts of devotional practices blossomed, piety grew, and the unity of God's people was enhanced," Witsius wrote.[11]

After serving Goes, Witsius went to his fourth pastoral charge, Leeuwarden, where he served for seven years (1668–1675) that were more mixed. Despite Witsius's peaceful nature and the good relationships he had with Wilhelmus à Brakel (1635–1711) and Johannes van der Waeijen (1639–1701), his ministerial colleagues at Leeuwarden, relationships in the consistory and classis were often divisive. Then, too, his new book, *Twist des Heeren*, which continued where his first publication left off, created some disturbance in various places, not just because Witsius failed to wait for ecclesiastical approval before publishing it, but especially because "it satirized Cartesian and Cocceijan positions as damaging new ideas."[12] In 1672, called the year of miracles because the Dutch Republic survived the onslaught of four enemies who had declared war on the Netherlands (France, England, and the German electorates of Cologne and Munster), Witsius became known for his faithful ministry in the midst of crisis.

Witsius proved to be a blessing wherever he pastored. Johannes à Marck, a future colleague, said of Witsius that he knew of no other minister whose labors were so owned of God.[13]

In 1673, Witsius again teamed up with a renowned colleague—this time, Wilhelmus à Brakel, with whom he served two years. At Leeuwarden, Witsius played a critical role mediating disputes between Voetius and Maresius.

Professorships

In 1675, Witsius was called to be a professor of theology. He served in this capacity for the rest of his life, first at Franeker (1675–1680), then at Utrecht (1680–1698), and finally at Leiden (1698–1707).

Shortly after his arrival at Franeker, the university there awarded Witsius a doctorate in theology. His inaugural address, "On the Character of a True Theologian" (1675), which was attended by scholars from all over the province, stressed the difference between a theologian who

---

11. Van der Haar, *Het blijvende Woord*, 244.
12 De Reuver, *Sweet Communion*, 265.
13. Fraser, "Memoir of Witsius," 1:xvii.

knows his subject only scholastically and a theologian who knows his subject experientially.[14]

Under Witsius's leadership the university began to flourish as a place to study theology, especially after the appointment of the twenty-year-old professor, Johannes à Marck (1656–1731), in 1676. It soon attracted students from all over Europe.

During his professorship at Franeker, tension between the Voetians and the Cocceians escalated, particularly after the appointment of van der Waeijen, who meanwhile had moved from a Voetian to a Cocceian position. Gisbertus Voetius, a renowned Reformed scholastic theologian and professor at Utrecht, represents the mature fruit of the Dutch Further Reformation, much as John Owen does for English Puritanism. Voetius unceasingly opposed Johannes Cocceius (1603–1669), the Bremen-born theologian who taught at Franeker and Leiden and whose covenant theology, in Voetius's opinion, overemphasized the historical and contextual character of specific ages. Voetius believed that Cocceius's new approach to the Scriptures would undermine both Reformed dogmatics and practical Christianity. For Voetius, Cocceius's devaluing of practical Christianity culminated in his rejection of the Sabbath as a ceremonial yoke no longer binding on Christians.[15] The Voetian-Cocceian controversy wracked the Dutch Reformed church until long after the death of both divines, splitting theological faculties into factions. Eventually both factions compromised, agreeing in many cities to rotate their pastors between Voetians and Cocceians.[16]

---

14. Herman Witsius, *On the Character of a True Theologian*, ed. J. Ligon Duncan, III (Greenville, SC: Reformed Academic Press, 1994).

15. H. B. Visser, *Geschiedenis van den Sabbatstrijd onder de Gereformeerden in de Zeventiende Eeuw* (Utrecht: Kemink en Zoon, 1939).

16. For further study, see Charles McCoy, "The Covenant Theology of Johannes Cocceius" (PhD diss., Yale University, 1957); Charles McCoy, "Johannes Cocceius: Federal Theologian," *Scottish Journal of Theology* 16 (1963): 352–70; Charles McCoy, *History, Humanity, and Federalism in the Theology and Ethics of Johannes Cocceius* (Philadelphia: Center for the Study of Federalism, Temple University, 1980); C. Steenblok, *Gisbertus Voetius: zijn leven en werken*, 2nd ed. (Gouda: Gereformeerde Pers, 1976); C. Steenblok, *Voetius en de Sabbat* (Hoorn, 1941); Willem van't Spijker, "Gisbertus Voetius (1589–1676)," in *De Nadere Reformatie: Beschrijving van haar voornaamste vertegenwoordigers* ('s-Gravenhage: Boekencentrum, 1986), 49–84; C. Graafland, "Structuurverschillen tussen voetiaanse en coccejannse geloofsleer," in F. G. M. Broeyer and E. G. E. van der Wall, ed., *Een richtingenstrijd in de Gereformeerde Kerk: Voetianen en Coccejanen 1650–1750* (Zoetermeer,

Witsius's concern about this controversy moved him to publish his most important work, *De Oeconomia Foederum Dei cum Hominibus* (1677), first printed in English in 1736 as *The Oeconomy of the Covenants between God and Man, Comprehending a Complete Body of Divinity.* It was reprinted numerous times and has become a classic in the fields of covenant and systematic theology. In governing his systematic theology by the concept of covenant, Witsius uses Cocceian methods while maintaining essentially Voetian theology.[17]

In his work on the covenants, Witsius argued against Roman Catholicism, Arminianism, Socinianism, and those Dutch Protestant theologians, who, with Hugo Grotius, had exchanged a *sola scriptura* theology for an institutionalized, sacramental view of the church based on traditions that paved the way back to Rome. Witsius opposed Grotians "who spoke of a 'law' which was not the law of Moses, a 'satisfaction' which was not through punishment and a 'substitution' which was not of necessity and not vicarious."[18]

Witsius next went to Utrecht, the cathedral city to which he said that he owed nearly everything, as he was deeply indebted both to the church and the academy there. His inaugural address, "The Excellence of Gospel Truth," stressed that personal knowledge of the truth enables the believer to experience profound inward joy. God Himself invites His people into this experiential joy, Witsius said.[19]

Witsius labored in Utrecht for eighteen years as professor and pastor. Students from all over the Protestant world attended his lectures; magistrates attended his sermons. On two occasions, his colleagues, the most famous of which were Petrus van Mastricht (1630-1706) and Melchior Leydekker (1642-1721), honored him with the headship of the university (1686, 1697).

In 1685, the Dutch Parliament appointed Witsius as a delegate to represent the Dutch government at the coronation of James II and to

---

1994); Willem J. van Asselt, "*Expromissio* or *Fideiussio?* A Seventeenth-Century Theological Debate between Voetians and Coccejans about the Nature of Christ's Suretyship in Salvation History," *Mid-America Journal of Theology* 14 (2003): 37-57.

17. Cf. Nicolaas Tjepko Bakker, *Miskende Gratie: Van Calvijn tot Witsius: Een vergelijkende lezing, balans van 150 jaar gereformeerde orthodoxie* (Kampen: J. H. Kok, 1991).

18. George M. Ella, *Mountain Movers* (Durham, England: Go Publications, 1999), 157.

19. Herman Witsius, *Miscelleanorum Sacrorum*, 4 vols. (Utrecht, 1692), 2:680-705.

serve as chaplain to the Netherlands Embassy in London.[20] While there, he met the archbishop of Canterbury as well as several leading theologians. He studied Puritan theology and enhanced his stature in England as a peacemaker. Later, the English church called on him to serve as a mediating figure between antinomians and neonomians—the former accusing the latter of overemphasizing the law, the latter accusing the former of minimizing the law. Out of this came his *Conciliatory Animadversions*, a treatise on the antinomian controversy in England. In this treatise, Witsius argued that God's starting point in His eternal decrees did not demean His activity in time. He also helped facilitate the translation into Dutch of some of the works of Thomas Goodwin, William Cave, and Thomas Gataker and wrote prefaces for them.[21]

Witsius's years at Utrecht were not free from strife. Though he grew increasingly irenic as the years passed, Witsius felt obliged to oppose the theology of Professor Herman A. Röell (1653–1718), who advocated a unique mixture of the biblical theology of Cocceius and the rationalistic philosophy of René Descartes (1596–1650).[22] Witsius felt that this combination threatened the authority of Scripture. He taught the superiority of faith over reason to protect the purity of Scripture. Reason lost its purity in the fall, he said. Though reason is a critical faculty, it remains imperfect, even in the regenerate. It is not an autonomous judge, but a servant of faith.

Clearly Witsius's understanding of who God is affected his understanding of how we know what we know and that Scripture is the final standard of truth rather than our reason. His knowledge of God through the Scriptures shaped all his thinking, as is evident in his defense of the penal substitution of Christ against the rationalist Faustus Socinus (1539–1604).[23]

Subsequently, Witsius opposed rationalism in the teachings of Balthasar Bekker (1634–1698) as well as the popular, separatistic ideas of Jean de

---

20. John Macleod, *Scottish Theology* (repr. London: Banner of Truth Trust, 1974), 140.

21. Cornelis Pronk, "The Second Reformation in the Netherlands," *The Messenger* 48 (Apr. 2001): 10.

22. See Thomas Arthur McGahagan, "Cartesianism in the Netherlands, 1639–1676: The New Science and the Calvinist Counter-Reformation" (PhD diss., University of Pennsylvania, 1976).

23. Herman Witsius, *The Economy of the Covenants between God and Man* (1822; repr. Grand Rapids: Reformation Heritage Books, 2010), 1.2.16; 2.5.8.

Labadie (1610–1674). He admitted that the Reformed churches were seriously flawed, but he strongly opposed separating from the church.

At Utrecht, Witsius published three volumes of *Exercitationes Sacrae* (*Sacred Dissertations*), two on the Apostles' Creed (1681) and one on the Lord's Prayer (1689). Second in importance only to his *Economy of the Covenants*, these books stress the truths of the gospel in a pure, clear manner. The three works birthed in a seminary setting are known as Witsius's trilogy.

In the midst of his busy years at Utrecht (1684), Witsius's wife died. His daughter Petronella, who never married, remained with her father, faithfully caring for him through twenty-four years as a widower.

When he was sixty-two years old, Witsius accepted a call to serve at Leiden University as professor. His inaugural address was on *De Theologo modesto* (Concerning Modesty in Doing Theology). At Leiden he trained men from Europe, Great Britain, and America, including several Native Americans who had been converted through the work of John Eliot (1604–1690).[24] He again worked with à Marck as well as with a Cocceian, Salomon van Til (1643–1713).

In the 1690s, Witsius again showed his skills of mediation by accepting an invitation to help resolve a debate that had arisen in and around London between Congregationalists and Presbyterians. Witsius responded in 1696 with a book titled, *Conciliatory, or Irenical Animadversions on the Controversies Agitated in Britain, under the Unhappy Names of Antinomians and Neonomians.*[25]

In 1699, Holland and West Friesland appointed Witsius inspector of the university's theological college, a position he held until he retired in 1707 because of ill health. He published his last book in 1703 (*Meletemata Leidensia*), in which he provided a summary of his life's work: "I am at liberty to say that in my work I have above all kept in mind God's honor and the purity of the gospel, the promotion of godliness, without which all scientific fame is idolatry, and the harmony of the brethren."[26]

---

24. Ella, *Mountain Movers*, 158.

25. Translated into English by a Scottish minister, Thomas Bell, and published in 1807; see Patrick Ramsey, "Meet Me in the Middle: Herman Witsius and the English Dissenters," *Mid-America Journal of Theology* 19 (2008): 143–64.

26. Van Genderen, *Herman Witsius*, 96.

In his last six years, Witsius suffered painful bouts of gout, dizziness, and memory lapses.[27] After a serious attack in October 1708, he told friends that his homecoming was near. Four days later, he died at the age of seventy-two, after nearly fifty-two years of ministry. During his last hour, he told his close friend, à Marck, that he was persevering in the faith that he had long enjoyed in Christ. À Marck, together with another of Witsius's close friends, Guiljelmus Saldenus (1627–1694), gave the memorial addresses.

All his life Witsius was a humble biblical and systematic theologian, dependent on the Scriptures. He was also a faithful preacher. For him, Christ—in the university, on the pulpit, and in daily living—took pre-eminence. "Free and sovereign grace, reigning through the person and righteousness of the great Immanuel, he cordially regarded at once as the source of all our hope, and the grand incitement to a holy practice," Fraser wrote of Witsius.[28]

Despite all his learning, Witsius remained concerned about the soundness and piety of the church. All his writing and learning was employed to promote the church's well-being. After his death, his writings were collected in six volumes. We shall briefly look at Witsius's trilogy, now being reprinted.

Economy of the Covenants

Witsius wrote his *magnum opus* on the covenants to promote peace among Dutch theologians who were divided on covenant theology. Witsius sought to be a theologian of synthesis who strove to lessen tension between the Voetians and the Cocceians. He wrote in his introduction, "the enemies of our church…secretly rejoice that there are as many and as warm disputes amongst ourselves, as with them. And this, not very secretly neither: for they do not, nor will ever cease to cast this reproach upon us; which, I grieve to say is not so easily wiped away. O! how much better would it be to use our utmost endeavours, to lessen, make up, and, if it could be, put an end to all controversy!"[29]

---

27. William Crookshank, biographical preface to Herman Witsius, *Economy of the Covenants*, 1:39.

28. Fraser, "Memoir of Witsius," 1:xxvii.

29. Witsius, *Economy of the Covenants*, 1:22–23.

Economy of the Covenants is not a complete systematic theology, though its title claims that it comprehends "a complete body of divinity." Several major doctrines not addressed here, such as the Trinity, creation, and providence, were dealt with later in Witsius's exposition of the Apostles' Creed.

For Witsius, the doctrine of the covenants is the best way of reading Scripture. The covenants are for him what J. I. Packer calls "a successful hermeneutic," or a consistent interpretative procedure yielding a proper understanding of Scripture, both law and gospel.[30] Witsius's work is divided into four books:

book 1: *The Covenant of Works* (120 pages)
book 2: *The Covenant of Redemption, or The Covenant of Grace from Eternity between the Father and the Son* (118 pages)
book 3: *The Covenant of Grace in Time* (295 pages)
book 4: *Covenant Ordinances throughout the Scriptures* (356 pages)

Throughout his exposition of covenant theology, Witsius corrected inadequacies of the Cocceians and infused Voetian content. He treated each topic analytically, drawing from other Reformed and Puritan systematicians to move the reader to clarity of mind, warmth of heart, and godliness of life.

In book 1, Witsius discusses divine covenants in general, focusing on etymological and exegetical considerations related to them (ברית and διαθήκη). He notes promise, oath, pledge, and command as well as a mutual pact that combines promise and law. He concludes that covenant, in its proper sense, "signifies a mutual agreement between parties with respect to something."[31] Then he defined *covenant* as "an agreement between God and man, about the method of obtaining ultimate blessedness, with the addition of a threat of eternal destruction, against anyone contemptuous of this blessedness."[32] The essence of the covenant, then, is the relationship of love between God and man.

Covenants between God and man are essentially monopleuric (one-sided) in the sense that they can be initiated only by God and are grounded in "the utmost majesty of the most high God." Though initi-

---

30. J. I. Packer, "Introduction: On Covenant Theology," in *Economy of the Covenants*, [27].
31. Witsius, *Economy of the Covenants*, book 1, chapter 1, paragraphs 3-5 [hereafter 1.1.3-5].
32. Witsius, *Economy of the Covenants*, 1.1.9.

ated by God, these covenants call for human consent to the covenant, to exercise the responsibility of obedience within it and to acquiesce in punishment in case of violation. In the covenant of works, that responsibility is partly gracious and partly meritorious, whereas in the covenant of grace, it is wholly gracious in response to God's election and Christ's fulfillment of all conditions of the covenant.[33]

Nevertheless, all covenants between God and man are dipleuric (two-sided) in administration. Both aspects are important. Without the monopleuric emphasis on God's part, covenant initiation and fulfillment would not be by grace alone; without the dipleuric emphasis of divine initiation and human responsibility, man would be passive in covenant administration. The attempt made by contemporary scholars to force seventeenth-century federal theologians into either a monopleuric or dipleuric concept of the covenant misses the mark, as Richard Muller has shown, both with Witsius as well as his popular younger contemporary Wilhelmus à Brakel (1635–1711), whose De Redelijke Godsdienst (The Christian's Reasonable Service) was first printed in Dutch in 1700.[34] Muller concludes, "It is not the case, as some have argued that covenant language cuts against election and grace and that covenant doctrine either relaxes the strict doctrine of the decrees or is itself rigidified by contact with the doctrine of predestination during the scholastic era of Reformed theology."[35]

According to Witsius, the covenant of works consists of the contracting parties (God and Adam), the law or condition (perfect obedience), the promises (eternal life in heaven for unqualified veneration to divine law), the penal sanction (death), and the sacraments (Paradise, the tree of life, the tree of knowledge of good and evil, the Sabbath).[36] Throughout, Witsius stressed the relationship of the covenant parties in terms

---

33. Witsius, Economy of the Covenants, 1.1.15; 1.4.

34. Wilhelmus à Brakel, The Christian's Reasonable Service, trans. Bartel Elshout, ed. Joel R. Beeke, 4 vols. (Morgan, PA: Soli Deo Gloria, 1992–95).

35. Richard A. Muller, "The Covenant of Works and the Stability of Divine Law in Seventeenth-Century Reformed Orthodoxy: A Study in the Theology of Herman Witsius and Wilhelmus à Brakel," Calvin Theological Journal 29 (1994): 86–87. Reprinted in Richard A. Muller, After Calvin: Studies in the Development of a Theological Tradition (Oxford: Oxford University Press, 2003), 175–89.

36. Stephen Strehle, Calvinism, Federalism, and Scholasticism: A Study of the Reformed Doctrine of Covenant (New York: Peter Lang, 1988), 288.

of the Reformed concept of covenant. Denying the covenant of works causes serious christological and soteriological errors, he said.[37]

For example, Adam and Eve's violation of the covenant of works rendered the promises of the covenant inaccessible to their descendants. Those promises were abrogated by God, who cannot lower His standard of law by recasting the covenant of works to account for fallen man's unrighteousness. Divine abrogation, however, does not annul God's demand for perfect obedience. Rather, because of the stability of God's promise and His law, the covenant of grace is made effective in Christ, the perfect Law Fulfiller. In fulfilling all the conditions of the covenant of grace, Christ fulfilled all the conditions of the covenant of works. Thus "the covenant of grace is not the abolition, but rather the confirmation of the covenant of works, inasmuch as the Mediator has fulfilled all the conditions of that covenant, so that all believers may be justified and saved according to the covenant of works, to which satisfaction was made by the Mediator," Witsius wrote.[38]

Witsius outlined the relationship of the covenant of works to the covenant of grace in his second book. He discussed the covenant of grace from eternity, or, the covenant of redemption as the *pactum salutis* between God the Father and God the Son.[39] In the eternal *pactum*, the Father solicited from the Son acts of obedience for the elect while pledging ownership of the elect to the Son. This "agreement between God and the Mediator" makes possible the covenant of grace between God and His elect. The covenant of grace "presupposes" the covenant of grace from eternity and "is founded upon it," Witsius said.[40]

The covenant of redemption established God's remedy for the problem of sin. The covenant of redemption is the answer for the covenant of works abrogated by sin. The Son binds Himself to work out that answer by fulfilling the promises and conditions and bearing the penalties of the covenant on behalf of the elect. Ratified by the covenant of redemption, "conditions are offered to which eternal salvation is annexed; conditions not to be performed again by us, which might throw the mind into

---

37. Witsius, *The Economy of the Covenants*, 1.2.13–15; 1.3.9–10; 1.4.4–7.
38. Witsius, *Economy of the Covenants*, 1.11.23.
39. Witsius, *Economy of the Covenants*, 2.2–4.
40. Witsius, *Economy of the Covenants*, 2.2.1.

despondency; but by him, who would not part with his life, before he had truly said, 'It is finished,'" Witsius explained.[41]

Richard Muller establishes several similarities in Witsius and Cocceius in their development of the *pactum salutis*.[42] Witsius, like Cocceius, found support for the *pactum salutis* in Zechariah 6:13 as well as in various psalms that reflect the worship of the messianic ruler (2:8; 22:3; 40:7–9; 45:8; 80:17) and several passages in Isaiah that tie the servant of Jehovah together with the redemption of God's people (Isa. 4:2; 49:4–6; 53:10–12). In addition, Witsius finds New Testament support for the *pactum salutis* primarily in Luke 22:29, Galatians 3:17, Hebrews 7:22–28, and 1 Peter 1:20. Interestingly, as Muller notes, Witsius also "parallels his formulation of the *pactum* with a discussion of the relationship between the divine and human natures of Christ and the decree of election."[43]

The covenant of grace worked out in time (book 3)[44] is the core of Witsius's work and covers the entire field of soteriology. By treating the *ordo salutis* within the framework of the covenant of grace, Witsius asserted that former presentations of covenant doctrine were superior to newer ones. He showed how covenant theology should bind theologians together rather than drive them apart.

Election is the backdrop of the covenant. Election, as the decree or counsel of God, is God's unilateral, unchangeable resolve that does not depend on human conditions. Here the covenant of grace parts ways

---

41. Witsius, *Economy of the Covenants*, 2.1.4; cf. Gerald Hamstra, "Membership in the Covenant of Grace," unpublished research paper for Calvin Theological Seminary (1986), 10.

42. Richard A. Muller, "Toward the *Pactum Salutis*: Locating the Origins of a Concept," *Mid-America Journal of Theology* 18 (2007): 23–25. For more on Witsius's views on the *pactum salutis*, see J. Mark Beach, "The Doctrine of the *Pactum Salutis* in the Covenant Theology of Herman Witsius," *Mid-America Journal of Theology* 13 (2002): 101–142; B. Loonstra, *Verkiezing–Verzoening–Verbond: Beschrijving en beoordeling van de leer van het pactum salutis in de gereformeerde theologie* ('s-Gravenhage: Boekencentrum, 1990), 193–218.

43. Muller, "Toward the *Pactum Salutis*," 23; cf. Witsius, *The Economy of the Covenants*, 3.4.2.

44. For the debate between the three-covenant and two-covenant view, see Sebastian Rehnman, "Is the Narrative of Redemptive History Trichotomous or Dichotomous? A Problem for Federal Theology," *Nederlands archief voor kerkgeschiedenis* 80, 3 (2000): 296–308. For Witsius's treatment of the Mosaic covenant as a covenant marked primarily by grace rather than a works principle, see J. V. Fesko, "Calvin and Witsius on the Mosaic Covenant," in *The Law Is Not of Faith: Essays on Works and Grace in the Mosaic Covenant*, ed. Bryan D. Estelle, J. V. Fesko, and David VanDrunen (Phillipsburg, NJ: P&R, 2009), 25–43.

with the covenant of works. In the covenant of works, God promised man life on the condition of complete obedience without promising that He would work that obedience in man. In the covenant of grace, God promised to give everything to the elect—eternal life and the means to it: faith, repentance, sanctification, and perseverance. Every condition of salvation is included in God's promises to His elect. Faith is not, properly speaking, a condition, but the way and means through which believers receive the promises of eternal life.[45]

Though the "*internal*, mystical, and spiritual *communion*" of the covenant is established within the elect, there is also an external economy or administration of the covenant. Those who are baptized and raised with the means of grace are in the covenant externally, though many of them "are not in the testament of God" in terms of being saved.[46]

Effectual calling is the first fruit of election, which in turn works regeneration. Regeneration is the infusion of new life in the spiritually dead person. Thus the incorruptible seed of the Word is made fruitful by the Spirit's power. Witsius argued that so-called "preparations" to regeneration, such as breaking of the will, serious consideration of the law and conviction of sin, fear of hell and despairing of salvation, are fruits of regeneration rather than preparations when the Spirit uses them to lead sinners to Christ.[47]

The first act of this new life is faith. Faith, in turn, produces various acts: (1) knowing Christ, (2) assenting to the gospel, (3) loving the truth, (4) hungering and thirsting after Christ, (5) receiving Christ for salvation, (6) reclining upon Christ, (7) receiving Christ as Lord, and (8) appropriating the promises of the gospel. The first three acts are called preceding acts; the next three, essential acts; the last two, following acts.[48]

In the last two acts, the believer promises to live in the obedience of faith and obtains assurance through the reflective act of faith which reasons syllogistically like this: "[Major premise:] Christ offers himself as a full and complete Saviour to all who are weary, hungry, thirsty, to

---

45. Witsius, *The Economy of the Covenants*, 3.1–4; 3.8.6.

46. Witsius, *The Economy of the Covenants*, 3.1.5.

47. Witsius, *The Economy of the Covenants*, 3.6.11–15.

48. Cornelis Graafland, *De Zekerheid van het Geloof: Een onderzoek naar de geloofsbeschouwing van enige vertegenwoordigers van reformatie en nadere reformatie* (Wageningen: H. Veenman & Zonen, 1961), 162–63.

all who receive him, and are ready to give themselves up to him. [Minor premise:] But I am weary, hungry, etc. [Conclusion:] Therefore Christ has offered himself to me, is now become mine, and I his, nor shall any thing ever separate me from his love."[49]

Witsius referred to this conclusion of faith, later called the practical syllogism, whenever he discussed assurance of faith. In this, he followed Puritan and Dutch Second Reformation thinking.[50] Aware of the dangers of relying upon personal sanctification for assurance—particularly the objections of the antinomians that syllogisms can provide no sure comfort and may lead to "free-will" thinking, Witsius took pains to keep the syllogism within the confines of the doctrines of grace. Like the Puritans, he taught that the syllogism is bound to the Scriptures, flows out of Jesus Christ, and is ratified by the Holy Spirit. The Spirit witnesses to the believer's spirit, not only by direct testimony from the Word but also by stirring up the believer to observe scriptural marks of grace in his own soul and in the fruits of his life. Those marks of grace lead to Jesus Christ. The syllogism is always scriptural, christological, and pneumatological.

For Witsius, assurance by syllogism is more common than assurance by the direct testimony of the Spirit. Consequently, careful self-examination as to whether one is in the faith and Christ in him is critical (2 Cor. 13:5). If justification issues in sanctification, the believer ought to reason syllogistically from sanctification back to justification—i.e., from the effect to the cause. That is what the apostle John does in his First Epistle General (2:2, 3, 5; 3:14, 19; 5:2).[51]

Concerning the doctrine of justification, Witisus speaks of the elect being justified not only in Christ's death and resurrection but already in the giving of the first gospel promise in Genesis 3:15. Applications of justification to the individual believer occur at his regeneration, in the court of his conscience, in daily communion with God, after death, and on the Judgment Day.[52]

---

49. Witsius, *The Economy of the Covenants*, 3.7.24.

50. Joel R. Beeke, *Assurance of Faith: Calvin, English Puritanism, and the Dutch Second Reformation* (New York: Peter Lang, 1991), 113–15, 124–26, 159–69, 247–48.

51. For the views of Calvin and the Puritans on the syllogisms in assurance, see Beeke, *Quest for Full Assurance*, 65–72, 130–42.

52. Witsius, *Economy of the Covenants*, 3.8.57–64.

Witsius went on to discuss the immediate results of justification: spiritual peace and the adoption of sonship. These chapters excel in showing the friendship and intimacy between the believer and the triune God. They place a large measure of responsibility on the believer to be active in preserving spiritual peace and the consciousness of his gracious adoption.[53]

Typical of Puritan and Dutch Second Reformation divines, Witsius devoted the longest chapter in his *ordo salutis* to sanctification. Sanctification is the work of God by which the justified sinner is increasingly "transformed from the turpitude of sin, to the purity of the divine image."[54] Mortification and vivification show the extensiveness of sanctification. Grace, faith, and love are motives for growing in holiness. The goals and means of sanctification are explained in detail. Nevertheless, because believers do not attain perfection in this life, Witsius concluded by examining the doctrine of perfectionism. God does not grant perfection to us in this life for four reasons: to display the difference between earth and heaven, warfare and triumph, toil and rest; to teach us patience, humility, and sympathy; to teach us that salvation is by grace alone; and to demonstrate the wisdom of God in gradually perfecting us.[55]

After explaining the doctrine of perseverance, Witsius ended his third book with a detailed account of glorification. Glorification begins in this life with the firstfruits of grace: holiness, the vision of God apprehended by faith and an experimental sense of God's goodness, the gracious enjoyment of God, full assurance of faith, and joy unspeakable. It is consummated in the life to come.

The focus of glorification is the enjoyment of God, Witsius said. For example, the joy in the intermediate state is the joy of being with God and Christ, the joy of loving God, and the joy of dwelling in glory.[56]

Book 4 presents covenant theology from the perspective of biblical theology. Witsius offered some aspects of what would later be called progressive redemption, emphasizing the faith of Abraham, the nature

---

53. Witsius, *Economy of the Covenants*, 3.9–11.
54. Witsius, *Economy of the Covenants*, 3.12.11.
55. Witsius, *Economy of the Covenants*, 3.12.121–24.
56. Witsius, *Economy of the Covenants*, 3.14.

of the Mosaic covenant, the role of the law, the sacraments of the Old Testament, and the blessings and defects of the Old Testament. Some of his most fascinating sections deal with the Decalogue as a national covenant with Israel rather than as a formal covenant of works or covenant of grace;[57] his defense of the Old Testament against false charges; his explanation of the ceremonial law's abrogation and the relationship between the covenant of works and the covenant of grace. He then explained the relationship between the testaments and the sacraments of the New Testament era. He was convinced by Romans 11:25-27 of the future restoration of Israel.[58] He set Christian liberty in the context of freedom from the tyranny of the devil, the reigning and condemning power of sin, the rigor of the law, the laws of men, things indifferent (*adiaphora*), and death itself. By including things indifferent, he dispelled the charge that the precisianism of the Puritans and Dutch Further Reformation divines allowed no room for the *adiaphora*.

In summary, Witsius was one of the first theologians among Dutch Further Reformation divines who drew close ties between the doctrines of election and covenant. He aimed for reconciliation between orthodoxy and federalism, while stressing biblical theology as a proper study in itself.

The Cocceians did not respond kindly to Witsius's efforts to reconcile them and the Voetians. They accused him of extending the covenant of grace back into eternity, thereby helping the Reformed orthodox negate the Cocceian principle of the historical development of redemption.[59]

Witsius's work on covenant theology became a standard in the Netherlands, Scotland, England, and New England. Throughout this work, he stressed that the motto "the Reformed church needs to be ever reforming" (*ecclesia reformata, semper reformanda*) should be applied to the church's life and not to doctrine since Reformation doctrine was foundational truth. His stress was on experiencing the reality of the covenant with God by faith and on the need for godly, precise living—often called

---

57. Here Witsius follows the minority of the seventeenth-century English Puritans, e.g. Samuel Bolton (*True Bounds of Christian Freedom* [Edinburgh: Banner of Truth Trust, 1994], 99) and John Owen (Sinclair Ferguson, *John Owen on the Christian Life* [Edinburgh: Banner of Truth Trust, 1987], 28).

58. Witsius, *Economy of the Covenants*, 4.15.7.

59. Charles Fred Lincoln, "The Development of the Covenant Theory," *Bibliotheca Sacra*, no. 397 (Jan. 1943): 161–62.

precisianism somewhat pejoratively by many historians. Few realize, how-ever, that precisianism avoids both the medieval ideal of perfection and the pharisaical ideal of legalism. Witsius's emphasis on precise living is characterized by the following:

- Precisianism emphasizes what God's law emphasizes; the law serves as its standard of holiness.
- Precisianism is accompanied by spiritual liberty, rooted in the love of Christ.
- Precisianism treats others mildly but is strict toward one's self.
- Precisianism focuses primarily on heart motivations and only secondarily on outward actions.
- Precisianism humbles the godly, even as they increase in holiness.
- Precisianism's goal is God's glory.[60]

For Witsius precisianism was essentially the practice of experiential piety, for its core was hidden, heartfelt communion with the faithful covenant-keeping God. In Witsius we have theology that is pious in itself rather than theology to which piety is added.[61]

Witsius emphasized Scripture, faith, experience, and the saving work of the Holy Spirit. Scripture was the norm for all belief. The true believer is a humble student of Scripture, reads Scriptures through the glasses of faith, and subjects all his experiences to the touchstone of Scripture for confirmation. True experience flows from the "star light" of Scripture and the "sunlight" of the Holy Spirit, both of which illumine the soul.[62] These two are inseparable from each other and are both received by faith. Students of Scripture are also students of the Holy Spirit.[63] They experience in the Spirit's heavenly academy the forgiveness of sin, adop-tion as sons, intimate communion with God, love of God poured into the soul, hidden manna, the kisses of Jesus' mouth, and the assurance of blessedness in Christ. The Spirit leads His pupils to feast with God and to know in His banqueting house that His banner over them is love.[64]

---

60. Adapted from van Genderen, *De Nadere Reformatie*, 206.
61. I. van Dijk, *Gezamenlijke Geschriften* (Groningen, 1972), 1:314.
62. Witsius, *Twist des Heeren*, 167.
63. Witsius, *On the Character of a True Theologian*, 35–38.
64. Herman Witsius, *Miscelleanorum Sacrorum tomus alter* (Lugd. Bat., 1736), 671–72.

The Apostles' Creed and *The Lord's Prayer*

More than a century after Witsius's death, two of his most significant works were translated into English: *Sacred Dissertations on What Is Commonly Called the Apostles' Creed*, translated by Donald Fraser, 2 vols. (Glasgow, 1823), and *Sacred Dissertations on the Lord's Prayer*, translated by Rev. William Pringle (Edinburgh, 1839). Both of these works are judicious, practical, pointed, and edifying. They are meat for the soul.

Witsius's two-volume work on the Apostles' Creed, originally published in Latin at Franeker in 1681, grew out of lectures he gave to his students at the University of Franeker on what he called "the principal articles of our religion." These lectures affirmed Witsius's maxim: "He alone is a true theologian who adds the practical to the threoretical part of religion." Like all of Witsius's writings, these volumes combine profound intellect with spiritual passion.[65]

Witsius's exposition begins with studies that discuss the title, authorship, and authority of the creed; the role of fundamental articles; and the nature of saving faith. The creed's authority is great but not supreme, Witsius said. It contains fundamental articles that are limited to those truths "without which neither faith nor repentance can exist" and "to the rejection of which God has annexed a threatening of destructions." It is scarcely possible to determine the number of fundamental articles. Some are not contained in the creed but are taken up in lengthier doctrinal standards.[66]

Witsius again addressed the acts of saving faith, affirming that the "principal act" of faith is the "receiving of Christ for justification, sanctification, and complete salvation." He stressed that faith receives "a whole Christ," and that "he cannot be a Saviour, unless he be also a Lord."[67] He reasserted the validity of obtaining assurance of faith by syllogistic conclusions and distinguished temporary faith from saving faith. Because temporary faith can remain until the end of a person's life, Witsius preferred to call it presumptuous faith. These kinds of faith dif-

---

65. Sinclair Ferguson, "Foreword," in Herman Witsius's *Apostles' Creed*.
66. Witsius, *Apostles' Creed*, 1:16–33.
67. Witsius, *Apostles' Creed*, 1:49, 51.

fer in their knowledge of the truth, their application of the gospel, their joy, and their fruits.[68]

The remainder of the work follows a phrase-by-phrase eight hundred-page exposition of the creed, accompanied by more than two hundred pages of notes added by the translator. Throughout, Witsius excels in exegesis, remains faithful to Reformed dogmatics without becoming overly scholastic, applies every article of the creed to the believer's soul, and, when occasion warrants, exposes various heresies. His closing chapter on life everlasting is perhaps the most sublime. His concluding applications summarize his approach:

- From this sublime doctrine, let us learn the divine origin of the gospel.
- Let us carefully inquire whether we ourselves have a solid hope of this glorious felicity.
- Let us labor diligently, lest we come short of it.
- Let us comfort ourselves with the hope of it amidst all our adversities.
- Let us walk worthy of it by leading a heavenly life in this world.[69]

Like Witsius's work on the Apostles' Creed, *Sacred Dissertations on the Lord's Prayer* was based on lectures delivered to his theological students. As such, it is a bit heavy with Hebrew and Greek words; however, Pringle's translation includes a rendering of most words of the original languages into English.

The Lord's Prayer contains more than its title reveals. In his preface to a 230-page exposition of the Lord's Prayer, Witsius devoted 150 pages to the subject of prayer: "First, to explain what is prayer; next, in what our obligation to it consists; and lastly, in what manner it ought to be performed."[70] Though parts of this introduction seem a bit dated (especially chapter 4), most of it is practical and insightful. For example, Witsius's "On the Preparation of the Mind for Right Prayer" contains valuable guidance on a subject seldom addressed today.

---

68. Witsius, *Apostles' Creed*, 1:56–60.

69. Witsius, *Apostles' Creed*, 2:xvi, 470–83.

70. Herman Witsius, *The Lord's Prayer* (1839; repr. Grand Rapids: Reformation Heritage Books, 2010), 1. The following summary is adapted from my preface in this reprint.

Throughout this introduction, Witsius established that genuine prayer is the pulse of the renewed soul. The constancy of its beat is the test of spiritual life. For Witsius, prayer is rightly deemed, in the words of John Bunyan, "a shield to the soul, a sacrifice to God, and a scourge for Satan."[71]

Witsius stressed the two-part channel of prayer: those who would have God hear them when they pray must hear Him when He speaks. Prayer and work must both be engaged in. To pray without working is to mock God; to work without praying is to rob Him of His glory.

Witsius's exposition of the individual petitions of the Lord's Prayer is a masterpiece. In many instances, the questions receive greater instruction from Witsius's pen than anyone else to date. For example, where else can such insight be found on whether the infant believer and the unregenerate should use the name Father in addressing God?[72]

Gifts and Influence

Witsius had many gifts. As an exegete, he exhibited scriptural simplicity and precision, though at times he leaned toward questionable typological and mystical interpretations.[73] As a historian, he measured movements against the ideal, apostolic church, bringing history and theology from numerous sources to bear upon his reasoning. As a theologian, he grounded spiritual life in regeneration and covenantally applied the entire *ordo salutis* to practical, experiential living. As an ethicist, he set forth Christ as the perfect example in probing the heart and guiding the believer in his walk of life. As a polemicist, he opposed Cartesianism, Labadism, antinomianism, neonomianism, and the excesses of Cocce-

---

71 Cited in John Blanchard, *Complete Gathered Gold* (Darlington, England: Evangelical Press, 2006), 458.

72. Witsius, *The Lord's Prayer*, 168–70.

73. J. van Genderen shows how Witsius revealed some mystical tendencies in his enthusiasm for speaking about contemplation, ecstasy, and mystical marriage with Christ, which surfaces especially in his exegesis of the Song of Solomon and some of the psalms (*Herman Witsius*, 119–23, 173–76, 262; cf. I. Boot, *De Allegorische Uitlegging van het Hooglied Voornamelijk in Nederland* [Woerden, The Netherlands: Zuijderduijn, 1971], 192–203); De Reuver, *Sweet Communion*, 266–80. See also Witsius's discussion of the "mystery" of the manna (*Economy of the Covenants*, 4.10.48).

ianism. As a homiletician, he, like William Perkins, stressed the marks of grace to encourage believers and convict nominal Christians.[74]

Throughout his life as pastor and professor, Witsius mediated disputes. Formally a Cocceian and materially a Voetian, he managed to remain friends with both sides. His motto was "In essentials, unity; in non-essentials, liberty; in all things, prudence and charity." He was noted for meekness and patience and stressed that, despite the church's condition, a believer had no right to separate from the church. One biographer wrote of Witsius: "With him it was a fundamental maxim, that Christ 'in all things must have the preeminence'; and free and sovereign grace, reigning through the person and righteousness of the great Immanuel, he cordially regarded as at once the source of all our hope, and the grand incitement to a holy practice."[75]

Witsius influenced many theologians in his lifetime: Campegius Vitringa and Bernardus Smytegelt in the Netherlands; Friedrich Lampe in Germany; Thomas Boston and the Erskine brothers (Ralph and Ebenezer) in Scotland. James Hervey commended him as "a most excellent author, all of whose works have such a delicacy of composition, and such a sweet savour of holiness, [like] the golden pot which had manna, and was outwardly bright with burnished gold, inwardly rich with heavenly food." John Gill described Witsius as "a writer not only eminent for his great talents and particularly solid judgment, rich imagination, and elegance of composition, but for a deep, powerful, and evangelical spirituality, and savour of godliness."[76]

In the nineteenth century, the Free Church of Scotland translated, published, and distributed a thousand copies of Witsius's On the Character of a True Theologian, free of charge to its divinity students.[77] William Cunningham said in a prefatory note to that work, "He [Witsius] has long been regarded by all competent judges as presenting a very fine and remarkable combination of the highest qualities that constitute a 'true' and consummate theologian—talent, sound judgment, learning, orthodoxy, piety and unction."[78] Witsius's translator, William Pringle, asserted

---

74. van Genderen, *Herman Witsius*, 261–63.
75. Fraser, "Memoir of Witsius," 1:xxvii.
76. Fraser, "Translator's Preface," in *Apostles' Creed*, ii.
77. Michael W. Honeycutt, "Introduction" in *On the Character of a True Theologian*, 7.
78. Honeycutt, "Introduction," 19.

that his writings "are destined to hold an enduring place among the stores of Christian theology.... In extensive and profound acquaintance with the doctrines of scripture, powerful defence of the truth against attacks of adversaries, and earnest exhortations to a holy and devout life, he has few equals."[79]

Rabbi John Duncan described Witsius as "perhaps the most tender, spiritually minded and richly evangelical as well as one of the most learned of the Dutch divines of the old school." He said Witsius had special influence upon him. Duncan's biographers stated "that the attraction proved so strong that for some time he could hardly theologize or preach out of that man's groove."[80]

Witsius's influence continues today. We trust that the influence of Witsius's writings, facilitated by this analysis, will have a God-glorifying influence upon each of us who "take up and read."

Witsius's trilogy is the cream of Reformed theology. Sound biblical exegesis and practical doctrinal substance abound. May God bless their reprints in the lives of many, so that Reformed covenant theology, the Apostles' Creed, and the Lord's Prayer acquire a new depth of meaning. Oh, to be more centered upon our covenant LORD Himself—confessing His truth, hallowing His name, longing for the coming of His kingdom, doing His will!

---

79. William Pringle, "Translator's Preface," in *The Lord's Prayer*, xiii.
80. Pronk, "The Second Reformation in the Netherlands," 10.

INTRODUCTION
ON COVENANT THEOLOGY
by
J. I. Packer

I

The name of Herman Wits (Witsius, 1636–1708) has been unjustly forgotten. He was a masterful Dutch Reformed theologian, learned, wise, mighty in the Scriptures, practical and "experimental" (to use the Puritan label for that which furthers heart religion). On paper he was calm, judicious, systematic, clear, and free from personal oddities and animosities. He was a man whose work stands comparison for substance and thrust with that of his younger British contemporary John Owen, and this writer, for one, knows no praise higher than that! To Witsius it was given, in the treatise here reprinted, to integrate and adjudicate explorations of covenant theology carried out by a long line of theological giants stretching back over more than a century and a half to the earliest days of the Reformation. On this major matter Witsius's work has landmark status as summing up a whole era, which is why it is appropriate to reprint it today. However, in modern Christendom, covenant theology has been unjustly forgotten, just as Witsius himself has, and it will not therefore be amiss to spend a little time reintroducing it in order to prepare readers' minds for what is to come.

II

What is covenant theology? The straightforward, if provocative, answer to that question is that it is what is nowadays called a hermeneutic—that is, a way of reading the whole Bible that is itself part of the overall interpretation of the Bible that it undergirds. A successful hermeneutic is a consistent interpretative procedure yielding a consistent understanding of Scripture that in turn confirms the propriety of the procedure itself.

Covenant theology is a case in point. It is a hermeneutic that forces itself upon every thoughtful Bible reader who gets to the place, *first*, of reading, hearing, and digesting Holy Scripture as didactic instruction given through human agents by God Himself, in person; *second*, of recognizing that what the God who speaks the Scriptures tells us about in their pages is His own sustained sovereign action in creation, providence, and grace; *third*, of discerning that in our salvation by grace God stands revealed as Father, Son, and Holy Spirit, executing in tri-personal unity a single cooperative enterprise of raising sinners from the gutter of spiritual destitution to share Christ's glory forever; and, *fourth*, of seeing that God-centered thought and life, springing responsively from a God-wrought change of heart that expresses itself spontaneously in grateful praise, is the essence of true knowledge of God. Once Christians have got this far, the covenant theology of the Scriptures is something that they can hardly miss.

Yet in one sense they can miss it: that is, by failing to focus on it, even when in general terms they are aware of its reality. God's covenant of grace in Scripture is one of those things that are too big to be easily seen, particularly when one's mind is programmed to look at something smaller. If you are hunting on a map of the Pacific for a particular Polynesian island, your eye will catch dozens of island names, however small they are printed, but the chances are you will never notice the large letters spelling PACIFIC OCEAN that straddle the map completely. Similarly, we may, and I think often do, study such realities as God's promises; faith; the plan of salvation; Jesus Christ the God-man, our prophet, priest, and king; the church in both testaments, along with circumcision, Passover, baptism, the Lord's Supper, the intricacies of Old Testament worship, and the simplicities of its New Testament counterpart; the work of the Holy Spirit in believers; the nature and standards of Christian obedience in holiness and neighbor love; prayer and communion with God; and many more such themes, without noticing that these relational realities are all covenantal in their very essence. As each Polynesian island is anchored in the Pacific, so each of the matters just mentioned is anchored in God's resolve to relate to His human creatures and have us relate to Him in covenant—which means, in the final analysis, a way for man to relate to God that reflects facets of the fellowship of the Son and the Spirit with the Father in the unity of the Godhead. From this, perhaps, we can begin to see how big and significant a thing the covenantal category is both in biblical teaching and in real life.

"The distance between God and the creature is so great," says the Westminster Confession (7.1), "that although reasonable creatures do owe obedience unto him as their Creator, yet they could never have any fruition of him as their blessedness and reward, but by some voluntary condescension on God's part, which he hath been pleased to express by way of covenant." Exactly! So biblical doctrine, first to last, has to do with covenantal relationships between God and man; biblical ethics has to do with expressing God's covenantal relationship to us in covenantal relationships between ourselves and others; and Christian religion has the nature of covenant life, in which God is the direct object of our faith, hope, love, worship, and service, all animated by gratitude for grace.

Our theme is the life-embracing bedrock reality of the covenant relationship between the Creator and Christians, and it is high time we defined exactly what we are talking about. A covenant relationship is a voluntary mutual commitment that binds each party to the other. Whether it is negotiated, like a modern business deal or a marriage con-tract, or unilaterally imposed, as all God's covenants are, is irrelevant to the commitment itself; the reality of the relationship depends simply on the fact that mutual obligations have been accepted and pledged on both sides. Luther is held to have said that Christianity is a matter of personal pronouns, in the sense that everything depends on knowing that Jesus died for *me*, to be *my* Savior, and that His Father is *my* God and Father, personally committed to love, nurture, uphold, and glorify *me*. This already is covenant thinking, for this is the essential substance of the covenant relationship: God's covenant is precisely a matter of these personal pronouns, used in this way, as a basis for a life with God of friendship, peace, and communicated love.

Thus, when God tells Abraham, "I will establish my covenant between me and thee and thy seed after thee...to be a God unto thee... I will be their God" (Gen. 17:6-8), the personal pronouns are the key words: God is committing Himself to Abraham and Abraham's seed in a way in which He does not commit Himself to others. God's covenant commitment expresses eternal election; His covenant love to individual sinners flows from His choice of them to be His forever in the peace of justification and the joy of glorification. The verbal commitment in which electing sovereignty thus shows itself has the nature of a promise, the fulfillment of which is guaranteed by God's absolute fidelity and trustworthiness—the quality that David Livingstone the explorer celebrated by describing God as "an honorable gentleman who never breaks his word." The covenant promise itself, "I will be your God," is an unconditional undertaking on God's part to be "for us" (Rom. 8:31), "on our side" (Ps. 124:1-5), using all His resources for the furthering of the ultimate good of those ("us") to whom He thus pledges Himself. "I will take you to me for a people, and I will be to you a God" (Ex. 6:7), the covenant promise constantly repeated throughout both testaments (Gen. 17:6-8; Ex. 20:2; 29:45-46.; Lev. 11:45; Jer. 32:38; Ezek. 11:20; 34:30-31; 36:28; 2 Cor. 6:16-18; Rev. 21:2-7), may fairly be called the pantechnicon promise, inasmuch as every particular promise that God makes is packed into it—fellowship and communion first ("I will be with you," "I will dwell among them," "I will live among you"), and then the supply of every real need, here and hereafter. Sovereignty and salvation, love and largesse, election and enjoyment, affirmation and assurance, fidelity and fullness thus appear as the spectrum of themes (the second of each pair being the fruit of the first as its root) that combine to form the white light, glowing and glorious, of the gracious self-giving of God to sinners that covenant theology proclaims.

The God-given covenant carries, of course, obligations. The life of faith and repentance and the obedience to which faith leads constitute the covenant-keeping through which God's people receive the fullness of God's covenant blessing. "I bare you on eagles' wings, and brought you unto myself. Now therefore, *if ye will obey my voice indeed, and keep my covenant*, then ye shall be a peculiar treasure unto me above all people" (Ex. 19:4-5, emphasis added). Covenant faithfulness is the condition and means of receiving covenant benefits, and there is nothing arbitrary in that; for the blessings flow from the relationship, and human rebelliousness and unfaithfulness stop the flow by disrupting the relationship. Israel's infidelity was constantly doing this throughout the Old Testament story, and the New Testament makes it plain that churches and Christians will lose blessings that would otherwise be theirs, should covenant fidelity be lacking in their lives.

III

From what has been said so far, three things become apparent. First, the gospel of God is not properly *understood till it is viewed within a covenantal frame.*

Jesus Christ, whose saving ministry is the sum and substance of the gospel, is announced in Hebrews the mediator and guarantor of the covenant relationship (Heb. 7:22; 8:6). The gospel promises, offering Christ and His benefits to sinners, are therefore invitations to enter and enjoy a covenant relationship with God. Faith in Jesus Christ is accordingly the embracing of the covenant, and the Christian life of glorifying God by one's words and works for the greatness of His goodness and grace has at its heart covenant communion between the Savior and the sinner. The church, the fellowship of believers that the gospel creates, is the community of the covenant, and the preaching of the Word, the practice of pastoral care and discipline, the manifold exercises of worship together, and the administration of baptism and the Lord's Supper (corresponding to circumcision and Passover in former days) are all signs, tokens, expressions, and instruments of the covenant, through which covenantal enrichments from God constantly flow to those who believe. The hope of glory, as promised in the gospel, is the goal of the covenant relationship (Rev. 21:2–27), and Christian assurance is the knowledge of the content and stability of that relationship as it applies to oneself (Rom. 5:1–11; 8:1–39). The whole Bible is, as it were, presented by Jesus Christ to the whole church and to each Christian as the book of the covenant, and the whole record of the wars of the Word with the church as well as the world in the post-biblical Christian centuries, the record that is ordinarily called church history, is precisely the story of the covenant going on in space and time. As artists and decorators know, the frame is important for setting off the picture, and you do in fact see the picture better when it is appropriately framed. So with the riches of the gospel; the covenant is their proper frame, and you only see them in their full glory when this frame surrounds them, as in Scripture it actually does and as in theology it always should.

Second, *the Word of God is not properly understood till it is viewed within a covenantal frame.*

Covenant theology, as was said above, is a biblical hermeneutic as well as a formulation of biblical teaching. Not only does it spring from reading the Scriptures as a unity, it includes in itself specific claims as to how this should be done. Covenant theology offers a total view, which it is ready to validate from Scripture itself if challenged, as to how the various parts of the Bible stand related to each other. The essence of the view is as follows. The biblical revelation, which is the written Word of God, centers upon a God-given narrative of how successive and cumulative revelations of God's covenant purpose and provision were given and responded to at key points in history. The backbone of the Bible, to which all the expository, homiletical, moral, liturgical, and devotional material relates, is the unfolding in space and time of God's unchanging intention of having a people on earth to whom He would relate covenantally for His and their joy. The contents of Scripture cohere into a single consistent body of truth about God and mankind, by which every Christian—indeed, every human being—in every generation is called to live. The Bible in one sense, like Jesus Christ in another, is God's Word to the world.

The story that forms this backbone of the Bible has to do with man's covenant relationship with God first ruined and then restored. The original covenantal arrangement, usually called the covenant of works, was one whereby God undertook to prolong and augment for all subsequent humanity the happy state in which He had made the first human pair—provided that the man observed, as part of the humble obedience that was then natural to him, one prohibition, specified in the narrative as not eating a forbidden fruit. The devil, presented as a serpent, seduced Adam and Eve into disobeying, so that they fell under the penal sanctions of the covenant of works (loss of good and corruption of nature). But God at once revealed to them in embryo a redemptive economy that had in it both the covering of sin and a prospective victory for the woman's seed (a human Savior) over the serpent and his malice. The redemptive purpose of this new arrangement became clearer as God called Abraham, made a nation from his descendants, saved them from slavery, named Himself not only their God but also their King and

Father, taught them His law (the family code), drilled them in sacrificial liturgies, disciplined their disobedience, and sent messengers to hold up before them His holiness and His promise of a Savior-King and a saving kingdom, which in due course became reality. The Westminster Confession summarizes what was going on in and through all this.

> Man, by his fall, having made himself uncapable of life by [the first] covenant, the Lord was pleased to make a second, commonly called the covenant of grace: wherein he freely offereth unto sinners life and salvation by Jesus Christ; requiring of them faith in him, that they may be saved, and promising to give unto all those that are ordained unto eternal life his Holy Spirit, to make them willing, and able to believe....
>
> This covenant was differently administered in the time of the law, and in the time of the gospel: under the law, it was administered by promises, prophecies, sacrifices, circumcision, the paschal lamb, and other types and ordinances delivered to the people of the Jews, all foresignifying Christ to come; which were, for that time, sufficient and efficacious, through the operation of the Spirit, to instruct and build up the elect in faith in the promised Messiah, by whom they had full remission of sins, and eternal salvation; and is called the old testament.
>
> Under the gospel, when Christ, the substance, was exhibited, the ordinances in which this covenant is dispensed are the preaching of the Word, and the administration of the sacraments of Baptism and the Lord's Supper.... In them, it is held forth in more fulness, evidence and spiritual efficacy, to all nations, both Jews and Gentiles; and is called the new testament. There are not therefore two covenants of grace, differing in substance, but one and the same, under various dispensations (7.3, 5, 6).

So the unifying strands that bind together the books of the Bible are, *first*, the one covenant promise, sloganized as "I will be your God, and you shall be my people," which God was fulfilling to His elect all through His successive orderings of covenant faith and life; *second*, the one messenger and mediator of the covenant, Jesus Christ the God-man, prophet and king, priest and sacrifice, the Messiah of Old Testament prophecy and New Testament proclamation; *third*, the one people of God, the covenant community, the company of the elect, whom God brings to faith and keeps in faith, from Abel, Noah, and Abraham through the remnant of Israel to the worldwide New Testament church of believing Jews and Gentiles; and *fourth,* the one pattern of covenant piety, consisting of faith, repentance, love, joy, praise, hope, hatred of sin, desire for sanctity, a spirit of prayer, and readiness to battle the world, the flesh, and the devil in order to glorify God, a pattern displayed most fully, perhaps, in Luther's "little Bible," the Psalter, but seen also in the lives of God's servants in both testaments and reflected more or less fully in each single one of the Old and New Testament books. Covenant theologians insist that every book of the Bible in effect asks to be read in terms of these unities and as contributing to the exposition of them, and is actually misunderstood if it is not so read.

Third, *the reality of God is not properly understood till it is viewed within a covenantal frame.*

Who is God? God is the triune Creator, who purposes to have a covenant people whom in love He will exalt for his glory. (*Glory* there means both God's demonstration of His praiseworthiness and the actual praising that results.) Why does God so purpose—why, that is, does He desire covenantal fellowship with rational beings? The most we can say (for the question is not one to which God has given us a direct answer) is that the nature of such fellowship observably corresponds to the relationships of mutual honor and love between Father, Son, and Holy Spirit within the unity of the divine being, so that the divine purpose appears to be, so to speak, an enlarging of this circle of eternal love and joy. In highlighting the thought that covenantal communion is the inner life of God, covenant theology makes the truth of the Trinity more meaningful than it can otherwise be.

Nor is this all. Scripture is explicit on the fact that from eternity, a specific agreement existed between the Father and the Son that they would exalt each other in the following way: the Father would honor the Son by sending Him to save lost sinners through a penal self-sacrifice leading to a cosmic reign in which the central activity would be the imparting to sinners through the Holy Spirit of the redemption He won for them; and the Son would honor the Father by becoming the Father's love-gift to sinners and by leading them through the Spirit to trust, love, and glorify the Father on the model of His own obedience to the Father's will. This covenant of redemption, as it is commonly called, which underlies the covenant of grace, clarifies these three truths at least:

1. The love of the Father and the Son, with the Holy Spirit, to lost sinners is shared, unanimous love. The tri-theistic fantasy of a loving Son placating an unloving Father and commandeering an apathetic Holy Spirit in order to save us is a distressing nonsense.

2. As our salvation derives from God's free and gracious initiative and is carried through, first to last, according to God's eternal plan by God's own sovereign power, so its ultimate purpose is to exalt and glorify the Father and the Son together. The man-centered distortion that pictures God as saving us more for our sake than for His is also a distressing nonsense.

3. Jesus Christ is the focal figure, the proper center of our faithful attention, throughout the redemptive economy. He, as mediator of the covenant of grace and of the grace of that covenant, is as truly an object of divine predestination as are we whom He saves. With Him as our sponsor and representative, the last Adam, the second "public person" through whom the Father deals with our race, the covenant of grace is archetypally and fundamentally made, in order that it may now be established and ratified with us in Him. ("With whom was the covenant of grace made?" asks question 31 of the Westminster Larger Catechism, and the prescribed answer is: "The covenant of grace was made with Christ as the second Adam, and in him with all the elect as his seed.") From the vital union that we have with Christ through the Holy Spirit's action flows all the aliveness to God, all the faith, hope, and love Godward, all the desire for Him and urges to worship Him and willingness to work for Him, of which we ever were, are, or will be conscious; apart from Christ we should still be spiritually dead (objectively, lifeless; subjectively, unresponsive) in our trespasses and sins. Christ is therefore to be acknowledged, now and forever, as our all in all, our Alpha and Omega, so far as our salvation is concerned—and that goes for salvation subjectively brought home to us, no less than for salvation objectively

obtained for us. The legalistic, sub-spiritual Roman Catholic theology of Mass and merit, whereby Christians are required by the Father, and enabled by the Son, to take part in the achieving of their own salvation, is a further distressing nonsense.

These three truths together shape the authentic biblical and Reformed mentality, whereby God the Father through Christ, and Christ Himself in His saving ministry, are given all the glory and all the praise for having quickened us the dead, helped us the helpless, and saved us the lost. Writes Geerhardus Vos:

> Only when the believer understands how he has to receive and has received everything from the Mediator and how God in no way whatever deals with him except through Christ, only then does a picture of the glorious work that God wrought through Christ emerge in his consciousness and the magnificent idea of grace begin to dominate and form in his life. For the Reformed, therefore, the entire *ordo salutis* [order of salvation], beginning with regeneration as its first stage, is bound to the mystical union with Christ. There is no gift that has not been earned by him. Neither is there a gift that is not bestowed by him and that does not elevate God's glory through his bestowal. *Now the basis for this order lies in none other than in the covenant of salvation with Christ.* In this covenant those chosen by the Father are given to Christ. In it he became the guarantor so that they would be planted into his body in the thought-world of grace through faith. As the application of salvation by Christ and by Christ's initiative is a fundamental principle of Reformed theology, this theology has correctly viewed this application as a covenantal requirement which fell to the Mediator and for the fulfilling of which he became the guarantor" (*Redemptive History and Biblical Interpretation*, ed. Richard B. Gaffin, Philadelphia: Presbyterian and Reformed, 1980, 248).

The full reality of God and God's work is not adequately grasped till the covenant of redemption—the specific covenantal agreement between Father and Son on which the covenant of grace rests—occupies its proper place in our minds.

Thus it appears that, confessionally and doxologically, covenant theology brings needed enrichment of insight to our hearts; and devotionally the same is true. Older evangelicals wrote hymns celebrating the covenant of grace in which they voiced fortissimos of the triumphant assurance of a kind that we rarely hear today—so it will be worth our while to quote some of them. They merit memorizing, and meditating on, and making one's own; ceaseless strength flows to those saints who allow these sentiments to take root in their souls. Here, first, is the eighteenth-century leader, Philip Doddridge:

> 'Tis mine, *the covenant of his grace*,
> And every promise mine;
> All sprung from everlasting love,
> And sealed by blood divine.
> On my unworthy favored head
> Its blessings all unite;
> Blessings more numerous than the stars,
> More lasting, and more bright.

And again:

> My God! *the covenant of thy love*
> Abides for ever sure;
> And in its matchless grace I feel
> My happiness secure.
> Since thou, the everlasting God,
> My Father art become,
> Jesus, my Guardian and my Friend,
> And heaven my final home;
> I welcome all thy sovereign will,
> For all that will is love;
> And, when I know not what thou dost,
> I wait the light above.

Also in the eighteenth century, Augustus Toplady wrote this:

> A debtor to mercy alone,
> Of *covenant mercy* I sing;
> Nor fear, with thy righteousness on,
> My person and offering to bring.
> The terrors of law and of God,
> With me can have nothing to do:
> My Savior's obedience and blood
> Hide all my transgressions from view.
> The work which his goodness began,

The arm of his strength will complete;
His promise is Yea and Amen,
And never was forfeited yet.
Things future, nor things that are now,
Nor all things below or above,
Can make him his purpose forego,
Or sever my soul from his love.

Then, a hundred years later, Frances Ridley Havergal gave us the
following:

Jehovah's covenant shall endure,
All ordered, everlasting, sure!
O child of God, rejoice to trace
Thy portion in its glorious grace.

'Tis thine, for Christ is given to be
The covenant of God to thee;
In him, God's golden scroll of light,
The darkest truths are clear and bright.

O sorrowing sinner, well he knew,
Ere time began, what he would do!
Then rest thy hope within the veil;
His covenant mercies shall not fail.

O doubting one, the Eternal Three
is pledged in faithfulness for thee;
Claim every promise, sweet and sure,
by covenant oath of God secure.

O feeble one, look up and see
Strong consolation sworn for thee:
Jehovah's glorious arm is shown,
His *covenant strength* is all thine own.

O mourning one, each stroke of love
A *covenant blessing* yet shall prove;
His *covenant love* shall be thy stay;
His *covenant grace* be as thy day.

> O Love that chose, O Love that died,
> O Love that sealed and sanctified!
> All glory, glory, glory be,
> O *covenant Triune God,* to thee!

One way of judging the quality of theologies is to see what sort of devotion they produce. The devotional perspective that covenant theology generates is accurately reflected in these lyrics. Readers will make up their own minds as to whether such devotion could significantly enrich the church today and form their judgment on covenant theology accordingly.

IV

Earlier it was said that the Bible "forces" covenant theology on all who receive it as what, in effect, it claims to be—God's witness to God's work of saving sinners for God's glory. *Forces* is a strong word; how does Scripture "force" covenant theology upon us? By the following four features, at least.

First, *by the story that it tells.* The books of the Bible, from Genesis to Revelation, are, as was said earlier, God's own record of the progressive unfolding of His purpose to have a people in covenant with Himself here on earth. The covenantal character of God's relationships with human beings, first to last, has already been underlined and is in fact reflected one way and another on just about every page of the Bible. The transition in Eden from the covenant of works to the covenant of grace and the further transition from all that was involved in the preliminary (old) form of that covenant to its final (new) form, brought in through the death of Jesus Christ and now administered by Him from His throne, are the key events in the covenant story. The significance of the fact that God caused His book of instruction to mankind to be put together with the history of His covenant as its backbone can hardly be overestimated. Covenant relationships between God and men, established by God's initiative, bringing temporal and eternal blessings to individuals and creating community among them so that they have a corporate identity as God's people, are in fact the pervasive themes of the whole Bible; and it compels thoughtful readers to take note of the covenant as being central to God's concern.

Second, Scripture forces covenant theology upon us by the *place it gives to Jesus Christ* in the covenant story. That all Scripture, one way and another, is pointing its readers to Christ, teaching us truths and showing us patterns of divine action that help us understand Him properly, is a principle that no reverent and enlightened Bible student will doubt. This being so, it is momentously significant that when Jesus explained the memorial rite for Himself that He instituted as His people's regular form of worship, He spoke of the wine that they were to drink as symbolizing His blood, shed to ratify the new covenant—a clear announcement of the fulfilling of the pattern of Exodus 24 (Jesus echoes directly the words of verse 8) and the promise of Jeremiah 31:31-34. It is also momentously significant that when the writer to the Hebrews explains the uniqueness and finality of Jesus Christ as the only source of salvation for sinners, he does so by focusing on Jesus as the mediator of the new covenant and depicts Him as establishing this prophesied relationship between God and His people by superseding (transcending and thereby cancelling) the inadequate old covenant institutions for dealing with sins and giving access to God. It is also momentously significant that when in Galatians Paul tells Gentiles that their faith in Christ, as such, has already made them inheritors of all that was promised to Abraham, he makes the point by declaring that in union with Christ, as those who by baptism have "put on" the Christ in whom they have trusted so as to become His own people, they are now the seed of Abraham with whom God has made His covenant for all time (Gal. 3), the covenant that brings liberty from law as a supposed system of salvation and full fellowship forever with God above (Gal. 4:24-31). Such Scriptures require us to interpret Christ in terms of God's covenant, just as they require us to interpret God's covenant in terms of Christ, and this fact also alerts thoughtful readers to the centrality of the covenant theme.

The third way in which Scripture directs us to covenantal thinking is by *the specific parallel between Christ and Adam* that Paul draws in Romans 5:12-18 and in 1 Corinthians 15:21-28, 45-49. The solidarity of one person standing for a group, involving the whole group in the consequences of his action and receiving promises that apply to the whole group as well as to himself, is a familiar facet of biblical covenant thought, usually instanced in the case of family and national groups (Noah, Gen. 6:18, 9:9; Abraham, Gen. 17:7; the Israelites, Ex. 20:4-6, 8-12; 31:12-17; Aaron, Lev. 24:8f.; Phinehas, Num. 25:13; David, 2 Chron. 13:5, 21:7; Jer. 33:19-22). In Romans 5:12-18 Paul proclaims a solidarity between Christ and His people (believers, Rom. 3:22-5:2; the elect, God's chosen ones, 8:33), whereby the law-keeping, sin-bearing obedience of "the one man" brings righteousness with God, justification, and life to "the many," the "all"; and he sets this within the frame of a prior solidarity, namely that between Adam and his descendants, whereby our entire race was involved in the penal consequences of Adam's transgression. The 1 Corinthians passages confirm that these are indeed covenantal solidarities; God deals with mankind through two representative men, Adam and Christ; all that are in Adam die, all that are in Christ are made alive. This far-reaching parallel is clearly foundational to Paul's understanding of God's ways with our race, and it is a covenantal way of thinking, showing from a third angle that covenant theology is indeed biblically basic.

The fourth way in which Scripture forces covenant theology upon us is by *the explicit declaring of the covenant of redemption*, most notably (though by no means exclusively) in the words of Jesus recorded in the gospel of John. All Jesus' references to His purpose in the world as the doing of His Father's will, and to His actual words and works as obedience to His Father's command (John 4:32-34; 5:30; 6:38-40; 7:16-18; 8:28f.; 12:49f.; 14:31; 15:10; 17:4; 19:30); all His further references to His being sent by the Father into the world to perform a specific task (John 3:17, 34; 5:23, 30, 36, 38; 6:29, 57; 7:28, 29, 33; 8:16, 18, 26; 9:4; 10:36; 11:42; 12:44; 13:20; 14:24; 15:21; 16:5; 17:3, 8,18, 21, 23, 25; 20:21; cf. 18:37); and all His references to the Father "giving" Him particular persons to save, and to His acceptance of the task of rescuing them from perishing both by dying for them and by calling and shepherding them to glory (John 6:37-44; 10:14-16, 27-30; 17:2, 6, 9,19, 22, 24) are so many testimonies to the reality of the covenant of redemption. The emphasis is pervasive, arresting, and inescapable: Jesus' own words force on thoughtful readers recognition of the covenant economy as foundational to all thought about the reality of God's saving grace.

V

Historically, covenant theology is a Reformed development: Huldreich Zwingli, Henry Bullinger, John Calvin, Zacharias Ursinus, Caspar Olevianus, Robert Rollock, John Preston, and John Ball were among the contributors to its growth, and the Westminster Confession and Catechisms gave it confessional status. Johann Koch (Cocceius) was a Dutch stormy petrel who, in a Latin work, *Summa doctrinae de foedere et testamento dei* (1648; The Doctrine of the Covenant and Testament of God), not only worked out in detail what we would call a biblical-theological, redemptive-historical perspective for presenting covenant theology (three periods—the covenant of works, made with Adam; the covenant of grace, made with and through Moses; the new covenant, made through Christ), but muddied his exegesis by allegorical fancies and marginalized himself by needless attacks on the analytical doctrine-by-doctrine approach to theological exposition that was practiced by his leading contemporaries in Holland: Maccovius, Maresius, and Voetius. It seems clear with hindsight that his method and theirs were complementary to each other and that both were necessary then, as they are now. (Today we name the Cocceian procedure biblical theology and that which he opposed systematic theology, and in well-ordered teaching institutions students are required to study both.) But for more than half a century following the appearance of Cocceius's book, clouds of controversy hung over Holland as Cocceians and Voetians grappled with each other, each side trying to prove the illegitimacy and wrongheadedness of what the other was attempting.

Within this embattled situation, Witsius tries to have the best of both worlds—and largely succeeds. His full title (*The Economy of the Covenants between God and Man: Comprehending a Complete Body of Divinity*) might seem to claim too much; but it is clearly a friendly wave to the Cocceians, who were insisting that the only way to organize theology and set out Christian truths was in terms of the historical unfolding of God's covenant dealings. His four books, the first on the covenant of works, the second on the covenant of redemption, the third on the covenant of grace, and the fourth on covenant ordinances at different times and on the knowledge and experience of God's grace that these conveyed, are a journey over Cocceian ground, in the course of which Witsius, excellent exegete that he is, manages to correct some inadequacies and errors that poor exegesis in the Cocceian camp had fathered. But he treats each topic analytically and draws with evident happiness on the expository resources produced by systematicians during the previous 150 years, including, be it said, much deep wisdom from the Puritan-Pietist tradition, which is particularly evident in the third book. This is a head-clearing, mind-forming, heart-warming treatise of very great value; we possess nothing like it today, and to have it available once more is a real boon. I commend it enthusiastically to God's people everywhere.

THE

ECONOMY OF THE COVENANTS

BETWEEN

GOD AND MAN:

COMPREHENDING

A Complete Body of Divinity.

BY HERMAN WITSIUS, D.D.

PROFESSOR OF DIVINITY IN THE UNIVERSITIES OF FRANEKER, UTRECHT, AND LEYDEN;
AND ALSO REGENT OF THE DIVINITY COLLEGE OF THE STATES
OF HOLLAND AND WEST FRIESLAND.

FAITHFULLY TRANSLATED FROM THE LATIN, AND CAREFULLY REVISED,

BY WILLIAM CROOKSHANK, D.D.

TO WHICH IS PREFIXED,

THE LIFE OF THE AUTHOR.

IN TWO VOLUMES.

VOL. I.

LONDON:

PRINTED FOR R. BAYNES, 25, IVY LANE; J. MAITLAND, ABERDEEN,
T. LOCHHEAD, GLASGOW; AND T. NELSON, EDINBURGH.

1822.

RECOMMENDATIONS.

THE famous HERMAN WITSIUS, Professor of Divinity at Utrecht, in Holland, and the Author of a treatise entitled, *The Economy of the Covenants between God and Man,* and various other learned and theological tracts, was a writer, not only eminent for his great talents, and particularly solid judgment, rich imagination, and elegancy of composition; but for a deep, powerful, and evangelical spirituality and savour of godliness: And we most heartily concur in the Recommendation of his works to serious Christians of all denominations, and especially to ministers and candidates for that sacred office.

JOHN GILL, D. D. JOHN BRINE,
JOHN WALKER, L. L. D. WILLIAM KING,
THOMAS HALL, THOMAS GIBBONS, M. A.

The late Reverend, learned, and pious Mr. JAMES HERVEY, in his *Theron and Aspasio*, Vol. II. p. 366. having mentioned a work of the above WITSIUS, adds, " *The* " *Economy of the Covenants*, written by the same hand, is a " body of divinity, in its method so well digested ; in its " doctrines so truly evangelical ; and (what is not very usual " with our systematic writers) in its language so refined and " elegant ; in its manner so affectionate and animating ; that " I would recommend it to every student in Divinity. I " would not scruple to *risk all my reputation* upon the merits " of this performance : and I cannot but lament it, as one of " my greatest losses, that I was *no sooner* acquainted with " this most excellent author, all whose works have such a " delicacy of composition, and such a sweet savour of holiness, " that I know not any comparison more proper to represent " their true character, than *the golden pot which had manna ;* " and was outwardly *bright* with burnished gold ; inwardly " *rich* with heavenly food."

EXTRACT OF A LETTER FROM A CLERGYMAN IN THE COUNTRY TO THE PUBLISHER.

THE sale of WITSIUS' *Economy of the Covenants*, increases among my friends. The translation is very just, and the excellency of the work merits a place in every Christian's library ; I shall do my utmost to recommend it at all times, and on all proper occasions. No pious person on earth can forbear reading the 3d Book without wonder, rapture, and devotion. It exceeds all commendation : Hervey might well say, " *I would not scruple to risk all my reputation upon the* " *merits of this performance.*" For my own part, I am not ashamed, nor afraid of any scorn and ridicule, that may be poured on me from any quarter, whilst I constantly aver, that the work has not its equal in the world, &c.

CONTENTS

OF

VOLUME FIRST.

BOOK I.

BOOK II.

A 2

BOOK III.

TO

WILLIAM III.

KING OF GREAT BRITAIN, FRANCE, AND
IRELAND,

Defender of the Faith, the Pious, the Auspicious, the August, Hereditary Stadtholder of the United Provinces, Commander-in-Chief of their Armies and
Fleets, the Father of his Country.

D. C. Q.

HERMAN WITSIUS.

WERE none permitted to approach your Majesty with any
other address but what was adorned with elegance of language, and the beauties of rhetoric, or with such as Pliny the
consul, lavishing all his eloquence, pleased the ears of Tra-
jan; a Dutchman, unaccustomed to familiar access to kings,
and ashamed on the first opening of his mouth, who bewrays
his ignorance of the world, and unacquainted with the methods
of courts, might well despair of access. But as that God, to
whose ministry I was so early devoted, is pleased, not so
much with the accuracy of the address of his worshippers, as
with the innocence and holiness of their lives, and has a greater
regard for him who brings to his temple a pure and sincere
heart, than with those, who present the most studied form of
words; in like manner your Majesty, who is the most lively
image of the supreme Being upon earth, most of all prefers
to the gaudy pomp of the most elaborate speech, the candour
of an ingenuous breast, recommending itself by no manner
of arts.

The wisest of kings has taught us in his Proverbs, that
there is a certain penetration in kings. This, if ever conspi-

cuous in any king, since the beginning of the human race, does certainly in a peculiar manner, display itself in your Majesty ; who, with an incredible, nay, almost a divine sagacity, penetrates into the inmost recesses, and most secret springs of the human breast, as scarce to be imposed upon by any kind of flattery.

These considerations have greatly emboldened me to address your royal person, entirely relying on your goodness, that you will grant me the same favour now you are king, which formerly you did when you was prince. For though, in point of eloquence, I be inferior to many in the learned world, nay, in respect of merit, to many of my fellow citizens, especially those of my own rank, yet I know of none, either in Holland or your British dominions, to whom I ought to yield in point of duty, submission, and veneration for your Majesty. Believe me, Royal Sir, such is my attachment to every thing that concerns your person, that I think myself so interested in all your deliberations, designs, and actions, that in my public and private prayers, I duly recommend them all to God ; being well assured, that all your desires and councils solely aim at the welfare of your country, whose guardian, and of the church, whose defender you are.

Wherever you fight for our security, commanding as a general, or acting as a soldier, you expose your person, not only to the wicked stratagems and treachery of your enemies, but also to their swords, and other weapons of war ; yet thither, though perhaps a mean attendant, I follow you, not in body, but in mind, and trembling at every explosion of greater or smaller machines, as if close by your side, ardently pray, that heaven may propitiously avert every disaster from so valuable a life. And whenever I behold you returned in safety, from so many dangers, or rather deaths, I think words then fail me, fail the whole Protestant church, fail all Europe in confederacy, duly to celebrate that divine providence, which exposed you so often to such extraordinary perils, in order to display to the world your bravery, your constancy, your uninterrupted composure of mind, never ruffled by any storms of adversity ; but which also so soon rescued you, in order to exchange our solicitude for your person, into joyful acclamations for your safety, and shew your very enemies, what a favourite of heaven you are.

Surely I shall never forget that day on which the river Boyne in Ireland had like to be distinguished by your fall, though, by the blessing of God, it was ennobled by your victory : for while, according to your wonted attention and care, you went

to take a nearer view of the enemy's camp, a cannon ball, levelled at your person, happened to graze your shoulder; a wound,
which gave matter of greater joy to your enemies, of apprehension to your own people, than of real harm to yourself;
a wound, which taught us you was a man, but a man above
the common rank of mankind, a man dear to heaven : a wound,
in fine, which, however great, prevented not your performing
all the parts of a brave general, nor suffered you to take repose
to your own person till you had procured it for others. O !
the wisdom and goodness of propitious heaven ! O ! a day for
ever memorable in our calendar ! How near were your enemies
to exult with solid joy, who now, deceived by the false reports
of your death, made themselves ridiculous to the world by a
theatrical and unmanly shew of indiscreet rejoicing? Great
Prince, with these eyes I saw, in these hands I held, to these
lips I applied that military tunick, whose wide rent testified
the greatness of your wound. Those precious spoils I saw
purpled with your blood, and I mixed my affectionate tears
with the royal gore.

Lately again, your Majesty gave new matter to our anxiety
in the battle of Landen. Being prevailed with by no entreaties of your British or Belgic nobility, to pay a greater regard
to your valuable life, on which all our safety depends, nor satisfied to have done the part of a general, by drawing up your
army in battle array, animating them to the fight, darting
every where your watchful eyes, commending the brave, chid-
ing the dastardly, calling back to the charge by promises, by
threats, by example, those that gave ground ; your Majesty set a
pattern to all, and required nothing from your soldiers but what
yourself performed before them ; being well acquainted, how
to blend the general and the fellow-soldier, without derogating
from the dignity of the former. And then, where clouds of
smoke intercepted not the view, they saw you rushing through
fire and sword, and amidst the enemy, turning aside their sa-
crilegious points with your drawn sword from your sacred side.
But further, that day gave us an illustrious proof of the divine
favour towards your person : for while, lavish of your own
safety, all your attention is employed in ours, or, (if I may be
allowed to speak out ; and why should I not, where every virtuous liberty is allowable?) while, for our safety you ha-
zard your own life, by exposing yourself to the cannon of the
enemy, it was not your prudence, in which, in other respects,
you may vie with the Fabii and the Scipios ; but, as others would
say, your good fortune, or, what I reckon a more religious way
of speaking, God's own hand, that interposed between your

royal breast and the fatal ball, and suffered it only to violate
your military coat, and make a slight contusion on your side,
to withdraw you from slaughter, and delivered our hearts from
grief, had it been possible for us to survive to grieve your fall.
Surely all our wishes unite to purchase your life at the expence
of our own, and if it could be done to take from our own days
to add to yours.   For what true-born Dutchman does not glow
with the warmest affection for a prince, whom God, by confer-
ring all manner of accomplishments, has rendered the delight
of mankind ?   Who, like an auspicious star has shined on the
world, deeply plunged and sunk in darkness.   Who, in a word,
from the ashes of his father, is providentially come forth to
light, as the genuine phœnix of our days, and appears to be
born only for the welfare of his country.

When the Netherlands were trodden under foot, distressed,
and just on the brink of ruin, then heaven appointed you to
relieve, to deliver them, and repel their calamities.   The distressed republic flies for refuge to your bosom, being only sure
to find an asylum there.   Your British subjects also, being
almost ruined by the wicked designs of their kings, had long
ago been chained, enslaved, and become the prey of lawless tyranny, had not your Majesty hastened to relieve them, while
spreading out their suppliant hands towards you, nay, and to
relieve them with that resolution, prudence and constancy, and
with that success which their annals shall declare, to the amazement of posterity, who will hardly believe it.   That expedition shall stand transmitted through ages, which was laid
with incredible secrecy, notwithstanding so many piercing and
watchful eyes, and undertaken with that resolution, in the winter and end of the year, amidst so many fearful dangers of a
tempestuous ocean, did preserve and maintain to the Queen of
Islands, her liberty, her laws, her religion, and whatever is
valuable and dear to generous breasts.   And is it to be
wondered, that Britain, thus rescued under God, by your Majesty's aid, now destitute of a ruler, her ill-advised king James
being expelled, not by your Majesty, nor by the people of
England, but by the stings of his own conscience ; neither forced away, but voluntarily flying, should gratefully submit to
her preserver and deliverer ?   Indeed to your Majesty, together
with your most religious consort, Mary Augusta, by right of
succession, the sceptre of the vacant kingdom devolved.   And
even in those circumstances, your Majesty had declined accepting it, though offered by both houses of parliament, had any
besides yourself, and faithful consort, been found worthy to govern Britain, and capable to settle her distracted state, to main-

tain her liberty, and quash the efforts of envy. So that, not
the pleasure and happiness of that station, but the thorns and
difficulties thereof: neither your ambition, but the public necessity, constrained you to take the reins of government. Of
this can there be a more evident proof, than that, when settled
on the throne of your kingdoms, you never suffered a day nor
an hour, to pass undistinguished by cares becoming a prince;
and managed with incomparable diligence, both at home and
abroad, whatever makes for the security of the public good?
Against private rivals of your happiness, who were unacquainted with your character, you adhered closely to your own virtue alone, and made use of oblivion, as the most certain remedy against injuries, instead of that revenge, which, if you pleased, was in your own power to take. Against the public dis-
turbers of the peace of Europe, you protect, not so much
yourself, as your people, by armies, fleets and confederacies,
and, which renders you most of all formidable to your enemies,
by your innate prudence and magnanimity. And did not
words, equal to your merit, fail me, as it gives me singular
pleasure to speak of it, your piety above all things ought to
be celebrated, whereby you readily and with justice, ascribe
all the honour and success you are favoured with, to the goodness of the supreme Being, and are ready, gratefully to lay
down your sceptre at the feet of him who, encircled with the
rain-bow, sits on his heavenly throne: while you govern with
no other view, but that Jehovah may reign, and Jesus rule
throughout all your dominions: whose empire you promote
and enlarge, not as others do, in support of their superstition
and cruelty, by imprisonment, exile and stripes, and every en-
gine of torture, the gibbet and fire; not by depopulating countries, not by the terror and dreadful blasphemies of dragoons,
but by meekness, and by the demonstration of the truth to
every conscience; and by what is most of all prevalent, your
own example; never offering any violence to the consciences
of those who differ in religious sentiments from yourself.
But, in fine, what language can set off, as it ought to be, that
sacred solicitude you discovered at your very accession to the
throne? That your subjects, laying aside their disputes about
some points of Christian worship and ecclesiastical government, might unite with the most desirable harmony of minds,
in brotherly fellowship, and uniformity of prayers and praises
to God. I own, indeed, that I very much doubt whether ever
this can be attained by any mortal, amidst the innate blindness
and obstinacy that are in the minds of men. But if there be
any means to bring this about, your Majesty seems to be the

only person, by whose authority, wisdom and moderation, such a happy coalition of different sentiments may be effected. May that day, which is the ardent prayer of so many pious persons, at length appear, when all names of distinction being taken out of the way, and buried in everlasting oblivion, the whole Christian world, from the rising to the setting sun, may with one heart and one mouth, worship and praise one God, and, as it is in the prophecy of Zechariah, Jehovah may be one, and his name one in all the earth ! As this certainly ought to be the earnest prayer of all Christians, in an especial manner it ought to be the endeavour of those to whom Jesus, the king, both of truth and peace, has committed the office of preaching the gospel.

And as I rejoice in being one of their number, so I imagine, I ought always to behave in such a glorious ministry of so great a king, so that, while I attempt to set up the light of truth in the minds of men, I at the same time ought to inflame their hearts with the fire of love. To stain the tongue with bitterness, to dip the pen in gall, to screen passion under a zeal for religion, to bring strange fire to God's altar, and under pretext, of maintaining the truth, to attempt what is unlawful for the ministers of peace ; I judged to be so contrary to the spirit of Christianity, that if I did not religiously guard against these things, I should certainly account myself not only an unprofitable, but also a perfidious servant, and not escape the punishment due to those who betray the cause of the Lord. I was willing to give some specimen of this disposition in those books which were formerly published concerning the *Economy of God's Covenants with men*, and which I now, with all due submission and veneration, offer to lay at your Majesty's feet.

What I may have contributed towards clearing up the truth, with respect to the controversies at this day, and what towards cementing a peace, interrupted by the violent designs of others ; with what moderation I may have treated every particular subject, by what means I may have lessened, removed and decided controversies, which others have multiplied without end, always consistently with the faith once delivered to the saints, I would leave to the judgment of your divines, such as your Majesty has of very distinguished characters, both in England and Holland.

Suffer me solemnly to declare this one thing, that it has been my sincere and utmost endeavour, to form my hearers, both by doctrine and example, not to litigious disputations, but to the evident knowledge of the most sacred truth, to the upright and sincere piety of ancient and apostolic Christianity, and to the constant practice of that sacred peace, which the dying Jesus both bequeathed to, and purchased for his people; and I have the pleasing hope, that those who come from under my instructions, not only the natives of Holland, but those of your kingdoms of England, Scotland, and Ireland, of whom there is not a few here, who will bring the same spirit and temper to the churches to be committed to their charge, shall, under your Majesty's government, remarkably enlarge the kingdom of Christ.

Accept therefore, Royal Sir, with your wonted goodness accept this pledge and token of a heart sincerely devoted to your Majesty ; and vouchsafe a place among your friends to him, who, next to the Great and Blessed God, would not choose to belong to any other. But, at the same time, accept the most ardent prayers sent from the bottom of my heart. May that God, at whose footstool you daily fall down as a suppliant, may that God, who is the King of kings, and Lord of lords, make you always happy at home, successful abroad, ever august, the guardian of justice, the maintainer of liberty, the defender of religion, the author of concord, the consolation of the oppressed, the umpire of the whole Christian world, and, at last, crown your Majesty his own vicegerent, with the glory of his everlasting kingdom.

Utrecht, }
Oct. 15th, 1693. }

PACIFIC ADDRESS.

To the very reverend, learned, and celebrated Professors of Divinity in the Universities of the United Provinces of Holland; Pastors of the Reformed Churches, and zealous Defenders of the Faith once delivered to the Saints.

THE present age furnishes such a number of books, that the world is almost weary of them, and the church certainly groans under their weight: as this never flourished more than when, in the pure simplicity of faith and love, and without any fondness for disputations, it regarded the doctrine of our Lord alone, and drew the pure and undefiled truth from those writings only which could " make David wiser than all his teachers, and the man of God perfect, thoroughly instructed to every good work." It is, indeed, very difficult to write any thing now-a-days which can please. For so great is every where the fruitfulness of learning, or the vain imagination of science; so obstinate the attachment to once received hypotheses, so fixed the study of particular parts, and so malevolent the judgment passed on other people's works, (which even sometimes affects the minds of good men against their wills,) that whoever thinks by his writings to satisfy your delicate minds, or those who are engaged in a more general search after knowledge, seems to attribute too much to his own capacity, and to be ignorant of the disposition of the times. But I am conscious of the slenderness of my own abilities: and it is impossible for a person not to know the world, who is at all conversant with it. It therefore seems proper to assign some reasons for my appearing in public again; and to shew the design of the work I now offer to the churches.

And to whom, reverend and learned Sirs, should I render these reasons rather than to you, who are competent judges of what I write; and by whom, next to God and my own conscience, I long to have my studies approved. In the first place, then, I sincerely declare, that it is not an incurable itch of

writing, a raging thirst after vain glory, an envious disposition
of mind, a detestable desire of widening the wounds already
made in the churches, the odious pleasure of blackening another's character, by giving a wrong turn to what is really right;
nor lastly, the infamous desire to make, increase, or continue
strifes which have occasioned my writing at this time. Besides my own declaration to the contrary, the whole work itself,
though but slightly attended to, will acquit me of acting on
such motives.

To see the minds of the godly disturbed by the inconsiderate assertions of some, and their uncommon interpretations of
the scriptures; or the suspicions of others, (not at all times
dictated by charity, whatever share prudence may have in the
case,) gave me indeed the greatest concern. And forasmuch
as the doctrine of the covenant of grace, by which the manner
of the reconciliation of sinners to God is shewn, and the manifold dispensation of that covenant, have been the unhappy object of controversy in the Netherlands, so that whatever points
are now disputed upon, (if we except the new method of interpreting the prophecies, and the opinions of the modern philosophy, which are imprudently introduced into the present system of divinity, may, and ought to be referred to this,) I have
thought this subject in the first place deserving my notice. But
I have treated it in such a manner as is agreeable to the truths
hitherto received in the churches; and without that levity or
severity, which is not consistent with the law of love. On
which account I have not confined myself to bare disputations,
which are generally unprofitable; and if it were not that they
were seasoned with a degree of acrimony, would be destitute of
every kind of elegance.

I have chosen to enter on this subject from its very beginning,
and have endeavoured, as far as I could, to explain it methodi-
cally and clearly, enlightening the obscurer passages of scripture, carefully examining the phrases used by the Holy Ghost,
and referring the whole to the practice of faith and godliness,
to the glory of God in Christ, that my exposition might be
the more useful and entertaining. And as nothing was more
profitable and delightful to myself, so nothing could more evidently and fully convince the minds of others, than a clear and
sober demonstration of the truth to the conscience; which, by
pleasing advances, beginning with plain and acknowledged
truths, and connecting them together, gradually leads to the
more abstruse points, and forces an assent to them not less
strongly than to those we are obliged to agree to at the first
view; and at the same time by its efficacy, presents some be-

fore unknown truths to the inmost soul, fixing it with a degree of astonishment on the contemplation of the admirable perfections of God.

I have found it absolutely necessary to oppose different opinions; either those of the public adversaries of the reformed churches, amongst whom I reckon first the Socinians and the Remonstrants, who, by their daring comments have defiled the doctrine of God's covenants; or those of some of our brethren, who have taken it into their heads to form new hypotheses, and thereby almost root out all true divinity. I persuade myself, it is not in the power of malice to deny that I have acted with candour and modesty: I have stated the controversy justly, not attributing to any one any opinion which he ought not to allow to be his own; and have made use of such arguments as had before satisfied my own conscience; as if these were not of themselves convincing, I could not think that any force would be added to them by great warmth: especially, I thought that the opinions of our brethren were to be treated with candour. And I have never sought after any inaccurate word, harsh phrase, or crude expression, in order to criticise on them; esteeming it much better to point out how far all the orthodox agree, and how the more improper ways of expression may be softened; remarking only on those sentiments which are really different: and these, I dare affirm, will be found to be fewer, and of less moment, than they are generally thought to be, provided we examine them without prejudice. Yet, I cannot pass over in silence some uncouth expressions, foreign interpretations, or contradictory theses: and sometimes I note the danger attending some of them; but without any malevolence to their authors. For, I confess, I am of their opinion, who believe that the doctrine of the covenant has long since been delivered to the churches on too good a foundation, to stand in need of new hypotheses; in which I cannot find that solidity or usefulness, as is necessary to establish their divinity.

The observation of the threefold covenant of grace; the *first*, under the promise, in which grace and liberty prevailed, without the yoke, or the burden of an accusing law; the *second*, under the law, when the Old Testament took place, subjecting the faithful to the dominion of angels, and the fear of death all their lives; and last of all, to the curse, not allowing to the fathers true and permanent blessings; the *third*, under the gospel, when the godly began to be set at liberty from the dominion of the angels, from the fear of temporary death, and the curse which an exact observance of the ceremonial law carried with it, and at length enjoyed true and lasting blessings, the circumcision of the heart, the law written there, the full and true remission of sins, the spirit of adoption, and such like things ; this observation, I say, does not seem to me worthy to be insisted on in so many academical lectures, so many sermons, and such a number of books, as have been published in the Latin and our own languages, as though the whole of theological learning consisted in these. For, in the following work I have shewn, that, however those doctrines are explained, they are horrible to be mentioned ; and are not to be defended without wresting the scriptures.

But I esteem much more dangerous the opinions of some men, in other respects very learned, who deny that a covenant of works was made with Adam ; and will scarce allow that by the death with which he was threatened, in case he sinned, a corporeal death is to be understoood ; and deny that spiritual and heavenly blessings, such as we now obtain through Christ, were promised to Adam on condition of perfect obedience : and by a musty distinction dividing the sufferings of Christ into painful and judiciary, affirm, that the latter only, or, as they sometimes soften the expression, chiefly were satisfactory : excluding by this means his sorrows in the garden, the sentence passed on him both by the Jewish council, and the Roman governor, the stripes with which his body was wounded, his being nailed to the cursed cross, and last of all his death itself. On these subjects I have given my mind freely and candidly, as became " a defender of the truth, and an opposer of falsehood :" which laudable character was given of the emperor Constantine the Fourth, by the sixth Oecumenical Synod, which met at Constantinople ; and which is what all of our order ought to endeavour to deserve.

I have also made remarks on some things of less moment, which did not seem to have a solid scriptural interpretation, or are less accurately conceived of than they ought to be. Nor has my labour been without profit. Amphilochius is justly commended by Basilius, because he thought that " no word which was used concerning God, should be passed over without the most careful inquiry into its meaning." But I have done this without rancour or raillery : " not with a view of reproving the authors, but that the studious reader might be benefited by having their errors shewn him," as I remember Polibius somewhere expresses himself. And I hope it will not be taken ill by the learned and ingenious, to whom I grant the same liberty I myself take, if, (to use nearly the same words which Augustine uses, when he declares his dissent from Cy-

prian) whilst "I cannot arrive at their degree of merit, acknowledge my writings inferior to many of theirs, love their
ingenuity, am delighted with what they say, and admire their
virtues; yet, I cannot in all things agree with them, but make
use of the liberty wherewith our Lord has called us." Especially when they see, that I have willingly adopted their own
ingenious inventions, what they have happily found out by
searching into the original languages, have learnedly recovered
from the reliques of hitherto unknown antiquity, have judiciously confirmed, or clearly explained; and have highly recommended them to the reader.

They will also find that, wherever I think them right, however they may be censured by others, I have cordially defended them, and have wiped off the stamp of absurdity and novelty. And this I have done so frequently and solicitously, that,
without doubt, some will say, I have done it too much. But
I cannot yet allow myself to be sorry for having dealt so inge-
nuously by them. For how could any one have done otherwise,
who is not attached to any faction, or is not a slave to his own
or another's affections, but has dedicated himself to truth alone,
and regards not what any *particular* person says, but *what* is
said. He who loves the peace of Jerusalem, had rather see
controversies lessened than increased; and will with pleasure
hear that several things are innocent, or even useful, which
had sometimes been made the matter of controversy.

All good men indeed are justly offended with that wantonness
of wit, which now-a-days, by dogmatical attacks, rashly aims
to overturn wise opinions; and insolently offers a bold, and
often ludicrous, interpretation of prophecy, ridiculously hawl-
ing into their assistance, what contains nothing but the doctrine of our common faith and holiness; by which the public
and our sacred functions are not a little abused: and it is not
to be wondered at, if the warmer zeal of some has painted this
wantonness as it deserves, or, perhaps, in too strong colours.
But yet, a medium is to be regarded in all things: and I do
not approve the pains of some, who, whilst they discourse on
their differences, not only name some decades of our controversies, but centuries of them; and frequently with cruel eloquence are very violent on some innocent subjects. Whether
this method of disputing greatly conduces to the promoting of
saving knowledge, or the edification of souls, I will not now
say: but I am certain of this; the enemies of our church are
hereby greatly delighted, and secretly rejoice, that there are
as many and as warm disputes amongst ourselves, as with
them. And this, not very secretly neither: for they do not,

nor will ever cease to cast this reproach upon us; which, I grieve to say, is not so easily wiped away.

O! how much better would it be to use our utmost endeavours, to lessen, make up, and, if it could be, put an end to all controversy! Make this reverend and learned Sirs, your great concern. This all the godly who mourn for the breaches in Joseph; this the churches who are committed to your care; this Jesus himself, the king of truth and peace, require and expect from you; in the most earnest manner they entreat it of you. "If therefore there be any consolation in Christ, if any comfort of love, if any fellowship of the spirit, if any bowels, and mercies: fulfil ye my joy, fulfil ye the joy of all saints, fulfil ye the joy of our Lord Jesus himself, that ye may be like-minded, having the same love, being of one accord, of one mind." There have been already more than enough quarrels, slanders, and suspicions; more than enough of contentions amongst brethren, which, I engage for it, will afford no just cause of triumph; more than enough intestine divisions, by which we destroy one another; and more than enough of passion. Let the love of divisions, a thirst after pre-eminence, and schismatical names be henceforward banished from amongst us. Let all litigious, satirical, and virulent writings be blotted out; " as they only serve to revive the fires of hurtful questions." But if we must write on those controversies, let us lay aside all evil dispositions, which are hinderances to us in our enquiries, and mislead our readers. Let us fight with arguments, not railings, bearing in our minds this saying of Aristophanes, "it is dishonourable, and by no means becoming poets, to rail at each other." How much less does it become Christians to do so! The streams of divinity are pure: they rise only from the fountain of sacred learning, and should be defiled with none of the impure waters of the ancient or modern philosophy. Let us abstain from harsh and unusual expressions, and from crude and rash assertions; from whence arise envy, strife, railings, evil surmisings. The instruments of both covenants should be handled diligently by all, but with sacred fear and trembling. Let none please himself with his commentaries, because they contain something new and unknown by our predecessors. Let him who thinks he has found out something preferable to the received opinion, offer it to the public with modesty, without vilifying the brethren; not asserting or determining rashly, but submitting his thoughts to the censure of the learned, and the judgment of the church; not forcing them on the common people to the distraction of their minds; nor hastily offering them to incautious youth, who are improper judges of such weighty matters. Nor let any reject, on account of its novelty, what is agreeable to the meaning of the words, to scripture phrases, to the analogy of faith, or to the relation the text bears to others. Cajetan, who is commended by our Chameir, has not badly expressed himself on this head: "If a new sense of the text offer itself, though it be different from that of divines in general, let the reader judge of it for himself." And in another place he says, "Let none refuse assenting to a new sense of sacred writ, because it differs from that given by the ancients; for God has not bound himself to the truth of their expositions of the scriptures." Let the depths of prophecy be also diligently searched into; but reverently, without wresting the scriptures, without violating those bounds wherewith it has pleased God to keep them from human intuition; lest he who attempts to search into the majesty should be overwhelmed by the glory.

Let no one, of however great name, by his authority bind the free consciences of the faithful: but, as Clemens Romanus once said, "Let the truth be taken from the scriptures themselves;" by these alone it should stand or fall in religious affairs; by these are all controversies to be settled. And it was by the sacred and undefiled gospels of our Lord Jesus Christ, that the ancient councils were influenced, nevertheless, let not any one inconsiderately on this pretence, withhold his assent to such forms of expression which are taken from the word of God, and are agreeable to the scriptures, are the bonds of church union, the marks of orthodoxy, the bars of heresy, and the limits of wanton wits; as though they were the remains of the Babylonish tower, which obliged men to think and speak alike in religion.

Let no one choose for himself a guide out of the modern divines; all whose dictates he is determined to receive and defend as celestial oracles; as one who is given as a new teacher and light of the world, as the ancients said of Basilius; and in comparison of whom, all others appear as little children or dwarfs; when he himself, perhaps, protests that he would not be thought the author of any thing new, and made the head of a sect. On the other hand, let no one despise such a man, as if nothing true or good, nothing useful to the understanding of the scriptures could be learned from him: for God has not put it into the heart of any pious persons to search the scriptures night and day, without opening to them those treasures of his sacred wisdom.

Let us preach the good tidings of the gospel, let us congratulate the church on account of them; and make the best use of them ourselves we can. Let no one who has in general expressed the truth in eloquent language, be heinously censured on account of an improper word, or harsh expression which has slipped from his pen: "Poison does not lie hid in syllables; nor does truth consist in sound, but in the intention: nor godliness in the tinkling of brass, but in the meaning of the things signified." Yet, let us all endeavour to express ourselves as accurately as possible; and not take upon us to defend what has been imprudently said by our friends, or ourselves, lest others blame us for it; but as far as ingenuousness, truth, charity, and all good men will allow of it, let us pass by, cancel or correct any mistakes; which has been the practice of some great men, both among the ancients and moderns, to their very great credit. Let none of our brethren be stigmatized with the brand of heresy, on account of what is supposed to follow from any of their expressions, when they themselves deny and detest the consequence. Solid learning, manners conformable to Christian sanctity, a peaceable disposition, and a faithful discharge of our duty without noise and confusion, will procure favour much more than inconsiderate warm zeal, and the violent efforts of a passionate mind; which are designed for the most part, to heighten our own glory and seeming importance, though the cause of God be made the pretence for them.

Let some liberty also be given to learned men, in explaining texts of scripture, in the choice of arguments for the defence of the common truth, in the use of phrases and terms, and in resolving problematic questions, (for in this our state of darkness, it is not to be expected that all men should think and speak alike): but let this liberty be confined within the bounds of modesty, prudence, and love; lest it degenerate into petulent licentiousness, and turn our Zion into a Babel.

These, reverend and learned Sirs, are my earnest wishes; these my sentiments which I recommend to your prudence, faith, and piety; as I do yourselves and your pious labours, to the grace of our Great God and Saviour, Jesus Christ; "Who can make you perfect to every good work, to do his "will, working in you that which is well pleasing in his "sight;" and, at last, "when you happily have fought the "good fight of faith, can bless you with an everlasting crown "of glory." This was long since, and is now, the most earnest wish of, Reverend and learned Sirs,

Your fellow-labourer, and

Utrecht, }   Servant in the Lord,

Oct. 20. 1693. }   H. WITSIUS.

AUTHOR'S LIFE.

HERMAN WITS (or, as he is commonly called, WITSIUS) was descended from reputable parents. His father, Nicolaus Wits, was a gentleman universally esteemed by his fellow-citizens at Enkhuysen, to whom he endeared himself by his fidelity, modesty, justice, benevolence, and unaffected piety, in every character he sustained, either in the church or in the city; for in the former he was first a deacon, and afterwards a ruling elder; and treasurer in the latter. His mother was Johanna, a gentlewoman of great piety and prudence, the daughter of Herman Gerhard; who, after many dangers and distresses, obtained a calm and secure settlement in the church at Enkhuysen, where he preached the gospel for upwards of thirty years, with great reputation; and such was the affection he bore to his church, that he rejected the most profitable offers that were made to him.

The parents of our Witsius, having vowed to devote a child to the ministry, did upon the birth of this son, call him after his grandfather, praying, that in Herman the grandson, might be revived the spirit of the grandfather; and that, endued with equal, if not superior talents, he might imitate his example.

Herman Witsius was born on the 12th of February 1636, at Enkhuysen, a town of West Friesland; one of the first that threw off the Spanish yoke, asserted their own liberty, and, once enlightened with the truths of the gospel, retained the purity of worship ever after, and in the very worst times of Arminianism, continued, above many, stedfast in the faith. And though it was a place noted for trade and navigation, yet it produced men famous in every branch of literature; so that Witsius, even in his native place, had illustrious patterns to copy after.

The care which these pious parents took of young Witsius during his tender infancy, was not intermitted as he began to grow; for, being still mindful of their vow, they brought him up in a very pious manner, instructing him in the principles and precepts of religion and Christian piety.   In his sixth year they sent him to the public school of the town, to learn the rudiments of the Latin tongue; from which, after spending three years, and being advanced to the highest form there, his uncle by the mother, Peter Gerhard, took him under his own private and domestic tuition; a person well skilled in Latin, Greek, Hebrew, and philosophy.   But his principal study had been divinity.   This man, then disengaged from all public business, and being as fond of his nephew as if he had been his own son, taught him with that assiduity, that, before he was fifteen, he made no small proficiency in Latin, Greek, Hebrew, and acquired such knowledge in logic and other parts of philosophy, that, when he was afterwards removed to the university, he could study without a master.   At the same time he learned the ethic compendiums of Wallæus and Burgersdicius, with so much care as to be able to repeat most of the sentences, very frequent in Burgersdicius, from the ancients, whether Greek or Latin.   He also perused his elements of physics, and dipped a little into metaphysical subtilties, and committed to memory most of the theological definitions and distinctions from Wendelin.   As his uncle was a man of exemplary piety, and was wont to apply almost to every common occurrence of life, some striking passages of both Testaments, which he often repeated either in Hebrew or Greek, while rising, dressing, walking, studying, or otherwise employed; so, by his example and admonitions, he stirred up his nephew to the same practice.   Whence it was, that at those tender years he had rendered familiar to himself many entire passages of the Hebrew and Greek Testament, which he was far from forgetting when more advanced in life.

Being thus formed by a private education, in 1651, and the fifteenth year of his age, it was resolved to send him to some university: Utrecht was pitched upon, being furnished with men very eminent in every branch of literature, with a considerable concourse of students, and an extraordinary strictness of discipline.   What principally recommended it were the famous divines, Gisbert Voetius, Charles Maatsius, and John Hoornbeekius, all of them great names, and ornaments in their day.   Being therefore received into that university, he was, for metaphysics put under the direction of Paul Voetius, then professor of philosophy; and being, moreover, much taken

with the study of the Oriental languages, he closely attended
on the celebrated John Leusden, who taught those languages
with incredible dexterity, and under him he construed almost
the whole Hebrew Text, as also the commentaries of Solomon
Iarchi, Aben Ezra, and Kimchi on Hosea, and the Chaldee
Paraphrase of Jonathan on Isaiah, and of Onkelos on a part of
the Pentateuch. Moreover, under the same master, he just
touched on the mysteries of the Masora, and the barbarous dic-
tion of the Talmud; namely, the parts published by John Cocceius, under the title of Sanhedrim and Maccoth, and by Constantine Lempereur, under that of Babha Bathræ: under the
same master he learned the elements of the Syriac and Arabic
languages, which last, however, he afterwards less cultivated
than the others. What proficiency he made in the Hebrew,
appeared from a public specimen he gave at the instigation of
Leusden, of a well written Hebrew oration about the Messias
of the Jews and Christians, in 1654. But, though almost
quite swallowed up in those studies, he by no means neglected the study of divinity, to which he knew all the others were
only subservient; but in that sublime science, he diligently
used, as masters, the greatest men, and best seen in the sacred
scriptures, whose most laudable memory no lapse of time
shall ever be able to obliterate; namely, Gisbert Voetius,
John Hoornbeekius, Gualterus Bruinicus, and Andrew Essenius. By whose instructions, together with his own extraordinary application, and true piety towards God, what proficiency he made, the reader may easily judge for himself.
However, he had a mind to see Groningen, to have the benefit of hearing the famous Samuel Maresius: whither he went
in 1654, after the summer vacation, chiefly applying to divinity: under whose direction, he made exercises in French, by
which he gave so much satisfaction to this great man, that,
notwithstanding his many avocations, he deigned to correct
and purge those declamations of Witsius from their solecisms
and other improprieties, before they were recited in the college. Having thus spent a year at Groningen, and obtained
an honourable testimonial from the Theological faculty, he
next turned his thoughts to Leyden. But the plague then raging there, he resolved to return to Utrecht, in order to build
farther on the foundation he had there so happily laid; and,
therefore, he not only carefully heard the professors in divinity at this time, as before, both in public and private, but
cultivated a peculiar familiarity with the very reverend Justus van den Bogaerdt, whose piety, prudence, and admirable
endowments he had such a value for, that he imagined, per-

haps from youthful inexperience, no preacher equal to him. From his sermons, conversation, and example, he learned the deeper mysteries of the kingdom of God, and of mystical and spiritual Christianity. From him he understood how great the difference is between any superficial knowledge, which scholastic exercises, books learnedly written, and a close application, may procure to minds quite destitute of sanctification, and that heavenly wisdom which is acquired by meditation, prayer, love, familiar converse with God, and by the very relish and experience of spiritual things; which, proceeding from the Spirit of God, internally illuminating, convincing, persuading, and sealing, gloriously transforms the whole man to the most holy image of Christ. In a word, he owns that by means of this holy person, he was introduced by the Lord Jesus to his most secret recesses, while before he too much, and too fondly pleased himself in tarrying in the porch, and there, at length, learned, disclaiming all vain presumption of science, humbly to sit down at the feet of the heavenly Master, and receive the kingdom of heaven as a little child. But that it may not be thought, he so applied to the forming of his mind to piety, as to neglect for the future all academical studies, the theses he wrote on the Sacred Trinity, against the Jews, from their own writings, may, and ought to be, a proof to the contrary; and which he published in the month of October, 1655, to be disputed under the moderation of the famous Leusden; which, though warmly attacked by the most experienced academicians, yet the moderator thought the respondent acquitted himself so well as to supersede his interposition on any account: and when, according to custom, he returned solemn thanks to the moderator for his trouble, this last very politely and truly made answer, He had stood in no need of his help.

The time now seemed to require, that our Witsius, very famous at two universities, should be employed in the public service of the church, and first, as usual, gave specimens of his proficiency. Therefore, in the month of May, 1656, he presented himself at Enkhuysen to a preparatory examination, as it is called, together with his then fellow-student, John Lasdragerus, with whom he had a familiarity from his youth, and whom he afterwards had for his most intimate colleague and faithful fellow-labourer, first in the church of Leovaarden, and then at Utrecht. And upon this occasion he was not only admitted to preach publicly, which he did with uncommon applause, and gave so general satisfaction, that there was scarce a country church in North Holland, where he then resided, which wanting a minister, did not put his name in the number of the three candidates, from which the election is usually made. And, at the instigation of the reverend John James le Bois, minister of the French church at Utrecht, he ventured, upon leave given, to preach publicly to the French church at Dort in their language. And from that time he often preached in French, both at Utrecht and Amsterdam; as also sometimes in the course of his ministry at Leovaarden. But because he imagined there was still something wanting to the elegance of his language, he proposed very soon to take a tour to France, and pay his respects to the great men there, and at the same time have the pleasure of hearing them, and improving in their language.

But providence disposed otherwise; for the following year, 1657, and the twenty-first of his age, being lawfully called by the church of West Wouden, he was ordained there on the 8th of July. This village lies almost in the mid-way between Enkhuysen and Horn, and is united with the parish of Binne-Wijsent. And here, for four years and upwards, he laboured with the greatest alacrity of a youthful mind, and with no less benefit: for, by frequent catechising, and with the greatest prudence suiting himself to the catechumens, both boys and girls, they who before were grossly ignorant, could not only give proper answers on the principal heads of our religion, but prove their assertions by suitable texts of scripture, and repeat a whole sermon distinctly, when examined on it, to the joy as well as shame of their parents and older people. The reputation of so faithful and dexterous a pastor, being thus widely spread, the church of Wormer, in the same tract of North Holland, sufficiently numerous and celebrated, but then too much distracted by intestine commotions, imagined they could not pitch upon a fitter guide to allay their heats, and form their minds. This call Witsius not only accepted, passing to that charge in October 1661, but spent there four years and a half, doing every thing in his power to promote Christian unanimity and the common salvation; and as he saw the extensive fruits of his labours among them, so he was universally beloved. Wherefore he could not bear to remove from them to the people of Sluice in Flanders, who offered him great encouragement to preach, but the people of Goese in Zealand succeeded in their call, and he repaired to them about Whitsuntide 1666, and was so acceptable to all by his doctrine, manners, and diligence, as to live there in the most agreeable peace and concord, with his learned, pious, and vigilant colleagues, two of whom he revered as his

fathers; and the third, who was younger, he loved as his brother. He was much delighted with this settlement, and often
wished to grow old in this peaceful retreat. But the people of
Leovaarden, in West Friesland, interrupted these thoughts;
who, in November 1667, called him with a remarkable affection, to that celebrated metropolis of his native country, that he
might prove a shining light, not only in the church, court, and
senate, of that place, but to all the people of Friesland, who
flocked thither from all parts to the assembly of the states;
but the people of Goese doing all they could to hinder his removal, it was April 1668, before he went to Leovaarden. And
it is scarcely to be expressed with what vigilance, fidelity, and
prudence he conducted himself; but at a time of such difficulty,
when the enemy, having made such incursions into Holland,
and made themselves masters of most of its towns, and struck
a panic into all, that a man of such spirit and resolution was
absolutely necessary. Nor do I know of any, before or since,
whose labours were more successful, and who was more acceptable to the church, the nobility, and the court. And therefore he was for some time tutor to Henry Casimir, the most
serene prince of Nassau, hereditary governor of Friesland, too
untimely snatched away by death; and with remarkable success he instructed, in the doctrines of religion, his most illustrious sister, Amelia, a very religious princess, afterwards married to the duke of Saxe-Eisenach; and he presided at the
profession of faith which both princes publicly made, to the
great edification of the church, in the presence of the princes'
mother, Albertina of Orange.

It is not, therefore, to be wondered, that when, through the
injury of the most calamitous times, and the decease, both of
the venerable and aged Christian Schotanus, and of John Melchior Steinbergius, scarce installed in the professorship, the
theological interests of the university of Franequer seemed to
be fallen to decay; and the extraordinary, and truly academical endowments of our Witsius were perfectly well known in
Friesland, by an experience of seven whole years; that, I say,
he was appointed to the ordinary profession of divinity, in the
year 1675, in the academy of his native country, thus happily to be restored. Which opportunity also the church of
Franequer prudently laid hold on, being then without a second
minister, very cheerfully to commit to him, now appointed
professor, that sacred charge. Having, therefore, accepted
both these calls, he came to Franequer; and after being declared Doctor of divinity in the academical assembly, by the
divine his colleague, he was, on the 15th of April, installed

professor of the same, after delivering a solemn oration, with the greatest applause of a concourse of people from all parts; in which he excellently expressed the character of a genuine divine; and as such he soon after demeaned himself, together with the venerable and aged Nicolaus Arnoldus, his most intimate colleague.

In the pulpit, Witsius addressed himself with so much gravity, elegance, piety, solidity, and usefulness, that the general inattention of the people was removed, and religious impressions made both on great and small. The academical chair also gained a warmth from his sacred fire, to which, from the different and most distant parts of Europe, the youth intended for the ministry, resorted in great numbers. And not to be wanting in his duty, or disappoint the intention of those who called him, in any particular, he no sooner entered the university, than, notwithstanding his many daily public and private labours, in both his offices, he set himself to write, and, in a very little time published, besides select academical disputations, mostly tending to establish the peace of the church, and a smaller dissertation, two works pretty large and learned, which went through several editions, and were spread over Europe; being every where read with universal approbation. And besides, there was nothing of extraordinary importance to be transacted, even with the schismastic followers of Labadie, who had then fixed their principal residence in West Friesland, which both the nobility and the overseers of the church did not think proper should be dispatched by this man.

About this time, Mr. J. Mark, on his return from his studies at Leyden, commenced his acquaintance with Witsius, who recommended him as pastor to the church of Midlumen, between Franequer and Harlingen; and afterwards procured him the degree of Doctor in divinity; and, by his interest with his serene highness, and others, Dr. Mark was appointed third ordinary professor of divinity.

But, the justly renowned character of our Witsius was such, that others, envying the happiness of the people of Friesland, wanted to have the benefit of his labours themselves. This was first attempted by the overseers of the university of Groningen, who, to procure a worthy successor to the deceased James Altingius, as well in the theological and philological chairs, as in the university church, about the close of the year 1679, sent to Franequer a reverend person, to offer the most honourable terms, in order to prevail on Witsius. But that attempt proved unsuccessful. For, communicating

the affair to his serene Highness the prince, and other overseers of the university, they protested his services were most
acceptable to them; and he excused himself in a handsome
manner to the people of Groningen, in the beginning of the
year 1680; when, upon the decease of the celebrated Bur-
mannus, they judged it necessary to have a great man, to add
to the reputation of their university, and to maintain the ancient piety of their church; and being well assured that none
was fitter for all those purposes than Witsius, who was formerly one of their own students, they therefore dispatched a
splendid deputation to Franequer, to entreat him to come and
be an ornament to their university and church, to which he
consented with little difficulty, notwithstanding the opposition
made by those of Friesland, who were loth to part with one
who had been so useful among them; for his obligations to
the university of Utrecht were such that he thought he could
not shew his gratitude more, than by accepting of their invitation. Accordingly, after a most honourable dismission from
the afflicted Frieslanders, he came to Utrecht, and was admitted into the ministry of that church, on the 25th of April,
and four days after, into the professorship of the university,
after delivering a most elegant oration on the excellence of
evangelical truth, which fully answered universal expectation.
And it can scarce be expressed, how happily he lived in credit, and laboured above full eighteen years of his most valuable life, with these celebrated men, viz. Peter Maestricht,
Melchior Leideckerus, and Hermannus, then Halenius, after
the example of the doctors, his predecessors, whom he always
had in the highest veneration. In the ministry he had several colleagues, men of learning, piety, peace, and zeal for
God; among whom were his ancient colleagues in the church
of Leovaarden, Peter Eindhovius, and John Lasdragerus. In
the university, besides the fore-mentioned divines, he had not
only his own John Leusden, an excellent philologist, but Gerard de Uries, and Luitsius, famous philosophers, who, for the
benefit of the church, prepared the youth intended for the ministry. Before his pulpit he had a Christian magistracy and
the whole body of the people, who admired and experienced
the power of his elocution, their minds being variously
affected with religious impressions. Before his academical
and private chair, he had not only a large circle of promising
youths from all parts of the world, who admired his most
learned, solid, prudent and eloquent dissertations; but doctors
themselves daily resorted in great numbers to learn of him.
And therefore, he declined no labour, by which, even at the

expense of many restless nights, he might be of service to
the university and church. Nor did he think it sufficient by
sermons, lectures, conferences and disputations, to produce his
various stock of learning, but he exposed his treasures to the
whole world, present, and to come, in many public and excellent writings, to last for ever, and never to decay, but with
the utter extinction of solid learning and true piety itself.
And to the commendation of the people of Utrecht be it spoken, that, not only in ecclesiastical assemblies, they always acknowledged his abilities and prudence, seasonably calling him
to the highest dignities in synods; but even the nobility, both
by deeds and words, testified, that his endowments were perfectly well known to, and highly esteemed of by them. And
therefore they honoured him twice with the badges of the
highest office in their university, in 1686 and in 1697. And
we must by no means omit, that when in 1685, a most splendid embassy of the whole united provinces was decreed to be
sent to James king of Great Britain, afterwards unhappily
drawn aside and ruined by the deceitful arts of the French and
Romish party; which embassy was executed by the most illustrious Wassenaar, lord of Duvenvorden, and the ordinary ambassador, his excellency, Citters, with the most noble and illustrious Weed, lord of Dykveld; that, I say, this last easily
persuaded his colleagues of legation to employ none but Witsius for their chaplain : a divine, whom, to the honour of the
Dutch churches, they might present in person to the English
nation, without any apprehension, either of offence or contempt. Nor was Witsius himself against the resolution of
these illustrious personages, for he went cheerfully, though
indisposed in body; and on his return, in a few months after,
owned, that having conversed with the archbishop of Canterbury, the bishop of London, and with many other divines,
both episcopal and dissenters in discipline, he observed not a
few things, which made an increase to his stock of learning,
and by which he was better qualified to act prudently on all
future occasions. And the English, from that time, owned,
that being thus better acquainted with Witsius, he ever after
justly deserved their regard and applause.

The reputation of Witsius, thus spread all over the world,
made the most illustrious overseers of the university of Leyden, with the Burgomasters, resolve to give a call to this great
man, in 1698, in order to make up the loss which was apprehended from the decease of the great Spanhemius, which seemed to be drawing near. And this resolution was approved of
by our gracious Stadtholder, William III. king of Great Bri-

tain, of immortal memory, from that constant piety he entertained towards God, and that equal fidelity and prudence he exercised towards our church and university. Nor was there the least delay, either in determining or executing that call to the professorship of divinity, or in his accepting thereof. For, though the people of Utrecht could have wished otherwise, yet our Witsius had several weighty reasons why he thought it his duty to comply with the Leyden invitation ; judging it was entirely for the interest of the church, equally as for his own, that hereafter exempted from the labours of the pulpit, he might, with the greater freedom, devote the rest of his aged life to the benefit of the university. But especially, as he was made acquainted with his majesty's pleasure, by the illustrious pensioner Heinsius. And when his majesty admitted him into his royal presence, he signified the satisfaction he had with his accepting the call to the chair of Leyden. He entered on his office the 16th of October, after delivering a very grave and elegant oration, in which he gave the character of the Modest Divine. And with what fidelity he discharged this office for the space of ten years; with what assiduity he laboured, with what wisdom and prudence he taught, with what elegance he spoke, with what alacrity he discoursed in disputations, with what piety he lived, with what sweetness of temper he demeaned himself, with what gracefulness he continued to write, with what lustre he adorned the university, are things so well known to all, as may supersede any particular enlargement.

But he had scarce passed a year at Leyden, when the high and mighty states of Holland and West Friesland did, on the recommendation of the overseers of the university, in the room of Mark Essius, the piously deceased inspector of their theological college, in which ingenious youths of the republic are reared for the service of the church, commit the superintendency thereof to our Witsius, as the mildest tutor they could employ for their pupils; without detriment to all the honour and dignity of his professorship, which he enjoyed in conjunction with the celebrated Anthony Hulsius. When he was installed in this new office, the illustrious president of the supreme court of Holland, and overseer of the university, Hubert Roosenboomius, lord of Sgrevelsrecht, did, in a most elegant Latin discourse, in the name of all the nobility, not only set forth the praise of the new inspector, but also exhorted all the members of that college to a due veneration for him, and to shew him all other becoming marks of respect. Witsius accepted, but with reluctance, this new province ;

for, had he not judged a submission to the will of the states, and his laying himself out for the service of the church, to be his duty, he would not have complied with it. However, he executed this great charge with the greatest fidelity and care, for the advantage of, and with an affection for his pupils, equally with that of his professorship in the university : till, in the year 1707, on the 8th of February, on account of his advanced age, and growing infirmities, he, with great modesty, in the assembly of the Overseers and Burgomasters, notwithstanding all their remonstrances and entreaties to the contrary, both in public and private, and all the great emoluments arising therefrom to himself, resigned this other office ; being at the same time also discharged, at his own desire, from the public exercises of his professorship in the university ; for executing which in the old manner his strength of body was scarce any longer sufficient ; the vigour of his mind continued still unaltered ; but as he often declared, he had much rather desist from the work, than flag in it.

And it is not to be thought, that Witsius would have been equal to so many and great labours, and the church and university have enjoyed so many and so great benefits by him, had he not found at home the most powerful cordials and supports ; particularly in the choicest and most beloved of wives, Aletta van Borkhorn, the daughter of Wesselvan Borkhorn, a citizen and merchant of good character, at Utrecht, and a worthy elder of the church, and of Martina van Ysen ; whom he married in the middle of the summer of 1660, after three years spent in the sacred ministry. She was eminent for meekness, and every civil and religious virtue ; she loved and honoured her husband, in a manner above the common ; with whom he lived in the greatest harmony and complacency, about four and twenty years, in North Holland, Zealand, Friesland, and at Utrecht ; at length, in the year 1684, after many great and long infirmities of body, was taken from him by a truly Christian death. He was no less happy in his offspring, especially in three surviving daughters, Martina, Johanna, and Petronella, who were endued with every accomplishment that can adorn the sex, but especially in their duty and affection to their father, which they shewed, not only before, but more especially after the death of their mother.

From what has been said, may sufficiently appear, the admirable endowments and virtues of this man. How great was the force of his genius, in apprehending, investigating and illustrating, even the most abtruse subjects; the accuracy of his judgment, in distinguishing, determining, and arranging them ; the tenacity of his memory, in retaining and recollecting them; what readiness of the most charming eloquence, in explaining, inculcating, and urging them home; were well known to those whoever saw or heard him.   Nor was his gracefulness in a Latin style, as is most apparent from all he wrote and said, less than his readiness in the Dutch ; in which, discoursing from the pulpit, with a peculiar decency of gesture and voice, he ravished the minds of the faithful to a holy assent, and unbelievers and the vicious themselves he filled with astonishment, shame, and terror.   And as none will be found, from reading his funeral discourse, to have with more dignity commended the deceased queen Mary, so his many sacred poems must have affected a mind so learned and so pious.   There was no branch of learning, necessary to adorn a divine, in which he did not greatly excel !   He so increased his knowledge of philosophy, when at the university, that none of the quirks or sophisms of infidels could ensnare him, nor any artifice induce him to make shipwreck of the faith, or embrace, or encourage any of the errors of the times.   He was master of the whole compass of sacred philology, Greek and Hebrew : he was well acquainted with the elegances of profane literature, Latin, Greek, and Oriental ; skilfully borrowing from thence whatever might serve to explain, in a becoming manner, the sacred scriptures; prudently avoiding every extreme.   He was perfectly well skilled in history, both ancient and modern, ecclesiastical and civil, Jewish and Christian, domestic and foreign : and from it he always selected, with the greatest care, what might principally be of present use.   He thoroughly learned divinity in all its branches, being as expert in the confirmation and vindication of doctrines, and in shewing their connection, as in confuting errors, discovering their origin, and distinguishing their importance.   Above all, he was in love with, revered, and commended the holy scriptures ; as that from which alone, true wisdom is to be derived ; and which, by long practice, he had rendered so very familiar to himself, as not only to have the original words, upon all occasions, very readily at command, but to be able directly, without hesitation, to explain the most difficult.   Nor did he, in this case, rest on any man's authority ; most rightly judging such a conduct to be inconsistent with the divine glory of the Christian faith, declaring and demeaning himself the most obsequious disciple of the holy Spirit alone.   Hence he had neither a disdain for old, nor an itch for new things ; nor an aversion to new, and a mad and indolent fondness for old things.   He would neither be constrained by others, nor constrain any one himself; being taught neither to follow, nor to form a party. That golden saying pleased him much: " Unanimity in things necessary ; liberty in things not necessary ; and in all things, prudence and charity;" which he professed was his common creed. Nor can we have the least doubt of his zeal for the *faith once delivered to the saints*, and for true piety towards God, which he expressed in his writings, when at Leovaarden and Franequer, against some dangerous opinions, then starting up both in divinity and philosophy; of which also he gave a proof at Utrecht and Leyden, when publicly testifying in writing, that he could not bear the authority of reason to be so extolled above scripture, as that this last should be entirely subject to its command, or be overturned by ludicrous interpretations. His zeal, in his latter days, was greatly inflamed, when he observed all ecclesiastical discipline against those, who would overthrow the Christian faith, and even right reason itself, publicly trampled upon under the most idle pretences, and every thing almost given up to a depraved reason, to the subverting the foundations of Christianity ; while some indeed, mourned in secret, but were forced to be silent, and therefore he declared his joy at his approaching dissolution, on account of the evils he foresaw were hanging over the church ; and often called on those who should survive, to tremble when the adversary was triumphing over the doctrines of salvation, and all true piety, to the destruction both of church and state ; and that by men, whom it least became, and who still artfully dissembled a regard for religion, and for ecclesiastical and civil constitutions; unless God, in his wonderful providence, averted the calamity, and more powerfully stirred up the zeal of our superiors against Atheism, Pelagianism, and the seeds of both. I do not speak of those smaller differences, observable for some time past, in the method of ranging theological matters, in some modes of expression. All are well apprized with what equity and moderation Witsius ever treated these differences in opinion, and if ever any was inclined to unanimity and concord with real brethren, he was the man who never did any thing to interrupt it, but every thing either to establish or restore it, and to remove all seeds of dissension. This is what that genuine Christianity, he had imbibed, prompted him to ; and what the singular meekness of his temper inspired ; by which he was ready to give way to the rashly angry, and either made no answer to injurious railers, or repaid them even with those ample encomiums, which, in other respects, they might deserve. Thus lived our venerable Witsius, giving uneasiness to none, but the greatest pleasure to all, with whom he had any connection, and was not easily exceeded by any in offices of humanity and brotherly love. There was at the same time in him a certain wonderful conjunction of religious and civil prudence, consummated and confirmed by long experience, with an unfeigned candour. Neither was any equal to him for diligence in the duties of his office, being always most ready to do every thing, by which he could be serviceable to the flocks and pupils under his care, for the benefit of the church. He did not withdraw from them in old age itself, nor during his indisposition indulge himself too much. His modesty was quite singular, by which he not only always behaved with that deep concern in treating the holy scriptures and its mysteries; but also, by which he scarce ever pleased himself in the things he most happily wrote and said: and when his best friends justly commended his performances, he even suspected their sincerity. Nor could any under adversities, be more content with his lot, even publicly declaring at Utrecht, that he would not exchange his place in the university and church, either with the royal or imperial dignity. And to omit other virtues, or rather in the compass of one to comprize all; he was not in appearance, but in reality, *a true divine*, ever discovering his heavenly wisdom by a sincere piety towards God and his Saviour. For, he was constant in the public acts of worship, unwearied in the domestic exercises of piety, giving, in this, an example for the imitation of others in the fear of the Lord, incessantly taken up in heavenly meditation, and continued instant in prayer, both stated and ejaculatory; and shone in them, when under the dictates and impulses of the holy Spirit: In fine, his chief care was, by avoiding evil and doing good, to demean himself both towards God and man, as became one who had obtained redemption through Christ, and, by divine grace, the hope of a blessed eternity in heaven; which he constantly panted after, with the utmost contempt for the things in the world.

His writings are numerous, learned, and useful: In 1660, almost at his entrance on the ministry, he published his *Judæus Christianizans*, on the principles of faith, and on the Holy Trinity. When at Wormer, he put out in Low Dutch, 1665, *The Practice of Christianity*, with the spiritual characters of the unregenerate, with respect to what is commendable in them; and of the regenerate, as to what is blameable and wants correction. At Leovaarden, he gave also in Low Dutch,

The Lord's Controversy with his Vineyard, and at the same time, briskly defended it against opponents. Of his Franequer labours, we have, besides smaller works, afterwards comprised in larger volumes, his *Oeconomia fœderum Dei cum hominibus*, translated into Low Dutch, by Harlingius; and his *Exercitationes sacræ in Symbolum Apostolorum*, translated also into Low Dutch, by Costerus. At Utrecht, came out his *Exercitationes Sacræ in orationem dominicam*; his *Ægyptiaca* and *Decaphylon*, with a dissertation on the *Legio fulminatrix Christianorum*, and the first volume of his *Miscellania Sacra*, and a good deal of the second; besides some smaller works also. And at Leyden, he published, at last, the second volume of his *Miscellania Sacra*, complete: and at this last place he set on foot what he calls his *Meletemeta Leidensia*, to be occasionally enlarged with a number of select dissertations. Indeed, all these writings are justly in great repute, their style being polite, the subjects useful, and the whole replenished with various branches of learning, and a beautiful strain of piety, all which may deservedly commend them to the latest posterity.

He had been often, formerly, afflicted with racking and painful diseases; whence sometimes arose the great apprehension of a far earlier departure by death. And nothing, under divine providence, but his vigour of mind, joined to his piety, could have preserved him so long to the world; and that with so perfect an use of his senses, that not long before his death, he could read, without hesitation, the smallest Greek characters by moon-light, which none besides himself could do. But with his advanced years, he sometimes had cruel fits of the gout, and stone in the kidneys; and once in the chair, in the midst of a lecture, a slight touch of an apoplexy. These disorders were, indeed, mitigated by the skill of the famous doctor Frederic Deckers; but now and then, by slight attacks, threatened a return: for his wavering and languishing state of health, indicating the past disorders not to be entirely extirpated, gave apprehensions of a future fatal distemper; which was occasioned by the sudden attack of a fever on the evening of the 18th of October. This fever, though very soon removed, left his body exceeding weak, and his mind in a state of lethargy, an indication that his head was affected. The good man himself, considering these symptoms, with great constancy and calmness of mind, told the physician, and his other friends then present, that they could not fail to prove mortal. Nor did the slightness of the disease make any change in his opinion as to its fatal issue; while he foresaw that the consequences of an advanced age, and of the greatest weakness, could admit of no other event. Nor indeed without cause: for his senses were gradually weakened by repeated slumbers; however, about his last hour, he sensibly signified to Doctor Mark, who attended him, his blessed hope, and his heavenly desires, as he had frequently done before, and then about noon, on the 22d of October 1708, he sweetly departed this life, in the 73d year of his age, and entered into the joy of his Lord.

ECONOMY

DIVINE COVENANTS.

BOOK I.

CHAP. I.

Of the Divine Covenants in general.

I. WHOEVER attempts to discourse on the subject and design of the Divine Covenants, by which eternal salvation is adjudged to man, on certain conditions equally worthy of God and the rational creature, ought, above all things, to have a sacred and inviolable regard to the heavenly oracles, and neither through prejudice nor passion, intermix any thing which he is not firmly persuaded is contained in the records which hold forth these covenants to the world. For, if Zaleucus made it a condition to be observed by the contentious interpreters of his laws, That " each party should explain the meaning of the lawgiver, in the assembly of the thousand, with halters about their necks: and that what party soever should appear to wrest the sense of the law, should, in the presence of the thousand, end their lives by the halter they wore:" as Polybius, a very grave author, relates in his history, Book xii. c. 7. And if the Jews and Samaritans in Egypt, each disputing about their temple, were admitted to plead before the king and his courtiers on this condition only, That " the advocates of either party, foiled in the dispute, should be punished with death," according to Josephus, in his Antiquities, Book xiii. c. 6. Certainly he must be in greater peril, and liable to sorer destruction, who shall dare to pervert, by rashly wresting the sacred mysteries of the Divine Covenants; our Lord himself openly declaring, that " whosoever shall break one of these least commandments, and thall teach men so, he shall be called the least in the kingdom of heaven," Matt. v. 19. It is therefore, with a kind of sacred awe I undertake this work; praying God, that, lay-ing aside every prejudice, I may demean myself a tractable disciple of the holy scriptures, and, with modesty, impart to my brethren, what I think I have learned from them: if hap-pily this my poor performance may serve to lessen the number of disputes, and help to clear up the truth; than which no-thing should be accounted more valuable.

II. As it is by words, especially the words of those lan-guages, in which God was pleased to reveal his sacred mys-teries to men, that we can, with hopes of success, come to the knowledge of things; it will be worth while, more ac-curately to enquire into the import both of the Hebrew word, בדית, and the Greek διαϑηχη, which the holy Spirit makes use of on this subject. And first, we are to give the true ety-mology, and then the different significations of the Hebrew word. With respect to the former, the learned are not agreed: some derive it from גדא, which, in Piel, signifies to *cut down*: because, as we shall presently observe, covenants were solemnly ratified by cutting or dividing animals asunder. It may also be derived from the same root in a very different signification: for, as ברא properly signifies to *create*; so, me-taphorically, to *ordain*, or *dispose*, which is the meaning of διατιϑεσϑαι. And hence it is, that the Hellenist Jews make use of το χτιζειν. Certainly it is in this sense that Peter, 1 Pet. ii. 13. calls εξεσια, *power appointed by men*, and for human purposes, ανϑρωπινη χτισις, *the ordinance of man;* to which, I think, Grotius has learnedly observed on the title of the New Testament. Others had rather derive it from בדה, as שבית from שכה, signifying, besides other things, to *choose*. And in covenants, especially of friendship, there is a choice of persons between whom, of things about which, and of con-dition upon which, a covenant is entered into: nor is this im-properly observed.

III. But בדית is variously taken in scripture: sometimes *improperly*, and sometimes *properly*. *Improperly*, it denotes the following things. 1st. An immutable ordinance made about a thing: In this sense God mentions his " covenant of the day, and his covenant of the night," Jer. xxxiii. 20. That is, that fixed ordinance made about the uninterrupted vicissitude of day and night; which, chap. xxxi. 36. is called חק, that is, *statute, limited,* or *fixed,* which nothing is to be added to, or taken from. In this sense is included the notion of a *testament,* or of a last irrevocable will. Thus God said, Numb. xviii. 19. " I have given thee, and thy sons, and thy daughters with thee, עילם חיא לחם עילם בדית מלח, by a statute for ever: it is a covenant of salt for ever." This observation is of use, more fully to explain the nature of the covenant of grace, which the apostle proposes under the similitude of a *testament,* the execution of which depends upon the death of the testator, Heb. ix. 15, 16, 17. To which notion both the Hebrew בדיח, and the Greek διαϑηϰη may lead us. 2dly. A sure and stable *promise,* though not mutual, Exod. xxxiv. 10. " Behold I make a covenant; before all thy people I will do marvels." Isa. lix. 21. " This is my covenant with them, my Spirit shall not depart from them." 3dly. It signifies a *precept,* and to cut or make a covenant, is to give a precept, Jer. xxxiv. 13, 14. " I made a covenant with your fathers——Saying, at the end of seven years, let ye go every man his brother." Hence appears in what sense the decalogue is called God's covenant. But *properly,* it signifies a mutual agreement between parties, with respect to something. Such a covenant passed between Abraham, Mamre, Eshcol, and Aner, who are called, *confederates with Abraham,* Gen. xiv. 13. Such also was that between Isaac and Abimelech, Gen. xxvi. 28, 29.: between Jonathan and David, 1 Sam. xviii. 3. And of this kind is likewise that which we are now to treat of between God and Man.

IV. No less equivocal is the διαϑηϰη of the Greeks: which, both singularly and plurally, very often denotes a testament: as Budæus shews, in his *Comment. Ling. Græc.* from Isocrates, Oeschines, Demosthenes, and others. In this sense, we hinted, it was used by the apostle, Heb. ix. 15. Sometimes also it denotes a *law,* which is a rule of life. For, the Orphici and Pythagoreans denominated the rules of living, prescribed to their pupils, according to Grotius. It also often signifies an *engagement* or *agreement;* wherefore Hesychius explains it by συνωμοσια, *confederacy.* There is none of these significations but will be of future use in the progress of this work.

V. Making a covenant, the Hebrews call, בדית בדיות, *to strike a covenant,* in the same manner as the Greeks and Latins, *ferire, icere, percutere fœdus.* Which doubtless took its rise from the ancient ceremony of slaying animals, by

which covenants were ratified. Of which rite we observe
very ancient traces, Gen. xv. 9, 10. This was either
then first commanded by God, or borrowed from some extant custom. Emphatical is what Polybius, Book iv. page
398. relates of the Cynæthenses, " over the slaughtered
victims they took a solemn oath, and plighted faith to
each other :" a phrase plainly similar to what God uses,
Psalm l. 5. " those that have made a covenant with me
by sacrifice." They also used to *pass in the middle* between
the divided parts of the victim cut asunder, Jer. xxxiv. 18.
Whoever wants to know more about this rite, may consult
Grotius on Matt. xxvi. 28. and Bochart in his Hierozoicon,
Book ii. c. xxxiii. p. 325. and Ouwen's Theologum, Book iii.
c. i. It was likewise a custom, that agreements and com-
pacts were ratified by solemn feasts. Examples of which are
obvious in scripture. Thus Isaac, having made a covenant
with Abimelech, is said to have made a great feast, and to
have eat with them, Gen. xxvi. 30. In like manner acted his
son Jacob, after having made a covenant with Laban, Gen.
xxxi. 54. We read of a like federal feast, 2 Sam. iii. 20.
where a relation is given of the feast which David made for
Abner and his attendants, who came to make a covenant with
him in the name of the people. It was also customary among
the heathen, as the learned Stuckius shews in his Antiquitates
Convivales, lib. I. c. xl.

VI. Nor were these rites without their significancy : the
cutting the animals asunder, denoted, that, in the same manner, the perjured and covenant-breakers should be cut asunder, by the vengeance of God. And to this purpose is what
God says, Jer. xxxiv. 18, 19, 20. " And I will give the men
that have transgressed my covenant, which have not performed
the words of the covenant, which they had made before me,
when they cut the calf in twain, and passed between the parts
thereof. I will even give them into the hands of their enemies,
and their dead bodies shall be for meat unto the fowls of the
heaven, and to the beasts of the earth." See 1 Sam. xi. 7.
An ancient form of these execrations is extant in Livy, Book i.
" The Roman people do not among the first break these conditions; but if they should avowedly, and through treachery,
break them, do thou, O Jupiter, on that day, thus strike the
Roman people, as I do now this hog; and be the stroke the
heavier, as thy power is the greater." By the ceremony of
the confederates passing between the parts cut asunder, was
signified, that being now united by the strictest ties of religion,
and by a solemn oath, they formed but one body, as Vatablus

has remarked on Gen. xv. 10. These feasts were tokens of a sincere and lasting friendship.

VII. But when God in the solemnities of his covenants with men, thought proper to use these, or the like rites, the significancy was still more noble and divine. They who made covenant with God by sacrifice, not only submitted to punishment, if impiously revolting from God, they slighted his covenant; but God likewise signified to them, that all the stability of the covenant of grace was founded on the sacrifice of Christ, and that the soul and body of Christ were one day to be violently separated asunder. All the promises of God in him are yea, and in him amen, 2 Cor. i. 20. His blood is the blood of the New Testament, Matt. xxvi. 28. in a far more excellent manner than that with which Moses sprinkled both the altar and the people entered into covenant, Exod. xxiv. 8. Those sacred banquets, to which the covenanted were admitted before the Lord, especially that instituted by the Lord Jesus, under the New Testament, do most effectually seal or ratify that intimate communion and fellowship there is between Christ and believers.

VIII. There are learned men, who from this rite would explain that phrase, which we have, Numb. xviii. 19. and 2 Chron. xiv. 5. of " a covenant of salt," that is, of a covenant of friendship, of a stable and perpetual nature. Which seems to be so denominated, because salt was usually made use of in sacrifices to signify that the covenant was made sure upon observing the customary rites, says Rivet on Genesis, Exercit. 136. Unless we would rather suppose, a regard to be here had to the firmness of salt, by which it resists putrefaction and corruption, and therefore prolongs the duration of things, and in a manner renders them everlasting. For that reason, Lot's wife is thought to have been turned to a pillar of salt: not so much, as Augustin remarks, to be for a seasoning to us, as a lasting and perpetual monument of the divine judgment. For all salt is not subject to melting: Pliny says, that some Arabs build walls and houses of blocks of salt, and cement them with water, Nat. Hist. L. xxxi. c. 7.

IX. Having premised these things in general about terms of art, let us now enquire into the thing itself, *viz.* the nature of the covenant of God with man; which I thus define: A covenant of God with man, is an agreement between God and man, about the way of obtaining consummate happiness; including a commination of eternal destruction, with which the contemner of the happiness, offered in that way, is to be punished.

X. The covenant does, on the part of God, comprize three things in general. 1st. *A promise* of consummate happiness in eternal life. 2dly. *A designation* and *prescription* of the condition, by the performance of which, man acquires a right to the promise. 3dly. *A penal sanction* against those, who do not come up to the prescribed condition. All these things regard the whole man, or ολοκληρος, in Paul's phrase, as consisting of soul and body. God's promise of happiness is to each part, he requires the sanctification of each, and threatens each with destruction. And so this covenant makes God appear glorious in the whole man.

XI. To engage in such a covenant with the rational creature, formed after the divine image, is entirely worthy of, and by no means unbecoming of God. For it was impossible but God should propose himself to the rational creature, as a pattern of holiness, in conformity to which he ought to frame himself and all his actions, carefully keeping, and always exerting the activity of that original righteousness, which he was, from his very origin, endowed with. God cannot but bind man to love, worship, and seek him, as the chief good; nor is it conceivable, how God should require man to love and seek him, and yet refuse to be found by man, loving, seeking, and esteeming him as his chief good, longing, hungering, and thirsting, after him alone. Who can conceive it to be worthy of God, that he should thus say to man, I am willing that thou seekest me only; but on condition of never finding me: to be ardently longed for above every thing else, with the greatest hunger and thirst; but yet, never to be satisfied. And the justice of God no less requires, that man, upon rejecting the happiness, offered on the most equitable terms, should be punished with the privation of it, and likewise incur the severest indignation of God, whom he has despised. Whence it appears, that from the very consideration of the divine perfections, it may be fairly deduced, that he has prescribed a certain law to man, as the condition of enjoying happiness, which consists in the fruition of God; enforced with the threatening of a curse against the rebel. In which we have just now said, that the whole of the covenant consisted. But of each of these we shall have fuller scope to speak hereafter.

XII. Thus far, we have considered the one party of the covenant of God: man becomes the other, when he consents thereto, embracing the good promised by God, engaging to an exact observance of the condition required; and upon the violation thereof, voluntarily owning himself obnoxious to

the threatened curse. This the scripture calls, עָבוֹר כִּבְרִית יְהוָה,
" to enter into covenant with the Lord," Deut. xxix. 12.
" and to enter into a curse and an oath," Neh. x. 29. In this
curse (Paul calls it, 2 Cor. ix. 13. ὁμολογια, professed subjection) conscience presents itself a witness, that God's stipulation or covenant is just, and that this method of coming
to the enjoyment of God is highly becoming; and that there
is no other way of obtaining the promise. And hence the evils
which God threatens to the transgressors of the covenant, are
called " the curses of the covenant," Deut. xxix. 21. which
man on consenting to the covenant, voluntarily makes himself
obnoxious to. The effect of this curse on the man who stands
not to the covenant, is called " the vengeance of the covenant,"
Lev. xxvi. 25. The form of a stipulation, or acceptance, we
have, Psal. xxvii. 8. " When thou saidest, Seek ye my face,
my heart said unto thee, Thy face, Lord, will I seek." Where
the voluntary astipulation or acceptance, answers to the stipulation or covenant, made in the name of God by conscience,
his minister.

XIII. Man, upon the proposal of this covenant, could not
without guilt, refuse giving this astipulation or acceptance.
1st. In virtue of the law, which universally binds him, humbly to accept every thing proposed by God: to whom it is
the essential duty of every rational creature to be subject in
every respect. 2dly. On account of the high sovereignty of
God, who may dispose of his own benefits, and appoint the
condition of enjoying them with a supreme authority, and
without being accountable to any: and at the same time enjoin man, to strive for the attainment of the blessings offered,
on the condition prescribed. And hence this covenant, as
subsisting between parties infinitely unequal, assumes the
nature of those, which the Greeks called *Injunctions*, or
covenants from commands; of which Grotius speaks in his
Jus. Bell. and Pacis, lib. ii. c. 15. § 6. Hence it is, that
Paul translates the words of Moses, Exod. xxiv. 8. " behold
the blood of the covenant which the Lord hath made with
you," thus, Heb. ix. 20. : " this is the blood of the testament
which God hath enjoined unto you." It is not left to man
to accept or reject at pleasure God's covenant. Man is commanded to accept it, and to press after the attainment of the
promises in the way pointed out by the covenant. Not to
desire the promises, is to refuse the goodness of God. To
reject the precepts is to refuse the sovereignty and holiness of
God; and not to submit to the sanction, is to deny God's justice. And therefore the apostle affirms of the covenant of

God, that it is νενομοθετηται reduced to the form of a law, Heb.
viii. 6. by which man is obliged to an acceptance. 3dly. It
follows from that love, which man naturally owes to himself,
and by which he is carried to the chief good; for enjoying
which there remains no method beside the condition prescribed by God. 4thly. Man's very conscience dictates, that this
covenant is in all its parts highly equitable. What can be
framed even by thought itself more equitable, than that man,
esteeming God as his chief good, should seek his happiness in
him, and rejoice at the offer of that goodness? Should cheerfully receive the law, which is a transcript of the divine holiness, as the rule of his nature and actions? In fine, should submit his guilty head to the most just vengeance of heaven,
should he happen to make light of this promise, and violate
the law? From which it follows, that man was not at liberty
to reject God's covenant.

XIV. God, by this covenant, acquires no new right over
man; which, if we duly consider the matter, neither is, nor
can be founded on any benefit of God, or misdemeanor of man,
as Arminius argues: nor in any thing without God; the principal or alone foundation of it being the sovereign majesty of
the most high God. Because God is the blessed, and self-
sufficient Being, therefore he is the only potentate, these two
being joined together by Paul, 1 Tim. vi. 15. Nor can God's
power and right over the creatures, be diminished or increased
by any thing extrinsic to God. A thing which ought to be
deemed unworthy of his sovereignty and independence: of
which we shall soon treat more fully. Only God, in this covenant, shews what right he has over man. But man, upon
his accepting the covenant, and performing the condition, does
acquire some right to demand of God the promise; for God
has, by his promises, made himself a debtor to man. Or, to
speak in a manner more becoming God, he was pleased to
make his performing his promises, a debt due to himself, to
his goodness, justice, and veracity. And to man in covenant,
and continuing stedfast to it, he granted the right of expecting and requiring, that God should satisfy the demands of his
goodness, justice, and truth, by the performance of the promises.
And thus to man as stipulating, or consenting to the covenant,
God says, that " he will be his God," Deut. xxvi. 17. That
is, he will give him full liberty to glory in God, as his God,
and to expect from him, that he will become to man, in covenant with him, what he is to himself, even a fountain of consummate happiness.

XV. In scripture, we find two covenants of God with man:

The Covenant of Works, otherwise called the Covenant of Nature, or the Legal; and the Covenant of Grace. The apostle teacheth us this distinction, Rom. iii. 27. where he mentions the law of works, and the law of faith; by the law of works, understanding that doctrine which points out the way in which, by means of works, salvation is obtained; and by the law of faith, that doctrine which directs by faith to obtain salvation. The form of the covenant of works is, " the man which doth those things shall live by them," Rom. x. 5. That of the covenant of grace is, " whosoever believeth in him, shall not be ashamed,". ib. ver. 11. These covenants agree, 1st. That in both, the contracting parties are the same, God and man. 2dly. In both, the same promise of eternal life, consisting in the immediate fruition of God. 3dly. The condition of both is the same, viz. perfect obedience to the law. Nor would it have been worthy of God to admit man to a blessed communion with him, but in the way of unspotted holiness. 4thly. In both, *the same end*, the glory of the most unspotted goodness of God. But in these following particulars they differ. 1st. The character or relation of God and man, in the covenant of works, is different from what it is in the covenant of grace. In the former God treats as the supreme law-giver, and the chief good, rejoicing to make his innocent creature a partaker of his happiness. In the latter, as infinitely merciful, adjudging life to the elect sinner consistent with his wisdom and justice. 2dly. In the covenant of works there was no mediator: in that of grace, there is the mediator Christ Jesus. 3dly. In the covenant of works, the condition of perfect obedience was required, to be performed by man himself, who had consented to it. In that of grace, the same condition is proposed, as to be, or as already performed, by a mediator. And in this substitution of the person, consists the principal and essential difference of the covenants. 4thly. In the covenant of works, man is considered as working, and the reward to be given as of debt; and therefore man's glorying is not excluded, but he may glory as a faithful servant may do upon the right discharge of his duty, and may claim the reward promised to his working. In the covenant of grace, man in himself ungodly is considered in the covenant, as believing; and eternal life is considered as the merit of the mediator, and as given to man out of free grace, which excludes all boasting, besides the glorying of the believing sinner in God, as his merciful Saviour. 5thly. In the covenant of works, something is required of man as a condition, which performed entitles him to the reward. The covenant of grace, with respect to us, consists of the absolute promises of God, in which the mediator, the life to be obtained by him, the faith by which we may be made partakers of him, and of the benefits purchased by him, and the perseverance in. that faith ; in a word, the whole of salvation, and all the requisites to it, are absolutely promised. 6thly. The special end of the covenant of works, was the manifestation of the holiness, goodness, and justice of God, conspicuous in the most perfect law, most liberal promise, and in that recompense of reward, to be given to those, who seek him with their whole heart. The special end of the covenant of grace is, the praise of the glory of his grace, Eph. i. 6. and the revelation of his unsearchable and manifold wisdom : which divine perfections shine forth with lustre in the gift of a mediator, by whom the sinner is admitted to complete salvation, without any dishonour to the holiness, justice, and truth of God. There is also a demonstration of the all-sufficiency of God, by which not only man, but even a sinner, which is more surprising, may be restored to union and communion with God. But all this will be more fully explained in what follows.

CHAP. II.

Of the Contracting Parties in the Covenant of Works.

I. W E begin with the consideration *of the covenant of works*, otherwise called, *of the law* and *of nature ;* because prescribed *by the law*, requiring *works* as the condition, and founded upon, and coeval with *nature.* This covenant is an agreement between God and Adam, formed after the image of God, as the head and root, or representative of the whole human race ; by which God promised eternal life and happiness to him, if he yielded obedience to all his commands ; threatening him with death if he failed but in the least point: and Adam accepted this condition. To this purpose are these two sentences, afterwards inculcated, on the repetition of the law, Lev. xviii. 5. and Deut. xxvii. 26.

II. The better to understand this subject, these four things are to be explained. 1st. The contracting parties. 2dly. The condition prescribed. 3dly. The promises. 4thly. The threatening.

III. The contracting parties here, are God and Adam. God, as sovereign and supreme Lord, prescribing with absolute power, what he judges equitable: as goodness itself, or the chief good, promising communion with himself, in which man's principal happiness lies, while obeying, and " doing what is well-pleasing to him :" as justice itself, or sovereignly just, threatening death to the rebel. Adam sustained a twofold relation. 1st. As man. 2dly. As head and root, or representative of mankind. In the former relation, he was a rational creature, and under the law to God, innocent, created after the divine image, and endued with sufficient powers to fulfil all righteousness. All these things are presupposed in man, to render him a fit object for God to enter into covenant with.

IV. Man therefore, just from the hands of his Maker, had a soul shining with rays of a divine light, and adorned with the brightest wisdom ; whereby he was not only perfectly master of the nature of created things, but was delighted with the contemplation of the supreme and increated truth, the eyes of his understanding being constantly fixed on the perfections of his God ; from the consideration of which he gathered, by the justest reasoning, what was equitable and just, what worthy of God and of himself. He also had the purest holiness of will, acquiescing in God as the supreme truth, revering him as the most dread majesty, loving him as the chief and only good ; and, for the sake of God, holding dear whatever his mind, divinely taught, pointed out as grateful, and like to, and expressive of his perfections : in fine, whatever contributed to the acquiring an intimate and immediate union with him ; delighting in the communion of his God ; which was now allowed him, panting after further communion, raising himself thereto by the creatures, as so many scales or steps ; and finally setting forth the praises of his most unspotted holiness as the most perfect pattern, according to which he was to frame both himself and his actions to the utmost. This is, as Elihu significantly expresses it, Job xxxiv. 9. " delighting himself with God." This rectitude of the soul was accompanied with a most regular temperature of the whole body, all whose members, as instruments of righteousness, presented themselves ready and active at the first intimation of his holy will. Nor was it becoming God to form a rational creature for any other purpose than his own glory; which such a creature, unless wise and holy, could neither perceive nor celebrate, as shining forth in the other works of God ; destitute of this light, and deprived of this endument, what could it prove but the reproach of his Creator, and every way unfit to answer the end of his creation. All these particulars the wisest of kings, Eccles. vii. 29. has thrown together with a striking simplicity, when he says; " Lo! this only have I found, that God hath made man upright."

V. What I have just said of the wisdom of the first man, ought, I think, to be extended so far, as not to suppose him, in the state of innocence, ignorant of the mystery of the Trinity. For it is necessary above all things, for the perfection of the human understanding, to be well acquainted with what it ought to know and believe concerning its God. And it may justly be doubted, whether he does not worship a God entirely unknown, nay, whether he at all worships the true God, who does not know and worship him, as subsisting in three persons. Whoever represents God to himself in any other light, represents not God, but an empty phantom, and an idol of his own brain. Epiphanius seems to have had this argument in view, when, in his Panarius, p. 9. he thus writes of Adam : " He was no idolater, for he knew God the Father, Son, and Holy Ghost : and he was a prophet, and knew that the Father said to the Son, Let us make man."

VI. These last words furnish a new argument: for since God, in the work of the creation, manifested himself a Trinity, " the Father made the worlds by the Son," Heb. i. 2. the Holy Ghost cherished the waters by brooding upon them ; and the whole Trinity addressed themselves, by mutual consultation, to the creation of man ; it is not therefore credible this mystery should be entirely unknown to the Protoplast or first parent; unless we can suppose Adam ignorant of his Creator, who was likewise the Son and the Holy Ghost. It cannot certainly be without design, that the scripture, when speaking of man's Creator, so often uses the plural number : as Is. liv. 5. בעליך עשיך, which literally signifies, *thy husbands, thy makers*, Psal. cxlix. 2. ישראל בעשיו ישמח, *Let Israel rejoice and his makers*. Nay, requires man to attend to this, and engrave it on his mind, Eccl. xii. 1. זכר את בוראיך, *remember thy creators*. It is criminal when man neglects it ; and says not Job xxxv. 10. איה אלוה עשי, *where is God. my makers ?* Which phrases, unless referred to a Trinity of persons, might appear to be dangerous. But it is absurd to suppose Adam ignorant concerning his Creator, of that which God does not suffer his posterity to be ignorant of at this time; especially as God created man to be the herald of his being and perfections in the new world. But it certainly tends to display the glory of God, that he should particularly celebrate, not only the divine perfections, but likewise how they subsist in the distinct persons of the Deity, and the manner and order of their operation. Admirably to this purpose speaks Basil of

Seleucia, serm. 2. Take particular notice of that expression, *Let us make man*; again, this word used plurally, hints at the persons of the Godhead, and presents a Trinity to our knowledge. *This knowledge therefore is coeval with the creation.* Nor should it seem strange, that afterwards it should be taught: since it is one of those things, of which mention is made *in the very first creation.*

VII. I own Adam could not, from the bare contemplation of nature, without revelation, discover this mystery. But this I am fully persuaded of, that God revealed some things to man, not dictated by nature. For, whence did he know the command about the Tree of Knowledge, and whence the meaning of the Tree of Life, but by God's declaring it to him? whence such a knowledge of his wife's creation, as to pronounce her flesh of his flesh, and bone of his bone, but from divine revelation? Seeing then God had revealed to man many things, and those indeed not of such moment, can we believe he would conceal from him a thing, the knowledge of which was so highly expedient to the perfection of man and the glory of God? That learned man therefore, was mistaken who insisted, that the knowledge of the Trinity *exceeded the happiness of Adam's state, which was merely natural.* For it was not so merely natural, that Adam only knew what the alone consideration of nature could suggest. The contrary we have just shewn. And it must be deemed natural to that state, that innocent man, who had familiar intercourse with his God, should learn from his own mouth what might render him fitter to celebrate his praises. The learned Zanchius observes in his book de Creat. Hom. 1. 1. c. 1. § 12. that most of the fathers were of opinion, that Adam, seeing he was such, and so great a friend of God before his fall, had sometimes seen God in a bodily appearance, and heard him speak: and adds, " but this was always the Son of God." And a little after, " Christ therefore is the Jehovah, who brought Adam and placed him in Paradise, and spoke with him." Thus the ancients believed, that the Son of God did then also reveal himself to Adam, and conversed with him.

VIII. And it seems rather too bold to affirm, " that the œconomy subsisting between the three persons, is so principally taken up in procuring the salvation of mankind, that the knowledge thereof could not pertain to the state of innocence; in which there was no place either for salvation or redemption." For Moses declares the œconomy of the divine persons at the very creation. And while the gospel explains that admirable œconomy, as taken up in procuring the salva-

tion of mankind, it, at the same time, carries our thoughts
up to that œconomy, manifested in the first creation of the
world. If now it is so useful and pleasant to think, that the
Son of God our Saviour, " is the beginning of the creation of
God," Rev. iii. 14. " By whom were created thrones and dominions, things visible and invisible; that he might have the
pre-eminence in all things," Col. i. 16, 18. both of the works
of nature and of grace : and that the holy Spirit, now fitting
up a new world of grace in our hearts, did at first brood on
the waters, and make them pregnant with so many noble
creatures ; and thus to ascend to the consideration of the same
œconomy in the works of creation and nature, which is now
revealed to us in the works of salvation and grace. Who
then can refuse that Adam in innocence had the same knowledge of God in three persons, though ignorant what each
person, in his order, was to perform in saving sinners ? Add
to this, that though in that state of Adam, there was no room
for redemption, yet there was for salvation and life eternal.
The symbol of which was the Tree of Life, which even then
bore the image of the Son of God : see Rev. ii. 7. For *in him
was life*, John i. 4. which symbol had been in vain, if the
meaning thereof had been unknown to Adam.

IX. In this rectitude of man principally consists that image
of God, which the scripture so often recommends; and
which Paul expressly places *in knowledge*, Col. iii. 10. *in
righteousness and true holiness*, Eph. iv. 24. In which places
he so describes the image of God, which is renewed in us by
the Spirit of grace, as at the same time to hint, that it is the
same with which man was originally created : neither can
there be different images of God. For as God cannot but be
wise and holy, and as such, be a pattern to the rational creature, it follows, that a creature wise and holy, is, as such,
the expression or resemblance of God. And it is a thing quite
impossible, but God must own his own likeness to consist in
this rectitude of the whole man ; or that he should ever acknowledge a foolish and perverse creature to be like him :
which would be an open denial of his perfections. It is finely
observed by a learned man, that *true holiness* is not only opposed to *hypocrisy* or *simulation*, or to *typical purity*, but
that it denotes a *holy study of truth*, proceeding from the
love of God. For, ὅσιος, to which answers the Hebrew חמיד,
signifies in scripture, *one studious in, and eager after good.*
This *true holiness*, therefore, denotes such a desire of pleasing
God, as is agreeable to the truth known of, and in him, and
loved for him.

X. But I see not, why the same learned person would have the *righteousness*, mentioned by Paul, Eph. iv. 24. to be a privilege peculiar to the covenant of grace, which we obtain in Christ, and which Adam was without; meaning by the word *righteousness*, a title or right to eternal life; which, it is owned, Adam had not, as his state of probation was not yet at an end. In opposition to this assertion, I offer these following considerations. 1st. There is no necessity, by *righteousness* to understand a right to eternal life. For that term often denotes a virtue, a constant resolution of giving every one his due, as Eph. v. 9. Where the apostle, treating of sanctification, writes, *for the fruit of the Spirit is in all goodness*, righteousness, *and truth.* The learned person himself was aware of this, who elsewhere speaks thus, (on Gen. v. § 9.) " Righteousness is, first, the rectitude of actions, whether of the soul, or of the members; and their agreement with sound reason : namely, that they may easily avoid condemnation or blame, and obtain commendation and praise." So Tit. iii. 5. " Works of righteousness." And hence the denomination of just or righteous, denotes a blameless, or a praiseworthy person." Since then, that word signifies elsewhere such a rectitude, why not here too? Especially as it is indisputable, that such righteousness belonged to the image of God in Adam. 2dly. It ought not to be urged, that here *righteousness* is joined with *holiness*, and therefore thus to be distinguished from it ; as that the latter shall denote an inherent good quality, and the former a right to life. For it may be answered, *first*, that it is no unusual thing with the holy Spirit, to express the same thing by different words. " It is to be observed," says Ursinus, Quest. 18. Catech. " that righteousness and holiness were in us the same thing before the fall; namely, an inherent conformity to God and the law." Nor does the celebrated Cocceius himself speak otherwise on Psal. xv. § 2. " But רמ.צ, *righteousness*, if you consider the law of works, signifies, in the largest sense, every thing that is honest, every thing that is true, every thing that is holy." Secondly, Suppose we should distinguish righteousness from holiness, it follows not, that it is to be distinguished in this manner ; for there are testimonies, in which no such distinction can take place : as Luke i. 74, 75.—*Serve him in* holiness and righteousness *before him :* and 1 Thess. ii. 10. *Ye are witnesses and God also*, how holily, and justly, and unblameably, *we behaved ourselves among you that believe.* And 1 Kings iii. 6.—*he walked before thee in truth and in* righteousness, *and in uprightness of heart.*

Where *righteousness*, though added to holiness, can signify
nothing but a virtue of the soul, and the exercise of it. Thirdly, But if we must absolutely distinguish these two things,
it may be done many ways, 1st. So as to refer holiness to
God ; righteousness to men. Thus Philo, concerning Abraham, says, holiness is considered as towards God ; righteousness as towards men : and the emperor Antonine, Book 7. §
66. says of Socrates, In human things, just, in divine, holy.
2dly. Or so as to say, that both words denote universal virtue, (for even righteousness is said of the worship of God,
Luke i. 75. and holiness referred to men ; Maximus Tyrius,
Dissert. 26. says of the same Socrates, Pious towards God,
holy towards men,) but in a different respect : so as holiness
shall denote virtue, as it is the love and expression of the
divine purity ; as Plato explains holiness by the love of God :
righteousness, indeed, may signify the same virtue, as it is a
conformity to the prescribed rule, and an obedience to the
commands of God. Whether it be δικαιον, right, righteous to
hearken unto God, Acts iv. 19. 3dly. Ursinus, quest. 6.
Catech. speaks somewhat differently, saying, " that righteousness and holiness, may, in the text of Paul, and in the
catechism, be taken for one and the same, or be distinguished ;
for *righteousness* may be understood of those internal and external actions ; which agree with the right judgment of mind,
and with the law of God ; *holiness* be understood of the
qualities of them." So that there is nothing to constrain us to
explain righteousness here of a right to life ;• but there are
many things to persuade us to the contrary. For, 1st. That
image of God, which is renewed in us by regeneration, consists in *absolute qualities* inherent in the soul, which are as so
many resemblances of the perfections of God : but a right or
title to life is a mere *relation*. 2dly. The image of God consists in something, which is produced in *man himself*, either
by the first, or the new creation : but the right to life rests
wholly on the righteousness and merits of Christ ; things entirely *without us*, Phil. iii. 9. *Not having my own righteousness.* 3dly. The apostle in the place before us is not
treating of *justification*, where this right should have been
mentioned ; but of *sanctification*, and the rule thereof ; where
it would be improper to speak of any such thing. 4thly.
They who adhere to this new explanation of righteousness,
appear without any just cause to contradict the Catechism,
quest. 6. and with less force to oppose the Socinians, who
maintain, that the image of God, after which we are regenerated in Christ, is not the same with that, after which

Adam was created. And yet these learned men equally detest his error with ourselves. These considerations make us judge it safer to explain righteousness, so as to make it a part of the image of God, after which Adam was created.

XI. But if we take in the whole extent of the image of God, we say, it is made up of these three parts. 1st. *Antecedently*, that it consists in the spiritual and immortal nature of the soul, and in the faculties of understanding and will. 2dly. *Formally* and principally, in these enduments, or qualities of the soul, *viz.* righteousness, and holiness. 3dly. *Consequentially*, in the immortality of the whole man, and his dominion over the creatures. The first of these was, as one elegantly expresses it, as precious ground on which the image of God might be drawn and formed : the second, that very image itself, and resemblance of the divinity : the third, the lustre of that image widely spreading its glory ; and as rays, not only adorning the soul, but the whole man, even his very body ; and rendering him the lord and head of the world, and at the same time immortal, as being the friend and confederate of the eternal God.

XII. The principal strokes of this image, Plato certainly knew ; who defines happiness to be ὁμοίωσιν τῳ Θεῷ, the resemblance of God : and this resemblance he places in piety, justice, and prudence ; this last to temper and regulate the two former : his words are excellent, and deserve to be here transcribed : τὴν δὲ δνητὴν φύσιν, καὶ τόνδε τον τόπον τό κακόν περιπολεῖ ἐξ ἀνάγκης διοκάι πειρᾶσθαι χρη ἐνθένδε ἐκεῖσι φεύγειν ὅτι τάχιςα φυγὴ δὲ ὁμόιωσις Θεῷ καλὰ τὸ δυνατόν Ὁμόιωσις δὲ δίκαιον καὶ ὅσιον μεῖλὰ φρονήσεως γενέσθαι. " This mortal nature, and this place of abode, are necessarily encompassed with evil. We are therefore, with the utmost expedition, to fly from it : this flight is an assimilation to God as far as may be : and this assimilation is justice and piety, accompanied with prudence." Vid. Lipsii Manuduct. ad. stoicam philosophiam, lib. 2. Dissert. 13.

XIII. God gave to man the charge of this his image, as the most excellent deposite of heaven, and, if kept pure and inviolate, the earnest of a greater good ; for that end he endued him with sufficient powers from his very formation, so as to stand in need of no other habitual grace. It was only requisite, that God, by the continual influx of his providence, should preserve those powers, and excite them to all and each of their acts. For, there can be no state conceived, in which the creature can act independently of the Creator ; not excepting the angels themselves, though now confirmed in holiness and happiness.

XIV. And thus, indeed, Adam was in covenant with God, as a *man*, created after the image of God, and furnished with sufficient abilities to preserve that image. But there is another relation, in which he was considered as the head and representative of mankind, both *federal* and *natural*. So that God said to Adam, as once to the Israelites, Deut. xxix. 14, 15. "neither with you only do I make this covenant, and this oath; but also with him that is not here with us this day." The whole history of the first man proves, that he is not to be looked upon as an individual person, but that the whole human nature is considered as in him. For it was not said to our first parents only, *increase and multiply*; by virtue of which word, the propagation of mankind is still continued: nor is it true of Adam only; *it is not good that the man should be alone*: nor does that conjugal law, *therefore shall a man leave his father and his mother, and they shall be one flesh*, concern him alone: which Christ still urges, Matt. xix. 5.: nor did the penalty, threatened by God upon Adam's sinning, *thou shalt surely die*, affect him alone, but *death passed upon all men*, according to the apostle's observation, Rom. v. 12. All which loudly proclaim, that Adam was here considered as the *head* of mankind.

XV. This also appears from that beautiful opposition of the first and second Adam, which Paul pursues at large, Rom. v. 15, &c. For, as the second Adam does, in the Covenant of Grace, represent all the elect, in such a manner that they are accounted to have done and suffered themselves, what he did and suffered, in their name and stead: so likewise the first Adam was the representative of all that were to descend from him.

XVI. And that God was righteous in this constitution, is by no means to be disputed. Nor does it become us to entertain doubts about the right of God, nor enquire too curiously into it; much less to measure it by the standard of any right established amongst us despicable mortals, when the matter of fact is evident and undisputed. We are always to speak in vindication of God; "that thou mightest be justified when thou speakest, and be clear when thou judgest." Psal. li. 4. He must, surely, be utterly unacquainted with the majesty of the Supreme Being, with his most pure and unspotted holiness, which in every respect is most consistent with himself, who presumes to scan his actions, and call his equity to account. A freedom this, no earthly father would bear in a son, no king in a subject, nor master in a servant. And do we, mean worms of the earth, take upon us to use such freedom with the Judge of the whole universe ! As often as our murmuring flesh dares to repine and cry out, *the ways of the Lord are not equal;* so often let us oppose thereto, *are not thy ways unequal?* Ezek. xviii. 25.

XVII. However, it generally holds that we more calmly acquiesce in the determinations of God, when we understand the reasons of them. Let us therefore see, whether here also we cannot demonstrate the equity of the divine right. For what if we should consider the matter thus? If Adam had, in his own, and in our name, stood to the conditions of the covenant; if, after a course of probation, he had been confirmed in happiness, and we, his posterity, in him, if, fully satisfied with the delights of animal life, we had, together with him, been translated to the joys of heaven.; none certainly would then repine that he was included in the head of mankind : every one would have commended both the wisdom and goodness of God : not the least suspicion of injustice would have arisen on account of God's putting the first man into a state of probation in the room of all, and not every individual for himself. How should that, which in this event would have been deemed just, be unjust on a contrary event? For, neither is the justice nor injustice of actions to be judged of by the event.

XVIII. Besides, what mortal now can flatter himself, that, placed in the same circumstances with Adam, he would have better consulted his own interest? Adam was neither without wisdom, nor holiness, nor a desire after true happiness, nor an aversion to the miseries denounced by God against the sinner ; nor, in fine, without any of those things, by which he might expect to keep upon his guard against all sin : and yet he suffered himself to be drawn aside by the craft of a flattering seducer. And dost thou, iniquitous censurer of the ways of the Lord, presume thou wouldst have better used thy free will? Nay, on the contrary, all thy actions cry aloud, that thou approvest, that thou art highly pleased with, and always takest example from that deed of thy first parent, about which thou so unjustly complainest. For, when thou transgressest the commands of God, when thou settest less by the will of the Supreme Being than by thy lusts, when thou preferrest earthly to heavenly things, present to future, when, by thine own choice, thou seekest after happiness, but not that which is true; and, instead of taking the right way, goest into by-paths; is not that the very same as if thou didst so often eat of the forbidden tree? Why then dost thou presume to blame

God for taking a compendious way, including all in one; well knowing that the case of each in particular, when put to the test, would have proved the same.

CHAP. III.

Of the Law, or Condition, of the Covenant of Works.

I. Hitherto we have treated of *the Contracting Parties:* let us now take a view of the condition prescribed by this covenant. Where first we are to consider *the Law of the Covenant,* then *the Observance* of that law. The law of the covenant is two-fold. 1st. *The law of nature,* implanted in Adam at his crea-tion. 2dly. *The symbolical law,* concerning the tree of know-ledge of good and evil.

II. The law of nature is the rule of good and evil, inscribed by God on man's conscience, even at his creation, and there-fore binding upon him by divine authority. That such a law was connate with, and as it were implanted in the man, ap-pears from the reliques, which, like the ruins of some noble building, are still extant in every man; namely, from those common notions, by which the heathens themselves distin-guished right from wrong, and by which "they were a law to themselves, which shews the work of the law written in their hearts, their conscience bearing witness," Rom. ii. 14, 15. From which we gather, that all these things were complete in man, when newly formed after the image of God.

III. Whatever the conscience of man dictates to be virtu-ous, or otherwise, it does so in the name of God, whose vice-gerent it is, in man, and the depositary of his commands. This, if I mistake not, is David's meaning, Psal. xxvii. 8. לְךָ אָמַר לִבִּי, *to thee,* that is, for thee, in thy stead, my heart says, or my conscience. This conscience therefore was also called a God by the heathen: as in this, Iambic, Βροτοῖς ἅπασιν ἡ συνείδησις Θεός; *In all men conscience is a God.* Plato in *Philebus,* calls rea-son *a God dwelling in us.* And hence we are not to think that the supreme rule in the law of nature is its agreement or disagreement with the rational nature, but that it is the divine wisdom manifested to, or the notion of good and evil engra-ven by God, on the conscience. It is finely said by the author of the book de Mundo, c. 11. "God is to us a law, tending on all sides to a just equilibrium, requiring no correction, admitting no variation." With this Cicero agrees,

de Legibus, lib. 2. " The true and leading law, which is proper both to command and to forbid, is the right reason of the
Supreme Being.

IV. That author appears not to have expressed himself
with accuracy, who said, We here call the law, the knowledge of right and wrong, binding to do what is right, and to
avoid what is wrong. For law properly is not any knowledge,
but the object of knowledge. This law, we say, is naturally
known to man, but it would be absurd to say, knowledge is
naturally known. Knowledge is our act, and is indeed to be
squared by the rule of the law. The law is a rule prescribed
by God for all our actions.

V. That other author is far less accurate, who thus determines : " Prior to the fall there was properly no law : for
then the love of God prevailed, which requires no law. There
(as the same author elsewhere explains himself) a state of
friendship and love obtained, such as is the natural state of a son
with respect to a parent, and which is what nature affects. But
when that love is violated, then a precept comes to be superadded : and that love, which before was voluntary, (as best
agreeing with its nature ; for that can scarcely be called love,
unless voluntary) falls under a precept, and passes into a law,
to be enforced then with commination and coercion ; which rigour of coercion properly constitutes a law.

VI. But this way of reasoning is far from being the effect of
thought and attention. For, 1st. It is not the rigour of the
enforcement properly, that constitutes a law, but the obligatory
virtue of what is injoined, proceeding both from the power of
the lawgiver, and from the equity of the thing commanded, which
is here founded on the holiness of the divine nature, so far as
imitable by man. The apostle James, i. 25. commends
" the perfect law of liberty." 2dly. Nor is there any absurdity
to affirm, that the natural state of a son with respect to a
parent, is regulated by laws. It is certain, Plato de Legib.
lib. 3. says, that *the first mortals practised the customs
and laws of their fathers*, quoting that sentence of Homer,
Θεμιςευει δε εχαςος παιδων, *every one makes laws for his children.*
3dly. Nor, is it repugnant to do a thing by nature, and at the
same time by a law. Philo Judæus de Migratione, explaining that celebrated old saying of the philosophers, says, that to
live agreeably to nature, is done when the mind follows God,
remembering his precepts. Crysippus in like manner, as
commended by Laertius, lib. 7. on Zeno, says, that person
lives agreeably to nature, who does nothing prohibited by the
common law, which is right reason. In a sublimer strain al-

most than one could well expect from a heathen, is what Hier-
ocles says on Pythagoras' golden verses : " To obey right
reason and God is one and the same thing.   For the rational
nature being illuminated, readily embraces what the divine law
prescribes.   A soul which is conformed to God, never dissents
from the will of God, but being attentive to the divinity and
brightness, with which it is enlightened, does which it does."
4thly. Nor can it be affirmed, that after the breach of love, or,
which is the same thing, after the entrance of sin, that then it
was the law was superadded ; seeing sin itself is ανομια the transgression of the law.   5thly. Nor is love rendered less voluntary
by the precept.   For, the law enjoins love to be every way
perfect, and therefore to be most voluntary, not extorted by the
servile fear of the threatening, 1 John iv. 18.   Nor does he
give satisfaction, when he says, that what is called love, scarce
deserves that name, unless voluntary ; he ought to say, is by
no means charity, unless voluntary.   For love is the most delightful union of our will with the thing beloved ; which cannot
be so much as conceived, without the plainest contradiction,
any other than voluntary.   If therefore, by the superadded
law, love is rendered involuntary and forced, the whole nature
of love is destroyed, and a divine law set up, which ruins love.
6thly. In fine, the law of nature itself was not without a threatening, and that of eternal death.   I shall conclude in the most
accurate words of Chrysostom, Homil. 12. to the people of Antioch ; " when God formed man at first, he gave him a natural
law.   And what then is this natural law? He rectified our conscience, and made us have the knowledge of good and evil,
without any other teaching than our own."

VII. It is, moreover, to be observed, that this law of nature is the same in substance with the decalogue ; being what
the apostle calls, την ενΊολην Ίην εις ζωην, *a commandment which
was ordained to life,* Rom. vii. 10. that is, that law by the
performance of which, life was formerly obtainable.   And
indeed, the decalogue contains such precepts, " which if a
man do he shall live in them," Lev. xviii. 5.   But those precepts are undoubtedly the law proposed to Adam, upon which
the covenant of works was built.   Add to this, what the
apostle says, that that law, which still continues to be the rule
of our actions, and whose righteousness ought to be fulfilled
in us, was made weak through the flesh, that is, through sin,
and that it was become impossible for it to bring us to life,
Rom. viii. 3, 4.   The same law therefore was in force before
the entrance of sin, and, if duly observed, had the power of
giving life.   Besides, God in the second creation inscribes the

same law on the heart, which in the first creation he had engraven on the soul. For, what is regeneration, but the restitution of the same image of God in which man was at first created? In fine, the law of nature could be nothing but a precept of conformity to God, and of perfect love; which is the same in the decalogue.

VIII. This law is deduced. by infallible consequence from the very *nature of God and man*, which I thus explain and prove. I presuppose, as a self-evident truth, and clear from the very meaning of the words, that the great God has a sovereign and uncontrolable power and dominion over all his creatures. This authority is founded primarily and radically, not on creation, nor on any contract entered into with the creature, nor on the sin of the creature, as some less solidly maintain; but on the majesty, supremacy, sovereignty, and eminence of God, which are his essential attributes, and would have been in God, though no creature had actually existed; though we now conceive them as having a certain respect to creatures that do or at least might exist. From this majesty of the divine nature the prophet Jeremiah, x. 6, 7. infers the duty of the creature. "For as much as there is none like unto thee, O Lord, thou art great, and thy name is great in might, who would not fear thee, O king of nations, for to thee doth it appertain." For if God is the prime, the supreme, the supereminent; it necessarily follows that all creatures do in every respect depend on that prime, supreme, and the supereminent God, for existence, power, and operation. This is of the essence of creatures, which if not entirely dependent, were not possible to be conceived without the most evident contradiction. But the more degrees of entity there are in any creature, the more degrees also of dependance on the Supreme Being are to be attributed to it. In the rational creature, besides a metaphysical and physical entity, which it has in common with the rest of the creatures, there is a certain more perfect degree of entity, namely, rationality. As, therefore in quality of a being it depends on God, as the Supreme Being; so also as rational, on God, as the supreme reason, which it is bound to express, and be conformable to. And as God, as long as he wills any creature to exist, he necessarily wills it to be dependent on his real providence (otherwise he would renounce his own supremacy by transferring it to the creature;) so, likewise, if he wills any rational creature to exist, he necessarily wills it to be dependent on his moral providence; otherwise he would deny himself to be the supreme reason, to whose pattern and idea every dependent reason ought to conform. And thus a rational creature would be to itself the prime reason, that is, really God ; which is an evident contradiction.

IX. It is in vain therefore, that frantic enthusiasts insist, that the utmost pitch of holiness consists in being without law ; wresting the saying of the apostle, 1 Tim. i. 9. *the law is not made for a righteous man, but for the lawless and disobedient.* Certainly that passage does not destroy our assertion, by which we evinced that the human nature cannot be without the divine law ; but highly confirms it. For, since the ungodly are here described as *lawless*, who would fain live as without law ; and *disobedient*, who will not be in subjection : it follows, that the acknowledging the divine law, and the subjection of the understanding and will to it, is the character of the righteous and the godly. In the law of God, since the entrance of sin, we are to consider two things. 1st. The rule and direction to submission. 2dly. The power of bridling and restraining by terror and fear, and lastly, of justly condemning. When therefore the apostle declares, that the law was not made for a righteous man, he does not understand it of the primary and principal work of the law, which is essential to it, but of that other accidental work, which was added to it on account of, and since the entrance of sin, and from which the righteous are freed by Christ.

X. Nor does it only follow from the nature of God and of man, that some law is to be prescribed by God to man in common, but even such à law, as may be not only the rule and guide of human actions, but of human nature itself, considered as rational. For, since God himself is in his nature infinitely holy, and manifests this his holiness in all his works ; it hence follows, that to man, who ought to be conformed to the likeness of the divine holiness, there should be prescribed a law, requiring not only the righteousness of his works, but the holiness of his nature ; so that the righteousness of his works is no other than the expression of his inward righteousness. Indeed the apostle calls that piety and holiness, * which he recommends, and which undoubtedly the law enjoins, *the image of God*, Col. iii. 10. But the image should resemble its original. Seeing God therefore is holy in his nature, on that very account it follows, that men should be so too.

XI. A certain author therefore has advanced with more

---

* N. B. I suppose there is here an error of the press ; because it is in Eph. iv. 24. that the new man is said to be after God created in righteousness and true holiness.

subtilty than truth: that *the law obliges the person only to active righteousness, but not the nature itself to intrinsic rectitude;* and consequently, that *original righteousness is approved indeed, but not commanded by the law: and on the contrary also, that original unrighteousness is condemned, but not forbidden by the law.* For the law approves of nothing which it did not command, condemns nothing which it did not forbid. The law is תורה, the doctrine of right and wrong. What it teaches to be evil, that it forbids; what to be good, it commands. And therefore it is deservedly called *the law of nature;* not only because nature can make it known; but also because it is *the rule of nature itself.*

XII. To conclude, we are to observe of this law of nature, that at least its principal and most universal precepts are founded not in the mere arbitrary good will and pleasure of God, but in his unspotted nature. For if it is necessary that God should therefore prescribe a law for man, because himself is the original holiness; no less necessary is it, he should prescribe a law, which shall be the copy of that original. So that the difference between good and evil, ought to be derived not from any positive law, or arbitrary constitution of the divine will, but from the most holy nature of God himself; which I thus prove:

XIII. Let us take the summary *of the first table; Thou shalt love the Lord thy God with all thy heart,* &c. Should this command be said to be founded in the arbitrary good pleasure of the divine will, and not in the very nature of God; it may with equal propriety be said, that God might dispense with the necessity of loving himself. A thing entirely impossible, as appears hence : it is natural to God to be the chief good: it is included in the notion of God, that he is the very best. Now it is natural to the chief good, to be supremely amiable; it is natural also to reason and will to be unable, without a crime, not to love what is proposed as worthy of the highest affection. Whoever therefore shall affirm, that the necessity of loving God, flows not from the very nature of God, advances the following contradiction : God is in his nature the chief good, and yet in his nature not supremely amiable. Or this other; God is worthy of the highest love; and yet it is possible, that he who loves him not does nothing unworthy of God.

XIV. But to proceed : if the command to love God is founded, not in his nature, but in his arbitrary good pleasure; he might have enjoined the hatred of himself. For, in things in their own nature indifferent, whoever has the right of commanding, has also that of forbidding, and of requiring the contrary. To assert, that God can command the hatred of himself, not only conveys a sound, grating on the ear, but labours under a manifest contradiction; as will appear from a proper explication of the terms. God, the chief good, supremely amiable, are terms equivalent; at least, the last is an explication of the preceding. To hate, is to esteem a thing not the chief good, nay, not so much as any good at all, and therefore so far from loving it, we are averse from it. Would it not therefore be a manifest contradiction, should any one suppose the great and good God thus speaking to his creature: I am really the chief good, but my will is, not to be esteemed a good in any respect: I, indeed, am worthy of the highest love, but it is my will, that you deem me worthy of your hatred. A man must be blind who sees not a contradiction here.

XV. Moreover, I would ask those, if any are otherwise minded, whether it is not naturally good, even antecedently to any free determination of the divine will, to obey God when he commands any thing. If they own this, we have gained our point: if not, I ask further, whence then the obligation to obey? They cannot say, it is from any command. For, the question is, What binds me to obey that command? Here we must necessarily come to that sovereign majesty and supreme authority of God, to whom it is a crime in nature to refuse obedience. Again, if not to obey God is good in nature, then, it follows, God can command, that none may obey him. A proposition not only inconsiderate, but also contradictory. For, to command, is to bind one to obedience. To say, Obey not, is to dispense with the bond of obligation. It is therefore most contradictory to say, I command, but do not obey.

XVI. What we have proved concerning *the love* of God, the summary of the *first table* of the law; namely, that it is good in nature, might be also proved from the summary of the *second table*, the love of our neighbour. For, he who loves God, cannot but love his image too, in which he clearly views *express characters* of the Deity, and not a small degree of the *brightness of his glory*. Again, whoever loves God, will, by virtue of that love, seriously wish, desire, study, and as much as in him lies, be careful, that his neighbour, as well as himself, be under God, in God, and for God, and all he has, be for his glory. Again, whoever loves God, will make it his business, that God may appear every way admirable and glorious; and as he appears such most eminently in the sanctification and happiness of men, 2 Thess. i. 10. he will exert himself to the utmost, that his neighbour make advances to holiness and happiness. Finally, whoever sincerely loves God, will never think he loves and glorifies him enough ; such excellencies he discovers in him, sees his name so illustrious, and so exalted above all praise, as to long, that all mankind, nay, all creatures, should join him in loving and celebrating the infinite perfections of God. But this is the most faithful and pure love of our neighbour, to seek that God may be glorified in him, and he himself be for the glory of God. Hence it appears, that the love of our neighbour is inseparably connected with that of God. If therefore it flows from the nature of God, to enjoin us the love of himself, as was just proved ; it must likewise flow from the nature of God to enjoin us the love of our neighbour.

XVII. To conclude, if we conceive all holiness to be founded on the arbitrary will of God, this greatest of all absurdities will follow, that God our lawgiver can, by commanding the contrary of what he had done before, without any regeneration or renovation of the inward man, make of the wicked and disobedient, for whom the law is made to condemnation, persons holy and righteous : a shocking position !

XVIII. From what has been said, it is astonishing, that a certain learned person should approve of the following assertion ; namely, that " on the will of God not only things themselves depend, but also every mode of a thing, the truth, order, law, goodness ; nor can any goodness of the object either move the divine will, or put a stop to it." It is indeed certain, that no bounds or rules can be set to the will of God, by any thing out of God himself ; that being repugnant to his sovereign pre-eminence. Yet something may, and ought to be conceived, flowing from God himself, and his intrinsic perfections, which hinders the act of the divine will, and this is not therefore good, because God wills it ; but God wills it, because it is good ; for instance, the love of God, as the chief good. And they do not consider things regularly, who make the holiness of God to consist only in the exact conformity of his actions with his will. *Which will*, say they, *is the rule of all holiness*, and so of the divine. On the contrary, as the natural holiness of God ought to be conceived prior to his will, so it is rather the rule of the will, than to be ruled by it. For, this holiness of God is the most shining purity of the divine perfections, according to which, agreeably to the most perfect reason, he always wills and acts.

By this opinion, which we are now confuting, every distinction
between what are called moral and positive precepts, is destroyed, and Archelaus' exploded paradox brought up anew;
namely, τὸ δίκαιον ἐῖνα, κὰι τὸ ἀισχρὸν ἐ φυσει, αλλὰ νομω. "The
distinction of good and evil was not from nature, but of positive
institution;" adopted by Aristippus, and Theodorus, surnamed
the Atheist. "Than which opinion," says Cocceius, in his
Summa Theolog. c. xxiv. § 6. "none can be devised more
pernicious, and none more effectual for undermining all religion,
striking at the very root of the divine justice, and the necessity of a Saviour, cutting out the vitals of piety."

XIX. And thus we have proved these three things concerning the law of nature, on which the covenant of works is founded: namely, 1st. That it flows from the nature of God and man,
that some law be prescribed to man. 2dly. Such a law, as to
be the rule and standard, not only of our actions, but also of
our nature. 3dly. That the most universal precepts thereof at
least are founded on the nature of God. Let us now consider
the other, the *symbolical law.*

XX. We find this law, Gen. ii. 16, 17. "And the Lord
God commanded the man, saying, Of every tree of the garden
thou mayest freely eat; but of the tree of knowledge of good
and evil thou shalt not eat of it: for in the day thou eatest
thereof, thou shalt surely die." Concerning this tree, three
things are chiefly to be taken notice of. 1st. That it is not
quite certain, whether it was a single tree; since a whole
species of trees might be forbidden to man: we shall afterwards repeat this remark, when we speak of the Tree of Life.
2dly. There seems to be a two-fold reason for this appellation. 1. In respect to *God,* who, by that tree would try and
know, whether man would continue good and happy by persevering in obedience, or swerve to evil by disobedience.
In which sense God is said to have tried Hezekiah, 2 Chron.
xxxii. 31. "that he might know all that was in his heart."
2. In respect of *man,* because, if from love to God he obeyed
this law of probation, he was to come to the fruition of that
beatific good, which is never perfectly known, but by the enjoyment: on the contrary, if disobedient, he was to know by
sad experience, into what plunge and abyss of evils he had
brought himself.

XXI. 3dly. The tendency of such a divine precept is to
be considered. Man was thereby taught, 1. That God is
lord of all things; and that it is unlawful for man, even to
desire an apple, but with his leave. In all things therefore,
from the greatest to the least, the mouth of the Lord is to be

consulted, as to what he would, or would not have done by us.
2. That man's true happiness is placed in God alone, and nothing to be desired, but with submission to God, and in order
to employ it for him.   So that it is HE only, on whose account
all other things appear good and desirable to man.   3. Readily
to be satisfied without even the most delightful, and desirable
things, if God so command : and to think, there is much more
good in obedience to the divine precept, than in the enjoyment
of the most delightful thing in the world.   4. That man was
not yet arrived at the utmost pitch of happiness, but to expect
a still greater good, after his course of obedience was over.
This was hinted by the prohibition of the most delightful tree,
whose fruit was, of any other, greatly to be desired ; and this
argued some degree of imperfection in that state, in which
man was forbid the enjoyment of some good.   See what follows, chap. vi. § XIX.

XXII. Thus far of *the Laws of the Covenant*, both that
of nature, and of this other symbolical and probatory one.
It now follows, that according to what we proposed, § I. of
this chapter, we consider the observation of those laws.   Accordingly, a most perfect obedience to all the commands of
God is required ; agreeable to that stated rule, Lev. xviii. 5.
" which if a man do, he shall live in them."   And as life was
likewise promised upon obedience to the symbolical law about
the Tree of Knowledge, which doubtless was a positive institution ; so, to observe by the way, it appears, that by this
representation, moral precepts, as they are called, cannot be
so distinguished from positive, as if to the former alone this
sentence belonged, *which if a man do, he shall live in them*,
and not to the latter.

XXIII. This obedience does in the first place, suppose the
most exact preservation of that *original* and primitive *holiness*,
in which man was created.   For, as we have already said,
God by his law does above all things require the integrity
and rectitude of man's nature to be cherished and preserved,
as his principal duty, flowing from the benefit he has received.
In the second place, from that good principle, *good works*
ought to be produced : " Charity, out of a pure heart, and of
a good conscience," 1 Tim. i. 5.   In the third place, there
ought to be a certain ready alacrity to perform whatever God
shall reveal to man as his good pleasure and appointment,
that in all things he may be ready to say, *Speak, Lord, for
thy servant heareth*.

XXIV. A threefold *perfection* is required.   1st. *Of Parts*,
both with respect to *the subject*, as that the whole man shall,

in soul and body, and all the faculties of both, employ himself in the service of God, 1 Thess. v. 23. (for man is then
םת *perfect*, when the outward man corresponds with the inward, the actions with the thoughts, the tongue and hands
with the heart, Psal. xvi. 3, 4. and Psal. xxxvii. 30, 31.)
and with respect to *the object*, as that all and each of the precepts are observed, without any sin of commission or omission, Gal. iii. 10. Jam. ii. 10. 2dly. Of *Degrees*, which to
make obedience truly valuable, excludes all επιἐκειαν pardon and
connivance, strictly requiring obedience to be performed
" with all the heart, with all the soul, with all the mind,"
Matt. xxii. 37. " With all our might," Deut. vi. 5. " Thou
hast commanded us to keep thy precepts diligently," Psal.
cxix. 4. In the third place, Of *Perseverance*, without in-
terruption or period. God insists upon this with rigour,
Ezek. xviii. 24. pronouncing, that " all his righteousness
that he had done, shall not be remembered, when the righteous turneth away from his righteousness," which was fulfilled in Adam. This is emphatically expressed, Deut. xxvii.
26. " Cursed be that confirmeth not all the words of this law
to do them."

XXV. Such a perfect observance of the laws of the covenant, quite to the period which God had fixed for probation,
had given man a right to the reward. Not from any intrinsic
proportion of the work to the reward, as the grosser Papists
proudly boast ; but from God's covenant, and engagement,
which was no ways unbecoming him to enter into. Nor had
man, before the consummation of his obedience, even in the
state of innocence, a right to life. He was only in a state of
acquiring a right ; which would at length be actually acquired,
when he could say, I have fulfilled the conditions of the covenant, I have constantly and perfectly done what was commanded ; now I claim and expect that thou my God will
grant the promised happiness.

XXVI. How absurdly again do the Papists assert, that
Adam, as he came from the hands of his Creator, had a right,
as the adopted son of God, to supernatural happiness, as to
his paternal inheritance, which, according to Bellarmine, *de
Justificat.* lib. v. c. 17. " is due to the adopted son of God,
in right of adoption, previous to all good works." But this
is truly a preposterous way of reasoning. For, the right of
adoption belongs to the covenant of grace in Christ Jesus :
" the adoption of children is by Jesus Christ," Eph. i. 5.
Besides, was this opinion true, good works could not be required, as the condition of acquiring a right to eternal life ;

but could only serve to prevent the forfeiture of the right of a son: by this means, the whole design of the covenant of works, and all the righteousness which is by the law, are quite destroyed. In fine, what can be more absurd, than the trifling manner in which these sophisters talk of the grace of adoption, as giving Adam a right to enter upon an heavenly inheritance, in a legal covenant: when on the other hand, they so stiffly contend for the merits of works, under a cove- nant of grace. It is only there (*to wit*, under the covenant of grace,) that we are to apply the above sentiment, that the inheritance is due to an adopted son of God, in right of adop- tion, previous to all good works.

CHAP. IV.

Of the Promises of the Covenant of Works.

I. Having thus considered the condition of the Cove- nant of Works; let us now enquire into *the Promises* of that covenant. And here first, the *Socinians* come under our notice, who obstinately deny all promises. For, thus *Volkelius, de vera Religione*, lib. ii. c. 8. says, *Scarce, if at all, was any general promise made to the men of that age: but rather threatenings and terrors were then set before them. Nor do we see God promising, upon Adam's abstain- ing from the fruit of that tree, any reward of obedience; but only denouncing destruction, if he did not obey,* Gen. ii. 17. For this he assigns the following reason: *Moreover, the rea- son why God at that time would be obeyed, without propos- ing almost any general reward, seems to be this; because, at the very beginning of the world, he would shew to all that he owed nothing to any, but was himself the most absolute lord of all.*

II. To this I answer, as follows: 1st. Man's natural con- science teaches him, that God desires not to be served in vain, nor that obedience to his commands will go unrewarded and for nought. The very Heathens were also apprized of this. Arian, in his Dissert. lib. i. c. 12. introduces Epictetus speaking thus: " If there are no Gods, how can it be the end of man to obey the Gods? But if there are, and they be yet regardless of every thing; how is the matter mended? But if they both are, and take care of human affairs; but men have no recompense to expect from them, and have as little; the case is still worse." Let us add, Seneca, Epist. xcv.

" God does not want servants. Why so? He ministers himself to mankind ; being every where present and at hand.
Whoever conceives not of God as he ought, dealing all things,
bestowing his benefits freely, will never make the proper
proficiency. Why are the Gods so beneficent? It is owing
to their nature. The first article of the worship of the Gods,
is to believe that they are: then to render them the honour
of their majesty, and of their goodness, without which there
is no majesty : to know, that they preside over the world,
govern all things by their power, take special care of mankind, without neglecting individuals." In like manner, we
find it among the articles of the Jewish faith, as a thing naturally known, that *there are rewards as well as punishments
with God*; according to that common saying, *God defrauds
no creature of its reward.* The worship of God presupposes
the belief of this : *For he that cometh to God must believe that
he is, and that he is a rewarder of them that diligently seek
him*, Heb. xi. 6.

III. 2dly. Besides, this faith is not merely a certain persuasion of the mind, arising from reasoning, and the consideration of the goodness of God: but to render it a genuine
faith, it must rest on the word and promise of God : *faith
cometh by hearing, and hearing by the word of God*, Rom.
x. 17. 3dly. This was the intent of the tree of life, which
the *Socinians* themselves, in *Compend. Socinian.* c. 2. § 5.
*allow to have been a kind of symbol, though obscure, of eter-
nal life.* But that symbol, proposed to Adam, could have
been of no use, unless he understood it, and considered it as
a seal of the promise made by God. It had been mere farce,
to have prohibited man from access to, and eating of this tree
after the fall; unless thereby, God had given him to understand, that he would forfeit the thing promised, and consequently become unworthy of the use of that symbol and sacrament. 4thly. If no promise had been made, they might
have lived without hope. For the hope which maketh not
ashamed, is founded on the promises. But this is the character of the woeful calamity of those *who are without God
in the world, that they have no hope*, Eph. ii. 12. 5thly.
God represents to Cain a thing known long before, even by
nature, much more by paternal instruction; *If thou doest
well, shalt thou not be accepted?* Gen. iv. 7. But did this
maxim begin to be true, and to be known only after the fall?
6thly. The very threatening infers a promise. The language
of which at least is, that he was to be deprived of that happiness, which otherwise he would continue to enjoy ; we may,

therefore, most certainly infer, that man had no occasion to be afraid of losing that happiness, as long as he kept himself from sin. 7thly. By this assertion of our adversaries, according to their own hypotheses, all the religion of the first man is destroyed. Seeing, as our author writes at the beginning of that chapter, " the promise of rewards, for well-doing, is closely interwoven with religion." 8thly. The reason he gives for this assertion, is foolish and to no purpose. For, do these many and liberal promises of eternal life, which God hath given us in Christ, make it now less evident, that God is indebted to none, and is the most absolute lord of all things? Does the supreme Being, by his gracious promises, derogate any thing from his most absolute dominion? Must it not be known in all ages, that God owes nothing to any? How then comes it, that God did not always equally forbear promising?

IV. Let this therefore be a settled point, that this covenant was not established without promises. We now enquire what sort of promises God made to Adam. Accordingly, we believe God promised Adam life eternal, that is, the most perfect fruition of himself, and that for ever, after finishing his course of obedience; our arguments are these:

V. 1st. The apostle declares that God, by sending his Son in the flesh, did what the law could not do, " in that it was weak through the flesh," Rom. viii. 3. But it is certain Christ procured for his own people a right to eternal life, to be enjoyed in heaven in its due time. This the apostle declares the law could not now do, not of itself, or, because it has no such promises, but because it was weak through the flesh. Had it not therefore been for sin, the law had brought men to that eternal life, which Christ promises to and freely bestows on his own people. This appears to me a conclusive argument.

VI. 2dly. It is universally allowed, that Paul, in his epistles to the Romans and Galatians, where he treats on justification, does under that name comprise the adjudging to eternal life: he in many places proves that a sinner cannot be justified, that is, lay claim to eternal life, by the works of the law; but never by this argument, because the law had no promises of eternal life; but because man is by the law brought to the acknowledgment of sin, and the confession of deserved damnation, Rom. iii. 19, 20. He insists on this point with great labour and pains, though otherwise he might have very easily cut short the whole dispute, by just saying, that a title to eternal life was to be sought for by faith in Christ; that it is in vain to rest upon any law, though kept ever so perfectly, in regard it has no promises of eternal life annexed to it. On the

contrary, the apostle teaches, that the commandment, considered in itself, was ordained to life, Rom. vii. 10. that is,
was such as by the observance thereof life might have once
been obtained ; which if the law could still bestow on the sinner, " verily righteousness should have been by the law,"
Gal. iii. 21. that is, the right to that same happiness which
now comes from faith in Christ. For the dispute was concerning κληρονομία, the inheritance of eternal life, which was to
be entered upon ; whether now, by means of the law, or by
the promise of the gospel, v. 18. And he owns, it would be by
the law, could the law ζωοποιῆσαι *make alive*. And this could
be done by that law which was ordained to life, Rom. vii. 10.
But when ? In innocence before it was made weak by the flesh.
If Adam therefore had persevered in obedience, the law would
have brought him to that same inheritance, which now in
Christ is allotted not to him that worketh, but to him that
believeth. And this argument, if I mistake not, is plain to
any person of thought and attention.

VII. 3dly. We are above all to observe how the apostle
distinguishes the righteousness, which is of the law, from the
evangelical. Of the first he thus speaks, Rom. x. 5. " Moses
describeth the righteousness which is of the law ; that the
man which doth those things shall live by them :" Of the second, he writes as follows, Rom. i. 17. " The just shall live
by faith." On both sides, the promise of life is the same, and
proposed in the very same words. Nor does the apostle in
the least hint that one kind of life is promised by the law,
another by the gospel. Which, if true, ought for once at
least to be hinted ; as the doing this would have ended the
whole dispute. For, in vain would any seek for eternal life
by the law, if never promised in it. But the apostle places
the whole difference, not in the thing promised, but in the
condition of obtaining the promise ; while he says, Gal. iii.
11, 12. " But that no man is justified by the law in the sight
of God, it is evident ; for the just shall live by faith. And
the law is not of faith : but the man that doth them, shall live
in them." That very life therefore is promised by the law
to the man that worketh, which he now receives through the
faith of Christ. But to what man, thus working, were the
promises made ? Was it to the sinner ? Was it not to man in a
state of innocence ? And was it not then, when it might truly
be said if thou continuest to do well, thou shalt be heir of that
life upon that condition ? And this could be said to none but
to innocent Adam. Was it not then, when the promise was
actually made ? For after sin, there is not so much a promise

as a denunciation of wrath, and an intimation of a curse, proposing that as the condition of obtaining life, which is now evidently impossible to be performed. I therefore conclude, that
to Adam, in the covenant of works, was promised the same
eternal life, to be obtained by the righteousness which is of
the law, of which believers are made partakers through Christ.
But let none object, that all these arguments are fetched, not
from the history of man in innocence, but from Paul's reasoning.   For it is no matter whence arguments are taken, if they
contain a demonstration to the conscience, which I think is
here evident.   Undoubtedly Adam knew a great deal more
than is contained in that very short account of him by Moses.
Nor does it appear to be without a mystery, that Moses is more
sparing on most of the particulars of that covenant, and throws
so little light on the shadow of a transient image, to denote that
it was to evanish.

VIII. Once more, 4thly. It was entirely agreeable, that
God should promise Adam, by covenant, something greater
and better to be obtained after finishing his course of obedience than what he was already possessed of. What kind of
covenant would it have been to have added no reward to his
obedience, and his faithful compliance with the conditions of
the covenant, but only a continuation of those blessings which
he actually enjoyed already, and which it was not becoming
God to refuse to man whom he had created ? Now, Adam
enjoyed in paradise all imaginable, natural, and animal happiness, as it is called. A greater, therefore, and a more exalted
felicity still awaited him ; in the fruition of which, he would
most plainly see, that *in keeping the divine commands, there is*
ברב קב μισθαπαδοσναι μεγαλην *great reward,* Psal. xix. 11.   Let
none object the case of the angels, to whom he may pretend
nothing was promised by God, but the continuance of that
happy state, in which they were created. We are here to keep
to the apostle's advice, in Col. ii. 18. " not to intrude
into these things we have not seen." Who shall declare unto us those things which are not revealed concerning the angels ? But if we may form probable conjectures, it appears to
me very likely that some superior degree of happiness was
conferred on the angels after they were actually confirmed,
and something more excellent than that in which they were at
first created : as the joy of the angels received a considerable
addition, upon beholding the divine perfections so resplendent
in the illustrious work of redemption ; and at the consummation of all things, the happiness of all the elect, both angels
and men, will be complete ; when Christ's whole body shall

appear glorious, and God be glorified and admired in all his saints.

IX. It still remains doubtful, whether the life promised to Adam upon his perseverance was to be enjoyed in *paradise*, or in *heaven*. The latter appears more probable. 1st. Because paradise is in scripture represented as a type of heaven, and heaven itself is called paradise, Luke xxiii. 43. by that exchange of names which is very common between a sacrament, or sign, and the thing signified thereby. But is it in the least probable, that paradise should be made a sacrament after man's ejectment? 2dly. Is it fit that man when raised to consummate happiness should reside there, where God does most brightly display the rays of his glorious majesty; which doubtless he does in heaven, where he has fixed his throne, Isa. lxvi. 1. 3dly. As the earthly paradise was furnished with all the delights and pleasures appertaining to this animal life, of which there is no necessity in that most perfect and immediate fruition of God, all that external entertainment being in the highest degree excluded thence; heaven ought to be deemed a much more suitable habitation for glorified man than the earthly paradise. However, we would not deny, that happiness does not depend on place; and there being scarce any thing to demonstrate this in scripture; therefore we ought not to contend strenuously about such a question.

X. This therefore is settled; God promised to Adam eternal life. But here it may be and is usually asked whence this promise flows, whether from the mere good pleasure of the divine will, so that God would have acted nowise unworthy of himself, had he made no such promise to man: or, whether God's making the covenant with man in this manner was from the divine nature, and from what was suitable to it? Here indeed, I think, we are to be modest; I shall therefore propose, what I imagine I know, or may reasonably think or believe concerning my God, with fear and trembling. O my God, grant that what I shall speak on this point may be managed with a holy awe, and in a manner becoming thy majesty!

XI. And first, I lay this down as an acknowledged truth, that God owes nothing to his creature. By no claim, no law is he bound to reward it. For all that the creature is, it owes entirely to God; both because he created it, and also, because he is infinitely exalted above it. But where there is so great a disparity, there is no common standard of right, by which the superior in dignity, can become under an obligation to give any reward, Rom. xi. 35, 36.

XII. I approve on this subject of Durandus' reasoning, which Bellarmine was unable to refute. " What we are, and what we have, whether good acts, or good habits, or practices, are all from the divine bounty, who hath given freely and preserves them. And because none, after having given freely, is obliged to give more, but rather the receiver is the more obliged to the giver; therefore, from good habits, and good acts or practices, given us by God, God is not bound by any debt of justice, to give any thing more; so as not giving, to become unjust, but rather we are bound to God."

XIII. Whatever then is promised to the creature by God, ought all to be ascribed to the immense goodness of the Deity. Finely to this purpose speaks Augustine, serm. xvi. on the words of the apostle, " God became our debtor, not by receiving any thing, but by promising what he pleased. For, it was of his own bounty that he vouchsafed to make himself a debtor." But as this goodness is natural to God, no less than holiness and justice; and equally becoming God to act, agreeably to his goodness, with a holy and innocent creature; so, from this consideration of the divine goodness, I imagine the following things may be very plainly inferred.

XIV. 1st. That it is unbecoming the goodness, I had almost ventured to add, and the justice of God, to adjudge an innocent creature to hell torments. A paradox which not only some scholastic divines, but, which I am very sorry to say, a great divine of our own, with a few followers, scrupled not to maintain. Be it far from us, to presume to circumscribe the extensive power of God over his creatures, by the limits of a right prescribed to us, or by the fallacious reasoning of a narrow understanding. But be it also far from us, to ascribe any thing to him which is unbecoming his immense goodness and unspotted justice. Elihu, with great propriety joins these together, Job xxxvii. 22, 23. " With God is terrible majesty. Touching the Almighty we cannot find him out: he is excellent in power and in judgment, and in plenty of justice: he will not afflict." For, if God could thus afflict an innocent creature, he would shew he was not pleased with the holiness of his creature; since he would not only deprive him of communion with himself, but also give him to the cruel will of his enemies. When he destroys the wicked, he makes it plainly appear, he is not delighted with wickedness, nay, in scripture phrase, Psal. v. 5. hates it. Should he therefore, in the same manner, torment the pious, he would testify by this that he did not delight in piety, but rather hated it. Which none without blasphemy can conceive of God. And what else.

are pains of hell? Are they not a privation of divine love?
A sense of divine hatred? The worm of conscience? Despair
of recovering God's favour? But how is it possible, without
a manifest contradiction, to conceive this ever to be the case of
an innocent creature? And I own, I was struck with horror,
when I observed the most subtle Twiss, in order to defend
this paradox, choose rather to maintain, it were better to be
eternally miserable, and endure the torments of hell, than not
to exist at all: and when he objected to himself the authority of
our Saviour, plainly affirming of Judas; "it had been good for
that man, if he had not been born," Matth. xxvi. 24. that he
did not blush to answer, "that many things are said in scripture in a figurative and hyperbolical manner, nay, a great deal
accommodated to the sense of the vulgar, and even to human
judgment, though erroneous;" all which he applies to this
sentence of our Saviour, de Elect. P. 2. l. 1. § 4. p. 178, 179.
To what length is not even the most prudent hurried, when
he gives too much way to his own speculations? I, for my
part, think Sophocles formed a sounder judgment than the
very acute Twiss, when he said, "better not be, than to live
miserable;" and Oeschylus, in Ixion, "I think it had been
better for that man who suffers great pains never to have been
born, than to have existed." Bernard speaks excellently to
the same purpose, ad Eugen. de Consider. lib. 5. "It is not
to be doubted, but it will be much worse with those who will
be in such a state [of misery] than with those who will have
no existence. For, as he says in his sermon, 35, on Solomon's
Song, "the soul, placed in that state, loses its happiness without losing its being: whereby it is always constrained to
suffer death without dying, failure without failing, and an end
without a period."

XV. 2dly. Nor can God on account of this his goodness,
refuse to communicate himself to, or give the enjoyment of
himself to, an innocent, an holy creature, or to love and favour it, in the most tender manner, while it has a being, and
continues pure according to its condition. For, a holy creature is God's very image. But God loves himself in the
most ardent manner, as being the chief good: which he would
not be, unless he loved himself above all. It therefore follows, he must also love his own image, in which he has expressed, to the life, himself, and what is most amiable in him,
his own holiness. With what shew of decency could he
command the other creatures to love such as are holy, did he
himself not judge them amiable? Or, if he judged them so,
how is it possible, he should not love them himself?

XVI. Further, God does not love in vain. It is the character of a lover, to wish well to, and to do all the good in his power to the object of his love. But in the good will of God, consists both the soul's life and welfare. And as nothing can hinder his actually doing well by those whom he wishes well to: it follows, that a holy creature, which he necessarily loves from the goodness of his nature, must also enjoy the fruits and effects of that divine love.

XVII. Besides, it is the nature of love to seek union and communion with thé beloved. He does not love in reality, who desires not to communicate himself to the object of his affection. But, every one communicates himself such as he is. God, therefore, being undoubtedly happy, makes the creature, whom he loves and honours with the communion of himself, a partaker of his happiness. I say, he makes the creature happy, in proportion to the state in which he would have it to be. All these things follow from that love which we have shewn God does in consequence of his infinite goodness, necessarily bear to the creature who is innocent and holy.

XVIII. The same thing may be demonstrated in another manner, and if I mistake not, incontestably as follows: The sum of the divine commands is thus; love me above all things: that is, look upon me as thy only chief good: hunger and thirst after me: place the whole of thy happiness in me alone: seek me above all: and nothing besides me, but so far as it has a relation to me. But how is it conceivable, that God should thus speak to the soul, and the soul should religiously attend to, and diligently perform this, and yet never enjoy God? Is it becoming the most holy and excellent Being, to say to his pure unspotted creature, (such as we now suppose it) look upon me as thy chief good; but know, I neither am nor ever shall be such to thee. Long after me, but on condition, never of obtaining thy desire: hunger and thirst after me; but only to be for ever disappointed, and never satisfied: seek me above all things; but seek me in vain, who am never to be found. He does not know God, who can imagine that such things are worthy of him.

XIX. After all, if it cannot be inferred from the very nature of the divine goodness, that God gives himself to be enjoyed by a holy creature, proportionable to its state; it is possible, notwithstanding the goodness of God, that the more holy a creature is, the more miserable. Which I prove thus: the more holy any one is, he loves God with the greater intenseness of all his powers: the more he loves, the more he

longs, hungers, and thirsts, after him : the more intense the
hunger and thirst, the more intolerable the pain, unless he
finds wherewith to be satisfied. If therefore, this thirst be
great to the highest degree, the want of what is so ardently
desired, will cause an incredible pain. Whence I infer, that
God cannot, consistent with his goodness, refuse to grant to
his holy creature the communion of himself. Unless we yield
this, it will follow, that, notwithstanding the goodness of God,
it is possible for the highest degree of holiness to become the
highest pitch of misery.

XX. But let it be again observed here, (of which we gave
a hint, § VIII.) that this communion of God, of which we
are speaking, which the goodness of the supreme Being requires to be granted to a holy creature, is not all the promise
of the covenant here ; which is at length to be given, upon
fulfilling the condition. For it is not to be reckoned among
the promises of the covenant, what God gives his creature
now, before he has confirmed the conditions of the covenant.
Another and a far greater thing is promised, after the constancy of his obedience is tried, to which the creature acquires
some right, not simply because it is holy, (for such it came
out of the hands of its Creator) but because it has now added
constancy to holiness, being sufficiently tried to the satisfaction of its Lord. The promises therefore of the covenant
contain greater things than this communion and fruition of
God, of whatsoever kind it be, which Adam already enjoyed
whilst still in the state of trial. A farther degree of happiness, consisting in the full and immediate enjoyment of God,
and in a more spiritual state, to last for ever, was proposed
to him, which the scripture usually sets forth under the title
of eternal life.

XXI. And this is the proper question ; whether the promise of eternal life, to be entered upon by all after a complete
course of obedience, flows from the natural goodness of God,
or, whether it is of free and liberal good pleasure ? Indeed, I
know not, whether the safest course be not to suspend the
decision of this, till coming to see God face to face, we shall
attain to a fuller knowledge of all his perfections, and more
clearly discern what is worthy of them. For, on the one
hand, it appears to me hard to affirm, and somewhat too bold,
for any one obstinately to insist, that it would have been unbecoming God and his perfections, to enter into covenant with
man in this manner: namely, if thou keepest my commands,
thou shalt certainly have my favour and most endearing love,
I will not only save thee from all uneasiness, but also load

thee with every benefit, and even bless thee with the communion of myself; till having performed thy part, and being
amply enough rewarded, I shall at length say, Now return to
that nothing out of which thou wast created, and my will is,
that this my last command be no less cheerfully obeyed than
the others, lest thou shouldst forfeit by this last act of disobedience, all the praise of thy former obedience. Has the
creature any cause to complain of such a stipulation? Nay,
rather, may it not give him joy, since it is far better to have
existed for a few ages in a state of holiness and happiness, than
never to have existed at all.

XXII. On the other hand, I can scarce satisfy myself in
my attempts to remove some difficulties. For since (as we
before proved) God does, by virtue of his natural goodness,
most ardently love a holy creature, as the lively image of
himself, how can this his goodness destroy that image, and
undo his own work? *Is it good unto thee that thou shouldst
despise the work of thine hands* without deserving such
treatment? Job x. 3. If it was good, and for the glory of
God, to have made a creature to glorify himself; will it be
good, and for the glory of God, to annihilate that creature,
who thus glorifies him? And thus in fact to say, thou shalt
not glorify me for ever? Besides, as God himself has created
the most intense desire of eternity in the soul, and at the same
time, has commanded it to be carried out towards himself, as
its eternal good; is it becoming God to frustrate such a desire, commanded and excited by himself? Further, we have
said, it was a contradiction, to suppose God addressing himself to a holy soul in the manner following: hunger after me,
but thou shalt not enjoy me. Yet in the moment we conceive the holy creature just sinking into annihilation, it would
in consequence of that divine command hunger and thirst
after God, without any hope of ever enjoying him again.
Unless we would choose to affirm, that God at length should
say to that soul, Cease longing for me any more, acquiesce in
this instance of my supreme dominion, by which I order thee
to return to nothing. But I own it surpasses my comprehension, how it is possible a holy creature should not be bound to
consider God as its supreme good, and consequently pant after
the enjoyment of him.

XXIII. O Lord Jehovah, how little do we poor miserable
mortals know of thy Supreme Deity, and incomprehensible
perfections! how far short do our thoughts come about thee,
who art infinite or immense in thy being, thy attributes, thy
sovereignty over the creatures! what mortal can take upon

him to set bounds to this thy sovereignty, where thou dost
not lead the way! Lord, we know that thou art indebted to
none, and that there is none who can say to thee, what dost
thou, or why dost thou so? That thou art also holy, and infinitely good, and therefore a lover and rewarder of holiness.
May the consciousness of our ignorance in other things kin-
dle in our hearts an ineffable desire of that beatific vision,
by which, knowing as we are known, we may in the abyss
of thy infinity behold those things which no thought of ours
at present can reach.

CHAP. V.

Of the Penal Sanction.

I. It remains that we consider *the Penal Sanction*, expressed
by God in these terms, Gen. ii. 17. " for in the day that thou
eatest thereof (the tree of knowledge of good and evil) thou
shalt surely die."

II. Several things are here to be distinctly noted. 1st. That
all that God here threatens is the consequence and punishment of sin, to be only inflicted on the rebellious and disobedient: and therefore Socinus and his followers most absurdly
make the death mentioned in the threatening, a consequence
not so much of sin, as of nature; but God's words are plain
to any man's conscience, that death flows from eating of
the forbidden tree. 2dly. That the sin here expressed is
a violation not of the natural, but of the symbolical law,
given to man for the trial of his most perfect obedience. But
even from this he might easily gather, that if the transgression of a precept, whose universal goodness depends only on
the good pleasure of God, is thus to be punished, the transgression of that law which is the transcript of the most holy
nature of God, deserves much greater. 3dly. That it is altogether agreeable to God's authority and most righteous
will, that there be a certain connection between the sin and
the punishment, denounced by these words. This also is
indicated by the ingemination in the original, *Dying thou shalt
die;* that is, thou shalt most certainly die. So that, it is not
possible for the sinner to escape death, unless perhaps a proper sponsor (of which this is not the proper place) should
undergo it in his stead. 4thly. That the words of the
threatening are general, and therefore by the term *death*, we
ought here to understand, whatever the scripture any where

signifies by that name. For who will presume to have a right
of limiting the extent of the divine threatening? Nay, the
words are not only general, but ingeminated too, plainly teaching us, that they are to be taken in their full emphasis or signification. 5thly. That they are spoken to Adam in such a
manner as also to relate to his posterity: a certain evidence,
that Adam was the representative of all. 6thly. That on the
very day the sin should be committed, punishment should be
inflicted on man: justice required this, and it has been verified
by the event. For in the very moment when man sinned, he
became obnoxious to death, and immediately upon finishing his
sin, felt *the beginnings* both of corporal and spiritual death.
These things are here expressed with far greater simplicity
than in the fictions of the Jewish doctors, according to Ben
Jacchi, on Dan. vii. 25. where he speaks thus: " A thousand
years are as one time, and one day, in the sight of the holy
and blessed God, according to Psal. xc. 4. For a thousand
years in thy sight are but as yesterday;" and our doctors of
blessed memory, said, " Gen. ii. 17. for in the day that thou
eatest thereof, thou shalt surely die, is to be understood of the
day of the holy and blessed; that therefore the first man did
not complete his day, (not arrive at his thousandth year;) that
of that day he wanted seventy years." But this is far fetched,
and savours of rabbinical dotage.

III. It will be far more useful a little more accurately to
examine what is here meant by the word *death*. And, first,
it is most obvious, that by that term is denoted that bad disposition of the body, now unfit for the soul's constant residence, and by which the soul is constrained to a separation
from it. By this separation the good things of the body,
which are unhappily doted on, the fruits of sin, and the sinner's ill-grounded hope, are snatched away at once. God intimates this, Gen. iii. 19. " till thou return unto the ground;
for out of it wast thou taken: for dust thou art, and unto
dust shalt thou return." That is, thy body which was formed
out of the earth shall return to its principles, and be reduced to earth again, unto which by its nature it is resolvable,
as being taken out of it. And the reason why it is actually
to be resolved unto earth is, because it really is what God
said, *thou art dust,* now corrupted with earthly desires, a
slave to a body prone to sin, and taken from dust. In this
sense Abraham confesses himself *to be dust and ashes,* Gen.
xviii. 27. that is, a mortal sinner. And David says, Psal.
ciii. 14. *he knoweth our frame,* (called, Gen. viii. 21. *an
evil frame,* which passage Kimchi directs to be compared with

this,) *he remembereth that we are dust*, attached to the ground,
and viciously inclined to the good things of the earth. From
this consideration, the prophet amplifies the mercy of God, in
exercising it towards sinners, in whom he finds nothing to deserve his love. And by *dust* is clearly signified, Isa. lxv. 25.
the sinful body. Where it is said of the serpent, the devil,
now overcome by the kingdom of the Messiah, *dust shall be
his food,* he shall only have the pleasure to destroy the body,
and men of carnal dispositions. Whereas then, after Adam
sinned, God condemned him to the death of the body for his
sin, it is not to be doubted, but he also comprised this death
in the commination. Unless we will venture to affirm, that
God has inflicted greater punishment on the sinner, than he
threatened before the commission of sin.

IV. There is nothing so suprising but what may be devised by a luxuriant fancy. There is a certain learned man,
who, in the words of Moses above explained, can find an extraordinary promise, and even clearer and more pregnant with
consolation, than the prophecy concerning the seed of the
woman. He thinks here is pointed out the period and boun-
dary of toils ; that the meaning is, *till thou shalt return to
this land,* paradise, the state of happy souls, from which לקחת,
thou wast carried captive. For, thus Solomon לקים למות,
captivated to death, and Jeremiah לקחו, *Thy children carried
unto captivity.* And he thinks, that the opinions of the Jews
concerning the gathering of the souls into paradise, has no
other passage or foundation to support it. But this is nothing but the sally of a wanton imagination. Whereas, for
our part, we take pleasure only in what is sound and sober,
and yields satisfaction to the conscience. But to return to
our subject.

V. It is no ways strange, that the Socinians, whose practice it is to wrest the scriptures, should contradict this truth,
and deny that the death of the body is the punishment of sin.
Their other perverse hypotheses make this necessary. For,
by denying this, they imagine they can more easily answer
our arguments for original sin, taken from the death of infants, and for the satisfaction of the Lord Christ, from his
death. And as they impiously deny the true Godhead of
Christ, they allege as the most excellent sign of his fictitious
divinity, that he was the first preacher, author, and bestower
of immortality ; but their blasphemies have been largely and
solidly refuted by others. But I am sorry that any learned
person of our own should deny, that by the death denounced,
Gen. ii. 17. the death of the body ought to be understood ;

and who thinks he grants a great deal when he writes as follows : " From which place, if any insist they can prove a manifold ' death, eternal, spiritual, and corporal, and other afflictions, I can easily bear their fighting with these weapons
against the enemies, so they can extort from them what they
want." These are none of the best expressions. Why, without necessity, grant so much to our adversaries ? Is it at all
commendable for us to weaken those arguments which have
been happily made use of in defence of the truth ? This learned person owns, that death is the punishment of sin, and that
it may be evidently proved from the sentence pronounced upon
Adam, Gen. iii. 19. What reason is there then not to believe,
that the same death was proposed to man in the preceding
threatening ? Are not the words general, and ingeminated to
give them the greater emphasis ? Is not the death of the
body expressly set forth by the very same phrase, 1 Kings
ii. 37. where Solomon tells Shimei, *thou shalt die the death?*
Is not the very sound of the words such as a man cannot but
have this death of the body come into his mind, unless a pre-
judiced person should refuse to understand here by death, what
every one else does when death is spoken of ? Is it not also
highly becoming the divine goodness and justice, to inflict nothing by a condemnatory sentence on man, which was not previously threatened against sin; lest haply man should plead
in excuse, he did not know that God would so highly resent,
and so severely punish sin ? And seeing this learned person
would have death eternal here meant, does not that include the
death of the body ? Is the former ever inflicted on man, but
after the latter, by raising him from that death, that the whole
man, soul and body, may be eternally miserable ? Why are thus
suspicions entertained, of which, alas ! we have but too many ?
I could wish we all spoke with caution, *with fear and trembling!* This learned person will, it is hoped, not take amiss,
if I here suggest to him the very prudent advice of Cocceius,
which in a like case he inculcates, on Gen. iii. § 190. " Those
of our party, says he, want we should employ stronger arguments against the Jews. And certainly, that admonition is
good; namely, when we have to do with infidels we are to
make use of cogent arguments; lest we become the derision
of infidels, and confirm them in error. But as to the inculcating that rule, it is neither safe nor prudent, readily and
frequently to oppose it to the arguments of Ecclesiastics. For,
if thereby we refute them, N. B. we then go over to the party
of the adversaries, and we arm them, and teach them to cavil. But if we do not refute them, but only inculcate that ad-

monition; an injury is certainly done both to the disputant and the hearer, and we seem to give our own opinion as an argument. Let every one therefore argue with the utmost solidity : and if any manifestly abuses scripture, let him be corrected in a brotherly manner, upon pointing out his fault. As for the rest, let the arguments of believers be thoroughly tried, and not hissed off the stage."

VI. Secondly. By death is here understood, all that lasting and hard labour, that great sorrow, all the tedious miseries of this life, by which life ceases to be life, and which are the sad harbingers of certain death. To these things man is condemned, Gen. iii. 16, 17, 18, 19. The whole of that sentence is founded on the antecedent threatening: such miseries Pharaoh himself called by the name, Death, Exod. x. 17. And David, Psal. cxvi. 3. calls his pain and anguish, חבלימזת, *the bands* (sorrows) *of death ;* by these death binds and fastens men that he may thrust them into, and confine them in his dungeon. Thus also Paul, 2 Cor. xi. 23. " In deaths often," and 2 Cor. iv. 11. " are always delivered unto death ;" ib. v. 12. " Death worketh in us." As life is not barely to live, but to be happy ; so death is not to depart this life in a moment, but rather to languish in a long expectation, dread, and foresight, of certain death, without knowing the time which God has foreordained. Finely to this purpose, says Picus Mirandula, in his treatise de Eute and uno. " For, we begin, should you haply not know it, to die then, when we begin first to live ; and death runs parallel with life : and we then first cease to die when set free from this mortal body by the death of the flesh."

VII. Thirdly. Death signifies spiritual death, or the separation of the soul from God. Elegantly has Isidorus, Pelusiota iii. 232. defined it ; " The death of the immortal soul is the departure of the holy Spirit from it." This is what the Apostle calls, Eph. iv. 18. " being alienated from the life of God," which illuminates, sanctifies, and exhilirates the soul. For, the life of the soul consists in wisdom, in pure love, and to have the rejoicing of a good conscience. The death of the soul consists in folly, and, through concupiscence, in a separation from God, and the tormenting rackings of an evil conscience. Hence the apostle says, Eph. ii. 1. " We are dead in trespasses and sins."

VIII. But I would more fully explain the nature of this death, not indeed in my own, but in the words of another, because I despaired to find any more emphatical. Both living and dead bodies have motion. But a living body moves by vegetation, while it is nourished, has the use of its senses, is delighted, and acts with pleasure. Whereas, the dead body moves by putrefaction to a state of dissolution, and to the production of lothesome animals. And so in the soul, spiritually alive, there is motion, while it is fed, repasted, and fattened with divine delights, while it takes pleasure in God and true wisdom, while, by the strength of its love, it is carried to, and fixed on that which can sustain the soul, and give it a sweet repose. But a dead soul has no feeling; that is, it neither understands truth, nor loves righteousness, wallows, and is spent and tired out, in the sink of concupiscence, breeds and brings forth the worms of impure and abominable thoughts, reasonings, and affections. Men therefore alienated from that spiritual life, which consists in the light of wisdom, and the activity of love, who delight in their own present happiness, are no better than living carcases, 1 Tim. v. 6. dead whilst living: and hence in scripture are said to be spiritually dead.

IX. The word, גבל, ἄφρων, which the scripture applies to such, is both emphatical and of a very fertile signification. For, it denotes, 1st. A fool, corrupt in all the faculties of the soul, void of that spiritual wisdom, the beginning of which is the fear of the Lord. " Nabal is his name, and folly is with him," is Abigail's character of her husband, 1 Sam. xxv. 25. This גבל is opposed to חכם, wise, Deut. xxxii. 6. " O foolish people and unwise." 2dly. It also denotes a wicked person, Psal. lxxiv. 18. " the foolish people have blasphemed thy name." 3dly, and lastly. It signifies one in a dead and withered state; the root גבל denoting " to wither and die away," Isa. xl. 7. " the flower fadeth :" גבלה is a dead body, Isa. xxvi. 19. " thy dead men shall live." All which conjointly denote a man devoid of the wisdom of God, overwhelmed with sin, and destitute of the life of God; in a word, faded and breeding worms, like a dead body. In all which spiritual death consists.

X. This spiritual death, is both sin and the natural consequence of the first sin, being at the same time threatened as the punishment of sin. For, as it renders man vile, and entirely incapable to perform those works which alone are worthy of him, as it makes him like the brute creatures, nay, and even like the devil himself, and unlike God, the only blessed being, and consequently renders him highly miserable, so it must be an exceeding great punishment of sin.

XI. Fourthly, and lastly. Eternal death is also here intended. The preludes of which, in this life, are the terrors and anguish of an evil conscience, the abandoning of the soul, deprived of all divine consolation, and the sense of the divine wrath, under which it is miserably pressed down. There will ensue upon this the translation of the soul to a place of torments, Luke xvi. 23—25. Where shall be the hiding of God's face, the want of his glorious presence, and a most intense feeling of the wrath of God, for ever and ever, together with horrible despair, Rev. xiv. 11. At last will succeed, after the end of the world, the resurrection of the body, to eternal punishment, Acts xxiv. 15.

XII. And here again, the Socinian divinity, adopted by the Remonstrants, thwarts the truth: maintaining, Ap. p. 57. that " by these words, thou shalt surely die, or by any others elsewhere, Adam was not threatened with eternal death, in the sense of the Evangelists (or Protestants), so as to comprise the eternal death of body and soul, together with the punishment of sense: but directly corporal death only, or a separation of soul and body; which, all the evils disposing to death do precede ; and upon which, at length, the eternal punishment of loss, that is, the privation of the vision of God, or of grace and glory, will ensue." Another of that class, who examined in French the doctrine of Amiraldus and Testard, violently contends, that " in the law there is no mention of the sense of infernal pains, but that it is peculiar to the gospel, and threatened at last, against the profane despisers thereof," p. 59. and 114. Though elsewhere he adds, those " who stifle the light of reason, or hold the truth in unrighteousness, the more freely to fulfil the lusts of the flesh." As to others, he thinks, a middle state is to be assigned them, into which they may be received, different from the kingdom of heaven, and the damnation of hell fire: such as perhaps, that they are for ever to remain in the dust, to which they are to be reduced, and from thence never to arise, Curcellæus, dissert. de necess. Cognit. Christian. § 5.

XIII. But this is the rankest poison. For, either they would insinuate that the soul of a sinner is to be cut off, destroyed and annihilated, like some of the Jews, and Maimonides himself, as quoted by Abarbanel, on Mal. iv. who place eternal death in this, that " the soul shall be cut off, shall perish, and not survive:" from which leaven of the Epicureans and Sadducees, the Socinians profess themselves not averse : or else they assert what is the most absurd, repugnant, and tends to weaken the authority and meaning of the whole scripture. For it is impossible to conceive the soul of man in a state of existence, excluded from the beatific vision of God, deprived

of the sense of his grace and glory, and not be most grievously
tortured with the loss of this chief good ; especially as conscience shall incessantly upbraid the soul, who, through its
own folly, was the cause of all this misery, and torment it
with the most dire despair of ever obtaining any happiness.
And seeing God does not exclude man from the vision of his
face, where is fulness of joy, without the justest displeasure,
a holy indignation, and an ardent zeal against sin and the sinner ; the privation of this supreme happiness arising from the
wrath of God, cannot but be joined with a sense of the divine
displeasure and malediction. These things flow from the very
nature of the soul, and deserve a fuller illustration.

XIV. The soul of man was formed for the contemplation
of God, as the supreme truth, truth itself, and to seek after
him, with all the affection of his soul as the supreme good,
goodness itself ; and it may be said truly to live, when it delights in the contemplation of that truth, and in the fruition
of that goodness. But when, by the just sentence of a despised Deity, it is excluded that most pleasant contemplation
of truth, and most delightful fruition of goodness ; then it must
certainly own itself to be dead. And as it is so delightful to
enjoy a good, most desirable and desired ; so it must be afflict-
ing and painful, to be disappointed of it. But since the soul,
which is a spiritual substance, endued with understanding and
will, cannot be without the active exercise of these faculties,
especially when let loose from the fetters of the body ; it must
necessarily perceive itself miserable, by being deprived of the
chief good ; and being conscious of its misery, most bitterly
lament the want of that good, which it was formed to seek
after. To suppose a soul that has neither understanding nor
will, is to suppose it not to be a soul. Just as if one supposed
a body without quantity and extension : again, to suppose a
soul sensible of its misery, and not grieved because of it, is contrary to the nature, both of the soul, and of misery. It is certainly, therefore, an absurd and contradictory fiction, to suppose
the human soul to be under the punishment of loss without the
punishment of sense at the same time.

XV. Further, as the soul cannot be ignorant that God is infinitely good, and that it is the nature of goodness to be com-
municative ; it thence certainly gathers, that something exceedingly contrary to God must be found in itself, which he
has the most perfect detestation of, and on account of which
he, who is infinitely good, can have no communion with his
creature : and that therefore that non-communion is the most
evident sign and sad effect of the divine displeasure, depriving

the man of the fruition of that good by which alone he could
be happy. And thus, in this punishment of loss there is an
exquisite sense of the wrath of God : with which no torments
of the body by material fire can be compared.

XVI. Besides, the soul being conscious to itself of having
by its sins been the cause of this misery, becomes enraged
against itself, accuses, abhors, tears itself, acts the tormentor
against itself, and under this lash more severely smarts, than
any criminal under the hands of the most unrelenting execu-
tioner. Add, that all hope of a happy restitution failing,
being racked with horrid despair, it is appointed to eternal
misery. All these things are so closely connected, as to make
themselves manifest to every conscience, upon the least attention.

XVII. The same things the scripture expressly teach, when
they speak of eternal punishment, Matt. xxv. 46. and torments,
Luke xvi. 23, 28. of " the worm that dieth not, and the fire
that is not quenched," Mark ix. 44. and the like; expressions
too strong to be understood of the punishment of loss only,
without that of sense.

XVIII. And it is absurd to say, that this punishment is
threatened only against the contemners of the gospel, seeing
Paul testifies, that Christ is to come " in flaming fire, taking
vengeance, not only on them that obey not the gospel, but
on them that know not God," 2 Thess. 1. 8. compare 1 Thess.
iv. 5. " the Gentiles which know not God." Such namely,
who would not know God even from the works of creation,
and " did not like to retain God in their knowledge," Rom. i.
28. The very power of truth obliged Curcellæus to say, in
the place above cited, " these are altogether inexcusable before
God, and therefore it is not to be wondered, if, hereafter, they
be consigned to the punishment of eternal fire." And our adversaries will not say, that the gospel was preached to those
of Sodom and Gomorrah, and the neighbouring cities. And
yet, concerning them Jude writes, ver. 7. that " they are set
forth for an example, suffering the vengeance of eternal fire."
Words not to be restricted to that fire wherewith those cities
were burnt, but to be extended to the flames of hell, with
which the lewd inhabitants of those cities are at this very day
tormented. These things are to be distinguished, which the
nature of the things teaches to be distinct. Thus, we are to
understand, " giving themselves over to fornication, and going
after strange flesh," of the inhabitants and not of the towns.
But it is true of both, that they were burnt with fire : which,
with respect to the towns, may in some measure be said to be

eternal, they being so consumed as that they never shall or can be restored. But it is truly eternal with respect to the inhabitants, who, by the vengeance of God, were not annihilated ; but at the time, when the apostle was writing, having been cast headlong into everlasting pain and torment, they suffered the punishment of that fire, of which " whoremongers shall have their part in the lake which burneth with fire and brimstone," Rev. xxi. 8. So these cities are an emblem or type of eternal fire, but their wicked inhabitants " suffer the vengeance of eternal fire," and so both are for an example (Peter says, 2 Pet. ii. 6. an example,) by which we are reminded, what whoremongers are to expect.

XIX. Christ also expressly declares to the same purpose, Matt. xxv. 41. that all who shall be placed on his left hand, and not declared heirs of eternal life, shall by a righteous sentence, be condemned to " everlasting fire, which is prepared for the devil and his angels," which fire, ver. 46. is explained to be κόλασιν αιώνιον " everlasting punishment." We cannot approve what Curcellæus, in the said dissertation, § 6. has written ; that in " Matthew is not described a judgment in every respect universal, of all who ever had existed, but only of those who made a profession of the Christian religion ; some of whom behaved becoming the gospel, others not." These are expressions not of the best stamp. For, shall not that judgment be universal, which our Lord extends to all nations ? Matt. xxv. 32. " To all the tribes of the earth ?" Matt. xxiv. 30. In which every eye shall see Christ the judge ? Rev. i. 7. In which, according to Paul, Acts xvii. 31. " he will judge the world ? In which both sea, and death, and hell will deliver up their dead to be judged ? Rev. xx. 13. In which shall be accomplished the prediction which God solemnly confirmed by oath, saying, " every knee shall bow to me, and every tongue shall confess to God ?" Rom. xiv. 11. In which even the men of Nineveh and the queen of the south, shall rise to condemn the wicked Jews ? Matt. xii. 41, 42. And their portion of torment be assigned to those of Tyre, and Sidon, and Sodom ? Matt. xi. 22, 24. In which shall be inflicted on that servant who knew not his master's will, and did commit things worthy of stripes, his due measure of stripes ? Luke xii. 48. In which, in fine, " they who have sinned without law, shall perish without law ?" Rom. ii. 12. To restrict all this to those to whom the gospel has been preached, is to make sport with scripture, but God will not be sported with.

XX. But should Curcellæus perhaps reply, that he denies

not an universal judgment to come, but that it is not described
either in Matt. xxv. or in those passages, in which the men
to be judged are divided into two classes, as John v. 28, 29.
2 Thess. i. 6, &c. I answer, 1st. That the scripture makes
mention but of one judgment to be held on the last day, and
no where teaches us, that a different tribunal is to be erected
for those to whom the gospel was not preached, and for those
to whom it was. Paul was preaching, Acts xxiv. 25. " of the
judgment to come," in the singular number ; in like manner,
Heb. vi. 2. " of eternal judgment." 2dly. The passages alleged, have the marks of universality affixed to them. For,
John v. 28. it is said, " all that are in the graves shall hear
the voice of the Son of man," and v. 29. this universality is
not to be divided into those who either by faith received the
gospel preached to them, or perversely rejected it ; but into
those, " who have done good or evil," without mentioning the
gospel in the least. And 2 Thess. i. 6, &c. the punishment
of eternal destruction will be inflicted, by the sentence of the
judge, not only on those who were disobedient to the gospel, but also on those who knew not God, viz. God the
Creator, to the knowledge and worship of whom nature alone
might have led men, unless they had extinguished its light
through their wickedness, as Curcellæus himself explains it.
3dly. Nor is it any thing singular to distribute the persons
to be judged into two classes, but common in every judgment
concerning all mankind : of which there are but two dissimu-
lar bodies, either of those to be acquitted, or those to be condemned. An intermediate state the scripture knows nothing of.

XXI. The only thing specious adduced by Curcellæus, is
this, that Christ cannot upbraid those who knew nothing of
his will, with these words, *I was an hungered*, &c. But we
answer ; 1st. That Christ, in what he here speaks, takes not
in the whole process of the judgment, but only mentions this
by way of example. For who can doubt that more things
are to be considered in this judgment even with respect to
those to whom the gospel was preached, than barely those
effects of charity towards the godly when afflicted ? 2dly. The
scripture declares that *all the actions* of all persons shall be
tried in this judgment, Eccl. xii. 14. 2 Cor. v. 10. Rom.
ii. 5, 6, &c. Even *words*, Matt. xii. 37. both *the idle and
hard*, Jude 15. nay, even *the secrets of the heart*, Rom.
ii. 15, 16. 1 Cor. iv. 5. 3dly. It is not our business to determine with what the Judge may justly upbraid the damned.
It is plain, he will upbraid them with those things at least,
which they shall hear with the most dreadful amazement.

And seeing all the damned have discovered many evidences of an unrelenting, unmerciful, and unbeneficial disposition; who of us shall dare to censure Christ, for interpreting this their conduct, as if they would have shewn himself no kind of compassion, had he come among them in person? 4thly, and lastly. Granting that Christ may not upbraid all the wicked with this, yet does it not follow, that they are not to come to judgment; because there are many other things that shall be tried in this judgment, and for which they shall be condemned, which the scripture elsewhere declares, though, in this summary, Christ makes no mention of them. There is nothing to constrain us to believe that every thing relative to this judgment is to be learned from this passage alone: other testimonies of scripture are to be consulted, which treat on the same subject.

XXII. It remains that we enquire whence this Penal Sanction is to be derived; whether from the mere good pleasure of the divine will only, or rather from the natural and immutable justice of God, to which it would be unbecoming to have ordered otherwise. I shall not now repeat what the antagonists of the Socinians have fully and happily illustrated, concerning vindictive justice, as an essential property of God, and the necessity of its exercise, in case of sin. First, I shall only propose some arguments, by which this general proposition may, I think, be most evidently demonstrated, that it is agreeble to God's very nature and immutable right, not to let sin go unpunished; and *then* more especially inquire into the eternity of punishment.

XXIII. And first, let us duly consider the infinite *majesty* of God, and his supreme authority over all things; which is so illustrious, that it obliges rational creatures capable of knowing it, to obey and serve him, as we proved, chap. ii. § VIII. As often then as they in the least deprive him of this obedience, they directly incur the guilt of high treason against the divine majesty, and consequently are bound over to a punishment adequate to this crime, for neglect of obedience. For *the sinner*, as Thomas [Aquinas] justly said, *as much as in him lies, destroys God and his attributes*, slighting that majesty of God to which it is necessary that all things be subject, from the consideration both of God and the creatures. But it is altogether impossible that God should not love in the tenderest manner, both himself, his majesty, and his glory. Now he cannot but resent an injury done to what he thus loves. And therefore he calls himself, אל קנא *a jealous God*, and declares that this is his name, Exod. xxxiv.

14. But קִנְאָה denotes *resentment for the dearest thing:*
and hence *jealousy* and *great fury* are joined together, Zech.
viii. 2. But above all things he is jealous for his *name,* that
is, that it be made known to men as it is, Ezek. xxxix. 25.
and will be jealous for my holy name. In which name even
this is contained, *and will by no means clear the guilty,* Exod.
xxxiv. 7.

XXIV. We may likewise argue from the majesty of God
in this manner: It is altogether *impossible* that God *should
deny himself,* 2 Tim. ii. 13. that is, that he should conceal
his own imperfections, or do any thing to make him appear to
be what he is not, or that he is not possessed of properties
truly divine: and that because he himself is the archtype and
exemplar of the intelligent creature; to whom he is to discover in his works, his nature, dignity, prerogative, and excellence. He would therefore deny himself, did he conceal
his majesty, much more did he suffer man to slight it, which
is done by every sin. For the sinner behaves so in his presence as if there was no God to whom he owed obedience:
nay, as if himself was God, who had a right to dispose of
himself, his faculties, and other things with which he sins, at
his own pleasure and without any controul, saying, *Who is
lord over me?* Psal. xii. 5. This is indeed to usurp the
majesty of the Supreme Being. But how can God suffer
this to go unpunished? Unless we can suppose he can bear
any to be equal to him, which would have been an open
denial of his supremacy, majesty, and excellency. But he then
appears glorious in the eyes of sinners, when he inflicts
punishment on those who throw contempt upon his majesty.
Thus, Numb. xiv. 20. he swears, that " all the earth shall be
filled with the glory of God;" namely, by destroying in the
wilderness, those who did not believe though they had seen
the glory of God and his signs. The *glory of God,* in this
passage, signifies the manifestation of his jealousy against
those who despised him, for he will not suffer himself *to be
mocked.* And therefore, as he cannot but seek his own
glory, so he cannot suffer any to profane his majesty and go
unpunished.

XXV. Secondly. There are also several ways by which
this may, as evidently, be made appear from *the holiness* of
God.

XXVI. 1. God's holiness is such, that he cannot admit a
sinner to union and communion with himself without satisfaction first made to his justice. For, τίς γὰρ μετοχὴ " what fellowship (participation) hath righteousness with unrighteous-

ness ?" 2 Cor. vi. 14. Whoever touches what is unclean
can have no communion with God, verse 17. Every one
whom God unites to himself, " he causeth to cleave to himself as a girdle," that he may be unto him " for a name, and
for a praise, and for a glory," Jer. xiii. 11. But was he thus
to unite the sinner to himself, without a previous satisfaction
made for removing the guilt of sin, holiness itself would, in
that case, be united to, clothed and attended with sin; which
is a plain contradiction. It is indeed true that God had set
all these things before sinful Israel ; but that was done by
virtue of the covenant of grace, which supposes a due satisfaction. Nor are we to imagine that this union which God
describes in such magnificent language, was the lot of any
others, in its full emphasis and spiritual import, but of those
who were internally in covenant. Compare Deut. xvi. 19.
Should any object, that though it is really unbecoming the
holiness of God to favour the sinner with a communion of
friendship, while he continues such; yet he may certainly,
out of his goodness, take away sin, and so admit to his fellowship him who was before a sinner : I answer, that without a satisfaction, it is not consistent with the holiness of
God, even to sanctify the sinner, and thereby prevent him
with that greatest effect of his love. For if the beginning
of such a communion of God with the sinner, be not unbecoming his holiness, why do all allow it as to the progress
thereof ? It is plain, it is not suitable to the holiness of God
to cultivate a friendship with the sinner, so long as he continues such. But before sanctification he is nothing but a
sinner, nay, he is sin itself. Nor can a greater instance of
friendship be given to man than that by which he is sanctified. And therefore it is not consistent with the holiness of
God, without any satisfaction, to grant so great a favour to
the sinner, who is most worthy of his wrath. If it be still
urged, that though God cannot, consistent with his holiness,
love the sinner with a love of complacency, yet nothing hinders him from loving him with a love of benevolence, which
may so transform him as to render him a fit object of the
love of complacency : I answer, that this is spoken at ran-
dom : for those effects of the love of benevolence, by which
we are regenerated, are proposed to us in scripture, as consequences of the engagement and satisfaction of Christ, and of
our reconciliation with God, Tit. iii. 4, 5. 1 Cor. vi. 11.
1 Pet. i. 3. Faith, without which it is impossible to please
God, is freely bestowed on the elect, " through the righteousness of God, and our Saviour Jesus Christ," 2 Pet. i. 1.

Whatsoever way you interpret this, it at last appears, that the gift of faith is founded on Christ and his satisfaction. If therefore the satisfaction of Christ was previously requisite to the sinner's being blessed with those effects of the love of benevolence; it is rashly asserted, that it was becoming the holiness of God to bestow them on the sinner without satisfaction. Besides, God must needs punish those to whom he cannot grant union with himself; for the greatest punishment consists in the want of this union. This is that death with which the law threatens the sinner, as we have already made appear.

XXVII. 2. The holiness of God is so unspotted, that *he cannot behold evil, and look on iniquity,* Hab. i. 13. that is, bear it in his sight. He cannot therefore, " lift up the light of his countenance upon him," Psal. iv. 7. in which the salvation of men consists: but the privation of this is the highest punishment. As long as David refused to admit his son Absalom into his presence, though almost reconciled to him, this appeared to Absalom more intolerable than any death, 2 Sam. xiv. 32. So that in a nature conscious of its unhappiness, a punishment of sense cannot but accompany a punishment of loss.

XXVIII. 3. From the holiness of God flows a mortal and implacable hatred of sin. It is as much the nature of holiness to " hate iniquity, as to love righteousness," Psal. xlv. 8. Sin is " an abomination to his soul," Prov. vi. 16. that is, to his very essence, and essential holiness: and neither *sin* only, but also the *sinner* is the object of his hatred. " For all that do such things, and all that do unrighteously, are an abomination to the Lord thy God," Deut. xxv. 16. He therefore separates from himself, and from his chosen people, all whom he cannot make partakers of his favour: and so he cannot but inflict upon them that punishment which is the effect of his hatred. According to Solomon's reasoning, Prov. xvi. 5. " Every one that is proud in heart, is an abomination to the Lord." And the consequence is, *He shall not be unpunished.* In the same manner David reasons, Psal. v. 4, 5, 6. " Thou art not a God that hast pleasure in wickedness." Thou hatest sin, and the sinner too, because of it. " Thou hatest all the workers of iniquity." And surely the fruit of this must be exceeding bitter: " Thou shalt destroy them that speak leasing." And thus from the holiness of God, arises a hatred of sin and the sinner; from hatred, punishment.

XXIX. 4. It is doubtless diametrically opposite to the

holiness of God, that he should become like unto the sinner. For, as his image consists in a holiness every way perfect, it is a contradiction that it should consist in sin; but if God was unwilling to punish sin, he would then become like unto the sinner. This is what we may learn from himself, Psal. l. 21. when he would tell the sinner, thou thoughtest that I would not punish thy sin, he thus expresses it; " thou thoughtest that I was altogether such an one as thyself." But, says he, I will shew the contrary. And how? *I will reprove thee*, or punish thee. And by that I will, in effect, shew, that I am not like unto thee. Whence I conclude, that not to punish sin, would very much resemble the sinner; on the contrary, to punish sin in its proper time, is to shew himself most unlike to the sinner. Unless then God reproves the sinner, he will be like unto him, and deny himself. For since God is a pattern to man, and man was made in order that God may be glorified in him; and every thing that God hath made, has a tendency to this, namely, that man may from them know what a God he is: if God should by no method shew that sin deprives man of communion with him and of his kingdom; nay, should he make the sinner eternally happy; while it is the highest degree of punishment to be accounted unworthy of it, God would certainly in that case testify himself not worthy to be loved, desired, and glorified, and that sin is not an object unworthy of man's delight. As it is then impossible that God should be altogether like unto the sinner, it is likewise so, that he should let sin go unpunished.

XXX. 5. Hence God says, he is sanctified when he punishes, Lev. x. 3. On which place, Crellius himself, *de Vera Relig.* lib. i. c. 28. makes this annotation, which some learned men explain (and himself agrees with them), " I shall appear holy, that is, shall inflict punishment on them." The same thing he owns in the same chapter, that " neither the holiness, nor the majesty of God, can in any respect bear to have his commands violated with impunity." Such is the power of truth, that even the most obstinate are constrained to confess it! And the sense of this word is very evident, Ezek. xxxviii. 16.: where the punishment of Gog is foretold in these words: " That the heathen may know me, when I shall be sanctified in thee," viz. by thy punishment, " before their eyes:" more clearly still, Isa. v. 16. " God that is holy, shall be sanctified in righteousness," by inflicting on sinners the punishments threatened in the foregoing verses, and by not pardoning the elect, but only on account of the righteousness of Christ, in whose sufferings and death he displayed his most unspotted holiness, and his hatred of sin, before the whole world, nay, even before hell itself. It is therefore as necessary, that God should punish sin, as that he should be holy, lest he should seem to give up with his holiness. I shall conclude in the words of Joshua, xxiv. 19. " for he is an holy God." What then? " He is a jealous God." And what does he infer hence? " He will not forgive your transgressions, nor your sins." And thus from his holiness flows his jealousy, from his jealousy his vengeance.

XXXI. Thirdly. This may also be inferred from that attribute of God, which is usually called, *vindictive justice.* That it is the property of this to punish sin, the scriptures tell us in a thousand places; and heretics impudently cavil, when they assert it to be the work, not so much of divine justice, as of wrath and passion. They unadvisedly disjoin, what the apostle has conjoined, who speaks of *the day of wrath, and of the righteous judgment of God,* Rom. ii. 5. And is God's wrath any other than that ready disposition of the divine mind to do that which his hatred of sin, justice towards the sinner, and his character as the supreme judge, do require? I omit a thousand other considerations which occur every where. I shall rather shew where the stress of the whole lies. First, That this perfection is as natural to God, as infinity, holiness, omnipotence. Secondly, That in virtue of it, God cannot suffer sin to go unpunished.

XXXII. The former of these I thus prove. That perfection must belong to the nature and essence of God, and cannot be referred to the good pleasure of his will, if what is opposite to it cannot be conceived without a contradiction. But it is contradictory to conceive of God under any character opposite to that of just, or, as unjust, Job xxxiv. 10. But it is not contradictory, if I conceive of God even contrary to those things which depend on the mere good pleasure of his will: for instance, it was from the free will and pleasure of God, that he chose Israel for his peculiar people: if therefore I conceive of God, as having never been the God of Israel, I shall doubtless have formed a false conception, but nothing that, by an evident contradiction, destroys the nature of God. For he might have been God, and yet not the God of Israel; but if he had so pleased, the God of the Egyptians or Chaldeans. But whosoever says, that God is, and asserts that he is unjust, speaks contradictory things. For the first conception of the Deity is to be perfectly and infinitely good. But justice, in giving to every one his due, by a suitable compensation, belongs to this goodness: especially when we consider, that as he is the Lord of rational creatures, so he cannot but be their judge. Whoever therefore says that any is unjust, or not just, denies such to be God, of whom he thus speaks.

XXXIII. The latter I make out thus: The justice of God requires, that whatever is his righteous judgment be done; for it is necessary that God do himself justice; who, properly speaking, owes nothing to any one but to himself. As that is *the judgment* (righteousness) *of the law*, Rom. viii. 4. which the law demands, and which, without injustice, cannot be denied the law: what God requires, is the judgment of God, and cannot be denied him, unless he would be unjust to himself. But it is *the (judgment) of God, that they which do evil, are worthy of death*, Rom. i. 32. And therefore there is a connection between sin, and worthy of death, not only in virtue of the will, but of the justice of God. Moreover, as *the judgment* of God *is always according to truth*, Rom. ii. 2. he must pronounce the person unworthy of life, and worthy of death, who is worthy of it, consequently condemn him, unless a satisfaction intervene. To act otherwise, would be unworthy the just God. The apostle intimates this, Rom. iii. 25, 26. declaring, that " God set forth Christ to be a propitiation through faith in his blood, to declare his righteousness, that he might be just, and the justifier of him which believeth in Jesus." By which words he shews, if God should justify the wicked, and admit them to happiness without the atonement of the blood of Christ, he would not be just, at least, his justice would not be displayed.

XXXIV. Jeremiah has a most memorable passage, in which God says, ch. ix. 29. " Shall I not visit for these things, saith the Lord, and shall not my soul be avenged on such a nation as this?" The meaning is, shall I be Jehovah, nay, shall I not deny myself, if I bear with those things in my people? It is impossible I should do this, and that in virtue of *my soul*, that is, of my very essential holiness and Deity. Should I have a divine *soul*, that is, a divine *nature*, and just, and not be avenged of sin? For *the soul* of God denotes *the most holy nature* of God, or, which is the same, *the essential holiness* of God. As appears from comparing Amos iv. 2. with Amos vi. 8. In the former it is said, *the Lord hath sworn by his holiness:* in the latter, *the Lord hath sworn by* (his soul) *himself.*

XXXV. Crellius therefore trifles, *de vera Relig.* lib. i. c. 28. when he ridiculously said, that to punish is God's foreign and strange work; as if to shew mercy was God's proper work, but to punish his strange work. To that end wresting, Isa. xxviii. 21. " that he may do his work," which he thus translates, " his strange works; that he may work his work, foreign (or strange) is his work to him." We freely own, that by that foreign and

strange work, we ought to understand his vengeance against
the rebellious Jews. But it is said to be strange and foreign,
in a quite different sense from what this perverter of scripture
would have it. It was *strange and foreign*, because altogether
uncommon and extraordinary. For, it was a *great tribulation,
such as was not since the beginning of the world to that time,*
Matt. xxiv. 21. Likewise, because any would think it strange,
that God should deal thus with his own covenant people, on
whom he had multiplied so many favours, and make examples
of them, in a manner he had not done to his enemies, who were
strangers to his covenant. What he had done in mount Pera-
zim against the Philistines, 2 Sam. v. 21. and in the valley
of Gibeon, could scarcely be compared to this. It is likewise
so called, because such an extraordinary punishment from God
(as strange and unusual things very commonly do) would fill
any with such astonishment as they would be obliged to take
notice of the hand of God in it. Thus the miseries of the
Jews struck Titus himself with horror; and, on viewing the
walls and towers of Jerusalem, confessed, that without God,
such a city could never be taken. It is very remarkable what
Philostratus relates in the life of Apollonius Tyanæus, lib. v.
c. 14. When the neighbouring nations came, according to
custom, to adorn Titus with crowns, for his conquest of the
Jews; he said, *that he deserved no such honour: that he did
not achieve those things, but only was the instrument of God,
who was then displaying his wrath.* In like manner also,
because it was strange and foreign to the Israelites; who, that
the Romans might not come and destroy their city, brought
upon themselves the guilt of that wickedness against the Lord
Jesus, which was the cause of so great a destruction. It was
therefore strange and foreign, not to God, (for the text says
no such thing,) but in itself and to men. Or if we would say,
that it was altogether strange and foreign to God; it must
be meant, because God delights not either in destruction, or
in the destruction of his creatures, as such, but, (to speak after the manner of men,) is rather inclined to acts of goodness
and mercy. But this is so far from being of service to the
heretic, that, on the contrary, it furnishes us with a new and
solid argument. Thus,

XXXVI. Fourthly. It is certain that penal evil, as such, is
not in itself desirable, even to God, because it is connected
with the destruction of his own work. " Is it good unto thee·
that thou shouldst oppress? that thou shouldst despise the
work of thine hands?" Job x. 3. Nay, God confirms by an
inviolable oath, that *he has no pleasure in the death of the*

wicked, Ezek. xxxiii. 11. It must then be something else, which renders it desirable, that God declares, that *he exults* in it, and *derives* great *consolation* from it, as being that alone which can, as it were, be sufficient to mitigate his grief, and appease his indignation occasioned by sin. Nothing can be imagined stronger than the scripture phrases on this subject, some of which I shall exhibit; Hos. x. 10. " It is *in my desire* that I should chastise them." Amos v. 9. " That *refreshes himself* by desolation, (strengtheneth the spoiled) against the strong." Deut. xxviii. 36. " The Lord will rejoice over you to destroy you." Isa. i. 24. " I will ease me of my adversaries, and avenge me of my enemies." God, you see, desires to punish sinners. Whenever he pours out desolation upon them, he refreshes *(strengtheneth)* himself ; nor slightly only, but he both rejoices and exults ; and that with such a joy as may be capable of mitigating the pain caused by sin, and consequently of yielding consolation to God. What can it be which makes that evil of the creature so desirable to the Creator ? What other but that by inflicting punishment, he preserves inviolable the glory of his supremacy, holiness, and justice, which sin would wholly obscure? For, all the usefulness of punishment (as Crellius himself speaks,) *must needs regard God.* But we can conceive here no advantage redounding to God, unless his rejoicing in the declaration of his glory, shining forth in that judgment, the justice of which the holy angels acknowledge with applause, Rev. xi. 17. and xvi. 5, 6. and even the damned themselves, though unwilling and gnashing their teeth, are constrained to confess. It is indeed impossible that God should set light by this his most excellent glory, of which he is so jealous. As it is then necessary, that God should prefer the destruction of his wicked creature to that of his own glory, so it is necessary that he should punish the wicked. God indeed loves his creatures, but he does, as he ought, much more himself. He would act inconsistent with that love, was he not to recover his glory, which his sinful creature has by horrible sacrilege robbed him of, by inflicting punishment upon it.

XXXVII. Fifthly, and lastly. We shall use arguments, *ad hominem.* Socinus owns, *de Servato*, P. i. c. 1. that " not to pardon the impenitent is certainly right and agreeable to *the divine nature*," and consequently to rectitude and equity. Crellius, in like manner, *de Vera Relig.* lib. i. c. 23. says, that " it is unworthy of God to suffer the crimes of the ob-

tinate to escape unpunished." Let us here a little examine
these concessions. They say, it is unworthy of God not to punish the obstinate: nay, it is due to the nature of God not to
pardon them. Why pray? Is it because they are stubborn and
obstinate? But obstinacy is not punished on its own account,
because there is a good and laudable obstinacy or constancy.
It is therefore only punished because of the evil that is in it;
it is then necessary that sin be punished on its own account,
and obstinacy only because of the sinfulness of it. And if it
be necessary to punish sin on its own account, therefore where-
ever it is to be met with, it must necessarily be punished. Besides, all men after having once sinned, obstinately persevere
in sin, unless they are brought to repentance by the preventing
grace of God. But how can they obtain this without a previous satisfaction, if it be a debt which the divine nature owes to
itself, not to grant them pardon.

XXXVIII. We likewise readily admit what Crellius advances in the very same chapter: " by the same claim of right
that we owe obedience to God, by the same also we become
liable to punishment for neglect of obedience and service: for,
punishment succeeds, as it were, in the place of the duty omitted, and if possible, ought to atone for it." But doubtless, by
a claim of natural right, obedience is due to God; and it would
be repugnant to the divine perfections, not to require it of a
rational nature. I speak without reserve, he is not God who
cannot demand obedience from his rational creature. And
the very same thing, according to Crellius' very just hypothesis, is to be affirmed of punishment. I am well aware, that
Crellius founds both claims as well to obedience as to punishment, on the dominion of God, as Lord; though this ought
rather to be founded on the essential majesty and supremacy of
God, which is the foundation of his sovereign dominion. But
he is forced to confess that this sovereign dominion is so natural
to God, that he cannot renounce it; nay, indeed, that without
it, " it is scarce intelligible how he can be God; since it is
on account of that very authority, and the power from which
it flows, he is said to be God." It therefore stands firm, that
the penal sanction of the covenant is founded in the supereми-
nent, most holy, and just nature of God, and not in the mere
good pleasure of the divine will only.

XXXIX. We might here further enquire, whether the
eternity of punishment is to be derived from this natural right
of God; or, which is the same thing, whether a punishment,
justly equivalent to each sin, ought necessarily to be eternal,

according to God's natural right; so that to maintain the contrary, would be unworthy of God, and consequently impossible. A difficult question this, because to determine concerning this absolute right of God in special cases, seems to be above human reach. " God is greater than man, he giveth not an account of his matters," Job xxxiii. 12, 13. Let us however try, whether from the consideration of the divine perfections, we may not gather what may in this case be worthy of God.

XL. I now presuppose there is in sin committed against the infinite majesty of God, a malignity *in its measure infinite*, and therefore a demerit of punishment *in its measure* infinite also. I say, there is in sin a malignity only, *in its measure* infinite. For it cannot be called infinite in an absolute sense: if we consider the entity of the act in itself, an act infinitely intense canot be produced by a finite creature; if the irregularity, and the privation of moral good, adhering to the act, it is a privation of a finite rectitude, which is all that can be found in a creature: if, in fine, we consider the whole complex, namely sin, in the concrete, as they speak; neither in that case will its malignity be absolutely infinite. For neither are all acts of sin equally vicious, there being a great difference among them, which could not be if they were infinite. However, the malignity of sin is *in its measure* infinite: 1st. Objectively, because committed against an infinite good. 2dly. Extensively, in respect of duration, because the blot or stain of sin endures for ever, unless purged away by the blood of Christ. There is not therefore in sin a desert of punishment absolutely infinite as to intenseness of torments. 1. Because such a punishment is absolutely impossible; for, a finite creature is not capable of infinite torments. 2. Because it would follow, that God could never satisfy his justice by inflicting condign punishment on the wicked, because they are incapable of this punishment. It is then absurd to say, that any punishment is of right due to sin, which God can never inflict. 3. Because it would follow, an equal punishment was due to all sins, or that all in fact were to be punished alike, which is an absurdity, and against Matt. xi. 22, 24. The reason of this consequence is, because there neither is, nor can be, any disparity between infinites. Nevertheless, there is in sin a desert of punishment *in its measure* infinite: namely, in the same manner that the malignity of it is infinite. That is, 1st. Objectively, so as to deprive man of the enjoyment of the infinite good, which is God. 2dly. Extensively, so that the punishment shall last for ever. And thus I consider this desert of eternal punishment, so far only as to conclude, that God does nothing contrary to equity and justice, when he punishes the sins of men with eternal torments, both of soul and body. Which the event shews, as I have made appear § XVII.

XLI. But I know not if it can be determined, whether this eternity ought necessarily to consist in the punishment of sense, or whether the justice of God may be satisfied by the eternal punishment of loss, in the annihilation of the sinful creature. This, I apprehend, may be said with sufficient probability and sobriety : If God should be pleased to continue for ever in existence the sinner, it is necessary (without a satisfaction) that he for ever inflict punishment on him, not only the punishment of loss, but likewise that of sense.   The reason is, because not only the guilt of sin always remains, but also the stain with which sin, once committed, infects the soul, and which can never be purged out, but by the blood of Christ. But it is impossible, as we proved, § XXII, XXIII, XXIV. that God should admit man, stained with sin, to communion with himself: and it cannot be that a rational creature, excluded the enjoyment of the divine favour, should not feel this indignation of God with the deepest anguish.   Conscience most severely lashes the wretches for having deprived themselves of the chief good.   Which with no small care we have also shewn, § XIII. and the following sections.

XLII. But whether it be necessary that God should continue for ever the sinful creature in a state of existence, I own I am ignorant. May it not, in its measure, be reckoned an infinite punishment, should God please to doom man, who was by nature a candidate for eternity, to total annihilation, from whence he should never be suffered to return to life? I know, God has now determined otherwise, and that with the highest justice.   But it is queried, whether agreeably to his justice, he might not have settled it in this manner: If thou, O man, sinnest, I will frustrate thy desire of eternal happiness, and of a blessed eternity; and on the contrary, give thee up to eternal annihilation.   Here at least let us hesitate, and suspend our judgment.

CHAP. VI.

Of the Sacraments of the Covenant of Works.

I. IT hath pleased the blessed and almighty God, in every economy of his covenants, to confirm, by some sacred symbols, the certainty of his promises, and, at the same time, to remind man in covenant with him of his duty: to these symbols ecclesiastical practice has long since given the name of Sacraments: this was certainly appointed with an excellent design by the all-wise God. For, 1st. What God has made known concerning his covenant, is, by this means, proposed to man's more accurate consideration; since he is not only once and again instructed in the will of God by a heavenly oracle, but frequently and almost daily beholds with his eyes those things which by heaven are granted him as pledges of the greatest blessings: what believers see with their eyes, usually sink deeper into the soul, and leave deeper impressions of themselves, than those only which they hear with their ears. Elegantly to this purpose says Herodotus, " men usually give less credit to the ears than to the eyes." 2dly. These symbols also tend to confirm our faith. For, though nothing can be thought of that deserves more credit than the word of God, yet, where God adds signs and seals to his infallible promises, he gives a twofold foundation to our faith. " Thus he more abundantly shews unto the heirs of promise the immutability of his counsel: that by two immutable things, in which it was impossible for God to lie, we might have a strong consolation," Heb. vi. 17, 18. 3dly. By means of this institution, a holy man does, by the sight, touch, and taste, of the sacred symbols, attain to some sense of eternal blessings, and accustoms himself under the symbols, to a contemplation and foretaste of these things, to the plenary and immediate fruition of which he will, one time or other, be admitted without any outward signs. 4thly, and lastly. The man has in these something continually to remind him of his duty: and as, from time to time, they present to his thoughts, and give a foretaste of his Creator, so at the same time they put him in mind of those very strong obligations, by which he is bound to his Covenant-God. And thus, they are both a bridle to restrain him from sin, and a spur to quicken him cheerfully to run that holy race which he has so happily entered upon.

II. God also granted to man such symbols under the Covenant of Works; concerning which we are now to speak, that nothing may be wanting in this treatise, and, if I mistake not, were four in all, which I reckon up in this order: 1. *Paradise.* 2. *The Tree of Life.* 3. *The Tree of Knowledge of Good and Evil.* 4. *The Sabbath.* In speaking of each of these I shall distinctly shew first, What good they signified and sealed to man, with respect to God. Secondly, What duty and obligation they reminded him of.

III. But I must previously observe, that it is altogether

foreign to this treatise, and out of its place, to propose such significations either of Paradise, or of the Tree of Life, or of the Sabbath, as relate to the gospel, the grace of Christ, and to glory, as freely given to the elect by the Mediator and Spirit of grace. For here, I observe, that men of learning in other respects, have stumbled, who, when explaining the nature of those Sacraments, too uncautiously blend things belonging to a quite different covenant. Nothing is here to be brought in which does not belong to the covenant of works, the promises of that covenant, and the duties of man under the same: all which are most distinct from the covenant of grace. Here we are to say nothing of Christ, nothing of justifying faith in him, nothing of our ceasing from our own works as impure, nor any thing of that rest after the miseries of this life. All these belong to another covenant. I do not however refuse, that the unsearchable wisdom of God did appoint and order these symbols in such a manner, that the remembrance of them after the fall might be able to instruct man in many things relating to the covenant of grace and its Mediator. As that according to Paul, the first Adam himself was a type of the second: Eve, curiously formed out of Adam's rib while asleep, was a type of the church, as it were, taken from Christ in virtue of his death, and that the first marriage represented that great mystery which regards Christ and the Church. These things, however, were neither known nor thought of in the state of nature; nor to be mentioned in a discourse on the Sacraments of the covenant of works. Having premised these things, let us now enquire into each particular with all the care possible, beginning with Paradise.

IV. It is far from our design, elaborately to enquire into the situation and topography of Paradise. Let it suffice to observe, that it was a garden, and a most agreeable enclosure, planted by God himself, toward the east, in Eden, a most fertile region, and abounding in all kinds of delights, as very learned men think, near Haran, the mart of Arabia, at the conflux of the Euphrates and Tigris, not far from Mesopotamia; which was watered with four rivers, washing, by many windings and meanders, the most fertile orchard. When man was formed from the earth without Paradise, he was introduced by God as a new guest to till the ground, and give an account of his stewardship and care. Here was every thing that could contribute to the proper pleasures of this life, God frequently revealing himself to man, and familiarly admitting him to the sweetest fellowship with himself. Moses also mentions the gold and the precious stones of that country, as of the best kind and in the greatest plenty. And what now was the meaning, or mystical signification of all these things?

V. First. In general, the pleasantness of this place, which every moment set before man the most profuse bounty of the Deity, exhibiting the same to the enjoyment of all his senses, assured him, that he was to expect another residence far more noble and grand; where he should not, as now, enjoy his God through and in the creatures, but immediately delight in his Creator, to his being fully satisfied with his likeness. For if God now conferred upon him such things while here, before the course of his appointed trial was finished; what might he not, nay, what ought he not to promise himself from that immense munificence, after he had acted his part well, when he had acquired a right to come with boldness to his rewarder, and ask for his most ample recompence? Was not the Lord amidst this abundance, that lacked nothing pertaining to this animal life, [as it were] frequently addressing him, How shall I one day place thee among my sons, if thou constantly continuest obedient to my voice? If there is so much sweetness in these created rivulets of my goodness, in which now thou swimmest with so much pleasure; what will there not be in myself, the unexhausted fountain, and the most plentiful spring? Ascend, O man, by the scale of the creatures, to me the Creator, and from a foretaste of these first fruits, conclude what I have prepared for thee against that time, when I myself shall be " thy exceeding great reward." And certainly, unless we suppose Adam to have been stupid and devoid of all divine light, such thoughts must needs have arisen in his mind.

VI. The scriptures declare, that by Paradise is signified a place of perfect bliss, when they call heaven, the habitation of the blessed, by the name of *Paradise*, Luke xxiii. 43. 2 Cor. xii. 4. A manner of expression commonly used by the Holy Ghost, by which the names of the sign, and the thing signified, of the type and antitype, are mutually exchanged. The Jews themselves saw this, with whom it is usual to call the place of absolutely perfect happiness, עֵדֶן and גַּן עֵדֶן *Eden* and *the garden of Eden;* and no wish was more frequent among them, than this, *Let his rest,* that is, the place of his rest, *be Eden.* There is also a most suitable analogy between Paradise and heaven, which we are now more expressly and particularly to shew.

VII. 1st. Paradise was a garden planted by God himself, to

be the residence of man, formed after the divine image. Heaven is a place made and prepared by God for the eternal abode of man, after he has added constancy to his other virtues, and so has in himself the full image of God, where his holiness shall be unchangeable. As therefore it was incumbent on him to acknowledge the hand and most munificent bounty of his God in this terrestrial habitation; so he was still more evidently to experience the same in the celestial abode of his heavenly Father. 2dly. Paradise exceedingly surpassed all the other parts of the earth in respect to the pleasantness of it; for it was planted in Eden, a place of all kinds of delight. Whence the most pleasant countries in the world are said to be *as the garden of God,* Gen. xiii. 10. And Ezekiel, xxxvi. 35. prophesying of the future extraordinary plenty of the earth, says, that the earth which before that was lying waste, should be *as the garden of Eden.* And what is grander than that promise of Isaiah, li. 3. " For the Lord shall comfort Zion; he will comfort all her waste places, and he will make her wilderness like Eden, and her desert like the garden of the Lord; joy and gladness shall be found therein, thanksgiving and the voice of melody." From which words it is clear, that nothing was wanting in Paradise, in its primitive state, to give the completest pleasure to man. But much less will any thing be wanting in heaven to the most absolutely perfect happiness. The pleasures of which will far more exceed those of this terrestrial garden, than heaven itself exceeds the earth in its height. For Paradise had those things, which discovered its imperfection, such as those things that belonged to this animal life, all which will be altogether excluded heaven, where is fulness of joys, Psalm xvi. 11. 3dly. In Paradise flowed the most limpid streams, watering and fertilizing the garden, wherever it was necessary. In heaven there is " a pure river of water of life, clear as crystal, proceeding out of the throne of God," Rev. xxii. 1. By which circumlocution are signified the gifts of the holy Spirit, a few drops of which are indeed granted here, but with which the blessed will be intoxicated to a perfect joy. 4thly. Moses also mentions gold, bdellium, and the onyx stone, which were found in that region, Gen. ii. 11, 12. In heaven there will be spiritual treasures, with which no gold, no topaz, nor any of the precious stones of the whole earth, can any ways be compared. 5thly. In Paradise there were trees, both beautiful and useful. In heaven there are precious things, both pleasant to the sight, and excellent for use. Above all, there were the two trees, of Knowledge, and of Life. But in the heavenly kingdom there is true and perfect knowledge, and that life which is really and emphatically so. 6thly. Man being first created in the earth was translated into Paradise, as the better residence. For, if I mistake not, the words of Moses intimate this, Gen. ii. 8. " And there he put the man that he had formed." Compare Gen. iii. 23. where after his sin, he is said " to be sent forth from the garden of Eden, to till the. ground from whence he was taken." In like manner also, man was in due time to be translated from that natural and animal state in which he was created, to another altogether supernatural and heavenly : of which this desirable translation from earth to Paradise reminded him, which Zanchius also observed on Gen. ii. 15. as also Musculus. 7thly. Had not man been innocent, he would have had no place in Paradise. This garden did not suffer him when once tainted with sin. So *nothing that defileth can enter into heaven*, Rev. xxi. 27. that being *the habitation of God's holiness and glory*, Isa. lxiv. 15. 8thly. In Paradise man enjoyed the familiar fellowship of his God : and in this sense Paradise might also be styled *the garden of God*, as God dwelt there, delighting himself in the work of his hands, and especially in man himself. As it was a pleasure to man to be thus near and familiar with his Maker, so it was a delight to God. But in heaven the habitation of his Majesty, God will be always present with man, and give himself, in the most familiar manner possible, to be seen and enjoyed by him.

VIII. As Paradise might set forth all these things to man, so in like manner the use of this pledge reminded him of several duties. And, *first*, he might hence learn that he ought not to seek for his good and felicity in any thing upon earth, which, when appearing even most perfect, discovers its own imperfections ; thus, this animal life in Paradise, was to be recruited continually with meat, drink, and a succession of sleeping and waking. By which means he was taught to aspire after a greater happiness, namely, the immediate fruition of his God ; in the seeking after this happiness the principal holiness of *a traveller* consists. For, you love God above all things, if you ardently pant after an intimate union with him.

IX. Secondly. As this Paradise was given man to be cultivated and kept, the Lord thereby reminded him, that he took no pleasure in a lazy idleness, but in an active industry. His will was, that man should employ his labour and care upon the garden, that he might have something to do, in which he might continually experience the goodness and providence of his Creator. He did not choose that angels themselves should be idle, whom he made ministering spirits. And so he assigned man the care of cultivating and keeping Paradise, that he might have something to employ himself in the works of God; just as a king's son has some office assigned him, lest he should become indolent by an excess of pleasures, honour, and riches. Thus it became him to be conformed to his God * by a most holy diligence, and be employed about the very work of God's hands, till he should come to enjoy an eternal sabbath with himself.

X. Thirdly. This also had a further respect to himself. For 1. As Paradise was the pledge of heaven, so the careful keeping of it reminded him to have heaven continually in his thoughts. 2. The labour and culture of Paradise taught him, that only he that labours and does that which is acceptable to God, can get to the heavenly habitation. 3. He was also instructed to keep his soul for God as a most pleasant garden cultivated like the Paradise of God, and shew forth those trees of virtues, which God planted as producing the most excellent fruits; that is, works proceeding from good habits: that so the Lord might come into this his garden, and eat his pleasant fruits, Cant. iv. 16. 4. It pointed out to him that he should, above all things solicitously keep his soul, that garden of God, lest any wild beasts of depraved passions should break in to lay every thing waste. And when God said to him, Keep this my garden, may he not at the same time be supposed to say, Keep thy heart with all diligence, or above all keeping, Prov. iv. 23. 5. The keeping of Paradise virtually enjoined him, of all things to be anxiously concerned not to do any thing against God, lest as a bad gardener he should be thrust out of the garden, and in that discern a melancholy symbol of his own exclusion from heaven. We then conclude, that when man was, with joy and exultation, admitted into Paradise, he was bound, and was willing to be bound, to perform all these things to God; and so upon entering into Paradise, he bound himself as by a sacrament to these duties.

XI. We now proceed to consider the Tree of Life: but whether a single tree, or an entire species of trees, is a question among the learned. Some think that the former, which is indeed the common opinion, is founded on no probable reason: and suppose it more suitable to the goodness of God, that such a beautiful, useful tree should be in the view of his favourite, in as many parts of the enclosure as possible. They

---

* There seems to be here something obscure, perhaps occasioned by a typographical error, *actui* instead of *actu*, I have therefore expressed what I apprehend to be the sense of the author.

also allege the divine benediction, Gen. i. 11, 12. by which
God conferred on all trees the virtue of multiplying themselves. But they chiefly insist on Rev. xxii. 2. where John
pitches the Tree of Life on each side of the river, which they
compare with Ezek. xlvii. 12. Others, on the contrary, do
not think it probable that it was an entire species: First, Because the universal particle בל *all*, is not added as before when
Moses would express many things of the same species, or
many species themselves. Next, Because it is said to have
been placed in the middle of the garden, so as to have the
other trees surrounding it in order. To the passages alleged
from the Revelations and Ezekiel, they answer, that John
speaks only in the singular number, both in that place and
Rev. ii. 7. and that one tree could properly be said to stand
in the midst of the street, and on both sides of the river, because the river run through the midst of the street, and because that single tree extended its roots and branches to each
side, so that there was no defect on either side. They likewise conclude from its being a type, that it must be a single
one; because Christ is one. But Ezekiel saw many on the
bank of the river representing the church militant; because,
though one Christ quickens the church, yet it is by several means
he now communicates life to the elect. These are the arguments on both sides: if any should desire our judgment, we
are of opinion, that the arguments of neither side have the force
of a demonstration: but from the consideration of its being a
type, we rather incline to the more common opinion.

XII. Whether this Tree was endowed with a singular virtue
above others, so as perfectly to cure the disorders of the body,
who, with certainty, can either affirm or deny? To ascribe to
it a medicinal virtue against diseases, does not appear suitable
to the state of innocent man. For diseases and such like infirmities are only the effects of sin. But nothing sure is more
ridiculous than the paradoxical and altogether untheological
assertion of Socinus, that Adam, by the benefit of that food,
would have prolonged his life to a much longer time than
God chose he should, had he not been deprived of the opportunity of reaching forth his hand to that Tree. As if God,
when he expelled man out of Paradise, and said, *lest he put
forth his hand, and take also of the Tree of Life, and live for
ever*, Gen. iii. 22. was apprehensive, that man upon tasting
again of that tree should live for ever, notwithstanding his
will and threatening, which is downright blasphemy. For by
these words, God only intended to restrain the vain thoughts

of man, now become such a fool as to imagine that, by the use
of that Tree he could repair the loss he had sustained by sin;
or, as if the use of the sacrament, or the *opus operatum*, as it
is called, could be of any advantage without the thing signified.
And by driving man from that outward sign of immortality,
he cut him off from all hopes of salvation by that covenant, of
which that Tree was a symbol.   However, there must be some
great reason why that Tree obtained this designation, which
we will now enquire into.

XIII. The Tree of Life signified the Son of God, not indeed as he is Christ and Mediator, (that consideration being
peculiar to another covenant,) but in as much as he is the life
of man in every condition, and the fountain of all happiness.
And how well was it spoken by one, who said, that it became
God from the first to represent, by an outward sign, that person whom he loves, and for whose glory he has made and
does make all things; nay, " to whom he sheweth all things
that he doth, that he may also do likewise," John v. 19. as
the author of life to man; that man even then might acknowledge him as such; and afterwards, when he was to be manifested as his saviour and physician, Adam and his posterity
might bring him to remembrance, as exhibited by a symbol
at the very beginning.   As in fact it has happened, that they
who believe Moses, the Prophets, and the Gospel, avow,
that in the beginning there was no life but in him, for whose
glory, to be displayed in the work of salvation, the earth was
also made.   Wherefore Christ is called *the Tree of Life*,
Rev. xxii. 2.   What indeed he now is by his merit and efficacy, as Mediator, he would have always been, as the Son of
God, of the same substance with his Father.   For, as by him
man was created and obtained an animal life, so, in like manner, he would have been transformed by him and blessed
with a heavenly life.   Nor could he have been the life of the
sinner, as Mediator, unless he had likewise been the life of
man in his holy state, as God; having life in himself, and being life itself.

XIV. The fruit of this Tree, charming all the senses with
its unparalleled beauty, signified the pleasures of divine love,
with which happy man was one day to be fully regaled, and
which never cloy, but, with their sweet variety, do always
quicken the appetite.   In this sense, wisdom is said to be *a
Tree of Life to them that lay hold of her*, Prov. iii. 18. because the study and practice of true wisdom, fill the soul with
an ineffable pleasure.

XV. Moreover, it was man's duty: 1st. Attentively to consider this tree *as pleasant to the eyes*, Gen. iii. 6. and to contemplate therein the perfections of the Son of God, whose brightest vision was one day to complete his happiness. 2dly. By the use and enjoyment of this tree, to testify his communion with the Son of God, and acknowledge him as the author of the life he longed for ; which, though innocent, he was to seek after, not in himself, but in God as a liberal rewarder. 3dly. He himself, in imitation of the Son of God, and as in communion with him, ought to be as a tree of life to his wife and posterity, by giving them holy advice and example, as a plant of the garden of God, a partaker of the divine life, and as ministering to the life of his neighbour. " The fruit of the righteous is a tree of life," Prov. xi. 30.

XVI. Besides the tree of life, Moses speaks of another tree, deriving its name from THE KNOWLEDGE OF GOOD AND EVIL, concerning whose name and use we began to speak, chap. iii. § XX, XXI. That it was designed for man's probation is undoubted: but whether it was also a symbol of the covenant is disputed. I freely own I see no reason why this should be denied. For all the requisites to constitute a symbol of a covenant here concur. We have an external and visible sign instituted by God : we have the thing signified, together with a beautiful analogy ; we have, in fine, a memorial of man's duty : all which fully constitute the nature of a sacred symbol or sacrament.

XVII. The external sign was a certain tree, " in the midst of the garden, good for food, pleasant to the eyes, and to be desired to make one wise," Gen. iii. 3, 6. The use of this sign was twofold : 1st. That it might be attentively viewed and considered by man, while he carefully meditates on the mystical signification of this tree. For that end it was so beautiful and so desirable to the view, and placed in the middle of the garden, where man most frequently resorted. 2dly. That from a religious obedience he should abstain from eating of it, and thereby acknowledge God's absolute dominion over him, and his expectation of another world, in which he should be forbid nothing truly desirable.

XVIII. The thing signified was in like manner twofold, the sealing both of the promise and the threatening of the covenant. For its being called *the tree of knowledge of good*, intimated, that man, if from a principle of love he obeyed this probationary precept, should come to the knowledge, sense, and fruition of that good which is truly and excellently so, and the full knowledge of which is only obtainable by sense and enjoyment. On the other hand, when called *the tree of the knowledge of evil*, thereby is signified, that man, if found disobedient, should be doomed to the greatest calamity, the exceeding evil and wretchedness of which he should at last know by experience. And even they, who, in other respects, would not have this tree called a symbol of the divine covenant, do confess,

XIX. There was here a very plain memorial of duty. For this tree taught, 1st. That man was sincerely to contemplate and desire the chief good, but not to endeavour after it, but only in the manner and way prescribed by heaven ; nor here to give in to his own reasonings, how plausible soever they might appear. 2dly. That man's happiness was not to be placed in things pleasing to the senses of the body. There is another and a quite different beatifying good, which satiates the soul, and of itself suffices to the consummation of happiness. 3dly. That God was the most absolute Lord of man, whose sole will, expressed by his law, should be the supreme rule and directory of all the appetites of the soul, and of all the motions of the body. 4thly. That there is no attaining to a life of happiness, but by perfect obedience. 5thly. That even man in innocence, was to behave with a certain religious awe, when conversing with his God, lest he should fall into sin. To these add what we have already observed, chap. iii. § XXI.

XX. That very accurate and great divine, Hieronimus Zanchius, after giving a history of these trees, expresses their mystical signification in these words ; *de creat. Hom. lib.* i. c. i. § 8. " Moreover, these two trees in the midst of Paradise, and near each other, were very evident types of the law and gospel, or of Christ. The law declares what is good, and what is evil: Christ is the true and eternal life. Both were in the midst of Paradise, because the law and Christ, in the midst of the church, are always to be proposed to the posterity of Adam. One near the other, because the law leads to Christ." I cannot fully express what regard I pay to this great divine, whose commentaries I exceedingly prefer to the new-fangled comments, with which the minds of students are at this day distracted and led astray. Nevertheless, these expressions seem to be more ingenious than solid and judicious. For under the covenant of works, Adam neither had, nor was it necessary he should have any sacraments which respected Christ, the gospel and grace. This however may be said in excuse of these and the like things, which often occur even in the most learned authors, that though these things were not proposed to man at first in innocence in order to represent to him the grace of Christ, yet they were so wisely ordered by God, that man, by reflecting upon them, could after the fall discover in them the dark resemblance of those things which God afterwards, by a new promise, was pleased to reveal.

XXI. Other learned men have not thought proper to reckon the tree of knowledge among the symbols and seals of the covenant of works, for these following reasons: 1st. Because all sacraments are given for use, but man was forbid the use of this tree. 2dly. Because sacraments are signs of a blessing which they seal to those who use them in a proper way; but this tree sealed no blessing to any who should use it, but rather a curse. These considerations, however, are not of that weight that we should therefore depart from the more received opinion. And it is easy to answer both these arguments, not only from the truth of the thing itself, but also from the very hypotheses of these learned men.

XXII. It is indeed true, that all sacraments were given for use; but it is also certain, that the external use of all sacraments is not after one and the same manner; all are not granted to the mouth and palate. There are sacraments whose use consists in the contemplation of the sign, and meditation on the thing signified. Some learned writers maintain, that the rainbow was not a symbol only of the œcumenical, or general covenant with the whole earth, but also of the covenant of grace in Christ, and they think that the colours of the rainbow, the red, the fiery, and the green, denote, that by blood, holiness and mercy are united. But we can conceive no other sacramental use of the rainbow, besides the contemplation of it. In like manner, they place the brazen serpent among the sacraments of the Old Testament, whose use consisted only in the beholding of it. Nay, they are of opinion concerning the tree of life itself, that it was not promiscuously to be used by man, since " to him alone that overcometh, it is given to eat of the tree of life," Rev. ii. 7. " Whence," say they, " it does not appear that Adam touched it before the fall; nay, the contrary is rather evident." And yet they say, that it was the first and most ancient representation of the Son of God, and of the life to be possessed through him. Why then may not the tree of knowledge also be called a symbol of the covenant, though proposed only to be looked at by man, though he was never to eat of it?

XXIII. I go a step farther, and say, that there is no absurdity, should such a sacrament be appointed whose use should consist in a religious abstinence. Nor should those learned men, if consistent with themselves, be averse to this opinion. The deluge, say they, from which *Noah was preserved, must needs be reckoned among the types.* But the use of the waters, in respect to Noah, consisted in this, that they were neither to touch him and his, to their hurt, nor force themselves into the ark in which he was shut up; the waters of the *Red sea* likewise signified the same thing in the same manner to *Israel.* Nay, what may seem strange, these learned men say, that the first sacrament of the covenant of grace was "the ejectment of Adam out of Paradise, and the barring up his access to the tree of life:" or, as one is pleased to express himself, "the first sacrament was the tree of life, which, though at first it regarded the covenant of works, and the exclusion from it was the punishment of fallen man; nevertheless, that very exclusion was at the same time a sign of the grace and goodness of God." I would beg of those very learned men, to explain in what the sacramental use of the tree of life was to have consisted under the covenant of grace, after man was expelled Paradise, and that tree was no longer to be in his view. There is here no other use but a mystical abstinence and deprivation. And thus we imagine we have fully answered the first argument.

XXIV. Let us now consider the second, and we say, it is not inconsistent with the nature of sacraments, to seal death and condemnation, to those who unduly and irregularly use them: for the covenant of God with man is ratified, not only by the promises, but also by certain threatenings belonging to it; but sacraments are the seals of the whole covenant, not excepting the threatenings to the profane abusers of them. When a man partakes of the sacraments, he comes under an oath and curse, and makes himself liable to punishment if he deals treacherously. To say nothing of the sacraments of the covenant of works, the very sacraments of the covenant of grace are *the savour of death unto death* to hypocrites and profane persons, who in the bread and wine of the Eucharist *eat and drink damnation to themselves,* 1 Cor. xi. 27, 29. But it is not true, that the tree of knowledge sealed only death; for it also sealed life and happiness. It was the tree of knowledge, not only *of evil* but *of good.* As these learned men themselves acknowledge, while they write, that "had Adam obeyed, he would upon his trial have come to the knowledge and sense of his good to which he was called, and had a natural desire after, even eternal life and consummate happiness." Whence we conclude, that notwithstanding these reasonings, we may justly reckon the tree of knowledge among the sacraments of the covenant of works.

CHAP. VII.

Of the First Sabbath.

I. We said, that the first Sabbath was the fourth sacrament of the covenant of works. In order to treat somewhat more fully on this, it will not be improper to make it the subject of a whole chapter: Moses gives us the history of it, Gen. ii. 2, 3. in these words: " And on the seventh day God ended his work, which he had made ; and he rested on the seventh day from all his work, which he had made : and God blessed the seventh day, and sanctified it, because that in it he had rested from all his work, which God created and made." The more fully to understand these words, and from them to answer our design, we shall distinctly discuss these three things: 1st. Enquire whether what is here said about *sanctifying and blessing the seventh day*, ought to be applied to that *first* day, which immediately followed upon the six days of the creation, and which was the first that shone on the works of God when completed ; or whether it be necessary to have recourse to *a prolepsis*, or anticipation, by which we may look upon those things as spoken of the day on which many ages after the manna was given in the wilderness. 2dly. We shall explain the nature of that first Sabbath. 3dly. and lastly, Point out in what respect it was a Sacrament.

II. There is no occasion to mention, that the first of these points has been matter of great dispute among divines, without coming to any determination to this day; nor do I choose to repeat what they have said ; I shall only observe, that perhaps the parties might easily agree, did we know what we are to understand by *sanctifying and blessing* the seventh day, mentioned by *Moses*, and which we shall presently consider. But if we suppose in general, that God *rested* on the seventh day from his work, that is, not only *desisted* from creating new species of creatures, but *acquiesced* and *took complacency* in the work which he had now finished, especially in man, who was formed after his image, and furnished with those faculties, by which he was enabled to acknowledge, and celebrate the perfections of God, shining forth in his works ; and that he set this his *resting* before man as a pattern, by

which he should be taught to acquiesce in nothing but in God,
for whom he was created, please himself in nothing but in glorifying God, which is the end of his creation; moreover, that
he *sanctified* this day, of which we are speaking, by commanding it to be employed by man for that sacred work, adding *a
promise*, that all that time, thus employed by man, should be
highly *blessed* to him: if I say, we thus in general suppose, as
all these things are evidently truth, there is good hope, that
all equitable judges will allow that we adhere to the simplicity
of the letter, and interpret this history of *Moses* as the narrative of a thing done at that time, which the holy Prophet was
then describing.

III. I am glad to find the celebrated *Cocceius* assents to this.
His words are these, on Gen. ii. § 6. " Some imagine, that
this verse (namely 3.) is put by way of anticipation.—But
it is not probable that Moses, in recording this blessing and
sanctification, did by no means speak concerning the original
Sabbath, but only concerning the Jewish Sabbath. This is
plainly doing violence to the text, if one day be understood,
which God blessed and sanctified, and another on which he
rested from his work." And the very eloquent Burman,
though inclining to an anticipation, yet owns, that " the
words of Moses may be understood of that perpetual Sabbath,
the seventh day after the creation, which first saw the works
of God perfected, and most auspiciously shone on the world;
whence it is said to be peculiarly blessed by God, and afterwards to be celebrated and sanctified by man, for all ages to
come." Synops. Theol. lib. 2. c. 5. § 11. See the same author;
de œconomia fœderum Dei, § 208, 209. We shall say no more
on this, as we could rather wish to see the orthodox agreeing
among themselves, than contending with one another. And
indeed this must be acknowledged, if we would properly explain, in what manner this Sabbath was a sacrament of the covenant of works.

IV. The best Hebrew authors, on whose authority those of
the opposite opinion are wont to build upon, agree with us
in this dispute. For in the Talmud they enquire, " why man
was created on the evening of the Sabbath," and of the three
reasons they give, this is the last; " that he might immediately
enter on performing the command." The famous Ludovicus
de Dieu, mentioning these words, on Gen. i. 27. adds by way
of explication; " for, since the Sabbath immediately succeeded
the creation of man, he immediately entered on the command
of sanctifying the Sabbath." Baal Hatturim, after various interpretations of this passage, also subjoins this other; " in the

hour, that he created the world, he blessed the Sabbath and
the world." Jarchi also mentions this opinion, though himself was otherwise minded; " what would the world have been
without rest; on the coming of the Sabbath came rest, and
thus at length the work was finished and completed." By
which he intimates, that the institution of the Sabbath was
joined to the completing of the works of God. There are
also some Jews, who will have Psal. xcii. whose title is, " a
Psalm or Song for the Sabbath-day," to have been composed
by Adam. For thus the Chaldee paraphrases: " a Hymn and
Song, which the first man said of the Sabbath." And R. Levi
in *Bereschit Rabba, sect. 22.* at the end : " the first man spoke
this Psalm, and from his time it was buried in oblivion, but
Moses came and renewed it." Now I bring these testimonies
to shew that they speak too confidently who assert that it is
running counter to the unanimous opinion of the Jews, for any
to insist that the precept of the Sabbath was enjoined on the
first man. Whoever wants more to this purpose, may consult
Selden de jure nature, &c. lib. 3. c. 13.

V. These things supposed, we are further to enquire in
what the nature of the first Sabbath did consist. Here again
the learned run into very different opinions. I now take it to
be my province, to lay down such propositions, to which it is
to be hoped that the orthodox, who are lovers of truth, will
without difficulty give their assent.

VI. We are to distinguish first between the rest of God,
and the rest of man, which God enjoined upon him, and re
commended by his own example: in this manner also, Paul
distinguishes, Heb. iv. 10. " he also hath ceased from his own
works, as God did from his."

VII. The rest of God consisted, not only in his ceasing from
the work of any new creation, but also in that sweet satisfaction and delight he had in the demonstration of his own attributes and perfections, which were gloriously displayed in
the work he had now finished, especially after he had added a
lustre to this inferior world, by bestowing upon it a most
excellent inhabitant, who was to be a careful spectator, and the
herald and proclaimer of the perfections of his Creator, and
in whom God himself beheld ἐμικρον τεδδοξης αυτε απαυγασμα, *no
small effulgence of his own glory.* Wherefore it is said, Exod.
xxxi. 17. " and on the seventh day he rested, and was refreshed ;" not as if he was fatigued, but as rejoicing in his work so
happily completed, and in which he beheld what was worthy of
his labour.

VIII. God having rested on the seventh day, sanctified it,

as well by example as by precept. By example, in as much
as he brought man, whom he had newly formed to the contemplation of his works, and revealed to him both himself
and his perfections, that he might love, thank, praise, and glorify him. And indeed, because God rested on the seventh
day from all other works, and was only intent upon this, we
may conclude, that he sanctified it in a most extraordinary manner. He likewise sanctified it by precept, enjoining man to
employ it in glorifying his Creator. " To sanctify, (as Martyr,
whom several commend, says well,) is to set apart something
for the worship of God," as it is also taken here. And it was
very justly observed by Calvin, that it was the will of God,
his own example should be a perpetual rule to us. Rabbenu
Nissim, quoted by Abarbanel, on the explication of the law,
fol. 21. col. 3. is of the same opinion : " and this is the sanctification of the Sabbath, that on that day, the soul of man
be employed on nothing profane, but wholly on things sacred.".

IX. God's blessing the seventh day may be also taken in a
twofold sense : First, for his declaring it to be blessed and
happy, as that in which he had peculiar pleasure to enjoy, by
observing all his works in such order as to be, not only to himself, but to angels as well as men, a most beautiful scene, displaying the glory of his perfections. This is what David
says, Psal. civ. 13. " the glory of the Lord shall endure for
ever, the Lord shall rejoice in his works." Thus, God himself rejoiced on that day, and consequently blessed it. For,
as to curse a day is to abhor and detest it, as unfortunate and
unhappy, as afflictive and miserable, Job ii. 14. Jer. xx. 14.
so, by the rule of contraries, to bless a day is to rejoice in it,
as delightful and prosperous. And indeed, what day more
joyful, more happy, than that which saw the works of God
perfected, and yet not stained by any sin either of angels or
probably of men ? There has been none like it since that time,
certainly not since the entrance of sin. Secondly, It was also
a part of the blessing of this day, that God adjudged to
man, if he religiously imitated the pattern of his own rest,
the most ample blessings, and likewise in that very rest, the
earnest of a most happy rest in heaven ; of which more fully
presently. Elegantly said the ancient Hebrew doctors that
the " blessing and sanctifying the Sabbath redound to the ob-
servers thereof, that they may be blessed and holy themselves."

X. The rest here enjoined and recommended to man, comprises chiefly these things : in general, that he shall abstain

from every sin, through the whole course of his life, that giving nothing but uneasiness, both to himself and his God. As the Lord complains, Isa. xliii. 22. " thou hast been weary of me, O Israel," and ver. 24. " thou hast wearied me with thine iniquities." By sinning, we dreadfully transgress against the rest of God, who cannot delight in a sinner, of whom and his work he says, Isa. i. 14. " they are a burthen to me, *I am weary to bear them." But more especially, it is likewise man's duty, that as he is the concluding part of the works of God, and the last of all the creatures, that came out of the hands of his Creator, not so to harass and fatigue himself about the creatures, as to seek his happiness and good in them, but rather, by a holy elevation of mind, ascend to the Creator himself, and acquiesce in nothing short of the enjoyment of his unbounded goodness, of the imitation of the purest holiness, and of the expectation of the fullest rest, and intimate union with his God. This indeed is the true and spiritual rest, always to be meditated upon, sought after, and to be observed by man.

XI. Moreover, as man, even in the state of innocence, was to perform solemn acts of piety, together with his consort and children, and to be their mouth in prayer, thanksgiving, and praises; it was necessary, at that time, that laying aside all other occupations, and all cares about what related to the support of natural life, and ordering those about him to rest, he might, without any hindrance from the body, religiously apply himself to this one thing: which I hope none of my brethren will refuse.   At least the celebrated Cocceius readily allows it.   Whose words are these, *Sum. Theol.* c. 21. § 10. " It is right in itself, and a part of the image of God, that man should, as often as possible, employ himself in the worship of God, (that is, laying aside the things pertaining to the body and its conveniencies, be wholly taken up in those duties which become a soul delighting in God, glorifying him and celebrating his praise,) and that too in the public assembly, for the common joy and edification of all.

XII. After man had sinned, the remembrance of God's resting and sanctifying the seventh day, ought to rouse him from his slowness and dulness, in the worship of God, in order to spend every seventh day therein, laying aside, for a while, all other employment.   But it will be better to explain this in Calvin's words: " God therefore first rested, and then he bless-

---

* N. B. This is not to be understood, as if the blessed God could be wearied, but only that if such a thing was possible, sin is of such a malignant nature, that it would do it.

ed that rest, that it might be ever' afterwards holy among men:
or, he set apart each seventh day for rest, that his own example
might be a standing rule." Martyr speaks to the same purpose: "Hence men are put in mind that, if the church enjoins
them to set apart a certain day in the week for the worship of
God, this is not altogether a human device, nor belongs only
to the law of Moses, but likewise had its rise from hence, and
is an imitation of God." All this is also approved of by Cocceius, whose excellent words we will subjoin from the place just
quoted, § 12. " The consequence of these things in the sinner
is,—that if encompassed with the infirmities of the flesh, and
exposed to the troubles of life, he may at least each seventh
day recollect, and give himself up to far preferable thoughts,
and then cheerfully, on account of that part of the worship of
God which cannot be performed without disengaging from business, abstain from the work of his hands, and from seeking,
preparing, and gathering the fruits of the earth." And as this
celebrated expositor approves of this, I know not why he should
disapprove the elegant observation of Chrysostom, Not. at Heb.
§ 13. That " hence, as by certain preludes, God hath enig-
matically taught us to consecrate and set apart for spiritual employment each seventh day in the week." If we all agree, as I
hope we may, in these positions, which seem not unhappily to
explain the nature of the first Sabbath; I truly reckon, that a
way is paved, and a great deal done, to compose those unhappy
disputes about the Sabbath of the decalogue, which for some
years past have made such noise in the Dutch universities and
churches.

XIII. Having thus explained the nature of the first Sabbath,
we proceed to enquire into its spiritual and mystical signification; from whence it will be easy to conclude, that we have
not improperly called it a sacrament; or, which is the same, a
sacred sign or seal (for, why should we wrangle about a word,
not scriptural, when we agree about the thing?) of the promises of salvation made by God to Adam. We have Paul's
authority to assert, that the Sabbath had some mystical meaning, and respected an eternal and happy rest, Heb. iv. 4, 10.
And this is justly supposed by the apostle, as a thing well
known to the Hebrews, and which is a corner stone or fundamental point with their doctors. It was a common proverb,
quoted by Buxtorf, in *Florilegio Hebræo*, 299. " The Sabbath
is not given but to be a type of the life to come." To the
same purpose is that which we have in Zohar, on Gen. fol. 5,
chap. xv. " What is the Sabbath day? A type of the land of
the living, which is the world to come, the world of souls, the

world of consolations." These things indeed, are not improper to be said in general; but as you will not readily find any where, [or in other authors] the analogy between the Sabbath and eternal rest specially assigned; can it be thought improper, if by distinguishing between the rest of God, the rest of man, and the seventh day, on which both rested, we should distinctly propose the mystical meaning of each.

XIV. The rest of God from the work of the creation, was a type of a far more glorious rest of God from the work of the glorification of the whole universe. When God had created the first world, so as to be a commodious habitation for man during his probation, and an illustrious theatre of the perfections of the Creator; he took pleasure in this his work, and rested with delight. For he bestowed upon it all the perfection which was requisite to complete that state. But he had resolved, one day, to produce a far more perfect universe, and by dissolving the elements by fire, to raise a new heaven and a new earth, as it were out of the ashes of the old; which new world, being blessed with his immutable happiness, was to be a far more august habitation for his glorified creatures; in which, as in the last display of his perfections, he was for ever to rest with the greatest complacency. And besides, as God according to his infinite wisdom, so very wisely connects all his actions, that the preceding have a certain respect to the following; in like manner, since that rest of God after the creation was less complete than that other, when God shall have concluded the whole, and which is to be followed by no other labour or toil; it is proper to consider that first rest of God as a type, and a kind of prelude of that other, which is more perfect. In fine, because it tends to man's greatest happiness, that the whole universe be thus glorified, and himself in the universe, that God may altogether rest in him, as having now obtained his last degree of perfection, he is said " to enter into the rest of God," Heb. iv. 10.

XV. This rest of God was after the creation, immediately succeeded by the rest of man. For, when he had formed man on the sixth day, (as possibly may be gathered from the simplicity of Moses' narrative,) he had brought him into Paradise on the seventh, *and put him*, or, as others think the words may be translated, " he made him rest in the garden of Eden," Gen. ii. 15. Was not this a most delightful symbol or sign to Adam, that after having finished his course of labour on this earth, he should be translated from thence into a place far more pleasant, and to a rest far more delightful than that which he enjoyed in Paradise? And when at certain times he ceased from tilling the ground in Paradise, and gave himself wholly up to the religious worship of God, with a soul delighting in God: was not this a certain earnest and a prelibation to him of that time, in which, exempted from all care about this animal life, he should immediately delight himself in the intimate communion of God, in being joined with the choirs of angels, and in doing the works of angels.

XVI. May not this rest both of God and man, falling upon the seventh day, after the six of creation, properly denote, that the rest of the glory of God is then to be expected, after the week of this world is elapsed? And that man is not to enter into rest, till he has finished his course of probation, and God upon strictly examining it by the rule of his law, finds it complete and in every respect perfect? And are we to reject the learned observation of Peter Martyr; that " this seventh day is said to have neither morning nor evening, because this is a perpetual rest to those who are truly the sons of God?"

XVII. It is indeed true, that upon Adam's sin, and violation of the covenant of works, the whole face of things was changed: but all these things [we have been speaking of] were such, as might have been signified and sealed by this Sabbath to Adam, even in the state of innocence, and why might it not really have been so? For the apostle expressly declares, that " God's resting from his works, from the foundation of the world," Heb. iv. 3. had a mystical signification. It is therefore our business to find out the agreement between the sign and the thing signified; for the greater analogy we observe between them, we shall the more clearly and with joy discover the infinite wisdom and goodness of God, various ways manifesting themselves. It cannot but tend to the praise of the divine architect, if we can observe many excellent resemblances between the picture given us by himself, and the copy. Indeed I deny not, that Paul, when discoursing of the Sabbath, leads us to that rest purchased for believers by the sufferings of Christ. But it cannot thence be inferred, that after the entrance of sin, God's Sabbath borrowed all its mystical signification from the covenant of grace. For, as to the substance of the thing, the glorious rest promised by the covenant of works, and now to be obtained by the covenant of grace, is one and the same, consisting in a blessed acquiescence or rest of the soul in God. As this was sealed to man in innocence by the Sabbath, under the covenant of works; so likewise it is sealed by the Sabbath under the covenant of grace, though under another relation, and under other circumstances. For God having perfect knowledge, that man would not continue in the first covenant, had from all eternity decreed to set on foot a quite different order of things, and bring his elect by a new covenant of grace to the most peaceful rest. Accordingly he settled in his unsearchable wisdom, whatever preceded the fall, in such a manner, that man viewing them after the fall with the enlightened eyes of faith, might discover still greater mysteries in them, which regarded Christ and the glory to be obtained by him. But we are not to speak of this here. Whoever desires a learned explanation of those mysteries, may consult Mestresat's sermons on the fourth chapter of the Hebrews.

XVIII. This Sabbath also put man in mind of various duties to be performed by him, which having pointed out above, § X, XI. I think needless to repeat now. And thus we have executed what we promised concerning the sacraments of the covenant of works.

XIX. And here I might conclude, did not a very learned man come in my way, whose thoughts on the first Sabbath being widely different from the commonly received notions, I intend, with his permission, calmly to examine. He therefore maintains, that Adam, on the very day of his creation, being seduced by the devil, had involved himself and the whole world in the most wretched bondage of corruption: but that God on the seventh day restored all things thus corrupted by the devil and by man, by his gracious promise of the Messiah: upon this restoration he rested on that very day: and that rest, upon the reparation of the world, being peculiar to the seventh day, may be the foundation of the Sabbath. Doubtless, " on the sixth day, the heavens and the earth were finished, and all the host of them," Gen. ii. 1. And God beholding the works of his creation so perfect, pleasantly rested in them. This was the rest of the sixth day. But, on the same day, Satan corrupted all; for, upon losing heaven, of whose host he was one, and which he greatly diminished by associating many other angels to himself, and so far rendered that habitation a desert; and on earth, by means of a calumnious lie, he rendered man, the prince of the terrestrial host, a subject to himself, a rebel to God, and destitute of life. This was the corruption of the earth. And thus heaven and earth so beautifully finished by God on the sixth day, were on the same basely defiled by Satan and by man. This occasioned God to be engaged in a new work on the seventh, even to restore what had been thus defiled and corrupted, and to complete them anew. Which he did on the seventh day, when the Mediator, God-man, was revealed by the Gospel, whom, in the promise, he appointed to triumph

over Satan the corruptor of all, and so to restore all things;
both of the earth, where he began the restoration, by delivering the elect of mankind from the bondage of corruption; and
of heaven, by bringing the same chosen people into the heavenly habitation, in order to its being again re-peopled with
that colony of new inhabitants: in this manner he will complete the restoration.   Which completion Moses intimates,
verse 2. " and on the seventh day God ended his work, which
he had made." *This finishing of the restoration*, signified,
verse 3. by the word *made*, is very distinct from *the
finishing of the creation*, mentioned verse 1.   When God had
done all this, upon giving his Son to men for a Mediator and
Redeemer, he himself rested in this his last work, as this is
" the man of his delight," Isa. xlii. 1.   And this rest was the
only foundation for instituting the Sabbath.   This institution
consists of a twofold act: the first is of *blessing*, by which
God blessed that very day, by a most distinguishing privilege,
to be the day devoted to the Messiah, who was revealed in it
by the Gospel.   For this is the honour of the Sabbath, that
it is " the delight, on account of the holy of the Lord being
glorified," Isa. lviii. 13.   The other act is that of *sanctification*, by which he set it apart for a sign and memorial of that
benefit, because through and for *the holy of the Lord*, he
chooses to sanctify the elect.   This is the sum of that opinion.
Let us now consider whether it be solid, and can be proved
by scripture.

XX. The whole foundation of this opinion is, that Adam
fell on the very day in which he was created: which the scripture no where says.   I know that some Jewish doctors, with
boldness, as is their way, assert this; and, as if they were perfectly acquainted with what God was about every hour, declare, that man was created the third hour of the day, fell the
eleventh, and was expelled Paradise the twelfth.   But this
rashness is to be treated with indignation.   The learned person
deems it his glory to be wise from the scriptures alone, and
justly, for thus it becomes a divine.   But what portion of scripture determines any thing about the first sin?   We have here
scarce any more than bare conjectures, which at best are too
sandy a foundation, on which any wise architect will ever presume to build so grand an edifice.

XXI. Nay, there are many things from which we rather
incline to think that man's sin happened not on the sixth day.
For it was after God had on that day created the beasts; after
he had formed Adam of the dust of the earth; after he had
prescribed him the law concerning the tree of knowledge of

good and evil; after he had presented to him the beasts in
Paradise, that, upon enquiring into the nature of each (which
also he performed with great accuracy, as the great Bochart
has very learnedly shewn, Hierozoic. lib. i. c. 9.) he might
call each by their proper names; after Adam had found there
was not among them any help meet for him, for the purposes
and convenience of marriage; and after God had cast Adam
into a deep sleep, and then at last formed Eve from one of
his ribs.   All these things are not of a nature to be performed like the other works of the preceding days, in the shortest
space of time possible, and as it were, in a moment; but succeeded one another in distinct periods, and during these, several things must have been done by Adam himself.   Nay,
there are divines of no small note, who insist that these things
were not all done in one day, and others postpone the creation of Eve to one of the days of the following week: but
we do not now engage in these disputes.   After all these
things the world was yet innocent, and free from all guilt, at
least on the part of man.   And God contemplating his works,
and concluding his day, approved of all as very good and
beautiful.   He had yet no new labour for restoring the fallen
world, which would have been no ways inferior to the work
of the creation.   But what probability is there, that in those
very few hours which remained, if yet a single hour remained, Adam should have parted from Eve, who had been just
created, exposed his most beloved consort to an insidious serpent, and that both of them, just from the hands of the Creator, should so suddenly have given ear to the deceiver? Unless one is prepossessed in favour of the contrary opinion,
what reason could he have, notwithstanding so many proba-
bilities to the contrary, prematurely thus to hurry on Adam's
sin? Since therefore the whole of this foundation is so very
weak, what solid superstructure can we imagine it is capable
of?

XXII. Let us now take a nearer view of the superstructure itself, and examine whether its construction be sufficiently
firm and compact.   The very learned person imagines he sees
a new labour, or work on the seventh day, and a new *rest*
succeeding that labour, which is the foundation of the Sabbath.   The *labour* was *a promise of the Messiah*, by which
the world, miserably polluted with sin, was to be restored;
and that Moses treats on this, chap. ii. 2. "and on the seventh day God ended his work, which he had made." The
rest was the satisfaction and delight he had in that promise,
and in the Messiah promised.   But let us offer the following

considerations in opposition to this sentiment: 1st. If God, on the seventh day, performed the immense work of recovering the world from the fall, a work, which if not greater, yet certainly is not less than the creation of the world out of nothing, and he was again to rest when he had finished it, certainly then, the seventh day was as much a day of work to God, and no more a Sabbath, or day of rest, than any of the preceding days. For God having finished the work of each day, rested for a while and delighted in it. 2dly. Moses in the second verse makes use of the same word by which he had expressed the finishing of the world in the first. But *the finishing* in the first verse, as the learned person himself owns, relates to the finishing of the creation; what necessity then can there be for giving such different senses to one and the same word, in the same context, when there is not the least mark of distinction. 3dly. Hitherto Moses has not given the least imaginable hint of the fall of our first parents: is it then probable that he would so abruptly mention the restitution of the world from the fall; and that in the very same words which he had just used, and was afterwards to use for explaining the first creation? What can oblige, or who can suffer us to confound the neatness of Moses' method, and the perspicuity of his words, by this feigned irregularity, and ambiguity? 4thly. It may be doubted, whether we can properly say, that by the promise of the Messiah all things were perfected and finished; since God, if we follow the thread of Moses' narrative, did, after this promise, punish the world with a deserved curse: and the apostle still says of the world, that " the creature was made subject to vanity, and groans under the bondage of corruption," Rom. viii. 20, 21. It is indeed true that the promise of the Messiah, which could not be frustrated, was the foundation of the comfort of the fathers; but the scripture no where declares, that by this promise, as immediately made after the fall, all things were finished, nay, even this promise pointed out that person, who after many ages, and by various acts, not of one and the same office, was to effect the true consummation.

XXIII. Our learned author urges the following reasons why those two finishings are not to be looked upon as the same: 1st. It would be a *tautology*, if not an *inexcusable battology*, or idle repetition, in such a compendious narrative; and either the first verse, or the beginning of the second, would be superfluous. 2dly. The finishing or ending of verse 2. is annexed to *the seventh day*, by a double article in the same manner as *the rest* is. " And on the very seventh day

God ended his work which he had made, and he rested on the very seventh day from all his work which he had made." So that if the former verb יִכַל be rendered by the preterpluperfect, *and he had ended*, the latter וַיִּשְׁבֹּת must be rendered so too, *and he had rested;* but this is incongruous. Nay, since on the other days we reject the preterpluperfect sense, lest the works of the following day should be referred to those of the preceding, contrary to historical truth; it ought not then here to be admitted on the seventh day. 3dly. When the third verse shews the cause of this rest, it speaks of distinct finishings, the latter of which is that of the seventh day, "and God blessed the seventh day and sanctified it, because that in it he had rested from all his work, which God בָּרָא created and made." By two verbs he describes two actions; בָּרָא denotes *to create*, and עָשָׂה, *to adorn, to polish:* these words are frequently of the same import, yet when joined together they are to be distinguished, as is owned not only by Christian, but by Jewish interpreters. (Thus it is, Isa. xliii. 7. where another word is added, יָצַר, *to form*, and, as to all the three, בָּרָא certainly signifies, the creation of the soul, but יָצַר, the formation of the body, and עָשָׂה, reformation by grace.) But these two actions are so described, that עֲשִׂיָּה *making*, immediately precedes *resting*, and was the work of the seventh day; but כְּרִיאָה, *creation*, the work of the six preceding days. 4thly. To the same purpose is the recapitulation of verse 4. which repeats and confirms the distinction just now mentioned: "these are the generations of the heavens and of the earth, when they were created; in the day that the Lord God made the earth and the heavens." Thus he recites the generations both of the first six days, (in which the heavens and the earth, with their respective hosts, were created) and of the beginning of that one day, namely, the seventh, which is that of operation, in which he made and polished, inverting the order; first the earth, then the heavens. Thus far our very learned author.

XXIV. But we cannot assent to these things, and therefore we answer each in order. To the first, I would earnestly entreat our brother, both to think and speak more reverently of the style of the Holy Ghost; nor charge those simple and artless repetitions of one and the same thing, even in a concise narrative, with an inexcusable tautology, if not a battology, or vain and useless repetitions. It does not become us, the humble disciples of the Divine Spirit, to criticise on the most learned language, and the most pure style of our adorable master. It is very frequent, in the sacred writings, more than once to repeat the same thing, in almost the same words, at no great distance asunder. This very second chapter of Genesis, of which we now treat, gives us various examples of this. The reason of the sanctification of the seventh day, namely, the rest of God upon that day, is proposed in nearly the same words, in the second and third verses. This learned person himself calls the fourth verse a recapitulation of what was just said. And what is the whole of the second chapter, but a fuller explication of the formation of man, which indeed we have plainly, but more briefly related in the first chapter, or the whole of the second, is in a great measure, superfluous? Or, shall we dare to charge God with tautologies, if not with inexcusable battologies? Is it not more becoming to tremble with awe at his words, and rather return him thanks, that on account of the dulness of our apprehension he has vouchsafed to propose two or three times the same truths, either in the same, or in a variety of words, having all the same meaning? For my own part I would act in this manner without any doubt of acting as becomes.

XXV. To the second, I would answer. 1st. The words of Moses may be taken in this sense; namely, that God finished the work of the sixth day, and consequently of all the six days, in the very moment in which the seventh began. Thus the ancient Hebrews, and after them, R. Solomon, explains this manner of speaking; as thereby to intimate that God, in the very moment in which he entered on the Sabbath, finished his work; for God alone knows the moments and least parts of time in another manner than men do. 2dly. Nor is it an improper observation of Aben Ezra, *that the finishing of the work is not the work itself,* but only means the ceasing from work, and that the text explains itself thus ; *and he finished,* that is, *and he rested ;* having finished his work, he worked no longer. 3dly. But we need not insist on this: Drusius speaks to excellent purpose on this place : " The preterperfect Hebrew may be as well rendered by the preterpluperfect as otherwise. It is really so : the Hebrews have only one preterperfect, which they use for every kind of past time ; and therefore according to the connection, it may be rendered sometimes by the preterperfect, and at other times by the preterpluperfect." Let it therefore be rendered here by the preterpluperfect, *and he had finished,* as the Dutch translation has also done, and all the difficulty will disappear. Our learned author may insist, that if this be granted, then the following ויִשְׁבֹת must be also rendered by the preterpluperfect. But it does not follow ; for we are to consider the nature of the subject and the different circumstances. The learned person insists, that the word *finishing,* is used in a different sense in the first, from what it is in the second verse ; and shall we not be allowed to interpret a pre-terperfect, which, by the genius of the language is indeter-minate, sometimes by the preterperfect, and at other times by the preterpluperfect, as the subject shall require? And if elsewhere we justly reject the preterpluperfect sense, it is not because the genius of the Hebrew tongue does not admit of it, but because, as the learned person himself observes, such an interpretation is contrary to the truth of the history. Which not being the case here, such a reason cannot be urged. I will only add, if Moses wanted to say, what we imagine he has said, *et consummaverat die septima*, &c. *et cessavit.* &c. and *on the seventh, God had finished*, &c. *and rested*, &c. could he possibly have expressed in other words, or more aptly, ac-cording to the genius of the language, this sense? Was the learned person himself to render into Hebrew, word for word, these Latin words, he would certainly have rendered them in the same tense and mood, as Moses has done.

XXVI. To the third reason, I reply, 1st. The word עשה is very general, and signifies, *to do a thing any how, well* or *ill.* It is said of penal or physical evil, Amos iv. 13. *who maketh the morning darkness;* and Ezek. xxxv. 6. *I will prepare (make) thee·unto blood.* And of moral evil, Mic. ii. 1. *when the morning is light they practise it;* we shall give more in-stances presently. Hence it appears, that the learned person too much restricts the meaning of this word, when he explains it by the words, *to adorn*, or *polish :* especially, if he would precisely confine it to *the reformation by grace.* 2dly. The same word is often expressive of the six days work ; as Gen. i. 31. *and God saw all that he had made;* and Exod. xx. 11. *in six days the Lord made heaven and earth :* likewise Ezek. xlvi. 1. *the six working days* are opposed to the Sabbath. Neither does the learned person deny, that the words ברא and עשה are often equivalent. And why not here also? Is there any neces-sity, or probable reason, for taking עשיה for *the work of the seventh day*, and בריאה for *the work of the six preceding days*. 3dly. I think he goes a little too far, when he asserts that both Christian and Jewish interpreters admit that these words, when joined together, have distinct significations. Truly for my own part, of the several interpreters, both Jewish and Christian, whom I have consulted, I never found one, who distinguishes the meaning of these words, as this learned au-thor has done. (See Fagius on Gen. i. 1. Manasseh-Ben-Israel, de Creat. Probl. 4. Cocceius Disput. select. p. 70. sect. 72.) Let us in this case hear the learned De Dieu, who thus com-ments on this passage : " It appears to be an usual hebraism,

whereby the infinitive, added to a verb, including a like action, is generally redundant;" such as Judges xiii. 19. and
acting, he acted wonderously, that is, *he acted wonderously.*
1 Kings xiv. 9. and doing, thou hast done evil, that is, *thou
hast done evil.* 2 Kings xxi. 6. and working, he multiplied
wickedness, that is simply, *he multiplied wickedness,* or *he
wrought much wickedness.* 2 Chron. xx. 35. he doing, did
wickedly, *he doing* is redundant. Psal. cxxvi. 2. the Lord
doing, has done great things for them, *doing* is again redundant. Eccl. ii. 11. on the labour, that doing I had laboured,
that is simply, *I had laboured.* Which last passage is entirely parallel with this in Genesis, for, whether you say, לעשרת
עכזל *he doing, laboured,* or בדא לעשנת *he making, created,* you
say the same thing: unless that בלא signifies to produce something new, without any precedent or pattern, and which had
no existence before;" therefore, he making, created, is no
other than, *he made something new.* These things neither
could, nor ought to be unknown to this learned person, considering his great skill in Hebrew learning. 4thly. He ought
not to have made such a distinction barely and without any
proof between the words בדא, יצד, and עשה, which are used by
Isaiah, xliii. 7. as if the first intends *the creation* of the soul;
the second, *the formation* of the body, and the third, *the reformation* by grace: there not being the least foundation for it in
scripture. For, 1. בדא sometimes signifies reformation by
grace, as Psalm. li. 10. Create in me a clean heart. 2. יצר is
sometimes applied to the soul, Zech. xii. ver. 1. and formeth
the spirit of man within him: and Psalm xxxiii. ver. 15. and
fashioneth their hearts alike; sometimes too it denotes formation by grace; as Isa. xliii. 21. this people have I formed for
myself, they shall shew forth my praise. 3. עשה is more than
once used *for the first formation* of man; as Gen. i. 26. *Let
us make man:* and Gen. ii. 18. *I will make him an help meet
for him;* Jer. xxxviii. 16. *that made us this soul,* says
king Zedekiah to Jeremiah, without having any thoughts of
a reformation by grace. As therefore all these words are so
promiscuously used in scripture, ought we not to look upon
him, who distinguishes them in such a magisterial manner,
as one who gives too much scope to his own fancy? And
what if one should invert the order of our author, and positively assert, that here denotes, reformation by grace, as Psalm
li. 10.: the production of the soul, as Ezek. xii. 1. and the
formation of the body, as Gen. ii. 8. What reply could
the learned person make? But these are weak arguments.
It is more natural to take these words in Isaiah, as meant of
the new creation and reformation by grace. And this ac-

cumulation or multiplying of words, is very proper to denote the exceeding greatness of the power of God, and his effectual working in the sanctification of the elect. There is a parallel place, Eph. ii. 10. *for we are his*, Heb. *(workmanship)*, Heb. *created in Christ Jesus unto good works, which God hath before ordained, that we should walk in them :* as Isa. xxii. 11. *fashioned it long ago*, which properly προητοιμασε he hath *before ordained.* From all this it appears, that this passage in Isaiah can be of no service to our learned author. 5thly. But if we must distinguish between and το ברא and το עשה, nothing, I think, is more to the purpose than the interpretation of Ben Nachman. " He rested from all his works which he created, by producing something out of nothing, to make of it all the works mentioned in the six days : and lo ! he says, he rested from *creating* and from *working; from creating*, as having created in the first day, *and from working*, as having completed his working in the remaining days."

XXVII. The fourth reason coincides with the foregoing, only that it is still more cabbalistical. 1st. It is a strange interpretation to say, that by *the generations of heaven and earth*, we are to understand not only their first creation, but their restoration by the promise of the Messiah ; for it is quite foreign to the subject, to tell us, that by the sin of the angels, a state of corruption was introduced into the heaven of heavens, and thereby the throne of the divine majesty was basely defiled ; for though by the angelic apostacy, corruption had been introduced into heaven, yet by their ejection, whereby they were hurled into hell, the heavens were purged from that corruption. Nor was there any new heaven made by the promise of the Messiah, that was given on the sixth day ; for that promise made no alteration there, but only foretold, that after many years some elect souls were to be received into that holy and blessed habitation. 2dly. As to the order in which the earth is put before the heavens, it is well known that the scripture does not always relate things in the same order ; nor from the mere order of the narrative, which is an arbitrary thing, can any arguments be formed : However, Junius' observation is not to be rejected : " Earth and heaven are mentioned in an inverted order, because the formation of the earth preceded that of the heavens ; for the earth was perfected on the third day of the creation, heaven on the fourth." 3dly. It is doing manifest violence to the text, if we understand the formation of the earth and heavens, of their reformation by grace, in virtue of the promise of the Messiah, made on the seventh day ; because Moses treats of that formation of earth and heaven, which was prior to that of plants and herbs, as appears from the connexion of ver. 3.

with ver. 4. For thus the words run: " These are the generations of the heavens and of the earth, when they were created,
in the day that the Lord God made the earth and heavens, and
every plant of the field, before it was in the earth, and every
herb of the field," &c. Or, as the learned De Dieu shews, they
may otherwise be very properly rendered, " in the day that
the Lord made the heavens and the earth, there was yet no
plant of the field created," &c. So that this formation of the
earth and heavens was prior to man's own creation, much more
to the fall, and to the restitution from the fall. And this verse
wholly overturns the distinction which this learned person has
invented.

XXVIII. And as we have thus shewn, that the words of Moses neither mention nor intimate any work by which God restored all things from the fall on the seventh day ; so neither of
any rest from the work of restoration, which is the foundation
of the rest of the Sabbath. For, 1st. It is irrational to suppose,
that when God promised the Messiah, he then rested from the
work of the gracious reformation of the universe ; because that
promise was a prophecy of the sufferings, conflicts, and at the last
of the death of Christ, by which that reformation was to be
brought about and accomplished. 2dly. How can it be said that
God rested, immediately after having made that promise, from
all his work, when directly upon it he pronounced, and executed sentence upon Adam, Eve, and the earth that was cursed for
their crime, and expelled them paradise ? which work (to speak
after the manner of men, compare Isa. xxviii. 21.) was truly a greater labour to God than the very creation of the
world. And thus, instead of a Sabbath which Moses describes,
this day is made one of the most laborious to God. 3dly. The
Sabbath day after the publication of the first gospel promise, was
doubtless sacred to the Messiah, and to be celebrated to his honour by the saints with a holy exultation of soul. Nor shall I
be much against the learned person, should he choose to translate, Isa. lviii. 13. that the Sabbath may be called, " a delight,
on account of the holy of the Lord being glorified ;" but it cannot with any probability be inferred from this, that the promise
of the Messiah was the foundation of the first Sabbath, since
the Sabbath, as well as other things, did not acquire that relation
till after the fall. 4thly. The scriptures in express terms declare, that the rest of God from the work of the first creation
which was completed in six days, was the foundation of the Sabbath. " In six days the Lord made heaven and earth, the sea,
and all that in them is, and rested on the seventh day ; wherefore the Lord blessed the Sabbath day, and hallowed it," Exod.
xx. 11. Which being plain, it sufficiently, if I mistake not,

appears, that it is much safer to go in the old and beaten path, which is the king's high way, than in that other new trodden and rough one, which the learned person, whose opinion we have been examining, has chosen to tread in.   And so much for this subject.

CHAP. VIII.

Of the Violation of the Covenant of Works on the part of Man.

I. As the scripture does not declare, how long this covenant, thus ratified and confirmed, continued unbroken, we are satisfied to remain in the dark.   And we would have a holy dread of presuming rashly to fix the limits of a time which is really uncertain.   It is however evident, that man, wickedly presuming to eat the fruit of the forbidden tree, incurred the guilt of violating the covenant.   Nor ought that to be deemed a small sin, (as the apostle, Rom. v. calls it, the *offence, disobedience,* and *transgression)* because it may seem to have been committed about a thing of no great importance :   For the meaner the thing is, from which God commanded to abstain, and for which man despised the promise of the covenant, makes his transgression of it the more heinous ; as may be illustrated by the profaneness of Esau, which was so much the greater, as the mess was of so little value, for which he sold his birth-right, Heb. xii. 16.   In that sin, as divines generally observe, there was, as it were, a kind of complication of many crimes.   But it is our chief purpose to shew, that this was the violation of the whole covenant : for not only that tree, as we proved above, was a sacrament of the covenant, the abuse of which ought to be looked upon as a violence done to the whole ; not only the precept concerning that tree, which was the trial of universal obedience ; but likewise the covenant in its whole constitution, was violated by that transgression ; the law of the covenant was trampled upon, when man, as if he had been his own lord and master in all things, did, in defiance of his Lord, lay hold on what was not his property, and throw off the yoke of obedience that was due to God : the promises of the covenant were set less by than a transitory gust of pleasure, and the empty promises of the seducer ; and that dreadful death which the author of the covenant threatened the transgressor with, not considered and thought of in all its dreadful effects, but he presumed to act in opposition to it.   And thus *Adam transgressed the covenant,* Hos. vi. 7.

II. Though Eve had the first hand in this crime, yet it is usually in scripture ascribed to Adam : *by one man sin entered into the world,* according to Paul, Rom. v. 12. whom ver. 14. he declares to be Adam : For Adam was the head of the covenant, with whom, even before the creation of Eve, God seems to have transacted.   Adam was the root of all mankind, and even of Eve herself, who was formed out of one of his ribs; neither is it customary to deduce a genealogy from a woman : nor was the covenant judged to be entirely broken, till Adam also added his own crime to that of his wife's.   Then it was that the Creator, first acting in the character of a judge, summoned to his bar the inconsiderate pair, already condemned by their own conscience.   But we are not to think that this inheritance of sin was so derived from our father Adam, as to excuse our mother Eve from that guilt: for as by marriage they were made one flesh, so far they may be considered as one man.   Nay, Adam is not considered as the head and root of mankind, but in conjunction with his wife.   To this purpose is what Malachi (ch. ii. 15.) says, that God, *seeking a godly seed, made one :* one pair, two into one flesh.

III. It was doubtless a wicked spirit who seduced man to this apostacy, and who, tormented with the horrors of his guilty conscience, envied man his happiness in God, and God the pleasure he had in man, and sought to have the wretched consolation of making one a partaker of his misery.   And, the more easily to insinuate himself into man's favour by his ensnaring discourse, he concealed himself in the serpent, the most subtle of all animals, and at that time not less acceptable to man, than the rest of the obsequious creatures.   The great *du Moulin, disput.* iii. *de Angelis*, § 44. conjectures this serpent was of a conspicuous form, with fiery eyes, decked with gold, and marked with shining spots, so as to draw the eyes of Eve to it, and that he had before that time more than once insinuated himself by his soothing sounds, into Eve's favour, in order that having preconceived a good opinion of him, she might be brought the more readily to yield to him.   In fine, he was such, that what Moses says of the subtilty of the serpent must be applied to him only, and not to the whole species.   To this conjecture it is also added, that Eve, perhaps such was her simplicity, did not know whether God had bestowed the use of speech on any other animals besides man.   Laurentius Camirez in his *Pentecontarch*, c. i. (quoted by Bochart, *Hierozoic*, lib. i. c. iv. p. 30.) goes a step farther, and feigns that Eve was wont to play with the serpent, and adorn her bosom, neck, and arms with it ; and hence at this day the ornaments for those parts have the resemblance of serpents, and are called ὄφεις, *serpents*, by the Greeks.

IV. But all this is apocryphal.   We are not to advance such romantic things without any scripture authority.   Whether this was the first, or the only apparition of the serpent, as having the use of speech, I shall neither boldly affirm, nor obstinately de-

ny. But what we are told as probable of some extraordinary
serpent so curiously spotted and set off, and now made familiar
to Eve, by an intercourse repeated several times, are the pleasing amusements of a curious mind.   The subtilty of serpents
is every where so well known, that among many nations they
are proposed as the distinguishing character and hieroglyphic
of prudence.   Bochart in his *Hierozoic*. lib. i. c. 4. has collected many things relating to this from several authors.   To this
purpose is what our Saviour says, Matt, x. 16. *Be ye wise as
serpents.*   It is also injurious and reproachful to our mother
Eve, to represent her so weak, and at so small a remove from
the brutal creation, as not to be able to distinguish between a
brute and a man, and to be ignorant that the use of speech was
the peculiar privilege of rational creatures.   Such stupid ignorance is inconsistent with the happy state of our first parents,
and with the image of God, which shone so illustriously also in
Eve.   We are rather to believe, that the devil assumed this or-
gan, the more easily to recommend himself to man as a prudent
spirit, especially as this looked like a miracle, or a prodigy at
least, that the serpent should speak with human voice.   Here
was some degree of probability, that some spirit lay concealed
in this animal, and that too extraordinarily sent by God, who
should instruct man more fully about the will of God, and whose
words this very miracle as it were seemed to confirm : for that
serpents have a tongue unadapted to utter articulate sounds, is
the observation of Aristotle, *de Part. anim.* lib. ii. c. 17.   See
Vossius de Idol. lib. iv. c. 54.

V. As this temptation of the devil is somewhat like to all his
following ones, we judge it not improbable, that Satan exerted
all his cunning, and transformed himself, as he usually does,
into an angel of light, and addressed himself to Eve, as if he had
been an extraordinary teacher of some important truth, not yet
fully understood.   And therefore does not openly contradict
the command of God, but first proposes it as a doubt, whether
Adam understood well the meaning of the divine prohibition ;
whether he faithfully related it to Eve ; whether she herself
too, did not mistake the sense of it ; and whether at least that
command, taken literally, was not so improbable, as to render it
unnecessary to think of a more mysterious meaning.   And
thus he teaches to raise reasonings and murmurings against the
words of God, which are the destruction of faith.

VI. Next, he undermines the threatening annexed to the command ; *Ye shall not surely die,* says he ; God never meant by
death what you in your simplicity are apt to suspect.   Could
death be supposed to hang on so pleasant and agreeable a tree ?
or do you imagine God so envious as to forbid you who are his

familiars and friends to eat the fruit of this delicious tree, under
the dreadful penalty of death? this is inconsistent with his infinite goodness, which you so largely experience, and with the
beauty of this specious tree and its fruit; and therefore there
must be another meaning of this expression which you do not
understand.   And thus he instilled that heresy into the unwary
woman, the first heard of in the world, that there is a sin which
does not deserve death, or, which is the same thing, a venial sin.
The false prophet, the attendant on Antichrist, *who hath horns
like a lamb, and speaketh as a dragon*, Rev. xiii. 11. does at
this very day maintain this capital heresy in the church of Rome,
and nothing is still more usual with Satan, than by hope of impunity, to persuade men to sin.

VII. He adds the promise of a greater happiness; *your eyes
shall be opened, and ye shall be as gods, knowing good and
evil*.   He presupposes what in itself was true and harmless,
that man had a desire after some more perfect happiness; which
he made to consist in his being made like to God, which John
affirms to be, as it were, the principal mark of salvation, that
we *shall be like God*, 1 John iii. 2.   He says farther, that this
likeness was to be joined with the opening of their eyes, and a
greater measure of knowledge.   Now this is not unlike the doctrines of the scripture, which affirm that we *shall see God*, and
that *as he is*, and *shall know him, even as we ourselves are
known*.   And thus far indeed it might appear, that Satan spoke
not amiss, blending many truths, and those evident to the conscience, with his own lies, the more easily to deceive under the
appearance of a true teacher.   But herein the fraud lies concealed: 1st. That he teaches them not to wait for God's appointed time, but unadvisedly and precipitantly lay hold on the
promised felicity.   Man cannot indeed too much love and desire perfection, if he does it by *preparation*, and *earnest expectation*; preparing himself in a course of holy patience and subjection to the will of God, desiring not to anticipate, even for a
moment, the good pleasure of God.   2dly. That he points out
a false way, as if the eating of that tree was either a natural, or,
more probably, a moral mean to attain the promised bliss; and
as if God had appointed this as a necessary requisite, without
which there was no possibility of coming to a more intimate
communion with God, and a more perfect degree of wisdom;
nor, in fine, of obtaining that state, in which, knowing equally
good and evil, they would be no longer in danger of any degree of deception.   And it is most likely he perverted the
meaning of the name of the tree.   But all these were mere
delusions.

VIII. At last this disguised teacher appeals to the knowledge of God himself; *God doth know.* Most interpreters,
both Jewish and Christian, ancient and modern, interpret these
words, as if Satan would charge God with open malignity and
envy, as if he forbade this tree, lest he should be obliged to admit man into a partnership in his glory. And indeed there is
no blasphemy so horrid that Satan is ashamed of. But we are
here to consider whether such bare-faced blasphemy would not
have rather struck with horror, man, who had not yet entertained
any bad thoughts of God, than recommended itself by any appearance of probability. For why? is it credible, that a man in
his right senses could be persuaded that the acquisition of wisdom, and a likeness to God, depended on a tree, so that he should
obtain both these by eating of it, whether God would or not?
and then, that God, whom man must know to be infinitely great
and good, was liable to the passion of envy, a plain indication of
malignity and weakness; in fine, that there was such a virtue
in that tree, that, on tasting it, God could not deprive man of
life: for all these particulars are to be believed by him who can
imagine, that out of envy God had forbid him the use of that
tree. It does not seem consistent with the subtilty of Satan to
judge it adviseable to propose to man things so absurd, and so
repugnant to common notions, and the innate knowledge which
he must have had of God. May it not be made more proper,
to take that expression for a form of an oath? as Paul himself
says, 2 Cor. xi. 11. *God knoweth.* And thus the perjured im-
postor appealed to God as witness of what he advanced.

IX. Some think that Adam was not deceived, and did not believe what the serpent had persuaded the woman to, but rather
fell, out of love to his wife, whom he was unwilling to grieve;
and therefore, though he was conscious of a divine command,
and not exposed to the wiles of Satan, yet that he might not
abandon her in this condition, he tasted the fruit she offered; probably believing, that this instance of his affection for the spouse
whom God had given him, if in any measure faulty, might be
easily excused. To this they refer the apostle's words, 1 Tim.
ii. 14. " For Adam was not deceived, but the woman being deceived, was in the transgression." But this carries us off from
the simplicity of the divine oracles; the design of the apostle is
plainly to shew, that the woman ought not to exercise any dominion over her husband, for two reasons which he urges: 1st.
Because Adam was first created as the head, and then Eve, as a
help meet for him. 2dly. Because the woman shewed she was
more easily deceived, for being deceived first, she was the cause
of deceiving her husband, who was likewise deceived (though not

first) but by her means : for we commonly find in scripture, that
some things seem to be absolutely denied, which we are to understand only as denied in a restrictive sense : John vi. 27. and
Phil. ii. 4. are instances of this.   Nor can we conceive how
Adam, when he believed that what he did was forbidden by God,
and that if he did it he should forfeit the promised happiness,
nay, incur most certain death, (for all this he must know and
believe, if he still remained uncorrupted by the wiles of Satan,)
would have taken part in the crime only to please his wife.   Certainly if he believed that the transgression of the divine command, the contempt of the promised felicity, and his rash exposing himself to the danger of eternal death, could be excused only by his affection for his wife, he no less shamefully erred, nor
was less deceived, if not more, than his consort herself.   Nor
can it be concluded from his answer to God, in which he throws
the blame, not on the serpent's deceit, but on the woman whom
God had given him, that the man fell into this sin, not so much
by an error in the understanding, as giving way to his affection ;
for this subverts the whole order of the faculties of their soul,
since every error in the affection, supposes some error in the
understanding.   This was doubtless an error, and indeed one of
the greatest, to believe that a higher regard was to be paid to
his affection for his wife, than to the divine command.   It was
a considerable error to think that it was an instance of love to
become an accomplice in sin ; because it is the duty of love to
convince the sinner, and as far as may be restore him to the favour of God, which certainly Adam would have done, had he
been entirely without error.   In whatever light therefore we
view this point, we are obliged to own that he was deceived :
the only apology Adam would make, seems to be, that his beloved consort had, by her insinuations which she had learned
from the serpent, persuaded him also, and that he was not the
first in that sin, nor readily suspected any error or deception by
her, who was given him as an help by God.

X. It cannot be doubted, that providence was concerned about
this fall of our first parents.   It is certain that it was foreknown
from eternity ; none can deny this, but he who sacrilegiously
dares to venture to deny the omniscience of God.   Nay, as God
by his eternal decree laid the plan of the whole economy of our
salvation, and preconceived succession of the most important
things, presupposes the sin of man, it could not therefore happen
unforeseen by God.   And this is the more evident, because,
according to Peter, " He (Christ) was foreordained before the
foundation of the world," and that as the Lamb whose blood was
to be shed, 1 Pet. i. 19, 20. which invincible argument Socinus

knew not how otherwise to elude, but by this ridiculous assertion, that " after men had sinned, Christ indeed came to abolish their sins, but that he would have come, notwithstanding, though they had never sinned." But as this idle assertion is unscriptural, nay, antiscriptural, so it is not apposite to this place ; for the order of Peter's words obliges us to interpret them, concerning Christ's being foreknown as a Lamb to be slain, and to shed his blood to be the price of our redemption. And he likewise speaks, Acts ii. 23. of this determinate counsel and foreknowledge of God, according to which Christ was delivered into the hands of wicked men. Since therefore Christ was foreknown from eternity, as one to be slain for the sins of men, man's sin was also necessarily foreknown.

XI. And if foreknown, it was also predetermined ; thus Peter, in the place just quoted, joins together *the determinate counsel and foreknowledge of God.* Nor can God's prescience of future things be conceived, but in connection with his decree concerning them.

XII. From all this may be inferred by a plain consequence, that man could not but fall on account of the infallibility of the divine prescience, and of that necessity which they call a necessity of *consequence ;* for it is inconsistent with the divine perfection, that any decree of God should be rendered void, or that the event should not be answerable to it. It is the prerogative of Jehovah to say, " My counsel shall stand," Isa. xlvi. 10. " His counsels of old are faithfulness and truth," Isa. xxv. 1. God himself has ratified the stability of his purposes by an oath, the more certainly to declare the immutability of his counsel, Heb. vi. 17. " The Lord of hosts hath sworn, saying, Surely as I have thought, so shall it come to pass, and as I have purposed, so shall it stand," Isa. xiv. 24.

XIII. The infallibility of the event, as to man's sin, may be proved by another argument ; if we only attend to that subordination, by which all creatures depend on God, in their operations. For, it is not possible that God shall by his almighty concurrence, influence any creature to act, and yet that creature suspend its acting. And if God shall not influence to the moral goodness of that natural action, the creature cannot, without that influx, perform that action morally good. This is evident from the nature of God and the creature ; as he cannot ineffectually influence his creatures to act, so they cannot but act, when under his influence. These things being supposed, as they are evident to any person of attention, it is impossible that man can abstain from reasoning, willing, and eating, where God influences to these acts by his almighty concurrence. Nor is it any

more possible that man can reason, will, and eat in a holy manner, if God by his almighty concurrence does not influence the
holiness of it.   Supposing therefore, that God had afforded his
influence to the natural act of reasoning, willing, and eating, as
he actually did, but not the moral goodness of those acts, as he
did not; it could not otherwise be, but that man should act at
that time, and perform his action wrong.   All this holds true,
not only of this first sin of man, but of all other sins.   I see
not, therefore, why we may not boldly maintain these things,
as they are most evidently true, and more especially as they
tend to the glory of God, and to demonstrate his supereminence,
and the absolute dependence of the creatures upon him, as much
in their operations as in their existence.   Should those of the
contrary Pelagian sentiments pervert these truths, it will be at
their peril.   Nor ought we so much to regard that, as on their
account to conceal the truth.

XIV. However, it will not be amiss to insist a little longer
on this subject, that all the apparent harshness of this doctrine
may be entirely removed by an evident demonstration of the
truth, which we think we shall be able to effect, by beginning
with the more evident truths in one continued chain of arguments, flowing from each other, in such a manner as to gain the
assent even of the most obstinate.

XV. And first, I think it will be readily granted, that there is
but one first cause; that all other causes so depend upon that,
both in existing and acting, as without it to be able neither to
exist nor to act.   Paul inculcated this upon the Athenians, Acts
xvii. 28. " in him we live, and move, and have our being."
Nor indeed can the most powerful monarch in the world, such
as the Assyrian was, in the time of Isaiah, any more move
without God, than " the axe without him that heweth therewith, or the saw without him that shaketh it," Isa. x. 15.

XVI. Reason in this concurs with scripture.   For if there
was any cause besides God, which could act independently of
him, it would follow, there were more first principles than one;
as Thomas Aquinas reasons well in his *Secundo sentent. distinct.* xxxvii. *quæst.* 2. *art.* 2. whose reasoning, as it is both
solid, and very much to the purpose, we shall not scruple to
give in his own words: " It is, says he, essential to the first
principle, that it can act without the assistance and influence of
a prior agent; so that if the human will could produce any action, of which God was not author, the human will would have
the nature of a first principle."

XVII. Though they endeavour to solve this, by saying, that
notwithstanding the will be of itself capable of producing an

action, without the influence of a prior agent, yet it has not its being from itself, but from another; whereas the nature of a first principle is to be self-existent. But it seems inconsistent to say that what has not its being of itself, can yet act of itself; for, what is not of itself, cannot continue of itself. For, all the power of acting arises from the essence, and the operation from the power. Consequently, what has its essence from another, must also have its power and operation from that other. Moreover, though this reply denies that it is simply the first; yet, we cannot but see, that it is the first agent, if its acting cannot be referred to some prior agent as the cause. Thus far Thomas Aquinas.

XVIII. Nor does God only concur with the actions of second causes when they act, but also influences the causes themselves to act. Because the beginning of actions depends if not more, at least not less on God, than their progress. This opinion is not unhappily expressed in the Roman Catechism, published by the decree of the council of Trent, at the command of Pope Pius V., part I. on the first article of the Creed, No. 22. to this purpose; " But God, not only by his providence, preserves and governs all things that exist; but he likewise, by a secret energy, so influences those that move and act, to motion and action, that though he hinders not the efficiency of second causes, yet he prevents or goes before it; seeing his most secret power extends to each in particular; and, as * the wise man testifies, reaches powerfully from one end to the other, and disposes all things sweetly. Wherefore it was said by the apostle, when declaring to the Athenians the God, whom they ignorantly worshipped; he is not far from every one of us; for in him we live, and move, and have our being."

XIX. Moreover, as a second cause cannot act, unless acted upon and previously moved to act, by the preventing and predetermining influence of the first cause: so, in like manner, that influence of the first cause is so efficacious, as that supposing it, the second cause cannot but act. For, it is unworthy of God to imagine any concurrence of his to be so indifferent, as at last only to be determined by the co-operation of second causes: as if the rod should shake him who lifts it up; or, as if the staff should lift up what is not wood, Isa. x. 15. for so the words properly run. And the meaning is, that it is highly absurd to ascribe to an instrument of wood, the raising and managing of what is of a more excellent nature, namely spirit. By this allegory is intimated the absurdity of that opinion, which makes God to be determined in his actions by the creature.

* N. B. This is a quotation from the apocryphal book of Wisdom, ch. viii. 1. where it is said, Wisdom reacheth from one end to another, mightily and sweetly doth she order all things.

XX. Didacus Alvarez, de Auxiliis divinæ gratiæ, lib. iii. disput. 21. p. 163. makes use of the following argument against this: namely, the manner of concurring by a will, of itself indifferent to produce this or the other effect, or its opposite, is very imperfect; because, in its efficacy, it depends on the concurrence of a second cause; and every dependence imports in the thing which depends, some imperfection and inferiority, in respect of him on whom it depends; and therefore, such a manner of concurrence cannot be ascribed to God, or agree with his will, which is an infinite and most perfect cause.

XXI. And then this insolvable difficulty likewise remains; if the second cause determines the concurrence of God, in itself indifferent; in that act of determination, it will be independent of God; and so become the first cause. And if in one action it can act independently of God, why not in a second? If in the beginning of the action, why not also in the progress? Since the transition from non-acting to acting is greater than the continuing an action once begun.

XXII. As these things are universally true, they may be applied to those free actions of rational creatures, in which there is a moral evil inherent: namely, that creatures may be determined to those actions by the efficacious influence of God, *so far as they are actions*, according to their *physical entity*. Elegantly to this purpose Thomas Aquinas, in the place just quoted. Since the act of sin is a kind of being, not only as negations and privations are said to be beings; but also as things, which in general exist, are beings because even these actions in general are ranked in that order, and if the actions of sin [as actions] are not from God, it would follow that there would be some being, which had not its essence from God: and thus God would not be the universal cause of all beings. Which is contrary to the perfection of the first being.

XXIII. Neither does God only excite and predetermine the will of men to vicious actions, so far as they are actions; but he likewise so excites it, that it is not possible, but, thus acted upon, it shall act. For, if upon supposition of that divine influx, it was possible for the created will not to act, these two absurdities would follow: 1st. That the human will could baffle the providence of God, and either give to, or take from the divine influx, all its efficacy. 2dly. That there could be some act in the creature, of such weight as to resist the divine influence, and be independent of God. Nor do I imagine, they will say, that God concurs to the production of that action, whereby his influx is resisted. But we have already refuted any concurrence as in itself indifferent, to be determined by the free will of the creatures.

XXIV. Further, the free will of man excited to actions cannot, according to its physical essence, give them a moral and spiritual goodness, without the divine providence influencing and concurring to that goodness. This is evident from what has been said. For, as moral goodness is a superior and more perfect degree of entity, than a physical entity alone, and man in the physical entity of his actions depends on God; so it is necessary he should much more depend on God, in producing the moral goodness of his actions, that the glory thereof ought to be rendered to God as the first cause.

XXV. If all these truths thus demonstrated be joined and linked together, they will produce that conclusion which we laid down § XIII. For if all creatures depend on God in acting; if he not only concurs with them, when they act, but also excites them to act; if that excitation be so powerful, as that upon supposing it, the effect cannot but follow; if God, with that same efficacy influences vicious actions, so far as they are physical; if the creature cannot give its actions their due moral goodness without God; it infallibly follows, that Adam, God himself moving him to understand, will, and eat, could not but understand, will, and eat; and God not giving goodness to those actions, man could not understand and will in a right manner. Which was to be proved.

XXVI. But it does not follow, that man was obliged to what was simply impossible. For, it is only a consequential and eventual infallibility and necessity, which we have established. God bestowed sufficient powers on man, even such as were proper for a creature, by which he could have overcome the temptation. But then he could not proceed to action without presupposing the divine concurrence. Who shall deny, that man has a locomotive faculty, so sufficient in its kind, that he requires no more? For, will any affirm, that man, by that locomotive faculty, can actually move independently of God, as the first cause, without discovering his ignorance both of the supremacy of God, and the subordination of man? In like manner, we affirm, that, though God granted man such sufficient abilities to fulfil all righteousness, that he had no need of any further habitual grace, as it is called; yet, all this ability was given him in such a manner that he should act only dependently of the Creator, and his influence, as we hinted, chap. ii. § XIII.

XXVII. Much less should it be said, that man, by the above-mentioned acts of divine providence, was forced to sin. For, he sinned with judgment and will; to which faculties, liberty, as it is opposed to compulsion, is so peculiar, nay essential, as to be neither judgment nor will without it. And when we affirm, that God foreordained and infallibly foreknew, that man should sin freely, the sinner could not but sin freely; unless we would have the event not answer to the preordination and prescience of God. And it is so far from the decree of God, in the least to diminish the liberty of man in his acting, that, on the contrary, this liberty has not a more solid foundation than that infallible decree of God.

XXVIII. To make God the author of sin, is such dreadful blasphemy, that the thought cannot, without horror, be entertained by any Christian. God, indeed created man mutably good, infallibly foresaw his sin, foreordained the permission of that sin, really gave man sufficient powers to avoid it, but which could not act without his influx; and though he influenced his faculties to natural or physical actions, without influencing the moral goodness of those actions, all which appear from the event; yet God neither is, nor in any respect can be, the author of sin. And though it be difficult, nay impossible for us, to reconcile these truths with each other; yet we ought not to deny what is manifest, on account of that which is hard to be understood. We will religiously profess both truths, because they are truths, and worthy of God; nor can the one overturn the other; though in this our state of blindness and ignorance of God, we cannot thoroughly see the amicable harmony between them. This is not the alone, nor single difficulty, whose solution the sober divine will ever reserve for the world to come.

XXIX. This is certain, that by this permission of sin, God had an opportunity of displaying his manifold perfections. There is a fine passage to this purpose in Clemens, *Strom.* lib. i. which with pleasure we here insert. " It is the greatest work of divine providence, not to suffer the evil arising from a voluntary apostacy, to remain unuseful, or in every respect to become noxious. For it is peculiar to divine wisdom and power not only to do good (that being, to speak so, as much the nature of God, as it is the nature of fire to warm, or of light to shine) but much more, to make the evil devised by others, to answer a good and valuable end, and manage those things which appear to be evil to the greatest advantage."

XXX. It remains now lastly, to consider how, as Adam, in this covenant, was the head of mankind ; upon his fall, all his posterity may be deemed to have fallen with him, and broken the covenant of God. The apostle expressly asserts this, Rom. v. 12. " By one man sin entered into the world, and death by sin ; and so death passed upon all men, for that all have sinned."

XXXI. To illustrate the apostle's meaning, we must observe these things: 1st. It is very clear to any not under the power of prejudice, that when the apostle affirms that all *have sinned*, he speaks of an act of sinning, or of an actual sin ; the very term, to sin, denoting an action. It is one thing to sin, another to be sinful, if I may so speak. 2dly. When he affirms *all* to have sinned; he under that universality likewise includes those who have no actual, proper, and personal sin, and who, as he himself says, *have not sinned after the similitude of Adam's transgression*, verse 14. Consequently these are also guilty of some actual sin, as appears from their death ; but that not being their own proper and personal sin, must be the sin of Adam, imputed to them by the just judgment of God. 3dly. By these words ἐφ ᾧ πάντες ἥμαρτον *for that all have sinned*, he gives the reason why he had asserted that by the sin of one man death passed upon all. This, says he, ought not to astonish us, for all have sinned. If we must understand this of some personal sin of each, either actual or habitual, the reasoning would not have been just and worthy of the apostle, but mere trifling. For, his argument would be thus, that by the one sin of one all were become guilty of death, because each in particular had, besides that one and first sin, his own personal sin : which is inconsequential. 4thly. The scope of the apostle is to illustrate the doctrine of justification he had before treated of. The substance of which consisted in this, that Christ, in virtue of the covenant of grace, accomplished all righteousness for his chosen covenant people, so that the obedience of Christ is placed to their charge, and they, on account thereof, are no less absolved from the guilt and dominion of sin, than if they themselves had done and suffered in their own person, what Christ did and suffered for them. He declares that in this respect, Adam was the type of Christ, namely, as answering to him. It is therefore necessary, that the sin of Adam, in virtue of the covenant of works, be so laid to the charge of his posterity, who were comprised with him in the same covenant that, on account of the demerit of his sin, they are born destitute of original righteousness, and obnoxious to every kind of death, as much as if they themselves, in their own persons, had done what Adam did. Unless we suppose this to be Paul's doctrine, his words are nothing but mere empty sound.

XXXII. The last words of this verse, ἐφ᾽ ᾧ πάντες ἥμαρ]ον, are differently explained by divines, because the Greek phraseology admits of various significations. The principal explanations are three : 1st. Some render them, *in so far*, or, *because all have sinned*. For, it is allowed, that ἐφ᾽ ᾧ frequently admits this sense ; and thus it seems to be taken, 2 Cor. v. 4. ἐφ᾽ ᾧ οὐ θέλομεν ἐκδύσασθαι,

" not for that we would be unclothed ;" as if written, as Fro-
benius prints it, ἐπειδη, though Beza here greatly differs.   2dly.
Others observe, it may be explained, *with whom*, i. e. *who sinning*,
all have sinned.   For ἐπι in a similar construction denotes a
time, in which something was done.   Thus we say in Greek,
ἐπ᾽ ἐμοὶ μειρακίω τῦτο γέγονε, *when I was a boy this happened*, and
ἐπὶ κυνὶ *in the dog days ;* and the apostle Heb. ix. 15. ἐπὶ τῇ πρώτῃ
διαθήκη, *under the first testament.*   And then the meaning would
be, that upon Adam's sinning, all are judged to have sinned.
3dly. Augustine, and most of the Orthodox have explained it,
in whom.   Which Erasmus in vain opposes, saying, that ἐπι when
signifying *upon*, or, *in*, is joined to the genitive case ; as ἐπ᾽
δικε και ἐπὶ της χώρας; also when denoting *time*, as ἐπὶ καίσαρος
῾Οκλαβίε.   In all this he is strangely mistaken.   For, not to say any
thing now of *time*, it is certain, that ἐπι when joined to the dative
denotes *in :* as Matt. xiv. 8. ἐπὶ πίνακι, *in a charger ;* and in this
very context of Paul, verse 14. ἐπὶ τῷ ὁμοιωμαλι, *in the similitude.*
And which is more, ἰὸ ἐφ᾽ ᾧ, cannot sometimes be otherwise explained, than by *in which*, [or in whom] : as Matt. ii. 4. ἐφ᾽ ᾧ ὁ πα-
ραλυλικος καλεκεῖλο, *wherein the sick of the palsy lay*, and Luke v. 25.
ἀρας ἐφ᾽ ᾧ καλεμεῖλο *took up that whereon he lay.* · Nor is it taken
in this light, in the sacred writings only, but he might learn from
Budæus, *Commentar. ling f. Græc.* p. 506. that Aristotle used
this phraseology in the same sense, ἐφ᾽ ᾧ μεν η θήλεια, ἐπι θαλέρω δὲ
ὁ ἄ῾ρην ἐπωάζει, *on the one the female, on the other the male broods.*
However, we reckon none of those explanations to be impertinent as they are almost to the same purpose ; yet, we give the
preference to the last, because most emphatical and very applicable to the apostle's scope; it is a bad way of interpreting
scripture to represent it as declaring what is the least thing intended.   For, the words are to be taken in their full import,
where there is nothing in the context to hinder it.

XXXIII. Grotius really prevaricates, when he thus comments
on the passage before us.   It is a common metonomy in the Hebrew, to use the word *sin*, instead of *punishment ;* and *to sin*,
instead of *to undergo punishment*, whence extending this figure,
they are said, by a metalepsis, אטח *to sin*, who suffer any *evil*,
even though they are innocent, as Gen. xxxi. 36. and Job vi. 24.
Where אטח is rendered by δυςπραγεῖ ιν *to be unhappy*, ᾽Εφ᾽ ᾧ here
denotes *through whom*, as ἐπι with the dative is taken, Luke v.
5. Acts iii. 36. 1 Cor. viii. 11. Heb. ix. 17.   Chrysostom on this
place says, *On his fall, they who did not eat of the tree, are
from him all become mortal.*

XXXIV. This illustrious person seems to have wrote without attention, as the whole is very impertinent.   1st. Though we

allow, that sin does sometimes metonomically denote the punishment of sin, yet we deny it to be usual in Scripture, that he
who undergoes punishment, even while innocent may be said to·
sin.   Grotius says, it is frequent, but he neither does nor can
prove it by any one example; which is certainly bold and rash.
Crellius confuting his book on the satisfaction of Christ, brings
in the saying of Bathsheba to David, 1 Kings i. 21.   *I and my
son Solomon shall be counted offenders ;* that is, says he, *we shall
be treated as offenders,* or, *be ruined.*   But *a sinner,* or even *sin*
and *to sin* are different things.   The former is said of Christ,
2 Cor. v. 21. : but not the latter on any account.   Moreover, to·
be a sinner, does not signify, in the passage alleged, to undergo·
punishment, without any regard to a fault or demerit, but to be
guilty of aiming at the kingdom, and of high treason, and as such
to be punished.   The testimonies advanced by Grotius are so
foreign, that they seem not to have been examined by that great
man.   For, neither in the Hebrew do we find אטח *to sin,* nor in
the Greek version, δυσπραγειν; nor do the circumstances admit,
that what is there said of sin, or mistake, can be explained of
punishment.   It is necessary therefore to suppose, that either
Grotius had something else in his view, or that here is a typographical error.   2dly. Though we should grant, which yet we
do not in the least, that to sin sometimes denotes to undergo
punishment, yet it cannot signify this here; because, the apostle in this place immediately distinguishes between death, as the·
punishment, and sin, as the meritorious cause, and death by sin.
And by this interpretation of Grotius, the apostle's discourse,
which we have already shewn is solid, would be an insipid tautology.   For, where is the sense to say, " So death passed upon
all, through whom all die."   3dly. Grotius discovers but little
judgment in his attempt to prove, that ἐφ' ᾧ signifies *through
whom :* certainly Luke v. 5. ἐπὶ τῷ ῥήμαλί σε, does not signify
through thy word, but *at thy word,* or as Beza translates, *at
thy command.*   And Heb. ix. 17. ἐπὶ νεκροῖς does not signify
through the dead, but *when dead,* and rather denotes a circum-
stance of time, Acts iii. 16. is alleged with a little more judgment; and 1 Cor. viii. 11. not improperly.   But it might be insisted, that ἐπ' ἐμόι ἐςὶ signifies, *it is owing to me,* that the meaning shall be, " to whom it was owing that all sinned."   Which
interpretation is not altogether to be rejected.   Thus the sholiast,
ἐφ' ᾧ Ἀδὰμ, δἰ ὃν.   And if there was nothing else couched under
this, I would easily grant Grotius this explanation of that phraseology.   4thly. It cannot be explained consistent with divine justice, how without a crime death should have passed upon Adam's
posterity.   Prosper reasoned solidly and elegantly against Coll-

lator, c. xx. " Unless, perhaps, it can be said, that the punishment, and not the guilt passed on the posterity of Adam, but to say this is in every respect false; for it is too impious to judge so of the justice of God; as if he would, contrary to his own law, condemn the innocent with the guilty. The guilt therefore is evident where the punishment is so, and a partaking in punishment shews a partaking in guilt; that human misery is not the appoinment of the Creator, but the retribution of the judge." If therefore through Adam all are obnoxious to punishment, all too must have sinned in Adam. 5thly. Chrysostom also is here improperly brought in, as if from Adam he derived only the punishment of death, without partaking in the guilt; for the homily from which the words are quoted begins thus: " When the Jew shall say, How is the world saved by the obedience of one, namely, Christ? you may reply, How was the world condemned by one disobedient Adam?" Where it is to be observed, 1st. That he supposes the miseries of mankind to proceed from God as a judge, who cannot justly condemn but for sin. 2dly. That he compares the condemnation of the world by Adam's disobedience, with its salvation by Christ's obedience. But this last is imputed to believers, and deemed to be theirs, and therefore Adam's sin is in like manner imputed to all. As also Gregory of Nazianzen, quoted by Vossius, *Hist. Pelag.* lib. ii. P. ii. p. 163. said, that Adam's guilt was his. " Alas! my weakness," says he, " for I derive my weakness from the first parent."

XXXV. But we only understand this of Adam's first sin. We no wise agree with those who absurdly tell us, that Adam's other sins were also imputed to us; for Paul, when treating on this subject, Rom. v. every where mentions *transgression* in the singular number; nay, expressly verse 18. *one transgression,* by which guilt passed upon all; and the reason is manifest, for Adam ceased to be a federal head when the covenant was once broken, and whatever sin he was afterwards guilty of, was his own personal sin, and not chargeable on his posterity, unless in so far as God is sometimes pleased to visit the sins of the fathers on the children. In which Adam has now nothing peculiar above other men. So much for the violation by the covenant of man.

CHAP. IX.

Of the Abrogation of the Covenant of Works on the part of God.

I. Having sufficiently considered the violation of the covenant by sin; let us now enquire whether, and how far it is made void, or abrogated by God himself.

II. And first, we are very certain, that there are many things in this covenant of immutable and eternal truth, which we reckon up in this order: 1st. The precepts of the covenant, excepting that probatory one, oblige all, and every one to a perfect performance of duty, in what state soever they are. 2dly. Eternal life, promised by the covenant, can be obtained upon no other condition, than that of perfect, and in every respect complete obedience. 3dly. No act of disobedience escapes the vengeance of God, and death is always the punishment of sin. But these maxims do not exclude a surety, who may come under engagements in man's stead, to undergo the penalty, and perform the condition. But we shall speak of this afterwards, and now proceed to what has been proposed.

III. It is indeed a most destructive heresy to maintain, that man, sinful and obnoxious to punishment, is not bound to obedience. For by no misconduct of man, can God forfeit his right and supremacy; but the right and supremacy of God requires, that man, and even every creature, be subject in all respects to God, so far as possible. Moreover, the rational creature, such as sinful man is, and does continue to be, can be subject, not only to the natural, but also to the moral providence of God; nor only to his vindictive justice, but also to his legislative authority; and as he can, so he ought to be subject to him, as to the obligation of obedience, because every possible subjection is essential to the creature.

IV. If the sinner who deserves punishment was not subject to the law, he could no longer sin, and therefore by one sin he would set himself free from the danger of farther sinning; for where no law is binding, there is no transgression, no sin, which John defines to be *the transgression of the law*, 1 John iii. 4. But nothing can be imagined more absurd, than that man by sin has acquired an impeccability.

V. Moreover, according to this hypothesis, all sinners would be equal, and an equal degree of punishment remain for every one; which is contrary, both to sound reason and scrip-

ture, where the inequality of sins and punishment, is so often
inculcated.

VI. There is a plain passage, Gal. v. 3. which confirms, that
even by the promulgation of the new gospel covenant, the
breakers of the covenant who are without Christ, are not set free
from that obligation of the law, which demands perfect obedience, but continue debtors to do the whole law.

VII. Nay, even in a human court, the penal compact is
deemed an additional compact, adding to the principal conven-
tion, and consequently not abrogating, but accumulating the
former obligation. Much less at the bar of God, can the obligation to punishment, arising from the violation of the covenant, abrogate the primary and principal obligation of the law,
whereby the covenant was ratified.

VIII. Arminius therefore, *(in Epist. Præstantium viro-*
rum, p. 173.) very basely refuses, that God, when man once
fell from the state of innocence, and became obnoxious to punishment, even of right required obedience of man, as if God
had forfeited his right by man's disobedience. He makes use
of these arguments : 1st. Because when man is in a state of
sin, he is not in covenant with God ; therefore there is no
contract between God and man, by which he can require
obedience ; for by what reward, what punishment, can he give
sanction to the law, since man, for the disobedience already
committed, has forfeited the reward, and is become obnoxious
to punishment ? 2dly. As God has, because of sin, deprived
man of ability and power to fulfil the law, so by this very
thing he has signified, that he will no longer require man to
fulfil it, unless he restore his ability, nay he cannot in justice
do it. If any shall say, Could therefore the creature be exempted from the right or authority of the Creator, as no longer
to be bound to obey him ? He answers, Yes, indeed, if the
creature be accursed, and the Creator reckon it unworthy to
require obedience from it ; for it is the highest punishment
so to conclude the sinner under sin, as not to require any more
obedience from him, that being an evidence of irreconcileable
anger, namely, in that state. 3dly. The law itself, to be performed, is such, as it would be unbecoming, it should be performed by a sinner who is out of the favour of God. He is
commanded to have God for his God, to love, honour, and adore
him, to put his trust in him, to use his name with reverence, &c.
is it probable that such an obedience is required of him who is
under the curse of God ? Thus far Arminius, whose arguments
deserve to be carefully examined.

IX. We begin with the first. Arminius supposes a great many things in this argument, which we cannot admit; such as, that all the obligation of man arises from the covenant, that the law does not oblige, but in so far as it is enforced by rewards and punishments; that God cannot threaten a greater punishment, after man is once become obnoxious to the penalty; now, since we deny all this, so if we prove them to be false, as we hope to do, there will not remain the least appearance of force in this argument. The obligation of man to obedience is not founded first and principally on a covenant, but in the supereminent sovereignty, majesty, and holiness of God; and every rational creature, from a consideration of these, is bound to be subject to his sovereignty, adore his majesty, and form himself according to the example of his holiness. God would not be the absolute sovereign, if any rational creature existed which was not bound to take the rule of its actions from him, and therefore in regulating its actions was not subject to God. God would not be the supreme Majesty, if there was any rational creature who was not bound to acknowledge, worship, adore, and be subject to him in every respect. God would not be perfect in holiness, if any rational creature existed, who was not bound to acknowledge that holiness as most worthy of imitation. As God is such a being, he cannot but require to be acknowledged to be so. The creature cannot acknowledge him in this manner, without owning its obligation at the same time to obey him, who is the first, the most high, and most holy God. Which we have here explained and proved more fully, chap. iii. § VIII. Moreover, it is not true that the law is not binding, but because of the sanction of rewards and punishments. The principal obligation of the law arises from the authority of the lawgiver, and the perfect equity of all his commands. Though God had enforced his law neither by rewards nor punishments, we had been no less bound to obedience; lest self-love, whereby we are led to obtain the reward, and avoid the penalty, should be the only motive to stir us up to obey God: the reverence of the Supreme Being, and the love of holiness are to hold the chief place here; in fine, it is also false, that no further punishment will be inflicted, after that man having once broken the covenant, is become obnoxious to the penalty; for there are degrees in condemnation. And if that was true, it would not take off the obligation to obedience. It would not be lawful for a robber, condemned to be burnt alive, or broken on the wheel, or to the most cruel death that man can devise, to commit, in the mean time, a new capital crime; for as we have said, the obligation arises neither primarily nor chiefly from the penal sanction, but from the authority of the lawgiver.

X. To the second, I answer, 1st. Man himself is not only the meritorious, but also the physical cause of his own impotence, which he brought upon himself by his misconduct; as if an insolent and naughty servant should put out the candle by which he ought to carry on his master's business, or by drinking to excess, willingly render himself unfit for the service of his master. In this case, the master does by no means forfeit his right of requiring every piece of service properly due to him, and of punishing that naughty servant for non-performance. 2dly. Though God as a just judge had deprived man of ability to fulfil the law, yet, on that account, he both will in point of right, and can require the performance of it by man. He can very justly, because no wickedness of man, justly punished by God, can diminish God's authority over him, otherwise it would be in man's power, at his own pleasure, either to extend or limit the authority of God, which is contrary to the immutable perfection and blessedness of God. He also does require this for wise reasons, of which this is one, that sinful man may by that means be convinced of his irreparable misery, upon finding such things justly required of him, which he has rendered himself incapable to perform. And since he is as unwilling as unable to obey God, he is the more inexcuseable, the more clearly the duty of the law is inculcated upon him. 3dly. It is absurd to say, that it is the greatest punishment that God inflicts on man, not to require obedience from the rebellious creature. It is indeed true, that the creature ought to reckon it a part of its happiness to have the glory of obeying. And it is the punishment of the creature, if, by the just judgment of God, it is condemned never to perform what is incumbent, and may be acceptable to God. But it is another thing to say, that God will not require obedience from it. If God requires not obedience, the creature owes none; if it owes none, it does not act amiss, by disobeying, and if it does not amiss by disobeying, that cannot be the highest punishment for it. And thus Arminius destroys his own argument; who would have spoke rightly, had he said, that it is, instead of the highest punishment to the creature, to be condemned by the just judgment of God not to perform that obedience, which God consistently with his justice and holiness requires of it. 4thly. Should we deal more closely with a bold disputant, we might say, that there is a contradiction in the adjunct, when he supposes God addressing himself thus : I will not have thee to perform any obedience to me : for if any calls for obedience, he presupposes not only some authority by which he can require it, but also a command, which requires obedience, and which must be obeyed. Whoever by his authority gives such a command, requires that obedience be yielded to it. If he should give another command to this purpose, I will not have you to obey me, he would then contradict himself ; nay, contradict the nature of the command, which consists in an obligation to obedience. 5thly. It is the highest absurdity imaginable, that a creature shall, by its sin, obtain exemption from the authority of the Creator, and be no longer bound to obey him. If this is true, then the first of all deceivers spoke truth, that man, by eating the forbidden fruit, would become as God. Whoever is exempted from the authority of the Creator, is under the authority of none, is at his own disposal ; in fine, is God. For to be at one's own disposal, is to be God. Ah ! how ridiculous is this !

XI. The third argument is no less weak. For, 1st. The sum of the law is to love God with all the heart, mind, and strength, and our neighbour as ourselves. As this is reasonable in itself, so it cannot but be proposed as such by God to man ; for conscience itself, even that of the most abandoned, will bear witness with God to the reasonableness of this. What ? is it not certain that God is the chief good, consequently the most amiable ? Can he be unwilling that any should acknowledge him as the chief good, or to be what he really is, what he cannot but be ? Is he not the supreme Majesty ? Can he be unwilling to be honoured as such with the most submissive reverence ? 2dly. Arminius urges, that the law also commands us to trust in God. It does so ; what can be more right, what more becoming, than that man, even a sinner, should be bound to believe the testimony of God, should give him this glory, namely, that he alone both can and will justify the ungodly, that he should seek him even when angry, hunger and thirst after his righteousness, and willingly endeavour to be for his glory ; namely, that God may be glorified and admired in him by his justification and glorification by free grace ; and that he should neither neglect the salvation which God has most surely revealed, and neither despise nor reject the Saviour ? This is to trust in God ; and will any pious person ever doubt of the probability, nay, even of the most infallible certainty of this, that man under the curse of God till now, is not called upon to this ? 3dly. He will still urge, that when he speaks of trusting in God, he means thereby that full assurance of mind, whereby we hold God to be our God; that at least this is also enjoined by the law. We are to consider this more distinctly. When the law enjoins us to take God for our God, it is to be understood in this manner, *viz.* to take him for our Creator, preserver, lawgiver, and Supreme Lord; this is absolutely and without distinction enjoined upon all men: but if we understand it thus, to take him for our saving good, this is enjoined upon none, but in that method which the revealed will of God prescribes. And this is the way; either that men shall obtain the salvation of God by a most personal obedience, as proposed to Adam in innocence, which is now impossible for the sinner; or, that sinful man be converted, and united by faith to Christ, then examine himself whether he be in the faith, and in Christ, which being discovered, he may then indeed glory and exult in God his Saviour; this is the way that is now proposed in the gospel. But the law enjoins us to embrace every truth by faith, which God either has revealed, or shall reveal, and to walk agreeably to that truth. But the law no where enjoins the impenitent sinner to look upon God as the God of his salvation. Nay, the law, as it was given to Adam himself, enjoins him to believe the contrary. And thus I imagine I have fully dispatched the quaint subtilties of Arminius, that it is of immutable right, that man, even under sin and guilt, is still under obligation to obey the law.

XII. We proceed a step farther, to shew that man, even after the violation of the covenant, continues bound, not only to obedience, but to a perfect performance of duty. Paul said of those who are without the covenant of grace, Gal. v. 3. that "they are debtors to do the whole law." Nor can it otherwise be; for the law of the covenant, as to the natural precepts, is immutable, being the transcript of the image of God, which is no less immutable than God himself: for if the image which had the nearest resemblance is changed, and yet continues still to resemble its archetype, or original, the archetype itself must also necessarily be changed. But the law of the covenant did undoubtedly require perfect obedience.

XIII. Besides, if we imagine any abatement and relaxation of the law after sin, we are to conceive, that God addressed sinful man after this manner: " I formerly commanded thee to esteem as the supreme truth, thy chief good, and thy sovereign Lord, and consequently to assent with the fullest assurance of faith to all my precepts, to love me with all thy soul, and all thy strength, and esteem nothing preferable to that which is acceptable to me, to employ thy all in my service, at all times and in all things, to be at my command and beck, and never venture on any thing that is not agreeable to my will. But now, since thou hast once presumed to disobey me, I require no more for the future, but that thou esteem me indeed to be the truth, but not infallible; to be thy good, but not the chief; to be thy Lord, but not the Supreme: and I allow thee to doubt of some of my testimonies, to love other things besides, and above me; to place thy happiness in other things besides my favour; in fine, to depend on me in some things, but in other things to act at thy own discretion." If all these be absurd and unworthy of God, as they certainly are; it is also absurd and unworthy of God, to abate and relax any thing of his law. But if these general propositions are of immutable truth; that as God is the chief good, he is, at all times, and by all persons, to be loved with the whole heart; as he is the supreme Lord, none can ever, under any pretence, act but according to his command ; now the most perfect performance of every duty, must be the manifest consequence of all this.

XIV. Again, to perform duty perfectly, as every one will allow, is better than to do it in a slight manner. For all the goodness of duty consists in its agreement with the rule and directory of it. There must therefore be a certain rule, enjoining that perfection, which is a greater degree of goodness. If God has prescribed such a rule, it must certainly bind man to conform himself to it.

XV. The conscience of man, upon due attention, cannot but assent to these things. To make this appear I shall adjoin two excellent passages, one from Epictetus, the other from the emperor Julian. The former speaks thus, Dissertat. lib. 2. c. xi. " Having found a rule, let us keep it inviolable, and not extend so much as a finger beyond it." The latter thus, Orat. 1. " There is an ancient·law given by him who first taught mankind philosophy, and which runs thus : that all who have an eye to virtue and to honesty, ought, in their words and actions, in society and in all the affairs of this life, both small and great, endeavour altogether after honesty." The law therefore of the old covenant continues to bind all mankind, without exception, to a perfect performance of duty.

XVI. The second thing, which we said, § II. was immutable in the covenant of works, was this; that eternal life was not obtainable on ony other condition but that of perfect obedience: as may thus be invincibly proved: for, by virtue of this general rule, it was necessary for Christ *to be made under the law*, Gal. iv. 4. and *fulfil all righteousness*, and that for this end, *that the righteousness of the law might be fulfilled*, Rom. viii. 4. But if this righteousness had not been sacred and inviolable, Christ would have been under no necessity to submit to the covenant of the law, in order to merit eternal life for his people. This therefore is evident, that there ought to be a merit of perfect obedience on which a right to eternal life may be founded. Nor is it material whether that perfect obedience be performed by man himself, or by his surety.

XVII. The third thing which we affirmed as an unchangeable truth, regards the penal sanction; for that immutable and indispensable justice which we already defended by so many arguments, chap. v. § XVIII. seq. certainly requires this, so that there is no occasion to add any thing further.

XVIII. Since then these three things, the law, the promise, and the threatening, constitute the entire nature of the covenant, as proposed by God, stand so firm; one may conclude, that though man has really on his part broken the covenant, yet no abrogation of the covenant is made on the part of God. But, on duly weighing the matter, we must also acknowledge some abrogation on the part of God: as may be evidently inferred from the substitution of the new covenant of grace. For thus the apostle has taught us to reason, Heb. viii. 13. " In that he saith a new covenant, he hath made the first old." For though the abrogation of the old does not necessarily infer the substitution of a new; yet the substitution of a new does certainly import the abrogation of the old. It is indeed true, that the apostle, in this place, does not speak precisely of the covenant of works, but of the old economy of the covenant of grace, which he says is abrogated. But yet we properly build on his reasoning, which we may also, and ought to apply to this subject; namely, that every substitution of a new covenant supposes the abrogation of an old one.

XIX. That abrogation on the part of God consists in this, that God has declared, That no man can, by virtue of this covenant, have friendship with him, or obtain eternal life; so that he has declared all to have forfeited the promise of the covenant, and the hope of enjoying that promise according to that covenant. This is what the apostle says; " there is not now a law, which can give life, as that righteousness should be by the law," Gal. iii. 21. To this purpose is *what the law cannot do*, which he inculcates, Rom. viii. 3.

XX. And that covenant is so really abrogated, that it can on no account be renewed. For should we imagine God saying to man, " If, for the future, thou canst perfectly keep my law, thou shalt thereby acquire a right to eternal life," God would not by such words renew this very covenant of works; for sin is now pre-supposed to exist, which is contrary to that perfection of obedience which the covenant of works requires. God would therefore transact here with man on a different condition, whereby forgiving the former sin, he would prescribe a condition of an obedience less perfect than that which he stipulated by the covenant of works; which, excluding all sin, knew nothing of forgiveness of sin. Nay, such a transaction would be so far from a renewal of the covenant of works, that it would rather manifestly destroy it. For the penal sanction makes a part of that covenant, whereby God threatened the sinner with death, so that if he forgave him without a due satisfaction, he would act contrary to the covenant and his own truth.

XXI. The law therefore remains as the rule of our duty; but abrogated as to its federal nature; nor can it be the condition by the performance of which man may acquire a right to the reward. In this sense the apostle says, " We are not under the law," Rom. vi. 14. Namely, as prescribing the condition of life. There is indeed still an indissoluble connection between perfect righteousness and eternal life, so that *the last* cannot be obtained without *the first*. But after that man, by falling from righteousness, had lost all his hope of the reward, God was at liberty either to punish the sinner according to his demerit, or give him a surety to fulfil all righteousness in his stead.

XXII. There are learned men, who, besides this abolition of the covenant of works, which regards the possibility of giving life and justification, enumerate four other degrees of abolition in this order. 1st. *Of condemnation*, by Christ being proposed in the promise, and apprehended by faith. 2dly. *Of terror*, or the power of the fear of death and bondage, by *the promulgation of the new covenant*, after the expiation of sin: which being once accomplished, they who are redeemed are under the law of the Redeemer. So that the same law, abolished in the Redeemer as the law of sin, becomes the law of

the Saviour, and adjudges righteousness to those who are
his. 3dly. *Of that war* or struggle with sin, by *the death of
the body.* 4thly. *Of all the effects* of it, by *the ressurrection*
from the dead.

XXIII. But let us give our reasons why we have hitherto
doubted whether these things are with sufficient accuracy
conceived and digested. 1st. All the particulars here mentioned belong to the covenant of grace. But the covenant of
grace does not abrogate, but supposes the abrogation of the
covenant of works: because there could be no place for this,
without the abrogation of the other in the sense now mentioned. 2dly. The covenant of grace is not the abolition, but
rather the confirmation of the covenant of works, in so far as
the Mediator has fulfilled all the conditions of that covenant,
so that all believers may be justified and saved, according to
the covenant of works, to which satisfaction was made by
the Mediator. This is the apostle's meaning, Rom. iii. 31.
" Do we then make void the law through faith? God forbid;
yea, we establish the law." And again, Rom. viii. 4. " That
the righteousness of the law might be fulfilled in us." Which
signifies, (as the learned person, whose opinion we are now
examining, comments on this place,) " that what the law accounts for righteousness, is fully bestowed on us; and consequently, that what merits the reward of the law, becomes perfectly ours." 3dly. The very law of the covenant which
gave up the human sinner to sin, when his condition is once
changed by union with Christ the surety, does now, without
any abolition, abrogation, or any other change whatever, absolve the man from the guilt and dominion of sin, and bestow
on him that sanctification and glorification, which are gradually to be brought to that perfection which he shall obtain at
the resurrection of the dead ; as being constrained to bear
witness to the justification of the covenant of grace. This is
what the learned person not improperly says in the words we
have just quoted: " So that the same law, abolished in the
Redeemer as the law of sin, becomes the law of the Saviour;
and bestows righteousness on those who are his:" which he
has at large and learnedly explained on Rom. viii. 2. In a
word, the same law which was to man in innocence a commandment to life, and is to man in sin, the law of sin, giving
him up to the dominion and guilt of sin, becomes again in the
Redeemer the law of the spirit of life, testifying that satisfaction was made to it by the Redeemer, and bestowing on man,
who by faith is become one with the Redeemer, all the fruits

of righteousness for justification, sanctification, and glorification. All the change is in the state of the man, none in the law of the covenant, according to which man, in whatever state he is, is judged. Which things seem not to have escaped the observation of the learned person himself; when, Summa Theolog. c. xxxi. § 1. he speaks to this purpose. Nevertheless, *when we say this*, we mean, that *this fourfold* abolition and removal of the covenant concerning works to be done, which is connected without our own happiness, *is founded on the same law: not that this could be done by virtue of the law in itself alone, but that the intervention of a surety and redeemer made it, at last possible to the law.* I allow that what he calls the abolition of the covenant concerning works, is founded in the law of works; but I leave it to the reader's consideration, whether it is not a strange way of talking, to say, that "the abolition and removal of the law, is founded on the law itself, and that the intervention of a surety and redeemer made it, at last, possible to the law;" namely, that itself should effect its own abolition and removal? From all which I conclude, that it will be more proper to treat of these things when we speak of *the fruits and effects of the covenant of grace,* than when considering *the abolition of the covenant of works:* which is on no account abolished, but in so far as it is become impossible for man to attain to life by his own personal works.

THE

ECONOMY

OF THE

DIVINE COVENANTS.

BOOK II.

CHAP. I.

Introduction to the Covenant of Grace.

I. WHEN *the covenant of works was thus broken by the sin of man, and abrogated by the just judgment of God,* wretched man was cast headlong into the deepest gulf of ruin, whence there could be no escape. For listening to the solicitation of the devil, and giving way to his own reasonings, *he, in a most violent manner, withdrew* himself from God, that he might *be at his own disposal;* and (like the prodigal son, Luke xv. 12.) throwing off his rightful subordination to God, *sold* and enslaved himself *to the devil.* All which were acts of the highest in-justice : for *man* had no right thus *to dispose of himself;* nor *the devil* to accept of what was God's. Yet God considering that by this rash and unjust action man was justly punished, did, by his righteous judgment, ratify all this for his further punishment, gave him up to *himself,* as the most wretched and foolish of masters ; and to *sin,* as a cruel tyrant, which would continually force him to every abominable practice. " And even as they did not like to retain God in their know-ledge, God gave them over to a reprobate mind, to do those

things which are not convenient," Rom. i. 28. He also " gave
them up unto vile affections," verse 26 ; that so " they might
receive that recompense which was meet," verse 27. In fine,
he delivered them up as slaves *to the devil*, to be " taken captive by him at his will," 2 Tim. ii. 26. And all this according
to that most equitable law ; " of whom a man is overcome, of
the same he is brought into bondage," 2 Pet. ii. 19.

II. Moreover, when a man was no longer in covenant with
God, he then became " without God and without hope in
the world," Eph. ii. 12. For it was impossible for him to
devise any method, becoming God, whereby, consistently with
divine truth, justice, and holiness, he could be reconciled with
God, and return again to his favour. The law of sin was also
just, by which man was enslaved to sin, to the dominion and
condemnation of it, and given up to the devil as his tormentor.
In which sense he is said to be not only *the captive of the devil,
of the strong man*, mentioned Matt. xii. 29. ; but also *the lawful
captive*, Isa. xlix. 24. For he had *the power of death*, Heb. ii.
14. and that by the law, 1 Cor. xv. 56. *the strength of sin is
the law.* Nor could man contrive any way, whereby sin, which
condemned, by the most equitable law, could itself be justly
condemned by God.

III. But it pleased God, according to the riches of his unsearchable wisdom, to lay this breach of the legal covenant
as a foundation for his stupendous works; for he took occasion to set up a new *covenant of grace ;* in which he might
much more clearly display the inestimable treasures of his
all-sufficiency, than if every thing had gone well with man
according to the first covenant : and thus he discovered what
seemed to surpass all belief and comprehension, that God,
who is *true, just*, and *holy*, could, without any diminution to,
nay rather with a much more illustrious display of, his adorable perfections, become *the God* and *Salvation of the sinner :*
for he found out that admirable way to reconcile the strictest
vindictive justice with the most condescending mercy. So that
the one should be no obstruction to the other. For so illustrious an exercise of these perfections, there could have been no
place under the covenant of works.

IV. If therefore any thing ought to be accounted worthy
of our most attentive consideration, certainly it is the covenant of grace, of which we now attempt to treat. Here the
way is pointed out to a Paradise far preferable to the earthly, and to a more certain and stable felicity, than that from
which Adam fell. Here a new hope shines upon ruined mor-

tals, which ought to be the more acceptable, the more unexpected it comes. Here conditions are offered to which eternal salvation is annexed; conditions, not to be performed again by us, which might throw the mind into despondency; but by him who would not part with his life before he had truly said, *It is finished.* Here with the brightest splendor, shine forth the wonderful perfections of our God, his wisdom, power, truth, justice, holiness, goodness, philanthropy, or good-will to man, mercy, and what tongue can rehearse them all? Never before displayed on a more august theatre, to the admiration of all who behold them. Whoever therefore loves his own salvation, whoever longs to delight himself in the contemplation of the divine perfections, he must come hither, and deeply engage in holy meditations on the covenant of grace, which I think may not improperly be thus defined:

V. *The covenant of grace is a compact or agreement between God and the elect sinner; God on his part declaring his free good-will concerning eternal salvation, and every thing relative thereto, freely to be given to those in covenant, by, and for the mediator Christ; and man on his part consenting to that good-will by a sincere faith.*

CHAP. II.

Of the Covenant between God the Father and the Son.

I. In order the more thoroughly to understand the nature of the covenant of grace, two things are above all to be distinctly considered. 1st. The covenant which intervenes between God the Father and Christ the Mediator. 2dly. That testamentory disposition, by which God bestows by an immutable covenant, eternal salvation, and every thing relative thereto, upon the elect. The former agreement is between God and the Mediator: the latter, between God and the elect. This last pre-supposes the first, and is founded upon it.

II. When I speak of the compact between the Father and the Son, I thereby understand the will of the Father, giving the Son to be the Head and Redeemer of the elect; and the will of the Son, presenting himself as a Sponsor or Surety for them; in all which the nature of a compact and agreement consists. The scriptures represent the Father, in the economy of our salvation, as demanding the obedience of the Son even unto death; and upon condition of that obedience, promising him in his turn that name which is above every

name, even that he should be the head of the elect in glory :
but the Son, as presenting himself to do the will of the
Father, acquiescing in that promise, and in fine, requiring, by
virtue of the compact, the kingdom and glory promised to
him.   When we have clearly demonstrated all these particulars from scripture, it cannot, on any pretence be denied,
that there is a compact between the Father and the Son,
which is the foundation of our salvation.   But let us proceed
distinctly.   1st. By producing such places of scripture, as
speak only in general, but yet expressly of this compact.· 2dly.
By more fully unfolding the particulars which complete or constitute this compact. 3dly. By invincibly proving the same
from the nature of the Sacraments, which Christ also made
use of.

III.   Christ himself speaks of this compact, in express Luke
xxii. 29. *and I engage by covenant unto you a kingdom, as my
Father hath engaged by covenant unto me.* In which words
the Lord Jesus says, that, by virtue of some covenant or disposition, he obtains a kingdom, as we also obtain it by virtue of
the same.

IV.   And, Heb. vii. 22. where he is said to be *a surety of
a better covenant* or *testament.* But he is called the surety
of a testament, not principally on this account, because he
engages *to us for God* and his promises, or, because he engages *for us,* that *we shall obey;* as Moses intervened as a
surety between God and the Israelites, Exod. xix. 3—8. For,
by how much Christ was greater than Moses, in so much he
was also a surety, in a more excellent manner. His suretiship consists in this, that *he himself undertook to perform
that condition,* without which, consistently with the justice of
God, the grace and promises of God could not reach unto us ;
but being once performed, they were infallibly to come to the
children of the covenant : unless then we would make void the
suretiship of Christ, and gratify the Socinians, the very worst
perverters of scripture, it is necessary, we conceive of some
covenant, the conditions of which Christ took upon himself ;
engaging in our name with the Father, to perform them for us ;
and that, having performed them, he might engage to us for
the Father, that we should certainly have grace and glory bestowed upon us.

V.   Moreover, Gal. iii. 17. Paul mentions a certain *covenant,* or *testament, that was confirmed before of God in
Christ.* Where the contracting *parties* are, on one side God,
on the other Christ ; and *the agreement* between both is ra-

tified. But lest any should think, that Christ is, here only
considered as the *executor* of the *testament*, bequeathed to us
by God, the apostle twice repeats, that Christ was not promised to us, or that salvation was not promised to us through
Christ, though that be also true; but that the promises were
made to Christ himself, v. 16. That Christ was that seed,
ᾧ επαγγηλίαι, to which he had promised, or to which the promise
was made; namely, concerning the inheritance of the world,
and the kingdom of grace and glory. It is evident therefore,
that the word διαθηκη does here denote some covenant or testament, by which something is promised by God to Christ. Nor
do I see what can be objected to this, unless by Christ we
should understand *the head*, together with *the mystical body*,
which with Christ is that one seed to which the promises are
made. This indeed we shall not refuse, if it also be admitted,
that Christ, who is the head, and eminently the seed of Abraham, be on no account excluded from these promises, especially
as the promises made to his mystical body ought to be considered as made to himself; since he also himself hath received gifts
for men, Psal. lxviii. 19.

VI. Nor ought those places to be omitted in which explicit
mention is made of the suretiship of Christ: as Psal. cxix.
122. *be surety for thy servant for good;* that is, as surety
receive him into thy protection, that it may be well with him.
In like manner, Isa. xxxviii. 14. *I am oppressed, undertake
for me,* be to me a surety and patron. And that none but
Christ alone could thus undertake, God himself says, Jer.
xxx. 21. *who is this, that engaged his heart,* or appealed his
heart by his suretiship, or sweetened his heart by a voluntary and fiducial engagement, or in fine, pledged his very heart,
giving his soul as both the matter and price of suretiship (for
all these things are comprised in the emphasis of the Hebrew
language) to approach unto me, that he may expiate sin?
These words also shew, what that suretiship, or undertaking
was, which David and Hezekiah sought for: namely, a declaration of will to approach unto God, in order to procure the
expiation of sins.

VII. In fine, we may refer to this point, Zech. vi. 13. "the
counsel of peace shall be between them both;" namely between the man, whose name is the Branch, and Jehovah:
for, no other two occur here. It will not be foreign to our
purpose, to throw some light on this place by a short analysis
and paraphrase. In this and the preceding verse, there is a
remarkable prophecy concerning the Messiah, whose person,
offices, and glory, the prophet truly describes in a short, but

lively manner, subjoining at last the cause of all these ; namely, why the Messiah appeared as such a person, executed such
offices, and obtained such a glory ; namely, because of that
counsel which was between him and the Father, the fruit of
which with respect to us, *is peace.* Of the person of the
Messiah he says, that he is איש, *the man,* that is, true man, see
Hos. ii. 15. and indeed, the most eminent among men ; not
אנוש or אדם, which words denote *wretched man,* but איש ימינך
" the man of thy right hand," Psal. lxxx. 17. Because Christ
is not here considered as in the abasement of his misery, but
as in the excellence of his glory. His name is the Branch,
because sprung from God, Isa. iv. 2. Zech. i. 12. A new
root of a new offspring, or of the sons of God, according to
promise and regeneration, the second Adam. And indeed, a
branch, which shall blossom under himself. Aben Ezra, מאליו
from itself, which shall not be produced, or propagated, by
any sowing, or planting of man's hand, but shall spring from a
virgin, by the peculiar power of the Deity. His office is to
build the temple of the Lord, that is, the church of the elect,
" which is the house of God," 1 Tim. iii. 15. which Christ
κατεσκευασε framed, Heb. iii. 4. and built, Matt. xvi. 18.
Laying the foundation in his cross, and cementing it with his
blood. But because, in the same breath, it is twice said, " he
shall build the temple of the Lord," it may suggest to our
minds, whether besides the building of the church, which is
the mystical body of Christ, the resurrection of Christ's own
natural body may not be intended, which is called, " the building of the temple," John ii. 19, 21. which being done, he
will receive majesty," a name above every name, and sit on
the throne of God, to execute his kingly and priestly office in
glory. For a king to sit on a throne is nothing strange, but
for a priest, very much so ; being contrary to the custom of
the ancient priests in the Old Testament, who stood daily,
often offering the same sacrifices ; because their labour was
ineffectual to remove the guilt of sin, Heb. x. 11. But Christ
having once offered up the one sacrifice of himself, and by it
obtained eternal redemption, sat down for ever at the right
hand of the Father, never to rise to offer a second time, Heb.
i. 3. and ix. 12, 14. He now does what his session gives him
a right to do, he makes intercession for his people, Rom. viii.
34. As was ingeniously observed by James Altingius, Hept.
3. Dissert. 6. § 49. But whence does all this proceed, and
what is the origin of such important things? The counsel
of peace, which is between the man whose name is the Branch,
and between Jehovah, whose temple he shall build, and on

whose throne he shall sit, Rev. iii. 21.   And what else can this counsel be, but the mutual will of the Father and the Son, which we said is the nature of the covenant?   It is called a counsel, both on account of the free and liberal good pleasure of both, and of the display of the greatest wisdom manifested therein.   And a counsel of peace, not between God and Christ, between whom there never was any enmity ; but of peace to be procured to sinful man with God, and to sinners with themselves.

VIII. It seems two things may be objected, to which we are briefly to answer. 1st. That by those two we are not to understand the Father and the Son, but the Jews and the Gentiles. 2dly. That here it is not the counsel, which is the original and cause of all these things, and which ought to have been expressed in the preterperfect or present tense ; •but the counsel, which is the fruit of Christ's intercession, of which the prophet speaks in the future tense. To the first, I answer, that this exposition is asserted but not proved. There is no distinct mention made of Jews and Gentiles in the preceding verses of this chapter, and it is not lawful for us to add any thing to the text. What others allege concerning a priest and king, or the office of priest and king, or about the Jews of Jerusalem and Babylon, is quite forced. Our explication, says the very learned De Dieu, who here is of the same opinion with us, appears simple and plain. Neither is it new, since Jerome tells us, that this verse was understood of the Father and the Son. To the second, I reply, that there is nothing can oblige us to assent to it ; as the words, by our analysis and explanation, yield a very just and profitable sense, and this covenant could not be expressed by a more significant term than that of a mutual counsel between the Father and the Son. What is added with respect to the difference of tenses, seems to be of small moment: for that the tenses in Hebrew are often put one for the other, and the future for the present, none can be ignorant of, but they who are indifferently skilled in that language : see Psalm xvii. 3. *Thou hast tried me ;* and *thou doest,* or *didst find nothing ;* literally, *thou shalt find.* Such changes of tenses often occur in the same Psalm. Besides something is then said to be done in scripture, when it is declared to be solemnly done ; of which instances are to be met with every where, see Acts ii. 36. We will therefore fully explain the words thus, *the counsel of peace is between both.* And if you entirely insist on the future tense, the meaning will be this : At the exaltation of Christ, and the peace advanced by him from heaven, there will be a manifest execution of this counsel. But we need not come to this: for if by this counsel, we understand that agreement which subsisted between the Father and Christ, God-man, when assuming human nature, he appeared as the surety; the prophet might and ought to speak of it in the future tense: and he does so in a beautiful order, ascending from the effects to the cause, in the following manner; Christ God-man shall build the spiritual temple of the Lord; for which he shall receive as a reward, glorious majesty, and shall sit on the throne of God. And this needs not seem strange: for Christ clothing himself with human flesh, will, by a certain compact, on which our peace is founded, promise to the Father that he will do all this. The Father, on the other hand, will promise thus to reward that service. In this manner every thing runs smoothly. See more of this, chap. iii. § II—IV.

IX. It is also a proof of this, that Christ, often in the Psalms and elsewhere, calls God the Father his God. See, among other places, Psal. xxii. 3. and xlv. 8. Isa. xlix. 4, 5. and John xx. 17. which is the form or manner of the covenant. In this sense Jacob promised that the Lord should be his God, Gen. xxviii. 21. that is, that he would so frame his whole life, as became one in covenant with God. The Israelites also, when they solemnly renewed the covenant, Josh. xxiv. 18. said, " we will serve the Lord, for he is our God." In like manner God promises in the covenant, that he will be the God of his covenant people; that is, display the riches of his all-sufficiency for their salvation; Jer. xxxi. 33. " This is my covenant, that I will make with the house of Israel. I will be their God." Deut. xxvi. 17. " Thou hast avouched the Lord, (thou hast made the Lord say) this day to be, that he will be thy God." The very meaning of the word, [which we render God] implies this: for, אלה, *Eloah*, derived from אלה, *he swore* or *adjured*, denotes him, whose prerogative it is to bind us by oath, to love and faithful obedience to him, and to whom we ought by oath, to give all obedience; and who on his part engages that he will be all-sufficient to his faithful servants for salvation. He therefore who professes *Eloah* to be his God, does, at the same time by virtue of the covenant of God, call himself the servant of God: For, עבד, *servant*, is the correlate of אלה *Eloah*, or אלהים, *Elohim*: and as in Psalm lxxxvi. 2. *preserve thy servant, O thou my God.* And in this manner the Father calls Christ, in many places, *his servant*, Isaiah xlix. 5, 6. Besides, such a one professes, that he only depends on the promise and testimony of that covenant:

in these things the whole nature and design of the covenant consists. As therefore Christ calls God the Father his God; and on the other hand, the Father calls Christ his servant, both of them do by that name indicate a compact of obedience and reward.

X. But we come now more particularly to discuss all the parts of this covenant, that it may not only appear there subsists some covenant between Christ and the Father, but what that covenant is and of what nature. The contracting parties are, on the one hand, the Father, whom Christ calls my Lord, Psal. xvi. 2. On the other hand, the Son, whom the Father calls his servant, Isa. liii. 2. The law of the covenant is proposed by the Father, John x. 18. " this commandment have I received of my Father ;" and John xii. 49, " the Father which sent me, he gave me a commandment." To that law a promise is added by the Father, Isa. liii. 10—12. " when thou shalt make his soul an offering for sin, (when his soul shall make itself an offering for sin) he shall see his seed," &c. and Isa. xlix. 6—8. " it is a light thing that thou shouldest be my servant, to raise up the tribes of Jacob," &c. On performing that law, the Son acquires a right to ask the reward, Psal. ii. 8. " ask of me, and I shall give thee the Heathen for thine inheritance, and the uttermost parts of the earth for thy possession." Thus far the proposal of the covenant on the part of the Father. The acceptance on the part of the Son consists in this : that he willingly submitted himself to the law of the covenant, Psal. xl. 7—9. mine ears hast thou (bored) opened ; that is, thou hast engaged me a willing servant to thyself, having agreed about the reward. " Then said I, lo ! I come. I delight to do thy will ; yea thy law is within my heart :" see also John xiv. 31. Nor did the Son only undertake this, but actually performed it, " being made of a woman, made under the law," Gal. iv. 4. John xv. 10. " I have kept my Father's commandments, and abide in his love:" and John viii. 29. " I do always those things that please him." Nor did he part with his life, till he had truly said, It is finished, John xix. 30. In the course of this obedience the Son comforted himself in the faithfulness of the Father, to accomplish his promises. " I said surely my judgment (reward) is with the Lord, and (the recompence of) my work with my God," Isa. xlix. 4. And when he drew near the end of his course, he claimed, with great confidence of mind, the promised reward, John xvii. 4, 5. " I have glorified thee on the earth : I have finished the work which thou gavest me to do. And now, O Father, glorify thou me with thine ownself, with the glory

which I had with thee before the world was." What then
can be supposed wanting to complete the form of a covenant,
which we have not here ?

XI. In fine, all these things may be confirmed from this,
that Christ likewise made use of the Sacraments; not only as
to the matter of these institutions, as they were divine commands, the observance of which was to him meritorious; but
as to the form, as they were signs and seals of the covenant;
God the Father, by the use of them, sealed the federal promise concerning justification from sins, not his own personal
sins, either of commission or omission, (for such he had none,
2 Cor. v. 21. 1 Pet. ii. 18.) but from those, which, by a
voluntary engagement, he took upon himself as his own, and
from which, as surety, he was justified in the Spirit, 1 Tim.
iii. 16; and also concerning life eternal, to be bestowed on
him and his; God the Son, in the use of them, acknowledged
himself a debtor to fulfil all righteousness: as these things
have been already observed and explained by the celebrated
Voetius, *disput. de fide Christi, ejusque sacramentorum usu.*
Disput. T. ii. p. 160. and Essenius, *de subjectione Christi ad*
legem divinam, c. 10. § 11. But let us illustrate this by
an example. In the baptism of Christ, there was an evident
sealing of the covenant of both sides. Christ declared, that
it was his province to fulfil all righteousness. To that he
bound himself by baptism;. telling John, upon his refusing to
baptize him, " suffer it to be so now, for thus it becometh us
to fulfil all righteousness," Matt. iii. 16. The Father declared,
that he accepted the suretiship: " in thee I am well pleased,"
Luke iii. 22. and put him in mind of the inheritance; " thou
art my Son." And all these things he sealed by the symbol of
the Holy Ghost descending upon him.

XII. As these things are evident, and contain a demonstration of the truth to the conscience, I would not have Psal.
xvi. 2. strained to this purpose: " thou hast said unto the
Lord, thou art my Lord: טוֹבָתִי בַּל עָלֶיךָ my goodness (is not
upon thee) extendeth not to thee." As if in these words there
was an address of God the Father to the Son, to this purpose :
I require nothing more of thee as a satisfaction to me, in
order to display my grace. For thus a learned author paraphrases these words. *Thou hast said to the Lord,* &c. Thou
Son of man hast acknowledged, that Jehovah is the Lord, and
hast engaged thy obedience to him. Thou by loving and
obeying as a servant, even unto death (to which thou offerest
thyself) hast declared me to be Lord, and honoured me with
a perfect obedience. As to any advantage to be obtained, *my*

goodness, that is, my grace, and the benefits depending thereon, *extendeth not to thee,* (is not upon thee) that is, *thou art*
τέθελειωμένος, an absolute and perfect Saviour. What was laid
upon thee, or what thou wast bound by suretiship to perform,
that my goodness might extend to mankind, that thou hast
performed, and I accept of the whole. Thus עַל generally denotes something new, both among the Hebrews, and in the
sacred writings.

XIII. But I think these things are strained, and do not
run with that smoothness one could wish. For, 1st. There
is nothing which obliges us to imagine, unless we incline so
to do, that there is in these words, *an address of God the
Father to the Son;* since the whole of this Psalm has not
the least appearance of a dialogue, but only represents a single person speaking in one continued discourse, whom Piscator, by weighty arguments, proves to be the Lord Jesus.
The learned person himself speaks thus : " It is certain this
discourse may be ascribed to the Son, as addressing himself."
And therefore I say it is certainly possible, that this discourse
cannot contain the approbation of the Father, acquiescing in
the obedience of the Son. For if the Son addresses his own
soul, which said to Jehovah, " thou art my Lord, and my
goodness extendeth not to thee ;" doubtless the Son said this
to the Father, and not the Father to the Son. 2dly. I own
that these words which the Son says to the Father, or the
Father to the Son, are so emphatical, that they cannot, in
their full signification, be supposed to be spoken by either of
them to the other, on account of *the peculiar excellence* which
is in the Son, Heb. i. 4. But I question whether any can be
easily persuaded that the approbation of the most perfect
obedience of the Son, and the acquiescence of the Father therein are expressed in such slender terms. *Thou hast said, thou
art my Lord.* I appeal to any who *teaches the good knowledge of the Lord,* as it is said of the Levites, 2 Chron.
xxx. 22. whether those words of scripture be such as *that
nothing can be devised more proper to illustrate that sense*
which the very learned person elsewhere requires, before he
acquiesces in the meaning assigned, Sum. Theol. c. 3. § 30.
3dly. It is very true, that עַל sometimes, among the Hebrews,
signifies something due. The very learned De Dieu, on Gen.
xvi. 5. has long ago observed this, from the writings of the
Hebrews and also of the Arabs. But that signification does
not seem proper to this place. For *Christ was neither indebted to God for his goodness* or grace, and the blessings
depending upon it : Nor *did he* properly *owe the grace* of

God to *believers.*   But it was by virtue of a compact that *he owed obedience* to God; on performing which, *God owed to Christ, and to them who are Christ's, the reward* promised by the compact, which is given to Christ as a due debt.   The signification *of being due* might be insisted upon, had it been said *my law,* or *satisfaction to my justice,* or something to that purpose, *is no more upon thee, no longer extendeth to thee.*   But we must fetch a strange compass to make these words, *my goodness extendeth not to thee* (is not upon thee) to signify, *Thou art no longer indebted to my goodness,* and again, that the meaning of them should be, *Thou hast done every thing to which thou wast bound, that my goodness might be extended to men.*   And I verily doubt whether it could ever come into any one's mind, that, " such an explication is the fullest, the most simple, and most suited to the connexion : In fine, that it is such, that none who compares it with the words of scripture can devise a more happy manner of expressing the thing; and that therein an inexpressible degree of light, truth, and wisdom, may be discovered."   For these are laws of interpretation which the very learned person himself has laid down.   Sum. Theol. c. 6. § 38.

XIV. 4thly. Another sense may be fairly brought from the words of the Psalm, which has nothing either harsh or strained, and contains what is becoming the wisdom of God, as thus : the Lord Jesus being deeply engaged in holy meditations, addresses his soul, or himself : and declares, that while in his meditation he said to Jehovah the Father, *thou art the Lord,* all-sufficient to and by thyself for all happiness ; and therefore by this whole work of my Mediation, and consequently by all my obedience, no accession of new or greater happiness is made to thee, nor canst thou be enriched by my satisfaction ; *my goodness extendeth not to thee :* Thou receivest no benefit thereby : all the fruit of my satisfaction redounds to thy pious and chosen people.   See Job xxii. 2. and xxv. 7.   The comment of Ben Nachman on the former place is elegant, agreeing very much with the phraseology in our text ; he declares, " That no addition of good is made to God, when any good is done."   All which words contain a salutary truth, instructing us concerning *the all-sufficiency of God,* to whom no new good can accrue from any quarter, and concerning *the fruit of Christ's satisfaction,* as redounding to the godly : and are most adapted to the words and analogy of the whole Psalm.   For עַל many times in scripture signifies the same as אֶל, *to.*   I shall produce a place or two which occurred to me when meditating on these things in reading

the scriptures : what Micah says, chap. iv. 1. נהרו עליו עמים,
and people shall flow unto it : This Isaiah expresses as
follows, chap. ii. 2. כהדרו אליו כל חנזים, *and all nations shall
flow unto . it.*   Where על and אל are taken in the same
signification.   In like manner, 2 Chron. xxx. 1.   *Wrote letters,* על אמרים, that is, to the Ephraimites ; it is still more to
the purpose, what we have, 1 Sam. chap. i. 10.   *prayed unto the Lord,* and Psal. xviii. 41.   *They cried unto the
Lord, but he answered them not.*   Sometimes it signifies the
same thing as עד up to, or quite to, as 2 Chron. xxxii. 5.
and raised (the wall) *up to the towers :* not that it is credible the wall exceeded the towers in height.   Jer. iv. 18. *it
reacheth unto thine heart.*   You may add other instances from
Glassius Phil. Sacr. p. 773.   As therefore the use of this
particle is very extensive, we have no reason to restrain its signification to *owing* or *being due,* which seems less adapted to
this place.

XV. I speak not these things with a view to detract any
thing from the due praises of the very learned interpreter, to
whom I profess myself greatly indebted, but because nothing
is dearer to me than to search out the true meaning of the
Spirit speaking in the scriptures.   And while I am wholly
intent upon this, I cannot avoid sometimes examining the
opinions of others ; even of those for whom I have otherwise
the greatest veneration.   Faith is none of those things which
may be imposed by any human authority : neither is any injury done even to the greatest of men, when we declare our
dissent in a modest manner : whether we have done so here
or not, must be left to the determination of the impartial
reader, who may also judge whether by these observations,
I have deserved that severe language which the very famous
person Dr. John van der Waeyen, was pleased to throw out
against me in Sum. Theol. Christ. lib. i. c. 4, 5. 267. Seq.
He very much complains that I called that explication of the
celebrated Cocceius *harsh* and *forced,* and that the words of
the Psalm *were wrested to that meaning.*   I own indeed, I
had formerly wrote in this manner out of my simplicity, nor
did I imagine there was either reproach or injury contained
in these words : But there is no force of argument in the
tartness of language : and that the least appearance of that
may not remain, I now alter it, and instead of *wrested,* say
harsh, not running so smoothly.   The rest I cancel.   I freely
forgive the ill language of my Reprover, as becomes a Christian.   It does not belong to him, but to our common Lord,
to pass a judgment on my intention.   As to the subject itself,

I beseech the reader to compare my reasonings with his; and
if he thinks that mine are solidly confuted, I am not against
his differing in every respect from me as I differ from him;
and the simple explication of the words which I maintain,
with the generality of expositors, began the more to please
me, the more I saw my reprover stand in need for the defence of his opinion of such a compass of words, and so far-
fetched and intricate subtleties: I have no inclination minutely to consider the rest. Each one has his own temper, his
own way of writing: which if I cannot commend, I endeavour to bear with. But I return from this unwilling digres-
sion.

XVI. As the doctrine of *the covenant between the Father
and the Son* is so expressly delivered in scripture, it is unjustly traduced as a new and a late invention. Though I find
few among the more ancient who have professedly handled
this subject, yet some of the greatest divines have sometimes
made mention of this covenant. I say nothing now of Arminius, who does not carelessly discourse on this covenant, in
his oration for the degree of doctor; from which the very
accurate Amesius produces and commends some things in
Rescriptione ad Grevinchovium, c. i. Amesius himself, in
Anti-Synodalibus, de morte Christi, c. 1. § 5. charges a certain distinction of the Remonstrants with this absurdity, that
" it denies that the covenant entered into with Christ (he
shall see his seed, and the pleasure of the Lord shall prosper
in his hand,) had been ratified." Gomarus, treating of the
baptism of Christ, on Matt. iii. 13. says, that it was the
" sign and seal of the covenant between God and Christ;
namely, that God would be his God, and the bestower of
salvation; but he himself was bound to perform obedience
from a principle of perpetual gratitude." In like manner, on
Luke ii. 21. of the circumcision of Christ, he says, that it
was " a sign and seal of the covenant with God: which covenant consisted in this; partly that God was the God of
Christ, according to the general promise, made also to him,
Gen. xvii. 7. as to the seed of Abraham, Gal. iii. 16. and
according to the singular character given of him, Psal. xlv. 7.
Heb. i. 9. partly, that Christ was bound to obey the will of
God," John vi, 38. Matt. v. 17. See his disput. de merito
Christi, § 1. The very learned Cloppenburgius, disput. 3.
de fœdere Dei, not only slightly mentions this subject, but
fully and accurately handles it. The very famous Voetius, Disput. T. ii. p. 266. says, " He (Christ) was subject for us to
a special law of paying our debt by a condign punishment, as

our Mediator and surety, according to the tenor of the coye-
nant entered into with the Father. Essenius, formerly his
scholar, and afterwards his colleague, *de subjectione Christi
ad legem*, c. x. § 2. says, " the federal sealing of the divine
promise did also really take place in Christ," according to
Isa. liii. 10, 11. Dr. Owen handles this very subject at large,
on Heb. T. 1. Exercit. iv. p. 49. Nor was this doctrine unknown to the popish doctors. Tirinus on Isa. liii. 11. thus
comments, that the prophet there explains " the compact
agreed on between God the Father, and Christ," by which, on
account of the sufferings and death of Christ, redemption, justification, and glorification, were appointed to be the rewards
of all those who faithfully adhere to Christ. Thus it appears,
that these sentiments concerning *the covenant between the Father and the Son*, are not to be treated with contempt.

CHAP. III.

*The nature of the Covenant between the Father and the Son
more fully explained.*

I. As the covenant between the Father and the Son is the
foundation of the whole of our salvation, it will not be improper to stop here a little, and, in our further meditation, enquire, 1st. From whence *the beginning* of this covenant ought
to be taken, and in *what periods* of time it was completed.
2dly. What the law of the covenant contains, how far, and to
what it binds the Son. 3dly. Whether the Son might *not
have engaged* in this *covenant*, or have *withdrawn himself
from it*, and had no more to do with it. 4thly. What and how
great a reward was promised to the Son, and which he was to
obtain in virtue of the covenant.

II. I consider *three periods*, as it were, of this covenant.
Its commencement was in the eternal counsel of the adorable
Trinity: in which the Son of God was constituted by the
Father, with the approbation of the Holy Spirit, the Saviour
of mankind; on this condition, that in the fulness of time he
should be made of a woman, and made under the law; which
the Son undertook to perform. Peter has a view to this when
he says, 1 Pet. i. 20. that Christ " was foreordained before the
foundation of the world." To this purpose is also what the
supreme Wisdom testifies concerning itself, Prov. viii. 23. *I
was set up* (anointed) *from everlasting*; that is, by my own

and the will of my Father, which is one and the same, I was appointed to the performance of the mediatorial office in time. Paul likewise declares, that " we were chosen in Christ before the foundation of the world," Eph. i. 4. And consequently, Christ himself *was constituted from everlasting the head* of those that were to be saved, and they were given unto him, John xvii. 6. for whom he was to merit salvation, and in whom he was to be glorified and admired. From this constitution, the Son, from everlasting, bore a peculiar relation to those that were to be saved. Hence the book of life is especially appropriated to *the Lamb*, Rev. xiii. 8. as containing a description of the peculiar people assigned to *the Lamb* from all eternity. Hence also it was that God, by his amazing wisdom, so ordered many things in màn's state of innocence, that the attentive remembrance of them after the fall, and the comparing them with those things which were afterwards revealed, might have reminded him of this divine counsel; as we have shewn, chap. vi. § III.

III. The second period of this covenant I place in that intercession of Christ, by which, immediately upon the fall of man, he offered himself to God, now offended, in order actually to perform those things, to which he had engaged himself from eternity; saying, thou hast given them to me, and I will make satisfaction for them: and so he made way for the word of grace to be declared to, and the covenant of grace to be made with them. Thus Christ was actually constituted Mediator, and revealed as such immediately upon the fall; and having undertaken the suretiship, he began to act many things belonging to the offices of a Mediator. As a prophet, and the interpreter of the divine will, he even then, by his Spirit, revealed those things relating to the salvation of the elect, and by his ministers published them, Isa. xlviii. 15. 1 Pet. i. 11. and iii. 19. Nay, he himself sometimes appeared in the character of an Angel, instructing his people in the counsel of God. As a King he gathered his church, and formed to himself a people, in whom he might reign by his word and Spirit. For it was the Son of God who said to Israel, Exod. xix. 6. " and ye shall be unto me a kingdom of priests," and who with more than royal pomp, published his law on mount Sinai, Acts vii. 38. and whom Isaiah saw sitting as king upon a throne, chap. vi. compared with John xii. 41. As a priest, he took upon himself the sins of the elect, that he might expiate them by the sacrifice of his body, which was to be prepared for him in the fulness of time. In virtue of this, as a faithful surety, he likewise interceded for the elect, by declaring his will, that they might be taken into favour, saying, " deliver them from going down to the pit, I have found a ransom," Job xxxiii. 24. But what angel could speak thus, but the Angel of the covenant? who even then was called an Angel, before his coming in the flesh, because he was accomplishing what depended upon that future mission. He is one of a thousand, the captain of the host of angels, that guards each believer, the chiefest of (the standard-bearer above) ten thousands, Cant. v. 10. In like manner, the archangel Michael, (and who is this but the Lord Jesus Christ?) Dan. x. 13. is called, *one of the chief princes*, that is, the unparalleled among the chiefs, because he is *the great prince*, Dan. xii. 1. It is he who declares to man his righteousness, both the righteousness of God and of man. It is he who is the *propitiation; whom God hath set forth as a propitiation*, Rom. iii. 25.; see also Zech. i. 12, 13.

IV. The third period of this covenant is that, when on his *assuming human nature* he suffered *his ears to be bored;* compare Psal. xl. 7. with Heb. x. 5. that is, engaged himself as a voluntary servant to God, from love to his Lord the Father, and to his spouse the church, and his spiritual children, (for the ears of such voluntary servants were bored, Exod. xxi. 5, 6.) " was made under the law," Gal. iv. 4. by subjecting himself to the law: which he solemnly testified by his circumcision on the eighth day after his birth, whereby he made himself " a debtor to do the whole law," Gal. v. 3.

V. The law, proposed to the Mediator, may be considered in a twofold view: 1st. As *the directory of his nature and office.* 2dly. As *the condition of the covenant.* The Mediator himself may be considered these three ways. 1st. As *God.* 2dly. As *Man.* 3dly. As *Mediator God-man.* We are distinctly to compare these things together.

VI. The Son, as precisely God, neither was, nor could be subject to any law, to any superior; that being contrary to the nature of Godhead, which we now suppose the Son to have in common with the Father. " He thought it no robbery to be equal with God." No subjection, nothing but the highest super-eminence can be conceived of the Deity. In this respect he is King of kings, and Lord of lords, 1 Tim. vi. 15. The emperors Gratian, Valentine, and Theodosius, said long ago, that " he is a true Christian, who believes that the Deity of the Father, Son, and Holy Ghost, is one in equal power; that under the same majesty, there is one Deity, and he who teaches the contrary, is a heretic," *Cod.* lib. i. Tit. 1.

VII. Nor is it any objection against this, that the Son, from eternity, undertook for men, and thereby came under a certain peculiar relation to those that were to be saved. For, as that engagement was nothing but the most glorious act of the divine will of the Son, doing what none but God could do, it implies therefore no manner of subjection: it only imports, that there should be a time, when that divine person, on assuming flesh, would appear in the form of a servant. And by undertaking to perform this obedience, in the human nature, in its proper time, the Son, as God, did no more subject himself to the Father, than the Father with respect to the Son, to the owing that reward of debt, which he promised him a right to claim. All these things are to be conceived of in a manner becoming God.

VIII. Nor ought it to be urged, that the Son, even before his incarnation, was called *the Angel*, Gen. xlviii. 16. Exod. xxiii. 20. For that signifies no inferiority of the Son, before the time appointed for his incarnation; but only a form resembling the appearances of angels, and prefiguring his future mission into the world.

IX. As man, he was doubtless subject to the moral law, as it is the rule, both of the nature and actions of man. For, it is a contradiction, as we proved before, to suppose a rational creature, such as is the human nature of Christ, to be without law: and in this manner he was really bound by the law: 1st. To preserve the holiness implanted into his nature from his first conception, unspotted and pure. 2dly. To express it in the most perfect manner in his life and actions, from all his heart, all his soul, and all his strength. 3dly. Constantly to persevere therein, without yielding to any temptations, to the end of his course.

X. And as Christ was not only a man, and a common inhabitant of the world, but also an Israelite, that is, a member of the church of the Old Testament, and a citizen of the commonwealth of Israel, he was also subject to the ceremonial and political laws, which were then still in force, according to the divine institution. By virtue of these laws, Christ made use of the Sacraments of the Old Testament, observed the festivals, repaired to the temple, and behaved as an obedient subject under a lawful magistracy. He initiated himself by circumcision to the obedience of the ceremonial law; declared his obedience to the political laws by paying tribute, Matt. xvii. 24, 25.

XI. It may be objected that as to the ceremonial laws, Christ declared himself *greater than the temple*, Matt. xii. 6. And *Lord of the Sabbath*, v. 8. As to the political, that being the Son of God, he was exempted from paying tribute, Matt. xvii. 26, 27. But this may be solved from the different relations which Christ sustained; for as God, and the Son of God, he was Lord of the law, the lawgiver himself, who, on account of his divine nature, had authority to dispense with precepts of a mutable and positive institution: and if, when he became man, he had insisted on his being the Son of God, and for that reason had acted as equal to God, in that respect neither the officers of the temple, nor the questors of the emperor, could have demanded any thing of him as an inferior. But Christ did not think proper to insist on this his right, but rather to behave as *a servant of Rulers*, Isa. xlix. 7.

XII. But further, as *Mediator* and *Surety*, he is under the law in another manner, and that two ways: 1st. As *enjoining the condition* of perfect obedience, upon which he and his were to partake of happiness. 2dly. As *binding* to the penalty, due to the sins of the elect, which he had taken upon himself.

XIII. As to the former, had the Son of God been pleased to appear in our nature, but not in the quality of *a Surety*, he would necessarily have been a holy person, and conformed to the law of God prescribed to the human nature. For every man, as such, is bound to be subject to God, in all righteousness and holiness, which is exactly described in the divine law. But by the *personal covenant-engagement* of the Mediator to that absolute subjection of nature, which is eternally to continue without end, there is another obligation to subjection, limited to a certain period of time, which the apostle, Heb. v. 7. calls *the days of his flesh;* during which Christ, when obeying the law, was meriting that happiness, which he was not in possession of; considering this law, not only as *a rule of life*, but also as *prescribing the condition* of acquiring happiness. For, if we seclude the procuring of our salvation, nothing hindered him from the possession of glory and happiness, from the very beginning of his conception. For, by being the Son, he was heir of all things. But it was owing to his voluntary covenant-engagement, *that though he was rich*, 2 Cor. viii. 9. and might have acted as equal to God from the very beginning of his incarnation, *yet for our sakes he became poor*. That this subjection to the law, as *enjoining the condition of happiness*, is to be distinguished from that other absolute subjection to it, as *the rule of holiness*, appears hence, that Christ has laid aside the first, while this last continues, and will continue, to eternity.

XIV. The usefulness of this distinction is considerable, in order to the solving that problem, *how the active obedience of Christ* so called, though not so properly, *may be imputed to us; seeing as man he owed it for himself.* For, besides that on our account he was *made man,* it was not barely from his being man that he was under the necessity of meriting eternal life by the legal covenant, nay, and considered as God-man, abstracted from his suretiship-engagement, he might have exempted himself from all indigence, and all necessity of meriting; and consequently might have gloriously exercised all power in heaven and in earth, in, and by the human nature, from the *first* moment of his incarnation: for this flows from the union of the humanity with the person of the Son of God. But his subjecting himself to the law, as prescribing the condition of happiness, is wholly from his voluntary covenant-engagement which he entered into on our account, which by every right or just title, may, and ought to be imputed to us. The very ingenious and judicious divine, Francis Gomarus, seems to have had this in his view when he thus comments on Phil. ii. 9. " For our sake, he also vailed his glory for a time, which he might justly enjoy, and submitted to the cursed death of the cross; which, if we consider his merit and power, he might have declined."

XV. Besides, the Son of God was in virtue of the covenant subject to " the curse of the law, being made a curse for us," Gal. iii. 16. For, as the law likewise required *punishment* to be inflicted on the transgressor, and Christ bound himself by his engagement, to fulfil the whole law; it was necessary " he should come in the likeness of sinful flesh, to condemn sin in the flesh," Rom. viii. 3. Which likeness of sinful flesh consists in this, that Christ, from his birth, was obnoxious to various miseries, both of soul and body, and at last to that death by which he concluded the course of his painful life, and in which the most evident signs of every kind of curse appeared: for it was just that the sinner should thus live and die. Now Christ considered simply as a righteous person, might have been exempted from these miseries, and from such a death; but after having once, by *a voluntary engagement,* submitted himself to the law for us, he became bound to satisfy also this sanction of the law, which threatened death to sinners; for all these things arise from the mediatorial *covenant,* and belong to Christ *as Mediator.*

XVI. But since in Christ, as *Mediator,* there is an union of the *divine* and *human* natures, this difficulty remains to be discussed, whether *both* natures were in some measure subject to the law. We may easily affirm this of *the human,* as we have

already so often shewn, but it seems from what we have confirmed, § VI. it must be denied with respect to *the divine*. However, as the human nature does not, without the divine, complete
the person of the Mediator, it does not appear, that the Mediator
as such, did not engage to be subject to the law, without bringing his divine nature likewise to share in that subjection.

XVII. In order to remove this difficulty, we are accurately
to distinguish between *both natures* considered *separately*, and
the same *natures united in the person of* God-man. It was
proper that both natures should act suitably to themselves and
their distinct properties. Since *the divine nature*, as subsisting
in the Son, could not *truly* and *really be subject;* therefore, by
virtue of the covenant, it did *not exert* or display all its majesty
in the assumed form of a servant; nor hinder that nature to
which it was united by the hypostatical union, from being truly
subject to the law, both as to the condition of the reward, and
as to the penal sanction, which indeed, was neither a real *re-
nunciation, nor degradation* of the divine superiority, but only
a certain *economical vailing* of it for a time.

XVIII. *The human nature* was *really* and *properly* subject
to the law: nay, from *the hypostatical union* there was superadded, a certain *peculiar* obligation upon the human nature of
Christ, considered in *relation* to *the suretiship* undertaken for
us as his brethren. For, as men are bound to love God in such
a manner as above all things to seek his glory, which shines
most illustrious in the justification and sanctification of the sinner, and so to love their neighbour, as to desire to deliver their
brother from sin and misery, even at their own peril, if possible.
But though no mere man can effect this, yet the man Christ,
who is likewise true God, and so able by his obedience and
suffering, to promote this glory of God and the salvation of his
brethren, was therefore obliged to undertake and undergo all
those things, in which he might shew forth this most intense
love of God and his neighbour: since he only could do this, so
he only was bound to do it. What others were obliged to do
conditionally, as we observe a spark of this love in Moses,
Exod. xxxii. 32. and in Paul, Rom. ix. 3. was incumbent on
the man Christ *absolutely;* because being *God-man*, he could
absolutely perform it.

XIX. We commonly ascribe *to the person God-man*, the relation of an inferior to a superior, by a constitution or appointment: that, both by doing and suffering, those things might be
accomplished according to the condition of each nature, which
were requisite to our salvation: so that the very obedience
and sufferings themselves, are not only to be appropriated

to the human nature, but to be considered as truly performed
and suffered by the God-man.   If this was not the case, they
would not be of infinite value and dignity, nor sufficient for our
redemption.   Hence, he who is in the form of God, *is said* to
have " made himself of no reputation, and become obedient
unto death," Phil. ii. 6, 7, 8.   And to be " the Lord of glory
who was crucified," 1 Cor. ii. 8.

XX. It is here usual to enquire, *whether Christ as Mediator, is inferior to the Father, and subordinate to him.*   But
this controversy, it seems, *may* be easily settled among the orthodox : if the Mediator be considered in the state of humiliation, and the form of a servant, he is certainly inferior to the
Father, and subordinate to him.   It was not of his human nature only, but of himself in that state, that he himself said,
John xiv. 28. *The Father is greater than I.*   Nay, we may
look upon the very *mediatorial office* in itself as importing a
certain *economical inferiority*, or subordination; as being to be
laid down, when all things shall be perfectly finished, and *God
himself shall be all in all*, 1 Cor. xv. 28.   Nevertheless this
undertaking and mediation, and the bringing of fallen man to
God, to grace and glory, is not so much beneath the excellency
of the Deity, but we may without the least hesitation affirm,
that this glory of mediation is incommunicable to any creature.
It is the glory of Jehovah to be the righteousness of Israel.
This glory he gives to none who is not God : to be Mediator
does not merely denote a servant of God, but the great God
and Saviour ; who as the first and principal cause of saving
grace, equal to the Father, works by his own power, our reconciliation with God, by means of the subjection and obedience
of his human nature, without which the co-equal Son could
neither perform his service, nor obey the Father.

XXI. The third thing we promised to enquire into was
this : " Could the Son refuse to undertake, or withdraw himself from this covenant ?" To which question we are again to
answer distinctly.   1st. If *the Son* be considered as *God*, the
whole of this covenant was of his own most free will and pleasure.   There neither was, nor could be any necessity to bind
the Son of God, as such, to this covenant.   Here is nothing
but mere *good pleasure, philanthropy unmerited*, and altogether liberal, pure, and unmixed grace.   2dly. If he be considered as *man*, though he indeed entered into this engagement
of his own accord, without being constrained ; yet he could
not, without sin, from which he is at the greatest distance,
withdraw from this agreement : which we prove in the following manner :

XXII. 1st. The human nature of Christ, as we have often said, could not be without law. The law under which it naturally is, is *the royal law of love ;* which does not indeed formally, as it was made for man in innocence, but yet eminently contain this precept which John inculcates, Eph. iii. 16. *That one lay down his life for the brethren.* I say, the law of love, as given to man in innocence contains not this precept formally ; death being inconsistent with that state, and perfect obedience, which is all summed up in love, frees man from all necessity of dying, according to the promise, *he who doth those things, shall live in them.* And therefore we have shewn, that if Christ be considered *in himself as a holy person,* without respect to the decree of God, and his own engagement for his miserable brethren, he was, by virtue of his perfect holiness, under no necessity of dying and suffering. But the law of love does, supposing the requisite circumstances, *eminently* contain the command of dying for our brethren. For, it enjoins us to love *God above all, and our neighbour as ourselves.* And he who *loves God above all,* does not only delight in God his *creator, benefactor, lord,* and *example ;* not only studies to please him, but endeavours to promote his glory, and direct all things that are God's to that end. And as he ought to have a tender regard for *the glory of God* above *his own advantage,* he also ought to be ready to undergo every thing, by which the glory of God may be most illustrated. And supposing, such a one has brethren in distress, from which he can deliver them by his death, so that God shall in an eminent manner appear glorious in them ; the love of our brethren together with the love of God, enjoins him not to decline dying for them ; especially if he himself, becoming a conqueror over death, shall thereby obtain a most distinguishing reward at last. Since therefore, Christ as man, could not but be under the law of love, and a holy man, as doubtless it became him to be, he cannot therefore be conceived as destitute of love, much less as having a contrary disposition ; it follows, that he could not, in such circumstances, withdraw himself from his agreement to satisfy for men ; because the law of love *eminently* contains such an obligation.

XXIII. 2dly. The Son of God had from eternity engaged to satisfy this covenant, by assuming human nature, and obeying in it, as we shewed above, § II. If the human nature, personally united to him, could have withdrawn itself from, and renounced the covenant, it was possible that the Son of God himself might have violated his covenant engagements. And in that case Christ would not be either the true and faithful God, who cannot lie, or not be God omnipotent : because he, who, from eternity, willingly engaged in this undertaking, could not, in time, induce the human nature to execute that for which it was assumed at first. Nor do I see what reply can be made to this argument, unless one shall venture to say, that it is contrary to the nature of liberty, that the will should be thus bent, or brought over, by a superior cause: and that, in such a case, the human nature declining to stand to that covenant, would be deprived of the honour of the hypostatical union, and another be assumed in its stead. But besides that this overthrows the inseparability of the hypostatical union, admitted on both sides, the same difficulty must recur with respect to the nature newly assumed; because, equal liberty is to be ascribed to it.

XXIV. 3dly. God had by an eternal and irrevocable decree, *appointed, promised, and confirmed by oath,* the inheritance of all blessings in Christ, Heb. vi. 13—18. Luke i. 73. But if Christ could have withdrawn himself from the covenant, then *the decree* of God would have become *void,* his *promises been deceitful,* and his *oath falsified;* and therefore the whole counsel of God concerning the œconomy of our salvation, so often inculcated in the prophetical writings, would have become of no effect; which is indeed blasphemy to imagine. There is no occasion to suggest, as one has done, that God could, without the payment of any price, have remitted the debt of sin, and among some thousand methods have found out another way of saving mankind, had this method proved unsuccessful. For as this is very much more than we can readily yield to, so it is nothing to the purpose. For God did not only in general decree, promise, and confirm by oath, salvation to his elect; but salvation to be obtained by Christ and his obedience; which decree, promise, and oath, could be accomplished no other way; not to say, how unworthy it is of God to be obliged to make new decrees, after the former have miscarried. And this is the very bone of the Remonstrant divinity.

XXV. 4thly. Let us suppose that the human nature of Christ, to speak plainly, could have withdrawn itself from this covenant; yet *it could not,* at least *without* a horrible *sin,* after the preordination of God, the eternal will of the Son, the promise and oath had been discovered to him. Nay, it had been a more dreadful sin than that of the first Adam, for him obstinately to oppose all these considerations, and prefer his own private advantage to the glory of God and salvation of the elect; and by this means, we should be reduced, by this hypothesis we are now contending against, to the shocking blasphemies of some schoolmen, who affirm that *Christ could have sinned, and consequently have been damned.* These are the depths of Satan, which all Christians ought to pronounce accursed.

XXVI. Hence we see what we are to think of the divinity of the Remonstrants on this head, who, in chap. xvii. p. 187. b. of their *apology* or remonstrance, say, that " the obedience of Christ was of a different nature from ours; but agreeing in this that it was altogether free. Christ obeyed the will of his Father, not as we obey the law of God, under the threatening of eternal death, in case of disobedience : God forbid ; but as an ambassador is said to obey his sovereign, or a beloved son his father, when his sovereign or father, confers on either an honourable office to be executed by them, adding the promise of some extraordinary reward, if they will freely, and on their account undertake it. Whoever obeys in this manner, that is, willingly takes that office upon himself, he indeed properly and freely obeys, not that he would properly sin, did he not undertake it; or when undertaken, lay it down again, with the good-will of the father ; much less that he would deserve eternal punishment, if he did not undertake it, or excuse himself from undertaking, or bearing the burden thereof ; as it is most certain, that when we disobey God and his law, we deserve punishment. But no such threatening of punishment was made to Christ ; but he could either not undertake it, or when he undertook it, resign his charge, and so not enjoy, or forfeit the promised reward."

XXVII. In this discourse there are as many faults, as sentences. We will now chiefly remark these following things. 1st. The leading error of the Remonstrants, from whence their other errors flow, is their making the liberty of the will *to* consist in *indifference,* so as one may, or may not obey; whereas it is to be placed in *the free good pleasure of the mind.* Unless one would affirm either of these things, that it was either possible or lawful, for the holy angels, and the spirits of just men made perfect, nay, Christ himself exalted, not to do the will of God. 2dly. They distinguish not *the person* of the Son of God, and *the grace,* by which he humbled himself to undertake obedience in the assumed human nature, from *the human nature* itself, and *obedience* of Christ, now in his state *of humiliation.* The grace of the Son of God was so free, that he could not be against this humiliation, or emptying of himself, that he might come under an obligation to obedience. There is no reason, but the most free good pleasure of the divine will, why this future humiliation was decreed by the adorable Trinity, and consequently by the Son himself. Yet, upon supposing this free decree, the human nature assumed by *the logos, or the Word,* could not decline, or draw back from the office assigned to Christ, and now undertaken by the *logos* himself, without sin and disobedience.

3dly. They do not consider, that *the human nature* of Christ was bound, by *an indispensable necessity, to that holiness* which is the image of God : since they compare the whole of Christ's obedience with *the undertaking of some office, which a sovereign confers on his ambassador, or a father on his son.* For, as an ambassador, in the quality of *a subject*, and a son, as *such,* are bound by *the law of nature* itself, to perform to a sovereign and a father, an obedience distinct from that which arises from their *willingly undertaking this honorary office ;* so in like manner, the human nature of Christ was and still continues to be, bound to perform obedience to God, in order to maintain this conformity with the holiness of God ; which obligation is distinct from his undertaking the mediatorial office. 4thly. They falsely place *the essential difference* between *the obedience of Christ* and *ours ;* in that we obey *being awed by the threatening of death ;* but Christ not so. For, that threatening does not properly belong to obedience, which really ought not to be extorted from us by the fear of punishment, but to come freely from a reverence to the divine command, and a love to holiness. Our obedience will be no less obedience in heaven when the threatening of eternal death shall no longer have any place. Moreover, the same law which is proposed to us was the rule of the life and actions of Christ. But that law had the sanction of eternal death, which it was incumbent on Christ to believe to be just and right ; tending to inform the conscience of God's hatred to sin, and to inflame it likewise with a hatred of sin and unrighteousness. And thus far, after Christ had humbled himself for us, he obeyed the law even under the threatening, and acknowledged the same to be just ; and that every threatening of the law, produced in Christ a sense of the wrath of God, when he suffered for us. 5thly. They absurdly pretend, that Christ could, *with the Father's consent, decline the office committed to him,* or, *resign it after he had undertaken it ;* as if one should say that a son could have the consent of a virtuous father to make him a liar and guilty of perjury. For God the Father had promised, and solemnly confirmed by oath, that he would procure our salvation by the Son. 6thly. Nor is it less absurd, that they perceive no inconvenience flowing from the nonsusception, or from the resignation of that office, but this one, that in that case Christ *would not enjoy,* or *would forfeit the promised reward ;* since the very salvation of all the elect, and, which is above all, the whole of the glory of God, would thence fall to the ground. I would also fain know, what reward Christ would, according to that hypothesis, have forfeited ; whether the honour of the hypostatical union, or eternal salvation itself, and the communion of the divine love and glory; or whether that sublime glory, in which he is now eminently placed above the rest of the creatures; also, whether it is not blasphemy to say, that either the hypostatical union is dissolved, or that any nature hypostatically united to the Son of God, can have no share in eternal salvation; or, if in a state of happiness, has not *a more excellent name* than the rest of the creatures: in like manner, whether the loss of so great a happiness, can, in an intelligent nature, be without an eternal sensation of the most bitter anguish: in fine, whether it is not much better and more worthy of God and his Christ, to believe that Christ could not but undertake the office assigned unto him by the Father, and never withdraw from it, than run headlong into such absurdities.

XXVIII. We shall briefly dispatch the fourth thing remaining; namely, *the reward which the Son was to obtain in virtue of this covenant*, by enquiring *first, what reward* was promised the Son: *and then what relation his obedience* had to this *reward*.

XXIX. The reward promised to the Son, is *the highest degree of glory*, John xvii. 1. " Father, glorify thy Son, that thy Son also may glorify thee." But this glory may be considered distinctly with respect to *the humanity*, to *the Deity*, and to the whole person. In the humanity, I observe these three degrees of glory. 1st. That, together with the elect, his fellows, Psal. xlv. 7. and co-heirs, Rom. viii. 17. it is blessed in the perfect fruition of God. 2dly. That it is exalted above all creatures, on account of the dignity of the hypostatical union. 3dly. That the glory of his Godhead shines forth therein, with a more illustrious refulgence than in the days of his flesh: so that the man Christ cannot be seen, but he must appear to be the glorious Son of God, and his glory be as " the glory of the only begotten of the Father," John i. 14.

XXX. As the Deity of the Son could not properly be humbled, so neither could it acquire any new increase of glory. For as *the humiliation* of Christ, with respect to his God-head, consisted in this, that under the human form of a servant, which he assumed, the brightness of his glory was covered as with a vail: so *the glorification of the Deity* consists in this, that all the magnificence of the glorious majesty of God beautifully discovers itself, and becomes more conspicuous. And this is what Christ prayed for, John xvii. 5. " And now, O Father, glorify thou me with thine ownself, with the glory which I had with thee, before the world was."

XXXI. *The whole person of the Mediator* obtains for a reward, 1st. That God hath ὑπερύψωσε over raised, " highly exalted him, and given him a name, which is above every name,"

Phil. ix. 2. " Far above all principality and power, and might
and dominion, and every name that is named, not only in this
world but also in that which is to come," Eph. i. 21. 2dly.
That the whole church is given him as his peculiar possession,
Ps. ii. 8. Is. liii. 10. And that he himself is given *as head over
all things to the church*, Eph. i. 22. and *all power given him in
heaven and in earth*, Matt. xxviii. 18. that he may govern all
things, for the benefit of the church. 3dly. That, on account of the
most intimate union of the church, as his mystical body, with himself, he received all those gifts which he merited, and on that account
are bestowed on the elect. For the church united to Christ, the body,
together with the head, is called *Christ*, 1 Cor. xii. 12. And thus
literally run the words, Psal. lxviii. 18. *thou hast received gifts
in men*, as the Septuagint also renders them, ἔλαβες δόμαῖα ἐν ἀνθ-
ρώποις. Instead of which the apostle, Eph. iv. 8. not literally, but
giving the sense of the words, says, ἔδωαε δοματα τοις ανθρώποις,
he gave gifts to men. For, as Christ is supposed to receive
them, when they are given to his members, so he gives his members what he received of the Father, Acts ii. 33. *therefore being
by the right hand of God exalted, and having received of the
Father the promise of the Holy Ghost, he hath shed forth this
which ye now see and hear.*

XXXII. *The obedience* of Christ bears to these *blessings*, not
only the relation of *antecedent* to *consequent*, but of *merit* to *reward :* so that his obedience is *the cause*, and *the condition* now
fulfilled, by virtue of which he has *a right* to the reward, as
several express passages of scripture declare; Ps. xlv. 7. *thou
lovest righteousness and hatest wickedness*, (which is a description
of the obedience of Christ) עַל כֵּן, THEREFORE *God, thy God,
hath anointed thee with the oil of gladness above thy fellows ;*
which words contain the reward, intimating the most joyful entrance of Christ into the kingdom of his glory and delight. The
relation of obedience to the reward is set forth by the word
therefore, which denotes the cause, and not a mere antecedent.
In like manner, Isa. liii. 12. לָכֵן, THEREFORE *will I divide him
a portion with the great*, and *he shall divide the spoil with the
strong*, תחת אשר BECAUSE *he hath poured out his soul unto
death*. Where the relative particles, תחת אשר and לכן expressly indicate that commutative justice, whereby the reward due,
bears a reciprocal relation to the obedience performed, Phil. ii. 8,
9. *he became obedient unto death, even the death of the cross :*
διὸ καὶ ὁ Θεος αὐῖον ὑπερυψωσε, WHEREFORE *God also hath highly exalted him.* Heb. xii. 2. ἀλλὶ της προκειμενης αὐτῶ χαρας ὑπέμεινε ςαυρόν,
who, FOR *the joy that was set before him, endured the cross.*

Where there is an express commutation, or interchange of obedience and reward.

XXXIII. And the thing speaks for itself. For as there is a covenant between the Father and the Son ; *when thou shalt make his soul* (if the soul of the Son shall devote himself) *an offering for sin,* Isa. liii. 10. upon performing the condition, the Son acquired a right to the reward, and so has a *merit* according to the *covenant.* Nay, as it is not the obedience of a mere man, but of Christ God-man, an infinite person, it is also of an infinite value, consequently bears the justest proportion to the greatest corresponding glory ; and thus far it is *a merit of condignity,* as it is called ; such as no mere creature is capable to acquire.

XXXIV. The passages of scripture which represent the humiliation of Christ as *the antecedent* to the subsequent glory, are not contrary to this doctrine. For every cause is an antecedent, though every antecedent is not a cause. And the merit of Christ *for himself* is so far from being prejudicial to his merit *for us,* that on the contrary, they are inseparably conjoined. For if he merited for *himself,* in order to be the head of the elect in glory, and to receive gifts for them, he certainly at the same time, merited for *the elect,* in order to their being glorified, and enriched with gifts becoming the mystical body of Christ. Neither by this doctrine is the excellency of the love of Christ towards us diminished, though in his state of humiliation, he had likewise an eye to his own exaltation. For he might have been glorious as to himself, without going to it by this way of death, and the pains of hell. Besides he looked upon his own glory as the beginning and cause of ours, and whose fruit was all to redound to us. And it was the highest pitch of love, that he would not be glorious without us. Nor should the word χαρίζεσθαί, *given* which the apostle uses, Phil. ii. 9. be urged too closely, as if the rewards there mentioned were of mere grace freely given to Christ, without any regard to his obedience, as the cause of his right or title to them. For Paul there expressly asserts, that they were given to Christ on account of his obedience. And that term does not always denote mere grace. Hesychius, that very excellent master of Greek, explains it by δρᾶν ἰὰ κεχαρισμένα, *to do what is acceptable.* But those things also are called acceptable, which are due ; the Greeks say, Θεοῖς κεχαρισμένα ποιεῖν, *to do what is acceptable to the gods.* Whence the same thing, which here, in respect to Christ is called χάρισμα, is Isaiah xlix. 4. called *his work,* or the reward of his work, adjudged to him by the just judgment of God. " My judgment is with the Lord, and my work with my God." So that the plain meaning of this passage in Paul is this ; because

Christ submitted himself to the Father, by free or voluntary obedience, the Father therefore also rewarded him by giving him a name above every name.

CHAP. IV.

Of the Person of the Surety.

I. Having with some degree of care explained the nature of the covenant between the Father and the Son, it is fit we treat a little more distinctly of *the Surety* himself, concerning whom these are the principal particulars; and *first* we shall consider *the* PERSON *of the* SURETY, and what is requisite to constitute such: and then that SATISFACTION which he undertook to make by his suretiship; *the* TRUTH, NECESSITY, EFFECTS, and EXTENT, of which we shall distinctly deduce from the scriptures.

II. These four things are required as necessary to *the* PERSON *of a* SURETY, that he might be capable to engage for us. 1st. That he be *true man*, consisting of a human soul and body. 2dly. That he be *a righteous* and *holy man*, without any spot of sin. 3dly. That he be *true and eternal God.* 4thly. That he be all this in the *unity of person.* Of each severally and in order.

III. That our Surety ought to be *true man*, is what Paul declares more than once, Heb. ii. 10, 11, 16, 17. Επρεπε, *it became him*, it behoved him, it was becoming God *that he who sanctifieth*, and *they who are sanctified, be all of one*, of one human seed, so that they might call each other brethren. *In all things it behoved him to be made like unto his brethren*, in order to be their *Goel* or kinsman-redeemer : *for verily he took not on him the nature of angels, but he took on him the seed of Abraham*, (did not take upon him to deliver angels, but to deliver the seed of Abraham.)

IV. This assumption, or taking, does not seem to me to denote the assuming human nature into personal union, but the assuming of the elect, in order to their deliverance. For, 1st. The causal conjunction *for*, indicates, that the apostle uses this middle term [or this as an argument] to prove, what he had said v. 14. about the partaking of flesh and blood, and which v. 17. he deduces by the illative particle, *wherefore.* But the middle term must be distinguished from the conclusion : and so there is no tautology in the apostle's very just inference. 2dly. Since the assumption of the human nature was long before the apostle wrote those things, he would not speak of it in the pre-sent tense, as he does here, but in the preterperfect, as he did ver. 14. 3dly. As it would be an uncouth expression to say, the Son of God assumed or took man, if we suppose he only meant, that the Son of God assumed human nature ; and in like manner this other expression would appear harsh, the Son of God did not assume angels, to denote that he did not assume the nature of angels. 4thly. In the scripture style επιλαμβανεσθαι signifies to deliver by laying hold of one: thus Matt. xiv. 31. " and immediately Jesus stretched forth his hand, and επελαρετο αμτ8 caught him :" and this signification is most apposite to the con-text. For, in the preceding verse, the apostle had said, that Christ *delivered them who through fear of death were all their lifetime subject to bondage,* alluding it seems to the bondage of Egypt. But God is represented to us in scripture, as with a stretched out hand laying hold on, and bringing his people out of Egypt, Jer. xxxi. 32. " in the day that I took them by the hand to lead them out of the land of Egypt." Which the apostle ex-presses by saying, " in the day when I took them by the hand, to lead them out of the land of Egypt :" where we have the same word επιλαμβανεσθαι. And in profane authors, it denotes, *to claim* something as one's property, and say, according to Virgil, *these are mine.* Thus Plato, XII. *de legibus,* ότι αν τας κεκλημέιος ή και μηδείς επιλάβηϊαι, " if one is in possession of any thing, and none claims it as his own." To this answers the Hebrew גאל. Which makes me, with many learned men, think that these words of the apostle, whose genuine sense we have been en-quiring into, rather contain an argument for the incarnation of Christ, than assert the incarnation itself.

ᚺ X. Moreover, it may be proved by invincible arguments, that it was necessary our Surety should be man. Let us pause a little here, and see whether we may not possibly search this truth to the bottom. The legal covenant entered into with the first man, is founded on the very nature of God ; at least with respect to the commands of the covenant, and the threatenings annexed to them. So that it would be a contra-diction if these precepts of the law of nature should not be proposed to man, or if man, after the violation of them, should be saved without a satisfaction ; which I now presuppose, as having proved it before, and shall further confirm it in the sequel. I therefore proceed : this satisfaction can be nothing else but the performing the same precepts, and the undergoing the same penalty with which God had threatened the sinner. Because, from our hypothesis, it appears to be unworthy of God to grant life to man but on condition of his obeying those

precepts; nor possible for the truth and justice of God to be
satisfied, unless the punishment which the sinner deserved
should be inflicted. I add, that as those precepts were given
to man, so no creature but man could perform them. This
appears, 1st. Because the law, which is suited to the nature of
man, requires, that he love God with all his soul, and serve
him with all the members of his body, seeing both are God's.
None can do this but man, who consists of soul and body.
2dly. The same law requires the love of our neighbour; but
none is our neighbour but man, who is of the same blood
with us. To this purpose is that emphatical saying of God
to Israel, Isa. lviii. 7. " that thou hide not thyself from thine
own flesh." And thus our Surety ought to cherish us, as one
does his own flesh, and consequently we ought to be *of his
flesh and of his bones*, Eph. v. 30. 3dly. It requires also,
that we lay down our lives for our brethren, which we have
shewn was contained in the royal law of love, and none but
man can do this. For who else is our brother? Heb. ii. 11.
or who besides could lay down his life for us. No other
creature but man could undergo the same sufferings, as hunger, thirst, weariness, death. It became God to threaten sinning man with these things: that even the body, which was
the instrument of sin, might also undergo its share of the
punishment. And after the threatening, the truth of God
could not but inflict these things, either on the sinner or the
Surety. The dignity of the sufferer might indeed sufficiently
compensate for the duration of the punishment. But the
truth of God admits of no commutation of the species of
punishment. Wherefore our Surety was " partaker of flesh
and blood, that through death he might destroy him that
had the power of death," Heb. ii. 14. All these things put
together, incontestably prove that our Surety ought to be man;
that he might satisfy the law for us.

VI. This is what the apostle means when joining these
two together by an inseparable connexion, Gal. iv. 4. " made
of a woman, made under the law." For he intimates, that
the principal and immediate scope and end of Christ's incarnation was, that in the human nature he might be subject to
the law, to which it is under obligation: and so that God,
according to the same right, might renew with him the same
covenant which he had before entered into with the first man;
which he could not have done with any other created nature,
without a contradiction.

VII. There is this further consideration: our Surety ought
to have such a nature, in order to our being united to him in

one body. For it is necessary that the satisfaction of one be as it were the satisfaction of all, and the Spirit who fits for a holy and happy life, should flow from him as the head to us as his members; and so that he become " the saviour of the body," Eph. v. 23. The Scriptures frequently call this mystical union *a marriage*. But it is the inviolable law of marriage that the persons married be of the same nature ; " and they two shall be one flesh," Gen. ii. 24. Paul hath taught us, that the mystery of the spiritual marriage of the church with Christ lies concealed in these words, Eph. v. 31, 32.

VIII. We observed that the second condition required in the Surety was, that he be " a RIGHTEOUS and HOLY MAN : in all things like unto his brethren, yet without sin," Heb. iv. 15. This holiness required that from the first moment of his conception he should be free from all guilt and stain of sin of his own ; and on the contrary, be endowed with the original rectitude of the image of God : that moreover, through the whole course of his life, he should keep himself from all sin, and perfectly fulfil all righteousness : and in fine, constantly persevere in that purity to the end, without yielding to any temptation.

IX. And this also is clear from what has been already said. For, seeing our Surety ought to save us, according to the first treaty of the covenant, whereby perfect holiness was required of man, it also behoved him to be perfectly holy. And as sin shut the gates of heaven, nothing but holiness could set them open again. This the apostle urges, Rom. v. 19. " for, as by one man's disobedience many were made sinners ; so by the obedience of one shall many be made righteous." But that obedience excludes all sin. And then, how could a sinner satisfy for others who cannot satisfy for himself, for by one sin he forfeits his own soul ? " For who is this (from among sinful men) that can engage his heart to approach unto me ?" says God, Jer. xxx. 21. Or who but one who is free from every sin can be our priest, familiarly to approach to God, and offer an acceptable sacrifice and prevalent intercession to him ? " Such an high-priest became us, who is holy, harmless, undefiled, separate from sinners," Heb. vii. 26. He then can offer himself, as a lamb " without blemish and without spot," 1 Pet. i. 19. whose offering may be to God " for a sweet-smelling savour," Eph. v. 2. For none else who cannot offer himself to God " without spot, can purge the conscience from dead works," Heb. ix. 14. This was formerly signified by the legal purity of

N 2

the high priest, without which, it was such a crime for any
to intermeddle in holy things that he was to be punished by
death ; and by the purity of the beasts, which were to be
without any blemish.　And seeing it is well known that
" God heareth not sinners," John ix. 31. whose " prayers
are an abomination to him," Prov. xxviii. 9. who else can be
the general intercessor and advocate of all with the Father,
but he who is eminently *righteous ?* 1 John ii. 1. In fine,
how could he who is himself impure, " sanctify the church,
and present it to himself a glorious church, not having spot
or wrinkle, or any such thing, but that it should be holy and
without blemish," Eph. v. 26, 27 : there cannot be more in
the effect than there is in the cause.　Since then all these
things ought to be done by the Surety, it appears necessary
that he be a holy man.

　　X. But here the adorable wisdom of our God shines forth :
our Surety ought not only to be man, but also taken from
among men, that he might be *the son of man ;* for if his human nature was created out of nothing, or out of the earth,
he would certainly be true man, yet not our kinsman, not our
brother.　In order to this therefore, it became him, like
other " children, to be a partaker of flesh and blood," Heb. ii.
14. and to be " born of a woman," Gal. iv. 4.　But it seemed inconsistent with the unspotted holiness of the Surety,
that he should be descended of the posterity of Adam, who
all derive hereditary pollution from him : for " who can
bring a clean thing out of an unclean ?" Job xiv. 4.　Here let
us adore the unsearchable wisdom of God.　Though he
would have a Surety to be born of a woman, yet she was to
be a virgin.　For this, if there was nothing else intended,
was at least an evidence of these two things : 1st. That the
Surety was not from Adam's covenant, as not being born
according to the law of nature, and consequently not under the
imputation of Adam's sin.　2dly. Nay that he could not be
so much as considered as existing in Adam when Adam sinned.　Seeing he was not born in virtue of that word whereby God blessed the state of marriage before the fall ; *increase and multiply ;* but in virtue of the promise concerning
the seed of the woman, which was made after the fall.　And
thus he was created a second Adam in opposition to the first.
" For the Lord hath created a new thing in the earth, נבר
נקבה תסובב a woman shall compass a man," Jer. xxxi. 22. We
are it seems to take this in the utmost signification the words
can admit of.　That *a woman,* who is only such, and without any thing of the woman but the sex, *should compass,* not

by embrace, but by conception. (For such a compassing is meant, as is the work of God alone, and not the voluntary operation of man.) *A male*, denoting the more excellent sex, as Rev. xii. 5. " and she brought forth a male child." This then is a *new thing*, and a *creation* altogether divine. On this depend the blessing of the earth, and the satiating the weary soul, which are promised in the following verses.

XI. It may here be enquired, whether the miraculous nativity from a virgin does of itself, and from the nature of the thing, secure to the human nature of Christ immunity from sin : or whether indeed it was only appointed by God as a symbol ? I shall here present the reader, for his more accurate meditation, with the words of two great men who conceive differently of this matter. One of them speaks thus : " That miraculous nativity from the virgin, really bears no other relation to the holiness of the conception and nativity of Christ, but that *of a symbol appointed by God*, whereby he was separated from sinners : nor could that miracle of itself alone, namely, the impregnation of the virgin's womb, secure in the least an exemption to the flesh of Christ from the inheritance of sin : for the origin of sin is not derived from the male sex alone, or male seed ; nor did the apostle, Rom. v. so understand one man Adam, as to exclude Eve : which is here the leading error of some." The other of these learned men reasons in this manner : " He could be born of the virgin without any pollution : because what is in the body of a sinner, as it is God's creature, is no wise under curse and pollution, but in so far as it is a part of the sinner when he is to be punished, or is the instrument of sin, or the means of the ordinary propagation of nature, as that something should be born resembling what generates. There might therefore be something in the virgin's body that was not under a curse ; as the sweats, and other evacuations from the human body are not under curse or guilt, nor a means of transferring guilt ; but are parts of matter created by God, and are no longer any part of man." Perhaps the same learned person has elsewhere expressed himself more clearly, as follows : " He who was born not of father and mother, but of a virgin, was not under guilt and condemnation. For he only received from his mother what was prepared by God : that thence the Son of God might take to himself the materials for building a temple. For though what belongs to the sinner is, on account of the sinner to whom it belongs, under the same condemnation with the sinner himself ; yet that which is so contained in the substance

of the sinner, as that it cannot be a part of his substance, but
prepared by God for an extraordinary generation, is not under
condemnation solely because the redeemer and redeemed partake of flesh in common. And therefore it is rightly said
to be *sanctified*, that is, *preserved from* the common *condemnation of the sons of Adam*. For the word *sanctified* cannot, in
that case, signify *purified*, or delivered from impurity; as it
signifies when applied to the other sons of Adam." Which
of these two opinions is the more simple and more solid, we
leave to the judgment of the prudent reader to determine.
The words of both seemed however to us worthy of being inserted here.

XII. Thirdly. It is further required in our Surety, that he
be *true and eternal God*. " I will help thee, saith the Lord,
and thy Redeemer, the holy One of Israel," Isa. xli. 14. " I,
even I am Lord, and there is no Saviour besides me," Isa. xliii.
11. Salvation is not such work, that it cannot be said, " and
the Lord hath not done all this," Deut. xxxii. 27. It is peculiar to the true Saviour to say of himself, what Isaiah prophesied, chap. xlv. 24. *surely in the Lord (he said to me*, or
concerning me, namely, the Father, who *beareth witness of
Christ*, John viii. 18.) *are righteousness and strength; even
to him shall men come :* and the reasons are evident.

XIII. None but God can restore us to true liberty. If
any creature could redeem and deliver us, we should become
the peculiar property of that creature. For he who sets us
free, makes a purchase of us for his property and possession.
1 Cor. vi. 19, 20. But it is a manifest contradiction to be
freed and to be free, and yet at the same time to be the property and servant of any creature. True liberty consists in
subjection to God alone; so that all things are ours, and we
belong to God, and Christ himself, 1 Cor. iii. 22, 23. Adam
before the fall was subject to none but God. If, by our deliverance from the fall, we were put under the dominion of any
creature, that would rather be a change of servitude than a deliverance. Therefore our Lord says, " if the Son shall make
you free, ye shall be free indeed," John viii. 36.

XIV. None but God can give us eternal life; which consists in the most intimate union with God; nay in having God
for our inheritance, possession, and treasure, and even *our
portion for ever*, Psal. lxxiii. 26. But what creature can
possibly bestow God upon any? None but God can give God.
He gives himself. Hence, these two are joined, " the true
God and eternal life," 1 John v. 20.

XV. None but God can give us ἐξουσίαν *power or right to be-*

come the sons of God; and even this belongs to the office of
Surety, John i. 2.   For, who but God can bestow the Spirit,
by whom we become the sons of God by regeneration; so
that of him the whole πατρία *family in heaven and earth may
be named,* Eph. iii. 15.   Who but God could " give us these
great and precious promises, by which we might be partakers
of the divine nature?" 2 Pet. i. 4.   Who else but God, who
alone is Lord of heaven, can bequeath by testament the heavenly inheritance? And who but God can give us that Spirit,
who is so the Spirit of the Father, as to be also the Spirit of
the Son: " by whom we may cry Abba Father," Gal. iv. 6.
and who beareth witness with our spirit concerning the future inheritance? Rom. viii. 16, 17.

XVI. In fine, for man to glory in any one, as his Saviour,
and give him the honour of the new creation, to resign himself to his pleasure, and become his property, and say to him,
thou art lord of my soul; is an honour to which no mere creature can have the least claim.   " In Jehovah shall all the seed
of Israel be justified, and shall glory," Isa. xlv. 25. " My
spirit hath rejoiced in God my Saviour," Luke i. 47.   Whom
we acknowledge to be our Saviour, we must likewise acknowledge to be our judge, our lawgiver, and our king, Isa. xxxiii.
22. A holy soul can only thus rejoice in God; " the Lord
reigneth, let the earth rejoice, let the multitude of isles be glad,"
Psal. xcvii. 1.

XVII. It appears then, that none but he who is true God,
could possibly be Surety; but the question is, was it absolutely necessary, that he should be Son of God, and the second
person in the Trinity?   And here we cannot commend the
rashness of the schoolmen, who too boldly measure the things
of God by the standard of their own understanding.   No better reason can be assigned for the *Son's* undertaking the suretiship than the holy good pleasure of the adorable Trinity.
But when it is revealed to us, it is our duty to observe, and
proclaim, the wisdom and goodness of God in this constitution.

XVIII. Did not God most wisely order, that he who created man should restore, and as it were, create him a-new?
That he who is the personal Word of God, who commanded
light to shine out of darkness, and by whom all things were
made, John i. 3. should be that great publisher of the word of
the gospel, whereby God shines in the hearts of the elect,
and new creatures, not yet existing, are effectually called, and
by that call brought, as it were, into being: further, as the
second person alone is the Son, and our salvation consists in

adoption, was it not proper, that the Son of God should become the son of man, that having obtained a right of adoption
by him, we might be made his brethren and co-heirs? Moreover, let it be observed, that the Son alone is called "the
image of the Father," Col. i. 15. Heb. i. 3. and by way of
eminence, "the beloved of the Father," Mat. iii. 17. Col. i. 13.
Seeing man therefore had, by sin, shamefully defaced the image
of God, which he received in the first creation ; and thereby
most justly exposed himself to the hatred of God: was it not
worthy of God to restore that image by his own essential
image, in the human nature he had assumed ; in order by that
means, to open a way for our return to the favour and love of
the Father? In fine, could the philanthropy and love of the
Father, be more illustriously displayed to us, than in giving
his only begotten Son to us and for us, that in him we might
behold the Father's glory? Christ himself lays this before us,
John iii. 16.

XIX. The last condition requisite in the Surety is, that he
should be God-man ; " God and man, at the same time, in
unity of person: one mediator between God and man," 1 Tim.
ii. 5. For as it was necessary he should be *man*, and also
God, and *one* Surety ; it was necessary he should be both these
in unity of person, " God manifested in the flesh," 1 Tim. iii.
16. " The Word made flesh," John i. 14. " Of the seed of
David according to the flesh," in such a manner, as at the same
time to be " the Son of God with power," Rom. i. 3, 4.
Which may be further made appear.

XX. Had he been God only he could neither have been subject, nor have obeyed, nor suffered : if mere man, his obedience, subjection, and suffering, would not have been of sufficient value for the redemption of the elect. Nay, a mere
creature is so bound to fulfil all righteousness for itself, that
its righteousness cannot be imputed and imparted to others :
and should we suppose a man truly and perfectly holy, but
yet a mere man, who, according to the law of love, offered
himself even to die for his brother, he himself would doubtless obtain a reward by his righteousness ; but could merit
nothing for a guilty person, unless perhaps exemption from
punishment at most. And therefore it behoved our Surety to
be man, that he might be capable to submit, obey, and suffer ;
and at the same time God, that the subjection, obedience, and
suffering, of this person God-man, might on account of his infinite dignity, be imputed to others, and be sufficient for saving
all, to whom it is imputed.

XXI. Moreover, a mere creature could not support under

the load of divine wrath, so as to remove it, and rise again, when he had done; " who knoweth the power of thine anger; even according to thy fear, so is thy wrath," Psal. xc. 11. see Nah. i. 6. It was therefore necessary for our Surety to be more than man, that by the infinite power of his Godhead, he might support the assumed human nature, and so be able to bear the fierceness of divine wrath, and conquer every kind of death.

XXII. I shall not conceal what is objected to this argument; namely, that God could have so supported the human nature, though not personally united to himself, by his divine power, as to have rendered it capable to endure and conquer all manner of sorrows. I dare not refuse this. But yet that would not be sufficient in the present case. Because, by that hypothesis, it would be God himself, by the Surety, who would have vanquished his enemies. But it is necessary, that our Surety should do this by his own power, that " his own arm should bring salvation unto him," Isa. lxiii. 5. and therefore be " the mighty one of Jacob," Isa. lx. 16. " the mighty God," Isa. ix. himself " stronger than the strong man," Luke xi. 21, 22. " having life in himself," John v. 26. and " having power to take his life again," John x. 18. To which is required " the exceeding greatness of his power," Eph. i. 19. and so should " be declared to be the Son of God with power," Rom. i. 4.

XXIII. These are the tremendous mysteries of our religion, " which were kept secret since the world began, but are now made manifest, and by the scriptures of the Prophets, according to the commandment of the everlasting God, made known to all nations for the obedience of faith," Rom. xvi. 25, 26. From hence, the divinity of the Christian religion appears with evidence. What penetration of men or angels was capable of devising things so mysterious, so sublime, and so far surpassing the capacity of all created beings? How adorable do the wisdom and justice, the holiness, the truth, the goodness, and the philanthropy of God, display themselves in contriving, giving, and perfecting this means of our salvation? How calmly does conscience, overwhelmed with the burden of its sins, acquiesce in such a Surety, and in such a suretiship; when here at length, apprised of a method of reconciliation, both worthy of God, and safe for man? Who, on contemplating these things in the light of the Spirit, would not break out into the praises of the most holy, the most righteous, the most true, the most gracious, and the most high God? O! the depth of the wisdom and knowledge of

God! O the height of mysteries, which angels desire to look into! Glory to the Father, who raised up, accepted, and gave us such a Surety! Glory to the Son, who clothing himself in human flesh, so willingly, so patiently, and so constantly performed such an engagement for us. Glory to the Holy Ghost, the revealer, the witness, and the earnest of so great happiness for us. All hail! O Christ Jesus, true and eternal God, and true and holy man, all in one, who retains the properties of both natures in the unity of thy person. Thee we acknowledge, thee we worship, to thee we betake ourselves, at thy feet we fall down, from thy hand alone we look for salvation. Thou art the only Saviour; we desire to be thy peculiar property, we are so by thy grace, and shall remain such for ever. Let the whole world of thine elect, with us, know, acknowledge, and adore thee, and thus at length be saved by thee. This is the sum of our faith, and hope, and this the top of all our wishes. *Amen.*

CHAP. V.

Of the Suretiship and Satisfaction of Christ.

I. Having thus spoken of the person of the Surety, so far as the nature of our design requires, now is the time and place to treat a little more accurately of the satisfaction itself, which, by his suretiship he undertook to give. For he is called the Surety of the Covenant, or Testament, Heb. vii. 22. Not only, nor principally, because he engaged to us in the name of God, to fulfil the promises contained in that testament if we obeyed his commands, as Curcellœus, treading in the footsteps of his master Socinus, artfully pretends: but, because he engaged to God for us, to perform all those conditions in our stead; upon which we were to receive the testamentary inheritance. When Hezekiah desired the saving fruit of this suretiship, he prayed, Isa. xxxviii. 14. " I am oppressed, undertake for me." And God himself, when he gives to his Son all the glory of this suretiship, expresses himself thus: Jer. xxx. 21. " for who is this that engaged his heart to approach unto me? saith the Lord." That is, what mortal, nay, what creature dares engage to perform all those things which are incumbent on the priest, who shall have a right to approach to me for himself and his people. Our surety therefore, thus engaged to God for us. To what purpose is such a surety, who should only engage to us in

the name of God ? If Christ be a mere man, such as they represent him, could his engagement give us a greater assurance
of the truth of the divine promises, than if we heard them
immediately from the mouth of God himself? Was it not
necessary that God, who cannot lie, should first of all engage
to us, that the man Christ would be true in all his sayings,
before we could with sure confidence rely upon them ? Is it
not much better and more safe, to rely upon the oath of the
infallible God, by which he has *abundantly confirmed to the
heirs of promise, the immutability of his counsel,* Heb. vi. 17.
than on the declaration of a mere man, let him be ever so true
and faithful ? And what peculiar excellency would Christ
have had above others in this case, to the honour of being the
alone Surety, had he only, by the publication of a saving doctrine, which he confirmed by his martyrdom, assured us of
the certainty of the promises of grace : seeing the other prophets and apostles of Christ did the very same, not scrupling
to undergo the most cruel death, in order to seal with their
blood the truth of God's promises, which they had declared ?
What can vilify Christ, or make void his suretiship, if this
does not ?

II. Christ therefore is called our Surety, because he engaged
to God to make SATISFACTION FOR US. Which satisfaction
again is not to be understood in the Socinian sense, as if it only
consisted in this, that Christ most perfectly fulfilled the will of
God, and fully executed every thing God enjoined him, on
account of our salvation, and so in the fullest manner satisfied
God, and that for us, that is, *on our account,* for our highest
and eternal *good :* as Crellius, when making the greatest concessions, would fain put us off with these fair words : but it consists in this, that Christ, in *our room* and stead, did both by
doing and suffering, satisfy divine justice, both the legislatory,
the retributive, and vindictive, in the most perfect manner, fulfilling all the righteousness of the law, which the law otherwise
required of us, in order to impunity, and to our having a right
to eternal life. If Christ did this, as we are immediately to
shew he did, nothing hinders why we may not affirm, he satisfied for us in the fullest sense of the word. For to what purpose is it superciliously to reject a term so commodious, because
not to be met with on this subject in scripture, if we can prove
the thing signified by it ?

III. We find his engaging to make this satisfaction, Psal.
xl. 6, 7, 8. expressed in these words by Christ : " Sacrifice
and offering thou didst not desire, mine ears hast thou opened : burnt-offering and sin-offering thou hast not required.

Then said I, Lo! I come: in the volume of the book it is
written of me: I delight to do thy will, O my God; yea, thy
law is within my bowels or heart." Where observe, 1st.
The covenant between the Lord Christ and the Father, by
virtue of which Christ calls the Father his God. 2dly. That
Christ freely, and of his own accord, entered into this covenant with the Father; since he compares himself to a servant,
whose ears were bored or digged through, in order voluntarily to serve his beloved Lord. 3dly. That by virtue of
this covenant, Christ presented himself to do the acceptable
will of his God. 4thly. That that will was expressed by a
law, which Christ has within his bowels or heart, which he
loves from his soul, and is to keep with all his heart. 5thly.
That that law requires, not only perfect righteousness, in order to obtain a right to eternal life, but also deserved punishment to be inflicted on the sinner. For all this was signified
by the sacrifices, gifts, burnt-offerings, and sin-offerings, of the
law. For when the sinner offered to God beasts or corn,
which were given to himself for food, and was careful to have
them consumed by fire, as it were in his own room, he thereby confessed that, on account of his sin, he deserved the most
dreadful destruction, and even the eternal flames of hell.
6thly. That these external ceremonies of sacrifice could never,
without a respect to the thing signified, please God, nor
purge the conscience from dead works: therefore, Christ offered himself, in order to accomplish that will of God, by which
we are sanctified, Heb. x. 10. both by fulfilling all the righteousness prescribed by the law, and by undergoing the guilt
of our sins, that he might atone for them as an expiatory sacrifice. All these things are contained in the suretiship of Christ
described by David.

IV. Christ could, without any injury, undertake such a
suretiship; 1st. Because he was the lord of his own life,
which, on account of his power over it, he could engage to
lay down for others, John x. 18. *I have power to lay it
down.* 2dly. Because being God-man in one person, he was
able to perform what he undertook, by enduring condign
punishment, by fulfilling all righteousness, and in both, performing an obedience of such value as to be more than equivalent to the obedience of all the elect. 3dly. Because by
that means, he gave an instance of an extraordinary and incomprehensible degree of love, both to the glory of God and
the salvation of men. 4thly. Nor has his human nature any
reason to complain, because a creature could have no greater
glory than to be hypostatically united with a divine person,

and be subservient to him for accomplishing the greatest work, which the whole choir of elect angels will with astonishment celebrate through eternity; especially seeing it was assured, that after its sufferings, which were indeed the greatest that could be, yet of a short duration, that which was *made a little lower than the angels*, should obtain a name above every name.

V. It was also worthy of God the Father, both to procure and accept of this suretiship of his Son; because in the execution of it, there is a manifestation of *the truth* of God, exactly fulfilling every thing he had promised in his law to his justice, and had threatened against sin; and of *the goodness* of God, reconciling to himself sinful and wretched man, on giving and admitting a proper Mediator; and of the justice of God, not clearing the guilty, without a sufficient satisfaction; nay, accepting a far more excellent satisfaction, than could ever be given by man himself, because of the more excellent obedience of Christ, and his more meritorious sufferings, Rom. iii. 25. and of *the holiness* of God, not admitting man unto a blessed communion with himself, unless justified by the blood, and sanctified by the Spirit of Christ; in fine, of *the all-sufficiency* of God, who, as what seemed almost a thing incredible, is, by this means, become, without any diminution to his perfections, the God and salvation of the sinner. Hence it is, that the Lord Jesus, in the execution of his undertaking, professes, he manifested *the name*, that is, the perfections of God, John xvii. 6. particularly those we have just now mentioned, Psal. lx. 10. " I have not hid thy righteousness within my heart, I have declared thy FAITHFULNESS and thy SALVATION : I have not concealed thy LOVING KINDNESS, and thy TRUTH, from the great congregation." As then nothing can be thought more worthy of God, than the manifesting in the most illustrious manner, the glory of the divine perfections, and these perfections shine forth no where with greater lustre, than in the satisfaction of Christ, it was altogether worthy of God to procure and admit his undertaking such a satisfaction.

VI. Nor by the admission of such suretiship is there any abrogation of, or derogation to the divine law; as little any contradiction of, or substitution of another, but only a favourable construction put upon it, because the law, as it stood, but only taken in a favourable sense, was most fully satisfied by the Redeemer, who was in the closest union with us, when he paid the due ransom. Whence the apostle said, Rom. viii. 4. *the righteousness of the law* was fulfilled by Christ. We shall not improperly conceive of the whole, in the following manner: the law declares, there is no admission for any to eternal life, but on the account of a most perfect and complete righteousness; also, that every sinner shall undergo the penalty of death, and be under its dominion for ever. However, it is a doubtful matter, not explained by the law, whether that perfect righteousness must necessarily be performed by the very person to be saved, or, whether a surety may be admitted, who shall perform it in his room. Again, it is doubtful, whether it was necessary the sinner should, in his own person, undergo the deserved punishment, or whether he could truly undergo it in the person of a sponsor. In fine, it is a matter of doubt, whether he who was to undergo the penalty, ought to do so to an infinite degree, with respect to duration, or whether, that dominion of death could be abolished by the sufficient dignity and worth of the person who should undergo it, and so death be swallowed up in victory: strict justice would, as the words seem to import, at first view, demand the former; but the favourable construction, which, according to Aristotle, Ethic. lib. v. c. 10. *is an amendment of the law, where it is deficient, on account of its universality,* admits of the latter, where it can be obtained; as really was, and is the case with Christ and Christians. Thus therefore, that in which the law seemed to be defective from its universality, comes to be corrected; not as to the intention of God the lawgiver, which is altogether invariable, and always most perfect; but as to the express form of the words: almost in the same manner, as if a father should be admitted to pay an equivalent fine for his son, and instead of silver, make payment in gold. This would be a favourable interpretation of the law.

VII. Nor was it unjust for Christ to be punished for us: seeing Socinus himself and Crellius own, that the most grievous torments, nay, death itself, might be inflicted on Christ, though most innocent; which also appears from the event. For God, in right of his dominion, could lay all those afflictions on Christ; especially with the effectual consent of the Lord Jesus himself, who had power over his own life. The whole difficulty lies in the formality of the punishment. But as Christ, most willingly took upon himself our transgressions, and the trespasses we had committed against the divine majesty, and offered himself as a surety for them; God, as the supreme governor could justly exact punishment of Christ in our room, and actually did so. And thus *the chastisement of our peace,* that *exemplary punishment* inflicted on Christ, in which God by the brightest example, shewed his implacable hatred to sin, " was upon him," Isa. liii. 5. who

brought pardon and peace unto us.   For מוסר *was upon him,*
here is that *exemplary punishment*, in which God's wrath
against sin is discovered, which is well adapted to deter others
from it.   Thus Jer. xxx. 14. *the punishment of a cruel one,*
and Prov. vii. 22. *the exemplary punishment of a fool,* and
Ezek. v. 15. *so shall it be a reproach and a taunt, an instruction* (example) and an *astonishment.*

VIII. But we certainly take too much upon us, when we
presume to examine the equity of the divine government, by
the standard of our reason : when the fact is plain, we are
always to vindicate God against the sophistry of our foolish
reasonings.   That man is certainly the author of a monstrous,
horrible, and detestable heresy, and discovers a profane arrogance, who like Socinus, is not ashamed to write as follows :
*As for my part, indeed, though such a thing should be found
not once, but frequently, in the sacred records, I would not
on that account believe it to be so.*   But modesty should teach
us rather to say ; ' That truly for my part, though my rea-
' son, which I know is blind and foolish, and apt to be cla-
' morous against God, should a thousand times gain-say it, I
' would not therefore presume to call in question, what I
' find but once in the sacred records ; or, by seeking some other
' interpretation, would I force on the words of scripture, any
' meaning more consonant to my reason.'   When therefore we
shall have proved from holy writ, that the Lord Christ has
made satisfaction to the justice of God, and consequently, that
there is no injustice in it : according to the maxim, which nature itself dictates, that all the ways of God are righteousness
and truth.

IX. No Christian questions that Christ fulfilled all righteousness.   The multitude of the Jews, Mark vii. 37. testified concerning him, *he hath done all things well.*   And he
declared this truly, as he did every thing else, concerning himself, " for, I do those things that please him," John viii. 29.
And hence he boldly appealed to his enemies, v. 46. " which
of you convinceth me of sin ?"   Nay, even to his Father himself, Psal. xcix. 5. " O God, thou knowest my foolishness,
and my sins are not hid from thee :" for I suppose this Psalm
contains a prayer of the Lord Christ, as appears from several
parts of it being often quoted in the New Testament.   And
these words, I think, contain a protestation of the Lord Jesus
to his Father of his own innocence ; of which *Theodorus in
Catena,* has given no improper paraphrase : " whether I have
been guilty of any fault against them, thou thyself knowest,
and art my witness, I have done nothing."   But I think the

meaning may be more fully expressed thus: it is true my
God, I have taken guilt upon me, and am made a curse; but
thou knowest all my sins, even to the slightest offence, for
which I suffer; that in all there is not the least fault of mine,
by which I have violated thy law, so as to *restore what I have
taken.* The truth of this protestation the Father attests, when
Isa. liii. 2. he calls Christ his *righteous servant,* and *justified him in the Spirit,* 1 Tim. iii. 16. declaring that as man he
was innocent of every crime falsely laid to his charge; on the
contrary, he honoured his Father by his perfect obedience; and
as Mediator so diligently executed his office, that he was deficient in nothing.

X. It is also allowed that the most holy obedience of Christ
was for our good: because therein we have, 1st. A confirmation of his heavenly doctrine; the works of his most perfect
holiness, no less than his miracles, being a demonstration that
he was a preacher of divine truth sent down from heaven.
2dly. A living law and most perfect pattern of holiness, worthy both of God and of the children of God, of which we
had an exact delineation in the written law; but its shining
forth in its lively image and native light in Christ and his actions, is fitted to stir up every man to love it, who beholds it
with a spiritual eye. Mankind wanted this even to discern
the unspotted image of the divine holiness in one of their
brethren; which at length they obtained in Christ, who " left
us an example that we should follow his steps," 1 Pet. ii. 21.
3dly. A pointing out of the way to heaven: Christ teaching us
not only by his words, but his actions, that " without holiness
no one shall see the Lord," Heb. xii. 14.

XI. But we must proceed a step further, and affirm, that
the obedience of Christ was accomplished by him *in our room,*
in order thereby to obtain for us a right to eternal life. The
law, which God will have secured inviolable, admits none to
glory, but on condition of perfect obedience, which none was
ever possessed of but Christ, who bestows it freely on his own
people. This is what the apostle declares, Rom. v. 16. " but
the free gift of Jesus Christ is of many offences unto justification:" though we want those works, for which the reward
may be due: nay, though for so many sins, we may have deserved an eternal curse; nevertheless there is something sufficient, not only for abolishing many offences, but likewise to
be the meritorious cause of righteousness; namely, the obedience of one; and it becomes ours by gratuitous gift. More
clearly still, verse 19. " for as by one man's disobedience many
were made [constituted] sinners, so by the obedience of one

shall many be made [constituted] righteous." The *former one man* was *Adam*, the root and federal head of mankind. By his disobedience, all mankind, as belonging to him, were involved in the guilt of the curse: and as he sustained the person of all, what he did amiss, is accounted as done by all. *The other* is *the one man* Christ, who neither sinned in, and with Adam, nor had the dominion of sin and death passed upon him, and who is worthy to be both lord and head, a second Adam, and the origin and source of the inheritance to be devolved on his brethren. He is possessed of an *obedience*, even to the whole law of God, which enjoined him to have a perfect love for the glory of his Father, and for the salvation of his brethren. By that obedience the collective body of those who belong to him *are constituted righteous ;* that is, are judged to have a right to eternal life, no less than if every one had performed that obedience in his own person.

XII. Nor should it be thought strange, that the obedience of Christ is sufficient to acquire to all a right to eternal life, even though it became him *as man* to yield obedience *for himself.* For we are here to consider *the dignity of the person* obeying; who being man in such a manner, as at the same time to be the eternal and infinite God, he is much more excellent than all the elect, taken together : and therefore his obedience is deservedly esteemed of such value as may be imputed to all, for obtaining a right to a blessed immortality. And although the divinity, in the abstract, did not obey, yet he who did is God; and thus the divinity of the person contributes very much to the dignity of the obedience. It is certain, that *as man,* he owed obedience *for himself,* but since he became man on our account, he also performed that obedience in our room. Moreover, as man he was not necessarily under the law, as *prescribing the condition of happiness ;* because if we set aside the consideration of the suretiship undertaken for us, he would have enjoyed all manner of happiness, from the first moment of his incarnation, on account of the union of the humanity with the Godhead, as we have more fully shewn, chap. iii. § XIII, XIV.

XIII. It would likewise be false to infer from this, that ' if Christ performed obedience for us, we ourselves are un- ' der no necessity of obeying; because no demand can be ' made on the principal debtor, for what the Surety has per- ' formed in his room.' Our obedience may be considered, either as it is *the duty* of the rational creature, with respect to his sovereign Lord; or as it is a condition of acquiring a right to eternal life : in the latter respect Christ accomplished it for us, and therefore under that relation, it neither is, nor can be required of us, as if for want of perfect obedience, we could be excluded from eternal life. But in the former respect, we by all means owe obedience, and the obligation to it rather increased than diminished by this instance of Christ's love. For what more proper than by this to shew our gratitude, and declare, not so much by words as actions, that we acknowledge him for our Lord, who has purchased us for himself? And in fine, that as adopted sons, we decline no obedience to our heavenly Father, whom his natural Son, and of the same substance with himself, so cheerfully obeyed.

XIV. But besides, Christ satisfied *the vindictive justice* of God, not only *for our good*, but also, *in our room*, by enduring those most dreadful sufferings, both in soul and body, which we had deserved, and from which he by undergoing them, did so deliver us, that they could not with the wrath and curse of God, as the proper punishment of our sin, be inflicted on us. If there is any point in our divinity accurately proved, and solidly defended against the exceptions of the Socinians, by illustrious persons in the church, it is certainly this ; which I choose not to repeat, desiring the reader to fetch the arguments from a Grotius, a Junius, a Turretine, a Hoornbeck, an Essenius, and the like renowned heroes ; which will baffle all the efforts of the adversaries properly to answer.

CHAP. VI.

What sufferings of Christ are satisfactory.

I. But it is really to be lamented, that in these our days, a new question should be started among the orthodox : namely, which of the sufferings of Christ ought to be deemed satisfactory in our room. There is one in particular, who seems to acknowledge none of the sufferings of Christ to be satisfactory for us, but those which Christ underwent during the three hours of the solar darkness, while he was upon the cross, and before he expired ; excluding from the number of satisfactory sufferings, that agony and horror which he endured in the garden of * Olivet the night in which he was apprehended, and that blood which he shed before, and when he was crucified, and after he expired on the cross. He had

---

* This was the garden of Gethsemane, which lay at the foot of the mount of Olives.

not, says he, commenced his satisfactory actions, when by a word he levelled his enemies with the ground, cured Malchus, and promised paradise to the thief: no expiation was yet made when an angel came to strengthen him. Nay, he affirms, that Christ did not suffer corporal death as our Surety, and in our room; and that consequently it belongs not to the satisfaction which he made to the justice of God, if indeed he then fully satisfied God when he died. But in case Christ should seem to have suffered all these things in vain, the learned person concludes, that they were done in order to satisfy the veracity of God, which had foretold that thus it *should* be, and to fulfil the types by which they were prefigured in the Old Testament; distinguishing, moreover, between *convincing* and *compensating* punishments, between *warlike* sufferings and *judiciary.* He calls those compensating and ·judiciary, which Christ endured during the three hours of darkness; the others only convincing and warlike sufferings; having this tendency, that Christ might learn to become a merciful High Priest.

II. But it will be worth while to trace the hypothesis of this very learned person from the foundation; which he has done himself very accurately, in a letter to a friend, published after the first and second editions of my work. For he maintains, 1st. That when God threatened man, if he sinned, with death, he meant that death which our first parents incurred on the very day they sinned, and which Christ the Surety underwent in the room and stead of some; and which the damned themselves, who are without a Surety, shall suffer and be forced to undergo for themselves. But that is *the death of the whole man;* because the subject of it is man, made up of soul and body united; and consists, not only in the privation of the sense of God's favour, and of communion with him, and of a joyful delight in the enjoyment of him; but it is also attended with all the torture and racking pain which the almighty wrath of God can inflict. 2dly. Our first parents underwent that death immediately upon their sin: for in the cool of the same day in which they sinned, when drawing towards the evening, they heard the voice of the Lord continually walking in the garden. It was not that articulate voice which Adam was before accustomed to hear, and was afterwards pleased with its sound: but such as was heard at Sinai, Exod. xix. 16, 17. and described Psal. xxix. and lxxvii. 18, 19. The voice of thunder and lightning, a token of God's powerful wrath, which the guilty creature could neither bear nor avoid, which made Adam and Eve hide themselves in the

thickest of the trees of the garden, just as the damned will desire to do, Rev. vi. 15. 3dly. While our first parents endured
this threatened death, satisfaction was made to the veracity of
God, but not to his justice, demanding a plenary and sufficient
compensation. But on account of the mediatorial covenant
between the Father and Son, there intervened the long-suffering of God, or a deferring of his wrath, which removed that
death from man, and deferred it to the day of wrath and the
last judgment. 4thly. Christ the Surety, in the fulness of
time, underwent this same death of the whole man, in soul
and body united, while on the cross he was forsaken of God,
and at the same time had the sensation of his most dreadful
wrath, who, while demanding payment of him, was pleased to
bruise him: a bruising not inflicted by men, but immediately
by God, who punished him with affliction and imprisonment,
which will be the punishment of the damned, as it was of
Christ, who is said to be מעֻנֶּה and עָצוּר afflicted and in prison,
Isa. liii. 4, 8. 5thly. Men were not able to behold this dreadful
part of his punishment; for a most horrid and outward darkness concealed Christ from every eye. His whole man suffered this death, till divine justice was satisfied; and it sufficiently appeared to have been satisfied, when God removed
the darkness, that the creature who had before acted as an
enemy against him, on whom God was taking vengeance,
might again refresh him, and when he likewise comforted
him with such a sense of his paternal love, as now to be
able to call God his Father, and commend his spirit into his
hands, &c. 6thly. Moreover he felt, and properly bore this
death on the cross, when he cried out, *My God! why hast
thou forsaken me?* He dreaded this death in the garden,
as he saw it coming upon him, and this therefore is called the
Antepassion; and he was delivered from it when he said, *It
is finished.* 7thly. The Mediator Christ was bound by his
covenant engagement to this alone, and neither to spiritual
death, which supposes a want of rectitude, nor to corporal
death. For when he was made known in the first gospel-
promise, Gen. iii. 15. no mention was yet made of corporal
death, till verse 19. He therefore could not be bound to
that by any vicarious title. The apostle tells us what his
corporal death was, Heb. x. 20. When the blood of the sacrifice was shed for sin, atonement was made: but in order to
present it to God, the priest carried the blood which procured
the atonement into the holy of holies, the vail, which denoted
separation by sin, being made to give way. In like manner
also, when Christ completed his death, or endured the whole

load of anguish and wrath, having obtained eternal redemption, which he testified by his saying, *It is finished*, he was to carry his blood, or soul, into the heavenly sanctuary. The vail standing in the way was his human nature, which, upon taking upon him the sins of the elect, kept him at a distance from God; but after satisfaction made, that vail was rent asunder, by the separation of soul and body, and conveyed his spirit by an open way to the presence of God. And thus *the corporal death* of Christ belongs not to the *meritorious*, (which may be done by the alone death of man, not separated with respect to his essential parts) but to the *representing satisfaction*. Thus far this learned person. And who can deny but these things are ingeniously devised, and learnedly connected? But whether they are as solid, as they are uncommon, I imagine I may, with the consent of the lovers of truth, modestly enquire.

III. I remember to have learned in the communion of the Reformed church to the following effect: 1st. That the death wherewith God threatened man for sin, comprises in its whole extent all that misery which, by the justest displeasure of God, has followed upon sin, and to which the sinner man is obnoxious all his life, and whose principal part consists in the want of the favour of God, and in the want of the keenest sense of the divine curse, to be chiefly inflicted when it shall so please God. 2dly. That Christ, by the interposition of his engagements for the elect, took upon himself all that curse which man was liable to on account of sin; hence it was, that in order to the payment of the debt he engaged for, he led a life in the assumed human nature, subject to many vicissitudes of misery, just like the life of a human sinner. 3dly. That as God uses much forbearance with respect to sinners, and moderates the bitterness of life with some sweetness of patience till the day of vengeance, and of the retribution of his righteous judgment, when the whole weight of the curse shall light upon the condemned sinner; so also Christ, when in the form of a servant, had not always a sense of the painful effects of the sins that were laid upon him, but sometimes rejoiced in an eminent mixture of favour; till the hour and power of darkness came, when being called to the bar, he had every thing dreadful to undergo. 4thly. That as the death which consists in the separation of soul and body, is inflicted on the sinner man as the sad effect of the wrath of God; so in like manner Christ underwent the same death, that in this respect also, making satisfaction to divine justice, he might remove all the curse of that death from the elect.

5thly. In fine, that as all those miseries taken together, are what sin deserves, so Christ, who by his engagement took upon himself all the debt of the elect, did by all these miseries, to which he was subject all his life, satisfy divine justice; so that taken all together, they constitute the ransom which was due for our sins. This, if I mistake not, is the common opinion of our divines, which our Catechism has also expressed, *quest. 37.*; namely, that all the sufferings which Christ endured both in soul and body through the whole course of his life, constitute his one and perfect satisfaction; though it be certain, that those were the most grievous sufferings with which he encountered on the last night and day; and that what he bore in his body, were far exceeded by those that oppressed his soul: just as the whole of Christ's most holy obedience is imputed to us for righteousness, though he gave an evident demonstration of it, when he was obedient to his Father *to the death, even the death of the cross;* which consisted in a voluntary submission of soul, rather than in any thing he endured in the members of the body, directed by his holy soul. Which we prove from scripture in the following manner:

IV. 1st. When the scripture speaks of the satisfaction of Christ, it ascribes it to the sufferings of Christ in general, as Isa. liii. 4. " surely he hath borne our griefs and carried our sorrows;" that is, he hath suffered all the pains and sorrows due to us for sin: and that not only for our good, but in our stead. For, ver. 5. " He was wounded for our transgressions, he was bruised for our iniquities;" so that these sins were the meritorious cause of the griefs and anguish of Christ; because the Lord " made them to light, or rush upon him," v. 6. and for these " he was afflicted," ver. 7. when *the iniquity was exacted* by God, as judge and avenger. But that affliction even then lay upon him, and our iniquity was exacted of him, when he was *brought as a lamb to the slaughter, and as a sheep before her shearers, was dumb:* which certainly happened before the three hours of darkness, ver. 7. He therefore gives too great scope to his fancy, who restrains the things which are affirmed of the afflictions, griefs, and anguish of Christ in general, to the three hours' sufferings.

V. Add what the apostle writes, Heb. ii. 10. " for it became him to make the Captain of their salvation perfect (to consecrate) through sufferings." So that those sufferings, which Christ endured, (and who shall pretend to except any, the apostle speaking in such general terms?) were requisite in order to Christ's being a perfect Saviour to us, and a sacrifice consecrated and acceptable to God: for this the τελείωσις or *perfecting* of Christ, signifies, the performing of all those things to which he bound himself by his suretiship, and especially of those required to the full accomplishment of his sacerdotal expiation. And the apostle applies the sufferings of Christ to this perfecting, or consecrating. Whence Chrysostom concludes well: "Wherefore the sufferings are the perfecting, and the cause of salvation." Nay, the sacred writer had here in view all those sufferings, "by which he learned obedience; for being made perfect by them, he became the author of eternal salvation unto all them that obey him," Heb. v. 8, 9. But he learned obedience not only by his three hours sufferings, but in general by all his suffering; from which he learned and experienced the full extent of that obedience, to which he voluntarily submitted: nay, indeed, he principally learned obedience from his foregoing sufferings, for by these, as by certain principles, he was trained up to undergo those that were extremely painful. And thus the cause of our salvation is ascribed to all the sufferings which Christ endured in the days of his flesh.

VI. Peter, 1 Pet. ii. 21. speaks the same language; "Christ suffered for us." *To suffer* here denotes to be in affliction; for all those sufferings are here intended, in which Christ has left us an example of patience. These sufferings he affirms to be for us, that is, undergone as well in our stead, as for our good. For this is ordinarily the signification of the word ὑπερ: as in Euripides in Alceste, μη θυησχ᾽ ὑπερ τᵹ δ᾽ ανδρύς, ᾿δ᾿ εγὼ πρό σᾶ *die not for this man, as little shall I for thee;* which is to be understood in no other sense, but that of substitution; as the subject of the tragedy, exhibiting the wife dying in the room of her husband, plainly shews. In the same manner, Demosthenes in Corona, says, ερῶἶησον τέτᵹς, μᾶλλον δὲ εγὼ τᵹθ᾿ ὑπερ σᾶ ποιήσω, *ask these, or rather I shall do it for you.* And that this is the true meaning of Peter, we conclude hence, that in chap. iii. 18. he says, Christ suffered *for sins;* namely, that he might be *the propitiation for our sins,* 1 John iv. 10. But the sufferings which Christ underwent in our room, I imagine, may be said to be satisfactory.

VII. In fine, as *the likeness of sinful flesh,* or the sorrowful and contemptible condition of Christ, runs parallel with the whole course of his life, and he took it upon him *for sin;* so that God did therefore *condemn sin,* and declare it had no manner of right over believers, either to condemn them, or reign over them, Rom. viii. 3. it is manifest, that the scripture ascribes the satisfaction of Christ to the whole of his humiliation; consequently they do not take the scriptures for their guide, who confine it to the sufferings only of those three hours.

.VIII. 2dly. The scriptures so expressly declare, that Christ's death, even his corporal death, is to be esteemed a part of his satisfaction, that it is astonishing how any one could deny it. Thus Isa. liii. 10. " when thou shalt make his soul (when his soul shall make itself) an offering for sin;" which Christ himself, Matt. xx. 28. calls, to give his life a ransom for many, and he says, John x. 15. I lay down my life for the sheep. But to give his life, is to die a corporal death, which the resurrection puts an end to. For, thus Christ explains it, v. 17. I lay down my life, that I may take it again. And John says, chap. xix. 30. when describing the corporal death of Christ, he gave up the ghost. The argument will still be stronger, if we consider, that here an allusion is made to that typical satisfaction, which was effected by shedding the blood of the victim, so separated from the body, as to be accompanied with death. But the blood is given for the life. And therefore, a true satisfaction was made by the separation of the soul from the body of Christ, in order to keep up the resemblance between the type and antitype.

IX. Add what Paul writes, Heb. x. 20. *by a new and living way, which he hath consecrated for us through the vail, that is to say, his flesh;* the flesh of Christ was doubtless the vail which hindered our access. For, while it still continued entire, it was an indication that sin was not yet abolished, nor the curse removed. It was therefore necessary, that the vail or flesh of Christ should be rent, which was done, when the spirit quitted the flesh: for then the body ceasing to be a system of organs, became a heap of dusty particles, soon to return to dust, unless a speedy resurrection prevented it. And thus a new way was consecrated for us, that is, complete liberty purchased, and full right to the heavenly sanctuary. This was signified and sealed by that rending of the vail in the temple, at the very instant of Christ's death, Matt. xxvii. 51. Hence the body of Christ is said to be broken for us, 1 Cor. xi. 24. It is not improperly observed by the learned person, that, upon shedding the blood of the sacrifice, expiation was made, which was afterwards to be presented to God by bringing the blood into the holy of holies. But I wish he would consider, what I have just hinted, the separation of the soul of Christ from the body answered to the shed-

ding of the blood, which is the rending of the vail, and breaking of the body; as the bringing the soul into heaven, to
present to God the satisfaction made by death, answers to the
introduction of the blood into the holy of holies.

X. And what is more evident than that passage, 1 Pet. iii.
18. *Christ hath suffered once for sins, being put to death in
the flesh;* that is, in the body: where the death of the body
is set forth as a part of those sufferings, which Christ endured
for sins, and Col. i. 21, 22. " he hath reconciled you in the
body of his flesh through death;" Rom. v. 10. " We were
reconciled to God by the death of his Son;" Heb. ix. 15.
" that by means of death for the redemption of the transgressions that were under the first testament, they which are called
might receive the promise of eternal inheritance." And what
death does Paul here mean? Doubtless that which must intervene for the confirmation of the testament, verse 16, 17. which
certainly is the death of the body, Rom. viii. 34. " Who is he
that condemneth? It is Christ that died." To explain all this
in such a manner as by death not to understand what in every
language, the death of a man signifies, namely, the separation
of soul and body, is harsh and unreasonable.

XI. 3dly. Besides, both Isaiah and Peter affirm, that our
healing is in a more especial manner, owing to the stripes of
Christ, as a part of his sufferings, Isa. liii. 5. 1 Pet. ii. 24.
while they say, " By, or with his stripes we are healed." For
by that cruel scourging, whereby the whole body of the Lord
Jesus was so mangled, as in a manner to become one continued stripe, together with his other sufferings, he merited, that
we should be delivered from the sufferings of Satan, and the
strokes of divine vengeance. And when we farther contemplate the sufferings of Christ, and among them that cruel
scourging, whereby the Lord Jesus was made a spectacle to
men and angels, we then understand what the holiness of God
is, what God requires in order to the remission of sins, what
the sinner must undergo if he would make satisfaction to God
and to his holiness, what a dreadful thing sin is, and how
much, in fine, we are indebted to Christ for enduring so much
for us. And this healing from sin is ours, if we dread the
wrath of God, are in love with his holiness, and make returns
of love to Christ. And thus it appears, though we say we
are healed by the stripes of Christ as by an example, yet there
is in the scourging of Christ a demonstration of the justice of
God, that we may know it, and by knowing it with due affection, be restored to the likeness of God. In these stripes

there is " an exemplary punishment bringing peace to us :" as we lately shewed that word imports.

XII. 4thly. Nothing can appear more absurd than to exclude from the satisfactory sufferings of Christ, by way of eminence, that sorrow of his soul, that great trouble and heaviness, that horror and amazement, that exceeding great sorrow, even unto death, those clots of bloody sweat, those prayers and supplications, with tears and strong cries, the result of all this agony ; which the Holy Ghost so circumstantially describes. This exceeding trouble and agony did not arise only from the sympathy of the soul with the body, nor from the mere horror of impending death ; it was something else that afflicted the soul of Christ, namely, his bearing the sins, not of one, but of all the elect; he had beheld the awful tribunal of God, before which he was presently to appear, in order to pay what he took not away ; he saw the Judge himself, armed with all the terrors of his incomprehensible vengeance, the law brandishing all the thunders of its curses, the devil, and all the powers of darkness, with all the gates of hell just ready to pour in upon his soul: in a word, he saw justice itself, in all its inexorable rigour, to which he was now to make full satisfaction ; he saw the face of his dearest Father, without darting a single ray of favour upon him, but rather burning with hot jealousy in all the terrors of his wrath against the sins of mankind, which he had undertaken to atone for. And whithersoever he turned, not the least glimpse of relief appeared for him, either in heaven or on earth, till with resolution and constancy he had acquitted himself in the combat. These, these are the things, which, not without reason, struck Christ with terror and amazement, and forced from him his groans, his sighs, and his tears. And if all this was not for the expiation and satisfaction for our sins, what reason can be assigned, why the other sufferings of Christ, within the three hours of darkness, should be accounted so ?

XIII. He certainly forms too slender a judgment of them, who affirms, that those horrors, and this anguish, were, in comparison of the more grievous tortures, which Christ endured on the cross itself, only to be deemed an *antepassion*, or a kind of prelibation or foretaste. But neither do the scriptures which represent these things with such a flow of words, nor our expositors on Heb. v. 7. speak in this manner, though a certain person perverts their words to that purpose. And it would be difficult to point out what the soul of Christ endured on the cross itself, which could so vastly exceed these horrors. There he complained of sorrow, here he was not silent; there he bore the curse due to us, here he almost sunk under it; there he complained of being forsaken of his Father, here he almost fainted away, on taking the most bitter cup of wrath: nay, greater signs of consternation could scarce be observed on the cross, than what appeared here. We shall presently reply to what we read about the comforting angel. It must indeed have been an exceeding great distress, at the first onset of which, resolution and constancy itself began to be " amazed, in heaviness, and exceeding sorrowful even unto death;" that made him offer prayers and supplications to him who could preserve him from death, with strong cries and tears; that made him struggle with so much agony, as rendered the appearance of a comforting angel necessary, and made his sweat trickle down his body, like clots of blood falling to the ground: this discovered a commotion of the spirits and blood, as we scarce, if ever, meet with a similar instance in history. Let us therefore beware that we take not upon us with too much confidence to determine, what sufferings of Christ, and in what degree some were more grievous than others: let us rather prize all of them, and acknowledge their proper weight and satisfactory value. This is far more suitable to the glory of Christ, and to the sincerity of our faith.

XIV. 5thly. and lastly, Christ endured all those sufferings, either as a Surety, or in some other respect. If as a Surety, then we have what we plead for; for he engaged to satisfy divine justice, not only for our good, but in our room, by undergoing the punishment of our sins, the guilt of which he voluntarily took upon himself. This is a fundamental point among the orthodox; nor will the learned person whose opinion we have taken in pieces deny it. If we seclude the consideration of a suretiship, Christ can be no otherwise considered than as innocent and perfectly holy. But it does not seem to be very consistent with the justice of God, that an innocent person, as such, should be punished to the shedding of his blood, to cruel and inexpressible agony of soul; in a word, to death itself. Or, should God at any time be pleased to expose an innocent creature to such dreadful tortures, in order to shew his incontestible authority, it is not likely he would choose to give such a proof of it in the person of his only beloved Son, who fully acknowledges the right or authority of the Father. And then, of what use were those sufferings of Christ, if not undergone in our room? was it in order to confirm his doctrine; or to give a pattern of patience, and shew us the way by which through straits and difficulties we might reach to things noble and divine? or was it that being

made a merciful high priest, he might readily afford assistance
to the tempted? or was it to fulfil the truth of the prophecies,
and answer the signification of the types? But all these particulars the blasphemous Socinus with his followers will easily
admit. And if we here stop short, we allow no greater value
to the sufferings of Christ than what has been done by these
worst perverters of our religion, and of the hope and consolation of believers.

XV. But the very learned person takes a far different
course, whose observations, which lately came to hand on
account of their late publication, deserve a particular hearing.
Seeing the sinner man, says he, was, according to what God
had threatened, become liable to death, till he had satisfied
divine justice, Gen. ii. 17. and was brought into that condition
by the devil, who conquered man, and thereby became his
lord, 2 Pet. ii. 19. under whose dominion and captivity man
afterwards lived. Now, in order to deliver, and perfectly
restore him, it was necessary, because he could do neither of
these things himself, both that another should undergo and
conquer for him the death which he deserved, and that another should rescue him from the power of the devil, and deliver him by force and military prowess. The former requires
a Surety, who, taking guilt upon himself in man's name, should
willingly and patiently undergo the just penalty from the
hands of the most righteous Judge to his full satisfaction. The
latter calls for a * redeemer, who by a just claim, may rescue
slaves out of the hands of an unjust tyrant, such as is he who
by fraud and violence acquires a dominion, and by opposition
and resistance injures the innocent. For both these purposes
God appointed his own Son, whom by an eternal covenant he
chose to the mediatorial office, and revealed in his word that
he should be the valiant conqueror of the serpent, and the deliverer of some men, Gen. iii. 15. also a vicarious Surety, and
afterwards a sacrifice, which was pointed out by clothing our
first parents with skins, verse 21. The sufferings of Christ
therefore are twofold; one *judicial*, which he endured as Surety,
justly on the part of God, for the debts of others, which
he had undertaken to pay, and which being done, a reconciliation is the consequence; the other *warlike*, which he endured
as deliverer, or redeemer, unjustly from the hands of his enemies, Satan and his instruments, because he will bring to sal-

---

* The word signifies an avenger, or deliverer; but the word rendered Redeemer
in scripture takes in all these.

vation those whom he redeems by his ransom. Both these kinds of sufferings belong to the perfecting of Christ.

XVI. In this discourse of the very learned person, every thing savours of learning, much also is genuine and solid, which I heartily approve. For it is certain, that Christ is not only our Surety, but also our deliverer; what merits our consideration here is only this, whether, when Christ by his judicial sufferings as Surety, fully satisfied divine justice, other sufferings are also requisite, by which, as Redeemer he might overcome Satan, and bring the redeemed to heaven by his ransom. To me the matter appears in this light; namely, as all the sufferings of men arise from the demerit of their sins, no matter, whether inflicted immediately by God, or by means of Satan and his instruments, Jer. ii. 15, 16, 17. so in like manner, all the sufferings of Christ arose from the demerit of our sins; and when he had satisfied divine justice for these, he merited for his own deliverance, not only from the wrath of God, but also from the tyranny of the devil; but in order to deliver his redeemed from these, there is no occasion for sufferings of another kind, but only for his power and authority. It is sufficient for this that he is the *mighty God*, Isa. ix. 6. *the mighty One of Jacob*, Isa. lx. 16. *stronger than the strong man*, Luke xi. 21, 22. I own Christ had to struggle with the devil, which he could not do without sufferings; but even this very thing was owing to the demerit of our sins. For when man had suffered himself to be overcome by Satan, and when God had by a just sentence delivered him up as a slave to his tyranny: it was necessary that Christ, as man's Surety, should be exposed to, and harassed by the devil, that in that respect also he might satisfy divine justice; nor could the devil and his instruments ever have been able to give any vexation to Christ, had he not been charged with the guilt of our crimes, and by God the most righteous Judge exposed to injuries from them, Acts ii. 23. But we are to speak more at large of this presently.

XVII. And thus we are come to the examination of those distinctions, by which the learned person explains and maintains his cause: namely, he distinguishes between *compensating* and *convincing punishments*, between *judicious* and *warlike sufferings*. The meaning of the distinctions, if I rightly take them, is this: *Compensating punishment* is that whereby satisfaction is made to divine justice, of which Rom. ii. 5, 6, 8, 9. and called *the wrath to come*, Matt. iii. 7. 1 Thess. i. 10. *Convincing punishment* is that which is only inflicted, in order thereby to convince man of his sin, though by undergoing it no satisfaction is

made to divine justice, nor any guilt removed, but still remains
to be further avenged. Such punishment the scriptures call
convictions of wrath, *furious rebukes*, Ezek. v. 15. of these it
is said, Psal. l. 21. *I will convince, reprove thee, and set them
in order before thine eyes.* Judiciary *sufferings* are those which
are inflicted by God as an impartial Judge, for a compensation,
or satisfaction to his justice, and in which there is wrath; and
thus they are the same with compensating punishments. *Warlike sufferings* are those to which Christ was exposed when
conflicting with the devil, who persecuted him immediately
upon his birth by means of Herod, afterwards tempted him in
the wilderness, and many ways reviled and mal-treated him by
the enraged ministers of his malice, according to what God says,
Gen. iii. 15. *And I will put enmity,* &c. In these, with respect
to Christ, there was no wrath of God; but rather tended to
grace and glory, as when one suffers for righteousness sake,
1 Pet. iv. 14.

XVIII. To this we reply as follows: No doubt, a distinction
is to be made between the calamities, whereby God brings believers and his elect, to the knowledge and sense of their sins,
and which spring from love, and are called Heb. xii. 6. *fatherly
chastisements;* and the calamities, which are inflicted on the wicked, who are under the wrath and curse of God. But to make
some of the punishments of the wicked only convincing, and others
compensating, has neither the countenance of scripture nor reason.

XIX. The scripture, indeed, speaks of *the wrath to come,*
which, doubtless, is compensating; but they also frequently
mention a present wrath and curse, Psal. lvi. 25. lix. 8. compare
2 Thess. ii. 16. John iii. 36. " the wrath of God abideth on
him." Wherefore unregenerate sinners are called, Eph. ii. 3.
τἐκνα ὁϱ ης *children of wrath,* not only because they are liable to
the wrath to come, but also on account of the wrath and curse
of God actually hanging over them, while they are not translated into the kingdom of his dear Son. " For the wrath of God
is revealed from heaven against all ungodliness and unrighteousness of men, Rom. i. 18. Which wrath of God against the
wicked, being very different from that with which he is said to
be angry against the sins of his own children, no reason can be
assigned why it may not be deemed compensating, as it is the
beginning of the eternal curse, from which it differs not in
essence, but only in degree.

XX. Add, that this present wrath is a judiciary punishment,
inflicted by the righteous sentence of God on the wicked. The
obstinate unbeliever ηδη κεχϱιται *is condemned already,* John iii.
18. God, in punishing the wicked in this life, *executes judg-*

ments in anger and in fury, Ezek. v. 15. As in Egypt, he
executed *great judgments*, Exod. vi. 6. and vii. 4. That all
may know, that *he is a God that judgeth in the earth*, Psal. lviii.
11. But why may not a judiciary punishment be also deemed
compensating ?

XXI. And then those punishments of the wicked, called in
scripture, *rebukes*, are sometimes so described, as that they must
be compensating. For what else is a compensating punishment, but the vengeance of an offended God on those that despise him, in order to manifest his hatred against them ? But
all this is contained in those convincing rebukes, which the
Lord denounces against the Philistines, Ezek. xxv. 17. *And I
will execute great* VENGEANCE *upon them with* FURIOUS RE-
BUKES ; *and they shall know that I am the Lord, when I shall
lay my* VENGEANCE *upon them.*

XXII. Convincing, or rebuking punishments are no less compensating. Who shall deny that it is a compensating punishment when God consumes the wicked in his fury ? For that, in
the highest degree, convinces them of their guilt. Psal. lix. 13.
" Consume them in wrath, consume them, that they may not
be ; and let them know, that God ruleth in Jacob, unto the
ends of the earth." And surely nothing can convince the wicked more of the heinousness of their sins, than a punishment
heightened to the greatest degree, as a compensating punishment is, and in which there is a most evident demonstration of
the wrath of God. Deservedly therefore we reject that distinction, which has not any foundation in scripture, and whose parts
are contrary to the rules of sound logic.

XXIII. But though we should admit that distinction in
general, how is it applicable to the sufferings of Christ ? Here,
I own, I do not fully understand the learned author's meaning.
To what purpose is this distinction of convincing and compensating punishments ? Is it, that as the punishments which the
wicked endure in this life, are only convincing, and a compensating punishment will at length be inflicted at the day of wrath
and judgment ; so also the sufferings which Christ underwent
during the whole time of his life, answer to those convincing
punishments, and the three hours sufferings, to the compensating
punishment ? But what necessity to exact convincing punishments of Christ, seeing he both perfectly owned, and voluntarily
confessed the guilt of those sins he had taken upon him, and
most willingly performed every thing by which he might expiate that guilt ? Was it perhaps with this view, that, from a
sight of the sufferings of Christ, believers might be convinced
of their sins ? But that cannot be done more effectually, than
when they consider them as punishments due to their sins, and

as a satisfaction for them. As therefore no punishments of
Christ can be said to be merely convincing, it remains, that all
of them are compensating or satisfactory : which is what we
contend for.

XXIV. The distinction between *judiciary* and *warlike sufferings* is no less impertinènt. For Christ incurred no sufferings but by the sentence of God, the Judge. When Christ *was
afflicted, the iniquity of us all* ונבן, *was exacted,* Isa. liii. 7.
But that was the exaction of the Judge. When Satan, with
his infernal powers, assaulted Christ, then was *the power of
darkness,* Luke xxii. 53. God, in consequence of a determinate sentence, permitted the prince of darkness to harass Christ.
And Christ, in preparing himself for that conflict, had in view
that sentence, or commandment of God, as he himself speaks
John xiv. 31.

XXV. What else is that very word of God, from which the
original of the warlike sufferings is derived, than the sentence
of God the Judge against the serpent, who was to be destroyed
by Christ, and against Christ's human nature, in which he trod
the earth, which was to be harassed and slain by the serpent ? I
would fain know, if what is foretold concerning the bruising of
his heel, does not also comprise those sufferings of Christ,.which
are judiciary. If not, the first gospel promise does not explain
the method of obtaining salvation by the satisfaction of a Mediator : and if the words contain an enigmatical summary of our
belief, we must then be obliged to believe that they signify less
than they can, or is proper that they should ; but if, as is certainly right, we allow that the satisfactory sufferings of Christ,
are comprehended in these words, it is wrong to build this new
distinction upon them.

XXVI. Let us dwell a little longer on this meditation. Whatever power the devil has to harass wicked men, before they
are dragged to eternal death, he has it by the righteous sentence
of the Judge ; * Peter mentions the consequence of this, 2 Pet.
ii. 19. The elect themselves as sinners, were also subject to
that power, and on that account are truly said to be not only the
prey of the mighty, but Isa. xlix. 24. are likewise called *lawful
captives,* he having a right over them by the sentence of the
supreme Judge. But as Jesus the Surety came in their room,
so in virtue of the same sentence, he became subject to the buf-

---

* The apostle, in the last quoted text, speaks nothing, as I apprehend, of Satan's
power, but only of the servants of corruption and of the bondage ; and therefore,
instead of saying what the author in his short way of expression, *which Peter has
expressed,* I have rendered it as above.

fetings of Satan. And by this means all he suffered from the devil, was in the most proper sense judiciary.

XXVII. It is no objection to this truth that those conflicts with Satan proved glorious to Christ, as having endured them, because of the justice and for advancing the glory of God. For all Christ's sufferings, even those which according to this new hypothesis, we shall call judiciary, if the cause and event be considered, were highly glorious to him. He never more gloriously displayed his love to God and man, he never undertook a more excellent work, which the whole choir of angels beheld with greater applause, and God the Father himself was never more pleased with it than when hanging on the cross, he resolutely struggled with the horrors of eternal death. But if we consider this thing as an evil, contrary to nature, which is earnestly bent upon its own advantage, certainly in these harassings of Satan, there was the wrath of God against sin, which Christ had taken upon himself.

XXVIII. And why should not those sufferings be called warlike, which according to this hypothesis are judiciary? For who will deny that Christ, when hanging on the cross, was as it were wrestling with the infernal powers, and the horrors of eternal death? Indeed Paul testifies that Christ had then " spoiled principalities and powers, made a shew of them openly, triumphing over them in the cross," Col. ii. 15. But who can refuse that there was first a conflict before such a noble triumph and victory? From all these things we conclude, that the distinction of punishments into convincing and compensating, and of sufferings into warlike and judiciary, is both unscriptural, antiscriptural, and irrational.

XXIX. Let us now come to the arguments of the opposite side, as far as they have come to our knowledge. Some of them are general against all the sufferings of Christ, and others more special against some parts of his sufferings. The general are partly taken from scripture, partly from the Apostle's Creed, and partly from the catechism.

XXX. From scripture they argue in the following manner : 1st. That the sin of the whole earth shall be removed in one day, according to Zech. iii. 9. And Paul several times affirms, that the one offering of Christ, once made on the cross, was that expiatory sacrifice, by which all the elect are perfected, Heb. ix. 28. and x. 10, 12, 14: and therefore the preceding sufferings of Christ were not satisfactory. 2dly. Further that Christ from the beginning of his life, was neither a priest who could offer an expiatory sacrifice, nor a sacrifice which could be offered. Not a priest, because he could not lawfully be one before the thirtieth year of his age : not a sacrifice, as a lamb could not be such before the seventh day. But the truth of the types ought to appear in Christ. 3dly. Moreover that Christ through the whole of his life, except for a few hours, was in the favour of God, Luke ii. 52. " increased in favour with God:" Matt. iii. 17. was declared to be the beloved Son of God, Matt. xvii. 2. was glorified in the mount : Luke x. 21. *rejoiced in spirit*. But at the time, in which he was in the favour of God and rejoiced, he did not bear the wrath of God.

XXXI. From the creed it is observed, that professing our faith concerning the satisfactory sufferings of Christ, we do not barely say, that he suffered, but that *he suffered under Pontius Pilate*, words never to be disjoined, to teach us, that only those sufferings were satisfactory which he endured under Pilate.

XXXII. From the [Heidelberg] catechism are quoted questions 31, 67, 70, 75, 80, where the impetration of our salvation is referred to the one offering of Christ, once made on the cross. But as to what is alleged to the contrary, from question 37. where it is said, that " for the whole time of his life which he lived upon earth, especially at the end thereof, he sustained the wrath of God against the sin of all mankind, both in body and soul ;" they answer, that to sustain the wrath of God there cannot signify to feel the wrath of God, but to be bound to endure it. They illustrate and prove this explication by question 84. where it is declared concerning unbelievers and hypocrites, that " the wrath of God and eternal damnation do lie on them so long as they go on in their sins :" which cannot be understood of a compensating punishment, unless we would suppose, that the wicked by suffering on earth, make satisfaction to divine justice, which is absurd. It therefore follows, that we explain this of their being obnoxious to divine wrath, and eternal damnation. Since in the same sense, our Lord declares, John iii. 36. " he that believeth not the Son, the wrath of God abideth on him," that is, he is obnoxious to wrath.

XXXIII. To these arguments we humbly reply, as follows: and to the *first* we say, that all Christ's sufferings together, ought to be esteemed one full accomplishment of that sacerdotal office, which our Lord undertook, in order to expiate our sins, which was at last fully completed, when Christ, dying on the cross, offered himself to the Father for a sweet smelling savour: then the utmost farthing was paid ; this being done, God declared, he was satisfied to the full, and on that day he blotted out the sins of the whole earth, and crossed them out of his book. But from this it cannot be inferred, that the preceding sufferings of Christ were not satisfactory ; but that then only the satisfaction was completed; of which completion this was the fruit, that on that very day, the sins of all the elect were blotted out. And this is the mind of God in Zechariah. But what Paul so often speaks of the one offering, by which we are perfected, is to be understood in the same sense; namely, since the sufferings of Christ, when on the cross, were the most grievous, and the complement of the whole, therefore the scriptures commonly ascribe the expiation of our sins to the cross of Christ; because without that his foregoing sufferings had not been sufficient, as the payment of the utmost farthing completes the satisfaction, which is immediately followed by tearing the hand-writing, and giving a discharge.

XXXIV. To the *second* we reply, that here are many things asserted which we can by no means yield to. 1st. It is not true, that Christ was not a priest from the beginning of his life. For from the beginning of his life he was the Christ, that is, the Lord's anointed, no less to the sacerdotal than to his other offices. And since, when he lay in the manger, he was saluted king by the wise men, and when twelve years old, he shewed himself a prophet amidst the doctors; who will, after all this, presume to deprive him of the honour of his priesthood? and as it belonged to the priests to stand in the house of the Lord, Psal. cxxxiv. 1. was there not some display of his sacerdotal office in that apology to his parents, " Wist ye not that I must be about my Father's business," Luke ii. 49. Nay, even before his incarnation, he exhibited some prelude of his sacerdotal function by his intercession for the church, Zech. i. 12, 13. We own indeed that Christ was publicly inaugurated in the 30th year of his age to his mediatorial office; but we can no more infer from that, that Christ was not a priest, than that he was not Mediator before that time.

XXXV. I cannot but here subjoin the very solid reasoning of the celebrated Cloppenburg, from his *Disputat. de vita Christi privata*, § 15, 16. " It could not be, but that in the daily practice of piety, and the obedience due to God, which he performed in the days of his flesh, Christ, who knew his unction from a child, (as appears from Luke ii. 49.) should offer prayers and supplications for the salvation of the church, whose King and Saviour he was born; compare Luke ii. 11. with Heb. v. 7. And there is no reason why we may not extend the words of the apostle to all the days of his flesh, and all the sufferings he endured from his infancy, because by these he learned obedience; and so it was altogether the constant apprenticeship or novitiate of the mediatorial office of Christ, who walked from a child with God; wherein he from day to day fulfilled, by a persevering obedience, the work which the Father had given him for the redemption of the church, which was to be fully completed by crowning his whole obedience with the offering up of himself a sacrifice, when he should be publicly called thereto," John xvii. 4. Acts ii. 23.

XXXVI. 2dly. Neither is it true, that Christ was not a sacrifice from the beginning of his life. For though his offering was completed on the cross, and by his death, yet he was even before that "the Lamb of God that taketh away the sin of the world," John i. 29. The iniquities of us all were laid upon him; and it was for no other cause that he took upon him the form of a servant, and the likeness of sinful flesh, and though he was rich, yet for our sakes became poor; and in fine, was exposed from his very infancy, to griefs, sorrows, and persecutions. All these calamities proceeded from this, that as both priest and sacrifice he took our sins upon himself, in order to their being at last fully abolished by his death.

XXXVII. 3dly. The proof of this paradoxical assertion, taken from the types of the Old Testament, is in many respects defective. For, 1. There is no solid foundation for that hypothesis, that all the circumstances of the types ought, in the same manner to be found in the antitype. For, then it would follow, that Christ must have been slain at a year old, according to the type of the paschal lamb. 2. It is also a rash assertion, that none could act as a priest before his 30th year. There is no such command in sacred writings. The Levites, indeed, were by the * annal law, not admitted before their 25th year, Num. viii. 24. nor before their 30th year, to the full exercise of their function, Num. iv. 3. " But indeed I find no where among the Rabbins," says Selden, *de succession. ad Pontificat. Ebræor.* lib. ii. c. iv. " that the years of the Levites as Levites, indicated the legal age of the priests. And I very much wonder great men should admit of this, even while they sharply criticise upon others." It is the constant tradition of the Hebrews, that a priest is fit for his office at his 13th year, after his years of puberty, though he is not bound to take his turn with the rest before his 20th year. See *Outram. de sacrific.* lib. i. c. v. sect. 3. Josephus relates of Aristobulus, " that when a young man, and out of his 17th year, he by the law ascended the altar to officiate." It is astonishing the very learned person did not attend to these things, which, from his skill in the Hebrew ritual, he could not be ignorant of. 3. If this argument is to be urged,

---

* The author seems to refer to the law which debarred candidates from an office till such an age. Cic. de Legg. iii. 3.

it would thence follow, that Christ could have been a sacrifice after the 7th day from his birth, and immediately upon his 30th year be a priest, which is contrary to what is supposed in the sentiment we here oppose.

XXXVIII. To the third we reply: 1st. That the question is not, Whether Christ did all his life long so endure the wrath of God, as in the mean time to be favoured with no consolation or joy of the comforting Spirit? none will affirm this. But the question is, Whether all those sufferings, which Christ at any time endured, and all that form of a servant which he assumed, belong to the perfection of his satisfaction? a thing that cannot be overthrown by some shining intervals of joy now and then. 2dly. To be the beloved Son of God, and at the same time to suffer the wrath of God, are not such contrary things, as that they cannot stand together. For as Son, as the holy One, while obeying the Father in all things, he was always the beloved; and indeed most of all when obedient even to the death of the cross; for that was so pleasing to the Father, that on account of it, he raised him to the highest pitch of exaltation, Phil. ii. 9. though as charged with our sins, he felt the wrath of God, burning, not against himself, but against our sins, which he took upon himself. Who can doubt that Christ, even hanging on the cross, was in the highest love and favour of God, so far as he was Son, though at the same time he was made a curse for our sins? 3dly. It has never been proved, that it was a thing improper and inconsistent, for Christ to have some mitigation granted him, while he satisfied for our sins, by means of some rays of consolation at intervals shining in upon him, by which he might be animated resolutely to acquit himself in the conflict. Nor is it credible, that he had always the sensation of divine wrath, or that it was always equally intense, even on the very cross itself; or that he was as much pressed down by his agonies, when he made a promise of paradise to the thief, and spoke so affectionately with his mother and John, as when he complained he was forsaken of God. See that kind address of God the Father to Christ, when " despised by every one, and abhorred by the nation, and a servant of rulers," Isa. xlix. 7.

XXXIX. What is argued from the creed, scarce deserves any answer; for when Christ is said to have suffered under Pontius Pilate, it was with no such intention as to distinguish the satisfactory sufferings of Christ from those which are not: a fiction I imagine, that none ever thought of: but simply to specify the time in which Christ completed his sufferings, and the person by whose authority he was condemned to the cross. Nor will the maintainer of this paradox affirm, that all the sufferings, which Christ endured under Pilate, or by his authority, were satisfactory, for if the satisfaction must be restricted to the three hours of darkness, then both the scourging and those indignities which Christ suffered in the pretorium, and his condemnation, nay his very crucifixion and death, must be excluded.

XL. It is certain a violence is done the catechism, which refers the impetation of our salvation to the one offering of Christ, with no other design, than what Paul does, whose meaning I have already explained. The words of question 37. appear to be perverted and misinterpreted. 1st. Because it is an answer to this question: "What believest thou when thou sayest, *he suffered?*" But that expression *he suffered*, does not signify the bare susception of guilt, but the enduring of sorrows. 2dly. If *to endure the wrath of God* does not there signify to *feel it*, but only to take its guilt upon himself, or be exposed to it, it would follow, that even at the close of his life he did not feel the wrath of God. For in the same sense the catechism affirms that very thing of the whole of Christ's life, and of the close thereof. 3dly. Ursinus is a more faithful interpreter of the catechism, when he writes, "under the appellation of suffering, are understood all the infirmities, miseries, griefs, racking tortures of soul and body, to which on our account Christ was obnoxious, from his nativity to his last breath," &c. 4thly. It is in vain to seek for any pretence to this forced sense from question 84. and John iii. 36. for it is not an obnoxiousness to the wrath of God that alone hangs over unbelievers and hypocrites; but they are really in a state of wrath and curse, and that curse which they are now under; is the beginning and a part of those pains which they shall suffer for ever.

XLI. The more special arguments or exceptions, either regard the death of Christ, or his agonies in the garden, or are taken from the beginning and end of the solar eclipse; which I shall set in such a light as at the same time to refute them.

XLII. If any shall say, that the scripture, when ascribing our redemption to the death of Christ, means by that death those very intense pains of eternal death, which Christ endured both in soul and body together, when he complained that he was forsaken of God; I answer, that indeed they are not, on any account to be secluded from the compass or extent of the word *death*, but the death of Christ is not to be confined to them, so as to exclude the death of the body, or the separation of soul and body. For Peter speaks expressly of his being put to death in the flesh, 1 Pet. iii. 18. and the whole scripture ascribes our ransom to that death, from which Christ arose by his resurrection, and in fine, Paul makes the sacrifice which Christ offered to consist in a death which is like to that which is appointed for all men once to undergo, Heb. xi. 27. and which, verse 26. is a sacrifice, and was shadowed forth by the slaying of the legal sacrifices.   And we have already mentioned several places which cannot without manifest violence be so explained, as to exclude the death of the body from being included in his death.

XLIII. If you object that Christ had before said, *It is finished*, I answer, it ought to be understood of his finishing all those things which he was to suffer and do in life, so that nothing remained but to conclude the whole by a pious death. Just as Paul said, 2 Tim. iv. 7. " I have finished my course."   And Christ himself, John xvii. 4. " I have finished the work which thou gavest me to do." Whence one would absurdly infer, that there remained for Christ on saying this, nothing further to be done or suffered; when he was still to be made perfect by his last sufferings. The meaning is evident; namely, that Christ in discharging his office, had perfectly performed all he was thus far to perform.

XLIV. If you insist upon it, that his death was calm and gentle, without the appearance of any pains of eternal death, having already undergone these, I answer, it was a gentle death indeed, in so far as the faith of Christ, now victorious over all temptations, was well apprized, that he had surmounted the greatest pains, and was secure about his resurrection and the promised reward; but yet he died a cursed death, inflicted by the wrath of God against sin, and the curse of it was typically figured by his hanging on the tree, which still continued in, and after death. For while he hung on the tree, so far he was doubtless under the curse, according to Gal. iii. 13. by which is signified, that his punishment ought to be taken as holding forth guilt, and the curse of God.

XLV. But say you believers are still to die; and therefore Christ did not satisfy for them by his death. I answer, the Catechumens have been taught to answer this objection from * question 42. of the Heidelberg catechism. By the death of Christ, death hath ceased to be what it was before, the punishment inflicted by an offended judge, and the entrance into the second death, and is become the extermination

---

* Q. But since Christ died for us, why must we also die ? A. Our death is not a satisfaction for sin, but the abolishing of sin, and our passage into everlasting life.

of sin, and the way to eternal life; and at the last day it shall
be altogether abolished. And if you go on to argue in this
manner, I shall easily make it appear from your own hypothesis, that even that very anguish of Christ when he complained of his being forsaken of God, was not satisfactory for
us; for believers themselves often complain of spiritual desertion: " But Zion said, the Lord hath forsaken me," Isa. xlix.
14. Where we have the very same word, which the Lord
Jesus uses, Psal. xxii. 2. And Zion says so truly, with respect to the sense of grace, and the influence of spiritual consolation. The difference between the desertion whereby Christ
was forsaken of his Father and that of believers, consists in this,
that in the former, there was the wrath and curse of God, and
the *formal* nature of punishment, which are not in the latter;
neither are these in their death.

XLVI. What is objected to our argument, taken from the
agonies of Christ in Gethsemane, is very inconsistent. They
say that these sufferings were not satisfactory, because then
an angel appeared to comfort him; whereas a good angel
could not have done this without a most grievous sin against
God, if Christ was then actually making satisfaction; especially as he was to tread this wine-press alone, and it was
foretold, that while making satisfaction, he should be deprived of all consolation, Psal. lxix. 20. " there is none to take
pity, comforters I found none;" for 1st. That angel did not
tread the wine-press together with the Lord Jesus, nor bear
any part of his sufferings, nor by any natural influence did he
assist Christ in carrying that burden. He strengthened Christ
only in a moral sense, by setting before him the glorious issue
of the conflict he had undertaken, and by other arguments to
the like purpose. 2dly. There is no reason why some small
share of comfort should not be administered to Christ while
in the act of making satisfaction; especially if with a view
to preserve him for more, and not fewer sufferings. The
words of Psal. lxix. are not to be taken in such a general
sense as to exclude all manner of consolation and pity; for,
" a great company of people and of women bewailed him,"
Luke xxiii. 27. as did also " all the people that came together to that sight, and smote upon their breasts," v. 48. and
the beloved disciple John, and above all his pious mother,
" whose soul then a sword pierced," Luke ii. 35. Nor is
there any thing in the words of the Psalm which obliges us
to confine these things to the three hours of darkness. It treats
of that time in which " they gave him gall for his meat, and
in his thirst gave him vinegar to drink," ver. 21. which was

not done during the darkness. 3dly. It cannot be inferred that God the Father, in sending that angel, had not then either begun to act, or that time ceased to act, as a strict and impartial judge; any more than it can be inferred, that the disposition of Christ's enemies was softened to pity, when they laid the cross on Simon of Cyrene, in order to carry it after him. For both were done with a view, lest Christ sinking under his present pains, should escape those that were to ensue. 4thly. We shall by this be better able to form a judgment of the incredible load of anguish with which that mighty lion of the tribe of Judah was so pressed down, that he appeared almost ready to sink under it, unless he was, in some manner at least, encouraged. 5thly. Nor on any pretence can that angel be accused of any sin in strengthening Christ while satisfying for us; since by that consolation, he neither intended to rob Christ of his glory, to whom alone the praise of satisfying remains entire; nor to oppose the decree of God; for he animated Christ to execute that with resolution; nor to put any bar in the way of our salvation, for he encouraged our Lord to acquire the right to that by constancy in his sufferings.

XLVII. To pretend to infer from the beginning and end of the solar eclipse, during the passion of Christ, the beginning and end of his satisfaction, is a cabalistical fancy, founded neither on scripture nor solid reason. I do not deny, that in that darkness there was a kind of type of the very thick darkness with which the greatly distressed soul of the Lord Jesus was then overwhelmed, without a single ray of consolation breaking in upon him, but what his unshaken faith, grounded on the inviolable promises of his Father, and not staggering as to the certainty of the future reward, darted in at times upon his trembling soul. But the question is not, whether Christ was then actually satisfying? This we all allow: the question is, whether then only?

XLVIII. But let us now conclude this debate; which has so much disquieted the mind of this very learned person, as his friends wanted the world should know from letters published after his death. But God and my conscience are my witnesses, that nothing but the love of truth, which is only to be derived from, and defended by the scriptures, obliged me to enter upon this subject. I know not in what I can be blamed, unless in the liberty I have taken to dissent from the author. But if, by taking a wrong path, I have strayed from the truth, how acceptable will the kind admonition be! How readily shall I own and correct the error! I heartily wish we could generally endeavour to please ourselves less, in order to please God more. I ever had a veneration for this learned person, though after our dispute I found he was much disgusted. But I thought this should be no hindrance to my profiting by his learned commentaries, which I own I did, with a just commendation of the author, as my other writings abundantly testify.

CHAP. VII.

Of the * Efficacy of Christ's Satisfaction.

I. THE *efficacy* of Christ's satisfaction is *twofold :* the *first* regards Christ *himself;* the other, *the elect.* Christ by his satisfaction, obtained for *himself,* as Mediator, a right to all the elect: which the Father willingly and deservedly bestows upon him, Psal. ii. 8. " Ask of me, and I shall give thee the Heathen for thine inheritance, and the uttermost parts of the earth for thy possession." This is Christ's work with his God, that he should not only be his servant, to raise up the tribes of Jacob, and to restore the preserved of Israel ; but that he should be given for a light to the Gentiles, that he might be God's salvation unto the end of the earth, Isa. xlix. 4, 6. It appears also from that promise, Isa. liii. 10. " if his soul shall make itself an offering for sin, he shall see his seed." And thus we become his " inheritance," Eph. i. 11. his " peculiar treasure," Psal. cxxxv. 4. his " peculiar people," Tit. ii. 14. and 1 Pet. ii. 9.

II. Besides, it is not possible but Christ should exercise that right which he acquired at so dear a rate. For when, according to the determinate counsel of God, the time of the gracious visitation of every one of the elect is come, he actually delivers them, as his property, by an outstretched arm. And why should he not, seeing he can easily effect it by the power of his Spirit, turning and inclining their heart ? Is it credible he should suffer those who are his lawful right, to be, and to remain the slaves of Satan ? Is it worthy of Christ that he should not be actually glorified in the sanctification and happiness of those for whom he underwent so much infamy ? Or should suffer any of those to perish whom he purchased for his own possession by his precious blood ? Christ himself hath taught us thus to reason, John x. 16. " And other sheep I

---

* I have rendered this *efficacy,* rather than *effect,* as that expresses all the effects of Christ's satisfaction, treated of in this chapter.

have, which are not of this fold; them also I must bring, and
they shall hear my voice." Because these sheep were of right
his property, it therefore became him actually to lay hold of
them as his own, and bring them into his fold. Nor can the
right of Christ be made ineffectual, or remain without actual
possession; especially as he was not promised by the Father a
bare right, but also a possession by right, upon his making satisfaction; as the places above quoted evince.

III. The Lord Jesus obtained for *the elect*, by his satisfaction, *an immunity from all misery*, and *a right to eternal life*,
to be applied unto them in effectual calling, regeneration,
sanctification, conservation, and glorification, as the scripture
declares. Thus Matt. xxvi. 28. " this is my blood of the
New Testament, which is shed for many for the remission of
sins." Gal. i. 4. " he gave himself for our sins, that he might
deliver us from this present evil world, according to the will of
God and our Father." Tit. ii. 14. " gave himself for us, that
he might redeem us from all iniquity, and purify unto himself
a peculiar people, zealous of good works." Eph. v. 25, 26, 27.
" Christ loved the church, and gave himself for it, that he
might sanctify it, that he might present it to himself a glorious,"
&c. In a word, " this is that faithful saying, and worthy of
all acceptation, that Christ Jesus came into the world to save
sinners," 1 Tim. i. 15. By these and many other passages to
the same purpose, which it would be needless to mention here,
it evidently appears, that the effect of Christ's satisfaction was
not a bare *possibility of the remission* of our sins, and of our
reconciliation with God, but an actual *remission* and *reconciliation*, an abolition of the dominion of sin, and at length salvation itself: and it is not possible the elect should have no share
in this, unless Christ should be deemed to have satisfied for
them to no purpose. It is certainly incumbent on us, never to
weaken the force of the words of the Holy Ghost, especially in
those places and expressions of scripture, where the subject of
our salvation is treated of; nor to detract in any thing, from
the value of the satisfaction of our Lord.

IV. This truth also appears from those places of scripture,
in which the satisfaction of Christ is called απολύτρωσις a redemption, made by the payment of λυτρε a ransom, or αντιλυτρε
a price of redemption. For, the proximate effect of redemption, and of the payment of a ransom, is the setting the captive at liberty, and not a bare possibility of liberty. It is neither customary, nor equitable, that after paying the price,
it should still remain uncertain, whether the captive is to be
set free or not. A true redeemer procures the restitution

of liberty to the miserable captive, wherever good faith and
an agreement are of force.   One may possibly be upon terms
about the price, though uncertain of the event, but it is neither
prudent nor just, to make any payment, before what is stipulated be made sure and firm.   The scripture itself declares,
that the proximate effect of redemption is the actual remission
of sins, and restoration to liberty, Rom. iii. 24. " justified freely
by his grace, through the redemption that is in Christ Jesus."
Eph. i. 7. " In whom we have redemption through his blood,
the forgiveness of sins, according to the riches of his grace;"
and Col. i. 14. to the same purpose : in like manner, Heb. ix.
12. " by his own blood obtained eternal redemption for us;"
the fruit or effect, which is eternal liberty and salvation.

V. Of the like nature are those phrases, by which the elect
are said to be " bought with a price, purchased with blood,
redeemed by Christ's subjection to the law :" as 1 Cor. vi. 20.
" ye are bought with a price." Acts xx. 28. " to feed the
church of God, which he hath purchased with his own blood."
Gal. iv. 4, 5. " made under the law, to redeem them that were
under the law." But whoever makes a purchase of any thing
has an unquestionable right to it, and it not only may, but
actually does become his property, in virtue of his purchase,
upon paying down the price.   And herein consists our liberty
and salvation, that we are no longer our own, nor the property
of sin, nor of Satan, but the property of Christ.   Whence it
appears, that the effect of Christ's satisfaction is not a bare
possibility of our salvation, but salvation itself.

VI. A right to all the benefits of the covenant of grace is
purchased at once to all the elect by the death of Christ, so
far as, that consistently with the truth and justice of God,
and with the covenant he entered into with his Son, he cannot condemn any of the elect, or exclude them from partaking
in his salvation; nay, on the contrary, he has declared, that
satisfaction being now made by his Son, and accepted by himself, there is nothing for the elect either to suffer or do, in
order to acquire either impunity, or a right to life; but only,
that each of them, in their appointed order and time, enjoy the
right purchased for them by Christ, and the inheritance arising from it.   And this is what the apostle says, 2 Cor. v. 19.
" God was in Christ reconciling the world to himself, not imputing their trespasses unto them." That is, seeing God accepted of the offering of his Son, when he gave himself up to
death for his people, he received, at the same time into favour,
not only the preserved of Israel, but all nations, and all families of the earth, which, in other respects, lay in wickedness,

and were liable to the wrath of God, declaring that satisfaction
was now made to him for their sins, and that these could no
longer be imputed to them for condemnation, nor for excluding from his saving grace.

VII. We have a further proof of this, Zech. iii. 9. " for
behold the stone which I have laid before Joshua; upon one
stone shall be seven eyes; behold I will engrave the graving
thereof, saith the Lord of hosts, and I will remove the iniquity
of that land in one day." The stone here is doubtless the
Lord Jesus Christ, as Dan. ii. 34. Psal. cxviii. 22. on. which
the church is built, on which it is founded, and by which it is
supported. It is laid before Joshua and his companions the
priests, as architects, to lay it for the foundation of faith, acknowledge it as the corner-stone, and build thereon both themselves, and other believers. This stone is but one : for other
foundation can no man lay, than that is laid, which is Jesus
Christ, 1 Cor. iii. 11. Upon this stone there are seven eyes,
either of God the Father, viewing it with care and pleasure,
or of the church universal, looking to it by faith. Its grav-
ings engraved by God, represent those very clear indications or
characters, by which he may, and ought to be distinguished,
as one given by the Father to be a Saviour : among these characters were those sufferings, by which he was to be made perfect. These things being done, to shew that all the signs of
the Messiah were in him, God declares, that *he would remove
the iniquity of all that land*, (clearly signifying the whole
world, according to the Synecdoche just explained,) *in one
day*, at once, in the last day of Christ's passion : and thus, by
Christ's satisfaction we are taught that deliverance from sin,
and all the happy effects of that immunity, were purchased at
once for all the elect in general.

VIII. It is, however, certain, that true saving benefits are
bestowed on none of the elect, before effectual calling, and actual union to Christ by a lively faith : nevertheless, Christ did
by his satisfaction purchase for all the elect at once, a right to
those benefits, that they might have and enjoy them, in their
appointed time. Nay, before actual conversion, and the possession of saving blessings, they are favoured with no contemptible privileges above the reprobate, in virtue of the right
which Christ purchased for them. Such as, 1st. That they are
in a state of reconciliation and justification * actively considered, Christ having made satisfaction for them, as we see from
2 Cor. v. 19. That is, that God considers them as persons

* See the last § of this chapter, where this is further explained.

for whom his Son has satisfied, and purchased a right to eternal life. 2dly. That God loves them with a peculiar love of
benevolence, according to the decree of election; which love of
benevolence will, at the appointed time, certainly issue in a
love of complacency. For, as it was from a love of benevolence, that Christ was given to be their Saviour; so satisfaction being made, God in consequence of the same love, will
form them, so as he may deservedly acquiesce in them, as fit
objects of his love of complacency. May we not refer to this,
what God says, Jer. xxxi. 3. " I have loved thee with an
everlasting love, therefore with loving-kindness have I drawn
thee ?" 3dly. To this also it is owing, that they have the
means of salvation, the preaching of the gospel, &c. with some
internal illumination, and some incitement to good, though
not yet saving; and yet for this end, that in their appointed
time, they may be effectually converted by those means. 4thly.
From all this it likewise follows, that God preserves them
while living under the means of salvation, from the sin against
the Holy Ghost; from which there is no conversion. 5thly,
and lastly. They have the Spirit rendering those means effectual, to their actual and complete regeneration, and to unite
them to Christ by working faith in them, that they may enjoy benefits truly saving.

IX. As matters stand thus, we may easily gather what
judgment we are to form of the notions of Arminius and his
followers, on this point. Arminius proposes his sentiments
in *Examine prædestin. Perkins*, p. 75, 76. as follows: " Let
us add to all these things, by way of conclusion, the proper
and immediate effect of the death and passion of Christ. But
it is not an actual removal of sin from this or that particular
person, nor actual remission of sins, nor justification, nor
the actual redemption of this or that person, which
none can have without faith and the Spirit of Christ.
But the reconciliation of God, the impetration of remission, justification and redemption from God : hence God
now may, notwithstanding his justice, which is satisfied, forgive the sins of men, and bestow the Spirit of grace upon
them ; though he was really inclined before, from his own
mercy (for from that he gave Christ to be the Saviour of the
world,) to confer these things on sinners, yet his justice prevented the actual communication of them. However, God
still has a right to bestow those benefits on whom he pleases,
and on what conditions he thinks proper to prescribe. But on
the contrary, if we agree to such a method of mediation, as
you, Perkins, seem to approve of; namely, that the sins of

all the elect were actually removed from them, and laid upon
Christ, who having suffered for them, did actually deliver them
from punishment; and that obedience was required of him,
who accordingly performed it, and thereby merited eternal
life, not for himself, but for them ; and that just as if we
ourselves had appointed this Mediator in our room, and by
him had paid our debts to God: nay, we must now likewise
believe, that according to the very rigour of God's justice and
law, impunity and eternal life are due to the elect, and that
they may demand those benefits from God, in right of payment and purchase made, and yet God have no manner of
right to demand of them faith in Christ, and conversion to God."
But all the absurdities of this opinion cannot easily be expressed.   I will confute it only by one argument, but a very
cogent one, and taken from the writings of the apostles.   The
righteousness wrought out by Christ is not ours, as wrought
out, but as imputed to us by faith, so that faith itself is said
to be imputed to us for righteousness, Rom. iv. 5.   Thus far
Arminius, whose very words almost we have exhibited, omitting only those which are not to the purpose in hand.   His
followers have things of the like nature, in their *Scripta Synodalia*, adding, that the impetration is such, that *from the
nature of the thing, it may remain entire, and be every way
perfect, though there were none to apply it to, or none to enjoy the benefit of it.*

X. There are many things in this discourse, which are
consistent neither with scholastic accuracy, nor with the
other tenets of the Remonstrants, nor with theological truth :
which we are now to shew in order.   1st. Arminius does not
speak accurately, in saying, that the proper effect of the death
and passion of Christ is not the actual remission of sins, nor
justification, nor actual redemption of this or that person, &c.
but the impetration of remission, justification, and redemption
from God.   For the members of this distinction are not properly opposed : to actual remission, and to actual justification,
is not opposed the impetration of remission and of justification ; but a possible remission, and a possible justification.
And this Arminius ought to have expressed himself, in order
to speak accurately and fairly.   2dly. Nor is it an accurate
way of speaking, to say, that the effect of the passion and
death of Christ is *impetration of remission and of justification*.
He ought to say, it is remission and justification itself, whatever that be.   For so Arminius himself hath taught us to
speak with accuracy, p. 72.   " A distinction may be made
between the act, by which reconciliation is obtained, and the

effect of that act, which is reconciliation. The act impetrating reconciliation, is the offering which Christ made on
the cross: the effect is the reconciliation itself." And so he
ought to have said here: in the death and passion of Christ,
the impetrating act is that voluntary susception of all kinds
of sufferings, which he undertook both from his love to God
and men. The effect is remission and justification. The impetrating act is the satisfaction of Christ. The effect is immunity from debt. In this manner Arminius spoke, before
he had degenerated to worse opinions, *Disput. privat.* xxxv.
§ 7. " The effects of the priestly office are reconciliation
with God, impetration of eternal redemption, remission of
sins, the spirit of grace and eternal life." 3dly. Nor has that
expression a just meaning, at least it is not accurate, that by
the passion of Christ, God can forgive sins: as if some new,
some greater and more extensive power of God, was the effect
of the sufferings of Christ. The power of God is infinite,
and altogether incapable of increase. And then what is impetrated from any one, ought previously to be in his power.
The Remonstrants have more accurately expressed their sentiments in their Synodalia, in these words: " the effect of reconciliation or propitiation, is the impetration of divine grace,
that is, restitution to such a state," &c. So that a change in
our state, and not an increase of God's power, is the effect
of the satisfaction of Christ.

XI. Besides, Arminius is in this discourse consistent neither with *himself*, nor with his *adherents*. Not with *himself:* for his whole design is to shew, that the proper and immediate effect of the death of Christ, is only a possibility of
remission of sins; and yet he asserts, that the proper effect of
the death of Christ is the reconciliation of God, and the impetration of remission, justification, &c. But how do those
things agree, seeing a possibility of remission of sins my
consist with a perpetual enmity between God and man?
What kind of reconciliation is that, when an eternal enmity
may notwithstanding subsist? What sort of impetration of
remission, if nevertheless, it be possible, that sins may never
be pardoned? Nor, does Arminius here better agree with
the hypothesis of *his followers;* who expressly deny, that
God cannot, on account of his vindictive justice, remit sins
without a previous satisfaction. I now omit mentioning the
laboured disputation of Vorstius on this head against *Sibran-
dus Lubbertus.* Thus the Remonstrants profess, in express
terms, in their apology, p. 466. drawn up in the name of all,
that " to suppose the vindictive justice of God to be so essen-

tial to him, that, in virtue of it, he is bound and necessitated to punish sins, is highly absurd and unworthy of God."

XII. From this also we may, by a very evident consequence, infer, that the death and sufferings of Christ were in vain, and without any fruit or effect: which I thus demonstrate: If there is in God, even before, and exclusive of the satisfaction of Christ, a power of remitting sins, notwithstanding his vindictive justice, Christ has therefore done nothing by suffering and dying in order to the existence of such a power in God. But the Remonstrants strenuously declare and maintain, that God can, without satisfaction, and without the violation of his essential justice, let sins go unpunished, and that the contrary is highly absurd: Christ therefore procured nothing by his death. For what he is said to have obtained by it did already exist without it. "God could have saved us without the satisfaction of Christ: but did not choose to do it," says Corvinus, in his Censura Anatom. Molinæi, p. 436.

XIII. In a word, this assertion of Arminius is inconsistent with theological truth. For, 1st. The scripture no where declares, that the fruit of Christ's death is a possibility of the remission of sins: nor does Arminius produce any passage of scripture to that purpose. But to speak of the fruit of Christ's death without scripture is untheological. 2dly. Nay, the scripture asserts the contrary, as we have at large shewn § III, IV, V. 3dly. It is also contrary to all reason to say, that the proper effect of Christ's most perfect satisfaction was, that God might let the captive go free, yet so that the captive might always remain in prison and be liable to pay the debt. How absurd! that God should receive full satisfaction by the death of his Son, for the sins of any particular person, and yet, notwithstanding this plenary satisfaction of Christ, that man is to be sent to eternal fire, there to satisfy, in his own person, for those very sins which Christ had fully satisfied for already? 4thly. Such a bare possibility of remission, which, from the nature of the thing, may never become actual, overturns the unchangeable covenant between the Father and the Son; the sum of which Arminius himself has well expressed in his oration de Sacerdotio Christi, p. 14. "God required of Christ, that he should make his soul an offering for sin, give his flesh for the life of the world, pay the price of redemption for the sins and captivity of mankind: and promised, if he did so, that he should see his seed, and become an eternal priest. The priest accepted this condition," &c. Christ, relying on this infallible promise, did willingly

give himself up to death. But from this assertion of Arminius and the Remonstrants, it was possible, that Christ, after
having paid the ransom, should see no seed, be a king without
any kingdom of grace, an everlasting Father without any children, a bridegroom without a bride, a head without a body.
All which are most abominable.

XIV. Arminius, however, defends his opinion by three arguments.   The first is this : *God has fully right to impart those
benefits to whom he thinks proper, and on what conditions
he is pleased to prescribe.*   Whence it follows, that Christ has
not merited the bestowing those benefits actually upon any one ;
for this is the tendency of these words of Arminius. I answer,
1st. We deny that God may not impart those benefits which
Christ has merited to those for whom he died.   God might indeed appoint the persons Christ was to die for : but this appointment being once settled, God is not at liberty not to give that
grace and glory which was purchased by the death of Christ
to those for whom he died.   2dly. Arminius is further mistaken, when he says that God had a full right to impart those
benefits on what conditions he pleased to prescribe, supposing
that the performance of these conditions, namely faith and
repentance, or the grace necessary to the performance of them,
was not among those blessings which Christ had merited for us
by his passion.   For, it was agreed in that covenant between
the Father and the Son, by which Christ gave himself up to
death, that all adult persons should, in the way of faith and repentance, come to the saving enjoyment of the other blessings
of it :   nor can any other conditions be now settled by agreement.   Besides, it was also fixed that the Father should, from
the consideration of Christ's merit, grant the Spirit of grace for
faith and repentance, to those for whom Christ had died, as we
have already seen Arminius himself orthodoxly reckoning the
Spirit of grace among the effects of the sacerdotal office of Christ.
For, seeing God *hath blessed us with all spiritual blessings in
Christ,* Eph. i. 3. that is, through and for the merits of Christ,
and the gift of faith is one of the most excellent of these blessings, Phil. i. 29. that likewise must certainly come to us on
account of his merits.   3dly. Nor is it agreeable to scripture
language, to say, that faith and repentance are requisite conditions, before any effects of Christ's death are communicated to
a person.   Certainly they are not required previous to our
regeneration and vivification from the death of sin, and our
deliverance from this present evil world, which are reckoned
among the effects of Christ's death by Paul, Eph. ii. 5. and
Gal. i. 4.   We may therefore say, if you will, that these are
conditions requisite for applying to our consciences that conso-

lation purchased by the death of Christ, yet, in such a manner, as it is from the merit of Christ, that the grace, that is powerfully and abundantly effectual to perform those conditions, must flow.

XV. Arminius' second argument is this: " If the actual remission of sins, &c. be the effect of Christ's death, we must then allow, that, according to the very rigour of God's justice and law, both an eternal life and an immunity from punishment, are due to the elect, and that therefore they are entitled to ask those benefits of God, in right of the payment and purchase made ; without God's having any right to require of them faith in Christ and conversion to God." I answer, 1st. We are wholly of opinion, that one who is renewed may come boldly to the throne of grace, and ask for those blessings at God's hand, in right of the payment and purchase made by Christ. For, why should we not venture to ask of God that he would perform for us what he was pleased to make himself a debtor to his Son and to his merits ? This is the παρρησία, or boldness of our faith, to expect the crown of righteousness from God, as a merciful and gracious giver, in respect of our unworthiness, but as a just Judge, in respect to the merits of Christ, 2 Tim. iv. 8. 2dly. It is an invidious reflection of Arminius, to say, " without God's having any right to require of us faith in Christ, and conversion to himself." For it is impossible for any who approach to, and ask those blessings from God, not to perform those duties. For how can any ask those benefits of God in the name of Christ, and without conversion to the Father and the Son ? 3dly. But to speak plainly. If we admit of Christ's satisfaction, and of the ratification of the covenant of grace, and New Testament, then God can by no right require faith and conversion from the elect, as conditions of the covenant of grace, in the sense of Arminius and the Remonstrants ; namely, 1st. To be performed by us, without grace working them in us supernaturally, effectually, and invincibly. 2dly. As, by some gracious appointment of God, coming in the place of that perfect obedience to the law, which the covenant of works required. For, in this manner Arminius explains these things ; that, instead of perfect obedience, which the covenant of works required, the act of faith succeeds in the covenant of grace ; to be, in God's gracious account, imputed to us for righteousness, that is, to be our claim of right to ask eternal life. But the nature of the covenant of grace admits of no such conditions, however framed, on which to build a right to life eternal, either from the justice, or the gracious estimation of God. And thus far Arminius concludes well, if the Mediator has so satisfied for us, as if we ourselves had by him paid our debts, no condition can, by any right, be required of us, which, in any respect, can be reckoned instead of payment. The whole glory of our right to eternal life, must be purely ascribed to the alone merit of our Lord ; and on no pretence be transferred to any one of our acts.

XVI. There is still one argument, which Arminius imagines to be very cogent. " The righteousness, says he, wrought out by Christ, is not ours as wrought out, but as imputed to us by faith." I answer, 1st. What does Arminius infer from this? Does he conclude that besides the satisfaction of Christ, faith is also necessary to salvation? And what then? Therefore Christ did not obtain for us the actual remission of sins. We deny the consequence. For, faith is not considered as impetrating, but as applying the impetrated remission. And as the presupposed object of saving faith is remission, already impetrated for all the elect by Christ, it must certainly be the proper effect of the death of Christ. 2dly. This righteousness of Christ, was really his, as it was wrought out *by him* ; and it is *ours*, as it was wrought out *for us:* therefore, in a sound sense, even ours before faith, being the meritorious cause of that grace which is effectual to produce faith in us. It is ours, I say, in respect of *right*, because both in the decree of God the Father, and the purpose of the Son, it was wrought out for us, and in the appointed time to be certainly applied to us. Though it was not yet ours by *possession*, as to our actual translation from a state of wrath, to a state of grace, and our acknowledgment and sense of so great a benefit vouchsafed unto us : * The distinction between active and passive justification is well known. *The former* is that sentence of God, by which he declares his having received satisfaction from Christ, and pronounces that all the elect are made free from guilt and obligation to punishment, even before their faith, so far as never to exact of them any payment. *The latter* is the acknowledgment and sense of that most sweet sentence, intimated to the conscience by the Holy Spirit, and fiducially apprehended by each of the elect. The one precedes faith, at least as to that general article which we just proposed ; the other follows it. And thus we have defended the value and efficacy of Christ's satisfaction against the cavils of Arminius.

---

* Others distinguish the justification of the elect, into that which is decretive, virtual, and actual. The first is God's eternal purpose to justify sinners in time, by the righteousness of Christ; but God's eternal purpose to justify the elect is one thing, and the execution of it another. There was also a *virtual* justification upon Christ's having made satisfaction; and justification is actual when the elect sinner is enabled to believe in the Son of God, and by faith is united to him. See Book III. chap. viii. §. 57, &c.

CHAP. VIII.

Of the Necessity of Christ's Satisfaction.

I. HAVING explained from scripture the value and efficacy of the satisfaction of our Lord Jesus Christ, to the glory of God, and for the consolation of the elect, it will not be unseasonable to treat of the necessity of this satisfaction; seeing what we have shewn, § XXI. from the apology of the Remonstrants, naturally leads to this. And here we choose not to state the controversy in the manner, we observe, the otherwise great Chamierus has done in his *Pancratia*; namely, "whether God could not, by an act of his absolute power, grant remission of sin, without any satisfaction." We are not willing to enter into any dispute about the absolute power of God; since the consideration of that seems not to suit this present controversy. For this debate is not to be explained, and finally determined from the attribute of the power of God, but from those of his holiness, justice, and the like. Some, when they consider the power of God alone, affirm every thing about it: not reflecting, that God can do nothing but consistently with his justice, holiness, veracity, wisdom, immutability, in a word, with all his other perfections. The lawyer *Papinian ff.* lib. xxviii. Tit. vii. Leg. 15. has said well concerning a good man; that we are to believe, that he "*neither does, nor can do,* any thing prejudicial to piety, reputation, modesty, and in general, that is contrary to good manners." This certainly ought much more to be affirmed of the Great God; that whatever is not a display of, or whatever throws a slur on any perfection or on the glory of God, cannot be the work of God. Origen has judiciously pleaded this cause against Celsus, lib. iii. p. 154. " According to us God, indeed can do all things, consistently with his Deity, wisdom, and goodness. But Celsus (not understanding how God may be said to do all things) affirms, he cannot will any thing unjust, granting he can do what is so, but not will it. But we say, that as what is capable of imparting its natural sweetness to other things, cannot imbitter any thing, because that would be contrary to its nature: nor as what naturally enlightens, can as such darken: so neither can God act unjustly. For *the power of acting unjustly is contrary to his very Deity,* and to every power that can be ascribed to God." And therefore we think it very unbecoming, on every question about the most sacred right of God, to appeal to his absolute power. We would ra-

ther state the controversy thus: namely, whether God's requiring Christ to give him satisfaction before he restore sinners
to his favour, was owing to the mere good pleasure of the divine will; or whether the essential holiness, the justice, and the
like perfections of God, which he cannot possibly part with, required a satisfaction to be made? We judge the last of these to
be more true and safe.

II. In the preceding book, chap. v. § XIX. seq. we proved at
large, that the very nature and immutable right of God, could
not let sin go unpunished: which we may now lay down as a
foundation. At present, we will subjoin other arguments more
nearly relating to the satisfaction of Christ itself.

III. And *first* we may certainly form no contemptible argument from *the event,* and *a posteriori.* For as God does not need-
lessly multiply beings; what probable reason can be assigned
why without any necessity, he should make his beloved Son, in
whom he was well pleased, a curse for us? Let us insist a little on this thought. The infinite wisdom of God contrived the
admirable union of the human nature with one of the divine
persons: so that God himself might be said to obey, to suffer,
to die; in a word, to make satisfaction; that person was *holy,
harmless, and undefiled,* the man of God's delight, his only begotten and only beloved Son. Him the most affectionate Father
exposed to the greatest reproaches, to the most cruel sufferings,
and to an accursed death, as a ransom for the redemption of
sinners. These sufferings were a long time before predicted
in various obscure ways, and also prefigured by the whole train
of sacrifices appointed by Moses. He permitted the world
after so many other crimes, to be stained with the guilt of deicide
(from the view of which the very sun shrunk back and withdrew his rays,) a crime, indeed, truly inexpiable, and in the
guilt of which the whole Jewish nation is involved. Would
not all this, to speak with reverence, seem a kind of solemn
farce, if God by a single breath, could dispel all our sins as a
cloud? Is it not contrary to the goodness, the wisdom, and the
holiness of God, without any necessity, and to speak so, in a
mere arbitrary way to proceed in this manner? If he could have
reached his end in a direct and compendious way, why did he
take such a wide and perplexed compass?

IV. I would not have any reply here, that God acted in this
manner, in order to manifest that his infinite right or authority
over the creature was such, that he might inflict the most grievous torments even on the innocent. If God could claim that
right and authority if he pleased; yet surely, he scarce, if ever,
has made use of it. And if at any time he has, it was in suffering of a far more gentle, and mild nature, than what Christ

Jesus our Lord underwent. In a word, if, for the display of that right, he might at times inflict such grievous torments, yet he would withhold his hand from his most beloved and only Son in whom he so clearly testified that he was well pleased.

V. To insist upon it, that the whole of this affair was otherwise ordered by the arbitrary will of God, for confirming the saving doctrine of Christ, by this exemplary martyrdom, is contrary both to reason, scripture, and experience. For God had many other means, of a far more easy nature, by which he could confirm the doctrine of salvation, than by the dreadful passion of his beloved Son. And the scripture shews us, that this was done by Christ's miracles accompanying his most effectual preaching: and the native demonstration of the truth, shewed the divinity of his doctrine. By these things he approved himself to John's disciples, Matt. xi. 5. and even to the whole multitude, Luke vii. 16. and John vi. 14. and lastly, we gather both from scripture and experience, that the cross of Christ was " unto the Jews a stumbling-block, and unto the Greeks foolishness, 1 Cor. i. 23.

VI. Nor are we to say, it was necessary we should be taught in so laborious a manner, or even by the very example of the Son of God, that it is through many tribulations we are to enter into the kingdom of heaven. For if nothing else was intended, we might have been sufficiently taught all this by the examples of other martyrs. And then further, there is scarce one in a thousand of those who are saved, who, in the way to salvation, secluding the curse of God, have been called to suffer so many dreadful and great indignities as Christ did. Why then were we all to be taught, by the example of the Son of God, that the gate of heaven is, on no other terms open, but by passing through those hard sufferings? Unless we say, that satisfaction was made to the justice of God by the sufferings of Christ, and that in no other way satisfaction could be made thereto; there can no other just, holy, and wise reason, and worthy of God, be ever assigned for them. Certainly, for my own part, I never remember to have heard of any.

VII. If any affirm, that no satisfaction was necessary on account of the justice of God, but that he exacted it on account of some other perfections, namely, to declare his power and will to punish sin, which he might suffer to go unpunished: I answer, such power and will are scarcely to be called perfections in God; seeing Christ, Matt. v. 45, 48. reckons God's mercy, long-suffering, and bounty towards men, even the unjust, among his perfections. Which would certainly be most laudable, if God could, at pleasure, let sin go unpunished, and if that impunity was no ways inconsistent with his most holy nature. Nay, if God can, consistent with his highest glory, not punish sin, it might be queried whether he can consistent with this inflict punishment at all : because, in that case, he seems to afflict the sinner without a reason, and ill-treat the work of his hands. But to do any thing without a reason, can on no account be for the honour of God.

VIII. Perhaps, some will judge it the safest course not to in-trude into the depths of the unsearchable wisdom, and infinite power of God, and to say, God indeed was pleased for wise and good reasons, though known to himself alone, on no other terms, to set us at liberty, but by the satisfaction of his Son: but yet could, in a far different way bring us to salvation, nay, and re-deem us by a word or sign. And indeed, the great Augustine formerly spoke in this strain, *de agone Christiano :* " God could have done all things, had he so willed : but did not, and that for wise reasons, though unknown and incomprehensible to us : but though he had done otherwise, yet he would equally have dis-pleased your folly." And again, *de Trinitate*, lib. 13. c. 12. " Let us maintain, that this method, by which God sees proper to deliver us, by a mediator between God and man, the man Christ Jesus, is perfectly good and for the honour of God : but also let us acknowledge that God was at no loss for his power ; but yet none was more adapted to deliver us from our misery, neither was any necessary." I am certainly much pleased with that extreme modesty by which we dare not determine any thing rashly concerning the reasons and ends of the actions of God ; and judge inconsiderately about his ways, because there is that in them, the reasons whereof our ignorance cannot unfold ; nay, which seems, to our presumptuous folly, to be against reason. But when we are able to know and give such reasons for the divine conduct, as tend to set the glory of his adorable justice, wisdom, holiness, and goodness in the clearest light ; it is no longer modesty, but rather tends to darken the glory of the per-fections of God, not to acknowledge them ; which is the case here. The reason why God, willing to save elect sinners, chose to do it by the satisfaction of his Son, is because in his wisdom, he saw no other way, by which satisfaction could be made to his essential holiness and justice. And by affirming this, we dero-gate nothing from the power of God, who doubtless cannot but act agreeably to his holiness and justice : and we admirably pro-claim his wisdom, which found a means, which appeared im-possible to every created understanding, whereby satisfaction might be made to his justice ; and the sinner, consistently with his holiness, be saved. In order the more clearly to illustrate, and, at the same time, the more firmly to establish all this, let us

attentively consider, what the scripture declares concerning the
impulsive and final cause of giving Christ.

IX. The sacred writers on several occasions inculcate, that
God's not sparing his own proper Son, but giving him to us,
and delivering him up to death for us, was the effect of his unspeakable love to mankind, John iii. 16. Rom. v. 8. 1 John iv.
10. But if we could be saved any other way, than by the sufferings of the Son of God, the love of God would not shine
with such lustre in that method. For love is truly great, and
inexpressible to the last degree, when implacable justice having
demanded the punishment of mankind, God's love to man, and
free purpose of salvation, have nevertheless prevailed, by finding out for that end, in the treasures of divine wisdom, an
amazing method of reconciling justice with mercy; but it was
such as could have no effect, without giving up the most beloved Son to the most cruel torments for us. But if, without
any prejudice to justice, our salvation could be procured many
other ways than this, and even by a single word or nod, what
ardency of love was there in his giving the Son? It would certainly have been an instance of a very singular and notable
mercy to have forgiven our sins. But to have effected this by
the death of his Son, when without any urgent necessity, with
equal advantage he could have scattered our sins, some other
more compendious way, by a nod or sign, as some affirm, why
is that urged by Christ and his apostles as an argument of such
inconceivable love?

X. The apostle declares, that the end of Christ's satisfaction was " a declaration of the righteousness of God," Rom.
iii. 25. " Whom God hath set forth to be a propitiation
(propitiatory mercy-seat) through faith in his blood, εισ ενδειξιν
της δικαιοσινης αυτε to declare his righteousness." *God set forth*
his Son both *to himself* delighting in him, Isa. xlii. 1. as having
appointed him, in his eternal counsel, to be the Mediator, and
viewing him as thus appointed; and *to us*, placing him in
open view, and setting him on a throne of grace and glory, in the
sight of all. He set him forth as *a propitiation* (propitiatory
mercy-seat); where the apostle alludes to the cover laid upon the
ark of the covenant, called ιλαστηριον the propitiatory *mercy-seat:*
signifying that by which God was reconciled to men, in which
he dwells and rests, and from which he gives gracious answers.
Moreover, it is not called the propitiatory mercy-seat, unless it
be sprinkled with blood, to be applied to us *by faith.* That is,
Christ reconciled us to the Father only by sufferings. In the
tabernacle was a mercy-seat in the blood of the goat, that is,
sprinkled with the blood of the goat, Lev. xvi. 15. So that here

nothing did avail but the blood of him who is set forth to be a propitiation, unless we would here translate *ἱλασαριο an atonement;* an appellation given to Christ, because he is the sacrifice to be offered for sin : which coming in the room of the guilty, was to bear their punishment, and not only merit their freedom from punishment, but reconcile God, who before was offended, satisfaction being made to vindictive justice by this vicarious punishment. But, to what purpose was all this ? " To declare the righteousness of God, *διὰ τήν πάρεσιν* for the remission of sins that are past, through the forbearance of God." God had so passed by, and not punished the sins of believers in former times, that notwithstanding these, he called them to enter upon the heavenly inheritance. But it was necessary to shew, that this was done without any injury to the justice of God. Now it is evident, that no satisfaction was made to divine justice, either by the repentance of believers, or the typical pomp of sacrifices, or by the blood sprinkled on the golden mercy-seat. It was therefore necessary, that the righteousness of God should be manifested in the propitiation and blood of Christ; by which was plainly shewn that God, agreeably to his justice, suffers not the sins of any to go unpunished. But if God, without injury to his justice, without any difficulty and trouble, and without a satisfaction, can pardon sins, the whole appears to have been an empty shew, and by no means worthy of God, without any necessity to appear with such terrible majesty in the most cruel death of his most beloved Son. Which being so horrid to think of, we conclude from this discourse of Paul, that it was not possible but God must punish sin, unless he intended to set forth Christ as a propitiation, and so declare his righteousness : because not to punish sin without a propitiatory atonement, would be a disapprobation of divine justice. For, when justice is not manifested, it is dissapproved of; especially in this grand work of our salvation. For so God himself speaks, Isa. lvi. 1. " My salvation is near to come, and my righteousness to be revealed."

XI. Some perhaps will say, that the *righteousness* of God here means, as in other places, his veracity and constancy in performing his promises; the apostle only intending, that God therefore set forth his Son to be a propitiation, in order to fulfil his prophecies and promises, and thus shewed himself just, that is, faithful. But it is quite otherwise, for the righteousness of God here denotes that rectitude by which, according to his law, by inflicting condign punishment, he discovers the demerit of sin, and his hatred to it, and how unbecoming it is for him to have fellowship with the sinner at the expence of his own glory. And that this is the meaning is plain, because the apostle

being to explain, in what manner God, without any injury to
his justice, had forborne sinners, and passed by their sins, most
beautifully shews, that all regard was paid to the honour of
divine justice, in the propitiation by Christ's blood, to be made
and revealed in due time. For it was in virtue of this, that
the sins of the believers in past times were forgiven. But the
other explication does not remove this difficulty just mentioned.
The design of the whole is to shew, that God is just when justifying the sinner for the merits of Christ.

XII. It likewise deserves our consideration, what the apostle
has expressly said, and often repeated, that the legal sacrifices
could never abolish the guilt of sin, Heb. x. 1, 4, 11. But why
might not a thing so easily to be removed without atonement be
expiated by the death of legal sacrifices? And it is to be carefully
observed, that the apostle denies this from a consideration of
the nature of the thing. It is said they could not do it, not
because it seemed otherwise to God, but because sin is of a nature, that no blood of bulls or of goats can wash out its stain;
which the light of nature itself will readily yield to as a thing
certain. And indeed the church of the Old Testament professed, that their sins could not be expiated by any blood of
calves or rams, not though multiplied to thousands; by any li-
bations of oil, though ten thousand rivers thereof were poured
out; nay, not by the death of their first-born, Mic. vi. 6, 7.

XIII. And we must not omit the apostle's inference, whereby from the inability of legal sacrifices to make satisfaction, he
concludes the necessity of the alone sacrifice of Christ. For,
after he had said, " it is not possible that the blood of bulls
and of goats should take away sins," he immediately subjoins,
" wherefore, when he cometh into the world, he saith," &c.
adding, *he taketh away the first;* namely, the offering of
beasts, *that he may establish the second;* namely, the offering of
the body of Christ. But that inference would not hold, could
there be some third way of expiation, or if no satisfaction was
necessary. But now the apostle argues, by supposing it a thing
granted by the Jews, that sins cannot be forgiven without a
proper atonement; but as this could not be effected by the
legal victims, it certainly follows, that it is to be sought for
in the offering of Christ, without which the stain of sin remains
for ever indelible. The justness of this inference of the apostle
arises from the nature of God, and of the thing itself; for if
we are to infer the necessity of the offering of Christ from the
free and arbitrary good pleasure of the divine will, the apostle's
reasoning would have been to no purpose, the good pleasure of
God only was to be insisted upon.

XIV. In like manner, the same apostle argues, Rom. iii. 19, 20, 21, &c. Where he lays it down as a fundamental truth, that the whole world is subject to condemnation before God. Whence he infers, that none can be justified by the works of the law. And from that concludes, that we can be justified no other way but by the blood of Christ, which is, doubtless, a very trifling way of arguing, if God, by his mercy alone, by his bare nod, can take away sin, and adjudge the sinner to life. For the Jews would very readily answer, that 'there is another far more compendious way of justification, in the infinite mercy of God, and in the most free act of his power, without exposing the Messiah to reproach. And, to mention it once more, we are not to have recourse to the most free disposition of the divine will, as if that was the alone cause of this necessity. For if the apostle makes any such supposition, there is an end of all further reasoning. He would have gained his point, just by mentioning that disposition. And if he does not suppose this, his argument is of no force. Which is far from being the case.

XV. We must not here omit that expression of the apostle, by which he cuts off those who have sinned against the Holy Ghost from all hope of salvation by this argument: because, having rejected Christ's expiation, *there remaineth no more sacrifice for sin*, Heb. x. 26. For when he would intimate, that there remained no more sacrifice, laying it down as an undoubted truth, that the offering of a sacrifice necessarily goes before pardon. If this was not the case, why might not man, who wanted a sacrifice, hope for pardon, without any satisfaction, from the infinite mercy of God?

XVI. To the same purpose is what the apostle says, Heb. vi. 6. "it is impossible to renew those again unto repentance, who crucify to themselves the Son of God afresh, and put him to an open shame." Which last words are variously explained by divines. But doubtless are intended to give a reason why those who have made the crucifixion of Christ of no use to themselves, are excluded from all hopes of salvation: because, without that, it is impossible to obtain salvation. The very learned Moses Amyraldus, in *Desputat. de peccato in spiritum sanctum*, § 40. thus expounds it; namely, since those apostates have no further interest in the sacrifice already offered, because they have rejected it, and therefore if they would be saved, they must look out for another. And because none could offer a true expiatory sacrifice, besides that of Christ alone; if they will be saved, it is necessary they give up Christ to be crucified afresh, and again exposed to open shame. But it is impious to design such a thing, which, on no account, can be obtained of God, Rom. vi. 9, 10. If this exposition be admitted, it presents us with a very strong argument for our opinion; because it supposes such an absolute necessity for the satisfaction of Christ, that if what he has already done be of no avail, a new satisfaction must be made before ever the sinner can have any hopes of mercy.

XVII. Moreover, our sentiment tends to display the glory of the divine perfections. It sets off his *holiness*, by reason of which he can in no respect become like a sinner, or without due satisfaction, allow him to have communion with himself, and the inhabitation of his Spirit. It exalts *the justice* of God, which is implacably inclined to punish sin. It preserves inviolable the majesty of God, which, as zealous for his honour, can suffer no contempt to be put upon it, as all sin does to go unpunished. It glorifies the unsearchable wisdom of God, which found out a way, above the reach of all created understanding, by which justice and mercy might be happily reconciled, and the honour of them both maintained pure. In a word, it magnifies the inestimable grace and love of our God, who, when there were no other means of our salvation, spared not his own Son, but gave up him for us all. And who would not heartily embrace an opinion, that displays, in such an eminent manner, the glory of God?

XVIII. Nor is it less subservient to the promotion of piety. It teacheth us to tremble before the majesty of the most high God, who, from his being God, cannot clear the guilty. It heightens the horror of sin, which it becomes us to believe is of so atrocious a nature, that nothing short of the blood of a most holy, and truly divine sacrifice, could wash it away. It sets before us the unspotted holiness of God for our pattern, that, like him, we may entertain a mortal hatred to sin, and have no manner of fellowship with it. In a word, it inflames our hearts with the most deserved returns of love, willingly to devote ourselves to his service, who, out of pure grace, delivered up his Son for us unto death, without which we should have remained miserable through eternity. And thus our opinion is that true doctrine, which is according to godliness.

XIX. And it does not derogate in the least from any of the divine perfections: not from his absolute *power*; because, doubtless, God cannot deny himself and his own perfections; nor, by his actions, testify sin not to be contrary to his nature; nor ever behave, as if he took pleasure in it, by communicating himself to the sinner; not from his most *free will*; as God neither wills, nor can will any thing but what tends to his glory, which requires his appearing as unlike the sinner as possible. Seneca spoke well, quest. Nat. lib. 1. *God is not hereby less free, or less powerful: For he is his own necessity.* Nor does it derogate from the liberty of those actions of God, which are called *ad extra*, or without him. For though he is, by no necessity of nature, constrained to external operations, considered in the gross, or together: yet, supposing the existence of one operation without him, many others necessarily follow. For instance, God was at liberty to create a world out of nothing: but having done it, it became necessary that he should govern the same in a way agreeable to his justice, holiness, wisdom, and goodness. In like manner, here God was at liberty to permit sin; but then having permitted it, his essential justice requires it to be punished. He was also at liberty to save some sinners; yet, having declared his will with respect to this, there was a necessity for a suitable satisfaction to intervene, on account of those immutable divine perfections, which he cannot in any of his actions disavow. As little does this derogate from the wise counsel of God, in ordering the punishment of it, as to the time, the degree, and the persons. For though we do not think that God inflicts punishment from his nature in such a manner as fire burns (though even in this respect, he compares himself to fire, Isa. xxvii. 4. and Deut. iv. 24.) yet his nature is a strong reason why he orders and inflicts punishment in a most wise manner. Now the nature of God requires, that he so display the glory of his justice, as he may likewise manifest the riches of his grace. Nor does it derogate from the infinite goodness of God, as if by that he could grant repentance to the sinner, and so receive him into favour without any satisfaction. For the bestowing of the Spirit of regeneration is an effect of the highest love. But that God should so much love a sinner, continuing still impenitent, without the consideration of a satisfaction, is a conduct inconsistent with his other perfections, as we have already so frequently shewn. God cannot but take his Spirit from him who maketh a mock of him. It is not becoming to grant repentance by means of the same Spirit, without the intervention of the sacrifice of the priest, whereby sin may be expiated.

XX. Seeing therefore both the nature and actions of God, and the reasonings of the sacred writers, teach us the neces-

sity of a satisfaction; since by that doctrine the eminent perfections of God are placed in the most shining light : seeing the
right observance thereof tends very much to promote piety :
And as thereby there is no derogation made from any of the
divine perfections, we conclude it is the safest course soberly to
embrace it.

XXI. Yet we must observe, when speaking in general of
the necessity of a satisfaction, or of such a punishment of sin,
wherein the righteous and holy God may be justified and sanctified, we set no bounds to the time, the degree, or the special manner of the punishment. The history of the life and
death of Christ, makes it very evident, that dispensations,
and mitigations, at least a compensation by an equivalent,
took place here, and consequently could justly take place.
And who will assert, or, if he should presume to say so, can
plainly prove, that it was impossible that Christ, in order to
make satisfaction, should undertake and submit to sufferings,
fewer in number, shorter in duration, less intense in quantity,
as to the parts of the body, and faculties of the soul, the
moments and periods of his life spent here upon earth ? And
here let that saying of Paul, Rom. xii. 3. be ever a rule to
us ; " not to think more highly than we ought to think, but
to think soberly."

CHAP. IX.

Of the Persons for whom Christ engaged and satisfied.

I. WE should have no certainty of all those things, which
it is proper for us to know, for the glory of our Lord
Christ, and our own consolation, concerning this suretiship
and satisfaction, did it not also appear, for whom he satisfied
according to his covenant-engagement. The solution of this
question is indeed of very great moment, but it does not
appear so very difficult, if we only carefully attend to the
nature of Christ's suretiship and satisfaction, which we have
already explained, proved, and defended. For since Christ
did, by his engagement, undertake to cancel all the debt of
those persons for whom he engaged, as if it was his own, by
suffering what was meet, and to fulfil all righteousness in
their room ; and since he has most fully performed this by
his satisfaction, as much as if the sinners themselves had en
dured all the punishment due to their sins, and had accomplished all righteousness : the consequence is, that he has en-

gaged and satisfied for those, and those only, who are actually
saved from their sins; as is evident to reason. For Christ
neither engaged, nor satisfied, but for those whose person he
sustained. Which Arminius himself, Adversus Perkinsum,
p. 72. frankly owns. Moreover, that any of those whose
person Christ sustained, and for whom he satisfied as their
Surety, should be obliged to satisfy for the same debt, by
eternal death, is most inconsistent with, and contrary to the
faithfulness and justice of God. Nor can we, on any account,
think it possible, that any one should in earnest plead, that
Christ died for all and every one in particular, till he has
weakened the force of that expression, *to die for any one*, by
which, as we lately made appear against the Socinians, is denoted a substitution in the place of another. But it is worth
while distinctly to set forth the true doctrine in these following positions.

II. We therefore conclude, 1st. That the obedience and
sufferings of Christ, considered in themselves, are, on account of the infinite dignity of the person, of that value, as to
have been sufficient for redeeming not only all and every man
in particular, but many myriads besides, had it so pleased
God and Christ, that he should have undertaken and satisfied
for them.

III. 2dly. That Christ as man, subject to the law of love,
did, in a holy manner, love all men without distinction, as
his neighbours, heartily wished them well, seriously lamented the ruin of those that perished, whom yet, as God, he
knew were reprobates, and for whom, as Mediator, he had
not engaged. Yet he submitted this human affection, commanded by the law, common to us and to Christ, to the divine appointment, and restricted it to the purpose of the de-
creeing will of God; in this manner proving the holiness of
his will, in the glorifying of the divine counsel, and in a due
subjection thereunto. This appears from the tears, which
Christ, as man, shed over the calamities that were coming
upon that abandoned city, which had partly slain, and partly
loaded with contempt and ignominy the prophets: nay, had
been the only butchery in the whole world for them; and
was at length, by a most horrid parricide, to devote itself,
with its unhappy posterity, to the lasting curse of God, Luke
xix. 41.

IV. 3dly. The suretiship and satisfaction of Christ, have
also been an occasion of much good, even to the reprobate.
For it is owing to the death of Christ that the gospel is

preached to every creature, that gross idolatry is abolished in many parts of the world, that wicked impiety is much restrained by the discipline of the word of God, that they obtain at times many and excellent, though not saving gifts of the holy Spirit, that " they have escaped the pollutions of the world, through the knowledge of the Lord and Saviour Jesus Christ," 2 Pet. ii. 20. And who can in short enumerate all those things which they enjoy, not through accident only, and beside the intention of God, and of Christ, but by the appointment of God? Not indeed with a design and purpose of saving them according to the Testament; but from a view to make known his long-suffering towards the vessels of wrath, that is, those who are to perish, who dwell among those who are to be saved. For nothing falls out by accident with respect to the intention of God; every thing being according to his determinate counsel.

V. 4thly. That the obedience and sufferings of Christ are of such worth, that all, without exception, who come to him, may find perfect salvation in him: and it was the will of God, that this truth should, without distinction, be proposed both to them that are to be saved, and to them that are to perish; with a *charge* not to neglect so great salvation, but to repair to Christ with true contrition of soul; and with a most sincere *declaration*, that all who come to him shall find salvation in him, John vi. 40.

VI. 5thly. That, however, Christ, according to the will of God the Father, and his own purpose, did neither engage nor satisfy, and consequently in no manner die, but only for all those whom the Father gave him, and who are actually saved. This is that truth which is controverted, and which we are now to confirm, in a concise but solid manner, from the sacred writings.

VII. The scripture declares, that Christ satisfied for the whole body of the elect, when it declares, that he *died for all*, and *by him reconciled all things*, as 2 Cor. v. 15. Heb. ii. 9. Col. i. 20. And as this is not to be understood of all and every man in particular, it must be meant of all and every one of the elect. That it cannot be understood of all and every individual, I prove from the passages quoted in the following manner. Those *all for whom* Christ is said to *have died*, 2 Cor. v. 15. are those who are also dead, namely, as to the old man, whom in virtue of the crucifixion of Christ, they have crucified, Rom. vi. 6. and who " live not to themselves, but to Christ," and to Christ indeed, who rose again for them. But these things can be applicable only to the elect. None

but they are dead to themselves, the world, and to sin :
none else live to Christ. In a word, according to the very
hypothesis of the Remonstrants, the efficacy of Christ's resurrection is restrained to believers alone. In like manner, those
all, for whom Christ is said by the grace of God to have
tasted death, Heb. ii. 9. are *sons brought*, or to be brought,
unto glory, who have Christ for the *captain of their salvation ;*
who *are sanctified*, whom *he calls his brethren, which God
gave him*, ver. 10, 11, 13. These things can be applied not
to the reprobate, but only to the elect. In like manner, those
all things which are said to be " reconciled to God by the
peace made through the blood of Christ," Col. i. 20. can only
extend to the elect. The thing is self-evident. For reconciliation and peace-making with God are peculiar to elect believers, Rom. v. 1. On the contrary, the reprobate are perpetual enemies to God, " the wrath of God abideth on them,"
John iii. 36. By those things which are on earth, are understood believers, who are still in the world ; as by *those things
which are in heaven*, are meant, not angels, but men in the
state of bliss, who enjoy, in the fullest manner, the fruits of
Christ's atonement and reconciliation.

VIII. Let us add that remarkable passage, 1 Tim. ii. 4, 6.
" God will have all men to be saved, and to come unto the
[acknowledgment] knowledge of the truth : Christ gave himself a ransom for all." Where by *all*, we are not to understand all and every one in particular, but the elect of whatever nation and condition ; which I make evidently to appear
in this manner : 1st. They for whom Christ gave himself a
ransom, are actually rescued from the dominion of Satan, are
brought to perfect liberty, and can never be thrust into an
eternal prison, in order to satisfy again for those debts which
Christ paid to the utmost farthing. This we must certainly
maintain, unless we would have Christ's payment go for nothing. But all, and every one in particular, are not set free
from the dominion of Satan. Many are, and do still remain,
" children of disobedience, in whom that impure spirit worketh," Eph. ii. 2. and who are for ever *held captive at his will,
in the snare of the devil*, and these shall be forced to satisfy
for their own guilt. Christ therefore did not give himself a
ransom for them. 2dly. Paul speaks of *all* those who have
Christ for their Mediator. But he is Mediator, both by *the
offering* of his body and blood, and by his *powerful intercession*. This latter part of his mediation can on no account be
excluded here, when the apostle is treating concerning our
prayers, of which we have a most perfect pattern in the

prayers of Christ. Besides the Remonstrants acknowledge, that Christ's intercession is not for all and every man in particular: therefore, he is not the perfect Mediator of all and every individual. 3dly. What is here spoken is concerning all those " whom God will have to be saved, and come to the [acknowledgment] knowledge of the truth." But this is not his will concerning every man in particular, because he will have unbelievers condemned, John iii. 36. And the acknowledgment of the truth, or *faith, is not the privilege of all*, 2 Thess. iii. 2. but of *the elect*, Tit. i. 1. Nor is it the will of God it should. *He hardeneth whom he will*, Rom. ix. 18. Besides, it is unworthy of the divine majesty, to imagine that there is an *incomplete, unresolved*, and *ineffectual volition* in God, Psal. cxv. 3. And it is mere trifling and mean, to understand a bare *will of precept*, enjoining all to work out their own salvation with fear and trembling, and with all diligence to seek the knowledge of the truth; or, a will of his good pleasure, approving what is according to the precept; they with whom we now argue do not take it in that light. 4thly. The persons here meant are all those for whom we are to pray: but we are not to pray for all and every one in particular: not certainly for those who are already damned: not for the salvation of all who are now alive, collectively taken; because we cannot do it in faith; and we are sure that many of them will be damned: nor in fine, for those *who have sinned the sin unto death*, 1 John v. 16. 5thly. and lastly, It is acknowledged that these words are made use of by the apostle, as a motive for the prayers which he requires, and which shall not be in vain. But the words of the apostle would infer no such thing, if they only meant that Christ has, by his satisfaction, obtained no more than a possibility for God to be reconciled to all and every one in particular, though by the nature of that impetration, it is possible none may be actually saved; because if that death has only procured a possibility of salvation, and if our desires after that salvation might be ineffectual, we could neither be sure of their being heard, nor have that hope of audience, which maketh not ashamed. We must then conclude, that Christ gave himself a ransom of redemption for all the elect, of whatever nation and condition, and that it is the will of God they all should be saved; consequently, that it is our duty to be subservient, by our prayers, to this counsel of God; and as we know not how to distinguish the elect from the reprobate, to pray indiscriminately for all, referring it to God to distinguish those who are his; especially, because we are certain, we shall not pray in vain for those whom God wills to be saved, and for whom Christ gave himself.

IX. The scripture inculcates the same truth, when it says, that " Christ gave his flesh for the life of the world," John vi. 51. that he is " the propitiation for our sins, and not for ours only, but also for the sins of the whole world," 1 John ii. 2. That " God was in Christ reconciling the world to himself," 2 Cor. v. 19. That Christ is " the Lamb of God that taketh away the sins of the world," John i. 29. And other passages to the like purpose. Where by the term *world* cannot, nay, ought not be understood the whole of mankind, but the elect. Which we prove by the following arguments:

X. It is clear that in scripture things are sometimes said of the world, as agree only to the elect and to believers. Thus Christ prays, John xvii. 21. " that the world may believe that thou hast sent me," and ver. 23. " that the world may know that thou hast sent me." But these things belong to that sacerdotal intercession of Christ, concerning which we may with the greatest certainty conclude, that it will never be rejected, says *Arminius*, in *Oratione de sacerdotio Christi*, and which, it is certain, is not made for the world of reprobates, Christ having expressly declared that, v. 9. and they with whom we argue do not refuse it. It is therefore necessary, that by the *world*, we here understand the *world of the elect*, who believe on Christ, and know him by faith, by virtue of the intercession of Christ, and by means of the ministry, together with the holy and glorious example of believers.

XI. Moreover, many texts which speak of salvation, not only as impetrated, but as applied, ascribe it to the world. Thus Christ declares, John iii. 17. " for God sent not his Son into the world to condemn the world, but that the world through him might be saved." But the intention of God, in sending his Son, is not to save all, but " that whosoever believeth in him should not perish, but have eternal life," as Christ explains himself in the foregoing verses. In like manner, John vi. 33. " the bread of God is he which cometh down from heaven, and giveth life unto the world." But Christ gives life only to the elect, to the sheep, and not to the goats, John x. 27, 28. Thus Christ in prosecuting his discourse above quoted, John vi. restrains the term *world*, to those " whom the Father gave him, who see the Son, and believe on him," v. 39, 40.

XII. These expressions likewise, the *father of those that believe*, and *the heir of the world*, denote the same thing in the promise made to Abraham, Rom. iv. 11, 12, 13. Abraham is *the father of those that believe*. 1st. As a pattern of

faith. 2dly. As a pattern of the blessing, or of justification
by faith. 3dly. On account of Christ who descended from
him, and by whose Spirit the elect are born again : hence
Christ, along with his mystical body, is called *the seed of
Abraham*, Gal. iii. 16. He is *the heir of the world*, that is,
of all the families of the earth, who are blessed in him as in
the pattern of faith and of the blessing by it, and in his seed
Christ, as the fountain of every blessing. For this is that
world which Christ receives for an inheritance ; as also Abraham, and consequently every believer who is his seed in Christ ;
or who becomes Christ's own possession, and with whom Abraham and every believer have communion, exulting in the good
things which are bestowed upon them, 1 Cor. iii. 21, 22. For
that strict union and sincere love which subsist between them,
are the reason that every one rejoices in, and glorifies God, on
account of the benefits bestowed on his neighbour, as if bestowed on himself. And thus we have made it appear that the
term *world*, sometimes in scripture, denotes *the collective body
of believers, or of the elect.*

XIII. We add, that the Holy Ghost speaks in this manner with great propriety for several substantial reasons. For
1st. The term *world*, generally in the common way of speaking, denotes any large body or multitude of men whatever.
Thus the Pharisees said among themselves, " perceive ye
how ye prevail nothing? Behold ! the world is gone after
him," John xii. 19. We have a like phraseology in Horajot,
c. 3. In Gemara, " when Rabbi Simeon the son of Gama-
liel entered (namely into the synagogue) the whole world
rose up before him ;" that is, all who were present in the
synagogue. Why then should not a very large and almost
infinite multitude of the chosen people from among all nations ;
" that great multitude which no man can number," Rev. vii.
9. be elegantly designed by the appellation *world?* 2dly. Elect
believers, considered in themselves, and *before effectual calling*, are a part of " the world lying in wickedness," 1 John
v. 19. " In time past they walked in trespasses and sins,
according to the course of this world," Eph. ii. 1, 2. ; and so
far they belong to that *world* " which is become guilty before God," Rom. iii. 19. But this tends to illustrate the
glory of the love of God and Christ, and to the humiliation
of believers ; that while they were a part of the wicked
world, Christ was given to be their Redeemer. 3dly. Elect
believers are, *after effectual calling*, considered as beautified
with divine grace, though *the less*, yet *the best* part of the
world. " The saints and the excellent that are in the earth,"

Psal. xvi. 3. " The holy seed, which is the substance (support) of the earth." Isa. vi. 13. And as the Jews are wont to speak, *the just are the pillars of the world.* But what is more usual, what more suitable, than that the whole should, by a synecdoche, signify the better, as sometimes the greater part ? It is therefore not without its emphasis, and yields useful instructions, when we hear *the collective body of the elect* designed by the name of the *world.*

XIV. Now let us apply these things to the passages we have already quoted, § V. Christ indeed says, when speaking of *impetration,* John vi. 51. that " he will give his flesh for the life of the world ;" but in the same chapter, verse 33. when speaking of *the application,* he says, that *he giveth life to the world ;* and so he explains what in the subject of redemption he would have us to understand by *the world.* But it is a capital truth, that the application of redemption extends no further than to believers and the elect.

XV. When John writes, 1 John ii. 2. that " Christ is the propitiation not only for our sins, but also for the sins of the whole world :" he shews us by these words who they are that can take comfort to themselves from the intercession of Christ, and the remission purchased by him. But elect believers alone can do this ; he is their advocate with the Father, and not that of the reprobate. To them, and not to the reprobate, " God hath set him forth to be a propitiation, through faith in his blood," Rom. iii. 25. Moreover this consolation belongs not only to the elect from among the Jewish nation, such as John was, but also to the elect from among the Gentiles, whom Paul expressly points out by the name of *the world,* Rom. xi. 12, 15. By a phraseology very usual among the Hebrew doctors, who call the Gentiles *the nations of the world.* Nor does this saving truth yield comfort to those believers only who *lived at that time,* and to whom, as to his children, John was writing ; but also to those who lived in *the antediluvian world,* and under the Mosaical pedagogy, whose sins were no otherwise expiated than by the blood of Christ ; and in fine, to those believers who from John's days were *to be brought* to Christ out of all nations whatever, *to the end of the world ;* which very great multitude is deservedly designed by the name of *the whole world.* For it is very certain that by the whole world is not denoted the collective body of all mankind ; for John expressly discriminates himself and those to whom he is writing from the whole world, and yet he could not seclude them from being a part of the collective body of mankind.

XVI. When Paul says, 2 Cor. v. 19. that " God was in Christ reconciling the world to himself," he immediately sub-joins, that this was *by not imputing their trespasses unto them ;* to teach us, that reconciliation, and non-imputation, are of equal extent. But the latter is the privilege of the elect and of believers alone, and of those in whose heart there is no guile. For David declares " those blessed, to whom God imputeth not iniquity," Psal. xxxii. 1, 2. Rom. iv. 6, 8. Therefore by the world, the world of the elect is signified.

XVII. John i. 29. Christ is called " the Lamb of God, which taketh away the sin of the world." But like that goat on which the iniquity of the children of Israel was laid, he taketh them away by taking them upon himself, by satisfy-ing for them as if they were his own, and by taking them away from his people, as to their guilt by justification, and as to their dominion and stain by sanctification: see 1 Pet. ii. 24. But as these things point to the impetration of salvation, so as at the same time to include its application, they can extend no farther than to the world of the elect believers. " Blessed is he whose transgression is taken away [forgiven]," Psal. xxxii. 1.

XVIII. And thus we have shewn, that though the scrip-ture, when speaking of the world of the redeemed, really de-signs some collective body, yet it is that of the elect only. Which Prosper elegantly expressed, de Vocat. Gent. lib. 1. c. 3. or in another edition, c. 9. " In the elect, even those foreknown, and discriminated from every generality, or col-lective body, there is deemed to be a certain peculiar kind of universality ; so as that a whole world seems to be delivered out of a whole world, and all men to be redeemed from among all men."

XIX. Let us now more especially shew that Christ made satisfaction for the elect only. To this purpose are those passages of scripture, in which the death of Christ is restrict-ed to *his sheep, his church, his people,* nay, and *his peculiar people,* John x. 15. Acts xx. 28. Eph. v. 25. Tit. ii. 14. from which we thus argue: what the scriptures restrict to some certain kind of men, to the manifest exclusion of the rest, ought not to be extended absolutely to all men. But the scriptures, in the passages quoted, limit the death of Christ to a certain kind of men, so as manifestly to exclude the rest. Therefore, &c. The truth of the major, or first proposition, is evident from the terms: that of the minor, from the passages quoted : In order to illustrate this, we are to shew these two things : 1st. That the subject matter is the

impetration of salvation, which is the act of Christ; and not
the fruition alone, which is our act. 2dly. That the death
of Christ is so restricted to those who are there described, as
to exclude the rest of mankind. The Remonstrants, not being
able otherwise to resist the force of this argument, deny both
these.

XX. As to the former, namely, that the impetration of
salvation is here intended, I thus prove: 1st. The very
terms which the Holy Spirit uses in the passages quoted,
" to lay down his life for some, to purchase some, to give
himself for some," import satisfaction, impetration, and acquisition. Nor do the scriptures usually speak in any other
strain, when the subject is evidently concerning impetration.
2dly. In the passages quoted we have a clear description of
what Christ has done both without us and without our concurrence; whereas the real fruition or enjoyment, concerning which
the Remonstrants will have those passages to be understood, is
our act. These two differ much both in *nature* and *time*. In
nature; for the one resembles a mean appointed for some
end; the other an external end, or rather the use or enjoyment of that for which that mean is appointed. In *time;* for
these propositions were completely verified the moment in
which Christ laid down his life; but the actual enjoyment or
application, is a thing accomplishing gradually for a long tract
of time in all the elect. 3dly. The Remonstrants themselves
produce similar phrases from scripture, of *dying for some,*
purchasing some, &c. when they contend, that the impetration of the grace of God reaches to others besides the elect;
with what colour or pretence then, do they deny that impetration is here the subject matter? 4thly. They shew that
they lay no stress on these passages, when they afterwards
affirm, they cannot refer to believers alone, and maintain that
by the church, we are not to understand the elect alone, or
that Christ gave himself for them only. Therefore, I say, to
purchase and give himself for a person cannot here be understood of real enjoyment, which is peculiar to believers only.
5thly. and lastly, By making this exception, the answer of
the Remonstrants comes only to a begging the question: for
we maintain, and are directly to prove it by the strongest arguments, that the application of saving grace is as extensive
as its impetration; and we own the question here is not concerning such an impetration as may have its plenary effect
though never applied. For such an impetration, we judge
absurd, untheological, and highly unworthy of Christ.

XXI. The second, namely, which respects the exclusion

of the rest of mankind, when distinct mention is made of the
sheep, the church, a peculiar people; I shall make evident,
first, by shewing, that by these appellations, sheep, church,
peculiar people, cannot be understood all men in general; and
then that what is here asserted of the sheep, church, peculiar
people, flows from that extraordinary love of Christ, which
he has not for the rest of mankind.   The first has no great
difficulty in it : for Christ expressly says to some, John x. 26.
" ye are not of my sheep."   And therefore, he divides mankind into sheep and goats; of whom the last are undoubtedly
reprobate, the former, certainly the elect, and heirs of eternal
life, Matt. xxv. 33.

XXII. Our opponents themselves will not affirm that all
belong to the church.   They indeed say, that the visible church
is meant, in which there are others besides the elect.   But, 1st.
It sufficiently answers our purpose, that all and every one in
particular cannot be understood.   2dly. That what is said of
the visible church, is sometimes of such a nature, as can be
understood only of the elect therein : as when the apostle, writing to the visible church of the Ephesians, i. 4. says, *he hath
chosen you in him :* and in like manner, 1 Thess. i. 4. and we
shall presently shew, that what is said of the church in the
places quoted, is of the same nature.

XXIII. In a word, the term *all* cannot be applied to the
people of God, for God himself makes this clear, when he ordered some to be called, עַמִּי לֹא *ye are not my people,* Loammi,
Hos. i. 9.   And they who dissent from us, take a wrong course,
when, by *people,* they understand the Jews; for there were
reprobates even among them.   Thus we learn from Paul, that
with respect to spiritual privileges, they are not all accounted
Israel, who are of Israel, and therefore not to be reckoned the
people, Rom. xi. 1, 2.*

XXIV. But it is not enough to have shewn, that the names
sheep, church, people, do not comprehend every individual of
mankind : for it is possible, that on a particular occasion,
something might be said of some persons, which certainly
agree to them, but not to them only.   The question is not,
whether Christ died for the elect, but whether for them only.
Our adversaries say, this cannot be concluded from those passages where the particle *only* is not added.   We must therefore shew, that these things are so appropriated to the elect,
as to exclude the rest of mankind; I prove it thus: all the
passages quoted tend to amplify the extraordinary love of

---

* To this quotation of the author's, may be added, Rom. ix. 6.

Christ towards his sheep, for whom he laid down his life, towards the church, which he purchased with his own blood, towards his people, for whom he gave himself. But if in this, the sheep, the church, and people of Christ, have nothing peculiarly distinguishing beyond all other men, what probable reason can be assigned, why that infinite love of Christ, in laying down his life, shedding his blood, and giving himself, should especially be appropriated to them?

XXV. To this reasoning our adversaries absurdly oppose Paul's gloriation, who while writing, Gal. ii. 20. that Christ was given for him, does not exclude others from a share in the same love. For in that text, Paul does not speak of any divine love, whereby God peculiarly distinguished him from others who had the like precious faith with himself; nor does he consider himself as Paul, but as an elect person, and a believer, proposing himself there, as an example, in the name of all believers: and we are so far from being able to infer from this, that what Paul affirms of himself was peculiar to him, that quite the reverse ought to be concluded: this instance therefore does not suit the case.

XXVI. But let us consider each passage apart: when Christ publicly declares, that " he lays down his life for his sheep," he thence infers, that " he must bring them to hear his voice, that there may be one fold and one shepherd," John x. 15, 16, 17. But it is certain, that these last assertions agree to elect believers only, and therefore also the first, from which the others are deduced. For it would not be a just inference to say, I lay down my life for my sheep, therefore I must bring them to hear my voice, &c. Did he lay down his life for some, whom he never brings, &c.

XXVII. When Paul said, that Christ purchased his church with his own blood, Acts xx. 28. he more distinctly explains in his epistle to the Ephesians, v. 25. what he means by the church, which Christ loved and gave himself for, namely, the spouse of Christ, whom alone he loves with a conjugal affection, and sanctifies, and presents glorious to himself. But that love of Christ which was the motive of his giving himself, and of the sanctification and glorification of the church, which is the fruit of that donation, belongs to elect believers only; therefore also the very giving itself, which is the consequence of that love, and the cause of the sanctification of the church. Moreover, that this conjugal love of Christ, whereby he purchased the church as his spouse, by his own blood, has the general assembly of the elect alone, for its object, to wave other considerations, may be hence also inferred, because Paul proposes it here as a pattern of the conjugal love of the husband for the wife. But this love ought doubtless to reach no farther than the wife.

XXVIII. Lastly, when Paul reminds his son Titus, that " Christ gave himself for us, that he might redeem us from all iniquity, and purify unto himself a people, zealous of good works," Tit. ii. 14. he evidently shews, what was the fruit of Christ's giving himself; namely, redemption from iniquity, and the purification of a peculiar people, &c. And consequently they, who are not redeemed from iniquity, nor purified, nor made his peculiar people, &c. cannot glory in this, that Christ gave himself for them.

XXIX. What the apostle writes in this chapter, ver. 11. that " the grace of God, that bringeth salvation hath appeared to all men, teaching us that denying ungodliness, &c. neither avails our adversaries, nor is any way detrimental to the truth we maintain. For, 1st. The preaching of the gospel by which the saving grace of God is offered, and which is here intended by that expression, had not reached all mankind without exception, nay nor every nation in the days of Paul. 2dly. The preaching of the gospel reaches the ears of a great many more than of those, who are the objects of that love of Christ which bringeth salvation? For it is only an external mean, by which the elect, out of every nation, are brought to the communion of Christ. And therefore the gospel is to be preached to every nation, without distinction, that the elect therein may hear it. 3dly. We should observe the apostle's scope, which is to encourage servants to the exercise of universal piety, that by their holy conversation, *they may adorn the doctrine of Christ in all things.* The reason he gives for this is, because the saving grace of Christ has appeared, both to masters and servants, teaching us, &c. As if he had said, ' That all men, of whatever rank, professing the gospel, ought ' to reckon it their duty to adorn its doctrine by the purity ' of their manners : for as to the doctrine itself, it so plainly, ' so expressly, and so efficaciously instructs us in all good- ' ness as none, but they who wilfully stop their ears, can be ' ignorant of. And therefore all the professors of it, as well ' masters as servants, should take care, lest they bring a ' scandal on this most perfect of all rules, by lives which have ' little or no conformity to it.' This is the full import of these words, so that any may see that they make nothing for the universal efficacy of Christ's death.

XXX. If we search the matter to the bottom we will most clearly discern, that it never was Christ's intention to satisfy for all in general. Certainly, he satisfied only for those he engaged for. But he engaged " to do the will of his Father," Psal. xl. 9. But this is the will of his Father, not that every man should be saved, but those that were given him, that is, the elect out of every nation, who are to receive the gift of faith. Those the Father gave him for an inheritance by an irrevocable testament. For thus Jehovah speaks, Isa. xlix. 6. " It is a light thing that thou shouldst be my servant, to raise up the tribes of Jacob, and to restore the preserved of Israel: I will also give thee for a light to the Gentiles, that thou mayest be my salvation unto the end of the earth." And Christ himself still more clearly, John vi. 39. " This is the Father's will, which hath sent me, that of all which he hath given me, I should lose nothing." But all are not given to Christ, only those that come to him, v. 37. " all that the Father giveth me shall come to me." He therefore only engaged for these, according to the will of the Father: took their sins upon him, carried them on his heart, when he offered himself to the Father; claims them as his peculiar property, in virtue of his merit, according to agreement, challenges them for his own, and will, at length in due time, present them holy and glorious to his Father, saying, " behold I, and the children which God hath given me," Heb. ii. 13. All those things naturally flow from the very nature of the covenant which subsists between the Father and the Son, as formerly explained.

XXXI. And these particulars may be further illustrated, and confirmed from Aaron's typical priesthood. The high priest, on the solemn day of expiation, slew one of the goats, on which the sins of all Israel were laid, and sent the other into the wilderness. All these things were typical. The high priest, the sacrifice, the scape-goat, all set forth Christ. But who were typically designed by Israel? Not indeed all men. For what is more absurd than that Israel should be a type of the Edomites and Egyptians, and of all that world out of which they were chosen, and from which, on so many accounts, they were distinguished? We therefore conclude that they were typical of the elect, who are the true Israelites, Jews inwardly, and in the spirit, and whom the apostle loves to distinguish by the name of *the Election*, Rom. xi. 7. For, the nature of the type, consisted in this, that the people of Israel, was chosen by an external pomp of ceremonies, was redeemed, and in their measure was a holy priesthood. They therefore prefigured those, who were truly chosen, redeemed and consecrated a royal priesthood to God; as Peter seems not obscurely to signify, 1 Pet. ii. 5. As therefore the high priest formerly offered an atoning sacrifice not for the Egyptians or Canaanites, but for the typical Israel only; So our high priest, according to the order of Melchizedek, offered himself once, not for abandoned reprobates, but for mystical Israel, that is, the truly chosen.

XXXII. This truth will appear very plain, if we attend to some of the inseparable effects of Christ's satisfaction. It would carry us too far to enumerate all: let us consider some of the principal. " If they who were enemies to God were reconciled by the death of his Son; much more being reconciled, they shall be saved by his life," Rom. v. 10. For whom God, not sparing his own Son, gave him up unto death, " with him freely he gives them all things," Rom. viii. 32. We may boldly say to them for whom Christ died, " who shall lay any thing to the charge of God's Elect ? It is God that justifieth. Who is he that condemneth ?" &c. v. 33, 34. They whom Christ *redeemed from the curse of the law* are not under the curse, but " the blessing of Abraham, cometh upon them," Gal. iii. 13, 14. But this is not true of all and every one, but of elect believers only, that they are saved by the life of Christ: that with Christ God freely gives them all things; that none can lay any thing to their charge, or bring an accusation against them; that upon them is come the blessing of Abraham. Therefore they alone are the persons of whom the foregoing things may be truly affirmed.

XXXIII. That fictitious satisfaction for the reprobate, and those who perish, is altogether a vain and useless thing. For, whom does it profit? Not certainly God, who by no act can be rendered happier than he is. Not Christ himself, who, as he never seeks them, so he never receives, for his peculiar property, and neither is he enriched by possessing them, though supposed to have purchased them at a dear rate. Not believers, who content with their portion in God and in Christ, and fully redeemed by Christ, enjoy a happiness in every respect complete. In fine, not those that perish, who are constrained to satisfy in their own persons, for their sins to the utmost farthing. But to affirm the satisfaction of Christ to be a vain and useless thing is absurd, and borders upon blasphemy. Remigius, formerly bishop of Lyons, said extremely well, when discoursing at large on this controverted point, " The blood of Christ is a great price; such a price can, in no respect, be in vain and ineffectual, but rather is filled with the super-abundant advantage arising from those blessings for which it was paid." See *Forbes. Instruct. Hist.* lib. 8. c. 16.

XXXIV. Nor are we to say, that therefore the reprobate have no benefit by the satisfaction of Christ, because the condition of faith and perseverance, which the reprobate do not perform, is necessary to that purpose. For first, it is not true that faith and perseverance are pre-requisite conditions, before a person can have any of the fruits of Christ's satisfaction. For regeneration itself and effectual calling which go before actual faith ; justisfication, adoption, and sanctification, which precede final perseverance in the faith, are the fruits of Christ's most excellent satisfaction. And then from the want of faith and perseverance in those that perish, we have a most effectual proof, that the blood of the new covenant was not shed for them ; for by that Christ has merited for his people the continuance of the new life in faith and love. Seeing he is " the Mediator of that better covenant, which was established upon better promises," Heb. viii. 6. But these promises are sanctification, ver. 10. " I will put my laws into their mind ;" and the continuance thereof, " I will be to them a God, and they shall be to me a people." For in the new covenant, to be a God to any, is to be an everlasting Saviour, as we gather from Matt. xxii. 32. and which the opposition made between the new and the old covenant, in like manner shews, Heb. viii. 8, 9. These promises, being graciously and actually conferred on the elect in virtue of Christ's satisfaction, would have certainly been conferred on the rest of mankind, had Christ equally satisfied for them.

XXXV. Nay, the satisfaction of Christ for the reprobate had not only been useless, but highly unworthy both of God and of Christ. Unworthy of the wisdom, goodness, and justice of God, to exact and receive satisfaction from his most beloved Son for those whom he neither gave nor wanted to give his Scn, and whom he decreed to consign to everlasting confinement, to suffer in their own persons, according to the demerit of their crimes. Unworthy of Christ to give his blood a price of redemption for those whom * he had not in charge to redeem. And, if we may speak freely, this also, in some respect, would be for Christ *to account the blood of the new covenant,* or the new covenant itself, *in which he was sanctified, a common* or unholy *thing.*

---

* There is a deficiency in this part of the paragraph in the first and third editions, which, by the favour of a particular friend, I got supplied from the second.

XXXVI. I should now refute the arguments of those on the other side of the question ; but this has been done at large, and with so much judgment, by very learned men, that we can scarce make any addition. The very accurate dissertation of Gomarus on this head, may especially be consulted, which is inserted in his commentaries on the epistle to the Galatians.

CHAP. X.

After what manner Christ used the Sacraments.

I. Thus far we have at large treated of those things that relate to the covenant between Christ and the Father, and might seem to have completely finished that subject, was it not proper to add something concerning the sacraments, by which that covenant was confirmed. The apostle has observed, Heb. vii. 20, 21. that *not without an oath,* Christ was made priest, and Surety of a better Testament. As this manifested the stability of the covenant, and the immutability of God's counsel ; so it likewise contributed to the full assurance of Christ the Mediator. It moreover pleased God, to confirm that covenant by certain external symbols, and indeed the very same by which the covenant of grace was sealed to believers under the different dispensations of it. We have already hinted something on this subject, which we are now to enlarge upon more distinctly.

II. It is evident that the Lord Jesus was *circumcised* on the eighth day from his birth, Luke ii. 21. that he kept *the passover* with his disciples, Luke xxii. 8, 11. and was *baptized* by John, Matt. iii. 13. Though the evangelists do not indeed expressly assert that he also partook of the holy *supper ;* yet they relate what we think may make it more than probable he did.

III. 1st. It is certain that our Lord, in the institution and use of the mystical supper, borrowed most of the rites from the Jewish passover. The very learned Joseph Scaliger, Ludovicus Capellus, and most particularly Buxtorf, in a peculiar dissertation, have made this as clear as noon-day. Thus our Lord took the bread and cup distinctly, separately blessed them both, and gave them to his disciples after the Jewish manner. It was besides, a custom among the Jews, for the master of the family to eat first of the bread after blessing : to this purpose *Maimonides* in *Hilcot Berachot,* chap. vii. says, " the guests were not to eat or taste any thing till he who broke had tasted first." Nor was it permitted, at festivals and solemn feasts, for any of the guests to drink of the cup, till after the master of the family had done it first, according to an express passage quoted by Buxtorf from the *Talmud*, where it is said, " to be an excellent precept, that he who sanctifies or blesses, should first taste, and after all the guests sitting down, tasted : every one took a draught;" see the above dissertation, sect. 76. In this manner Christ acted at the paschal supper, Luke xxii. 15, 17. and why not so at this new mystical supper?

IV. 2dly. This observation will be more cogent, if we consider that the same phraseology used by Christ of the paschal cup, Luke xxii. 18. *I will not drink of the fruit of the vine, until the kingdom of God shall come,* is also, according to Matt. xxvi. 29. made use of concerning the cup at the holy supper. Whence we infer, that then Christ likewise drank of the cup with his disciples.

V. 3dly. We may add, that no reason can be assigned why Christ should not partake of the supper, as he did of baptism, and consecrate, in his own person, these two Sacraments of the New Testament.

VI. 4thly. Nay, this seems requisite from the mutual union between Christ and believers, and that intercourse of intimate familiarity, which among other things, was sealed in this mystical feast, and which our Lord himself has very elegantly proposed, under the similitude of a mutual supper, Rev. iii. 20. " I will sup with him, and he with me."

VII. This also was the opinion of the fathers : As of Jerome in epist. ad Hedibiam, quest. 2. " Not Moses, but the Lord Jesus gave us the true bread : he himself at once the entertainer and the entertainment; the eater and the food." Of *Augustine de Doctrina Christiana,* lib. 2. cap. iii. " And having first tasted the sacrament of his body and blood, he signified his meaning." Of *Chrysostom, Homil.* 83. *in Matth.* " He also drinks thereof, lest on hearing his words they should say, And do we then drink blood and eat flesh ? And therefore, in order to prevent this, he himself sets them an example," &c.

VIII. This use of the Sacraments was not a matter of choice to Christ, but *a part of his righteousness,* and *a duty* incumbent upon him. For he himself declared when John refused to baptize him, *suffer it to be so now ; for thus* πρέπον ἐστίν *it becometh us to fulfil all righteousness,* Matt. iii. 15. Where by *righteousness,* he means the obedience due to the command of God, and it became both John and Christ, to fulfil *all,* and consequently this part. The part of Christ was to present himself to be baptized by John: and John's duty not to deny Christ in this: thus it became both of them: nor was it a matter of mere *fitness* in this place, as if baptism was a thing unnecessary; (it being, as I have already said, a part of the righteousness which Christ was to fulfil) but it signified every duty incumbent, and the performance of every such duty is an ornament to the saints, and renders them beautiful in the eyes of God: as the Psalmist sings, Psal. xciii. 5. *holiness* [is the beauty of] *becometh thine house* [or those that frequent thy house]. In this sense Paul said; Eph. v. 3. *as πρέπει becometh saints*, and 1 Tim. ii. 10. *ὅ πρέπει which becometh women professing godliness*, and Heb. ii. 10. *for ἔπρεπε it became him.* *The rectitude, beauty, or comeliness of God, who is adorned with rectitude and beauty, Psal. lxxxix. 8. (which rectitude he can neither deny nor act contrary to) required, that the captain of our salvation should be made perfect by sufferings; *such a High Priest became us*, Heb. vii. 26. From which it appears, that the baptism of Christ was a part of his duty, by which he rendered himself comely both in the eyes of God and men.

IX. But besides this, the Sacraments which Christ made use of had still a further respect. They are not only to be considered as *acts of obedience*, enjoined by the law, but also as *signs and seals of the covenant*, whereby the mutual engagements of the contracting parties are sealed. For God did not institute the Sacraments with a view that any should place virtue and holiness in the bare exercise of those acts, but that they might be seals of spiritual things. Nor does he make a proper use of the Sacraments, who does not apply them to that end. But, doubtless, Christ made use of these institutions agreeably to the intention of God who appointed them, as was proper to be done by that most perfect and excellent servant in whom God was well pleased. There was therefore, in the use of the Sacraments, a confirmation of the promises, both of those made by the Father to the Son, and by the Son to the Father.

X. But then, the promises made to Christ were of various kinds: some were made to him as a particular man, born holy, who was to be justified and made happy upon constantly persevering in the course of his commenced purity. For Christ was indeed a holy creature, but to make a holy creature happy who preserves its holiness untainted, is so agreeable to the divine goodness, that it is scarce, if at all possible, it could be other-

---

* The author here uses a word of a very general signification, signifying every thing that is suitable to the perfections of God. And as the divine rectitude, holiness, or righteousness, is his beauty, so this, I apprehend, is what the author means here by *decentia Dei.*

wise, as we have proved at large, Book I. chap. iv. § XII. seq.
And these promises are legal, and belong to *the covenant of
works :* but there were other promises made to him as *Surety*
and *Mediator*, by which his *person*, and his *office*, and *work*, as
Mediator, should be acceptable to God, and very successful:
and a twofold effect was certainly to ensue, *one for himself*, viz.
a most excellent degree of glory; *the other for the elect*, who
were to be united to him, namely, their salvation.   And these
last are properly the promises of the covenant we are now upon,
of which we have given a specimen, chap. iii. § XXIX. seq.

XI. We may now enquire, whether both these kinds of promises were sealed to Christ, by the ordinary Sacraments of the
Old and New Testament, which he partook of.   But we must
not determine any thing rashly with respect to this: and therefore I shall modestly propose what I think most probable.
There is indeed no reason why Christ, as a holy man, and who
as such, was to be made happy, might not be confirmed in the
faith of this promise by some certain Sacraments, as appears
from the Sacraments of the covenant of works given to Adam
before the fall.   But that such Sacraments were for that purpose granted to Christ, does not appear from scripture.   Moreover, I dare not affirm, that the ordinary Sacraments, which
Christ made use of, were subservient to the confirming the legal
promises belonging to the covenant of works, because they are
Sacraments of the covenant of grace.   And it does not seem
consistent, that the promises of the covenant of works should
be sealed by the Sacraments of the covenant of grace.

XII. I cannot indeed refuse, that there is a great difference
in some circumstances, relative to the signification of the Sacraments, as made use of by Christ, and as used by believers.   For
to the latter they seal regeneration, the mortification of the old,
and the vivification of the new man, the remission of sins.   But,
as there neither was, nor could be any occasion for these with
respect to Christ, the holy One of God, so they could not, in
this manner, be seals to him.   Christ also, by the Sacraments,
engaged to perform obedience otherwise than believers do; for
he engaged to perform the most perfect obedience, without any
defect, and bound himself to bear the curse of the law, in order
to satisfy divine justice.   But though believers, in the use of
the Sacraments, engage to perform obedience, yet not that which
is absolutely perfect (for that would be to be guilty of a formal
life), neither do they bind themselves to bear the curse, nor promise any thing, by which of themselves they may satisfy the
justice of God.   So that all the same things, at least not in the

same manner, were not sealed to Christ by the Sacraments, which by these are sealed to believers.

XIII. That very accurate divine, Gomarus, having duly examined these things, has presented us with a certain general signification of the Sacraments, which he maintains to have been applicable to Christ, and, according to him, was this: namely, " a sign and seal of his covenant with God, and communion with the church, that God should be his God, and the bestower of salvation: and he himself bound to perform perpetual, grateful obedience to him, and joined in communion with the church." On Matt. iii. 13. Though there is no impropriety in these things, and they were doubtless signified in the Sacraments which Christ made use of, yet they do not seem to come up to the full signification of the Sacraments; because the proper, proximate, and principal end, and consequently the very nature of these Sacraments, is especially to be a seal of the new covenant. And here holds what is commonly said in the schools, the principal act specifies, as the great Voetius, Disput. Tom. ii. p. 161. has accurately observed,

XIV. I therefore conclude, that the promises made to Christ as Mediator, were principally sealed to him by the Sacraments; Christ indeed obtained these in virtue of his merits, or to speak with Paul, because he fulfilled the righteousness of the law; yet in themselves, and as they relate to believers, they are promises of the covenant of grace. By them it was declared, that Christ should be highly exalted, and become the head of believers, and that they should be redeemed by his satisfaction, justified by his merits, and at length made perfectly happy with him, that so he might for ever exult for joy with them, and in them, as his glorious inheritance.

XV. The justification of the Lord Jesus is contained in these promises, concerning which he himself says, Isa. l. 8, 9. " he is near that justifieth me, who will contend with me? Who is he that shall condemn me?" and Paul, 1 Tim. iii. 16. " he was justified in the Spirit." This justification does not only consist in his being declared innocent of those crimes with which he was falsely accused, and for which he was condemned by men; nor in the Father's declaring him to be holy and righteous, and worthy of his favour, on account of the perfect holiness of his nature and actions; but in his being, as Mediator, declared to have performed every thing he was bound to for the payment of the debt he had taken upon himself. So that he who had before appeared in *the likeness of sinful flesh*, Rom. viii. 3. was now to be seen χωρίς ἀμαρτίας *without sin, by those that look for him unto salvation.*

XVI. Yet I dare not say with a certain divine, in other re-spects very sound, that the remission of those sins which Christ as Surety took upon himself was sealed to him. For the scrip-ture no where speaks in this manner; besides, the remission of sins is the forbearance, or removal, of the punishment due to them. Which cannot be said of Christ, because he suffered the punishment due to us, and in the fullest manner satisfied the justice of God. Our sins are forgiven us, on account of the satisfaction of Christ. But neither scripture nor reason will authorise us to say, that sin was forgiven to Christ.

XVII. However, agreeably to both we may say, that the regeneration of the elect, the remission of their sins, their sanc-tification and glorification, in a word, all those benefits, which by virtue of the covenant of grace, are bestowed upon them, were promised and sealed to Christ by the Sacraments. For since, by virtue of the mystical union, founded on the decree of God, Christ and the elect are one spiritual body, he received those gifts in the elect which are given to them; as we have several times hinted from Psal. lxviii. 18.

XVIII. May we not here also refer what Paul writes, Eph. i. 23. that the church is πλήρωμα τȣ τὰ πάνⲧα ἐν πᾶσι πληρȣμένȣ *the fulness of him that filleth all in all?* Fulness, I say, not only to be completed by Christ, but also in its measure which makes Christ complete, who himself seems not to be completed with-out his whole body. So that the promises made to the elect may so far be looked upon as made to Christ, and thus sealed to him by the Sacraments.

XIX. Moreover, Christ on the other hand, promised the Father, in the use of the Sacraments, faithfully and persever-ingly to perform all he bound himself to by agreement. For, in the use of the Sacraments, there is, as it were, a kind of re-newal of the covenant, and, if we may thus speak, a repeated solemnization thereof. Christ therefore, by that act, publicly protested before God and the church, that he would not fail in any part of his duty.

XX. Some perhaps may think, to what purpose this mutual sealing of the promises by Sacraments: for neither was the faith of Christ subject to any vicious flaw of weakness, to render such a confirmation necessary; nor the Father under any doubt as to the fidelity of his engaging Son. But the answer is easy. 1st. The institution and use of Sacraments do not from the nature of the thing, presuppose sin, or any weakness of faith, as appears from the Sacraments instituted before the fall. And are not therefore to be esteemed a vain institution; for that would be injurious to the wisdom of God, who appointed them. 2dly. Though the faith of Christ had no stain, yet it was but human, and depended on the influence, support, and corroboration of the Deity, and as he usually does this by the means he has appointed for that purpose, it was the duty of the man Christ, to obey this will of the Deity, and carefully apply the means adapted to that end, some of which are the Sacraments. 3dly. None, I imagine, will deny, that Christ preserved, exerted, and strengthened his own faith by devout prayers, pious meditation on the word of God, an attentive observation of the ways of God towards himself and other believers, the contemplation of the divine perfections, and by a full exercise of instituted worship. For as these are things inseparable from the duty of a pious man, so they very much contribute to preserve and strengthen faith. Why should we not then believe, that they had the same effect on Christ as what, by their nature they are adapted to have? And if, by these means, the faith of Christ was supported, why not also by the Sacraments? 4thly. Nay, as often as a more bitter temptation, or dreadful affliction assaulted him, he was confirmed in the faith of the promises by extraordinary means; such as the appearance of God at Jordan, the descent of the Holy Spirit, Matt. iii. 16, 17.; the ministry of angels, Matt. iv. 11.; the glorious transfiguration on the holy mountain, Matt. xvii. 1, &c. A voice from heaven, John xii. 28. And an angel strengthening him in his agony, Luke xx. 43. So from this, I conclude, that since it was fit, Christ should at times be confirmed in faith by extraordinary means, it was no ways unfit to allow the ordinary means of the Sacraments to be applied for the same purpose.

XXI. Nor was it less proper, that Christ should so solemnly reiterate his engagements in the use of the Sacraments, though the Father was fully persuaded of his veracity and fidelity. For, 1. That free and often repeated profession of Christ's alacrity to perform every thing he engaged for, contributed to the glory of the Father. 2. The zeal of Christ himself, though never viciously languid, was yet roused and kindled to a flame by that repetition of his obligation. 3. It was highly useful to believers, who either were eye witnesses of his actions, or otherwise acquainted with them attentively, to consider that open declaration of Christ. For thus they were both strengthened in the faith of Christ, and excited to a like alacrity of zeal. Whence we conclude, that the use of the Sacraments was neither a vain, nor an empty thing to Christ.

XXII. Having premised these things in general, concerning

the Sacraments which Christ used, let us briefly take a view of
each.   And the first is his CIRCUMCISION, intimated, Luke ii.
21.   Which signified and sealed to Christ, 1st. That he was
acknowledged by the Father as the promised seed of Abraham,
in whom all the nations of the earth were to be blessed.   2dly.
That his death and cutting off out of the land of the living, Isa.
liii. 8. should be the means of the preservation and life of his
whole mystical body, as the cutting off of the foreskin, in the
Jews, was a mean for the preservation of the whole person.   For
they who neglected this were threatened to be cut off from among
their people, Gen. xvii. 14. 3dly. That his people were to derive from him the circumcision made without hands, consisting
of putting off the body of the sins of the flesh, to be begun in
regeneration, carried on in sanctification, and consummated in
the glorification both of body and soul, Col. ii. 11.

XXIII. On the other hand, Christ promised in circumcision,
1st. That he would in general perform all righteousness, see Gal.
v. 3.   And on his coming into the world he proclaimed this
by this solemn token, " lo ! I come to do thy will, O God,"
Psal. xl. 8, 9. 2dly. More especially, that he was ready and
prepared to shed his blood, and undergo those sufferings by
which he was under obligations to satisfy the justice of God.
For he entered upon life by undergoing pain and shedding his
blood on the eighth day.   And, 3dly. Most of all, that being now
made flesh of our flesh, Eph. v. 30. he would willingly, at the
appointed time give himself up to death, and to be cut off out
of the land of the living, in order thereby to be the Saviour of
his mystical body, Eph. v. 13.

XXIV. Of a like nature is the consideration of the BAPTISM
of Christ.   In which 1st. The Father openly declared, that he
acknowledged the Lord Jesus for his Son, whose person and
offices were most acceptable to him.   2dly. That Christ should
be filled with the gifts of the Spirit, not only to be furnished
with them, in the fullest manner for the executing his office, but
for believers to derive abundantly from his fulness.   This was
signified both by the water of baptism, Ezek. xxxvi. 25, 27.
and by the symbol of the descending dove.   3dly. That in the
appointed time Christ should by a glorious resurrection, come
out of the waters of tribulation, and lift up his head, Psal.
cx. 7. and xl. 3. as the baptized person ascends out of the
water.   4thly. On the other hand Jesus declared his readiness
to plunge into the torrents of hell, yet with an assured faith and
hope of a deliverance.

XXV. In the PASSOVER was signified to the Lord Jesus, 1st.

his being acknowledged by the Father the Lamb without spot or blemish, and separate from sinners.   2dly. That by his blood, he was certainly to obtain for believers deliverance from the destroying angel, as the Israelites in Egypt, by the blood of the passover.   On the other hand, Jesus made a declaration of his readiness to undergo the most bitter things for his people, prefigured by the bitter herbs of the passover, and to shed his blood and be slain and scorched in the fire of the divine anger burning against our sins; in a word, to give himself wholly for us, as the Gospel Lamb was all of it to be consumed.

XXVI. Here I cannot omit what the celebrated Buxtorf has observed in the dissertation above quoted, § 54. that the circumcision of Christ and his death on the cross, were very elegantly and exactly prefigured, by the manner of slaying the paschal lamb, as described in the Talmud on the passover, chap. v. in Mischna, in these words: " How do they hang up and excoriate, or flea off the skin of the lamb to be slain? Iron hooks or nails, were fixed in the walls and pillars; on which nails they hanged up and excoriated, or flead the lamb. If, on account of the number of the slayers, there was not room enough on the nails, they had recourse to slender smooth sticks; upon one of these a person took up the lamb and laid it on his own and his neighbour's shoulders; thus they hung up and excoriated the lamb." And much to the same purpose is what Bochart has remarked in his Hierozoicon, lib. 2. c. v. from Maimonides in his book *de Paschate*, c. viii. sect. 13. " When they roast the paschal lamb, they transfix it from the middle of the mouth to the pudenda, with a wooden spit or broach, and placing fire underneath suspend it in the middle of the oven." In order therefore to roast it, they did not turn it on an iron spit, in the manner used by us, but suspended it transfixed with one made of wood, which, in some measure, represented Christ hanging on the cross. Especially, if what Justin Martyr mentions is true in his dialogue with Trypho the Jew. " The roasted lamb was made into the figure of a cross, by empaling, or spitting it, from head to tail, and then from one shoulder to the other with a skewer, on which last were extended the fore feet, and thus it was roasted." And why may we not give credit to this relation of a man not only pious, but also well skilled in the Jewish customs, having been born at Sichem, and the son of a Samaritan? Since then the passover presented such a clear resemblance of the crucifixion, Christ, when he partook of it, promised an obedience even unto the cross.

XXVII. The signification of the *Holy Supper* is much the same:

by it was sealed to Christ, 1st. That he should be to the elect the sweetest food, meat and drink, for their spiritual and eternal life.   2dly. That the virtue of his merits should be celebrated by believers till his return again to judgment, 3dly. That, together with believers, he should enjoy a heavenly feast, never to have an end.   But then again, Christ promised the breaking of his body and the shedding of his blood,   And thus in all, and each of the Sacraments, which Christ made use of, there was a solemn repetition and a sealing of the covenant entered into between him and the Father,

THE

ECONOMY

OF THE

DIVINE COVENANTS.

BOOK III.

CHAP. I.

Of the Covenant of God with the Elect.

I. THE plan of this work, formerly laid down, has now brought us to treat of GOD's COVENANT WITH THE ELECT, founded on the compact between the Father and the Son. The nature of which we shall *first* unfold in general, and *then* more particularly explain it in the following order, as first to speak of *the* CONTRACTING PARTIES: then enquire into *the* PROMISES of the covenant, and moreover, examine whether, and what, and how far, any thing may be required of the Elect, by way of a CONDITION in the covenant; in fine, to debate whether this covenant has its peculiar THREATENINGS.

II. *The* CONTRACTING PARTIES are on the one part, GOD; on the other, *the* ELECT. And God is to be considered, 1st. As truly *all-sufficient*, for all manner of happiness, not only to himself, nay, nor only to the innocent creature, but also to guilty and sinful man. He himself impressed this upon Abraham at the renewal of the covenant, when God emphatically called himself *the Almighty God*, or God all-sufficient, Gen. xvii. 1. denotes *powerful*, and sometimes too in the abstract, *power*, as Prov. iii. 27. אל ידיך, *power of thine hand.*

it therefore denotes him who is endowed with such power,
as " that he is able to do exceeding abundantly above all
that we ask, or think," Eph. iii. 20.   Without whom we can
do nothing, and in whom we can do all things: שדי signifies
sufficient; whether we suppose it compounded of the relative ש, and די, so as to denote *one who is sufficient ;* or whether derived from שד, signifying both a pap or breast, and
desolation or *ravage.*   If we join each of these together and
say, that God is so powerful and so *sufficient,* as that himself
is in want of nothing, and from his *plentiful breast* all things
derive their being, their life, and their motion : which breast
being once withdrawn, all things relapse into *desolation.*
This is what he declares himself to be, to his chosen people,
in the covenant of grace, for whose benefit he is possessed of
this most powerful all-sufficiency.   That name therefore is
often repeated to the patriarchs, as the fountain of every
blessing, Gen. xxviii. 3. xxxv. 11. and xliii. 14.   2dly. As
most *merciful* and *gracious,* rejoicing to communicate himself
to the sinful creature, Exod. xxxiv. 6, 7.   3dly. And at the
same time as most *'just,* not entering into a state of friendship
with the sinner, but in a way consistent with his holiness,
and after having obtained full satisfaction to his justice: for
he will by no means clear the guilty.   4thly. and lastly, As
most *wise,* having found out an admirable mixture of his
mercy and justice, without infringing the rights of either.
For by this means, " unto the principalities and powers in
heavenly places, is made known by the church the manifold
wisdom of God," Eph. iii. 10.

III. But here men are considered, 1st. As *sinners,* miserable and lost in themselves, who could not be restored by
their own, or by any other created power ; in a word, possessed of nothing, on account of which they can please God,
Ezek. xvi. 1—6. Tit. iii. 3, 4.   2dly. As *chosen* by God to
grace and glory, according to his most absolute good pleasure,
and so appointed heirs of eternal life, and are that " little
flock, to whom it is the Father's good pleasure to give the
kingdom," Luke xii. 32.   3dly. As those for whom Christ
engaged or made satisfaction : for this ought to be considered
as necessary, before ever it could be worthy of God to make
mention of his grace to sinful man.

IV. The economy of the Persons of the Trinity in the covenant of grace, claims also our attention.   The FATHER is
held forth as the principal Author of it, " who was in Christ
reconciling the world to himself," 2 Cor. v. 19. and appoint-

ed the Elect to be heirs of himself, and joint heirs with his Son, Rom. viii. 17. The Son is not only *Mediator*, and executor of the covenant, but is himself also *the testator*, who by his death ratified the testament of grace, Luke xxii. 29. Heb. ix. 16. and the *distributer* of all the blessings of it. " I give unto them eternal life," John x. 28. The Spirit brings the Elect to Christ, and, in Christ, to the possession of the benefits of the covenant, intimates to their consciences τα ὁσια τȣ̃ Δαϱιδ τα πιϛα *the holy pledges, the sure mercies of David*, and is the seal and earnest of their complete happiness, 1 Cor. xii. 3, 11, 12. Eph. i. 13, 14.

V. Moreover, as we restrict this covenant to the Elect, it is evident we are speaking of the *internal*, mystical, and spiritual *communion* of the covenant. For salvation itself, and every thing belonging to it, or inseparably connected with it, are promised in this covenant, all which, none but the Elect can attain to. If, in other respects, we consider the *external* economy of the covenant, in the communion of the word and sacraments, in the profession of the true faith, in the participation of many gifts, which, though excellent and illustrious, are yet none of the effects of the sanctifying Spirit, nor any earnest of future happiness ; it cannot be denied, that, in this respect, many are in covenant, whose names, notwithstanding, are not in the testament of God.

VI. And thus we come to mention some things concerning *the promises* of the covenant, which, in general, may be included under the names of GRACE and GLORY, as is done by the Psalmist, Psal. xlviii. 9, 11. " the Lord will give *grace* and *glory*." Which are commonly so distinguished by divines, so as to refer grace to this life, and glory to that which is to come ; though the grace of this life be glorious, and the glory of the future life gracious. We may likewise not improperly say, that in the covenant of grace are promised both salvation itself, and all the means leading to it, which the Lord hath briefly comprised, Jer. xxxi. 33. " but this shall be the covenant, that I will make with the house of Israel, after those days, saith the Lord, I will put my law in their inward parts, and write it in their hearts, and will be their God, and they shall be my people:" and again, chap. xxxii. 38, 39, 40. " and they shall be my people, and I will be their God : and I will give them one heart and one way, that they may fear me for ever, for the good of them, and of their children after them. And I will make an everlasting covenant with them, that I will not turn away from them, to do them good : but I will put my fear in their hearts, that they shall not depart from me."

VII. Here we are to observe a remarkable difference between *the promises of the covenant of works*, and those of *the covenant of grace.* The same eternal life is promised in both, which can be but one, consisting in the communion and enjoyment of God ; but it is promised in a manner quite different in the one, from what it is in the other. In the covenant of works God promised life to man, on condition of perfect obedience, but he did not promise to produce, or effect this obedience in man. In the covenant of grace he not only promises life eternal, but also at the same time faith and repentance, and perseverance in holiness, without which life cannot be attained, and which being granted, life cannot but be obtained. And even in this sense it may be said that the covenant, of which Christ is the Mediator, is " more excellent, and established on better promises," Heb. viii. 6 ; because it does not depend on any uncertain condition, but is founded on the suretiship and actual satisfaction of Christ, does infallibly secure salvation to the believer, and as certainly promise faith to the Elect.

VIII. Divines explain themselves differently as to the CONDITIONS of the covenant of grace. We, for our part, agree with those who think, that the covenant of grace, to speak accurately, with respect to us, has no conditions properly so called : which sentiment we shall explain and establish in the following manner :

IX. *A condition* of a covenant, properly so called, is *that action, which, being performed, gives a man a right to the reward.* But that such a condition cannot be required of us in the covenant of grace, is self-evident ; because a right to life neither is, nor indeed can be founded on any action of ours, but on the righteousness of our Lord alone ; who having perfectly fulfilled the righteousness of the law for us, nothing can, in justice, be required of us to perform, in order to acquire a right already fully purchased for us. And indeed, in this all the orthodox readily agree.

X. Further, the apostle, more than once, sets forth the covenant of grace, under the appellation of a TESTAMENT, which is God's immutable purpose, not suspended on any one condition : and as it is founded on the unchangeable counsel of God, and ratified by the death of the testator, so it is not possible it should be made void by any unbelief of the Elect, nor acquire its stability from any faith of man : for in this very testament God has as immutably determined concerning faith as salvation. Thus, Gal. iii. 15. we see *the covenant of God* with Abraham is called *a testament*; the ratification of which must also be the same with that of a testament. And the covenant to be made with Israel, Jer. xxxi. has the same appellation, Heb. viii. 10. As also that covenant with Israel mentioned by Moses, Exod. xxiv. and the declaration of the manner of enjoying the love of God through faith in Christ, Heb. ix. 15, 20. And likewise the compact of the Father with the Son, Luke xxii. 39.; in which passage, first, the will of God is published, by which he decreed, that the Son should, by the divine power of the Father, obtain the inheritance of the world, and a kingdom: secondly, the will of Christ, that the apostles and others given him, should, through faith, become heirs of righteousness, and of the heavenly kingdom, and of that of the world. Compare Gal. iii. 8. But why should the apostle call the covenant of Abraham, and that mentioned Heb. viii. 10. a *testament*, and whether it ought not to be so taken, Matt. xxvi. 18. and in other places shall be considered in its place, *Cocceius de Fœder.* § 4. And, in a word, I know not whether Paul, when speaking of the covenant of grace, did at any time, or in any passage, give it any other name than that of a testament. " But at that time (at least if we give into Cocceius' opinion) that word signified, neither to Greeks, nor Hellenist Jews, nor to the Hebrews, any other thing but a testament," Cocceius ad Gal. 3. §. 134. I do not· assert these things as if I wanted to confound the notions of a covenant and a testament; but to shew that the covenant of grace is *testamentary*, and to be distinguished from a covenant, founded on a compact, agreement, or law. Nor do I conceal that I found this in Cocceius de fœd. § 87. Which made me wonder that a certain learned person, who is a great admirer of Cocceius, should find fault with these things.

XI. The famous Cloppenburg, formerly the ornament of the university of Friesland, has accurately observed the same thing, whose words I shall subjoin from Disputat. 3. de fœderibus, Thes. 29. " The other disposition of the covenant (which regards us) is testamentary, whereby the grace by which we are saved, comes to us from the most perfect merit of Christ the Surety. For we are reckoned to be in covenant with God by the new covenant of grace, without having superadded to the covenant confirmed with Christ the Surety, by the renewal of the old agreement, any condition, by which God should transact with us, but giving a gratuitous call to the inheritance of the promises, whose testament Christ rati-

fied by his death, and whose mediator he now is in heaven;
namely, of full reconciliation with God and of eternal life."
Junius, in like manner, in his Theses, Disputat. 25. § 29.
" The conditions being fulfilled by the angel of the covenant,
the catholic church was, through, and for him, constituted
heir of eternal life, without any condition."

XII. Besides, when God proposes the form of the covenant of grace, his words, to this purpose, are mere promises,
as we have lately seen, Jer. xxxi. and xxxii. Our divines
therefore, who, in consequence of the quirks of the Socinians
and Remonstrants, have learned to speak with the greatest
caution, justly maintain, that the gospel strictly taken, consists of pure promises of grace and glory.

XIII. And indeed if we were to take the promises of the
covenant of grace altogether without exception, we could not,
so much as in thought, devise any thing in us, as the condition of these promises. For whatever can be conceived as a
condition, is all included in the universality of the promises.
Should God only promise eternal life, there might be some
pretence for saying, that repentance, faith, and the like, were
the conditions of this covenant. But seeing God does in the
same breath, as it were, ratify both the beginning, progress,
uninterrupted continuance, and in a word, the consummation
of the new life; nothing remains in this universality of the
promises which can be looked upon as a condition of the
whole covenant. For we here treat of the condition of the
covenant, and not concerning any thing in man, which must
go before the actual enjoyment of consummate happiness.

XIV. It is, however certain, that God has in a very wise
and holy manner, so ordered it, that none should come to salvation but in a way of faith and holiness, and so ranged his
promises, that none should attain to the more principal, or
more perfect happiness, but they who should first be made
partakers of the preceding promises. Whence we gather,
that none can take comfort in the infallible hope of happiness,
who has not sincerely applied himself to the practice of faith
and godliness. And the scripture now and then assures us,
that it is impossible for any to please God without faith, or
see him without holiness. From this, many were induced to
call faith, and a new life, the conditions of the covenant:
whereas, to speak accurately, and according to the nature of
this covenant, they are on the part of God, the execution of
previous promises, and the earnest of future happiness, and
on the part of man, the performance of those duties, which
cannot but precede the consummate perfection of a soul de-

lighting in God. Or if we will insist upon it, to call these things *conditions :* they are not so much conditions *of the covenant,* as *of the assurance* that we shall continue in God's covenant, and that he shall be our God. And I make no doubt, but this was exactly the meaning of those very learned divines, though all of them have not so happily expressed themselves.

XV. Let us again hear our own Cloppenburg on this subject, to whose accuracy on this point I have nothing to add. *Disputat.* 4. *de Foeder. Thes.* xxvi. 27. Nor do *the conditions of the new covenant, enjoined by a law* adapted thereto, as repentance, faith, and the practice of love to God and our neighbour, destroy this *evangelical* display of the grace of *the new covenant,* which the testamentary donation, made on account of death, demands. For, these conditions of the new covenant are inserted in such a manner in the testament, as to exclude the impenitent, the unbelieving, and the ungodly, from inheriting the promises, but not as if the dispensation and donation of salvation depended on these; or that by our works of obedience to the law-giver, we obtain a right to the promise of the inheritance.—What then? Conditions of new obedience are inserted into the testament of the new covenant, under *a legal form,* indeed, *as* the *rule of our self-examination,* and of becoming gratitude, lest, without having the undoubted characters of the sons of God, we should without any ground, think ourselves sure of the inheritance. However, repentance itself, consisting in the mortification of sin, and the practice of good works, is also promised under *another form,* to wit, as the gift of God, which he himself works in us, that, by this sign, or evidence, we may, from the time of our truly repenting and believing, perfectly hope in that grace, which is brought to us, at the revelation of Jesus Christ, 1 Pet. i. 13. having eternal life already begun in ourselves, together with the new creation of the new spiritual life, by the Spirit of God. Thus far Cloppenburg, the accuracy of whose dissertation nothing can exceed.

XVI. We are not to think, that by this sentiment, the nature of a covenant is destroyed, which consists in *a stipulation,* and *restipulation.* For, there is no absurdity, should we maintain, that that disposition of the new covenant, which was made to the Surety, retained the proper notion of a covenant, signifying a compact between two parties of mutual faith; but that the other disposition made *to us,* comes nearer to the form of a testament, and is rather unilateral, or appointed by one party. Nor is the word ברית any obstacle, which we have shewn, B. I. chap. i. § III. is of various significations, and often denotes the same as פח, *a constitution*, or signifies a certain promise, though not mutual.

XVII. Moreover, God, by a certain wonderful act of condescension, publishes the promises of his grace to his covenant people, in this manner; to shew that it was his will, that they seek for, and expect from him, what he promises, just as if it was a promise of reward, and proceeded from covenant and agreement, and was irrevocable on the account of the right of him who sues for the performance of it. Which is indeed, an astonishing degree of the Lord's goodness; nevertheless, we are not to use it as an argument for conditions of the covenant of grace, properly so called.

XVIII. But, which is the principal thing, we imagine, the best way to conceive of this constitution of the covenant, is as follows: since the covenant of grace, or the Gospel, strictly so called, which is the model of that covenant, consists in mere promises, prescribes nothing properly as duty, requires nothing, commands nothing: not even this, believe, trust, hope in the Lord, and the like. But declares, sets forth, and signifies to us, what God promises in Christ, what he would have done, and what he is about to do. All prescription of duty belongs to the law, as, after others, the venerable Voetius has very well inculcated, *Disput. Tom.* 4. p 24. *seq.* And we are, by all means, to maintain this, if, with the whole body of the Reformed, we would constantly defend the perfection of the law, which comprehends all virtues, and all the duties of holiness. But the law, adapted to the covenant of grace, and according to it, inscribed on the heart of the elect, enjoins to receive all those things which are proposed in the Gospel, with an unfeigned faith, and frame our lives suitably to that grace and glory which are promised. When God, therefore, in the covenant of grace, promises faith, repentance, and consequently eternal life, to an elect sinner, then the law, whose obligation can never be dissolved, and which extends to every duty, binds the man to assent to that truth, highly prize, ardently desire, seek, and lay hold on those promised blessings. Moreover, since the admirable providence of God has ranged the promises in such order, as that faith and repentance go before, and salvation follows after, man is bound, by the same law, to approve of, and be in love with this divine appointment, and assure himself of salvation only according to it. But when a man accepts the promises of the covenant, in the order they are proposed, he does, by that acceptance, bind himself to the duties contained in the foregoing promises, before he can assure himself of the fulfilment of the latter. And in this manner the covenant becomes mutual. God proposes his promises in the Gospel in a certain order. The man, in consequence of the law, as subservient to the covenant of grace, is bound to receive the promises *in that order*. While faith does this, the believer at the same time, binds himself to the exercise of a new life, before ever he can presume to entertain a hope of life eternal. And in this manner it becomes a mutual agreement.

XIX. But let none here object, that life is promised in the new covenant to him that believes and repents, no less than it was in the old covenant to him that worketh; in order thence, to conclude, that faith and repentance are now, in the same manner, conditions of the covenant of grace, that perfect obedience was the condition of the covenant of works. For when life is promised to him that doeth any thing, we are not directly to understand a condition, properly so called, as the cause of claiming the reward. God is pleased only to point out the way we are to take, not to the right, but to the possession of life. He proposes faith, as the instrument, by which we lay hold on the Lord Jesus, and on his grace and glory: good works, as the evidences of our faith, and of our union with Christ, and as the way to the possession of life.

XX. But we must not forget to observe, that faith has quite a different relation with respect to the blessings of the covenant of grace, from what the other works of the new life have. In this indeed they agree, that both conjointly are the way to the promised bliss; but faith has something peculiar. For, as faith is an astipulation, or assent given to the divine truth, it includes in it the acceptance of the benefit offered by the covenant, and makes this promise firm and irrevocable. Here is my Son, says God, and salvation in him. I offer him to whoever desires him, and believes that he shall find his salvation in him. Who desires him? Who believes this? I do, says the believer, I greatly long for him. I believe my salvation to be laid up in him. I take him as thus offered to me. Be it so, saith the Lord. And in this manner the promise is accepted, the truth of God sealed, the donation of Christ, and of salvation in him, becomes irrevocable. From all which it is evident, that faith has a quite different relation in the new covenant, from what works formerly had in the old. What the difference is between *giving* and *receiving*, such seems to be the difference between a condition of works and of faith: which the celebrated Hoornbeck has not unhappily explained in *Socin. Confut. Tom.* ii. *p.* 280.

XXI. Let us now lastly consider the *threatenings*, whether there be any such in this covenant. It cannot indeed be denied, but that, in the doctrine of Christ and the apostles, we frequently meet with very many comminations, which have their peculiar respect to the covenant of grace, and which could not have thus been set before us, if there had been no such covenant. For instance, " whoever shall not believe in Christ, whoever shall despise the counsel of God against his own soul, whoever shall not obey the Gospel, shall be condemned." And these threatenings seem to be distinguished from those, which are evidently *legal*, such as the following: " cursed is he that continueth not in all things," &c. Yet, if we would weigh the matter narrowly, the covenant of grace has no threatenings so peculiar to itself, but what may well be referred to the law from which every curse proceeds.

XXII. Which I would explain thus: we no where hear of any threatenings, which may, and ought not to be deduced from that threatening, which doubtless is purely legal, " cursed is every one that continueth not in all things," &c. In this most general threatening are included the other more particular ones. Moreover, when salvation by Christ alone is proposed, in the covenant of grace, as the principal truth, the law, which enjoins man to embrace every truth, made known to him by God, with a firm faith, obliges him to receive this truth in particular, and be delighted with the glory of God, shining forth in it, and that his own salvation is connected with the glory of God. Should we deny, that the law lays us under this obligation, we should then affirm, that the law does not enjoin us, to acknowledge God as true, and that there is a holy love of God, and of ourselves, which the law does not command: all which are most absurd. I go further: when man, as the law prescribes, receives the truth of the Gospel with a lively faith, then not the law, but the Gospel, promises salvation to him. For the law knows of no other promise than what depends on the condition of perfect obedience. But should man slight, and obstinately reject that truth proposed to him, he sins against the law, and so incurs its curse, according to the general rule so often inculcated. And since we have supposed the Gospel declaring, that salvation flows from the faith of Christ alone, the law enjoins, that all, who desire salvation, should seek it by the faith of Christ alone, and consequently it cannot but thunder the curse against those who, rejecting the Gospel, believe not on Christ.   As therefore, unbelief, or the rejecting the Gospel, is a sin against the law which is the only perfect rule of all virtue (it can be called a sin against the Gospel, only objectively) so every threatening of the curse and of wrath against unbelievers, and the despisers of the Gospel, must come from, and be reduced to the law, but then it is to the law as now subservient to the covenant of grace.

XXIII. In the discourses of the prophets, Christ and his apostles, there is a certain mixture of various doctrines, which, indeed, are closely connected, and mutually subservient; each of which ought to be reduced to their proper heads; so that the promises of grace be referred to the Gospel; all injunctions of duty, and all threatenings against transgressors, to the law.

CHAP. II.

Of the Oneness of the Covenant of Grace, as to its Substance.

I. IT is a matter of the greatest moment, that we learn distinctly to consider the covenant of grace, either as it is in its *substance* or essence, as they call it, or as it is in divers ways proposed by God, with respect to *circumstantials*, under different economies.   If we view *the substance* of the covenant, it is but only *one*, nor is it possible it should be otherwise.   There is no other way worthy of God, in which salvation can be bestowed on sinners, but that discovered in the Gospel.   Whence the apostle, Gal. i. 7. has beautifully said, *which is not another.*   And that testament, which was consecrated by the blood of Christ, he calls *everlasting*, Heb. xiii. 20. because it was settled from eternity, published immediately upon the fall of the first man, constantly handed down by the ancients, more fully explained by Christ himself and his apostles, and is to continue throughout all ages, and, in virtue of which, believers shall inherit eternal happiness. But if we attend to the circumstances of the covenant, it was dispensed *at sundry times and in divers manners*, under various economies, for the manifestation of the manifold wisdom of God.   In considering this, we are first to discourse on those general things, which appertain to the substance of the covenant, and have continued in every age: and then explain the different economies, or dispensations, and the new accessions made to each, which we will first do in a general and concise

T 2

manner, in this and the following chapter ; then gradually descend to the more special considerations.

II. We therefore maintain, agreeable to the sacred writings,
that to all the Elect, living in any period of time, 1st. *One* and
the same *eternal life* was promised. 2dly. That Jesus Christ
was held forth as the *one* and the same *author* and bestower
of salvation. 3dly. That they could not become partakers of
it any other way, but by a true and lively *faith* in him. If
we demonstrate these three things, none can any longer doubt,
but that the covenant of grace must be, as to its substance, only
one from the beginning. For, if the salvation be the same,
and the author of it the same, the manner of communion with
him the same, it is certain the covenant itself cannot be more
than one.

III. The scriptures so plainly declare, that eternal life was
promised to the Elect from the beginning, that it is astonishing any Christians could venture to deny it; who indeed are
much blinder than the Jews themselves, of whom our Lord
testifies, John v. 39. Ye do search the scriptures, for in them
ye think ye have eternal life: and that they were neither rash
nor erroneous, in thinking that the promises of eternal life,
and the manner of enjoying them, were contained in the scriptures they had, we prove by the most cogent arguments.
1st. Because, not only the Lord Jesus does not charge them
in this respect with the least error, but makes use of that as
a reason to recommend to them the search of the scriptures.
But it is very inconsistent with the great sincerity of the Lord
Jesus, and the divine dignity of the scriptures, to recommend
them by arguments not genuine, or to recommend their value
and usefulness from Jewish forgeries. Nay had the Jews
falsely persuaded themselves, that the promises of eternal life
were contained in the Old Testament records, our Lord ought
not, by any concession, to have cherished that mistake,
which would have hindered them from acknowledging the excellence of his doctrine, and consequently the divinity of his
person: but rather to have exclaimed against them ; " in vain
do you search the scriptures, in hopes of finding eternal life
in them; attend rather to me and my doctrine, who am the
first who came into the world as a preacher of eternal life."
But every one may see, how inconsistent this was from the
design of the Lord Jesus. 2dly. To this we add, that Paul's
hope was founded on the law and the prophets, as well as the
expectation of the Jews, Acts xxiv. 14, 15. " believing all
things, which are written in the law and the prophets: and
have hope towards God, which they themselves also allow,

that there shall be a resurrection of the dead, both of the just and unjust." He testifies, that the Jews expected a resurrection of the dead : he professes the same belief and hope with them : and that he did not do so out of a vain presumption, but from a faith resting on the law and the prophets, which they also, in their manner, carefully read, and from which they had derived the same expectation with him. 3dly. The Jews were so far from judging amiss in this respect, that on the contrary, the Lord Jesus reproved the Sadducees, as ignorant of the scriptures, because from them they had not learned life eternal, and the resurrection, Matt. xxii. 29

IV. But let us argue from the very books of the Old Testament : and first, after the example of our Lord, who, Matt. xxii. 31, 32. speaks to this purpose; " but as touching the resurrection of the dead, have ye not read, that which was spoken unto you by God, saying, I am the God of Abraham, and the God of Isaac, and the God of Jacob ? God is not the God of the dead but of the living." This inference appeared so evident to the multitude, that they were astonished at his doctrine, and the Sadducees were put to silence, verse 33, 34. And indeed, if the words of Moses, quoted by Christ, be accurately weighed, the evidence of this argument will easily appear to the attentive reader.

V. For, 1st. That expression, *to be God to any*, in its full import, includes life eternal. For when God becomes the sinner's God, he then becomes to him, what he is to himself. But what is he to himself ? Doubtless, the fountain of eternal and complete blessedness. When God, out of his grace, gives himself to man, he gives him all things. For himself is all things. Such a man finds in God *a shield* against every evil, and an *exceeding great reward*, Gen. xv. 1. And what can he desire more in order to his perfect happiness ? Accordingly, the apostle joins these two, Heb. xi. 16. *God to be the God of any one, and to have prepared for them a city.* And seeing the *gifts of God's grace*, especially when he gives himself, *are without repentance*, Rom. xi. 29. hereby also the eternity of this happiness is established.

VI. 2dly. Moreover, this covenant is not made with the soul, but with the man ; and God, not only requires the worship of the soul, but also the submission of the body, as redeemer of both, in order to his being glorified in both . accordingly he appointed a sign of his covenant to be in the body, Gen. xvii. 13. And consequently, when he calls himself the God of the whole man, he promises his salvation not to the soul alone, but to the body also.

VII. 3dly. These considerations will be more cogent, if we reflect that the words from which our Lord argues, were spoken of the patriarchs, who had been dead long before, Exod. iii. 6. But as God is not the God of persons who have no existence; it was first evident, that their souls survived, and enjoyed the beatific vision of God; and since, as we have just said, their body also was comprehended in the covenant, it followed, that, at the appointed time, their very body, when raised from the dust, should be re-united to the soul, in order to partake of the same happiness.

VIII. 4thly. To be the God of any one, signifies in the usual style of scripture, deliverance from enemies; compare Psal. iii. 7, 8. But death is our greatest and last enemy, 1 Cor. xv. 26. As therefore God delivers those, whose God he is, out of the hand of their enemies, he cannot be the God of those who always remain under the power of death; but all who have him for their God, must, after death is swallowed up, exultingly sing that song of triumph, *O death! where is thy victory?*

IX. 5thly. It is beyond all controversy, that God promised to those illustrious patriarchs, when he called himself their God, something highly excellent, and by which they were to be peculiarly distinguished above others, who were not so eminent in the service of God. But they obtained nothing so very distinguishing above other men, in this world, that could equal the greatness of this promise. Many wicked men lived more happily in the land of Canaan, and elsewhere. It follows then, that these things regard concerns of a superior nature, and belong to eternal life in heaven.

X. 6thly. and lastly, If we are benefactors to any here, for the sake of another, we will much more do good to him on whose account we do good to them, if it is in our power. But God wants no power. And he declares he will be a benefactor to the posterity, for the sake of Abraham, Isaac, and Jacob, much more then he is, and will be * a benefactor to themselves. But they could not be capable of receiving any good, if they did not exist, nor of the highest benefit, if they were, for ever, to be under the power and dominion of death. It therefore follows, that, when these words were spoken, their souls were in being, and at the time appointed, were to be restored to life, that God, in a distinguishing manner, might be their benefactor. All these things follow from the words of Moses by an easy consequence.

XI. What Volkelius says is to no purpose, when being

---

* The author here, seems plainly to intimate, that *to be a God to any,* is to be a benefactor.

pinched by this passage, he requires us, lib. iii. c. 11. to produce testimonies, in which *this benefit is promised to us* [viz. in
the old] *in as clear and evident terms,* as in the New Testament; for he refuses that the passage we are now treating of
can on any account be of that number, as appears from this,
that, " before Christ explained it, none ever ventured so much
as to suspect it contained any such thing.   Nor is it credible
that the Pharisees, who were very well skilled in the divine
law, and who, as it seems, frequently and warmly disputed with
the Sadducees, about the resurrection of the dead, would have
passed over this place in silence, if they had imagined it to
contain a testimony to that purpose."

XII. All this is trifling, for, 1st. The question is not, whether the testimonies concerning eternal life are expressed in
such plain and clear words in the Old Testament as in the New,
which none of us affirm, who own that these economies differ
exceedingly in the degrees of their clearness; but whether any
testimonies at all concerning eternal life are to be found in the
Old Testament; which the Heretics obstinately deny.   For
Volkelius, at the beginning of the same chapter, says, *it appears that that promise* (of eternal life) *was not at all made in
that old covenant.*   How unfair then is it to require us to produce such plain and clear testimonies?

XIII. 2dly. He is of a different opinion from Christ, in
commending the Pharisees for being very skilful in the divine
law, for he reproves them, Matt. xxiii. 16, 17. as blind and
foolish guides, and charges them with taking away the key of
knowledge, Luke xi. 52. and of whom Paul testified, " a vail
was upon their heart, that in reading Moses and the Old Testament, they did not understand," 2 Cor. iii. 14, 15.

XIV. 3dly. And we are little concerned after what manner,
or from what topics, they formed their arguments; since it appears, that Christ, which impudence itself will not dare to deny,
reasoned judiciously.   Nor will our adversary be able, in any
manner, to shew, that they never argued from this passage.
For who has given us a history of all their disputations?

XV. 4thly. Whatever it be with the Pharisees, certainly
Philo, an ancient Jew, seems to have had something like this
in his mind; whose words the illustrious Grotius, a name no
ways unacceptable to our adversaries, adduces in his commentaries on Matt. xxii. 32. to this purpose: " To say, that God
is eternal, is the same, as to say, he is one who bestows
grace, not at some certain times only, but incessantly at all
times."   The celebrated Lightfoot, in his Specilegia in Exo-
dum, § 5. has observed, that our Lord's argument would

appear with greater evidence, if compared with the mind and
doctrine of the Jews. For Rabbi Simeon Ben Jochai said,
" the blessed and holy God does not put his name on the righteous who are alive, but on those who are dead." As it is
said, Psal. xvi. 3. to the saints that are in the earth. " When
are they saints? When they are laid in the earth. For the
holy and blessed God does not put his name upon them all
the days they live. Why so? Because the holy and blessed
God does not confide in them, as if they could not be turned
away from the right path, by evil affections : but when they
are dead, the holy and blessed God puts his name upon them."
See Tanchum on Gen. xxviii. and Menachem on Exod. iii. which
comes to this purpose, that God, in a far more excellent
manner, is said to be the God of those who are dead, than
of those who still live in the mortal body. And what reason can possibly be assigned for this, but that the separate
soul enjoys a more excellent life? Aben Ezra, among the
moderns, had the same view of this, who, on Lev. xviii. 4.
explains those words, *I am the Lord thy God*, as containing
a promise of *life in both worlds*. And Manasseh Ben Israel,
de resurrect. Mortuor. lib. i. c. 10. uses our Lord's very
argument.

XVI. What can be more evident than that testimony, by
which the apostle, Heb. xi. 10. recommends the faith of
Abraham? " He looked for a city, which hath foundations,
whose builder and maker is God :" adding the other Patriarchs ; " for they that say such things, declare plainly that
they seek a country," v. 14. " but now they desire a better
country, that is, a heavenly," v. 16. The perverting of these
things to a bare expectation, and a vain persuasion, founded
only on conjectures, as Smalcius expresses it, does an injury
to these pious heroes, and contradicts Paul, who in this respect, celebrates their faith. But it would not have been a
faith, founded on the word of God alone, but a culpable te-
merity, to hope for so great things to themselves without a
promise from God. Franzius, Disput. 7. Thes. 55. uses here
a most excellent climax or gradation. " How could they have
hoped, had they not believed? How could they have believed,
what they had not heard? How could they have heard, unless
it had been preached to them? But how could any have
preached to them, had not God sent them for that purpose,
and expressly commanded them to preach this very thing?"
As the apostle of the Gentiles, Rom. x. argues in a like
case.

XVII. But lest they should cavil, that we borrow our

arguments only from the New Testament (though none can better instruct us in the contents of the Old Testament than Christ and his apostles) we shall consider some passages of the Old Testament, and free them from the misconstructions of our adversaries. And first we have that swan-like song of Jacob, Gen. xlix. 18. יחוה קויתי לישועתך *I wait for thy salvation, O Lord.* The aged Prophet was now at the point of death, and being full of the Spirit of God, he, in the midst of his prophecies, in which he foretels what was to befal his children and latest posterity, breaks out into these words; which were not spoken without the Spirit of God, so as, with Smalcius, to be referred to a vain persuasion, nor possibly to be wrested to any other, but this spiritual and eternal salvation.

XVIII. Here again let a certain Jew put the followers of Socinus, if possible, to the blush: in opposition to whom we produce this paraphrase of the Jerusalem Targumist: "Our father Jacob said, my soul does not expect the redemption of Gideon the son of Joaz, that being only momentary; nor the redemption of Samson, because a transient redemption; but the redemption thou hast mentioned in thy word, or by thy word, which is to come to thy people, the children of Israel; my soul, I say, expects this thy redemption." Is not this a very clear testimony of the most certain persuasion, and the fullest assurance of their salvation?

XIX. Nor must we omit the celebrated passage of Job, xix. 25, 26, 27. where in very clear terms, he declares his belief of a future resurrection: " for I know that my Redeemer liveth, and that he will stand at the latter day [over the dust] upon the earth. And though after my skin worms destroy this body, yet in my flesh shall I see God; whom I shall see for myself, and mine eyes shall behold, and not another, though my reins be consumed within me." On this confession of faith I would make the following remarks:

XX. 1st. That it is something very great that Job here treats of, appears both from the sacred loftiness and majesty of the style, and the preface with which he ushers them in; namely, his earnest desire, that these his words might be " written and printed in a book, and graven with an iron pen, and lead, in the rock for ever." And nothing was more becoming such a desire than the profession of his faith in the Messiah, and his hope of a blessed resurrection.

XXI. 2dly. Job clears his innocence against the accusations of his friends, who condemned him as " a wicked person, *and one* who did not acknowledge the strong God," Job xviii.

21. " I am so far, says he, from being such as you reproach-
" fully represent me, that on the contrary, I am fully pos-
" sessed of the hope of the righteous, and know both God
" and my Redeemer, and expect greater blessings at his hands
" than all the things of this world can possibly afford." This
indeed was far more powerful to silence the accusations of his
friends, than if he had spoken of some extraordinary happiness
in this life.

XXII. 3dly. He speaks of a thing he was certain of, and
which therefore ought to be built on the infallible promise of
God. But it does not appear, any promise was made him of
being restored in this life to his former state. Nor are there
any general promises, from which this could be certainly concluded. Nay, there are not a few things which persuade us,
that Job had such expectation. For he wishes, Job vi. 8, 9,
11. and vii. 7, 8. that it would please God to grant him the
thing he longed for, that is, *death*, and to destroy him. For,
says he, " what is my strength that I should hope out, or,
what is mine end, that I should prolong my life ?"

XXIII. 4thly. All the words of the text direct us to the
blessed resurrection of believers in Christ. He speaks of his
Goel, who, as the Redeemer of believers, and, as Theodotion
translates it, their next of kin, had the right of consanguinity
to redeem them. He declares, that he *liveth*, being the *true
God and eternal life*, 1 John v. 20. And who has taught us
to reason from his life to our own, John xiv. 19. " Because I
live ye shall live also." Though he was really once to die, nevertheless he says, " I am he that liveth, and was dead, and,
behold ! I am alive for evermore," Rev. i. 18. And this is
what Job adds, " he shall stand at the latter day upon the earth
[over the dust]." After having triumphed over all his enemies,
he will manifest himself in the field of battle, both alive and a
conqueror : or, he shall stand upon the earth, or over the
dust, the receptacle of death, as an enemy prostrate under
his feet, as 1 Cor. xv. 26, 27. " The last enemy that shall
be destroyed is death. For he hath put all things under his
feet." He considered this resurrection of Christ as an earnest
of his own. " And though after my skin, worms destroy
this body," which he pointed to with his finger, " yet in my
flesh shall I see God," *namely*, that " great God and Saviour
Jesus Christ," at that time to be manifested in his glory, 1 John
iii. 2. Whom he was to see *for himself*, for his own salvation and consummate joy, in like manner also, as David foretold, Psal. xvii. 15. " As for me, I will behold thy face in
righteousness ; I shall be satisfied when I awake with thy like-

ness." This vision therefore was different from that of which
he speaks chap. xlii. 5, 6. Which affected him with grief,
and humbled him to dust and ashes. Nor was it possible,
but such a firm hope of so great a happiness must excite an ardent longing after the enjoyment of it. And this is what he
adds, *my reins are consumed*, that is, are wasted and languish
through my longing, (see the signification of this word כלה
Psal. lxxxiv. 2. and cxix. 81.) *within me.* In the same
manner also as the apostle ardently longed " to know the
power of Christ's resurrection; if by any means he might attain unto the resurrection of the dead," Phil. iii. 10, 11. All
these things most exactly agree with Job's design, with the
force and magnificence of the style, with the whole tenor of
scripture, and was it not for prejudices, could never be perverted to any other meaning.

XXIV. We therefore conclude in the words of Jerome to
Pammachius, concerning the error of John of Jerusalem.
" What is more evident than this prophecy? None after Christ
speaks so plainly of the resurrection, as he before Christ."

XXV. Let us subjoin the prophecy of Daniel xii. 2. " And
many of them that sleep in the dust of the earth shall awake,
some to everlasting life, and some to shame and everlasting
contempt." On this place I observe these following things:
1st. That a general resurrection of all, and among these of
the righteous to life eternal, can scarce be described in more
evident terms. Indeed, under the New Testament, the Lord
Jesus, speaking of this very mystery, uses almost the very
same words, John v. 28, 29. I appeal to any conscience,
had Daniel been appointed to prophesy of the resurrection of
the dead, whether he could have described it in clearer language?

XXVI. 2dly. It is no objection, that Daniel says, *many*
of them that sleep shall be raised. For, not to mention, that
many sometimes signifies the same thing as *all*, (as Rom. v.
15. compared with 12.) it is evident, that Daniel divides the
whole collective body of those that sleep in the dust of the
earth into two classes, one of which shall rise again to life,
the other to shame.

XXVII. 3dly. And this most august prophecy cannot be
explained to signify nothing but a temporal and corporal deliverance from the oppression of *Antiochus.* For how did
transgressors rise out of the dust after Antiochus, seeing they
were then rather dead, and rendered contemptible? For, during the life of Antiochus, they even flourished. And how
were the pious and persevering delivered to eternal life, for

they all doubtless died again? Will you affirm with Volkelius, that this is to be understood of those *who constantly adhered to the law of God, and to whom that deliverance was to turn to an eternal glory?* Then, I say, we have an evident promise of eternal life in the books of the Old Testament, which is what we contend for. But if we allow eternal glory to have been promised to them, why not too the resurrection of the dead, which precedes consummate glory?

XXVIII. 4thly. Nor ought it to be urged, that these things agree not with the time, of which Daniel prophesied, namely, the tyranny of Antiochus, and the deliverance therefrom. For should we grant that Daniel speaks, in the verses immediately preceding, of Antiochus, yet it does not follow, that he could not in this speak of the resurrection of the dead. For, the Prophet was here shewing, that God, after having displayed so illustrious an instance of his glorious power, would proceed in the extraordinary deliverance of his people, till all should terminate in the happy resurrection of the dead. If you insist, that the things here foretold, were to exist at *that time,* about which he had hitherto been speaking, I answer first, that this is not in the text. This verse, indeed, is connected with the foregoing by the particle י *and,* where the words concerning *that time* are found. But nothing is more frequent in the prophets, than thus to join two things, which are to exist at very different times: of which we have unexceptionable instances, Matt. xxiv. It has likewise been observed by very learned men, that the particle י sometimes signifies *at length,* or *afterwards.* Secondly, It may also be said, that בעת ההיא denotes *after that time:* as Josh. v. 5. בצאתם signifies, *after they came forth.* And therefore the promise of the resurrection ought not to be thought a thing foreign to the times of Antiochus: because it is certain, that they who continued stedfast in the ways of piety, might comfort themselves by that hope, under all their dreadful torments, as may be seen, 2 Maccab. vii. 6, 11, 14. and Heb. xi. 34.

XXIX. But nothing hinders us, with very excellent expositors, to refer the things which Daniel prophesies of, towards the close of this chapter, to the New Testament Antichrist, or to the Roman emperors, subservient to Antichrist, in promoting the mystery of iniquity. Cunradus Graserus has very learnedly handled this sentiment in a peculiar treatise. And thus the resurrection of the dead would be joined with the destruction of Antichrist, as is likewise done Rev. xx. 10, 13.

XXX. This being the case, we may justly be surprised that a person, in other respects very learned and orthodox in the main of this inquiry, could not find the general resurrection of the just, in the second verse, when he could find, in the first, the war of the English with the Dutch, of the Danes with the Swedes, of the * Tartars in China, and of the Chinese in Florida, of the Portuguese with the Castilians, and a great many other things of a modern date. But let these things suffice to shew, that even under the Old Testament, eternal life was promised to believers.

XXXI. Our writers have distinctly answered whatever heretics have advanced to the contrary. The whole comes to this : when the apostle, Heb. viii. 6. calls *the promises* of the New Testament *better*, that may be understood in various respects : if referred to eternal life, it does not regard so much the thing promised, as the plainness and certainty of the promise, which is not now wrapt up in certain obscure words, shadows, and ceremonies, but distinctly proposed ; does not depend on some uncertain condition, but in the fullest manner, is confirmed by the blood of the testator, as the apostle himself suggests, v. 9, 10.

XXXII. When it is said, 2 Tim. i. 10. That Christ " hath abolished death, and hath brought life and immortality to light through the gospel," it cannot be understood of the first promise of eternal life, unless any shall say, that it was not made before the resurrection of Christ, which is what is here spoken of. But none will say so. The plain meaning is, that the Lord Jesus being risen from the dead, shewed to the whole world, both Jews and Gentiles to whom the gospel was preached, that he was the true author of life and immortality : namely, that on his coming forth out of the grave, the light of this truth was very widely diffused, even among those who before sat in darkness, and in the shadow of death.

XXXIII. When the same apostle affirms, that " our salvation at the first began to be spoken by the Lord," Heb. ii. 3. it is clear, he speaks of the gospel completed, and of the Messiah, the author of salvation, already exhibited ; which gospel the Lord first published, with respect to the apostles, evangelists, and the other ordinary preachers that followed them. For otherwise who can deny that Zacharias, the father of John the Baptist, and Mary the mother of our Lord, and the angels who proclaimed his nativity, and the aged Simeon, and John the Baptist, were preachers of salvation before the Lord ?

* There is certainly here a most egregious blunder in the author to whom Witsius refers.

Of the fathers the apostle himself affirms, that they were
ευαγγελισμενοι *gospelised*, or that *the gospel was preached unto
them as well as unto us*, Heb: iv. 2.

XXXIV. When it is written, Heb. ix. 8. " That the way
unto the holiest of all was not yet made manifest, while as
the first tabernacle was yet standing ;" the apostle indeed in‑
timates, that the manner of obtaining salvation was, in some
measure hid, in comparison of the brighter lustre of the gos‑
pel.   For then, doubtless, the way to life was clouded with
much pomp of ceremonies and figures ; which being now dis‑
pelled, we behold with open face, and ardently desire, heavenly
and spiritual things.   But from this it no ways follows, that
those, under the Old Testament, had no knowledge of salva‑
tion, any more that it can be concluded we know nothing of
our glorious state, because John says, " it doth not yet ap‑
pear what we shall be," John iii. 2.   We may almost in the
same manner, answer the other objections advanced by our
adversaries.   But it is no part of our design to examine each
in particular.

XXXV. Now let us proceed to the *second thing*, which we
undertook to prove ; that *in Christ*, and in virtue of his sure‑
tiship, the fathers of the Old Testament also obtained salva‑
tion even as we.   Which Peter declares almost in so many
words, Acts xv. 11. " but we believe, that, through the grace
of the Lord Jesus Christ, we shall be saved even as they."
Where the pronoun *they* is to be referred to the fathers, on
whose neck an insupportable yoke of ceremonies was put, as
appears both from the grammatical consideration of‑the gen‑
der, and from the connection and the force of the apostle's argu‑
ment.   For, since κἀκεῖνοι is masculine, and Ία ἔθνα, *the Gen‑
tiles*, mentioned v. 7. is neuter, it is not so properly referred
to the Gentiles, as to *the fathers*.   And we are not here,
without necessity, to have recourse to an enallage of gender.
And then too, what method of commenting is it, to imagine
so wide an hyperbaton, or transposition, and to bring from
verse 7. a noun, to which, after the interposition, of so many
other things, a pronoun shall at length answer in the 11th
verse, and which yet does not answer ; because, in the words
immediately preceding, you may find a noun with which
the pronoun in question may be very well joined ?   In fine,
it will either be nonsense, or very inspid, if the words be so
constructed.   For, what manner of reasoning is it, if we sup‑
pose the apostle to have said, " The yoke of ceremonies
ought not to be put on the necks of the Gentiles, because we
Jews and apostles believe, that we shall be saved in the same

manner as they, by the alone grace of the Lord Jesus Christ?"
For besides this, it was improper to propose the Gentiles, to
the Jews and apostles, as a pattern of salvation, because it
appears, that the contrary should be done; and we could only
conclude from that position, that the apostles and Jews were
not bound to circumcision, and the other ceremonies any
more than the Gentiles. But that was not the thing in dispute. But according to our interpretation, the apostle argues
in the strongest manner: " You ought not to put the yoke
of ceremonies on the necks of the disciples, who are converted from among the Gentiles, because the fathers themselves,
who were under that yoke, really felt the uneasiness of it, but
did not find salvation in it, and yet they were saved, not in
consequence of these ceremonies, but by the grace of our
Lord Jesus Christ. Neither are we, nor any of the human
race, to take any other way to attain salvation. They therefore are under a mistake who tell the disciples, if you will
be saved, you must be circumcised, and keep the law of Moses." To sum up the whole, then, in short, the apostle here
declares three things. 1st. That the fathers *were saved*. 2dly.
By the very same covenant that we are. 3dly. *Through the
grace of our Lord Jesus Christ:* intimating likewise by all
this reasoning, that there can possibly be but *one* way of salvation.

XXXVI. This is likewise confirmed by that famous passage, Heb. xiii. 8. " Jesus Christ the same yesterday, and to-
day, and for ever." In the foregoing verse the apostle admonished them, to keep fresh in their memory " the word
which their guides had spoken unto them, whose faith they
should follow." Now, he gives this for the reason of that
admonition, because " Jesus Christ is the same yesterday, and
to-day, and for ever;" constantly preached by all the teachers of the truth, believed on by all, and to be believed on by
those that come after, if they will imitate the faith of their
predecessors. The same doctrine therefore is always to be
retained, because Christ, who was always both proposed, and
believed, as the author of salvation changeth not. But the
particles, *yesterday, to-day, and for ever*, denote all the differences of times. Nor does *yesterday* here signify something of a late date, as we usually say, *yesterday* or *lately;*
but *all the time past:* as the phrase *to-day*, denotes *the time
of grace under the New Testament.* For this is compared to
some one present day, as chap. iii. 13. " while it is called to-
day:" and chap. iv. 7. again, *he limiteth a certain day, saying in David, to-day;* of which 2 Cor. vi. 2. " behold,

now is the accepted time, behold, now is the day of salvation."
As therefore Christ is to-day, under the New Testament, acknowledged the alone author of salvation, and will be acknowledged as such for ever ; so in like manner, *yesterday*, under
the Old Testament, which day is now past, he was the same,
and as such was declared and acknowledged.

XXXVII. Let us also add what we have in Heb. ix. 15.
" and for this cause he is the mediator of the New Testament,
that, by means of death, for the redemption of the transgressions that were under the first testament, they which are called might receive the promise of eternal inheritance." Where
we have an open declaration, that the death of Jesus Christ
was effectual for the redemption of transgressions committed
under the Old Testament. For thus the apostle proceeds.
He supposes that the fathers of the Old Testament were saved notwithstanding their sins, which Socinus with his followers dare not deny. He says further, that the blood of
bullocks, and of goats, and consequently of all sacrifices whatever, could not really, and before the tribunal of God, expiate
sin, and purify the conscience. Yet, since as he declares,
without shedding of blood, there can be no remission, verse
22. he concludes, it was necessary, that the death of Christ
should indeed be undergone, in order not only to the establish-
ment of the New Testament, but by virtue of which the redemption of former sins might also be obtained. This is the
genuine meaning of the sacred writer.

XXXVIII. And indeed Grotius shamefully shuffles, when
to favour the Socinians, he thus writes on this place ; " His
death intervened for this end, that men might be delivered
from those sins which generally prevailed before Christ
among those called God's people." Is it really so ? Would
thus " the redemption of the transgressions that were under
the first testament," denote such an action of Christ, whereby succeeding ages would abstain from the like sins as were
formerly committed ? God forbid we should ever pervert
scripture thus. Redemption is כפר an expiation of sin, upon
paying a ransom. Christ paid this for all the sins of his
Elect, at whatever time they lived. And upon the credit
of that payment, to be made at the appointed time, believers,
even under the Old Testament, obtained redemption.

XXXIX. Moreover, since it is evident, that Old Testament saints were saved, it must likewise be evident that they
were saved through Christ. For our Saviour himself says, John
xiv. 6. " no man cometh unto the Father but by me." And
Peter, Acts iv. 12 ; " neither is there salvation in any other ;

for there is none other name under heaven given among men, whereby we must be saved." Nothing can be plainer than these words, which seem to be written as with a sunbeam. Yet the itch of contradiction has found something to say, but that something is less than nothing.

XL. Our adversaries except, that these passages should be understood of those who live under the New Testament, and therefore that both Christ and Peter speak in the present, and not in the past time, of us, and not of the Old Testament saints; of the times when Christ was exhibited, and not of the Old Testament times. We answer, 1st. As both texts are expressed in universal terms, they are not to be limited without cause and necessity, as there is none in this case. For if salvation could be obtained formerly without Christ, equally as now through Christ, what need had we of Christ's coming? Or, what so very great matter do we obtain in Christ? 2dly. There are very solid reasons why they neither ought nor can be thus restricted. Because they who were " without Christ, were strangers from the covenants of promise, having no hope, and without God in the world." Eph. ii. 12. 3dly. The quibbling about the verbs being of the present time is idle, because verbs of that time, or tense, may equally refer to all times. And whatever expression had been used, whether denoting the future, or past time, there might always be room left for such cavils. Besides, no reason can be assigned why the past time should be excluded any more than the future, if that verb of the present tense is thus to be racked. If this is not false reasoning against the Supreme Being, and a childish abuse of one's genius and parts, what can be called so?

XLI. That which in the third and last place, we promised to prove, namely, that there is no other means of communion with Christ but FAITH, appears from that very noted passage of Habakkuk, so often quoted by the apostle, *but the just shall live by* HIS FAITH, or the faith of HIM, namely, of the promised Messiah, Hab. ii. 4. From which Paul, at different times, proves our justification, who live under the New Testament, through faith. And then Moses declares concerning Abraham, " and he believed in the Lord, and he counted it to him for righteousness," Gen. xv. 6.; which the apostle quotes for the same purpose, Rom. iv. 3. David likewise declares the man " blessed that putteth his trust in him" (the Son), Psal. ii. 12. And Isaiah counsels the sinner to *take hold of the strength of the Lord,* and thus *make peace with him,* Isa. xxvii. 5. But what is it to take

hold of the fortress of the Lord, but to believe in the Lord?
And finally, Paul by a long enumeration of examples, which
he took from the Old Testament fathers, attempts to prove
this general truth, Heb. xi. 6. " without faith it is impossible
to please God."

XLII. Our adversaries object, that the passages above-
mentioned treat only of a general faith in God, and not of a
special faith in Christ. We deny not that as Christ was
then more obscurely revealed, so believers had likewise a less
distinct knowledge of him ; yet we boldly affirm, that they
had some knowledge, and sufficient for their time, upon the
authority of our Lord, who says, " Abraham saw my day
and rejoiced," John viii. 56. and of Paul, who testifies concerning Moses, Heb. xi. 26. " that he esteemed the reproach of Christ greater riches than the treasures in Egypt ;"
and concerning the other fathers, ver. 13. " that they saw the
promises afar of, and embraced them," and lastly of Peter, who
tells us, 1 Pet. i. 11. that the prophets " searched what, or
what manner of time, the Spirit of Christ which was in them
did signify, when it testified before hand the sufferings of
Christ, and the glory that should follow." Since then, these
things were said of the heroes of that time, it will not be
hard to determine, what we are to judge concerning other believers according to their rank and station. And the patriarchs and prophets had not acted the part of honest men, if
they had enviously concealed from other believers such an excellent talent, which was committed to their trust.

XLIII. The apostle writes nothing in opposition to this
truth when he says, Gal. iii. 23. " but before faith came, we
were kept under the law." For it is far from the apostle's intention to deny, that faith in Christ prevailed before
his coming in the flesh, because, in the same chapter, he had
highly commended the faith of Abraham, and proposed it as
a pattern to us all, ver. 6, 7, 9. But by *faith* we here understand either the object of *faith*, the doctrine of the gospel,
as chap. i. 23. and the Lord Jesus himself, believed on in the
world, 1 Tim. iii. 16. or, *the faith of the redemption* already
actually *wrought out*, as contradistinguished from *the hope* of
the Old Testament saints, who with earnest longing, as it
were, expected the coming of the Lord, " waiting for the consolation of Israel," Luke ii. 25. And thus we have now
shewn, that the Old Testament saints had the same promises
of eternal life with us, to be obtained by the same Christ and
the same faith in him, and consequently also had the same covenant of grace with us.

CHAP. III.

Of the different Economies or dispensations of the Covenant of Grace.

I. IT nevertheless pleased God, at sundry periods of time, and in divers manners, to dispense the same covenant of grace. We shall exhibit, in this chapter, a short representation of these dispensations in such a method, as *first* simply to explain what in this matter seems to us most exactly agreeable to the whole tenor of scripture; *then* freely, but calmly weigh the reflections of other learned men.

II. This diversity of economies is comprised under two principal heads, which the apostle calls by the names of the OLD and NEW TESTAMENT, where we are to note, that by *the Old Testament,* we are by no means to understand *the legal covenant,* obtaining salvation by our own works; that being very different from the covenant of grace. But according to us and Paul, the Old Testament denotes the testament [or covenant] of grace, under that dispensation, which subsisted before the coming of Christ in the flesh, and was proposed formerly to the fathers under the vail of certain types, pointing out some imperfections of that state, and consequently that they were to be abolished in their appointed time ; or as Calvin has very well expressed it, Institut. lib. 2. chap. xi. § 4. " the Old Testament was a doctrine involved in a shadowy and ineffectual observation of ceremonies, and was therefore temporary, because a thing in suspense, till established on a firm and substantial bottom." *The New Testament* is the testament [or covenant] of grace ; under that dispensation, which succeeded the former, after being consecrated and established by the blood of Christ. For this reason Christ calls the cup, which he reached to his disciples in the supper, " the cup of the new testament in his blood," Mat. xxvi. 28. To signify that then at length the New Testament would be perfected when sealed by the blood of the testator, which he shed at his death.

III. It is carefully to be observed, that the difference of these testaments is not to be placed in the substance of the promised inheritance ; as if, under the Old Testament, was allotted the inheritance of the land of Canaan, and the inheritance of heaven under the New. Nothing can be imagined less accurate and just. The allotment of the heavenly inheritance proceeds from the testament of grace, absolutely considered, which remains invariably one and the same under every economy. Only the same inheritance is proposed in a different manner. In the Old Testament, under shadows, and in a certain period thereof, under the pledge of the land of Canaan, and which at the appointed time was to be purchased by the death of the testator. In the New Testament clearly, without a pledge to which any regard was to be had, and as now purchased by the death of the testator. The promise of the common salvation which is in Christ, whether formerly made to the fathers, or to us at this day, does not belong to the Old and New Testament as such, but absolutely to the testament or covenant of grace. The difference of the testaments consists in the different manner of dispensing and proposing the same saving grace, and in some different adjuncts and circumstances. Whatever was typical in that dispensation, and denoted imperfection, and an acknowledgment that the ransom was not yet paid, belongs to the Old Testament. Whatever shews that the redemption is actually wrought out, is peculiar to the New Testament. Without carefully adverting to this, it is not possible, we can have a distinct knowledge of the nature of both testaments.

IV. But let us insist a little further on this point, if possibly we may advance what may set the truth in a clear light. Three things are to be distinguished : the testament of grace, the Old and New Testament. To each its own inheritance is to be assigned : That of the testament of grace is eternal salvation, with every thing belonging to it, through Jesus Christ ; which is equally common to believers in all ages. The Old and New Testament being different economies of this one testament of grace which they comprise, suppose also and include the same heavenly inheritance. But in so far as they are different, the inheritance also attributed to each, is different : but that difference consists chiefly in two things, first, in the different manner of proposing it, which I hope I have now clearly explained : then in the circumstantial adjuncts of the principal inheritance ; which, in the Old Testament are, the inheritance of the land of Canaan, as a pledge of heaven, with a bondage to the elements of the world, and the exclusion of the Gentiles, and a less measure of the Spirit of grace. In the New Testament the inheritance of the Gentiles, with liberty, and a more plentiful measure of grace.

V. We begin the economy of the Old Testament immediately upon the fall, and the first promise of grace, and end it in Christ ; as both the nature of the thing and scripture direct us to do. We argue from the nature of the thing in this manner ; since believers had the covenant of grace proposed and confirmed to them, immediately after the fall, by such signs, as contained a confession that guilt was not yet expiated ; and which therefore were, at the time appointed, to be abrogated by the introduction of the New Testament ; there can be no reason, why the promise thus proposed and ratified should not be the Old Testament.   We do not reckon the promise of the seed of the woman bruising the serpent's head, and of the enmity established between the seed of both, as belonging to the Old Testament, for these things absolutely belong to the covenant of grace in general, but the sacrifices, which were added, and by the blood of which that testament was confirmed, belong indeed to the Old Testament.   It appears more than probable to us, with some very learned men, from the Mosaic history, that immediately upon the promulgation of the covenant of grace, Adam, at the command of God, slew beasts for sacrifice, whose skins were, by the favour of God, granted to him and his wife for clothing: which was not without its mystical signification, as shall be explained in its proper place.   It is certain, we have an express account of sacrifices, Gen. iv. 2. seq. which account, in the opinion of chronologers, happened about the year of Adam, 129.   Seeing therefore these sacrifices belong to the testament [or covenant] of grace, and typically seal the blood of Christ, which was to be shed in due time, and likewise reminded of guilt not yet expiated, they can be referred to nothing but the Old Testament.   For, whatever is thus joined to the covenant of grace, cannot possibly be referred to the New Testament, the very force of the words requires its being said of the Old Testament.   To this argument a certain very learned person objects as follows : " Adam, the deluge and the rain-bow were types, and previous to the actual performance of redemption, and yet they belong not expressly to the Old Testament. For, this last was abrogated with all its shadows.   But those others cease not to be types of greater and spiritual things to us."   But the answer seems to be easy.   The deliverance of the Israelites out of Egypt, the passage through the Red sea, their wonderful support in the wilderness by manna, and water from the rock, the fall of Jericho, the expulsion of the nations out of Canaan, the carrying away of the Israelites into Babylon, their return from Babylon, and many other things of the like nature (for it would be endless to recount all), do they not all belong to the Old Testament economy ? But these very things certainly cease not according to the sentiments of very learned men, to be all of them types of the greatest things to the Christian church.   The city of Jerusalem itself, the very temple with its whole pomp of ceremonies, though no longer in being, any more than Adam and the deluge, yet ought also to be considered by us Christians as types of the heavenly city and temple not made with hands. In a word, the whole of the Mosaic law, though abrogated as to any obligation of observance, ceases not to exhibit to us, for our instruction, a type of spiritual things.

VI. There is another reason taken from Paul, who reduces all these institutions of God to the Old Testament, Heb. viii. 13. *Which decay and wax old, and are ready to vanish away.* But it is certain, that not only those things which were first ordained by Moses, but those also, which were in force, long before Moses, as sacrifices and circumcision, were abrogated by the introduction of the New Testament. But these were not abrogated, because, as the learned person would have it, they were reduced by Moses, with the rest of his constitutions, into one obscure system, but because they were of the same nature with the Mosaical; namely, shadows, which were to give place to Christ the substance. And they were so, not from their being renewed by Moses, but from their first institution.

VII. Nor do we speak without scripture, when we reckon all that time, from the fall to the coming of Christ, to the Old, or former Testament. For thus we have the apostle's authority, Heb. ix. 15. " And for this cause he is the mediator of the New Testament, that by means of death, for the redemption of the transgressions that were under the FIRST TESTAMENT, they which are called, might receive the promise of eternal inheritance." But it is evident, that, by the death of Christ, the transgressions not only of those believers who lived under the Mosaic economy, but also of the elder patriarchs, were expiated from the foundation of the world ; to which the apostle's reasoning leads us, as by the hand, ver. 26. And therefore to their time also THE FIRST TESTAMENT belongs. And no reason can be given, why the apostle should make particular mention of any determinate period, seeing the efficacy of Christ's death equally extends to all believers backward. Which was also finely observed by Cocceius himself, in his comment on this place ; " those very sins therefore, which *have been*, and were not remitted under the first testament, seeing that sin, which all men have in common, because all are said to have sinned, when Adam sinned, Rom. v. 12. and all other sins his children were guilty of, as also the sins of those, who expected Christ, in order that the testament, which gives remission and the inheritance, might be ratified, ought to be expiated by the death of the Mediator, as by a ransom."

VIII. We will again consider and examine the very learned person's exception ; and thus he speaks ; " from the time that sin was imputed, to wit, from the time of the law, there being made, by the law of Moses and the Mosaic institution, a commemoration and exprobation or charge, or accusation of sin, and a hand writing exacted, Heb. x. 3. Col. ii. 14. ; hence all the preceding sins committed during all the time ανοχης of the forbearance, are said to HAVE BEEN, in a peculiar manner, under the Old Testament. Not that the Old Testament was from the time in which sin was first committed, but that those committed before the Old Testament, are said in a peculiar manner, *to have* then chiefly *existed* when they were imputed, commemorated and exprobated or charged. Nor did it contribute a little to heighten the virtue of Christ's death, expressly to have observed, that sins not only not imputed when there was no law, but also very often imputed and charged, were yet, by the death of Christ, entirely removed, so that there is no more remembrance of them."

IX. These things are so subtle (for I hardly dare call them obscure and perplexed, lest the learned person should be offended) that I own I do not understand them all ; I will however attempt it. He supposes with me, and with all the orthodox, that the virtue of Christ's redemption extends to the removing all the sins of all the Elect from the beginning of the world. This being so, he enquires, why Paul called those sins *the transgressions that were under the first testament.* The reason of which he will not have what we contend for; namely, that the Old Testament was from the time, in which sin was to be expiated by Christ, but that all the preceding sins, committed from the beginning of the world, are said, in a peculiar manner, to HAVE BEEN and to HAVE EXISTED *under the Old Testament*, or Mosaic economy. But why did those very old sins exist under the Old Testament? Because then they were imputed and charged by that remembrance of sin, that was made by the law of Moses. From this reasoning I first assert, that, by the transgression under the first testament, are understood all the preceding sins which were committed during the whole time of *the forbearance.* Whence by a very easy consequence it follows, that the times of *the forbearance,* in the sense the learned person uses that expression, that is, the ages which went before the coming of the Messiah, and of *the first testament,* are of equal extension. No, says he : But the very old sins, suppose of Adam, Enoch, Noah, are said to *have existed* under the Mosaic covenant or testament. Where, learned sir ? Where, I say, is it said, that the sins committed before the Old Testament *existed* in a peculiar manner upon the introduction of the law of Moses? Not certainly in these words of Paul. For the very word, *existing,* is not to be found there, much less, in the sense you frame to yourself. I imagine the learned person had in his eye, Rom. v. 13. *for until the law, sin was in the world.* But in what manner soever this may be explained, the apostle never and no where says that I know, that the sins, for instance, committed by the inhabitants of the first world, existed, in a peculiar manner, under the economy of the Mosaic testament. And in what sense, pray, should they be said to have then existed? Because, says he, they were then imputed and charged. But to whom? Not certainly to those very persons who, dying in the faith, were received into heaven. And how imputed and exprobated by the introduction of the Mosaic testament? Seeing it was so much later than their death and salvation, it does not greatly regard those departed pious and happy persons, at least as to its rigour. I refuse not, that the Israelites were convinced of their sins by the Mosaic law, and that a remembrance of sin was made, and that all mankind was condemned in the Israelites: but that the sins of the more ancient believers were then imputed and charged, and then in a peculiar manner existed, is neither asserted in scripture, nor consonant to reason.

X. But this also deserves consideration, that he would have the apostle expressly mention the Mosaic testament, because that tended to amplify the virtue of Christ's death, as peculiarly shining forth therein; seeing it has removed all remembrance of those very sins which were often imputed and charged upon them by the law. Which does not indeed appear to me to be very pertinent to that matter. For, since the commemoration and remembrance of sins are made in the repeated offering of the same sacrifices which could not take away sins, and seeing sacrifices of that kind began to be used immediately upon the promulgation of the testament of grace; these very sins were commemorated and charged by sacrifices, before the Mosaic economy took place. But if, on the introducing the law of Moses, that exprobation or charging of sin was more frequent and strong; the promise, in the same law, was likewise more frequent and strong, as likewise the sign and seal of the remission of sins, which the Messiah was to procure. For, the same institution which commemorated sin, signified also and sealed the future expiation of it by the Messiah. If therefore, on one hand, it may seem strange, that those very sins were also expiated by Christ, which were so often commemorated and charged; on the other hand, the expiation of those sins, which was so often signified and sealed, appears less strange. But the pious meditation of the redemption purchased by Christ stands in no need of any such subtleties of idle disputation. It is sufficient to say with Paul, that the efficacy of the death of

Christ, who is the Mediator of the New Testament, is such that it has purchased for the elect, in every age, the redemption of those transgressions, which could never be expiated by any blood of bulls or goats. Our argument therefore remains in its full force, and is in vain attacked by the windings and mazes of a perplexed discourse. *The transgressions under the first Testament*, are sins committed from the most ancient period of the world; therefore *the first Testament* comprises all the ages from the first origin of the world.

XI. Moreover, in this economy of the Old Testament several periods are distinctly to be observed. For " God at sundry times and in divers manners spake unto the fathers," Heb. i. 1. *The first* period reaches from Adam to Noah, and comprehends the whole time of the first world, in which every thing was very simple and plain. The first gospel promise was published by God, received by faith by our first parents, was inculcated on their children by incessant catechising, or instruction, sealed by sacrifices offered in faith. The death of the Messiah, the righteous one, the most beloved of God, who was to be slain by his envious brethren, was prefigured in the person of Abel, who was murdered by Cain; his ascension into heaven, with all his faithful people, was foreshewn in the type of Enoch, who also, according to Jude ver. 14. prophesied of his return to judgment with ten thousands of his saints: and in fine, the separation of the sons of God from the sons of men for the pure worship of God.

XII. *The second* period begins with Noah, in whom his father Lamech seems to have beheld a certain type of the Messiah, when he said, " this same shall comfort us concerning our work and toil of our hands," and therefore he called his name Noah, which signifies *rest*, Gen. v. 29. He was a just and upright man in his generation, and *a preacher of righteousness*, 2 Pet. ii. 5. By him Christ *preached to the spirits in prison*, 1 Pet. iii. 19. He was not only *heir of the righteousness of faith*, Heb. xi. 7. but the head and restorer of a new world, and in that respect an eminent type of Christ. For the same purpose the ark was built by him; the sacrifice of a sweet-smelling savour offered to God; God's gracious covenant, entered into with the habitable world after that sacrifice, and sealed by the rain-bow; and many other things of the like kind, full of mystical sense, which shall be explained in due time. This second period reaches down to Abraham.

XIII. To this succeeds *the third* period from Abraham to Moses. There were indeed very great and precious promises made to Abraham; as of the multiplying his seed, of giving that seed the land of Canaan, of the Messiah to spring from his

loins, of the inheritance of the world, and the like.   The covenant of grace was solemnly confirmed with him, and sealed by
the new sacrament of circumcision : and himself constituted the
father of all the faithful both of his own seed according to the
flesh, and of the Gentiles, Rom. iv. 12. Melchizedek, priest and
king of righteousness and peace, meets him fatigued after the
overthrow and pursuit of his enemies, who also blessed him, and
presented to him in himself, as in an eminent type, a view of the
Messiah.   Hence was kindled in Abraham a desire of seeing
still more clearly the day of Christ, which he both saw and rejoiced at, John viii. 56.   This favour of the Supreme Being
was continued to Abraham's son and grand-son, Isaac and Jacob,
to whom he often made himself known by repeated revelations
which confirmed to them the promises made to that great patriarch, and proposed them to future generations as the chiefs of
his covenant.   And thus the old promises of the covenant of
grace were enlarged with many additions, and enriched with a
fuller declaration.

XIV. But things put on a quite different aspect under *the
fourth* period, which was introduced by the ministry of Moses.
The people were delivered out of Egypt by an out-stretched
arm and by tremendous prodigies.   The Son of God, before all
the congregation of the people, declared himself to be the king of
Israel, by the solemn manner in which he gave the law from
mount Sinai, amidst thunderings and lightnings.   The tabernacle and the ark of the covenant with propitiatory, or the
mercy-seat, the gracious residence of God, were constructed
with wonderful art.   An incredible number of ceremonies was
added to the ancient simplicity.   So many myriads of men
(strange to relate) were fed with manna from heaven in the
horrid and scorched deserts of Arabia for forty years, and supplied with water from the rock, which Moses struck with his
rod.   Whole nations were cast out before them and devoted to
destruction.   Israel, as the favoured inheritance of God, was
introduced, after a very great destruction of their enemies, to
the promised possession of Canaan ; and who can pretend to
enumerate all the things with which this period was ennobled
above the others; of which we cannot now speak particularly,
Heb. ix. 5.

XV. Seeing all the institutions of former ages were renewed
under the direction of Moses, and enlarged with very many additions, and reduced to a certain form of worship, and as it were,
into one body or system ; and the covenant was solemnly renewed with Israel both at mount Sinai, and in the plains of
Moab ; therefore it is that in the sacred writings the Old Tes-

tament covenant is ascribed to Moses, and to his ministry and times, Heb. viii. 9. from Jer. xxxi. 32. Not that either at that time all these things on which the Old Testament depended were first instituted, or that on no account it is to be referred to the preceding times; for the religion of both times, namely, both before and after Moses, was the same ; and many rites the very same, as sacrifices, the distinction of clean and unclean beasts, circumcision, and many others: but that then the confirmation both of old and new rites was reduced into a certain form of a ritual, and that period was so distinguished by a solemn renovation of the covenant, and by many additions, that it seemed to swallow up as it were all that went before. We likewise at other times read, that something is said to be given by Moses, which was long before Moses' time. Our Lord says, John vii. 22. " Moses therefore gave unto you circumcision, not because it is of Moses, but of the fathers." God also is said, Ezek. xx. 11. to have " given Israel in the wilderness his statutes, which if a man do he shall even live in them." Yet we could not from thence conclude, that the origin of those statutes was only to be derived from that time: seeing it is plain that they were cotemporary with man, and from the beginning made known to all believers by the teaching of the Spirit of God. This Mosaic period lasted, though under the kings David and Solomon, there was a great accession of magnificence made to the public worship, by the superb structure of the temple, and the appointment of its ministry, even to the Lord Jesus, or his forerunner John. For thus we are taught, John i. 17. " the law was given by Moses, but grace and truth came by Jesus Christ;" and Luke xvi. 16. " The law and the prophets were until John ; since that time the kingdom of God is preached."

XVI. When the Old Testament evanished, the New succeeded ; whose beginning and epocha divines do not fix in one and the same point of time. Some begin the New Testament *from the birth* of Christ, because of that expression of the apostle, Gal. iv. 4. in which he asserts the fulness of time was come, when God sent his Son made of a woman : to which they add, that oh that very day the angels proclaimed the Gospel concerning Christ manifested, Luke ii. 10, 11. Others begin the New Testament *from the year of Christ's preaching*, alleging Mark i. 1. where the evangelist seems to refer the beginning of the Gospel to that year in which John and Christ began to preach, which is more clearly taught in that passage just cited from Luke xvi. 16. Others again place the beginning of the New Testament *at the moment of Christ's death*, upon the authority of the apostle, who says, that the New Testament was ratified by the death of Christ the testator, Heb. ix. 17. Some in fine, on the day of Pentecost, or the effusion of the Holy Spirit on the apostles, on which the New was as it were sealed, and its law came out of Zion, Isa. ii. 3.

XVII. But all these things are easily reconciled, if we allow some latitude to that fulness of time, in which the New succeeded the Old Testament. God indeed began to prepare for the New Testament from the very birth of Christ, on which very day the Gospel of Christ exhibited, began to be preached to the shepherds; but those beginnings were very small, but were soon after more illustrious by the preaching of John proclaiming the kingdom of heaven to be at hand, Matt. iii. 2. and of Christ himself, asserting it was already come, and even among the people of the Jews, Luke xvii. 21. Yet the kingdom of heaven did not directly and all at once attain to its full state of maturity, but by slow degrees acquired strength till Christ having finished the work which the Father gave him to do, completed all by his death, and ratified the New Testament. By this death of Christ, the Old Testament was of right abrogated. Yet there was an accession of greater solemnity to the New, when after the death, resurrection, and ascension of our Lord, upon the plentiful effusion of the Spirit on the apostles, the doctrine of salvation was proclaimed over all the habitable world, God at the same time, bearing witness by signs and wonders, and various virtues and gifts of the Holy Ghost. Nevertheless, the church did not enjoy the full liberty of the New Testament, till after God had rejected the people of Israel, who stiffly adhered to their ceremonies, till their temple was burnt, and their whole land was smitten with a curse, which time of full liberty the apostle in his day, Heb. ii. 5. called *the world to come.*

XVIII. Hence we see, that the close of the Old Testament gradually vanishing away, and the beginning of the new gradually gaining ground, both centered in one point of time. For, as on the birth of Christ, a more joyful period shone forth, and the songs of the pious were heard, concerning the truth of God's covenant confirmed by the accomplishment of the promises; so Christ acknowledged himself to be subject to the laws of the Old Testament by his circumcision, and the rites following upon it. And as the kingdom of heaven, which is a kingdom of liberty, was preached by our Lord, John iv. 21, 23. so he ordered, in the mean time, the person cleansed of his leprosy to offer the sacrifices enjoined by the law of Moses, Matt. viii. 4. Which is an evident indication of the Old Testament still maintaining its ground. Of right it was entirely abrogated, when, upon Christ's death, the vail of the temple was rent, and the holy of holies, before hid and concealed, was then set open to all; and by the blood of a dying Christ, the New Testament was sealed. However, for some time the apostles themselves apprehended that there was a sanctity in the ceremonies, till Peter was better taught by a heavenly vision, Acts x. 11, &c. In fine, the church struggled with the observation of these ceremonies, now in pangs of death, till Jerusalem was taken and destroyed by the Romans, and the temple set on fire; together with these, all remains of the Old Testament, which were long before condemned to death, quite expired, and made way for a New Testament, then at last blazing forth in the full lustre of its liberty.

XIX. And here again we are to observe various periods, which are distinctly described in the prophetic writings, especially in the mystical revelation of John; the church has already experienced some of them, and expects the rest with faith and patience. Periods, I say, not relating to any new worship either instituted, or to be instituted by God, after the preaching of the everlasting gospel ; but respecting very different vicissitudes in the church, and times either more adverse, or more prosperous, in which truth and piety were either oppressed, and forced to conceal themselves in deserts, being wounded and spent by many persecutions, or then victoriously triumphed over their enemies, and were placed on an illustrious throne, which dazzled the eyes with the refulgent beams of their light. Of all these we are to speak in their place.

XX. And though we imagine we have reckoned up properly enough, and agreeably to the sacred writings, the economies of the times, yet some very learned men have thought otherwise, who are better pleased with the *trichotomy*, or threefold division, than with the received *dichotomy*, or twofold distribution. They therefore consider the administration of the covenant of grace, 1st. *Under the* PROMISE and before the law, which they contend to have been a promise of mere grace and liberty, without any yoke, or burden of an accusing law. 2dly. *Under the* LAW, where they will have the Old Testament begin. 3dly. *Under the* GOSPEL, where the New begins. This diversity would not have been of that importance as to oblige us therefore to throw up the cause we plead for, if it consisted only in the computation of times. But seeing a vast difference is made between these economies, it will not be from the purpose more minutely to examine these thoughts.

XXI. It appears that the fathers living before the Mosaic
law, were loaded with a much lighter burden of ceremonies
than the Israelites were under after Moses; yet it does not appear, that they enjoyed full liberty, without any yoke and burden of an accusing law.   For, not to mention the law of nature,
which, with its appendages of curses, was handed down by constant instruction, they had precepts concerning sacrifices, not indeed binding them to a certain time and place, but yet enjoining
sacrifices (which indeed were not will-worship) and distinguishing clean from the unclean beasts.   This I imagine the very
learned persons will not deny.   At least the celebrated Cocceius
finds fault with Grotius, who affirms, that the offering of Abel
was made " without any command of God, from the dictates of
reason only," and he insists, that Abel could not have offered
in faith *without the word of God;* and that he did not offer
" according to his own pleasure and fancy, but by the direction
of the Holy Spirit, Adam doubtless being the interpreter, and
setting an example here."   The same thing he proves at large,
in *Sum de foed.* § 305. on Gen. iv. § 14, 19, 20.   And
another of those, whose opinion we are now examining, writes
to this purpose: " the sacrifices of believers were doubtless
of divine institution:" which after he had proved by various
arguments, he thus concludes: " in fine, if God made a distinction between clean and unclean animals before the deluge, which
was done on account of sacrifices, doubtless God also appointed
sacrifices."   But in every sacrifice there was a *remembrance* of
sins not expiated, and, as Athanasius speaks, ὀνειδ ισιηιος, *a reproaching* of, and a handwriting against the sacrificers.   For,
the reproaching with sin consists not only in this, that the offering of sacrifices was limited to a certain time and place, as
was done under Moses, but in the very offering of the sacrifices; for when a man slew and burnt the animals which God
granted him for food, he thereby signified, that he himself deserved destruction; nay, and to perish in avenging flames for
ever; and that he who by the one offering of himself was truly
to expiate the sins of all the elect, was not yet come: and that
when he offered frolicsome animals, who are apt to go astray
from the flock, unless kept by the shepherd, thereby were signified the guilt of sin and our going astray, as very learned
men have observed from Isa. liii. 6.

XXII. It is therefore strange that a great man, in answer to
this question, whether Abel's sacrifice was propitiatory, or eu-
charistical? should say, that " before Moses' time sacrifices for
sins were not instituted by God, the design of which was to accuse of sin."   That this is said without proof, appears plain,

1st. Because, in that case no sacrifices were instituted before Moses to be types of the propitiatory sacrifice of Christ. For, as it was necessary there should be an agreement between the type and antitype, those sacrifices which shadowed forth the propitiatory sacrifice of Christ were also in their measure propitiatory; that is, they so expiated sin to the cleansing of the flesh, as at the same time to condemn sin, and to shew that they were not sufficient for its real expiation, because they were to be often repeated. Neither do the learned doubt, but that the sacrifices even of the oldest patriarchs were sacraments and types of Christ's sacrifice, for they write, in express words, that " the fathers offered before Moses' time the same sacrifices with Moses, and apt to signify the same things." 2dly. It also appears that Job, who it is probable lived before, certainly without the Mosaic polity, offered burnt-offerings for his children and friends, in order to expiate the sins they had committed, Job i. 5. and xlii. 8. But the end of a burnt-offering is to " be accepted for him that offers, to make atonement for him," Lev. i. 4. And by such sacrifices the believers of that time testified, (which is the learned person's own observation) that " they acknowledged, that such a satisfaction was due to God, which was not possible for themselves to make:" this was a charge of guilt and inability; which the same great man could not conceal, when he treats of the burnt-offerings offered by Job, at the command of God, for his friends, and expresses himself thus: " For though many sacrifices were slain, and the man indeed, upon offering a beast, was no longer deemed a sinner, but a righteous person among men, yet CONSCIENCE WAS ACCUSED OF SIN, and consequently offerings were to be accumulated and repeated without end." See the same author on Job ix. 28. but especially on Job vii. 1. " Job complains not, says he, of that servitude whereby we obey God; but of that laid on the fathers, which is a heavy yoke of fear, and of the terror of the law, with the greatest incumbrance of ceremonies.—But though Job seems to have lived before the law of Moses, and not to have been loaded with so many ceremonies as the Israelites, yet his condition was no better than theirs." There were therefore in the sacrifices which God enjoined from the beginning, a reproaching with, and an accusation of sin : and consequently a yoke, not consistent with that liberty of the fathers, which these learned men imagine.

XXIII. And what will they say with respect to circumcision ? Was not that also a yoke ? since it was *not to be performed without blood, and mixed with much pain and shame.* Was there not in it an accusation of sin ? " When the new born in-

fant could not enter into God's covenant without first shedding
his blood.   Hence this sacrament was performed on the genital
member, to denote the original stain ; and by the cutting off a
small part of the flesh, the whole man was declared to be worthy of death." Let the learned persons here acknowledge their
own words.   And what is more plain from the writings of the
New Testament, than that circumcision was considered by the
apostles as the principal part of the heavy yoke ? Acts xv. 5.
compared with ver. 10.   Nevertheless, it does not appear that
Moses made any addition of rigour to it ; having been long before enjoined upon Abraham at first under pain of being cut off.
We conclude therefore, that the condition of the ancient patriarchs is too much extolled above that of the Jewish church,
when it is insisted that they lived in liberty, without any charge
of sin, without any yoke ; though we readily grant, that the
servitude was heightened, and the yoke made heavier by the
Mosaic polity.   And this is what we had to say on the first
period.

XXIV. They make *the law* to be the second period, under
which they would have the Old Testament to begin ; which
they define, to be " the will and purpose of God, whereby he
determined to give to some of Abraham's posterity, as his own
people, the inheritance of the land of Canaan, as his own land ;"
adding, that this Testament " commenced from the Exodus
out of Egypt, and from Mount Sinai."   Which a very learned
person endeavours to prove by several arguments briefly joined
together in the following manner.   The scripture says, Jer.
xxxi. 32. that God made the Old Testament with the fathers
when he brought them out of Egypt ; that is, called them to
the inheritance of the land as of a pledge, &c.   In like manner
Paul, Gal. iv. 24. says, that the two Testaments were signified
by Hagar and Sarah, and that the first was truly from mount
Sinai.   The same Paul says, Heb. ix. 18. *Neither the first
Testament was* [instituted] *dedicated without blood.*   He has
his eye on Exod. xxiv. 8.   He says ἐλκεκάινιςαι it was [initiated],
therefore that Testament then became καινη *new.*   Consequently, that Testament was then introduced.   Nay, Deut. v. 2, 3.
it is said, " the Lord our God made a covenant with us in
Horeb : the Lord made not this covenant with our fathers."
How can we conceive that the fathers had that which we are
told had not been intimated to them ?

XXV. We shall make the following reflections on this
subject, which we submit to the examination of the learned :
1st. They seem to confine the Old Testament within too
narrow bounds, who define it only by the destination of the
land of Canaan as a pledge of heaven ; as we shewed § II.

Doubtless according to the Old Testament, the inheritance of the land of Canaan was given to the Israelites: but this does not complete the whole substance of the Old Testament. Paul clearly enough declares, Gal. iv. and Heb. ix. without speaking any thing of the land of Canaan, that it consisted in a typical exhibition of the heavenly inheritance, and comprised every thing that imports a typical servitude, and was to be abolished upon the introduction of the New Testament.

XXVI. 2dly. When learned men say, that the Old Testament commences from the exodus out of Egypt, and from mount Sinai, and call it the will and purpose of giving the land of Canaan, they understand not by that will, or that purpose, the counsel or decree of God from eternity; nor the execution of that decree, which was not effected at mount Sinai, but forty years after, when, under the conduct of Joshua, they were introduced into the land: but they understand the declaration of the counsel of God by an irrevocable promise. But that promise was not first made at mount Sinai, but long before, even to the patriarch Abraham, four hundred and thirty years before the giving of the law, Gen. xii. 7. *Unto thy seed will I give this land.* And it was confirmed by solemn signs, and sealed by the blood of sacrifices, Gen. xv. 7. We therefore conclude, that, if the Old Testament be the declaration of the will of God about giving the land of Canaan, it did not commence from Moses, but from Abraham.

XXVII. 3dly. Hence it appears, what answer ought to be given to Jer. xxxi. 32. and Gal. iv. 24.: namely, that the first institution of the Old Testament is not treated of in these places, but the solemn renewal and confirmation of it, and the accession of many new rites, which we mentioned § XVIII. For, God himself often testified concerning that time, that he did those things in virtue of his covenant entered into with Abraham, Exod. ii. 24. " And God remembered his covenant with Abraham," &c. and chap. viii. 8. " And I will bring you into the land, concerning the which I did swear to give it to Abraham, Isaac, and Jacob, and I will give it you for an inheritance." It therefore remains, that the Testament, about giving the land of Canaan, was not then first published, but solemnly renewed, when God was now about to accomplish it. And this is what Jeremiah and Paul intend in the places quoted.

XXVIII. 4thly. What the apostle says, Heb. ix. 18. *Neither the first Testament was* [initiated] *dedicated without blood,* is very general, and may be extended to the sacrifices, which were slain at God's command. The very learned

Cloppenburg in Schola Sacrificiorum, Problem. 1. § 3.
would prove from the same passage of Paul, that there was
no interval of time between the first promise of the future
seed of the woman, and the first sacrifice. " The apostle, says
he, confirms this our opinion, when he says that the Old Testament was not dedicated without blood, and that without shedding of blood there is no remission of sins. For hence it
follows, that, with that promise about the future seed of the
woman, there was either no solemnizing of the spiritual covenant of God with man, by which he might hope for, and
believe the remission of sins, or that there was none without
shedding of blood." The apostle, indeed, mentions what we
have in Exod. xxiv. as an example. But it does not follow,
that no other example of that truth could be given before that,
or that any would mistake the subject, who should add to the
apostle's argument, what we find Gen. xv. about the beasts
which were slain by Abraham.

XXIX. And the term *dedicated* ought not to be so insisted upon, as if that necessarily inferred, that the testament
thus dedicated was entirely new. For, even that may be said
to be dedicated, which is again solemnly dedicated, though
the thing itself was in being long before. Thus the author of
the 1 Maccabees, chap. vi. writes about the temple profaned by Antiochus, χαι ενεκαινισθη το αγιασμα ως το προτερον *and the
sanctuary was dedicated as before.* Yet Antiochus had only
profaned, but not destroyed the sanctuary, so as to make it
necessary to build one entirely new, which Judas Maccabeus
purified, chap. iv. 43. and thus dedicated it to God. From
this was τα εγκαινια *the feast of the dedication,* John x. 22.
On which place Grotius comments; εγκαινιζειν " to dedicate,
whence the appellation, εγκαινια, and feast of dedication, in Hebrew חנך is used of any dedication, whether the first, or that
which is renewed. And indeed, when the apostle was saying,
Heb. x. 20. that Christ ενεκαινισε, *consecrated a way* to heaven,
he by no means intimated, that there was no way to heaven
before that time.

XXX. But let us allow, the Old Testament was then new;
and that this may be proved by the word εγκεκαινισαι, let us also
allow, that the apostle, speaking of the shedding of blood,
with which the testament was dedicated, does not look back
to any time prior to that described Exod. xxiv. Yet nothing
will be concluded in favour of the hypothesis. For, the Old
Testament was certainly new at that time, not absolutely and
in its whole substance, but only with respect to those circumstances under which it was proposed to Israel, promising them

the immediate possession of the land of Canaan, for an inheritance, together with the imposition of so many new rites. We ought to be upon our guard against being guilty of the sophism, called arguing from what is hypothetical to what is absolute. As these things are neither unskilfully nor improbably observed by very learned men, I could have wished that hard saying had not dropt from the learned person, that they, who thus proceed, *wrest this passage contrary to the meaning of the Holy Ghost.* Cannot such a dispute as this be determined, without such warmth and vehemence of language?

XXXI. On Deut. v. 2, 3. many things have been taken notice of by interpreters. I imagine nothing appears more simple and solid, than what the very learned Dutch interpreters have observed, to the following purpose: that this covenant was not entered into with the fathers, in the same manner with all its circumstances and particular laws, and in that form (as we use to speak) in which it was revealed to Israel at Sinai or Horeb. For, even the believing patriarchs had the substance of the moral and ceremonial law, and, by the grace of God, managed their religious worship according to it. This exposition is confirmed chiefly by two reasons: 1st. That it is no new thing in the sacred writings, for something to be said not to be mentioned before, and to be revealed at that time, when it is more clearly discovered, and some new addition made to it. Thus the apostle writes Rom. xvi. 25, 26. " Which was kept secret since the world began, but now is made manifest;" and yet the same apostle says, *preached before the Gospel to Abraham,* Gal. iii. 8. and to the other ancient fathers, Heb. iv. 2. It was therefore kept secret not simply, but in a comparative sense: not preached in the same manner as now. The apostle himself thus explains the matter, Eph. iii. 5. " Which in other ages was not made known unto the sons of men, as it is now revealed to his holy apostles." What God here says may be taken in the same sense; that he did not make this covenant with their fathers, namely, in the same manner and form, by speaking to them from the midst of thunderings and lightnings, giving them the law of the covenant written with his own hand, with an addition of so many ceremonies. 2dly. It also appears that these words of God not only may, but ought to be explained in this manner. For since the decalogue, which constitutes the principal part of the federal precepts, was likewise, with respect to its substance, given to the ancient patriarchs, as God's covenant-people, for a rule of gratitude and a new life: and the sum of it was comprised in those words spoke to Abraham, which God, when he formerly entered into covenant with him, said, Gen. xvii. 1. " I am the Almighty God, walk continually before me and be thou [sincere] perfect:" it cannot therefore absolutely be denied, that that covenant, whose first and principal law is the decalogue, was also entered into with the ancient patriarchs. Neither, as has been often hinted, do all the ceremonies owe their original to Sinai or Horeb. From the whole I conclude, that it cannot be proved from the alleged passages, that the Old Testament took its first commencement from the exodus out of Egypt or from mount Sinai, and that it is more probable, and more agreeable to the analogy of scripture, to adhere to the received opinion. But how great the difference between the economy of the Old and New Testament, and what prerogatives the last has above the first, we shall carefully explain in its time and place.

CHAP. IV.

Of Election.

I. WE are now first of all to consider those benefits which belong to the covenant of grace, taken absolutely and in itself, and therefore common to all those in covenant, under what economy soever: which we enumerate in the following order : 1. Election. 2. Effectual calling to the communion of Christ. 3. Regeneration. 4. Faith. 5. Justification. 6. Spiritual peace. 7. Adoption. 8. The Spirit of Adoption. 9. Sanctification. 10. Conservation, or preservation. 11. Glorification. The devout meditation of all these things cannot fail to be glorious to God, agreeable, delightful, and salutary to ourselves.

II. The beginning and first source of all grace is *election*, both of *Christ the Saviour* and of *those to be saved* by him. For even Christ was chosen of God, and by an eternal and immutable decree, given to be our Saviour; and therefore is said to be " foreordained before the foundation of the world," 1 Pet. i. 20. And they whom Christ was to save were given to him by the same decree, John xvii. 6. They are said to be " chosen in Christ," Eph. i. 4. That is, not only *by Christ as God*, and consequently the elector of them; but also *in Christ as Mediator*, and on that account the elected, who by one and the same act, was given to them to be their head and lord, and at the same time they were given to him to be his members and property, to be saved by his merit and power, and to enjoy communion with him. And therefore the book of election is called " The book of life of the Lamb," Rev. xiii. 8. Not only because life is to be obtained in virtue of the Lamb slain, but also, because the Lamb takes up the first page of that book, is the head of the rest of the Elect; "the first born among many brethren, and joint-heirs with him," Rom. viii. 17, 29. But we before treated of this election of Christ the Mediator, B. II. chap. iii. § VIII. and now we are to speak of the election of those to be saved.

III. We thus describe it: " *Election* is the eternal, free, and immutable counsel of God, about revealing the glory of his grace, in the eternal salvation of some certain persons. Most of the parts of this description are in these words of the apostle, Eph. i. 4, 5, 6. " according as he hath chosen us in him, before the foundation of the world, that we should be holy, and without blame before him in love : having predestinated us unto the adoption of children, by Jesus Christ to himself, to the praise of the glory of his grace, wherein he hath made us accepted in the beloved."

IV. We call Election, *the counsel of God*, by which term we mean that which is commonly called decree. Paul on this subject calls it the *purpose* of God. This term appears very familiar to the apostle, which he very frequently makes use of, and denotes a sure, firm, and fixed decree of God, which he can never repent of, and which depends on nothing out of himself, but is founded only in his good pleasure. All this is intimated, 2 Tim. i. 9. " who hath saved us, and called us with an holy calling, not according to our works, but according to his own purpose and grace." To this purpose also, Eph. i. 11. " we are predestinated according to the purpose of him who worketh all things after the counsel of his own will." And elsewhere the same apostle also speaks of *the purpose* of Election, Rom. viii. 28. " who are called according to his purpose, and Rom. ix. 11. " the purpose of God according to Election." And thus we distinguish this *internal* election, and *of counsel*, from *the external* and *of fact*, which signifies the actual separation of believers from unbelievers, by effectual calling. In this sense the Lord Jesus said to his apostles, John xv. 19. " but I have chosen you out of the world, therefore the world hateth you." But the eternal and internal decree of God could not be the cause of this hatred, but only as it discovered itself by the event, and by the actual separation of the apostles from the world. To this we may also it seems apply what the apostle writes, 1 Cor. i. 26, 27. " ye see your calling brethren, how that not many wise men, &c. But God hath chosen the foolish things of the world, to confound the wise," &c. Where he seems to take calling and election for the same thing. Nor does this internal Election and of counsel, differ from the external and of fact, but only in this, that the last is the demonstration and execution of the first.

V. It is likewise clear, that we are not here speaking of an election to any political or ecclesiastical dignity, 1 Sam. x. 24. and John ix. 70. nor even to the privilege of an external covenant with God; in the manner that God chose all the people of Israel, Deut. iv. 36. " he loved thy fathers, and chose their seed," compared with Deut. vii. 6, 7. But of that election which is the designation and enrolment of the heirs of eternal salvation : or as Paul speaks 2 Thes. ii. 13. by which " God hath from the beginning chosen you to salvation through sanctification of the Spirit and belief of the truth."

VI. For this purpose *the book of life* is so frequently mentioned in scripture: it will not then be improper here to enquire what is intended by that appellation. That God has no book properly so called is self-evident : but as men write down those things in books which they want to know and keep in memory ; so the book of God denotes the series of persons and things, which are most perfectly known to God. Moreover, the scripture speaks of several books of God. 1st. God has *a book of common providence*, in which the birth, life, and death of men, and every thing concerning the same are inserted, Psal. cxxxix. 16. " in thy book all my members were written." 2dly. There are also *books of judgment*, in which the actions, good or bad, of every man in particular, are written, Rev. xx. 12. " and the dead were judged out of those things which were written in the books according to their works." These books are mentioned in the plural number, as if each particular person had his own peculiar book assigned him, lest the good, or bad behaviour of one should be put to the score of another, and thence any confusion should arise. By which is signified the most exact and distinct knowledge of God. And because, in other respects, God knows all things at one intuitive view of his understanding, this very book is mentioned in the singular number, Mal. iii. 16. " a book of remembrance was written before him." 3dly. There is also *the book of life*, which is three-fold. 1st. Of this natural life of which Moses speaks, Exod. xxxii. 32. Where entreating the face of the Lord, who had said, he would consume Israel in the wilderness, and make Moses a great nation. Moses prays, that God would preserve his people, and bring them into the inheritance of the land of Canaan, offering himself at the same time, instead of the people: " yet now, if thou wilt, forgive their sin: and if not, blot me, I pray thee, out of thy book which thou hast written." As if he had said, " I accept not the condition offered of preserving me alive, and increasing me greatly after the destruction of Israel: I choose rather to die an untimely death, than that Israel should be destroyed in the wilderness." 2. *Of a federal* and *ecclesiastical life,* consisting in communion with the people of God. Which is the register not only of those internally, but of those externally in cove- nant, mentioned Ezek. xiii. 9. " they shall not be in the as- sembly of my people, neither shall they be written in the writ- ing of the house of Israel;" and Psal. lxxxvii. 6. " The Lord shall count, when he writeth up the people, that this man was born there." 3. *Of life eternal,* mentioned Isa. iv. 3. Dan. xii. 1. Phil. iv. 3. Luke x. 20. Rev. iii. 5. xiii. 8. xx. 12. and xxi. 27. which book signifies the register of those predestinated to life eternal.

VII. Further, as the book of God denotes not one and the same thing; so the writing of persons in any of these is not always the same. The writing of some is only *imaginary,* consisting in a fallacious judgment concerning ourselves or others, too easily presuming either our own, or the election of others, such as was that of those who cried out, Jer. vii. 4. " the temple of the Lord, the temple of the Lord, the temple of the Lord are these;" and of the people of Sardis, who were said to live, though they were really dead, Rev. iii. 1. There is another inscription which is indeed *true,* but it is only *human,* in the book of the federal life, done either *by the man himself,* by a profession of the faith, sub- scribing as with his own hand, *I am the Lord's,* Isa. xlv. 5. or *by the guides of the church,* inserting such a person in the list of professors, and acknowledging him for a member of the church, of the visible at least. There is, in fine, a writing of *God* himself, made by his eternal and immutable decree; of which the apostle says, 2 Tim. ii. 19. *the Lord knoweth them that are his.* The observation of these things throws much light on many places of scripture, and will immediately prove also of use to us.

VIII. This election to glory is not some *general de- cree* of God about saving the faithful and the godly, who shall persevere in their faith and piety to the end of their life; but *a particular designation* of certain individual per- sons, whom God has enrolled as heirs of salvation. It is not consistent with the perfection of God to ascribe to him general and indeterminate decrees, which were to receive any

determination or certainty from men. We read, Acts ii. 23.
of *the determinate counsel of God*, but never of a general
and indeterminate decree. Neither does the scripture ever
describe election as *the determination of any certain condition*,
by and without which salvation is, or is not obtained. It
is no where said that faith is chosen by God, or written
down in the book of life, or any thing like that ; but that
men, indeed, are chosen by God. Let us refer to Rom. viii.
29, 30. " for whom he did foreknow, he also did predestinate.
Whom he did predestinate, them he also called," &c. It is
not said in the text, *persons so qualified*, that it might
be applied to the designation of any condition, but *certain
persons* are appointed as the objects of the acts there mentioned.

IX. The very term, προορίζειν *to predestinate*, which the
apostle more frequently uses on this subject, does not obscurely discover this truth. For, as ὁρίζειν signifies to point out,
or ordain a certain person, Acts xvii. 31. *by that man
whom* ὥρισε *he hath ordained*, and pointed out by name; and
Acts x. 42. ὁ ὡρίσμενος, *which was ordained of God to be the
judge ;* and Rom. i. 4. ὁρισθέντος υἱὸς θεοῦ, *declared to be* [*determin-
ately marked out as*] *the Son of God*, who was, by name, and
particularly declared to be so by God, by a public nomination ;
so προορίζειν, as applied to the heirs of eternal life, must signify,
to enroll, or write down some certain persons as heirs in the
eternal Testament.

X. This is what Christ said to his disciples, Luke x. 20.
rejoice because your names are written in heaven. Where he
speaks to them by name, and assures them of his election,
and bids them rejoice on that account. Which is certainly
of much greater import, than if he had said in general, " rejoice because God has established, by an eternal decree, that
he would make all believers happy in heaven, though he has
thought nothing of you by name :" for in this manner, according to the opinion of our adversaries, these words were to
be explained.

XI. What the apostle, Phil. iv. 3. expressly asserts concerning Clement and his other fellow-labourers, that their
names were in the book of life, ought to be sufficient for determining this enquiry : since impudence itself dares not
wrest that to a general decree of some condition. For, 1st.
The name of a person is one thing, *the condition of a thing*
another. He who determines to inlist none but valiant men
for soldiers, does not write down the names of some soldiers
in the roll. 2dly. The condition of salvation is but one, but

the scripture always speaks in the plural number of the names written in the book of life. Therefore the writing down of the names is one thing, the determination of some condition another. 3dly. It is certain, that the apostle, and other sacred writers, when they say, that some men, or the names of some, are written in the book of life, do always, by that very thing, distinguish them from others who are not inserted. But, according to the opinion of our adversaries, the appointment of this condition imports no actual distinction between men. Because notwithstanding that decree, about saving believers and those who obey it, it may be possible, according to their principles, that none should believe, obey, or be saved. 4thly. All these things will be more cogent, if we attend to the original of this metaphorical expression. The similitude is taken from a genealogical catalogue or register, especially among the people of God; in which the names of every particular person, belonging to any family, was written: and, according to this catalogue, at the time of the jubilee, or other solemnity, when the paternal inheritance was restored to any family, every one was either admitted, or rejected, according as his name was, or was not found there. We have an example of this, Ezra ii. 61, 62. when after the Babylonish captivity, the posterity of Habaiah, Koz, and Barzillai, not being able to prove their descent by the genealogical registers, were put from the priesthood. In the same manner, the book of life contains the names of those who belong to the family of God; in which he who is not written, whatever he may presume, or pretend, will be deprived of the inheritance.

XII. To conclude, I would ask our adversaries, when the apostle says, 2 Tim. ii. 19. " the Lord knoweth them that are his," and the Lord Jesus, John xiii. 18. " I know whom I have chosen," whether there is nothing ascribed to God or to Christ, in these words, but what the least in the school of Christ knows, that they who believe in, and obey Christ, are the peculiar property of God and of Christ? Has not that language a grander sound, and does it not intimate, that God has the exactest account of all, in whom he will be glorified, as his peculiar people? We yield to what our adversaries declare in *Compend. Socin.* c. iv. § 1. " Admitting the infallible prescience of all future contingents, Calvin's doctrine of the predestination of some by name to life, of others to death, cannot be refuted." But that prescience of God has as many witnesses, as he has constituted prophets. It follows therefore, that election is a designation or appointment of some certain persons.

XIII. This designation was made from ETERNITY; as were all the counsels or decrees of God in general; for, " known unto God are all his works from the beginning of the world," Acts xi. 18. " who worketh all things after the counsel of his own will," Eph. i. 11. And all the foreknowledge of future contingencies is founded in the decree of God: consequently he determined with himself from eternity, every thing he executes in time. If we are to believe this with respect to all the decrees of God, much more with regard to that distinguishing decree, whereby he purposed to display his glory in the eternal state of men. And I shall add what ought in the fullest manner to establish this truth, that " we are chosen in Christ Jesus before the foundation of the world," Eph. i. 4.

XIV. And hence appears the gangrene of the Socinian heretics, who, distinguishing between *predestination*, which they define the general decree of God, concerning the salvation of all those who constantly obey Christ, and between *election*, which is of particular persons; they say, indeed, that the former is from eternity, but the latter made in time, when a person performs the condition contained in the general decree of predestination. And they make the excellence of the Lord Jesus, and a part of his divinity to consist in this, that he was foreknown by name from eternity. But as Peter writes, 1 Pet. i. 20. that Christ " was foreordained before the foundation of the world;" so we have just heard Paul testifying by the same expression, that " we were chosen before the foundation of the world." But neither the subject, as we have just shewn, nor the apostle's words, which describe not an election of holiness, as the condition of life, but an election of some certain persons to holiness, which in virtue of that election, they had already in part obtained, and were afterwards in the fullest manner to obtain, will not suffer us to pervert this to some general decree of saving saints.

XV. We are here to explain what our Saviour declares he will pronounce on the last day of judgment, Matt. xxv. 34. " inherit the kingdom prepared for you ἀπὸ καταϐολῆς κοσμȣ from the foundation of the world:" he does not say, " before the foundation of the world," as is said, Eph. i. 4. If by this preparing we understand God's decree, we must say with many expositors, that this phrase *from the foundation of the world*, is equivalent to that other, *before the foundation of the world*: just as, *from the beginning of the world*, Acts xv. 18. and *before the world*, 1 Cor. ii. 7. denote the very same thing. Similar expressions of eternity may be compar‑ ed, Prov. viii. 23. " from everlasting; from the beginning; or ever the earth was." Or if we would rather distinguish these, and explain that expression, *from the foundation of the world*, to signify, not eternity, but the remotest period of time, (as it is taken Luke xi. 50. " the blood of all the pro‑ phets which was shed from the foundation of the world," that is, from the remotest antiquity, beginning with the blood of Abel, ver. 51. and Heb. iv. 3.) we shall say, that by pre‑ paring the kingdom, is meant the formation of heaven, which is the throne of glory; and that the Elect are invited to en‑ ter upon the inheritance of that habitation which was created at the very beginning of the world, in order to be their eternal residence. And who can doubt, but what God creat‑ ed in the beginning, in order to be the blessed abode of the Elect, was appointed by him from eternity for that pur‑ pose.

XVI. And we must not omit that illustrious passage, Rev. xiii. 8. " whose names are not written in the book of life of the lamb slain from the foundation of the world." The last of these words are so placed, that they stand in a threefold connection with the preceding. For, *first*, they may be joined with the immediately preceding, as to mean, that Christ was *the lamb slain from the foundation of the world;* that is, either from all eternity, in the decree of God, which importing a certain futurition of events, to use a scholastic term, is the reason that things future may be considered as already exist‑ ing; or from the remotest antiquity of the world, not only in the members of his mystical body, but also in the promise of God, in the type of sacrifices, and of Abel, slain by his en‑ vious brother; and in fine, in the efficacy of his death, which extended itself to the first of the human race. For unless the death of Christ, which he was once to undergo in the fulness of time, could have extended its virtue to the first men in the world, " Christ must often have suffered since the founda‑ tion of the world," Heb. ix. 27. God did many things be‑ fore Christ could die, which could not decently have been done unless with a view to Christ's death, which was to en‑ sue in its appointed time, and with respect to these, he is said to be slain from the foundation of the world. Nay, the foun‑ dation of the earth itself was not laid without a view to the death of Christ. For since the manifestation of his glorious grace in man through Christ, was the chief end of God, in creating man, we must look upon the foundation of the earth to be an habitation for the good as a mean to that end. Nor

would it have been consistent with God, to form the earth for
a habitation of sinful man, unless that same earth was one
time or other to be purged by the blood of Christ, as the
sanctifier and glorifier of his Elect. For all these reasons, the
slaying of Christ, and the foundation of the world, are not
improperly connected. Secondly, Those words, *from the
foundation of the world*, may be referred to what goes before,
are written; to signify, whose names are not written from the
foundation of the world in the book of life of that lamb slain.
Which appeared more simple to Junius, Piscator, Gomarus,
and other great divines. And indeed, we observe, Luke iv.
5. an instance of a transposition not unlike this. And John
himself is found to have so ranged these very words, as to
omit entirely what is here inserted about the lamb slain, Rev.
xvii. 8. " whose names were not written in the book of life
from the foundation of the world." And then this phrase
would denote the eternity of the divine decree, as we shewed
in the foregoing paragraph it might be explained. Thirdly,
and lastly, The words may be so construed, as to point to men,
who have lived since the foundation of the world, and whose
names are not written in the book of life. And then the usual
and most common sense of that phraseology will be retained,
so as to denote the first times of the world.

XVII. We are also to enquire into the genuine sense of that
saying in 2 Tim. i. 9. and which is commonly brought as a
proof of the eternity of election; " saved us according to his
own purpose and grace, which was given us in Christ Jesus
before the world began." Two things are here especially to
be enquired into. 1st. What is to be understood by *the
giving of grace?* 2dly. What by *before the world began?* The saving grace of the New Covenant is given to
those who are to be saved, 1. In the decree of God. 2. In
the promise. 3. In the actual gift of it. The decree of God
is the original source of grace: the promise is the manifestation of the decree: the actual gift is the execution of both.
But because it is impossible for the decree of God to fail, or
the promise of God to deceive, the person to whom God decrees and promises to give any thing, may be so certain that
it shall be given, as if he was already in the actual possession
of it. And, on account of that certainty of the decree and
promise of God, the benefit decreed or promised, may be considered as already given. But it is plain, that the apostle
speaks not here of actual bestowing: therefore it ought to be
understood of giving, either in the decree or in the promise.
But which of these explications is to be preferred, depends on

the meaning of the following phrase, πρὸ χρόνων ἀιωνίων *before the world began.*

XVIII. If there be any, who by χρόνες ἀιωνίες, *before the world began,* understand absolute eternity, such refute themselves. For, seeing Paul here relates something done before the world began, something must be imagined more eternal than eternity itself, than which nothing can be more absurd. It is better, we thereby understand all that time, which commenced with the creation of the world (when ἀιῶνες ἐκλίσθησαν, *the worlds were framed,* Heb. xi. 3.) which then run on, and will run through all ages, without end and limit. But what is it, *before the world began?* Is it what precedes all time, and so eternal, as most divines think, who from hence directly conclude the eternity of our election, and interpret this giving of the giving contained in the decree? But we are to consider, whether we can firmly maintain that exposition against the exceptions of those of the opposite opinion. Indeed, the very subtlé Twiss himself, *in Vindiciis Gratiæ,* lib. i. p. 1. *Digress.* 2. § 4. p. 64. cavils, " that it is not necessary directly to believe, that what is said to be before the foundation of the world, signifies to be before all time; but only before many ages." But that very learned person, as frequently on other occasions, so also on this, appears to have given too much scope to his wit and fancy. If this exposition of his be retained, there is nothing of which it may not one time or other, be said that it was done *before the foundation of the world,* a regard being had to following ages. Which is, in a remarkable manner, to weaken the force and majesty of the apostle's expression. And I would not willingly make such concessions to our adversaries. Since χρόνοι ἀιώνιοι *the beginning of the world,* commenced at that beginning, in which αἰῶνες ἐκτίςθησαν *the worlds were framed;* what was done, πρὸ χρόνων ἀιωνίων *before the foundation of the world,* seems altogether to have been done before the creation of the world, and consequently from eternity; unless we should be under a necessity to limit that phrase. And none can doubt, but in its full import it may signify this. Why then may it not be explained in its full emphasis, if there be nothing to hinder it? But what is here said of giving grace, is no such hindrance; " For, because all things are present to God, and that what God has decreed to be future, shall certainly come to pass; therefore God is said to have done from eternity, what is revealed to us in its appointed time:" as the venerable Beza has well observed on Tit. i. 2. And let this be said for those who understand this giving of the giving

in the decree, and explain that expression, *before the foundation of the world*, so as to mean the same thing as from eternity.

XIX. Yet other divines explain it of *the giving* in *the promise*; or comparing Tit. i. 2. in hope of eternal life, which God
that cannot lie, promised, πρὸ χρόνων ἀιωνίων, *before the world began.*
" Hence we see, says a celebrated expositor of our day, *that the
promise which was made in the beginning of ages*, Isa. xli. 4.
" before any age had passed away; and so when there was no
secular time, or time of this world, when the second age was
not yet called forth. We see, I say, that the promise was
said to be given forth before the world began. Here therefore we do not only understand a giving by decree, or purpose, but also by promise, that is, by assignation." Which
is given unto us, that is, " the effect of which grace is assigned to us by promise, which is almost coeval with this world."
These things are much more plausible than what we just
heard from Twiss. Indeed, from that passage in Titus, it
seems that we might conclude, that πρὸ χρόνων ἀιωνίων, *before
the world began*, neither always, nor necessarily, denotes absolute eternity. For, because the apostle there treats of the
promise, he does not so comprehend all ages, as to lead us beyond the creation of the world, as Calvin himself has observed; but he points out the beginning of the first age, in which
the promise of salvation was made to our first parents immediately upon the fall, which our Dutch commentators have
also adopted. Whence it appears, that they are guilty of no
absurdity, who so explain this giving, as to include the promise of grace, made before the flux of any age. And then,
in the apostle's discourses, there are these three things proposed in order; first, *the purpose* of God, which is the source
of all grace; then *the promise* made from the remotest antiquity, which he expresses by the term, *giving*; and lastly,
the actual *bestowing* and *manifestation* by the glorious coming of our Saviour Jesus Christ. Nor would I make much
opposition, if any should explain the apostle's expression in this
manner.

XX. But whatever way you interpret, there is a strong argument in the said passage of Paul for the eternity of election. For if you explain the *giving*, of the decree, and say,
that *before the world began*, is equivalent to *eternity*: you
will conclude directly: and I think both may be defended.
For indeed, the phrase, *before the world began*, in its full emphasis, signifies so much: nor can it be much weakened by
Tit. i. 2. For, the subject is different; in the one place the

apostle speaks of the purpose of God, and of giving from his purpose : in the other, of the promise. But the same predicate is often to be differently explained, according to the diversity of the subjects. For instance, when Peter says, Acts xv. 18. *known unto God are all his works*, ἀπ᾽ ἀιῶνος, *from the beginning of the world*; ἀπ᾽ ἀιῶνος, doubtless signifies *from eternity*. For, if all his works, certainly also that of the first creation, prior to which was nothing but eternity : but when the same apostle, Acts iii. 21. says, *which God hath spoken by the mouth of all his holy prophets*, ἀπ᾽ ἀιῶνος, *since the world began*; he means nothing by these words, but the most ancient times, in which the prophets existed. Why therefore may not προ χρονων ἀιωνίων be explained one way in 2 Tim. i. 9. and another Tit. i. 2. But let us grant, that the apostle, by the giving of grace before the world began, understands the promise made in the beginning of the first age ; seeing he says, that the *purpose of God was the source of it*, certainly that *purpose* was prior to the promise. But none, I imagine will say, that it was made when God created man : it must therefore have been from eternity. " According to the eternal purpose, which he purposed in Christ Jesus our Lord," Eph. iii. 11. That must certainly *be an eternal purpose*, since the effect of it is grace, given *before the foundation of the world.*

XXI. Let us add another passage of Paul, which we think is a testimony to the eternity of Election : namely, 2 Thes. ii. 13. " but we are bound to give thanks always to God for you, brethren, beloved of the Lord, because God hath ἀπ᾽ ἀρχῆς from the beginning chosen you to salvation." The apostle distinguishes that Election, of which he speaks, from the call by the Gospel, v. 14. And therefore, with great propriety, we understand it of the Election of counsel and purpose. This, he says was ἀπ᾽ ἀ᾽ρχῆς *from the beginning*, that is, from eternity. For that phrase is often taken in that sense : thus what John i. 1. says in his Gospel, ἐν ἀρχῇ ἦν *in the beginning was*, in 1 John i. 1. he says, ἀπ᾽ ἀρχῆς *was from the beginning*. But to have been already in the beginning, signifies to be from eternity. For, what was already ἐν ᾽ἀρχῇ *in the beginning* when all things were made, must have been self-existent, and from eternity. But, lest any should cavil, that the new world of grace was here intended, John speaks of the beginning of things made, because he speaks of the existence of him by whom the world was made, and that very world which knew him not, v. 10. By comparing the alleged passages it appears, that *in the beginning* and *from the beginning* are equivalent terms. We have this sense more clearly, Mic. v. 2. Where the prophet

describes at least a twofold going forth of the Messiah: the one
from Bethlehem which is after the flesh, and relates to his being
born of the virgin Mary: the other which is after the Spirit,
and is expressive of his eternal generation; of which last he says,
whose goings forth have been from of old, from everlasting.
Which the Septuagint translate, *and his goings forth from
the beginning, from everlasting.* What can be more evident,
than that απ' 'αρχης there denotes eternity? The son of Sirach
also Ecclesiasticus xxiv. 9. may shew us in what sense the Hel-
lenists were wont to use this expression, when he joins as
synonymous, προ τε αιωνος and 'απ' 'αρχης. As then, the apostle
speaks of the election of purpose, as distinct from that of execution, which is made by effectual calling, and since απ αρχης signifies eternity, we very properly infer the eternity of election.

XXII. Here again Twiss comes in our way, who confidently
affirms, that there is no place in all the scripture where this
word signifies eternity: nay, he thinks it may be put out of all
controversy, that it never is, or can be, so used in the sacred
writings, according to right reason, *l. c. p.* 60. And he applies the election mentioned here, to some external declaration
of internal election, and thinks the apostle alludes to that remarkable promise made to Adam after the fall, of the seed of
the woman bruising the serpent's head. For, says he, God
himself has pointed out, in that place, a remarkable difference
between the elect and the reprobate: " and I will put enmity
between thee and the woman, and between thy seed and her seed,"
&c. p. 63. I cannot but wonder at the confidence of this very
learned person. It is, indeed, true, that *from the beginning,*
does not always denote eternity; as John viii. 44. and 1 John
iii. 8. where the signification is to be determined by the subject treated of. But from the places above quoted it is plain,
that sometimes it can admit of no other sense. And I hope, the
learned person did not desire to wrest out of our hands those
passages, by which our divines have so happily defended the
eternity of the *logos,* or Word, against the Socinians. I would
rather believe, that he did not attend to the places we have
mentioned. Besides, I could wish, he could shew, where in the
sacred writings the first promise of grace is called *election;*
which I imagine, he will never be able to do: we are not to forge
significations. Moreover, though in that promise there is
some general indication of a difference made between the elect
and reprobate; yet it is not credible the apostle here had any
eye to that; who gives thanks to God, not because he chose
some men; but most especially because he chose the Thessalonians. But the election of the Thessalonians cannot be infer-

red from that declaration of God, the truth of which might have remained, though none of those who then dwelt at Thessalonica had been chosen. We therefore conclude, that the received explication of divines is perfectly well grounded.

XXIII. There is another learned person, who asserts that this place of Paul is to be understood " of that beginning in which God began to make the Gentiles heirs of salvation ; seeing the Thessalonians were almost among the first of these, they are said to be chosen, separated from the beginning. Or also the beginning of the gospel may be understood, of which Mark i. 1. Phil. iv. 15. or of the salvation which was preached by Jesus, Heb. iii. He hath chosen you from the beginning : that is, from the beginning of preaching the gospel, and of salvation manifested and proclaimed." But even these things are not satisfactory : for, 1st. We have shewn, that Paul treats here of election in purpose or intention, and not in execution. 2dly. It is indeed true, that the term *beginning*, ought to be explained in a way suitable to the subject it treats of; but I do not think that, *from the beginning*, absolutely taken, does any where signify the beginning of the gospel preached, much less the beginning of the inheritance of the Gentiles ; nor do the places alleged prove it. 3dly. Nor does it agree with history, that the Thessalonians were the first-fruits of the Gentiles brought to the inheritance of salvation : for, the people of Antioch, both in Syria and Pisidia, and the people of Lystra and Derbe, and the Philippians, had already received the gospel, and the apostles had acquainted the brethren at Jersualem with the conversion of the Gentiles, Acts xv. 3. before ever Paul preached the gospel at Thessalonica, as appears from the Acts of the Apostles, Nor do I think, the learned person was unacquainted with this ; and therefore he said, the Thessalonians were *almost* among the first ; which diminutive particle does not a little weaken the force of the expression *from the beginning*. 4thly. Much less can it be said, that the Thessalonians were separated from the beginning of that salvation which Jesus published ; which beginning Paul makes prior to the confirmation of the gospel made by those who heard it from the mouth of Jesus himself, that is, to the preaching of the apostles, Heb. ii. 3. For it is plain, Christ was the minister of circumcision, and did not preach the gospel to the Gentiles. Nothing therefore appears more easy and solid than that explication we have already given.

XXIV. Having said enough concerning the *eternity* of election, let us now consider its *freeness* ; which consists in this, that God, as the absolute Lord of all his creatures, has chosen, out of mankind, whom and as many as he pleased ;

and indeed, in such a manner, as that no good which he
foresaw in such a man, was the foundation of that choice, or
the reason why he chose one rather than another. This appears, 1st. Because the scripture asserts, that the most free
will of God was the supreme reason or cause of election,
Mat. xi. 26. " even so, Father, for so it seemed good in thy
sight." Luke xii. 32. " it is your Father's good pleasure to
give you the kingdom." Above all, the apostle is full in
vindicating this absolute power of God, Rom. ix. Where
among other things he says, ver. 21. " Hath not the potter
power over the clay, of the same lump to make one vessel
unto honour, and another unto dishonour ?" 2dly. At the
same time also, that the scripture refuses the consideration
of any good foreseen in man, it maintains this most free and
gracious good-pleasure of God, Rom. ix. 11. " for the children being not yet born, neither having done any good or evil,
that the purpose of God according to election might stand,
not of works, but of him that calleth," &c. 2 Tim. i. 9. "not
according to our works, but according to his own purpose."
3dly. Neither faith, nor holiness, nor any thing truly good
can be considered in man, unless bestowed out of divine grace,
Phil. i. 29. *unto you is given to believe on Christ*, Eph. ii. 8.
faith, not of yourselves, it is the gift of God. But the bestowing of this favour can proceed from no other cause than
the election of grace, and the benevolent good pleasure of
his will. And consequently these benefits cannot be presupposed
as preparatory to divine election. 4thly. The scriptures expressly declare, that we are chosen to faith, holiness, and to
perseverance in both, which being the consequents and fruits
of election, cannot be the antecedent conditions of it, Eph. i.
4. " he hath chosen us, that we should be holy and without
blame," or have it begun on earth, and consummated in heaven. John xv. 16. " I have chosen you and ordained you,
that you should bring forth fruit." I have chosen you from
eternity, called and ordained you in the appointed time.
2 Thess. ii. 13. " God hath from the beginning chosen you
to salvation, through sanctification of the Spirit, and belief of
the truth." Election is as well to the means, as to the end.
All these passages, and many others of a like nature, have been
so fully and solidly defended by our divines against the objections of the Remonstrants, that I have scarce any thing to add.

XXV. This counsel of God, as it is free, so it is also *Immutable* from eternity. 1st. Immutability belongs to all the
decrees of God, in general, Is. xiv. 27. " The Lord of hosts
hath purposed, and who shall disannul it ?" Is. xlvi. 10. " my

counsel shall stand, and I will do all my pleasure." Rom. ix. 19.
" who hath resisted his will ?" To affirm with Crellius, that
these things are to be understood of the absolute decrees of
God, not of his conditional, is begging the question. For we
deny that any decree of God depends on a condition : if the
thing decreed be suspended on a condition, the condition itself
is at the same time decreed. These texts speak nothing of Crellius's distinction, nor lay any foundation for it : and even reason
is against it. For, if any decree of God could be changed, it
would be because God either would not, or could not effect
the thing decreed, or because his latter thoughts were wiser
and better than his first : all which are injurious to God.
You will answer ; God, indeed, wills what he has decreed to
be done, but on condition the creature also wills it, whose
liberty he would no-wise infringe. I answer, Is God so destitute either of power, or of wisdom, that he cannot so concur
with the liberty of second causes, which he himself gave and
formed, as to do what he wills, without prejudice to, and
consistently with their liberty? God is far more glorious, in
our opinion, and more to be had in reverence, than for us
to believe any such thing of his power and wisdom. And
here the very heathen poets and philosophers themselves, who,
at times, have spoken more devoutly of their gods, may put
the heretics to the blush : for thus Homer introduces Jupiter,
saying,

——'Ου γὰρ ἐμὸν παλινάγρετον ἠδ' ἀπαληλὸν,
'Ουδ' ἀτελεύτητου ὅτι κ'εν κεφαλῇ κατανεύσω.

——Nec enim mutabitur unquam
Quod capite annuero, nec falsum fine carebit.

" Nor is it mine to recal, nor to be false in, nor leave
unfinished whatever I .shall have signified by my awful
nod." And Maximus Tyrius, who quotes these words of
Homer, Dissert. 29. adds of his own in the following dissertation ; " to be changeable, and to repent, is unworthy, not to
say, of God, but even of an honest man." And he argues
much in the same manner as we. 2dly. More especially the
scriptures ascribe immutability to the divine Election, Rom.
ix. 11. " that the purpose of God according to Election might
stand ;" 2 Tim. ii. 19. " The foundation of God standeth sure,
having this seal, the Lord knoweth them who are his;" Isa.
xlix. 15, 16. " Can a woman forget her sucking child, that she
should not have compassion on the son of her womb? Yea,
they may forget, yet I will not forget thee. Behold ! I
have graven thee on the palms of my hands;" Rev. iii. 5.

" I will not blot out his name out of the book of life;" Isa. iv. 3. " And it shall come to pass, that he that is left in Zion, and he that remaineth in Jerusalem, shall be called holy, even every one that is written among the living in Jerusalem." Our adversaries have scarce any thing to oppose to such express passages, but their stale musty distinctions, of Election peremptory and not peremptory, and the like, which are contrary both to the glory of. God, and to the simplicity of the scriptures.

XXVI. But we must say something on Psal. lxix. 28. Where the Lord Jesus denounceth a curse against the Jews, the obstinate despisers of his grace, and his sworn enemies; " let them be blotted out of the book of the living, and not be written with the righteous." And it cannot be doubted but this imprecation of our Lord had its full effect: and hence it is concluded, that some are blotted out of the book of the living. But we have already § VI and VII, spake somewhat largely on this head, which may throw no small light on this passage. For, 1st. By the *book of life* here, we may very well understand the list of those who live on earth with respect to this animal life. For the wicked Jews were blotted out of that book by the tremendous judgment of God, when, in their last wars with the Romans, many myriads of them were slain in a shocking manner; whose number *Lipsius de Constant. lib. 2. c.* 21. has collected to amount to *twelve hundred and thirty thousand*, who were cut off in less than full seven years. 2dly. By the book of the living may be understood, *the book of God's covenant-people*, out of which the Jews were erased, when God publicly disowned and rejected them; and it was said to them lo-Ruhama and lo-Ammi, according to the prophecy of Hosea, i. 6, 9. This was done when the Gospel, which the Jews rejected, was preached to the Gentiles, and eagerly received by them; and the wretched remains of the Jews were dispersed among the nations. 3dly. If we should understand it of the *book of election*, it may be said, they were blotted out of that book, as to that *writing*, by which they presumptuously *wrote themselves down* therein, falsely boasting, that they were the dearly beloved children of God and of Abraham; our Lord Jesus justly imprecates against them, that this their boasting may be found actually vain. 4thly. But if this blotting out is to be absolutely understood of *the writing of God himself* in the book of election; we shall say, that the blotting out was not privative but negative, and that the latter part of the verse is an explication of the former: so that the blotting out is a declaration of their not being written down. Kimchi, among the Jewish doctors, also observed this, who writes, *the verse is double, the same sense being proposed in different words.* And he adds, LET THEM BE BLOTTED OUT, *signifies let them not be written in the book of life.* From which it appears, that our adversaries argue falsely from this passage, against the immutability of God's election.

XXVII. As this is fixed and settled with respect to God, so the believer may also attain to a certain assurance thereof, and from infallible marks, know that he is one of the chosen. If it was not so, Peter had to no purpose admonished believers, " to make their calling and election sure," 2 Pet. i. 9, 10. That is, to endeavour by evident signs to be fully persuaded in their own mind. Vain also would have been Paul's glorification, 1 Thess. i. 4. " knowing brethren beloved your Election of God." For by the same evidences Paul could have known this of the Thessalonians, the Thessalonians could have known it with respect to themselves. In fine, they could not possibly, in faith, give thanks to God for their Election, unless they could be assured of it in their own mind. And yet they do give thanks to God for it, Eph. i. 3, 4.

XXVIII. But in what manner do believers attain the assurance of their Election? Who hath ascended into heaven? Or who, with a prying eye, hath perused the volumes of God's decrees and secrets? Who hath looked into the heart of God? We are here, indeed, to guard against rash presumption. But what God has, from eternity, determined about the salvation of his people, he declares to them in time by signs that cannot deceive them. He has given them two books, from which they may gather what is sufficient to know, that they are written in the book of life : namely, *the book of scripture, and the book of conscience.* In the book of scripture, the distinguishing marks of Election are drawn out with great exactness. In the book of conscience, every one may read, if he gives that proper diligence, as a matter of such importance requires, whether these marks are with him. The scripture shews, that the marks of Election are, 1st. Effectual calling by the word and Spirit of God, Rom. viii. 30. 2dly. Faith in God and Christ, 2 Thess. ii. 13. 3dly. Hatred and eschewing of evil, 2 Tim. ii. 19. 4thly. The sincere and constant study of holiness, Eph. i. 4. 2 Thess. ii. 13. And when it is well understood and known, what effectual calling is, what faith in God and Christ, what eschewing of evil, and what the study of genuine godliness are ; the conscience is then to be examined, whether these can be found in itself; and upon discovering that they are, the believing soul may, from these undoubted fruits, be assured of his Election. And it frequently happens, that God favours his chosen people with the ravishments of his most beneficent love, that while they are inebriated with those spiritual and unspeakable delights, which earthly souls can neither conceive nor relish, they are no less persuaded of their Election, than if they had seen their names written by the very hand of God himself. These things make them, with exultation, cry out to their infernal enemies, who in vain resist their faith, " know that the Lord hath set apart him that is godly for himself," Psal. iv. 3. Especially if, what then is not usually wanting, the internal witness of the Spirit to their adoption is superadded, of which in Rom. viii. 16. and which is by way of seal, Eph. i. 13. But there will be occasion to speak of this hereafter.

XXIX. And it is the interest of believers to endeavour earnestly after this assurance of their Election. For, 1st. It is not possible they should have a life of joy and exultation in the Lord while they are ignorant of this. They may, no doubt, happily fall asleep in the Lord, and through death, reach to eternal life, though they are not assured of their Election. For our salvation depends not on this *full assurance* of faith: but on our union and communion with Christ, which may remain safe and secure without that. But a man who has his salvation at heart as he ought, cannot live in secure joy, so long as he doubts of his Election. 2dly. Nor does this assurance greatly contribute to our joy only, but also very much to the glory of God. For then it is, that we properly value the riches of divine love, and are sweetly swallowed up in the immense ocean of his goodness, when we ascend in our minds, and in our praises, to the original fountain of all grace; and in imitation of Paul, celebrate his free love, by which " he hath chosen us in Christ Jesus, to the praise of the glory of his grace, wherein he hath made us accepted in the beloved," Eph. i. 6. 3dly. Nay this certainty of the Election, which we preach, likewise promotes the careful study of piety, and kindles a fervent zeal therein; so far is it from opening a wide door to ungodliness and carnal security; which none dare assert, but they who are ignorant of the good ways of God, or malignant perverters of them.

XXX. Here then is the meditation of one who is thus fully persuaded, and this is his language to his God, " Didst " thou, O Lord, from eternity, entertain thoughts of glorifying

" me, a miserable wretch, who am less than nothing; and
" shall I not again carry thee for ever in my eyes, and always
" in my bosom? shall I not delight in meditating on thee?
" shall I not cry out, *how precious also are thy thoughts unto*
" *me, O God! how great is the sum of them!* Psal. cxxxix.
" 17. Shall I not, with the most sincere repentance, bewail
" that time, in which so many hours, days, weeks, months,
" and years, have passed over my head, without one single
" holy and pleasing thought of thee? Didst thou, out of mere
" love, choose me to salvation? And shall not I again choose
" thee for my Lord, my king, my husband, for the portion
" of my soul, for my chief, or rather mv only delight? Didst
" thou choose me from among so many others who being
" left to themselves, have eternal destruction abiding them?
" And shall not I exert myself to the utmost, to excel others
" in love, in thy worship, and in all the duties of holiness?
" Didst thou predestinate me to holiness, which is so amiable
" in itself, and so necessary for me, that without it there
" can be no salvation? And shall not I walk therein? Shall
" I presume to cavil with thee, thou brightest teacher of
" truth; that separating the end from the means, I should
" securely promise myself the end, as being predestinated
" thereto, in a neglect of the means, to which I was no less
" predestinated? Is thy purpose concerning my salvation,
" fixed and unchangeable? And shall I change every hour; at
" one time, giving my service to thee, and another time to
" the devil? Shall I not rather cleave to thee with such a
" firm purpose, as sooner to choose a thousand deaths rather
" than perfidiously forsake thee? Shall I not be *stedfast,*
" *immoveable, always abounding in the work of the Lord,*
" *for as much as I know, my labour shall not be in vain in*
" *the Lord?* 1 Cor. xv. 58. Wilt thou by thy Spirit, assure
" me of thy love, which passeth all understanding? And I not
" love thee again with all my heart, all my mind, and all my
" strength? Wilt thou give me the assurance of my salva-
" tion? And shall not I, *having this hope, purify myself as*
" *thou art pure?*" 1 John iii. 2. Who, that understands
these things, can deny, that the doctrine of Election, as we
have explained it, affords ample matter to a pious soul for
these and such like meditations? And who also can deny
that in the practice of these meditations consists the very ker-
nel of piety and holiness?

CHAP. V.

Of Effectual Calling.

I. THE first immediate fruit of eternal election, and the principal act of God by which appointed salvation is applied, is *Effectual Calling.* Of which the apostle, Rom. viii. 30. " Whom he did predestinate them he also called." And this *calling* is that act by which those, who are chosen by God, and redeemed by Christ, are sweetly invited, and effectually brought from a state of sin to a state of communion with God in Christ, both externally and internally.

II. The term *from which* they are called, is a state of sin and misery, in which all men are involved, ever since the sin of our first parents ; " having the understanding darkened, being alienated from the life of God, through the ignorance that is in them, because of the blindness of their heart," Eph. iv. 18. For we are brought to such a pass, that we are wholly excluded from the saving communion of God and Christ. Being sunk in the deep gulf of misery, and having lost all notion of true happiness, we wallow in the mire of the wickedness and vanities of this world without end and without measure, and are enslaved to the devil, to whom we have submitted as conquered captives, " for all have sinned and come short of the glory of God," Rom. iii. 23. But out of this darkness of ignorance, sin, and misery, God calleth us unto his marvellous light, 1 Pet. ii. 9. and delivers us from this present evil world, Gal. i. 4. And we are never to forget our former state ; " remember that at that time ye were without Christ, being aliens from the commonwealth of Israel, and strangers from the covenants of promise, having no hope, and without God in the world," Eph. ii. 12. The meditation of this tends to humble us the more deeply before God, who calleth us ; the more to prize the riches of his glorious grace, and the more to quicken us to walk worthy of our calling, and of God, by whom we are called.

III. The term *to which* we are called, is Christ, and communion with him. For this he calls out, Isa. xlv. 22. " Look to me," or, Incline yourselves to me, " and be ye saved, all the ends of the earth." In this communion with Christ consists that mystical and most delightful marriage of the elect soul with Christ, to which he invites him with all the allurements of his gospel, and whose exalted nuptial song Solomon sung; " Wisdom hath builded her house.—She hath sent forth her maidens, she crieth upon the highest places of the city, Turn in hither: come eat of my bread, and drink of the wine which I have mingled," Prov. ix. 1—5.

IV. From this communion results the communication of all the benefits of Christ, both in grace and in glory, to which we are likewise called. " Hearken diligently unto me, and eat that which is good, and let your soul delight itself in fatness. Incline your ear and come unto me; hear and your soul shall live, and I will make an everlasting covenant with you, even the sure mercies of David," Isa. lv. 2, 3. Thus he calleth us to his kingdom and glory, 1 Thess. ii. 12.

V. And since Christ cannot be separated from his Father and his Spirit, we are at the same time called to the communion of the undivided Trinity. " That our fellowship may be with the Father, and with his Son Jesus Christ," 1 John i. 3. to which Paul joins the communion of the Holy Ghost, 2 Cor. xiii. 14. And it is the very top of our happiness, to exult in God as ours, and sing aloud to him, *My God,* while he himself calls to us, *My people,* Hos. ii. 23.

VI. Moreover, as all the elect are partakers of one and the same grace, they are all likewise called to mutual communion with one another, " that ye also may have fellowship with us," 1 John i. 3. Believers of the New Testament with those of the Old; the Gentiles with the Jews, being all of the same body, Eph. iii. 6. in Christ, who hath made both one, Eph. ii. 14. Nay, those on earth with those in heaven; " For all things are gathered together in one in Christ, both which are in heaven, and which are on earth: even in him, in whom also we have obtained an inheritance," Eph. i. 10, 11. And this is that blessed state to which, by the holy and heavenly calling, we are invited, namely, communion with Christ, and by him with the undivided Trinity, and consequently with all the saints, both militant and triumphant, not even excepting the praising assembly of angels, in order with them to exult in the most delightful fruition of all the blessings of God. For all who obey this call, " are come unto Mount Zion, and unto the city of the living God, the heavenly Jerusalem, and to an innumerable company of angels, to the general assembly and church of the first-born which are written in heaven, and to God the Judge of all, and to the spirits of just men made perfect, and to Jesus the Mediator of the New covenant," Heb. xii. 22, 23, 24. What grander things can be spoken, what more noble and divine can be conceived than these?

VII. But this calling is given, partly externally by a persuasive power, called moral suasion; partly internally, by a real supernatural efficacy, which changes the heart. The external call is in some measure published by the word of nature, but more fully by that of supernatural revelation, without which every word of nature would be insufficient and ineffectual. The internal comes from the power of the Holy Spirit working inwardly on the heart, and without this every external revealed word, though objectively very sufficient, as it clearly discovers every thing to be known, believed, and done, yet is subjectively ineffectual, nor will ever bring any person to the communion of Christ.

VIII. Nature itself is not silent, but many ways calls on man to lay aside his too eager care and pursuit of earthly things, and of this animal life, and to endeavour after the far better things of heaven and eternity. For when with attentive eyes he surveys that glittering canopy on high, bespangled with so many constellations, and sparkling with so many stars, above which, according to the general belief of mankind, the throne of the supreme Being is placed, he feels a certain strong desire excited in his breast, that when he leaves this earthly dross, he may hereafter ascend on high, be admitted into the inmost recesses of nature, and received into fellowship with God. And when his thoughts pursue the several beauties of the starry heavens, he then takes a secret pleasure to look down with contempt on the pavements of the rich, nay, on this whole earth, with all its gold, not only that which it has already produced, but that which still lies concealed for the avarice of posterity. And when he further traverses the whole universe, he learns to despise the most stately porticos, ceilings inlaid with ivory, woods formed by art, and rivers conveyed home, and looking down from on high on this small terrestrial globe, a great part of which is covered with the sea, and much of what remains greatly uncultivated, many places being either scorched with heat, or frozen with cold, he thus says to himself; " Is this that insignificant spot which so many nations divide among themselves by fire and sword? When thou hast been engaged in the contemplation of these things truly great, then as oft as thou shall espy armies with banners displayed, and as if some great event was in agitation, the horse now advancing to gain intelligence, again pouring forth from the flanks, you may well say, The deadly squadron marches over the plain. This is but the excursion of ants, toiling within a scanty compass. Whereas there are vastly extensive regions above, into the possession of which the soul is admitted, and thus, although it has suffered some inconvenience from the body, yet if by being content with little, it has dropt all its dross, it is now light and ready to depart: unless then I be admitted into these regions, my birth has been in vain.

For why should I rejoice for being numbered among the living ? Without this inestimable good, life is not of such value, that I should sweat and fatigue myself therein. O ! how contemptible is man, unless he is advanced above what is human." Thus the book of nature, thus the contemplation of the heavens, taught Seneca both to think and speak. In Præfat. Quest. Natur.

IX. But seeing the same nature teacheth us that God is far more excellent than those very heavens, which are his throne and the work of his hands, that he is both the Creator and ruler of the heavens, the same works invite man to seek after the communion of God himself above all things. For happiness cannot consist in barely dwelling in heaven unless one enjoys the fellowship and communion of God there. Thus by the voice of nature men are invited to seek God if haply they might feel after him, Acts xvii. 27. " He left not himself without witness in that he did good," Acts xiv. 17. and that by discovering himself to be the fountain of all good, both the greatest and the best of beings, whose communion alone can render any perfectly blessed. "It is therefore an old saying, and handed down from our ancestors to mankind, that all things were both framed by God, and in him consist ; and that no nature can be sufficient for its own safety, which is only entrusted with its own preser-vation, without God." Thus the author of the book *De mundo*, extant among Aristotle's works, c. xi. and who concludes with these excellent words, " Whoever would attain to a blessed and happy life, must partake of the Deity from the very beginning."

X. But God not only invites men by the light of nature to seek him, but also gives some hope of enjoying him. For why else should he forbear sinners with so much long-suffering, un-less he had decreed to take pity on some of them ? Would it be worthy of the most pure Deity to have preserved now for so many ages the world, subjected to vanity by the sins of men, un-less there were some of mankind to whom he was willing to shew himself glorious in their happiness ? " The Lord is long-suffer-ing to us-ward, not willing that any should perish, but that all should come to repentance," 2 Pet. iii. 9. And as this consi-deration of the divine patience and forbearance, shining forth in the whole government of the world, yields some hope of salva-tion, and the long suffering of our Lord ought to be accounted salvation, ib. ver. 15. So this goodness of God should lead every one to repentance, Rom. ii. 4.

XI. For nature also teaches, that it is not possible any one can enjoy converse and familiarity with God, who does not sin-cerely endeavour after purity and holiness, and, as the emperor

Mark Antony speaks, lib. 2. § 5. labours not to live a life resembling God. For, like delights in like, and rejoices to communicate itself thereto. *Plato de Legibus,* lib. iv. says well, " what practice is it that is agreeable to, and in imitation of God? This and that ancient one ; that like delights in like." Thus man is invited to the practice of the strictest purity, by the voice of nature herself, in order to the enjoyment of God. I cannot forbear adding the gradation of Agapetus, which is really fine, and strictly true. Thus he says to the emperor Justinian ; " for, he who knows himself shall know God. But he who knows God, shall be made like to God. He shall be like God, who is worthy of God. He shall be worthy of God, who does nothing unworthy of God, but meditates on the things of God, and what he thinks he speaks, and what he speaks he acts."

XII. All these things the royal prophet, Psal. xix. 1—4. has exhibited in a concise but very strong manner. " The heavens declare the glory of God ;" for as they are his throne curiously framed, so they display his power, majesty, greatness and holiness, before which the heavens themselves confess they are not clean : however, their very excellence invite men, within their circuit to endeavour, to the utmost, after the enjoyment of communion with the great and good God. " And the firmament sheweth his handy-work," proclaiming, that by his word only, it was framed together. " Day unto day uttereth speech, and night unto night sheweth knowledge." These vicissitudes of light and darkness mutually corresponding in so exact and constant an order, prove a most wise director. And there is no day nor night but speaks something of God, and declares it to the next as the scholar of the preceding and the master of the following. " There is no speech nor language where their voice is not heard." If they were words, the instruction would cease with their sound ; but now what the heavens declare, they do it always, and in the same manner. If speeches, and sentences deduced with much subtlety from their reasons and causes, they would labour under obscurity ; if their voice was heard it would stun us with its noise. But now the heavens instruct both constantly, clearly and sweetly. For, though their voice is not heard, yet they have a voice, no less strongly adapted to strike the mind, than the sound of a trumpet, or of thunder ; seeing they exhibit to the eyes of all the magnificence of their Creator, so clearly as to escape the observation of none but the wilfully blind. Or possibly this may be the meaning ; " There is no speech nor language, where their voice is not heard." Though people differ in languages, and the Greek understands not the barbarian : yet the heavens have a common language adapted to

the instruction of all alike : and nothing but a culpable carelessness can hinder the most distant people from improving by the
instruction, as it were, of one teacher. " Their line is gone out
through all the earth." The instruction of the heavens resembles that of schoolmasters, who teach children their letters,
namely, by drawing their strokes before them. Thus-the heavens draw lines, or strokes, with their rays, and as it were, letters of the alphabet, from which combined and variously joined together, an entire volume of wisdom is formed. This is the
signification of קו, as Isa. xxviii. 10. *line upon line :* from which
the Greek φθογγος, which the apostle uses, Rom. x. 18. does
not differ much, denoting not only a *sound*, but also a letter of
the alphabet, as *Plutarch in fabio* notes, as Scapula has observed in his lexicon. Nor is it necessary, we say, that the text is
here corrupted, or that the Septuagint read קולם *their voice.*
And this line " is gone out through all the earth, and their
words to the end of the world." All mankind whether in a
habitable or desert country are taught by this master. There
is no corner of the world, where the figures of the heavens, as
so many arguments of the divine perfections, are not to be seen.
And this is the reason why I have just now proposed the reasonings of those (if you except the quotation from Agapetus, a
deacon of the church of Constantinople,) who had no other
master but nature.

XIII. But though the invitation which nature gives to seek
God be sufficient to render them *without excuse*, who do not
comply with it, Rom. i. 20. yet it is not sufficient, even objectively, for salvation. For it does not afford that lively hope
which *maketh not ashamed;* for this is only revealed by the
gospel; whence the Gentiles are said to have been " without
hope in the world," Eph. ii. 12. It does not shew the
true way to the enjoyment of God, which is no other than
faith in Christ. It does not sufficiently instruct us about
the manner in which we ought to worship and please God,
and do what is *acceptable to him.* In short, this call by nature never did, nor is it even possible that it ever can, bring
any to the saving knowledge of God: " the gospel alone is
the power of God unto salvation, to every one that believeth,"
Rom. i. 16.

XIV. We cannot agree with those, whether they be ancients, a list of whom Casaubon, *Exercit.* I. *ad Apparat. Annal. Baronii,* and after him Vossius, *Histor. Pelag.* lib. iii. p.
3. Thes. 11. have drawn up; or whether they be moderns, who
maintain that good men, among the Gentiles, were brought to
salvation by this call of nature, without the knowledge of Christ.

And we think, some of our brethren ascribe too much to nature, who tell us, That " men, if not wilfully blind, could, by
what is known of God, have attained to some knowledge of
the divine mercy, by which they might obtain salvation in a
manner perhaps unknown to us; though destitute of the distinct knowledge of some mysteries which they could no way
discover of themselves," *Amyraldus, Specim. Animad. in Exerc.
de Gratia. Univ.* P. ii. p. 133.   For we are persuaded, there
is no salvation without Christ, Acts iv. 12. no communion of
adult persons with Christ, but by faith in him, Eph. iii. 17.
no faith in Christ, without the knowledge of him, John xvii. 3.
no knowledge, but by the preaching of the Gospel, Rom. x.
14. no preaching of the Gospel in the works of nature.   For,
it is that " mystery which was kept secret since the world began," Rom. xvi. 25.

XV. To what purpose then, you will say, is this call by
the light of nature?   Not to speak of the being *without excuse* just now mentioned, which indeed may be the end of
him who calls, though not of the call itself, that calling serves
to pave the way for a further, a more perfect, and a more ex-
plicate call by the Gospel, and as a prelude of a fuller instruction.   For, as grace supposes nature, and makes it perfect;
so the truths revealed in the Gospel are built on those made
known by the light of nature.   When a person under that
glimmering light has discovered, that there is a God, that
happiness consists in his communion with him, and in comparison of him all things are nothing, and that he is the rewarder of those who seek him; and that, if he is sought in a
proper way and manner, he is not sought in vain; he has now
a foundation laid, on which to build the gospel, which declares
what that God is, in what manner he becomes propitious to
men in Christ, how he is to be sought, and in what method
he will certainly be found.   And thus that knowledge, he
learns from nature, being sanctified by the Spirit, better prepares the mind for embracing those truths which though they
surpass, are yet so far from destroying, that they perfect nature.
And it is very expedient for believers, who live under the
Gospel, to have always the book of nature before their eyes:
which furnishes them with useful instructions, and lashes the
conscience with continual reproaches, unless they love, worship,
and celebrate the Deity, who is every where present.   Which
the heathens themselves, as Epictetus and others, have represented in their own way.

XVI. We must therefore add the other call by the word of
God, supernaturally revealed, either immediately from God's

own mouth, as was formerly done to the patriarchs, prophets, apostles, and others; or mediately by the ministers of God, whether they preached it by word of mouth, or consigned it to writing. Thus Paul says, Rom. x. 14. " how shall they believe in him of whom they have not heard? And how shall they hear without a preacher?" And here indeed both parts of the word are to be made use of; thus the law convincing man of sin, Rom. iii. 20. awakens him to a sense of his misery, drives the sinner out of himself, stirs him up to desire deliverance, and makes him sigh and cry in this manner, " O wretched man that I am, who shall deliver me from the body of death!" Rom. vii. 24. Therefore the law ought certainly to be preached in its full vigour and force, that " knowing the terror of the Lord we may persuade men," 2 Cor. v. 11. But yet the principal part is performed by the Gospel, which revealing Christ, and the fulness of all grace and salvation in him, allures, by its endearing sweetness, awakened and concerned sinners to communion with God. Nothing more powerfully sinks into the inmost soul, than that most alluring invitation of Jesus, " Come unto me all ye that labour and are heavy laden, and I will give you rest," Matt. xi. 28. " Let him that is athirst come, and whosoever will, let him take the water of life freely," Rev. xxii. 16. This is " the power of God unto salvation, to every one that believeth," Rom. i. 16. If the law only was preached, it would, by its horrors, harden souls, driven to despair, into a hatred of God, as a severe avenger of sin. But by adding the gospel, which makes a bright hope of grace to shine, even on the most abandoned and wretched sinner, if displeased with himself, he heartily desires it: obstinate hearts come to relent, and to be melted down into a love of God, and of his Christ. And therefore nothing ought to be more sweet and dear to us than the most delightful word of the Gospel, in which are brooks of honey and butter, *Job xx. 17.

XVII. This word of grace was published in the world from the very first sin of man, though variously dispensed, Heb. i. 1. But in such a manner, as to be sufficient for the instruction of the Elect to salvation, in all ages, according to that measure of grace and knowledge, which the providence of God distributed in each period of time. When the revelation was more sparing and obscure, God being satisfied with a less measure of knowledge, did, by the secret power of his

---

* The author's quotation of Isa. lii. 7. seems to be a mistake of the press, and therefore I have given this, to which he appears to have referred.

Spirit, unite the Elect to Christ, and keep them united by an almost invisible band, which yet no force could break asunder. But when he had more brightly discovered himself, he called for a more exact knowledge and faith. And as he clearly teaches his people, " how they ought to walk, and to please God, so he also requires them to abound more and more," 1 Thess. iv. 1.

XVIII. We do not agree with those, who think, that by the unwritten word of God, those only were called to salvation through faith in Christ, who were eminent for the spirit of prophecy, but the rest of the church was so rude and ignorant, that they were brought to an unknown Christ, by the help of the law of nature alone, without the spirit of faith. For, down from Adam, the true church had one and the same precious faith, and the same common salvation with the prophets. God did not only speak to the prophets for their private use, but by the prophets to the fathers, Heb. i. 1. The prophets would have acted perfidiously, had they put the candle that was lighted for them under a bushel, and indolently wrapt in a napkin the talent entrusted with them. Nor is it consistent with the piety of the ancient fathers, not to have inculcated with care and diligence upon their children, what they themselves had learned about the promised seed of the woman. So that though we are not to determine any thing rashly, as to the manner and measure of knowledge, yet we are not to doubt, but that the revelation of a Saviour was made to the Elect from the beginning.

XIX. This gospel call was never given universally to all men ; unless in the beginning of the world, just springing from Adam, or rising again from Noah. Though even then, God gave warning of the seclusion of some from his grace by the distinction he made between the seed of the woman and the seed of the serpent ; and by separating Ham from his brethren by a dreadful curse, and the ancient prophecy of alluring, in after times, the posterity of Japhet into the tents of Shem, which insinuated, that the posterity of Japhet should, for some time, be aliens from the communion of the people of God. Afterwards, the greatest part of mankind were left to themselves, and though God vouchsafed the word of his grace to the posterity of Abraham, yet not to them all. In fine, when he claimed Israel to himself for a people, he rejected the other nations, and suffered them all to go on in their own ways, Acts xiv. 16. And though, upon breaking down the wall of partition, the apostles were enjoined to preach the gospel to every creature, without distinction, yet it was never so universally preached, but that there were always very many nations, and still are at this day, whom the report of the Gospel never reached. They are therefore mistaken who, having feigned an universal redemption by Christ, and an universal objective grace, as it is called, have at the same time devised, for supporting it, an universal call to Christ.

XX. This call contains the command of faith, by which all men without exception, to whom God vouchsafes the same, are enjoined to believe in Christ, in that way and manner which is revealed in the Gospel, Isa. xlv. 22. " look unto me and be ye saved all the ends of the earth." But the method of believing is this : *first*, that a person do heartily acknowledge all men, without exception, and himself among the rest, to be liable to condemnation because of sin : and *then*, that he embrace the principal truths of the Gospel ; namely, that there is no salvation, but in Christ, nor any communion with Christ, but by a true and lively faith : *moreover*, that he do not neglect so great salvation, but renouncing all earthly enjoyments, and every false remedy for his sins, he only desire the righteousness of Christ, receive him as his Saviour, give himself up wholly to him, not doubting but in so doing he shall find rest to his soul. All and every one in particular therefore, to whom the Gospel is preached, are not commanded directly to believe that Christ died for them. For that is a falsehood : but are commanded to proceed in that method I have now described ; and not to take comfort to themselves from the death of Christ, before having acknowledged their own misery, and renounced every thing but Christ, they have given themselves up sincerely to him. We cannot therefore conclude from this general call, who they are for whom Christ died : but only this, that there is no other name given under heaven, in which we can be saved ; and that in him, as an all-sufficient Saviour, every believer shall have life.

XXI. But that *external* call will bring none to communion with Christ, unless it be accompanied with the *internal*, which is accomplished not only by persuasion and command, but by the powerful operation of the Spirit. There is a certain call of God, whereby he makes the things he calls to exist by that very call. By such a call, *he calleth those things which be not, as though they were*, Rom. iv. 14. For, when he said, *let there be light*, immediately *there was light*, Gen. i. 3. Not unlike this is that internal call of the Spirit, of which the apostle writes, 2 Cor. iv. 6. " God who commanded the light to shine out of darkness, hath shined in our hearts." But when he says to the Elect, in the hour of their happy visitation, " awake thou that sleepest and arise from the dead, and Christ shall give thee light," Eph. v. 14. it is no more possible for them to remain any longer in the sleep of death, than it was possible for Lazarus to continue in the grave, after Christ had said to him, *Lazarus, come forth*, John xi. 43.

XXII. Here God exerts his infinite power, by which he converts the soul no less powerfully than sweetly. While the Gospel is externally proposed to his chosen people, " he gives them the eyes of their understanding to be enlightened, that they may know what is the hope of their calling, and what the riches of the glory of his inheritance in the saints," Eph. i. 18. he " openeth their heart, that they may attend unto the things which are spoken," Acts xvi. 14. and causes them " to receive the word with all readiness of mind," Acts xvii. 11. He writes his laws on their heart, Jer. xxxi. 33. puts the reverence of himself there, Ezek. xi. 20. And not only calls them from darkness to his marvellous light, but also, by the call, draws them, not to stand still in the path of doubtful deliberation, but to *run after him*, Cant. i. 4. Not only puts them in an equal poise, but *turns them*, Jer. xxxi. 18. Not only advises, but persuades, and *he is stronger and prevails*, Jer. xx. 7. Nor does he solicit, but *translate*, Col. i. 13. Not by an ordinary, but by that mighty power by which he raised Christ from the dead, Eph. i. 20. Let * changeable human nature put on what form it will, it must be obliged to confess, that in this matter, these are so many displays of divine omnipotence, like so many thunderbolts thrown out to bring down its pride.

XXIII. Nevertheless, God deals here with the rational crea- ture in such a manner, that the liberty of the human will is not in the least affected : which he is so far from destroying by the energy of his power, that, on the contrary, he rescues and main- tains it. *He put*, indeed, *into the heart of Titus the earnest care of going*, yet so as to *undertake the journey of his own accord*, 2 Cor. viii. 16, 17. It is a violence indeed, but that of heavenly love, the greater the sweeter. A certain kind of com- pulsion, but that of the most charming friendship ; to the end, that the soul being loosed from the chains of sin and Satan, may rejoice in the most delightful liberty. God does not drag along the unwilling, by head and shoulders, but makes them willing, Phil. ii. 13. bringing his truths so clearly to their understanding,

---

* The author's words are *humani ingenii vertumnus*, alluding to *Vertumnus*, a God worshipped by the *Romans*, under several shapes, because he was thought to be the *God of change*, and to be graceful under every form, and therefore I have rendered it *changeable human nature.*

that they cannot but assent, so effectually gaining upon their will by the charms of his goodness, that they are not able to reject them; but yield themselves conquered, and that with the highest complacency; exulting with joy, ' " O Lord, thou hast enticed me, and I was enticed, thou art stronger than I, and hast prevailed," Jer. xx. 7.   I may well exult in this victory and triumph over the devil, for that I myself am conquered by thee.'   And who can be so rude, as to complain of any violence done to human liberty, by this winning power (so to speak) of the Deity?

XXIV. It was certainly inconsistent with the power and majesty of God to attempt any thing and leave it in suspense, and not bring it to a final issue; it was likewise unworthy both of his goodness and wisdom, so to vex and distress a man endowed with reason and will, as, in a matter of the far greatest moment, to act, without .knowledge or against his will, by a certain fatal and blind instinct of his own.   He therefore employs the highest degree of force, thereby to conquer the highest degree of the corruption of nature; but a pleasant force, a force under the direction of wisdom, as became an intelligent and rational nature; which is so willingly overcome as not only not to resist because nothing can resist God, when he comes to convert the soul; but also because, should it resist, it would think itself most unhappy.   But yet we are here to distinguish between the beginning and accomplishment of the call; as also between the object and the end, or that in which it terminates. For, at the beginning of the call man necessarily resists, and cannot but resist, because the object is an unbelieving and rebellious sinner and a child of disobedience: but in the consummation, he necessarily makes no resistance, and cannot now resist, because the end of this call, or that in which it terminates, is a believer, who owns himself conquered, and glories in the obedience of faith.   This is, what the Greek authors emphatically call, πειθανάγκη, the contracting persuasion of God, who calls.

XXV. The many admonitions, promises, and threatenings, by which we are invited, make nothing against this truth: for as they inform us of our duty, so they are made effectual to conversion by the internal operation of the Spirit.   Nor ought the complaints of God and of Christ, of the unwillingness of people, to be converted, be objected to it; because these do not speak of any inward power that would bring about their conversion, as if they were able to weaken that, but of the external ministry of the word, against which the wicked harden their heart.   Neither are we to urge, what we elsewhere find about grieving the Spirit of God: because we are to distinguish between the common operations of the Spirit of God, and the special operations of the Spirit of grace; between the moral and the supernatural actions of the Spirit of grace: between some more feeble impulses to certain exercises of virtue and piety, and that grand attempt of the Spirit, when he goes to convert an elect person. They grieve the Spirit of God, because they rather choose to obey the impulses of the flesh and of the devil, than his holy admonitions, which are partly proposed externally by the word, partly insinuated into their mind by conscience. Believers themselves also grieve the Spirit of grace, whereby they are sealed, as often as they refuse to comply with his holy admonitions; and though conscience, in which the Spirit has set up his throne, in vain struggles with them, yet they suffer themselves to be carried away by the flesh and the world; and likewise every time, that, with a becoming reverence of soul, they refuse to receive, cherish, follow his holy impulses, when he quickens them to duty. Whence nothing can be concluded against the invincible efficacy of God, when he calls internally, and effectually undertakes the conversion of his people.

XXVI. We ought then attentively to consider, carefully hearken to, and willingly comply with the call of God, both the external by the light of nature and revelation, and the internal by the Spirit, so that upon being brought to communion with God and Christ, " we may shew forth the praises of him who hath called us out of darkness into his marvellous light," 1 Pet. ii. 9.

CHAP. VI.

Of Regeneration.

I. By that same word, whereby the Elect are called to communion with God and his Christ, they are also regenerated to a far more excellent life. For thus James saith, chap. i. 18. " of his own will begat he us with the word of truth, that we should be a kind of first fruits of his creatures." It is therefore proper, we proceed from the subject of *effectual calling*, to that of *Regeneration*.

II. But here all things are deep, and wrapt up in mystery. Who can unfold to us the secrets of his own corporal birth? Who can distinctly declare, in what manner he was poured out like milk, and curdled like cheese within the bowels of his mother? The prophet himself, as if he was seized with a holy amazement, cried out, " I will praise thee, for I am fearfully and wonderfully made; marvellous are thy works, and that my soul knoweth right well. My substance was not hid from thee, when I was made in secret, and curiously wrought in the lowest parts of the earth. Thine eyes did see my substance yet being unperfect," Psal. cxxxix. 14, 15, 16. But if these things, which regard the origin of our body, and the beginnings of this animal life, are involved in such darkness as to frustrate the enquiries of the most sagacious; how much more involved are the things that constitute our spiritual regeneration, which none can doubt to be mystery all over?

III. But yet this is so necessary, that our Saviour declares, that without it there is no entering into the kingdom of heaven, John iii. 3, 5. It therefore deserves to be enquired into; that if we have perhaps attained to it, we may celebrate with becoming praises the glorious perfections of God our Father which shine so conspicuous in this illustrious work, and properly valuing our happiness, we may frame the whole tenour of our lives in a manner suitable to it.

IV. We give this definition of it; " *Regeneration* is that supernatural act of God, whereby a new and divine life is infused into the elect person spiritually dead, and that from the incorruptible seed of the word of God, made fruitful by the infinite power of the Spirit."

V. We are *all dead in* Adam, 1 Cor. xv. 22. through the poison of the tempting serpent. *This murderer from the beginning*, John viii. 44. had such success attending his endeavours, that all men who now exist are by nature *dead in trespasses and sins*, Eph. ii. 1. That is, 1st. They are separated at the greatest distance from God and his Spirit, who is the soul of their soul; and life of their life; or in the language of Paul, *alienated from the life of God*, Eph. iv. 18. 2dly. They are spiritually insensible of all spiritual things, and destitute of all true feeling: they do not rightly consider the load of their sins, because they are in them as in their element: nor have a right knowledge of their misery, *being past feeling*, Eph. iv. 19. nor any relish for divine grace, because it has not yet been conferred upon them; nor any longing after heavenly things, being ignorant of their worth. 3dly. They are wholly incapable of every act of true life; " not sufficient of ourselves to think any thing as of ourselves," 2 Cor. iii. 5. The understanding is overspread with dismal darkness, Eph. iv. 18. " hath not set God before it," Psal. lxxxvi.

14. " receiveth not the things of the Spirit of God, neither can
it know them," 1 Cor. ii. 14. The will has no tendency to
things unknown; and thus all the things of God are despised
by it as mean. And if, at times, it seem to perform any things
that have some appearance of vital actions, this proceeds not
from a principle of life, but resembles those automatical or
artificial motions by which statues, ingeniously framed, counterfeit living animals.

VI. But as a dead carcase swarms with vermin, arising
from putrefaction, in which the briskest life is observed, though
of another order and kind from that life which was formerly
in that body; so in like manner, there is a kind of life in a
man spiritually dead, but it is carnal, hellish and diabolical,
at the greatest distance from true life, and the more vigorous it is, it gives the more evident signs of the most deplor-
able death. The apostle has elegantly joined this death and
life, Eph. ii. 1, 2. " when ye were *dead* in trespasses and
sins, ye walked in them, as in *the life* of this world:" so Beza
translates. In the Greek it runs κατὰ τὸν αἰῶνα τȣ κοϛμȣ τȣτȣ.
Elegantly *Philo Alleg.* lib. 1. defines this death : " when
the soul is dead as to virtue, it lives the life of vice." Not
unlike to what Macarius says, *Homil.* 12. " when Adam began
to entertain evil thoughts and devices, he perished as to God ;
we say not, he perished altogether, was destroyed and quite
dead; but that, though as to God he was dead, yet he was
alive as to his own nature." What Macarius affirms of Adam
is universally true of all : for in a man spiritually dead, there
is really a natural or animal life, which though not active in
that which is good, is doubly active in that which is evil. The
understanding not apprehending the wisdom of God, looks
upon it as foolishness, 1 Cor. ii. 14. and yet, when it would
find wisdom in the things of God, it so transforms them by its
mad presumption, and compels them, even against their nature, to a conformity to the notions of its trifling presumptuous
self-wisdom, that while it impiously presumes to correct
the wisdom of God, it transforms it in a dreadful manner into
downright folly. The will, not finding any thing in God
wherewith it can take delight, seeks it either in the creatures
without God, or which is more abominable, in the very per-
petration of wickedness. The affections, shaking off the
reins of reason, rush on in full career. The body, with all
its members, is the throne of mad and furious lusts. And
the whole man, being so averse from God, and infatuated
with the fond love of himself, sets himself up for an idol,
makes his own advantage his supreme end, his own pleasure

his most infallible law.   This is the life of the soul, which *is
dead while living*, 1 Tim. v. 6.

VII. And thus it is with the elect before regeneration :
but by regeneration a new life is put into them, resulting
from a gracious union with God and his Spirit.   For, what
the soul is to the body, that God is to the soul.   Moreover,
this spiritual life may be considered, either by way of *faculty*,
and in the *first act*, in the usual language of the schools ;
or by way of *operation*, and in the *second act*.   In the former
respect, it is that inward constitution of the soul whereby it is
fitted to exert those actions which are acceptable to God in
Christ, by the power of the Spirit uniting it to God : whether
such actions immediately flow from that principle, or whether
they lie concealed for some time, as fruits in their seed.   In the
latter respect, it is that activity of the living soul by which
it acts agreeably to the command of God and the example of
Christ.

VIII. If we consider this first principle of life, there is not
the least doubt, but regeneration is accomplished in a moment.   For there is no delay in the transition from death to
life.   No person can be regenerated, so long as he is in the
state of spiritual death : but in the instant he begins to live,
he is born again.   Wherefore no intermediate state between
the regenerate and unregenerate can be imagined so much as
in thought, if we mean regeneration in the first act : for one
is either dead or alive ; has either the spirit of the flesh and
the world, or the Spirit of God actuating him ; is either in
the state of grace, or in the state of malediction ; either the
child of God, or of the devil ; either in the way to salvation,
or damnation.   There neither is, nor can be any medium here.
The holy scripture divides all mankind into two classes, *sheep
and goats*, Matt. xxv. 2, 3. and compares their goings to *two
ways*; whereof the one, which is broad, leads to destruction ;
the other, which is narrow, to life, Matt. vii. 13, 14. and
there is none who does not tread in one or other of these
ways.   And what if he, whom some imagine to be in an intermediate state, should depart this animal life before he be
fully brought to the spiritual life, would such a one be received into heaven ?   But heaven is open only to the actually regenerate, John iii. 3.   Or thrust into hell ?   But hell is allotted
only for the goats, and for those who, all their life long, have
walked in the broad way : or perhaps such will be received
into some intermediate place where being free from the pains
of hell, and deprived of the joys of heaven, they will delight
themselves in I know not what degree of natural happiness ;

as some Popish doctors, discoursing in the council of Trent,
of infants dying without baptism, pleased themselves with
these fond sportings of their imagination; which the author
of the history of that council, lib. ii. p. 159. has not dismiss-
ed without a good deal of acrimony and sharpness. Or you
will say perhaps, it is a case which never happens, that any
one should die in that intermediate state. But produce me
the vouchers of such an assertion, whereby security is given to
those, in this intermediate class, of spinning out their lives
till they have declared of what class they choose to be. I do
not remember to have read any thing on that head in scripture. And if that intermediate state has such an indissolva-
ble connection with salvation, it will be no longer intermediate,
but a state of grace. For it is grace alone to which the
attainment of glory is infallibly assigned. I own there are various degrees of regeneration in the second act; and that the
seed of it sometimes lies hid under the earth, or at most exerts
some slender and initial, and as it were, infantile operations,
differing very much with respect to perfection from those
which a more advanced spirit of sanctification produces: yet
seeing the former also have their rise from the fountain of
the new life, it is plain, that they who exert them are to
be ranked among the regenerate. For we must say one of
these two things; either, that these operations ascribed to the
intermediate state, proceed from the powers of nature and
common grace; and thus there is nothing in them which may
not be found in the reprobate, and those entirely unregenerate: or, that they proceed from the indwelling Spirit of
grace, and so are effects of regeneration, to which the beginnings of the new life are owing.

IX. Hence it appears, there are no preparations antecedent
to the first beginning of regeneration; because previous to
that, nothing but mere death in the highest degree is to be found
in the person to be regenerated. " When we were *dead in sins,*
he hath quickened us together with Christ," Eph. ii. 5. And
indeed the scripture represents man's conversion by such simili-
tudes as shew, that all preparations are entirely excluded; sometimes calling it a *new generation,* to which certainly none
can contribute any thing of himself: but yet, as natural generation presupposes some dispositions in the matter, so
that we may not imagine any such thing to be in ourselves
but from God, we have this held forth by the similitude of
a resurrection; in which a body is restored from matter,
prepared by no qualifications: yet because here certainly is
matter, but in the resurrection of the soul there is nothing

at all, therefore we have added the figure of a creation, Psal.
li. 10. Eph. ii. 10.; by which we are taught that a new creature exists from a spiritual nothing, which is sin : but as
there was not something in nothing to assist and sustain creation ; so there was nothing to oppose and resist ; but sin is
so far from submitting to what God does, that it is reluctant
thereto, and in a hostile manner at enmity with him ; accordingly, the other images did not fully complete the idea of
this admirable action, till at length it is called the *victory* of
God : victory, I say, over the devil, who maintains his palace,
Luke xi. 21. and effectually worketh *in the children of disobedience*, Eph. ii. 2. All these operations of God, which Alex-
ander More has, in an elegant order, ranged one after another,
de victoria Gratiæ, Diss. 1 *Thess.* 10. tend to exclude, as
far as possible, all preparations from the beginning of our
regeneration.

X. The Semi-pelagians therefore of Marseilles were mistaken, who insisted, that a man comes to the grace whereby
we are regenerated in Christ by a natural faculty ; as by asking, seeking, knocking ; and that, in some at least, before
they are born again, there is a kind of repentance going before, together with a sorrow for sin, and a change of the life
for the better, and a beginning of faith, and an initial love of
God, and a desire of grace : it is true they did not look on
these endeavours to be of such importance as that it could be
said, we were thereby rendered worthy of the grace of the
Holy Spirit ; as Pelagius and Julian professed : but yet they
imagined, they were an occasion by which God was moved
to bestow his grace ; for they said, that the mercy of God is
such, that he recompenses this very small beginning of good
with this illustrious reward ; as Vossius hist. pelag. lib. iv. p.
1. Thess. 1. has refined this their opinion. The Remonstrants are likwise mistaken, in Collatione Hagiensi, editi-
onis Brandianæ, p. 302. when they write, " some work of
man therefore goes before his vivification ; namely, to acknowledge and bewail his death, to will and desire deliverance from it ; to hunger, thirst, and seek after life : all which,
and a great deal besides, is required by Christ in those whom
he will make alive." But there is little accuracy in the reasonings of these men. For, 1st. Since our nature is become
like an evil tree, after having eaten of the forbidden fruit, it
can produce no fruit truly good and acceptable to God, and
do nothing by which it can prepare itself for the grace of regeneration ; unless a person can be thought to prepare himself for grace by sin. 2dly. It has been found that they who

in appearance were in the best manner disposed for regeneration, were yet at the greatest distance from it, as the instance
of that young man, Mark. xix. 21, 22. very plainly shews.
He appeared to be full of good intentions, and inflamed with
a desire after heaven, and a blameless life before men, to a
degree, that Jesus himself beholding him loved him; but,
notwithstanding all these dispositions, he parted with our
Lord sorrowful.   3dly. And on the other hand, they who
had not even the least appearance of any preparation, as the
publicans and harlots, went into the kingdom of God before those
who were civilly righteous and externally religious; " for
these last believed not John, declaring the way of righteousness; but the publicans and the harlots truly believed,"
Matt. xxi. 31, 32. 4thly. and lastly, God testifies, that in
the first approach of his grace, " he is found of them that
sought him not, and asked not for him," Isa. lxv. 1. *Fulgentius, lib.* 1. *de veritat prædest.* p. 62. says extremely well :
" We have not certainly received grace, because we are willing, but grace is given us while we are still unwilling."

XI. There have been likewise some among ourselves who
have spoken of preparations to regeneration or conversion ;
but in a quite different sense from the favourers of Pelagianism,   In persons to be regenerated they have assigned, 1st.
A breaking of the natural obstinacy, and a flexibility of the
will. 2. A serious consideration of the law. 3. A consideration of their own sins and offences against God. 4. A legal fear of punishment, and a dread of hell, and consequently
a despairing of their salvation, with respect to any thing in
themselves. For in this order, Perkins, Cos. Conscient. c.
5. quæst. 1. § 1. reckons up these preparations; and
Ames in the same manner, Cas. Conscient. lib. 2. cap. 4. And
the British divines explained themselves almost to the same
purpose in the synod of Dort, p. 139, of the Utrecht edition,
1620, fol. 1st. " There are some external works ordinarily
required of men before they are brought to a state of regeneration or conversion, which are wont sometimes to be freely
done, sometimes freely omitted by them : as going to church,
hearing the word preached, and the like. 2dly. There are
some internal effects, previous to conversion, or regeneration,
excited by the power of the word and Spirit in the hearts of
those who are not yet justified; as the knowledge of the
will of God, sense of sin, dread of punishment, anxiety
about deliverance, some hope of pardon." But they differ
from the favourers of Pelagianism in this manner. 1st. That
they are not for having these things to proceed from nature,

but profess them to be the effects of the spirit of bondage, preparing a way to himself for their actual regeneration. 2dly. That they are not for God's bestowing the grace of regeneration from a regard to, and moved by occasion of, these preparations, much less by any merit in them; but they imagine that God, in this manner, levels a way for himself, fills up vallies, depresses mountains and hills, in order the better to smooth the way for his entrance into that soul. Nay, the British divines add, Thess. vi. " That even the Elect themselves never behave in these acts preceding regeneration, in such a manner as that on account of their negligence and resistance, they may not justly be abandoned and forsaken of God." Yet they call them rather preparations for grace, than the fruits and effects of grace; because they think that even the reprobate may go as far as this: and they affirm, " that these antecedent effects, produced by the power of the word and Spirit in the minds of men, may be, and in many usually are, stifled and entirely extinguished through the fault of the rebellious will." Ibid. Thess. v. But we really think they argue more accurately, who make these, and the like things in the Elect, to be preparations to the further and more perfect operations of a more noble and plentiful spirit, and so not preparations for regeneration, but the fruits and effects of the first regeneration: for as these things suppose some life of the soul, which spiritually attends to spiritual things, and are operations of the Spirit of God when going about to sanctify the Elect, we cannot but refer them to the Spirit of grace and regeneration. Nor is it any objection, that the like, or the same be also said to be in reprobates; for they are only the same materially, but not formally. Reprobates also have some knowledge of Christ, some taste of the grace of God, and of the powers of the world to come. Yet it does not follow, that the knowledge of Christ, as it is in believers, and that relish of grace and glory they have, is not the gift of the Spirit of grace and of glory. And indeed, the things mentioned by Perkins, and the other British divines, are no preparations for regeneration in the reprobate; either from the nature of the thing, or the intention of God. Not the former: for however great these things may appear to be, yet they are consistent with spiritual death; and the reprobate are so far from being disposed thereby to a spiritual life, that, on the contrary, deceived by those actings which counterfeit spiritual life, they are the more hardened in a real death, and fondly pleasing themselves, are at a greater distance from enquiring after true life, which they falsely imagine they have obtained. Not the latter : for no intention of God can be rendered void. It is therefore necessary that all these things be in another manner in the Elect than in the reprobate.

XII. If this matter be more closely considered, we shall find that the orthodox differ more in words, and in the manner of explaining, than in sense and reality. For the term *regeneration*, is of ambiguous signification : sometimes it is blended with sanctification, and by regeneration is understood that action of God, whereby man, who is now become the friend of God, and endowed with spiritual life, acts in a righteous and holy manner, from infused habits. And then it is certain, there are some effects of the Spirit, by which he usually prepares them for the actings of complete faith and holiness ; for, a knowledge of divine truths, a sense of misery, sorrow for sin, hope of pardon, &c. go before any one can fiducially lay hold on Christ, and apply himself to the practice of true godliness. God does not usually sanctify a man all at once, before ever he has had any thought about himself and God, and any concern about his salvation. And this is what the British divines seem to have intended ; when *in confirmatione Secundæ Theseos*, they thus speak : " Divine grace does not usually bring men to a state of justification, in which we have peace with God through our Lord Jesus Christ, by a sudden enthusiasm, but first subdues and prepares them by many previous acts by the ministry of the word." By which words they sufficiently shew, that, by regeneration, they mean the state of passive justification. But sometimes regeneration denotes the first translation of a man from a state of death to a state of spiritual life ; in which sense we take it. And in that respect none of the orthodox, if he will speak consistently with his own principles, can suppose preparatory works to the grace of regeneration. For, either he would maintain, that these works proceed from nature ; and so, by the confession of all the orthodox, are but dead and splendid sins. But none in his right mind will affirm, that any can be disposed for the grace of regeneration by those things which are sinful. Or he would maintain, that these works proceed from the Spirit of God. But if thus far he does not operate in another manner in the Elect than in the reprobate : these works, notwithstanding this his operation, may be reckoned among dead works, for the orthodox look upon all the actions of the reprobate to be sinful, let them be ever so much elevated by divine assistance. Thus the British divines, l. c. p. 143. " an evil tree, which naturally brings forth evil fruit, must itself be first changed to a good tree, before ever it can yield any good fruit. But the will of an unregenerate person is not only an evil, but also a dead tree." I now infer, the reprobate are never regenerated, and therefore continue evil trees, without ever producing any other than bad fruit. And so there can be no preparation in such works for regeneration, for the reason above explained. If you say, that these works which you call preparatory are different in the Elect: I ask, in what respect? No other answer can be given but this, that they proceed from the Spirit of grace and life: right, but then they are not preparations for the first regeneration, but effects of it; for regeneration is the first approach of the Spirit of grace and life, effectually working in the Elect.

XIII. You will say then, are there no preparatory dispositions to the first regeneration? I confidently answer, there are none: and agree with *Fulgentius, de Incarnat et Gratia Christi*, c. 19. " with respect to the birth of a child, the work of God is previous to any will of the person that comes into the world; so also in the spiritual birth whereby we begin to put off the old man." I own, indeed, spiritual death has its degrees, but with a distinction: what is privative therein, or what it is destitute of, namely, the want of the life of God, is equal or alike in all; and in this respect there are no degrees less or more. But what is positive, or, as it were, positive therein; namely, those evil habits, these indeed are very unequal. In infants there are only those evil habits which come into the world with them: in the adult there are others contracted and deeply rooted by many vicious acts, and a course of wickedness. These again greatly differ, according as, by the secret dispensation of God's providence, the affections of men are more or less restrained. For though every kind of wickedness, like * a certain hydra, lurks in the heart of all; yet God suffers some to give loose reins to their vices, and to be hurried on as by so many furies; while he moves others with a sense of shame, and a reverence for the laws, and some kind of love to honour and honesty; who, in that respect, may be said not to be at such a distance from sanctifying grace, as they who are guilty of horrid crimes, which are more opposite thereto than a civil and external honesty of life. But yet whatever length any before regeneration has advanced in that honesty, he nevertheless remains in the confines of death, in which there is no preparation for life.

XIV. Nor do we agree with those who so inconsiderately assert, that man is no more disposed for regeneration than a stone or an irrational animal. For there are naturally such faculties in the soul of man, as render him a fit subject of regeneration, which

---

* The author's phrase is *quædam velut lerna;* and therefore I have rendered it like a certain Hydra, which was supposed to be a water serpent in the lake of Lerna, having several heads, which grew again as fast as they were cut off. This monster was killed by Hercules.

are not to be found in stones or brutes. Thus a man *can* be regenerated, but a brute or a stone *cannot*. In that sense *Augustine de Predest. sanct. c. 5.* said, " the capacity of having faith and love is of the nature of man, but to have them, of the grace of believers." Vossius has proved by proper arguments, that this is to be understood, not of the proximate, but remote capacity, in so far as man has naturally those faculties, in which faith and love may be wrought: *Histor. Pelag.* lib. iv. P. I. p. 418.

XV. But we must not here omit, that the Elect, before their actual regeneration, are honoured by God with various, and those indeed very excellent privileges above the 'reprobate, which are intended, according to the purpose of God, to be subservient for promoting their regeneration in his appointed time. For as God has a love of special benevolence for them, according to the decree of election; and they are redeemed by Christ, and in a state of reconciliation with God, and of justification, actively taken, it follows, 1st. That God often preserves them from those base and scandalous crimes which are repugnant to common humanity, and that by some assistance of light, of divinity, of conscience, and civil honesty, with an accession of * some grace operating internally, and laying a restraint on the wickedness of their nature. 2dly. That all and every one of them, who are brought to the acknowledgment and the common illumination of the truth of the Gospel, are kept from the sin against the Holy Ghost. 3dly. That by the ministry of the word, and other operations of God's special providence towards them, many evident principles of divine truth are understood by the natural mind, and also imprinted on the natural memory, the meditation of which, immediately after they are regenerated, conduces very much to the confirmation of their faith. And thus, without knowing it, they have collected a very valuable treasure, the excellence and genuine use of which they come not to see, till they are born again. But as these things do not, of their own nature, dispose man for regeneration, though, by the appointment of God, they are so disposed, as that regeneration is certainly to follow, they cannot but very remotely be called preparations, and they will be such more from the intention of God, than from the virtue of the thing.

XVI. Now after a principle of spiritual life is infused into the elect soul by regeneration, divine grace does not always proceed therein in the same method and order. It is possible that for some time, the spirit of the life of Christ may lie, as it were, dormant in some (almost in the same manner, as vegetative life in the seed of a plant, or sensitive life in the seed of an

---

* This is what is generally called *restraining grace.*

animal, or a poetical genius in one born a poet), so as that no
vital operations can yet proceed therefrom, though savingly
united to Christ, the fountain of true life, by the Spirit.   This
is the case with respect to elect and regenerate infants, whose
is the kingdom of God, and who therefore are reckoned among
believers and saints, though unqualified through age, actually
to believe and practise godliness.

XVII. Moreover, this spirit of a new life will even sometimes exert itself in vital actions in those who have received it
in their infancy, as they gradually·advance in years, and are
qualified to raise their thoughts above the objects of sense.
Accordingly it has often been observed, that, in children of
five or six years of age, some small sparks of piety and devotion have shone forth in holy longings, ardent little prayers,
and in a certain extraordinary tenderness of conscience, not
daring to do any thing with respect to God, themselves, or
their neighbour, which they have been taught to be displeasing
to God : as also it appears in their discourses concerning God
and Christ, which have been full of a holy and unfeigned love,
and breathing something heavenly, which I have not words to
express.   Thus sometimes God is pleased, " out of the mouth
of babes and sucklings to ordain strength," Psal. viii. 2.   This
has been especially observed in some dying children, to the
great astonishment of all present.

XVIII. But when the foundation is laid, divine grace does
not always grow up in the same manner.   It often happens
that this principle of spiritual life which had discovered its
activity in the most tender childhood, according to, and sometimes above, the age of the person, God, by his singular grace
preventing the full maturity of the natural faculties, grows up
by degrees with the person, after the example of our Lord,
who " increased in wisdom and stature, and in favour with
God and man," Luke ii. 52. and of John the Baptist, who
grew and waxed strong in spirit, Luke i. 80.   Such persons
make continual progress in the way of sanctification, and grow
insensibly " unto a perfect man, unto the measure of the stature of the fulness of Christ," Eph. iv. 13.   We have an illustrious example of this in Timothy, " who from a child had
known the holy scriptures," 2 Tim. iii. 15. and who in his
tender youth, to Paul's exceeding joy, had given evident signs
of an unfeigned faith, with tears of the most tender piety burst-
ing out at times, 2 Tim. i. 4, 5.

XIX. On the other hand, sometimes those sparks of piety,
especially which more sparingly shone forth in childhood, when
in a manner covered with the ashes of I know not what, worldly
vanities, and carnal pleasures of youth, will appear to be almost

extinguished. The allurements of the deceitful flesh, and the sorceries of a tempting world, assaulting the unadvised unwary heart with its deceitful pleasures, almost stifle these small beginnings of piety; and for months, sometimes for years together, so violently overpower them, that all their attempts against them seem to be in vain. Yet there are still, in these persons, remorses of conscience, awakening them at times, languid resolutions, and vanishing purposes, of reforming their lives, till by the infinite efficacy of divine grace, insinuating into the languid and decaying breast, they awake as from a deep sleep, and with the greatest sorrow for their past life, and utmost seriousness, apply to the careful practice of piety; the warmth of their zeal then breaks forth being exceedingly desirous to shew, by brighter flames, its having been unwillingly kept smothered under the ashes. Augustine has given us in his own person, a representation of this state in the excellent book of his confessions.

XX. But the Elect are not all favoured with regenerating grace in their infancy. There are some adult persons whom God regenerates, and at once effectually calls, and converts, in the second act, from a worldly and hypocritical condition, or even from a state of profligate wickedness. Thus it is with those, who are born and brought up without God's covenant, or even of those who, living where this covenant is dispensed, have sold themselves wholly to sin, Satan and the world. The regeneration of these is usually followed with great consternation of soul and sorrow for sin, with a dread of God's fiery indignation and incredible desires after grace, together with an inexpressible joy, upon finding salvation in Jesus, and a wonderful alacrity in the service of the Lord, which they can scarcely contain. All this may be observed in the jailor of whom we read, Acts xvi.

XXI. On this depends the solution of that question, whether we are to look upon any as born again, but those who can specify the time, manner and progress of their regeneration? None indeed are here to be flattered or soothed, as to think it lawful for them securely to presume on their regeneration: but then the consciences of believers are not to be racked with too severe a scrupulosity. We cannot determine this point without a distinction: we have just shewn, that the progress of regeneration is various. Adult persons, who are brought altogether from a carnal to a spiritual life, indeed may, and ought exactly to know the beginning and manner of so great a change. They who, though regenerated in infancy, have yet been carried away by the entanglements of the world, and for some time have struggled, as it were, with destruction, but afterwards have been roused by the grace of God, made to renounce the world, and give themselves wholly to piety, such as we described, § XVII. These may, and it is their duty to recollect, not so much the beginning of their very first regeneration, as the process of that actual and thorough conversion. But it would be wrong to require those, who, being regenerated in their infancy, have grown up all along with the quickening Spirit, to declare the time and manner of their passage from death to life. It is sufficient if they can comfort themselves, and edify others, with the fruits of regeneration, and the constant tenour of a pious life. It is, however, the duty of all to recollect, not in a careless manner, the operations of the Spirit of grace on their hearts : which is highly useful, both for our glorifying God, and for our own comfort, and excitement to every duty.

XXII. There cannot be the least doubt of God's being the author of our regeneration. For we become his sons by regeneration, which were born of God, John i. 13. And even in this respect, *the sons of God by grace*, bear some resemblance to him who is *the Son of God by nature*: observing only the difference between the infinite excellency of our Lord, and that dark resemblance of it in us. Why is the Lord Jesus called the Son of God? Because begotten of the Father, Psal. ii. 7. Wherein consists that generation of the Father? In this, that " as the Father hath life in himself, so he hath given to the Son to have life in himself," John v. 26. And why are we in communion with Christ, called the sons of God? because his Father is our Father, John xx. 17. How is he our Father? " He hath begotten us," James i. 18. 1 John v. 4, 11. Wherein does that generation consist? " He hath made us partakers of a divine nature," 2 Pet. i. 4. Thus we are even transformed into his likeness, and have upon us no contemptible effulgence of his most glorious holiness.

XXIII. But there is here a special consideration of Christ, who, *as God*, is, together with the Father and Spirit, the principal, but *economically* considered, the meritorious and *exemplary* cause of our regeneration. For when he cast a vail over the majesty of the Son of God, took upon him human form, and came in the " likeness of sinful flesh," Rom. viii. 3. he thereby merited for all his elect, their advancement to the illustrious dignity of the sons of God ; sons, I say, not only by adoption, but by a spiritual and heavenly generation. The holy and glorious life of Christ is also the most perfect of our new life, all the excellence of which consists in a conformity with the life of Christ, who is the " first-born among many brethren," Rom. viii. 29. And we may add, that Christ, as the second Adam, is become not only by merit, but also by efficacy, *a quickening spirit,* 1 Cor. xv. 45. So that the regenerate do not so much live themselves, as feel, acknowledge and proclaim Christ living in them, Gal. ii. 20. Phil. i. 21.

XXIV. What Christ declares of the Spirit, the author of regeneration, deserves our consideration, John iii. 5. "except a man be born of water and of the Spirit, he cannot enter into the kingdom of God." Here interpreters enquire, what we are to understand by *water*, and what by *the spirit ?* There is one who by *water* understands the origin of our natural birth ; comparing with this place what we have Isa. xlviii. 1. where the Israelites are said " to have come forth out of the waters of Judah," and Psal. lxviii. 26. " from the fountain of Israel :" and then the meaning will be; besides that birth, whereby we are born men, there is still another requisite, whereby we are born the sons 'of God ; which appears both simple and agreeable to scripture language. There is another, who understands by *water, Christ's obedience ;* we doubt not but that is the meritorious cause of our regeneration ; but we question whether it is ever called water in scripture. For no such thing appears from the scriptures they bring to prove it, Heb. x. 22. 1 John v. 6, 8. Ezek. xxxvi. 25. By water in these places we are more properly to understand the Holy Spirit with his operations. And it is evident, our Lord himself explains the passage in Ezekiel in this manner. The common explication therefore is to be preferred, that one and the same thing is meant by *water* and the *spirit,* as it is by the spirit and fire, Mat. iii. 11. For, nothing is more common in the sacred writings, than to represent the Holy Spirit under the emblem of water. See among other passages, Isa. xliv. 3. " I will pour water upon him that is thirsty, and floods upon the dry ground ; I will pour my Spirit upon thy seed;" where the former figurative expression is explained by the subsequent one, that is plain.

XXV. The seed of regeneration is the word of God. For thus 1 Peter i. 23. *born again not of corruptible seed, but of incorruptible,* δια λογȣ ζωνȷος Θεȣ και μενονȷος εις τον αιωνα, which may be translated, " by the word of God, who liveth and abideth for ever ;" or, " by the word of God, which liveth and abideth for ever." But this seed does not operate always in the same manner : for adult persons are born again by the word of God, laying before them the deformity, horror and misery of their natural life, or rather of their living death ; and at the same time, the excellence of that spiritual life, of which Christ is the author, fountain and pattern; pressing them also by the most powerful exhortations, that, denying all carnal lusts and appetites, they may give themselves up to be new moulded and formed by the Spirit of God. And in this manner, the word is to them a moral instrument of regeneration, by teaching and persuasion. But the case is otherwise with elect infants, being incapable of teaching and persuasion. If they also be thought to be regenerated of the seed of the word, it is to be understood, not of the word externally propounded, which they understood not, but of the truths contained in the word, the efficacy of which is imprinted by the Holy Spirit upon their minds, which they will come to the actual knowledge of when they grow up; but the word operates effectually in none unless when impregnated by the efficacy of the Spirit. To the external word must be added the internal, which is no less effectual than that word of God, whereby he commanded light to shine out of darkness.

XXVI. It is therefore incumbent on every person who would not profanely despise his salvation, diligently to read, hear and meditate on the word of God, and constantly attend on the public worship and assemblies of his people. For though before his regeneration, he cannot savingly hear, read or meditate on the word of God, yet how does he know which may be the happy hour of his gracious visitation; which part of holy scripture, what sermon, and by whom, the Lord is to render effectual for his regeneration, by the supernatural efficacy of his Spirit? Experience teaches this, that men are born again there where the word of God is preached; a thing which is not the case in those parts of the world which God favours not with the preaching of the gospel. And though we dare not assure any one, that if he continues in hearing the word, he shall certainly be born again: yet we justly insist upon this, that there is a brighter hope of the wished-for conversion for those, who in the best manner they can, use the means which God has prescribed, than for such as frowardly neglect them. While Ezekiel was prophesying to the dry bones, behold, a shaking was observed among them, and *the breath* (spirit) *came and they lived,* Ezek. xxxvii. 10.

XXVII. Let none think it absurd that we now speak of means for regeneration, when, but a little before, we rejected all preparations for it. We have above sufficiently proved, that none can contribute any thing to his own regeneration: yet God commands every one to " make himself a new heart, and a new spirit," Ezek. xviii. 31. to " awake from sleep and arise from the dead," Eph. v. 14. and to " flee from the wrath to come," Mat. iii. 7. And what then? Shall we insignificant mortals, pretend to reply to God, as if by our sophistry we could catch and entangle the Almighty ? shall we say, to what purpose are we enjoined to what none of us can comply with ? Shall we exclaim against the counsel of God, and cry out, " since we can contribute nothing to our regeneration, is it not the best course we can take to put our hands in our bosom, and securely wait till he himself regenerate us ?" But would not this be, with our vain and carnal reasonings, to argue with God, whose foolishness will be ever found wiser than our most exalted wisdom ? How much better is it, when one hears these commands of God, and at the same time is sensible of his own incapacity, that he learn a holy despair of himself, and in sorrow, anxiety, and a longing desire of soul, and in the use of the means, patiently wait for the coming of the grace of God ?

XXVIII. Moreover, when a person touched with an unfeigned sense of his misery, and a sincere desire after his salvation, cries out with the jailor, " what must I do to be saved ?" Acts xvi. 30. even then some pious emotions begin to arise, which proceed from an inward, but a very tender principle of new life, and which are solicitously to be cherished. For which purpose it is expedient, 1st. That he frequently, and in as affecting a manner as possible, set before his eyes the most wretched condition of all unregenerate persons, and how himself also, while he continues in the state of nature, has nothing to expect but eternal destruction, a deprivation of the divine glory, and intolerable torments both of soul and of body ; and all this unavoidable, unless he be born again in the image of God. 2dly. That, affected by this consideration, he cry, pray to, be earnest with God, and not give over crying till he has obtained his grace. Let him often represent himself to himself, as now standing on the very brink of the infernal lake, with the devil standing by him, who, should the supreme Being permit, would instantly hurry him headlong into hell : and in this anguish of his distressed soul, importune God, and as it were, extort pardon by the warmest prayers, sighs and tears. 3dly. Let him, however, go on to hear, read and meditate on the word of God, expecting the farther motions of the Spirit, as the diseased waited for the angel to move the waters of Bethesda. 4thly. Let him join himself in society with the godly, and in the exercise of piety, endeavour to catch the flame of devotion from their instruction, example, and prayers.

CHAP. VII.

Of Faith.

I. W<small>E</small> now proceed to explain the nature of true *Faith* in God by Christ, which is the principal act of that spiritual life implanted in the elect by regeneration, and the source of all subsequent vital operations. But it is not any one particular act, or habit, nor must it be restricted to any one particular faculty of the soul; for it is a certain complex thing, consisting of various acts which, without confusion, pervade, and by a sweet and happy conjunction, mutually promote and assist one another; it imparts a change of the whole man, is the spring of the whole spiritual life, and in fine, the holy energy and activity of the whole soul towards God in Christ. And therefore its full extent can scarcely be distinctly comprehended under any one single idea.

II. And we need not wonder, that under the name of one Christian virtue, so many others are at once comprehended. For as when any person speaks of life, he signifies by that term something that, diffusing itself through the whole soul, and all its faculties, is also communicated to the body, and extends itself to all the actions of the living person : so when we speak of faith, which is the most fruitful spring of the whole spiritual life, we understand by it that which pervades all the faculties, and is well adapted to unite them with Christ; and so to enliven, sanctify and render them blessed.

III. There are many things both in *naturals* and *morals,* which are almost by general consent allowed to extend to the whole soul, without being restricted to any one faculty. In *naturals*, free-will, which as *will* is referrred *to the understanding ;* as *free*, rather to *the will :* so that as Bernard somewhere speaks, " let man be his own free man on account of his will; his own judge on account of his reason." In *morals* the image of God, and original righteousness ; which are to be placed neither in the understanding alone, nor in the will alone, but may justly belong to both these faculties.

IV. Should we not then at last see every difficulty removed, and the whole of that controversy among divines about the subject of faith, settled, if, as we justly may, we should refuse, that there is any real distinction of understanding and will, as well from the soul, as from each other? For, what is the understanding, but the soul understanding and knowing? What else the will, but the soul willing and desiring? We must on no account conceive of the soul as of a thing in itself brutish and irrational, which at length becomes intelligent and rational when something else is given to it. What some affirm, that the understanding comes from the soul by a certain kind of emanation is what we can scarcely conceive. For if the soul, in its proper and formal conception, does not include the power of reasoning, it can never produce it; for we are in vain to expect from a cause what it contains neither formally nor eminently. If the soul is of itself endowed with the faculty of reasoning, no necessity requires, that some other faculty be superadded to that wherewith the soul is of itself endowed. The like holds with respect to the will, which is not really distinct from the soul any more than the understanding, but is the very soul itself, as God has given it a natural aptitude to desire good. Since both these faculties are only modally [or in our manner of apprehension] distinct from the soul, so they are also from each other. For if the will be so distinct from the understanding, as in itself to be blind, it is not possible to explain how it can perceive, and so rationally desire, the object discovered by the understanding, as good. And for what reason, pray, should we make a real difference between these two? Is it, because the object is different? But the object of both is really the same: namely, a *true good*, though the manner of our considering it differs. For the understanding considers the good as *true*: and the will desires this *true* thing as it is *good*. And do not the objects of the speculative and practical understanding differ far more among themselves? And yet philosophers generally agree, that they are but one and the same power of the soul. Is it because their acts are different? But every difference of acts does not infer a difference of power. Indeed, simple apprehension differs from judgment and discourse or reasoning; which yet are all the acts of the same faculty.

V. This ought not to be looked upon as a new assertion. Scotus long ago maintained, that the understanding and will differed neither among themselves nor from the soul, *in 2. dist.* 15. *qu.* 1. Scaliger, in like manner, whose words we shall not scruple to transcribe from his *Exercitat.* 307. sect. 15. Although " the understanding and will, *says he*, are one thing, yet they are distinguished by the manner in which we conceive them. For they are proper and not accidental affections of the soul, and one thing with it. As *one*, *good*, and *true*, are the affections of entity or being; nay, one and the same thing with being itself. But they are distinguished from it, and among themselves by definition, in this manner : because being itself is placed in the first *nature* or *essence*, which nature does in some measure display itself, and is the cause of that *one*, *true*, and *good*. Which is a formality different from the first formality. Because the notion of being is one thing, as it is being, and another as it is one. For the latter follows and arises from the former ; but not without it, for it is one thing. Thus soul, understanding and will, are one thing. Yet the soul denotes the essence : the understanding that very essence, as it apprehends : the will, the same with that intelligent essence tending to enjoy the thing known, or understood." Thus far Scaliger. Durandus was of opinion, that indeed the faculties differ really from the soul, but not from each other. An opinion, which Vossius is above all pleased with, *de Idololat. Lib. 3. c.* xlii. Which is sufficient for our present purpose : as we are not then to separate those faculties, no wonder though we place faith in both.

VI. Mean while we observe, that among those things which we are about to describe, there is one principal act in which, we apprehend, the very essence and formal nature of faith consists, as it unites us with Christ and justifies us. This is to be carefully taken notice of in the matter of justification, lest any one should look upon some acts of love, which in different ways are implied in the exercise of faith, as the causes of justification.

VII. Moreover, we are likewise to maintain, that those things which we shall, for the greater accuracy, explain distinctly in particular, stand various ways mutually connected in the very exercise of faith. While the whole soul is engaged in this work of God, very many actions may all at once tend towards God and Christ, without observing any certain method ; and which the believer, engaged in this work itself, has neither leisure nor inclination to range in their proper order ; nay, sometimes it is impossible to do it. Yet it is expedient, that we attend to the natural process of faith, whereby its entire nature and manner may be the more thoroughly perceived.

VIII. The first thing which faith either comprehends or presupposes, is *the knowledge* of the thing to be believed. This appears in opposition to Popish triflers, I. From express passages of scripture, which so speak concerning faith

as manifestly to intimate, that knowledge is included in its
very notion and exercise, Isa. liii. 11. John xvii. 3. compared
with Heb. ii. 4. John vi. 69. 2 Tim. i. 3.   II. From the nature of faith itself, which, as it doubtless means an assent
given to a truth revealed by God, necessarily presupposes the
knowledge of these two things.   (1.) That God has revealed
something.   (2.) What that is to which assent is given, as
a thing divinely revealed.   For it is absurd to say, that a person assents to any truth which he is entirely ignorant of, and
concerning which he knows of no testimony extant worthy of
credit.   III. From the manner in which faith is produced in
the elect; which is done *externally* by preaching and hearing
of the Gospel, Rom. x. 27. revealing that which ought to be
believed, with the demonstration of the truth to every man's
conscience, 2 Cor. iv. 2. and *internally* by the teaching of
God the Father, John vi. 45.   If therefore faith be generated
in the heart by a teaching both external and internal, it must
of necessity consist in knowledge: for knowledge is the proper and immediate effect of such instruction.   IV. From the
consequence annexed, which is confession and απολογιά, or giving an answer, Rom. x. 9, 10. 1 Pet. iii. 15.   But it is impossible, that this should be without knowledge.   Hilary
saith well, "For none can speak what he knows not; nor
believe what he cannot speak."

IX. But indeed it must be confessed, that in the present
dark state of our minds, even the most illuminated are ignorant of a great many things; and that many things are believed with an implicit faith, especially by young beginners and
babes in Christ, so far as they admit, in general, the whole
scriptures to be the infallible standard of what is to be believed;
in which are contained many things which they do not understand, and in as far as they embrace the leading doctrines
of Christianity, in which many other truths concenter, which
are thence deduced by evident consequence, and which they
believe in their foundation or principle, as John writes concerning believers, that they *knew all things*, 1 John ii. 20.
because they had learned by the teaching of the Spirit, that
foundation of foundations, to which all saving truths are reduced, and from which they are inferred.   But I go a step
farther: it is possible that one, to whom God, who distributes his
blessings as he pleases, has measured out a small degree of
knowledge, may yet be most firmly rooted in the faith, even
to martyrdom.   But then it no ways follows, that faith is
better described by ignorance than by knowledge: or that
they do well who cherish ignorance among the people as the

mother of faith and devotion, contrary to Col. iii. 16. for we can by no means believe what we are quite ignorant of, Rom. x. 14. And all should strive to have their faith as little implicit, and as much distinct as possible; as becometh those who are *filled with all knowledge*, Rom. xv. 14. For the more distinctly a person sees by the light of the Spirit a truth revealed by God, and the rays of divinity shining therein, the more firm will be his belief of that truth. Those very martyrs, who, in other respects, were rude and ignorant, most clearly and distinctly saw those truths for which they made no scruple to lay down their lives, to be most certain and divine; though perhaps they were not able to dispute much for them.

X. Moreover those things which are necessary to be known by the person who would believe, are in general, the divinity of the scriptures, into which faith must be ultimately resolved; more especially, those things which regard the obtaining of salvation in Christ; which may summarily be reduced to these three heads: 1st. To know, that by sin thou art estranged from the life of God, and art *come short of the glory of God*, Rom. iii. 23. That it is not possible, that either thou thyself, or an angel from heaven, or any creature in the world, nay, or all the creatures in the universe, can extricate thee from the abyss of misery, and restore thee to a state of happiness. 2dly. That thou shouldst know Christ this Lord to be *full of grace and truth*, John i. 14. who is that only name given under heaven, whereby we can be saved, Acts. iv. 1. and in the knowledge of whom consists eternal life, John xvii. 3. 3dly. That thou shouldst know, that, in order to thy obtaining salvation in Christ, it is necessary that thou be united to Christ, by the Spirit and by faith, and give up thyself to him, not only to be justified, but also sanctified, and governed by his will and pleasure, *proving what is that good, and acceptable, and perfect will of God*, Rom. xii. 2.

XI. To this knowledge must be joined *assent*, which is the *second* act of faith, whereby a person receives and acknowledges as truths those things which he knows, *receiving the testimony of God*, and thus *setting to his seal, that God is true*, John iii. 33. This assent is principally founded on the infallible veracity of God, who testifies of himself and of his Son, 1 John v. 9, 10. On which testimony revealed in scripture, and shedding forth all around the rays of its divinity, the believer relies with no less safety than if he had been actually present at the revelation of these things. For when the soul, enlightened by the Spirit, discerns those divine truths,

and in them a certain excellent *theoprepy*, or beauty worthy of
God, and a most wise and inseparable connection of the whole, it
cannot but assent to a truth that forces itself upon him with
so many arguments, and as securely admit what it thus knows,
for certain, as if it had seen it with its own eyes, or handled
it with its own hands, or had been taken up into the third
heavens, and heard it immediately from God's own mouth.
Whatever the lust of the flesh may murmur, whatever vain
sophists may quibble and object, though perhaps the soul
may not be able to answer or solve all objections, yet it per-
sists in the acknowledgment of this truth, which it saw too
clearly, and heard too certainly, as it were from the mouth of
God, ever to suffer itself to be drawn away from it by any
sophistical reasonings whatever: " For, I have not followed,
says the believing soul, cunningly devised fables, when I believed the power and coming of our Lord Jesus Christ, but in
the Spirit was eye witness of his majesty, and heard his voice
from heaven," 2 Pet. i. 16, 18.   And thus faith is accompanied
with 'υποϛασις, *substance*, and βεγχος, *evidence*, Heb. xi. 1. *and*
πληροϑορία, *full persuasion* or *assurance*, Rom. iv. 21.   It will
not be unprofitable to consider a little the meaning of these
words.

XII. The apostle speaks more than once of πληροφορία *plerophory* or *full assurance ;* as Col. ii. 2. πληροφορία συνεσεως, *the
full assurance of* understanding ; Heb. vi. 11. πληροφορία της ελ-
πίδος, *the full assurance of hope*, Heb. x. 22. πληροφορία πίσεως, *full
assurance of faith.*   According to its etymology the word
plerophory, denotes *a carrying with full sail*, a metaphor, as
it should seem, taken from ships when all their sails are filled with a prosperous gale.   So that here it signifies the ve-
hement inclination of the soul, driven forward by the Holy
Spirit, towards an assent to the truth it is made sensible of.
Hesychius, that most excellent master of the Greek language,
explains it by Βεβαίοτητα, *firmness*.   And in that sense, πληροφορία
πίσεως, plerophory of faith, is nothing but ςιρεωμα της εις χρισον
πισεως, *the stedfastness of faith in Christ*, as the apostle varies
those phrases, Col. ii. 2, 5. ; and πεπληροφορημένα πράγμαla, *are
things most surely or firmly believed*, Luke i. 1. So firm therefore must the believer's assent be to divine truth.

XIII. The term υποϛασις, *hypostasis substance*, is also very
emphatical, which the apostle makes use of when he speaks
of faith, Heb. xi. 1.   Nor have the Latins any word that can
fully express all its force and significancy.   1st. 'Υπόϛασις *hypostasis* denotes *the existence*, or, as one of the ancients has

said, the *extantia*, the standing up of a thing; in which sense
philosophers say that a thing that really is has an ὑπόϛασις, that
is, *real existence*, and is not the fiction of our own mind.
And indeed faith makes the thing hoped for, though not actually existing, to have, notwithstanding, an existence in the
believer's mind, who so firmly assents to the promises of
God, as if the thing promised was already present with him.
Chrysostom had this in his mind when he thus explained this
passage : ἡ ἀνάϛασισ 'ὐ παραγέγονεν, 'ὐδέ ἐϛιν 'εν ὑποϛάσει, αλλ' ἡ ἐλπὶς
ὑφίϛησεν ἀυτὴν εν ἡμετέρᾳ ψυχῇ, *the resurrection does not yet exist in
itself, but hope* (let us say faith) *presents it to, and makes it extant in our soul.* A Greek scholiast, cited by Beza, has most
happily expressed the same thing : Ἐπειδὴ γὰρ τὰ ἐν ἐλπίσιν ἀν ὑπόϛα-
ϡά ἐϛιν ὡς τέως μὴ παρόνϡα, ἡ πίϛις ἐσιά τις ἀυτῶν Καὶ ὑπόϛασις γίνεται ἔιναι
ἀυτὰ Καὶ παρεῖναι τρόπον τίνα παρασκευάζὐσα, διὰ τὐπιϛεύειν ἔναι, *as
things hoped for, are not yet extant, as not being present, faith
becomes a kind of substance and essence of them, in some measure, extant and present with us, in that it believes them to be.*
2dly. Ὑπόϛασις also signifies a *base* or *foundation*, in which sense
Diodorus Siculus, quoted by Gomarus, has said, ὑπόϛασις τὐ
πάφὐ, that is, the *foundation of the Sepulchre.* And Calvin's
interpretation looks this way ; *faith*, says he, is *hypostasis*, that
is, *a prop or possession on which we fix our feet.* 3dly. It also
denotes *subsistence*, or *constancy*, without yielding to any assault of the enemy. Thus Plutarch in Demetrius, ἐδενὸς ὑφιϛμένὐ
τῶν ἐναντίων, ἀλλὰ φευγόντων, *none of the enemy standing their
ground, but all giving way.* And Polybius in his description of
Horatius Cocles, they feared, ἐχ' ὐτω την δύναμιν, ὡς την ὑποϛασιν
ἀυτὐ, *not so much his strength, as his firmness and resolution*, not
to give way. And indeed there is something in faith that can
with intrepidity sustain all the assaults of temptations, and not
suffer it to be moved from an assent to a truth once known.
Now if we join all this together, we may assert, that faith is so
firm an assent to divine truth, as to set things future before us
as if they were present, and that it is a prop to the soul on
which it fixes its foot without yielding to any assault whatever.

XIV. Nor ought it to be omitted that the apostle calls
faith ἔλεγχος, ὐ βλεπομενων *the evidence of things not seen.* But
ἔλεγχος denotes two things. 1st. *A certain demonstration.*
Aristotle, Rhetoric. c. 14. says, ἔλεγχος δε ἐϛιν, ὁ μὲν μὴ δυνατὸς
ἄλλως ἔχειν, αλλ' ὕτως ὡς ἡμεῖς λέγομὐνε ; *demonstration is what cannot possibly be otherwise, but must necessarily be as we affirm.*
2dly. *Conviction of soul* arising from such a demonstration of the
truth : as Aristophanes in Pluto, σὐγ ἐλέγξαι μ' ὐπω δύνασαι παρὶ

τίτε, *you cannot convince me of that.* There is therefore in faith, if it be *ἔλεγχος* [an elenchus] *a demonstration,* a certain conviction of soul, arising from that clear and infallible demonstration. But this demonstration of truth rests on the testimony of God who cannot deceive: from which faith argues thus: whatever God, who is truth itself, reveals, cannot but be·most true and worthy of all acceptation, though perhaps I may not be able to see it with my eyes, or fully conceive it in my mind.

XV. All this tends to instruct us that the assent which is in faith has a most certain assurance, which no certainty of any mathematical demonstration can exceed. Wherefore they speak very incautiously who maintain there may be falsehood in divine faith, since the proper object of faith is the testimony of God, which is necessarily true and more certain than any demonstration. Nor can any places of scripture be brought in which any thing that is not true can be man's belief.

XVI. But we are here to remove another difficulty : if faith is such a certain and firm assent, are those then destitute of true faith who sometimes waver even with respect to fundamental truths? I answer, 1st. We describe faith, considered in the idea, as that Christian virtue or grace, the perfection of which we all ought to aspire after : and not as it sometimes subsists in the subject. 2dly. There may at times be waverings, staggerings, and even inclinations to unbelief in the best of believers, especially when they are under some violent temptation, as is evident from the waverings of Asaph, Jeremiah, and others, about the providence of God : but these are certain defects of faith arising from the weakness of the flesh. 3dly. Faith presently wrestles with those temptations, it never assents to those injections of the devil, or the evil desires of the carnal mind, nor is ever at rest, till having entered the sanctuary of God, it is confirmed by the teaching Spirit of faith in the contemplation and acknowledgment of those truths about which it was staggered. There at length, and no where else, it finds rest for the soles of its feet.

XVII. That which follows this assent is the *love* of the truth thus known and acknowledged; and this is the *third* act of faith, of which the apostle speaks, 2 Thes. ii. 10. For since there is a clear manifestation of the glory of God, in saving truths, not only as he is true in his testimony, but also as his wisdom, holiness, justice, power, and other perfections shine forth therein, it is not possible but the believing soul, viewing these amiable perfections of the deity in those truths, should break out into a flame of love to exult in them and glorify God. Hence the believer is said *to give glory to God*, Rom. iv. 20. and *to love his praise* (glory), John xii. 43. Above all, the soul is delighted with the fundamental truth concerning Christ. Loves it as an inestimable treasure, and as a pearl of great price; it is *precious* to believers, 1 Pet. ii. 7. yea, *most precious*. It is indeed true, that love, strictly speaking, is distinguished from faith; yet the acts of both virtues, or graces, are so interwoven with one another, that we can neither explain nor exercise faith without some acts of love interfering; such as is also that of which we now treat: this also is the observation of some of the greatest divines before me; as, not to mention others at present, Chamierus, Panstrat. T. 3. lib. 12. c. 4. No. 16. Wendelin, Theol. lib. 2. c. 24. ad Thes. 8. And both of them cite Augustine in their favour, who asking *what is it to believe in God?* answers, *It is by believing to love.* See also le Blanc, a divine of Sedan, in Thes. de fidei justificantis natura, &c. § 95. But if any will call this love, according to the gloss of the schools, *an imperate*, or *commanded act* of faith, he is indeed welcome to do so for us; if he only maintain that it is not possible but the believing soul, while in the exercise of faith, must sincerely love the truth as it is in Christ, when known and acknowledged, rejoicing that these things are true, and delighting itself in that truth: far otherwise than the devils and wicked men, who, what they know to be true, they could wish to be false.

XVIII. Hence arises a *fourth* act of faith, *a hunger and thirst after Christ.* For the believing soul knowing, acknowledging and loving the truths of salvation, cannot but wish that all those things which are true in Christ may also be true to him, and that he may be sanctified and blessed in and by those truths: And he seriously desires, that having been alienated from the life of God through sin, he may be again sealed unto the glory of God by free justification, and in that by sanctification. This is that *hunger* and *thirst after righteousness* mentioned Mat. v. 6. And pray what reason can be given why he who believes and feels himself a most miserable creature, and is fully persuaded that he can be delivered from his misery by nothing either in heaven or on earth; who sees, at the same time, the fulness of that salvation which is in Christ; and is assured he can never obtain salvation unless he be united to Christ; who from his very soul loves that truth that treats of the fulness of salvation

which is in Christ alone, and in communion with him; how
is it possible, I say, that such a person should not seriously
and ardently desire to have Christ dwelling in him, seek and
pant after this, and indeed with such longings, as nothing
short of the possession of the thing desired can satisfy: as
hunger and thirst are only allayed by meat and drink.

XIX. This hunger and thirst are followed by *a receiving
of Christ the Lord* for justification, sanctification, and so for
complete salvation: which is the *fifth*, and indeed the formal and principal act of faith. Thus the heavenly Father
freely offers his Son to the sick and weary soul; and Christ
the Lord offers himself with all his benefits, and the fulness
of salvation which is in him, saying, *behold me, behold me*,
Isa. lxv. 1. And the soul now conscious of its own misery,
and with joy and hope observing the fulness of salvation that
is in Christ, and earnestly desiring communion with him, cannot but lay hold on and receive, with the highest complacency
of soul, that extraordinary blessing thus offered, and thus by
receiving, appropriate or make it his own. And by this
act, at length Christ becomes the peculiar property of the
believing soul. Thus it lays claim to whatsoever is Christ's,
which is offered at the same time with Christ, and above all
the righteousness of Christ, which is the foundation of salvation. And in this manner, by apprehending Christ, he is
united to him; and being united to him, he is judged to have
done and suffered what Christ, as his Surety, did and suffered
in his room and stead. And thus it is easy to understand
how we are justified by faith on Christ.

XX. The scripture more than once represents this act of
faith in express terms. Remarkable is the passage, John i.
12. " as many as received him," which is equivalent " to
them that believe on his name;" and Col. ii. 6. " as ye have
therefore received Christ Jesus the Lord;" to which may be
added what the Lord has very emphatically said, Isa. xxvii.
5. " let him take fast hold of my strength," or my tower,
so as not to let it go. For *take fast hold of*, and *let go*,
are opposed, Prov. iv. 13.

XXI. But because the soul thus apprehending Christ for
salvation, does at the same time *recline* and *stay itself upon*
him, therefore this act of faith is explained by this metaphor
also, as Psalm lxxi. 6. " by thee have I been holden
up" (stayed). Isa. xlviii. 2. " stay themselves upon the
God of Israel," pretending to and feigning a true faith:
he is stayed, is another term used, Isa. l. 10. *stay upon his
God;* add Isa. x. 20. 2 Chron. xvi. 7, 8. If you would sub-

tily distinguish this act of the believing soul, thus reclining and thus staying itself upon Christ, from the act of receiving Christ, and make it posterior thereto, I shall not oppose it. Let us therefore call this the *sixth* act of faith.

XXII. Which we think is very significantly expressed by the Hebrew word האמין, which properly signifies, *to throw one's self in order to be carried*, on the truth and power of another; as an infant throws itself to be carried on the arms of its nurse. For it is derived from אמן, which properly signifies *to carry*: hence, *a carrier, a nursing father*, Numb. xi. 12. " carry them in thy bosom, as a nursing father beareth the sucking child:" and האמן signifies *to be carried*, Isa. lx. 4. " thy daughters shall be nursed (carried) *at thy side*." Instead of which it is said, Isa. lx. 12. *ye shall be borne upon her sides.* And Christ really *carries* believers as nurslings, *in his bosom*, Isa. xl. 11. for Moses also uses that similitude, " the Lord thy God bare thee, as a man doth bare his son," Deut. i. 31. " underneath are the everlasting arms," Deut. xxxiii. 21. האמין therefore in virtue of its signification denotes *to give up one's self to be carried* by Christ, and so to cast himself into his bosom and arms. By which similitude the activity of the believing soul towards Christ is most elegantly expressed.

XXIII. Moreover, when the believer so receives Christ and leans upon him, he not only considers him as a Saviour but also as a Lord. For he receives a *whole* Christ, and receiveth him just as he is: but he is no less Lord than a Saviour. Yea, he cannot be a Saviour unless he be likewise a Lord. In this doth our salvation consist, that we neither belong to the devil, nor are our own, nor the property of any creature, but of Christ the Lord. Faith therefore *receives Christ the Lord*, Col. ii. 6. Nor does Christ offer himself as a husband to the soul upon any other condition, but this, that he acknowledge him as his Lord, Psal. xlv. 10, 11. And when the soul casts himself upon Jesus, he, at the same time, renounces his own will, and surrenders himself up to the will of Jesus, to be carried whithersoever he pleaseth. Whence there is also in faith a humble surrender and giving up one's self, whereby the believer, as in duty bound, yields himself, and all that is his, to Christ, who is freely given him. " I am my beloved's, and my beloved is mine," Cant. vi. 3. 2 Cor. viii. 5. " gave their own selves to the Lord." Almost in the same form as Amasai, with his companions gave themselves up to David, 1 Chron. xii. 18. " thine are we, David, and on thy side, thou son of Jesse." And this our surrender to Christ, which we account the seventh act of faith, is the continual fountain and spring of all true obedience, which is therefore called *the obedience of faith*, Romans i. 5.

XXIV. After the believing soul has thus received Christ, and given himself up to him, he may, and ought, thence to conclude, that Christ with all his saving benefits are his, and that he shall certainly be blessed by him, according to this infallible syllogism or reasoning of faith : " Christ offers himself as a full and complete Saviour to all who are weary, hungry, thirsty, to all who receive him, and are ready to give themselves up to him : but I am weary, hungry, &c. Therefore Christ has offered himself to me, is now become mine, and I his, nor shall any thing ever separate me from his love." This is the eighth, and the reflex act of faith, arising from consciousness or reflexion, Gal. ii. 20. 2 Tim. i. 12. Rom. viii. 38.

XXV. Hence, in fine, the soul, now conscious of its union with Christ by faith, obtains trust or confidence, tranquillity, joy, peace, and bold defiance to all enemies and dangers whatever, a glorying in the Lord, a glorying in adversity ; while the soul *leans (stays itself) with delight on its beloved ;* with stretched out arms throwing itself, or with its elbow sweetly leaning upon him (מַרְפֵּק signifies according to the Talmudists the *arm-pit*), being assured of mutual communion and mutual love, while it sings, " I am my beloved's, and his desire is towards me," Song vii. 10. it piously exults and delights itself in its Lord, is inebriated with his love, rejoices " with joy unspeakable and full of glory," 1 Pet. i. 8. and savingly melts at the glowing flames of reciprocal love ; in one word, " rejoices in the hope of the glory of God," Rom. v. 2.

XXVI. We shall now briefly compendize, as it were, in one view, what we have so largely explained. Faith comprehends the knowledge of the mystery of God, and of Christ in the light of grace, the truth of which mystery the believer acknowledges with full assent of mind, on the authority of the testimony of God. And not only so, but he is also in love with that truth, exults therein and glorifies God ; he likewise ardently desires communion with Christ, that the things which are true in Christ, may be also true to him for salvation : wherefore, when Christ is offered to him by the word and Spirit, he receives him with the greatest complacency of soul, leans and rests upon him, and gives and surrenders himself to him ; which done, he glories that Christ is now his own, and most sweetly delights in him, reposing himself under the shadow of the tree of life, and satiating himself with its most delicious

fruits. This is the faith of God's elect, Tit. i. 1. an inva-
luable gift, the bond of our union with Christ, the scale of
paradise, the key of the ark of the covenant, with which its
treasures are unlocked, the never ceasing fountain of a holy
quiet and blessed life.

XXVII. If any imagines that he speaks more exactly when
he distinguishes these acts of faith, so as to think some of
them precede or go before faith strictly so called, as the knowledge of revealed truth, to which some excellent divines add,
a pious affection of the will towards God; that other acts belong to the very form or essence of faith, as assent, hunger
and thirst after righteousness, the receiving Christ as Lord
and Saviour, and the soul's flying to him for refuge; and that
others are accidental, which agree only to a confirmed and
strengthened faith; as the certainty or assurance that Christ
is now become mine, and the most delightful reliance upon
him as mine, joined with exultation and glorying in him; we
see no reason why such a person may not enjoy his accuracy
without any displeasure to us: for we only intended to shew
that all these things concur in the full practice and exercise of
faith.

XXVIII. From what has been said it is evident, that the
faith usually called *historical* and temporary, though I question
the propriety of that name, very widely differs from *saving* faith,
which we have thus far described. They call an *historical*
faith " a naked assent to the things contained in the word of
God, on the authority of God, by whom they are asserted, but
without any pious motion of the will." But since this assent
may be given not only to the historical parts of scripture, but
also may extend to the precepts, doctrines, promises and threatenings, the character *historical*, given to that faith, seems to be
too restricted. Unless perhaps it be so called, with respect to
the manner in which it is conversant about its object. For as
he who reads histories of transactions with which he has no
concern, barely contemplates them without being inwardly moved or affected by them; so they who have that kind of faith
do only, in an idle or careless manner, observe and think of
those things which are taught in the word of God, but do not
reduce them to practice; though it is not universally true, that
even the most ancient histories, and the things which concern
another world, are read without any affection, emotion and application. It had therefore been better to call this faith *theo-
retic*, or a naked assent.

XXIX. Our Lord, Mat. xiii. 21. calls that a *temporary*
faith, which, besides that general assent, exults in the known

and acknowledged truth, makes profession thereof, and stirs up many emotions in the heart, and actions in the life, which exhibit some appearance of piety ; but for a time only, while every thing is prosperous under the gospel, but falls off when the storms of persecution assault it. This is wisely called by our Lord πρόσκαιρος *temporary*, or for a while. But as it may, and even does frequently happen, that in the prosperous state of the church, men may persevere to the end of their life in this profession of faith and imaginary joy, and in such a course of life as they suppose to be sufficient for the purposes of piety ; so this being a constant, but not saving, is not so properly called temporary faith, that being the title which our Lord only gave to the faith of apostates. We might rather perhaps better call it a *presumptuous* faith.

XXX. But it is needful for our consolation, that we distinctly know how this may be distinguished from a true, lively, and saving faith, which it boldly though falsely resembles. And, *first*, there is no small difference in the *acknowledgment* of revealed truths ; to which as to truths, this presumptuous faith really assents ; but as it is destitute of the true light of the Spirit, it sees not the proper form or beauty of these truths, and as they are truths in Christ ; it does not observe the perfections of God shining in them, does not rightly estimate their value : when it begins first to know them, it is indeed taken with the novelty and rarity of them, but neither burns with an ardent love to them, nor labours much to have them not only impressed upon the soul, but also expressed in the life and conversation : and as often as other things present themselves to the mind, which flatter it with a great pretended shew of pleasure or profit, it easily suffers the ideas of those truths, which oppose that advantage, to be blotted out, and almost wishes these were no truths, which in spite of itself, it is constrained to acknowledge for such. But these things are quite the reverse in true faith, as we shewed, Thes. XVII.

XXXI. *Secondly*, There is a great difference in the application of the promises of the gospel : For presumptuous faith does not proceed in the right method ; it rashly imagines that the salvation promised in the gospel belongs to itself ; but this is either upon no foundation, or upon a false one. For sometimes these persons, without any trial or self-examination, which they avoid as too troublesome, and inconvenient to their affairs, foolishly flattering themselves, proudly lay claim to the grace of our Lord ; and securely slumber in this vain dream, without either enquiring, or being willing to enquire, what foundation they have for this their imagination. Sometimes again they lay for a foundation of their confidence, either that perverse notion concerning the general mercy of God, and easy way to heaven, of which nothing that I know of is mentioned in the gospel covenant, or an opinion of the sufficiency of their own holiness, because they are not so very vicious as the most profligate, or the external communion of the church in religious worship, or the security of their sleeping conscience, and the pleasing fancies of their own dreams, which they take for the peace of God and the consolation of the Holy Spirit. With these and the like vanities of their own imagination they deceive themselves, as if these things were sufficient marks of grace. But true believers, from a deep sense of their misery, panting after the grace of the Lord Jesus, and laying hold of it with a trembling humility, dare not boast of it as already theirs, till, after a diligent scrutiny, they have found certain and infallible evidences of grace in themselves. It is with a profound humility, a kind of sacred dread, and a sincere self-denial, that they approach to lay hold on the grace of Christ. Nor do they boast of having laid hold of this, till after an exact examination, first of the marks of grace, and then of their own hearts. But it is otherwise in both these respects with presumptuous persons, who rashly lay hold on what is not offered them in that order, (for God does not offer security and joy to sinners, before the soul is affected with sorrow for the guilt of his past sins, and a due solicitude about salvation,) and then presumptuously boast of their having laid hold on grace ; but they cannot produce any necessary arguments to make the same appear.

XXXII. The *third* difference consists in that joy which accompanies or follows both sorts of faith, and that is twofold ; 1st. In respect to the rise. 2dly. In respect of the effect of that joy. In presumptuous faith, joy arises partly from the novelty and rarity of the things revealed, (for the knowledge of a truth, which is more rare and abstruse, gives delight to the understanding ; as the enjoyment of a good does to the will;) partly from that vain imagination, that the good things offered in the Gospel belong to them ; of which they have, from the common gifts of the Holy Spirit, some kind of taste, but a very superficial one, affecting only the outside of their lips. But in a living faith, there arises a joy much more noble and solid, from a love of those most precious truths, by the knowledge of which the soul, taught of God, rightly esteems itself most happy ; from a hope that maketh not ashamed, and a sure persuasion of its own spirit, with the super-added testimony of the divine Spirit

concerning the present grace of God and future glory; and
lastly, from a most sweet sense of present grace, and a real
foretaste of future glory. And as the causes of both these
joys are so diverse, no wonder though the effects are very different too. The first makes the soul full of itself, leaves it
empty of the love of God, and, by a vain tickling of its own
imagination, heightens the sleep of carnal security. But the
latter strikes believers with an incredible admiration of the
unmerited philanthropy, or love of God to man, inflames them
with a mutual return of love to the most kind and bounti-
ful Jesus, and inspires them with a solicitous care, lest
they commit any thing unworthy of that infinite favour of
God, or grieve the Spirit of grace who hath dealt kindly with
them.

XXXIII. The *fourth* difference consists in the *fruits*. For
presumptuous faith either sinks men in the deep sleep of security, which they increase by indulging the flesh; or brings
with it some outward change of conduct for the better, and
makes them, in a certain measure, to " escape the pollutions
of the world through the knowledge of the Lord and Saviour
Jesus Christ," 2 Pet. ii. 20. or when it operates in the brightest manner, it excites some slight and vanishing purposes, and
endeavours after a stricter piety, but does not purify the
heart itself nor introduce new habits of holiness; and whenever either the allurements of the world and flesh, or some
inconveniences attending gospel piety, assault them more
strongly than usual, they immediately grow weary in that
course of goodness they had entered upon, and return as
" swine that were washed, to their wallowing in the mire."
By that superficial knowledge of evangelical truth, and of a
good, so pleasing and useful, as well as honourable, which is
held forth by the gospel, and which is not deeply imprinted
on their minds, they are indeed stirred up to some amendment
of life: but when the matter stands either upon the acquisition
of some present good, or the avoiding some imminent calamity, the ideas of true and of good, which the gospel had
suggested to them, are so obliterated and defaced, that they
prefer the obtaining a present pleasure or advantage, or the
avoiding a present impending evil, to all the promises of the
gospel, and all evangelical piety. But a living faith impresses
on the soul, in such deep characters, the image of what is
right and good, that it accounts nothing more lovely than to
endeavour after it to the utmost of its power; it paints in
such lively colours, the most shining holiness of the Lord
Christ, that while the soul beholds it with the supreme affection,

it is transformed into its image, 2 Cor. iii. 18. it so patheti-
cally represents the love of a dying Christ, that the believer
accounts nothing dearer than in return, both to live and die to
him, Gal. ii. 20. the meditation of the promised happiness is
so deeply engraved on his mind, that he is ready, for the sake
of it, to try all things, to bear all things, 2 Cor. iv. 16, 17,
18. and thus it purifies the heart itself, Acts xv. 9. in order
to the practice of a sincere and constant piety; which, in
consequence of a more lively or more languid faith, is itself
either more lively or more languid.

XXXIV. Having considered these things concerning the
nature of a living faith, and how it differs from that which is
presumptuous, let us now further enquire, how a person may
be conscious of his own faith. Now that it is both possible and
frequent for believers to have a consciousness of their own faith,
Paul not only teacheth us by his own example, 2 Tim. i. 12.
" I know whom I have believed," but also by that admonition
directed to all, 2 Cor. xiii. 5. " examine yourselves, whether
ye be in the faith, prove your ownselves." Which admonition
would have been in vain, was it impossible for them, by examining and proving themselves, to attain to the knowledge of
what they search after. Yea, that it is possible, he expressly
enough insinuates, by adding, " know ye not your ownselves,
how that Jesus Christ is in you !"

XXXV. Nor is it difficult to understand how this consciousness of faith may arise in believers: for first it becomes
them to be well instructed, from the word of God, about the
nature of saving faith. Nor is it necessary to harass the minds
of the weak with a multiplicity of marks: only let the principal and essential acts of a true faith be explained to them in
a simple and clear manner; let the difference between a strong
and weak faith be inculcated; between a lively and a languid;
between a calm faith, and that shaken by many temptations;
and let them be put in mind, that not only a weak, a languid,
and a shaken faith is nevertheless genuine and true; but also
that in examining themselves, a weak faith is not to be tried by
the idea of a strong faith, nor a languid by that of a lively, nor
that which is shaken by the idea of a calm and quiet faith;
but that each is to be compared with its own proper idea. This
being well observed, let every one examine himself, whether he
puts forth acts agreeable to what we have now described.
Which none who attends to himself can be ignorant of: as every
one is immediately conscious to himself of what he thinks and
wills, for this very reason that he thinks and wills it: for faith
is an act of the understanding and will.

XXXVI. But one perhaps may reply, if it is so very easy

to have a consciousness of one's own faith, whence then is it
that very many believers are tormented with such troublesome waverings about this matter? There is more than one
reason for this: 1st. It often happens that they have either
formed to themselves a wrong notion of saving faith, or unadvisedly taken up with what others have as uncautiously
drawn up to their hand. Thus we have learned by experience,
that not a few afflicted souls have thought that the essence of
faith consists in the assured persuasion and delightful sense
of divine love, and in the full assurance of their own salvation.
And not observing these things in themselves, they have, by
an unfavourable sentence, crossed themselves out of the roll
of believers. But these very persons being better informed
of the nature of faith, and taught that these things were
rather glorious fruits of an established than essential acts of a
true faith, have gradually returned to a more composed mind.
2dly. It also sometimes happens, that believers being tossed
with so many storms of temptations, do but little, nay, are
unable, to distinguish the proper acts of their own souls: for
while they are in that case, they perform every thing in such
a confused, such a feeble and inconsistent manner, that during
that disorder, they cannot clearly discern the state and frame
of their own heart; while the thoughts of their mind, and the
emotions of their will, succeed and cross each other with a surprising variety. 3dly. Sometimes too it is difficult, especially
in an afflicted state of soul, to compare their own actions with
the description of true faith, or, to speak more clearly, to compare the rule with that which they want to bring to it, especially
when one has proposed to himself the idea of a lively faith, and
finds in himself only a languid one. In that case, it can scarcely
be otherwise, but that when he sees so little agreement, nay,
the greatest difference between the two, he must form a less favourable judgment of his own faith.

XXXVII. It is not indeed absolutely necessary to salvation, that one should know that he believes: for the promise
of salvation is annexed to the sincerity of faith, Mark xvi. 16.
John iii. 16. not to the knowledge one may have of his faith.
Yet it is nevertheless expedient, that every one should, by an
accurate scrutiny, enquire into the sincerity and truth of his
faith, 1st. In order to render due thanks to God for this in-
valuable gift. For if Paul did so often return thanks to God
for the faith of others, Eph i. 15, 16. Phil. i. 3. Col. i. 3, 4.
1 Thes. i. 2, 3. 2 Thes. i. 3. How much more incumbent is
it to do so for one's own faith? But he cannot do this unless he knows that he does believe. 2dly. That he may have

strong consolation in himself; for, the consciousness of our faith gives us assurance of salvation ; thus the apostle joins these two together, 2 Tim. i. 12. " I know whom I have believed, and I am persuaded he is able to keep that which I have committed unto him against that day." 3dly. That with the greater alacrity, he may run the race of piety : for he who is assured that he acts from faith, is also assured, that *his labour shall not be in vain in the Lord;* and this assurance makes the believer *stedfast, immoveable, always abounding in the work of the Lord,* 1 Cor. xv. 58.

CHAP. VIII.

Of Justification.

I. **T**HAT faith which we have in the last chapter treated of as *saving,* is usually also called *justifying* in the divinity schools.   And since *justification* is its first memorable effect, it will by no means be improper to speak of it now, and that with the greater accuracy, as it so nearly concerns the whole of religion, that we stumble not in explaining this article.   The doctrine of justification diffuseth itself through the whole body of divinity, and if the foundation here is well laid, the whole building will be the more solid and grand ; whereas a bad foundation or superstructure threatens a dreadful ruin.   The pious Picardians, as they were called in Bohemia and Moravia, valued this article, at its true price, when in their confession of faith, Art. vi. speaking of justification, they thus write : " this sixth article is accounted with us the most principal of all, as being the sum of all Christianity and piety.   Wherefore our divines teach and handle it with all diligence and application, and endeavour to instil it into all."   Let us to the utmost of our power imitate them in this, beginning with its name.

II. To *justify,* in Hebrew הִצְדִּיק, in Greek δικαιῦν, is very frequently and ordinarily used in a *declarative* sense, and signifies to *account, declare, prove* any one *just.*   Which is manifest from those places of scripture, where it occurs, as the act of a judge, as Psal. lxxxii. 3. " do justice to *(justify)* the afflicted and needy ;" and this is especially the case, when it is opposed to condemnation, as Deut. xxv. 1. Prov. xvii. 15. Isa. v. 22, 23.

III. And doubtless this word has such a signification when God is said to *be justified,* as Psal. li. 4. " that thou mightest be justified when thou speakest ;" that is, that thou mightest be declared, proved, acknowledged to be just, when thou pronouncest sentence.   In like manner, Matt xi. 19. " wisdom is justified of her children," that is, they who are truly regenerated of God by the Gospel, have accounted the wisdom of God, which

the Scribes and Pharisees falsely accounted foolishness, to be, as
it really is, the most consummate wisdom, and cleared it from
the calumny of folly, with which it was branded. In the same
sense it is said, Luke vii. 29. " all the people and the publicans
justified God."

IV. Nor can this word have any other than a forensic signification, when Christ is said to be *justified*, 1 Tim. iii. 16. and
still more fully Isa. l. 8. where the Lord himself thus speaketh :
" he is near that justifieth me, who will contend with me? Let us
stand together ; who is mine adversary ?" Almost in the same
manner as the apostle speaks of the elect, Rom. viii. 33, 34.
How was Christ justified ? 1st. When the Father declared that
he was holy and without spot, according to his mind and will,
and even such " in whom he was well pleased," Matt. iii. 17.
and xvii. 5. 2dly. When he pronounced him innocent of all the
crimes with which he was falsely accused, and for which he was
unjustly condemned. 3dly. When he declared, that he had
made full satisfaction to his justice, and was no longer under
the guilt of those sins which as Surety he took upon himself.
The two former acts of justification respect Christ as man ; the
last as Mediator. And in this view he is called " the righteous
or just servant of God," Isa. liii. 11. not only as holy and without
sin in himself, but as one who had also fulfilled all that righteousness to which he bound himself by his voluntary engagement, whereby, though he was the Son, yet he became the servant of God, and by his resurrection was declared to have performed the whole, and so was exalted to that state, that he
might be able to justify many, or procure righteousness for
many, by virtue of his own righteousness.

V. But we are not to imagine we have accomplished any
great matter, when we have shewn that justification is often
taken in a forensic or law sense. For scarce any who love to
be called Christians, have such a bold front or stubborn mind
as to deny it. Certainly the Popish doctors themselves generally own it; *Bellarm. de justificat. Lib.* 1. *c.* i. *Becan. Sum.
Theol. T.* 2. *Tract.* 4. *c.* iii. *Tirin. Controvers.* 15. *No.* 1. Nor
do they deny that Paul himself sometimes treats of justification
in that sense : *Estius in Comm.* ad Rom. ii. 13. observes,
that to be *justified* there is the same thing as to be " adjudged,
declared, accounted righteous, according, *says he*, to the most
usual language of scripture." Which interpretation Ruardus
Tapperus also approves, *ad Art.* 8. p. 32. I will do my *
townsman the honour to quote his words. " As to what was
a foresaid, *says he*, it is to be considered, that in scripture, to be

---

* ENCHUSANO meo. For it seems, Tapperus was born at Enkhuysen as well as
Witsius.

justified, not only signifies, to be endowed and adorned with righteousness; but sometimes also to be pronounced, declared, adjudged, allowed, and esteemed just or righteous. According to which interpretation, blessed Augustine explains the apostle Paul's expression. The doers of the law shall be justified, " that is, *says he*, shall be accounted and esteemed just." In like manner, Cornelius a Lapide on Rom. viii. 33. " it is God that justifieth," thus comments; " it is God that acquits these elect persons, namely, his faithful people and true Christians, from their sins, and absolves from the charge brought against them by sin and the devil, and pronounces them just," or righteous. The state of the controversy therefore between us and the doctors of the church of Rome, is not whether justification be sometimes taken in a forensic or law sense: for that is confessed on both sides.

VI. What then? Are we thus to state the question, namely, whether the term to justify has *always* in scripture a forensic sense? But the most eminent Protestant divines do not affirm this, and therefore it would be too harsh and inhuman to charge them with prevarication on that account. Beza on Tit. iii. 7. thus comments; " I take the term justification in a large sense, as comprehending whatever we obtain from Christ, as well by imputation, as by the efficacy of the Spirit in our sanctification, that we may be αρτιοι, that is, perfect and complete in him. Thus also the term justify is taken, Rom. viii. 30. Much to the same purpose *Thysius in synops. Purior. Theolog. Leyden. Disput. 23. sect. 3.* Nor yet do we deny, that, on account of their very great and close connection, justification seems sometimes to comprise sanctification also, as a consequent, Rom. viii. 30. Tit. iii. 7, &c. I shall add one testimony more, namely, *Chamierus Panstrat. T. 3. Lib. 10. c. 1. No. 6.* who speaks to this purpose: " We are not such ridiculous judges of words as not to know, nor such impertinent sophisters, as not to allow that the terms *justification* and *sanctification*, are put one for the other: yea, we know that they are called saints principally on this account, that in Christ they have remission of sin. And we read in the Revelations, ' let him that is righteous, be righteous still;' which can only be understood of the progress of inherent righteousness; and we deny not, that there may be a promiscuous use of the words perhaps in other places."

VII. And indeed this ingenuity of these very great men is not to be too much canvassed, who, though they have granted so much to their adversaries, have yet, in the main question, happily triumphed over them. Nevertheless we see no suffi-

cient reasons why they should have been so liberal to them.
There had been no violence put on the alleged passages, if in
them the term justification should be taken in the sense in which
Paul commonly takes it : nor doth it appear that all things
would have flowed less agreeably.

VIII. What should hinder us from explaining Rom. viii. 30.
in this manner? *Whom he did predestinate*, that is, whom, by
his most free and immutable decree, he has chosen to grace and
glory, *them he also called*, that is, by his word and Spirit he
sweetly invited, and powerfully drew them from a state of sin
and misery to communion with Christ, and being endowed with
faith, regenerated them : *and whom he called, them he also justified;* that is, as soon as they were united to Christ by the
Holy Spirit and by faith, he, on the account of the merits of
Christ, imputed to them, acquitted them from the guilt of sin,
and adjudged them to have a right to all the good things of
Christ, as well in grace as in glory : *and whom he justified, them
he also glorified;* that is, he not only gave them a right, but
also put them in actual possession of the greatest blessings,
1st. By sanctifying them, and transforming them more and more
to his own image, and making them partakers of a divine nature,
which doubtless is a great degree of glory. 2dly. By plentifully pouring in upon them the sweetest consolations of his Spirit,
which are, as it were, the preludes of joy and gladness. 3dly.
and lastly, By making them perfectly happy, first in soul, and
then in soul and body together.

IX. But we think it far more proper to comprise *sanctification* under *glorification* than to refer it to *justification*. For,
it is familiar to the Holy Spirit, to delineate holiness under the
names of *beauty, ornament, and glory.* Thus Psal. xciii. 5.
holiness becometh thine house. Psal. cx. 3. *thy people shall be
willing in the day of thy power, in the beauties of holiness.*
Nay, by the very term *glory*, holiness and righteousness are expressed, Psal. xlv. 13. *the king's daughter is all glorious within:*
But what else is meant there by that glory, but the genuine holiness of believers? Or as Peter speaks, 1 Pet. iii. 4. " the hidden
man of the heart, in that which is not corruptible, even the ornament of a meek and quiet spirit, which is in the sight of God
of great price :" add Isa. lxii. 2. *and the Gentiles shall see thy*
RIGHTEOUSNESS, *and all kings thy* GLORY; where these two
words are used alternately one for the other : and justly, for
the highest pitch of our glory consists in a perfect conformity to
God, 1 John iii. 2. But holiness is the image of God, Eph. iv. 24.
so that saints who accurately express, or resemble that image,
are on that account called the *glory of Christ*, 2 Cor. viii. 28.

Why then should we not account our conformity to God in holiness as no contemptible first fruits of glory? Certainly Paul calls the progress made in sanctification, *a transformation*, or a *being changed from* GLORY *to* GLORY, 2 Cor. iii. 18.

X. It is plain, that with the same propriety we may understand by justification, Tit. iii. 7. absolution from guilt, and an adjudging to eternal life. For the first work of a man who is regenerated by the Holy Spirit, is the work of faith, the infallible consequent of which is, the remission of sins; this is either succeeded by, or attended with, the hope of the inheritance of eternal life. What probable reason is there then to make us to depart from this sense? And if we would have sanctification contained in any of the words which the apostle makes use of, why shall we not rather refer it to *regeneration, and the renewal of the Holy Ghost?* For really, sanctification differs no otherways from the first regeneration and renovation than as the continuance of an act differs from the beginning of it. And we are sure, that the apostle exhorts the Romans who had been, for some time regenerated, to a progress in sanctification, when he writes, Rom. xii. 2. *be ye transformed by the renewing of your minds;* and in like manner, Eph. iv. 23. *be renewed in the spirit of your mind.* As the beginning of this renovation goes before justification strictly so called, so the progress of it serves to promote the certainty and the sense of justification; and in both respects it was excellently well said by the apostle, that the elect are regenerated by the Holy Spirit, shed on them abundantly; that being thus justified by his grace, that is, acquitted from sin, and conscious to themselves of absolution, they might lawfully, yea, in full assurance, hope for the inheritance of eternal life.

XI. As to Rev. xxii. 11. *he that is righteous, let him be righteous still;* it does not appear that any fuller sense can be put on these words, than if we thus explain them: whoever is reputed righteous before God by faith on Christ, should think it his duty, or concern, to verify by his actions this his justification before men and to his own conscience; and so by faith and the exercise of it, and by studying the word of God, he may have a more abounding consolation concerning his righteousness. And by this reasoning too the forensic use of this term is still retained.

XII. Others also allege, 1 Cor. vi. 11. " but ye are washed, but ye are sanctified, but ye are justified in the name of the Lord Jesus, and by the Spirit of our God." But even this testimony does not prove that justification is equivalent to sanctification, rather the contrary. For after the apostle

had said that the *Corinthians were washed*, that is, delivered
from the power of sin, he more particularly shews wherein
that washing consisteth. Now the power of sin over man is
twofold. 1st. That it compels him to the servile works of
wickedness. 2dly. That it condemns him. The *dominion*
is destroyed by *sanctification: the power of condemning*, by
justification. Both these are bestowed on the Elect *in the
name of the Lord Jesus;* that is, on account of his merits,
and by his authority and will; *and by the Spirit of our God*,
who is the author of sanctification, and sweetly insinuates the
sentence of justification into the minds of believers. Both these
benefits are sealed in baptism, to the washing of which there is
here an evident allusion. Nor should it offend us, that sanctification is here put before justification; a diligent enquirer cannot but know that the scripture does not always exactly observe
that order, as that things first in time are set in the first place.
Thus even Peter puts vocation before election, 2 Pet. i. 10.
Besides, justification consists of various articles, as we will shew
more distinctly in its place.

XIII. However, I cannot conceal that there are two places in
which the term *justify* may seem to denote something more
than a mere declaration of righteousness, though that be also
included. The first is, Isa. liii. 11. " by his knowledge shall
my righteous servant justify many." It is indeed true that
our Lord Jesus Christ is constituted judge by the Father, and
consequently empowered to absolve his Elect who were given
him: but here he is not represented as a judge pronouncing
sentence, but as the cause which, both by merit and efficacy,
brings and gives to his own people that righteousness on account of which they may be absolved at the bar of God: and
the unusual construction of the word with the particle of the
dative case calls for our notice. It is therefore the same as if
the prophet had said, *he will make a righteousness unto many*,
that which he himself performed as the cause of righteousness,
he will communicate to many: and thus δικαιωμα *his righteousness will redound to many*, and *unto justification of life*, as the
apostle speaks, Rom. v. 18. which I would have to be compared with this passage.

XIV. The other testimony I hinted at is, Dan. xii. 3.
where the faithful preachers of the Gospel are said to be *justifying many*. None doubts that it belongs to the office of
the ministers of the Gospel to publish, in the name of God,
absolution from sin to the contrite in heart. But the compass of their function is much more extensive, namely, that
by their preaching, example, and prayers, they may bring as

many as possible to such a state as remission of sins may be preached, and that with special application unto them, who by faith and repentance are reconciled unto God, and are diligent in the practice of holiness. The ministry of reconciliation with which they were entrusted comprises all this. They who are diligent in the performance of these things, are said to *justify many*, because they stir them up to repentance, which is the beginning of righteousness or holiness; to faith, where-by they lay hold on the righteousness of Christ, on account of which they may be pardoned; to the practice of a holy life, which when they prove by their works, they may obtain fuller assurance of their justification by the ministers in the name of God.

XV. We have been the fuller on the signification of this word *justify*, that, at the same time, we might shew the force of various testimonies of scripture, nothing being more pleasant and useful than the study of this. But when treating of justification we shall always take that term in the *declarative* sense. Which being observed once for all, let us now address ourselves to the more distinct examination of the thing itself.

XVI. The declaration of God concerning men either regards some of their *particular actions*, or their *whole state*. The *actions* of men are considered, either in *relation to the rule of the divine will*, or *in comparison with the actions of others*, whether more or less evil. God pronounces absolutely on actions when he declares them either *evil* condemning man in them; as Nathan said to David in the name of God, 2 Sam. xii. 9. " thou hast despised the commandment of the Lord, to do evil in his sight:" or *good*, justifying a man in them; in which sense David, having his eyes intent on the justice of his cause against his enemies, prays, Psal. vii. 8. "judge me, O Lord, according to my righteousness, and according to mine integrity that is in me." Thus God justified Job when he declared that he " spoke of him the thing which is right." Job xlii. 8.

XVII. The example of Phinehas is here very memorable, Psal. cvi. 30, 31. " then stood up Phinehas and executed judgment; and so the plague was stayed. And that was accounted unto him for righteousness, unto all generations for ever more." The fact of Phinehas was thus: Zimri, one of the princes of the tribe of Simeon, brought into his tent, with an incredible impudence, Cozbi, a daughter of the king of Midian, in the sight of the princes of his people, with an intent to pollute her and himself with whoredom; while Mo-

ses, with the whole congregation, stood in tears, at the door
of the tabernacle, to deprecate the vengeance of God already
broke out. Phinehas, son of Eleazar, the high priest, and
himself a priest, *could not bear this sight;* but being inflamed with a mighty zeal, and moved with the indignity of the
action, rushed from amidst the congregation, and taking up a
javelin, thrust them both through in the very act of their
whoredom.

XVIII. There were many things in this action which, to
outward appearance, were faulty. 1st. Phinehas was a priest,
whom it did not become to imbrue his hands in human blood.
For if it brought guilt on a priest, to be expiated by sacrifice,
to have touched a dead body, much more to have made a living
man a dead carcase. 2dly. He was none of the judges of Israel,
whom Moses, at the command of God himself, deputed to
punish the guilty, by hanging them up before the Lord, Numb.
xxv. 4, 5. 3dly. He did not observe the due order or course of
justice, because he began with the execution. 4thly. The whole
seemed to breathe an enraged passion of mind, rather than a
zeal tempered with due lenity. For these reasons, Phinehas
might be thought to have been guilty of a horrid murder;
and on that account, to have forfeited the honour of the priesthood.

XIX. But it is plain, it appeared otherwise in the sight of
God, who pronounced the action right, commending this zeal
of his, and declaring, that he was so pleased with it, that therefore he averted his great wrath from the children of Israel.
And Phinehas was so far from being divested of the priesthood
on that account, that, on the contrary, God adjudged to him and
his seed after him a perpetual priesthood, by a covenant of
peace that was to last for ever, Numb. xxv. 11, 12, 13. And
this is what David sings, " it was counted unto him for righteousness," that is, it was judged that he had acted in a due and
regular manner, and was therefore more worthy of praise and
reward, than of blame and punishment.

XX. And as this man was justified in that absolutely, so
others are justified in their actions, *comparatively,* or when
compared with the actions of others which are far worse. In
this sense it is said, Jer. iii. 11. " the backsliding Israel hath
justified herself more than treacherous Judah." That is, by
her works hath shewed herself more righteous and innocent,
professing according to the sentiments of her heart, and not acting so hypocritically and deceitfully, as the prevaricating and
dissembling Judah, who would appear, as if she was converted
to me, while in the mean time, she profanes my name. In like

manner, Ezek. xvi. 31. " thou hast justified thy sisters in all thine abominations which thou hast done." Thou hast behaved in such a manner, that in comparison of thee, they may seem to be innocent.

XXI. Thus much for the declaration of God concerning the *actions* of men. On the other hand, his declaration as to their state is of several kinds. For either God considers them as *they are in themselves*, according to inherent qualities, either *vicious* through corrupt *nature*, or *holy* and laudable through reforming *grace;* or *as they are reputed in Christ the surety.*

XXII. God can neither consider nor declare men to be otherwise than as they really are. For " his judgment is according to truth," Rom. ii. 2. and therefore they, who are still under the dominion of sin, and walk with delight, according to their depraved lusts, are judged and declared by God to be unregenerate, wicked, and slaves of the devil, as they really are; for, " by no means does he clear the guilty," Exod. xxxiv. 7. but they who are regenerated by his grace, created anew after his image, and heartily give themselves up to the practice of sincere holiness, are by him absolved from the sin of profaneness, impiety, and hypocrisy, and are no longer looked upon as dead in sins, slaves to the devil, children of the world; but as true believers, his own children, restored to his image, and endowed with his life. It was thus he justified his servant Job, declaring, " that there is none like him in the earth, a perfect and an upright man one that feareth God and escheweth evil," Job i. 8.

XXIII. And this is still the case of all believers. The devil indeed, who is the accuser of the brethren, frequently charges them with hypocrisy before God, as if they did not serve him in sincerity; and he not only thus accuses them before God, but he also disquiets their conscience, as if all their faith and piety were only a mask and outward shew, by which they have hitherto imposed not only on others, but also on themselves. In order to calm the consciences of believers, when thus shaken by the false accuser, they have need to be absolved from this accusation, and justified from this false testimony before God; which God also daily does, assuring the elect of the sincerity of their conversion, by the testimony of his Spirit, and thereby shewing, that " the praise of a true Jew is of him." Rom. ii. 29. This justification is indeed very different from that other, of which we shall presently treat, wherein the person is absolved from sins, whereof he is really guilty, and which are forgiven him on Christ's account. In this we are

speaking of he is acquitted of sins, which he is not chargeable
with, and is declared not to have committed.

XXIV. The foundation of this justification can be nothing
but inherent holiness and righteousness. For, as it is a declaration concerning a man, as he is *in himself*: by the regenerating and sanctifying grace of God, so it ought to have
for its foundation, that which is found in man himself: *He
that doth righteousness is righteous*, says John, 1 John iii.
7. and Peter says, Acts x. 34, 35. " of a truth, I perceive,
that in every nation he that feareth him and worketh righteousness is accepted with God." And Luke in the name of
God, gives this testimony to the parents of John the Baptist,
that " they were righteous before God, walking in all the commandments and ordinances of the Lord blameless," Luke i. 6.
But yet inherent righteousness is not the foundation of this justification, from its own worthiness, or because it is a holiness
exactly commensurate with the rule of the law, but because it
is the work of the Holy Spirit in the elect, which God cannot
but acknowledge and delight in as his own, and because the
failings with which it is always stained in this world are forgiven
for Christ's sake.

XXV. In this sense we think the apostle James speaks of
justification in that much controverted passage, James ii. 21,
24. where he declares, that " Abraham was not justified by
faith only, but also by works," and insists upon it, that every
man ought to be justified in this manner. For the scope of the
apostle is to shew, that it is not sufficient for a Christian to
boast of the remission of his sins, which indeed is obtained by
faith only, but then it must be a living faith on Christ; but
that besides he ought to labour after holiness, that being justified by faith only, that is, acquitted from the sins he had been
guilty of, on account of Christ's satisfaction, apprehended by
faith, he may likewise be justified by his works, that is, declared
to be truly regenerated, believing and holy; behaving as becomes those who are regenerated, believing and holy. Thus our
father Abraham behaved, who having been before now justified
by faith only, that is, obtained the remission of his sins, was
afterwards also justified by his works. For, when he offered up
his son to God, then God said to him, " now I know that thou
fearest God, seeing thou hast not withheld thy son, thine only
son, from me," Gen. xxii. 12. And James insists upon it, that this
last justification is so necessary to believers, that, if it be wanting,
the first ought to be accounted only vain and imaginary.

XXVI. These things are evident from scripture: but lest
any after the manner of the world should ridicule this, I in-

form the more unskilful, that this is no invention of mine, but that the most celebrated divines have, before me, spoken of such a "justification according to inherent righteousness and of works." *Bucerus in altero Colloquio Ratisbonensi,* p. 313. says, " we think that this begun righteousness is really a true and living righteousness, and a noble excellent gift of God ; and that the new life in Christ consists in this righteousness, and that all the saints are also righteous by this righteousness, both before God and before men, ' and that on account thereof the saints are also justified by a justification of works,' that is, are approved, commended and rewarded by God." Calvin teaches much the same, *Instit.* lib. iii. c 17. § viii. which concludes with these words, " The good works done by believers are counted righteous, or which is the same, are imputed for righteousness." The very learned Ludovicus de Dieu has at large explained and proved this opinion, in *Comment. ad* Rom. viii. 4. And he quotes, as agreeing with him herein, Daniel Colonius, formerly regent or professor of the French college at Leyden. The same is also maintained by the Rev. Dr. Peter de Witte, that very able defender of the truth, *in Controversia de justificatione adversus Socinianos.* And Triglandius explains the passage of James to the same purpose with us, making use of the very same distinction of justification, *Examine Apologiœ Remonstrantium,* c. 21. p. 316.

XXVII. Let us now at length proceed to treat of the justification of man as a sinner, but considered as in Christ the Surety. As this subject is the foundation of all solid comfort, so it is full of mysteries and perplexed with many controversies : nevertheless it is clearly delivered in the scriptures, if men would only be satisfied with their simplicity, and not shut their eyes against the light, which so freely shines upon them, nor give way to curious niceties, and the roving of a luxuriant fancy. We thus define the gospel justification of a sinner : " It is a judicial, but gracious act of God, whereby the elect and believing sinner, is absolved from the guilt of his sins, and hath a right to eternal life adjudged to him, on account of the obedience of Christ, received by faith."

XXVIII. This is evident, that all men, considered in themselves, are abominable sinners before God, and obnoxious to eternal death. Paul before proved both Jews and Gentiles to be all under sin ; so that every mouth may be stopped, and all the world may become guilty before God, Rom. iii. 9, 19. But since, as we observed before, the judgment of God is always according to truth, it cannot be otherwise, but that God declare those who in themselves are sinners, and liable to death, to be really so in themselves. Yet the scripture declares, that God *justifies sinners*, that is, *acquits* them from sin and from being liable to eternal death, and *adjudges* them a right to eternal life. And unless this was the case, the salvation and hope of all mankind had been at an end. But certainly God does this agreeably to his truth and justice. It is therefore necessary, that they who are sinners in themselves appear in another light to a justifying God, namely, as considered in another, whose perfect righteousness may be so imputed to them, as in virtue thereof they may be reputed righteous. And this is the mystery of our justification in the faith of Christ.

XXIX. After all had sinned in Adam, and come short of the glory of God, the only begotten Son of God offered himself as Surety to the Father, and promised, that, at the time appointed, he would fulfil all the demands of the law for the elect. And he also executed this with all fidelity: he was born of a virgin, without any spot of sin, being conceived by the Holy Ghost, and endowed with original righteousness, in order to remove the guilt of original sin, and make up the defect of original righteousness which the elect are born without. Besides, from his very infancy, and through the whole course of his life, especially at the close thereof, he endured all manner of sufferings, both in soul and in body, humbling, nay, emptying himself, and being obedient to the Father unto death, even the death of the cross, that he might bear, in their stead, the punishment due to the sins of his chosen people; the dignity of the person who suffered, abundantly compensating what was wanting in the duration of the punishment, which otherwise must have been eternal. In fine, he fully performed for his people all that the law required, in order to obtain a right to eternal life. Had the elect themselves, in their own persons, performed what Christ did for them, there is no doubt but they would have obtained that for which they might have been justified by God, nay, and ought to have been so, at least according to the * covenant.

XXX. Moreover, since whatever of this kind Jesus performed, he did it by a voluntary undertaking, with the Father's approbation, *in the room and stead of the elect*, it is deservedly *imputed* to them, and *declared to their account*: just as what a surety pays for a debtor, or in his stead, is accounted as

* The author, I suppose, means that covenant, which says, " the man which doth those things, shall live by them," Rom. x. 5.

paid by him to the first creditor. Paul, in the fifth chapter of his epistle to the Romans, has handled this point in an excellent and divine manner : the sum of which is contained ver. 19. " as by one man's disobedience many were made [*constituted*] sinners ; so by the obedience of one, shall many be made [*constituted*] righteous."

XXXI. Moreover, to set the ground of this imputation in a clearer light, we must observe that Christ, according to the eternal counsel of the Father, not only undertook all these things for the elect, and fulfilled them agreeable to his undertaking, but also, that the elect, before the righteousness of Christ is imputed to them for justification of life, are so closely united to him by faith, as to be *one body*, 1 Cor. xii. 13. and which is still more indivisible, or indissoluble, *one spirit with him*, 1 Cor. vi. 17. nor are they only *united*, but he and they are *one*, and that by such an unity or oneness, in which there is some faint resemblance of that most simple oneness, whereby the divine persons are one among themselves, John xvii. 22, 23. But in virtue of this union or oneness, which the elect have with Christ by faith, they are accounted to have done and suffered whatever Christ did and suffered for them.

XXXII. Elect sinners, destitute of any righteousness of their own, that is, not having in themselves that for which they can have a right to eternal life, are by faith " found in Christ, having that righteousness which is through the faith of Christ, the righteousness which is of God by faith," Phil. iii. 9. and that in this manner, namely, they are acquitted from obnoxiousness to eternal death, on account of the voluntary sufferings of Christ, which were completed by a most cruel and dreadful death. Original sin is pardoned, and the soul presented unspotted before God, on account of his most pure nativity, being conceived by the Holy Ghost, born of the virgin. Eternal life is adjudged to be communicated to them in certain degrees of it, on account of the most perfect obedience of his whole life. This is the sum of this mystery, which being comprehended in a few words, we have thought proper thus to lay before the reader's contemplation, as it were, in one view. But there are not a few things which require a fuller explication.

XXXIII. The JUDGE in this cause *is God*, Rom. viii. 33. Isa. xliii. 25. For he is " that one law-giver, who is able to save and to destroy," Jam. iv. 12. And as he alone has a right and power to inflict due punishment on the sinner, so likewise he alone has a right to acquit him ; because he is " the judge of the whole world," Rom. iii. 6.

XXXIV. What is in general said of God, *essentially* considered, is especially appropriated to the Father, *hypostatically* or personally, who is " the justifier of him which believeth in Jesus," Rom. iii. 26. and " who was in Christ reconciling the world unto himself, not imputing their trespasses unto them," 2 Cor. v. 19. Where the distinction made of *God from Christ* sufficiently shews, that God the Father is there meant. Reason also requires, that justification be especially ascribed to God the Father. For Jesus Christ, the *Son of God*, appears in judgment in behalf of the guilty, as *Surety*, as *Advocate*, and in fine, as furnishing them with those *evident proofs*, by which they may be able to demonstrate that divine justice has been satisfied for them. The *Holy Ghost*, by working faith in the guilty, makes them to lay hold on, and present the Surety and his satisfaction in judgment. And in this respect both stand on the side of the guilty. But the *Father* acts as *judge*, who righteously, and at the same time mercifully, absolves the guilty, on account of the satisfaction of the Son, apprehended by the power of the Holy Spirit.

XXXV. But a certain person has rashly asserted, that the *Son and Holy Ghost* cannot, for the reasons above mentioned, *act the part of judge*, and pronounce sentence. For, in the economy of our salvation, the persons in the Trinity sustain various relations, which are to be reconciled with and not placed in opposition to each other. He who sometimes is described as *Surety*, is at other times represented as *judge*, John v. 22, 27. And indeed Christ himself claims the power of forgiving sins, Mat. ix. 2. And in the day of the general judgment, himself will peremptorily pronounce the *justifying* sentence upon the elect. Nor is it inconsistent for one and the same person to be both the *meritorious cause* of justification, and the *advocate* of the guilty, and at the same time the *judge* of the cause. All these relations agree in one Christ, and teach us that fulness of salvation which is to be found in him.

XXXVI. The Holy Ghost also hath his own proper parts in this matter, for it is he who brings in and seals that sentence of absolution pronounced in the court of heaven, to and upon the believing soul in the court of conscience, and so pacifies and cheers it; he shews it " the things that are freely given to it of God," 1 Cor. ii. 12. and " bears witness with the spirit of believers," Rom. viii. 16. that they are reconciled to God. Hence it appears, that none of the divine persons are to be excluded from pronouncing sentence.

XXXVII. That thing for which we are justified, and which some call the *matter* of our justification, is the perfect righteousness of Christ alone: this Christ finished for his elect, " for their sakes sanctifying himself," John xvii. 19. The Father *imputes* the same to his chosen people, as he imputed their sins to Christ: " he hath made him to be sin for us, who knew no sin; that we might be made the righteousness of God in him," 2 Cor. v. 21. But it is impossible to explain how Christ was made sin for us, unless in that sense in which our sins are imputed to him, that he might suffer for them; and we are made righteousness in him in the same manner that his righteousness is imputed to us, that on account of it we may receive the crown. It is evident that in scripture, the righteousness of Christ is called *our* righteousness: for he is *the Lord our righteousness,* Jer. xxiii. 6. *He of God is made unto us righteousness,* 1 Cor. i. 30. Now it is ours either *inherently,* or by *imputation,* for there can be no third way: it is not ours *inherently;* for in that sense Paul opposes it to ours, Phil. iii. 9. nor does the nature of the thing admit that acts performed by Christ can *inherently* be ours. It therefore remains, that it is ours by *imputation;* God *imputing* to man *righteousness without works,* Rom. iv. 6.

XXXVIII. Arminius by his subtlety, frames vain empty quibbles, when he contends that the righteousness of Christ cannot be imputed to us for righteousness, because it is his very righteousness; laying this down as a foundation, that which is imputed to us for righteousness is not properly our righteousness. Which none will admit, who has considered that every judgment of God is according to truth; whence it follows, that nothing can be imputed to any one for righteousness which is not really righteousness. But it is imputed to us, that is, put to our account, as if it was ours: for, though it was not performed by us, yet it was performed by Christ for us, and in our room. Nor in doing this, does God judge otherwise than as the thing is; for he judges not that we in our own person have fulfilled that righteousness, which is not true; but that Christ has so fulfilled it for us, as that by the merit thereof we may justly be rewarded, This is so true, that it is the sum of the whole Gospel.

XXXIX. And whereas that righteousness of Christ is in every respect complete, and God has acknowledged, that full satisfaction was made to his law to the very utmost, when he raised Christ from the dead, and called him *his righteous servant;* it is not necessary that any thing to come from us should acquire either freedom from punishment or a right to life. I add, that it could not in justice be demanded of us. For as the least farthing cannot be demanded by the principal creditor after the surety has paid him in full for the debtor, it therefore appears, that they do injury, both to the satisfaction of Christ, and to the justice of God, who contend, that any thing is to be done by men, that is, to be added to the merits of Christ, as the matter of our justification. For if, by the satisfaction of Christ, the demand of the law, which prescribes the condition of life, is perfectly fulfilled, nothing can, or ought to be joined thereto; that the glory may remain pure and entire to Christ alone. If there was but the least thing wanting in Christ's satisfaction, which the law required for righteousness, it would not deserve even the name of satisfaction; nor would Christ have merited any thing, either for himself or for us. For nothing is admitted in this judgment but what answers all the demands of the law.

XL. The scripture confirms this truth, when it sets the grace of Christ in diametrical opposition to our works, maintaining, that there can be no mixture of the one with the other. *If righteousness comes by the law*, saith the apostle, that is, if, by our works, we can acquire a right to life eternal, *then Christ is dead in vain*, Gal. ii. 21. And more clearly, Rom. xi. 6. "and if by grace, then it is no more of works; otherwise grace is no more grace. But if it be of works, then is it no more grace, otherwise work is no more work." In order clearly to discern the force of the apostle's inference, it is to be observed, that there are but two ways by which we can come to the possession of salvation, according to the two covenants entered into between God and man. For, either one has a right to life, because he has fully satisfied the demand of the law, according to the covenant of works; and to him that thus *worketh*, *is the reward reckoned of debt*, Rom. iv. 4. Or he hath a right to life, because the Surety of a better testament has made satisfaction for him, which, of pure grace and most unmerited favour, is imputed to him, who worketh not in order to acquire that right, ver. 5. according to the covenant of grace. As these covenants do, in the whole essence of them differ, and, in this respect, are contradistinguished from, and set in opposition to each other, it is evident, they conjoin inconsistencies, who would join together our works with the grace of God, our righteousness with the righteousness of Christ, in the matter of justification.

XLI. And indeed the apostle expressly declares that there
is nothing in us that can here come into the account, Rom. iii.
24. *justified freely by his grace.* In respect of *God* it is *of
pure grace*, which, as we just said, admits of no partnership
with our works. *In respect of us*, it is *freely*, without any
thing in us as the cause of it. For the adverb δωρεὰν *freely*, signifies this: not so much hinting here that justification is a *free
gift*, as the apostle calls it, Rom. v 16. (for that the following
words denote, τῆ ἀυτȣ χαριτι *by his grace*,) as that there is nothing in us, by which to obtain it. The Greek word δωρεὰν, *freely*,
answers to the Hebrew םנח, that is, *without a cause*, which, in
that case is found to be false and feigned; as Psal. lxix. 4.
they that hate me without a cause, which is the same thing
as *my lying enemies.* The former is translated by the Septuagint, or Greek interpreters, μισȣν7ες μὲ δωρεὰν. Just as John xv.
25. ἐμίσησάν με δωρεὰν, *they hated me without a cause.* In like
manner, Psal. xxxv. 7. δωρεὰν, *without a cause have they hid for
me their net into a pit.* Where δωρεὰν does not signify any donation or gift, but the absolute denial of any cause which could
render a man deserving of such treatment. When the apostle
therefore says, we are justified δωρεὰν, *freely*, he teaches us that
there is nothing in us, upon which to found the gracious sentence of our justification, or for which we can be justified. Excellently well, says the Greek scholiast, δωρεὰν τȣτεϛιν ἀνευ σων
κα7ορθωμα7ων, *freely*, that is, *without any merit in thee.*

XLII. And this reason may be added, that nothing can avail
in the business of justification but what is entirely perfect, and
can answer the law of God in all things. For in justification
there is *a declaration of the righteousness of God*, Rom. iii. 25,
26. But that requires *the righteousness of the law to be fulfilled*, Rom. viii. 4. The righteousness of the law cannot be
fulfilled, but by a perfect obedience. Chrysostom speaks finely on this place, " what is righteousness? It is the end, the
scope, the righteous action. For, what does the law want, what
does it always command? To be without sin." But no person
pretends to this, but the presumptuous and the liar, 1 John i.
8. We therefore conclude, that a sinner cannot be justified by
any act of his own.

XLIII. The *Form* of justification consists in these two acts.
1st. The *discharging* of unrighteousness. 2dly. The *adjudging* of righteousness.

XLIV. Unrighteousness or sin, has a double power over the
sinner. 1st. A power of *condemnation*. 2dly. A power of
dominion. The law defends both these powers: the former, by
declaring him who sins to be guilty of death, Rom. i. 32.

The other, by giving up the conquered, by a just sentence, to
the conqueror, 2 Pet. ii. 19. Wherefore it is said that the *law
is the strength of sin*, 1 Cor. xv. 56. Because sin has its power
from the law, which pronounces the sinner accursed, and the
servant of corruption. Nay, the most holy law of God itself,
is called by Paul the *law of sin and of death*, Rom. viii. 2.
Not as if it allowed of any sin, much less commanded it; but because by its righteous sentence it gives up the sinner and his
children to sin, that it may tyrannize over them as unworthy of
the life of God both in holiness and glory. Now sin does this
both by pushing the sinner on to further degrees of wickedness,
and by hastening and aggravating his condemnation. Who can
doubt but all these things are justly determined by God against
the sinner? Why should not then this sentence, which is founded on the law of the covenant of works, be called *a law?* And
seeing sin exercises, according to this law, a dominion over the
sinner, and condemns him to death, very appositely and emphatically has Paul called it *the law of sin and death*. Sin therefore, in the judgment of God, insists upon two things against
the sinner, that it may condemn him, and for ever have dominion over him; and alleges for itself the righteous law of God.
And indeed the law, as long as satisfaction is not made to it,
cannot, in this action, or process, condemn sin, that is, silence
or extenuate its accusation, lay aside its claim, and pronounce it
partial or unjust.

XLV. But now the satisfaction of Christ being substituted
and apprehended by faith, by which the whole righteousness of
the law is fulfilled, the man is then justified, and sin condemned,
both its claims being rejected. God declares, 1st. That there
is no condemnation to them who are in Christ Jesus, that all
their sins are pardoned, and that none of them shall avail to condemnation; because the Surety has, in the fullest manner, undergone the punishment due to them. And in that respect, *forgiveness of sin is* called *justification*, Rom. iv. 6, 7. 2dly. That
sin shall no longer reign in their mortal body; for since Christ
did also, of his own accord, subject himself to those laws which
were the hand writing of sin; they are no longer under the law
of sin, but under grace, Rom. vi. 14. This justifying sentence
of man, and condemning sentence of sin, are founded on the same
law of God, which, if the satisfaction of Christ be set aside, is
the law of sin and death; but if that satisfaction be supposed,
it is *the law of the Spirit of life in Christ Jesus* delivering
man with a liberal hand. For after Christ has once obeyed *in
the likeness of sinful flesh* for the elect, God declares, that every
thing was done which sin could possibly demand, according to
the law, and pronounces a sentence of liberty from sin to those

who by faith receive this grace of the Lord Christ, both with respect to its *condemning* and *domineering* power, as the apostle divinely illustrates, Rom. viii. 1, 2, 3.

XLVI. This deliverance from the guilt and dominion of sin has, indeed, an indissoluble connection with happiness ; therefore they, *whose iniquities are forgiven*, are declared *blessed*, Rom. iv. 7. nevertheless this alone is not sufficient to happiness. For he who now is set free from sin, has not immediately a right to life : as is manifest in Adam while innocent, who, as long as he continued such, had no condemnation to fear, nevertheless had not yet acquired a right to eternal life. It is therefore necessary, that that right be also adjudged to man in justification. Which God does on account of a perfect obedience, agreeably to that promise of the law, *the man that doth these things shall live in them*, Lev. xviii. 5. But what Christ has done for his people, they are accounted, as we have already often said, to have done in their own person. And in this manner, " grace reigneth through righteousness unto eternal life, by Jesus Christ our Lord," Rom. v. 21.

XLVII. The *Mean* by which we receive the righteousness of Christ, and justification depending thereon, is *faith*, and that *only*. For, if there was any thing besides faith, it would be our own works, proceeding from the other Christian virtues. But Paul will have them entirely excluded, Gal. ii. 16. " knowing that a man is not justified by the works of the law, but by the faith of Jesus Christ, even we have believed in Jesus Christ, that we might be justified by the faith of Christ, and not by the works of the law : for, by the works of the law shall no flesh be justified," Rom. iii. 28. " therefore we conclude, that a man is justified by faith without the deeds of the law." All the Christian virtues or graces are contained in these two, *faith* and *love*, which comprehend every affection of a pious soul. It is the property of *love* to *give up*, and offer oneself and all he has to God : of *faith* to *receive* and accept of God freely giving himself to us. And therefore faith alone is adapted to receive and appropriate the righteousness of Christ, on account of which we are justified. And this is a truth so certain and clear, that not a few of the doctors of the school of Rome, and they the principal and of greatest reputation among them, have acknowledged it, from the very same passages of scripture which we have advanced. Titelmannus in his paraphrase on Gal. ii. says, " we then firmly believe, that none can be justified before God by the works of the law, *but only by faith in Christ.*" Estius in like manner : " It is evident, that the particle *but* is in scripture often taken adversatively, to denote *but only ;*"

adding, that all the interpreters, both Greek and Latin, agree in this interpretation, and that it is gathered from what follows, and from Rom. iii. 28. Sasbout is also express to the same purpose, who maintains, that Paul's expression is an Hebraism, and that, according to the Hebrews, the negative particle *not* is to be repeated from what went before. " A man is not justified by works, not but by faith." And he adds : " if you ask, whether it may be rightly concluded from that proposition, a man is not justified but by faith, therefore we are justified by faith alone ? We are to say, it may." A little after he adds ; " in this our day, the Catholic writers can, on no account, bear that proposition, imagining that there is poison concealed in that particle *only*, and therefore to be disused, Yet the ancients had no such aversion to that particle, nor Thomas Aquinas : if any, says he, were righteous under the old law, they were not righteous by the works of the law, but *only* by the faith of Jesus Christ. Paul's true meaning is, not unless by faith, that is, by no merits of our own." Thus Sasbout on Gal. ii. 16.

XLVIII. But we are farther to enquire, how faith justifies. Not certainly in that sense, as if God graciously accepts the act of faith, and new gospel obedience flowing therefrom in the room of the perfect obedience, which, from the rigour of the law, we are bound to perform in order to justification : as the Socinians, and Curcellæus, who imitates them in this respect, explain it ; understanding by faith the observance of the precepts of the Gospel, which God has prescribed by Christ. For this is to make void the whole Gospel. The Gospel has not substituted our faith, but Christ's obedience, by which the righteousness of the law is fulfilled, in the room of that perfect obedience, which the law required in order to justification. It is also false, that faith and new obedience are one and the same thing. I own that faith is a virtue or grace, commanded by the law of God, and that a believer, by his very believing, obeys God. I likewise con fess, that we are to look upon nothing as a true and living faith, which is not fruitful in good works. But yet faith is one thing, and the obedience flowing from it quite another, especially in the matter of justification, of which we now speak, where Paul always contradistinguishes the obedience of all manner of works to faith. For it is a rash attempt to confine to a certain species or kind of works what the apostle says concerning them all in general. The force of truth extorted from Schlichtingius this assertion : " faith, in its strict and proper signification, bears the same relation to obedience as the cause to the effect, as the tree to the fruit, as the mother to the daughter," *contra Meisnerum*, p. 325. In fine, neither the truth nor the justice of God allow our faith and our obedience, which are imperfect, to be admitted as perfect. For, it is the will of God, that the righteousness of the law be fulfilled in our justification, and not that any thing be derogated from it, as we proved § XLII.

XLIX. Others think proper to say, that faith is here considered as a condition which the covenant of grace requires of us, in order to our justification. A certain learned divine of ours, in a volume of disputations lately published, speaks thus: " Nothing can be said with greater probability, simplicity, and more agreeable to scripture, than that justification is therefore ascribed to faith, because faith is the condition which the gospel requires of us in order to our being accounted righteous and innocent before God." And a little after; " yea, since we affirm that faith alone justifies, we do not intend, that the alone act of believing, taken precisely, as it is opposed to acts of love and hope, and distinguished from repentance, is the condition which the new covenant or the gospel requires, in order to obtain remission of sin, and be absolved from them on account of Christ. For, the hope of pardon, and love to God, sorrow also for sin, and purpose of a new life; in a word, all the acts, requisite to a genuine and serious conversion, are also somewhat necessary, and altogether prerequisite, in order for any to be received into the favour of God, and from thence forward to be accounted a justified person, yea, that a living faith that works by love, which we affirm alone to justify, includes and implies all these things." And the learned person imagines these are such truths, as the doctors both of the Romish and reformed schools receive with common consent. He also adds: " As often as the apostle affirms, that we are not justified by works, but by faith, he intends nothing else, but that none can, on any account, be justified by such observance of the law, as the legal covenant requires, in order to obtain life thereby, and escape the curse of God; but that God accounts as righteous, and out of mere grace, freely forgives all the sins of those, who with sincerity receive the gospel, and from faith perform obedience thereto." These things justly call for our animadversion.

L. 1st. With this very learned person's leave, I doubt whether he can persuade any who is not altogether unskilled in theological matters, that what he has proposed is the received opinion of the reformed school. I find nothing of this in their confessions and catechisms; but there is a great deal

which does not differ much from the words of the learned
person, in the writings of those, whose unhappy names and
heretical principles, I from my very heart believe are detestable to him.

LI. 2dly. When the discourse is about the relation which
faith bears to justification, the learned person does not seem
with sufficient caution to repeat so often *the act of believing.* For it is well known that the reformed churches condemned Arminius and his followers, for saying that faith
comes to be considered in the matter of justification as a
work or act of ours: whereas the Dutch confession speaks far
more accurately; namely, that faith is here instead of
an instrument, whereby we are joined together with
Christ in a partnership or communion of all his benefits. I
am well aware, that this is not very agreeable to the learned
person, who maintains, that faith can be said to be the instrument of justification no other way but as it is a kind of
condition, prerequisite on our part thereto. But when the Remonstrant apologists, in order to be relieved from that
troublesome expression of our confessions, by their softening
interpretations wrote, that faith is therefore said to be the instrument of justification, " as it is a work performed by us
according to the command, and by the grace of God. For, a
condition, so far as it is performed, may in some measure be
said to become a mean or instrument, whereby we obtain the
thing promised on such a condition," Apolog. p. 112. a. The
Reformed protested, that they were displeased with this explication. They deny not, that our master, Christ himself
says, John vi. 29. that faith is a work: neither do they refuse
that in the matter of justification, the apprehending and receiving Christ is an act of faith: and that faith ought to be
so far considered as active. Yet they deny, that faith justifies as it is an act prescribed by God (for thus it would stand
in the same relation with the other works enjoined by the
law) but they affirm, that we are justified by that act, as by
it we apprehend Christ, are united to him, and embrace his
righteousness. Which they usually explain by this similitude; a beggar's stretching forth his hand, by which, at the
command of a rich man, he receives the free gift of his charity, is the act of the beggar prescribed by the rich; but it
does not enrich the beggar, as it is an act, but as by this
means he applies the gift to himself, and appropriates, or
makes it his own. These things are too evident to be ob-
scured by any quibbles or subtleties whatever.

LII. 3dly. Nor do I think it an accurate way of speaking,

that faith is the condition, which the gospel requireth of us
in order to be accounted righteous and without guilt before
God. The condition of justification, properly speaking, is
perfect obedience only : this the law requires ; nor does the
gospel substitute any other : but declares that satisfication
has been made to the law by Christ our Surety ; moreover, that
it is the office of faith to accept that satisfaction offered to it,
and by accepting appropriate the same. Which is quite a
different thing from saying (as the Socinians and Remonstrants
do, and which I know not whether the learned person would
choose to say), that in the room of perfect obedience, which
the law prescribed as the condition of justification, the gospel now requireth faith, as the condition of the same justification. Though some of the Reformed have said, that faith is a
condition, sine qua non, without which we cannot be justified :
yet they were far from being of opinion, that faith is a condition properly so called, on performing which, man should,
according to the gracious covenant of God, have a right to justification as to a reward. This is very far from the mind of
the truly reformed. See what the celebrated Triglandius
has fully, solidly, and perspicuously reasoned against the subtle trifling of the Remonstrants *in Examine Apologiæ*, c. 20,
21. and Isaac Junius in *Antapologia*, p. 236.

LIII. 4thly. Neither is it according to the mind of the reformed church, that the acts of hope and love, nay, all those
which are required to a true and serious conversion, are included in justifying faith as justifying, and concur with faith,
strictly so called, to justification. When the Remonstrants said
in their confession, that " faith contains in its compass the
whole of a man's conversion prescribed by the gospel : nay,
the prescript of faith can here be considered in no other light,
than as, by its natural propriety, it includes the obedience of
faith, and is as a fruitful parent of good works, and the fountain and source of all Christian piety and holiness," c. x. § 2, 3.
The Leyden professors in their censure remarked, " that the
adversaries, who write in this manner, and throw off the mask,
ascribe to faith the *Socinian-Popish* faith of justification,
which Peter Bertius, a principal asserter of this, found to be
the way to popery." And this assertion of theirs they make
out by solid arguments. And when the Remonstrant apolo-
gist, foolishly said, that this his opinion differed not from the
common doctrine of the reformed churches, the venerable
Triglandius replied, that " it was clearer than noon day, that
this was too barefaced an assertion." The whole comes to this,
that no faith justifies, but that which is living and fruitful

in good works; that acts of love and holiness are required, as fruits of faith, as testimonies of Christ dwelling in us, as marks of our regeneration, as what go before salvation, and without which there can be no full assurance of it. But that those acts of love, holiness, and conversion, concur with faith to justification, and are included in justifying faith, as such, is a strange way of speaking to reformed ears, nor agreeable to scripture, which always, in the matter of justification, sets faith in opposition to all works whatever.

LIV. 5thly. Some time ago *I read* in Socinus, before the sentiments of this celebrated person came to hand, the same exception which he makes, that, by the works which Paul excludes from justification, is understood the perfect observance of the law, such as the legal covenant requires. For thus he says *de servat.* P. 4. c. 11. " the works to which faith is opposed are not every kind of works, nor taken and considered in every light, but, as we have observed elsewhere, these works denote an absolute and perpetual observance and performance of the divine law, through the whole course of life." But our divines openly declared against this exposition; who contend that all works, however considered, are opposed to faith. The apostle's words are plain, *he that worketh not, but believeth*, and his mind or intention, as Lubbertus has learnedly observed, is to be considered from the state of the controversy, then in debate. But the state of the controversy was not, whether a man could be justified by a perfect observance of the law, if there was any one who could keep it perfectly? Which none in his senses will deny: or whether there are many, who, since Adam's first sin, have, for the whole of their life, done nothing amiss, but have attained to every perfection both of parts, degrees and perseverance? Which none in his right mind will affirm. But the matter in question was, whether the Jews could be justified by that observance of the law which they were able to perform. They certainly thought that they could be justified if they only observed the moral law to the utmost of their power, and gave these satisfactions for their failings which the ceremonial law had prescribed. But the apostle denies this, resting his argument on that maxim, that the righteousness which can be valid at God's tribunal, must be perfect in all its parts: but since none can pretend to any such works, he concludes, that no works, of what kind soever, can contribute any thing to obtain justification. The apostle, doubtless, excludes those works in which they commonly trusted, who endeavoured to establish their own righteousness. But it is not credible, that any of them could say, that he kept himself pure, through the whole course of his life from every even the least stain of sin. These things are evident.

LV. But I would not have it wrested to the worst sense, in that I have in some things compared the opinion of this celebrated person with that of Socinus and the *Remonstrants.* It was not with the view to rank a man, in other respects orthodox, and usefully employed in the service of the church of God, with those perverters of our faith.   This of all things is farthest from my mind and manner : but my design was only to warn those under my care, and who may reap benefit by the very learned labours of this person, with considerable increase of knowledge, against these and the like expressions; in which, through a disgust for controversy, and a too eager desire of laying disputes aside, he seems to yield rather too much to our adversaries.   Peace indeed is to be pursued, but by no means at the expense of truth.

LVI. The genuine opinion of the reformed is this : that faith justifies, as it is the bond of our strictest union with Christ, by which all things that are Christ's become also ours, as we explained § XXXI.   Or, which is the same thing, as it is the acceptance of the gift offered, rendering the donation firm and irrevocable.   And this is what the apostle intended when he wrote Rom. iv. 5. that *faith is counted for righteousness*, that is, faith is judged to be that with which the right of demanding the reward is connected ; a way of speaking borrowed from merchants : thus in the book of God's accompts is set down what he hath given to us, and what we are indebted to him.   But when in the other page, our complete obedience, and the payment of the debt could not be inserted, what then is written there, viz. to balance the account ? In the first place, our righteousness or the righteousness of Christ wrought out for us : then * our faith by which we receive that righteousness offered to us, and present it to God as ours.

LVII. It is, moreover, to be observed, that justification, if we take in whatever can be comprised under that name, consists of various † *articles*, or periods, which we will describe in the most pointed manner we can.   And first, God's sentence

---

* The author does not here mean, that faith, as an act of ours, justifies : for he has sufficiently explained himself on that head ; he only mentions faith here as the instrument by which we lay hold on Christ's righteousness whereby our debt, both of duty and punishment, is fully paid.

† The word *articulus* is of various significations ; but it is plain from the sequel, that the author here uses it, for a moment or period, so that he here gives us a very distinct account of the *Time* of justification.

of absolution regards either all the elect in general collected into one mystical body ; or relates to each in particular. I observe *two articles* with respect to that general sentence: the
first of which commenced immediately upon the fall; when
Christ, having entered into suretiship engagements for elect
sinners, obtained by his covenant, which the Father was assured
he would most faithfully perform, that Satan should be condemned in the serpent, his right over man, which he acquired by
wicked arts, be made void as to the elect: and the elect, on the
other hand, who are comprehended under the seed of the woman,
be declared, in Christ their head, no longer friends or subjects,
but enemies and conquerors of the devil. For, all these things
are contained in the first gospel promise; which presupposes that
suretiship of Christ, whereby he took upon himself all the sins
of the elect, and on account of which God declared, he never
intended to exact them from any of his chosen; because, on admitting a Surety, the principal debtor is freed from all obligation to make satisfaction. And this is the first effect of Christ's
suretiship, the declaration of that counsel of God, by which he
had purposed to justify the ungodly ; and not to impute sin to
those who are inserted as heirs in the testament.

LVIII. The *other* article of this general justification relates
to the time in which God declared that full satisfaction was
made to his justice by a dying Christ. Of which Paul treats
2 Cor. v. 19. " God was in Christ, reconciling the world unto
himself, not imputing their trespasses unto them." He, together and at once reconciled to himself the whole world of his
elect ; and declared that he would not impute their trespasses
to any of them, on account of the perfect satisfaction of Christ.
For, when he raised Christ from the dead, he gave him a discharge, in testimony that the payment was made; and when he
rent the vail of the temple, he also tore the hand writing consisting in ordinances, which, till that time, loudly proclaimed
that payment was not yet made. But who can doubt, that a
creditor, tearing the hand writing or bond, and giving a discharge to the Surety, declares, he will not, and even in law
cannot, demand any satisfaction of the principal debtor ?

LIX. But justification is not confined to these bounds. Besides that *general* declaration of God, there is also another, applied to every believer *in particular*. And this again has its
distinct articles. The *first* is, when the elect person, who is
redeemed, regenerated and united to Christ by a living faith, is
declared to have now actually passed from a state of condemnation and wrath, to a state of grace or favour. For, the elect
sinner, though redeemed by Christ, and so far reconciled to

God, as that he declares, he is never actually to be condemned; yet that right, purchased by Christ, is not applied to him till he is regenerated and united to Christ by faith. Till then he is in " the present evil world," Gal. i. 4.; " alienated and an enemy, and under the power of darkness," Col. i. 13, 21. But immediately, on his receiving Christ by faith, God declares in the court of heaven, that he is no longer under wrath, but under grace; though perhaps the justified person may yet be ignorant of it. And in this sense God is said to *justify the ungodly*, Rom. iv. 5.; him who is so in himself, and actually continues such till he is born again, when that faith is freely bestowed on him for which he is immediately justified.

LX. The *second* article is, when that sentence of God, which was pronounced in the court of heaven, is *intimated* and *insinuated to the conscience* by the Holy Spirit; so that the believer knows, feels, and experiences, that his sins are forgiven. To this David has an eye, Psal. xxxii. 5. " and thou hast taken away, or thou forgavest the iniquity of my sin," that is, thou madest me to know and experience this, by speaking to my heart.

LXI. The *third* article is, when the sinner, being actively and passively justified, is admitted to *familiar converse with God*, and to the mutual participation of the most delightful friendship. For it may happen, that God may have removed the tokens of his anger from the elect sinner, and given him assurance of it, and yet not directly admit him to an intercourse of familiarity. In the same manner almost, as David had forgiven Absalom's parricide, and declared it by Job, by ordering his return from Geshur to Jerusalem; yet he did not immediately admit him to court, much less to his presence chamber, and least of all to the kisses of his mouth, 2 Sam. xiv. David himself is an example of this. Nathan had told him, in the name of God, " the Lord hath put away thy sin," 2 Sam. xiii. 13. and yet, for some time, he was racked with grievous sorrows, crying out from the bottom of a contrite heart, and a sense of broken bones; " have mercy upon me, O God, according to thy loving kindness; according unto the multitude of thy tender mercies blot out my transgressions," Psal. li. 1. That is, as he explains it, ver. 12. " restore unto me the joy of thy salvation." This near and intimate access to God, as the author of his most joyful exultation, is the real declaration of his justification. And it is to be observed, that such a declaration is often repeated. For instance, when a believer happens to fall into some grievous sin, or into a languid and drowsy frame of soul, then his familiarity with God is not a little interrupted; but after he is roused out of that sin, or from that drowsy frame by the preventing grace of God, and has been sufficiently exercised with the stings of conscience, then God applies that general sentence of the pardon of all his sins, which was pronounced immediately upon his regeneration, to this particular act, or state, and suffers himself to be prevailed on at length to renew this most delightful friendship.

LXII. The *fourth* article is immediately *after death;* when God assigns to the soul, on its departure from the body, an eternal mansion in his own blessed habitation, Heb. ix. 27. " it is appointed unto men once to die, but after this the judgment."

LXIII. The *fifth* and last article is *at the last day*, which is therefore called *the day of judgment*, Mat. xii. 36. when the elect shall be publicly justified, and, in the view of the whole world, declared heirs of eternal life. Which justification indeed, may be called *universal*, as all those, who are to be justified, shall appear together before God's tribunal, nevertheless it will be most *particular*, as every one shall be recompensed according to his works; " we must *all* appear before the judgment seat of Christ, that *every one* may receive the things done in his body, according to that he hath done, whether it be good or bad," 2 Cor. v. 10.

LXIV. Let us briefly explain the whole manner of this justification in the *next world*. Christ, *the judge*, being delegated to that office by the Father, Acts x. 42. Acts xvii. 32. will pronounce two things concerning his elect. 1st. That they are truly pious, righteous and holy. And so far this justification will differ from the former; for by that *the ungodly is justified*, Rom. iv. 5. Whereas here, God, when he enjoins his angels to summon one of the parties to be judged, says, " gather my *saints* together," Psal. l. 5. if, as many suppose, these words refer to the last judgment. See Mat. xiii. 40, 41, 43. 49. 2dly. That they have a right to eternal life, Mat. xx. 35.

LXV. The ground of the *former* declaration is *inherent righteousness*, graciously communicated to man by the Spirit of sanctification, and good works proceeding therefrom. For on no other account can any person be declared pious and holy, but because he is endowed with habitual holiness, and gives himself to the practice of godliness, Mat. xii. 37. " by thy words thou shalt be justified," that is, be declared just or righteous, because words are indications of the mind, and signs either of the good or bad treasure of the heart; " when the Lord will bring to light the hidden things of darkness, and will make manifest the counsels of the heart; and then shall every man have praise of God," 1 Cor. iv. 5.

LXVI. The *foundation of the latter* can be no other than *the righteousness of* Christ the Lord, communicated to them according to the free decree of election, which is succeeded by adoption, which gives them a right to take possession of the inheritance. The very sentence of the Judge himself leads us to this: *come, ye blessed of my Father,* whom, on my account, he freely loved (for, in Christ all the nations of the earth are blessed, Gen. xxii. 18. Eph. i. 3.), *inherit, possess by hereditary right,* as the adopted sons of God, who, *because ye are* sons, are *also heirs,* Rom. viii. 17. " the kingdom prepared for you from the foundation of the world;" ordained for you from eternity, whose palace was fitted up in the beginning for that purpose, by the hands of God the Creator.

LXVII. Mean while, in this respect too, there will be room for mentioning good works, for they shall be produced, 1st. As *proofs of faith,* of the union of believers with Christ, of their adoption, and of that holiness, without which none can see God, and of friendship with God, and brotherhood with Christ. 2dly. As signs of that sacred *hunger* and *thirst,* with which they desired happiness, and of that strenuous endeavour, by which, not regarding the advantages of this life, and despising carnal pleasures, they had sought the kingdom of heaven and its righteousness; and it is inconsistent with the perfection of the infinitely holy God, to disappoint this hunger and thirst, and seeking after his kingdom. 3dly. As *effects of divine grace,* to which, the *communication of divine glory* will answer, in the most wise proportion, when it shall come to crown his own gifts. For the more abundant measure of sanctification any one has obtained in this life, and the more he has gained by the talent entrusted to him, it is also credible, that the portion of glory will be the more exuberant, which the divine bounty hath appointed for him. And in this sense, we imagine, it is so often said in scripture, that every one shall be recompensed according to his works, not that these works are, on any account, the cause of any right they will have, to claim the reward; but as they are evidences of our adoption and of our seeking the chief good, and as they shew that proportion of grace, according to which the proportion of future glory will be dispensed.

LXVIII. In this judgment, therefore, there will also be *grace mixed with justice. Justice* will appear because none will be admitted to the possession of the kingdom of heaven, but he who can shew by undoubted evidences, that he is a partaker of Christ and his righteousness. *Grace* also will appear, because eternal happiness will be adjudged to him, who has done nothing to acquire a right to it; because works, stained with so many infirmities, as justly make believers themselves blush, will then be celebrated with so great an encomium by the Judge. And indeed the apostle does in express words make mention of the *mercy* that will be shewn on *that day*, 2 Tim. i. 18. " the Lord grant unto him, that he may find mercy of the Lord in that day." It is certainly true, that by mercy is there understood *the reward of that mercy* which Onesiphorus had shewn to Paul: but the reward of our mercy is not reckoned of *debt, but of grace*, Rom. iv. 4. And as it is not merited on the part of him who receives it, so neither is it due from him who bestows it. For what doth God owe to man, but what he hath made himself a debtor to man by his gracious promises; or rather was willing to owe to his own goodness and truth, that man might expect from him a retribution for his holiness? Which debt is not opposed to, but supposes grace; it is to be derived from the " alone *gracious will* and truth of God the Father, who hath promised an unmerited reward to the labour of obedience which is the duty of all, and will have this to be only due on account of his promise." As becomes a reformed teacher to speak who returns to his sound mind.

LXIX. Whence it appears, that they do not speak right, who affirm, that in the *last justification mere justice will take place without any mixture of grace*. It is said indeed, Heb. vi. 10. *God is not unrighteous to forget your work*, &c. But that the reward of our works is of mere justice, without any mixture of grace, is language which sounds harsh in reformed ears, and is diametrically repugnant to our catechism, * quest. 63. Ludovicus de Dieu, on Luke i. 2, 57. and on Luke xvi. 19. and on Rom. iii. 4. has proved at large, that in the Hebrew, Syriac, and Arabic languages, justice and truth denote one and the same notion, and generally are put one for the other. Thus צדקה, justice, or righteousness, when affirmed of God, in many places denotes his *truth*. But also אמת *truth*, is translated by the Septuagint, δικαιοσύνη, *justice*, or *righteousness*, Gen. xxiv. 49. Isa. xxxviii. 19. And Grævius has proved, that the same phraseology obtained among the ancient Greeks, in his Lec-

---

* Q. How is it, that our good works merit nothing, since God promises that he will give a reward for them both in this life and the life to come?
  A. That reward is not given out of merit, but of grace.

tiones Hesiod. And what is more suitable than by *the mammon of unrighteousness*, Luke xvi. 9. to understand not the true riches, such as the spiritual and heavenly are, for ver. 11. *the unrighteous mammon* is opposed to *the true riches*. Is not that signification of the word clear from 1 John i. 9. " if we confess our sins, he is faithful and just to forgive us our sins :" that is, faithful and true ? For, who will say that God owes the pardon of sins in justice, without any mixture of grace, to him that confesseth them ? So also in the place just quoted; *God is not unrighteous*, that is, deceives not in his gracious promises by which he has adjudged a reward of grace, to our labours of love. The celebrated Iac. Altingius gives us an excellent commentary on this place as follows : " the obligation to the reward depends on the truth of the promiser, who is a debtor to himself, that what he was once pleased, in the promise, to determine the consequence of the work and reward, might always please him in the performance : thus the just and righteous God forgives the sins of the penitent, 1 John i. 9. is the justifier of him that believeth," Rom. iii. 26. And a little after : " every consideration of merit therefore is at an end : but a debt remains, which justice will have discharged in respect of what God has promised ; who, on account of his truth, which is without repentance, or unchangeable, is debtor to himself to perform his promises, Rom. iii. 3, 4. Deut. vii. 9. *This is the justice meant in this place, and God is denied to be unrighteous to forget good works ; though he has decreed and promised, out of mere grace and mercy, that recompence :*" all this is judicious, solid, and orthodox.

LXX. This manifestation of mere justice is not more strongly concluded from that day being called *the day of the righteous judgment*, Rom. ii. 5. For, 1st. It is there called *the day of wrath*. And yet wrath will not be exercised only, without a manifestation of mercy. 2dly. Even in the justification of a sinner, in this world, there is *a declaration of the righteousness of God*, Rom. iii. 25.; where notwithstanding, as Paul expressly affirms ver. 24. and all own, grace has the principal place : so also here *grace reigneth through righteousness unto eternal life*, Rom. v. 21. 3dly. As God will justly inflict punishments on the impenitent, so in like manner, agreeably to his justice, he will distribute rewards, and shew grace to the godly, as we explained § LXVIII. Justice and grace are here not to be opposed but joined together.

LXXI. What is asserted Rom. ii. 11. viz. that with God there is no *respect of persons*, is still less sufficient to confirm this opinion. For because God does all things without respect of persons, does it follow that he exercises no grace ? When Peter took notice of the piety and faith of Cornelius, and said, *Of a truth I perceive, that God is no respecter of persons*, Acts x. 34. did he ever intend by these words to deny that grace was shewn to Cornelius ? A non-respect of persons excludes, indeed, injustice, and the consideration of these things which ought to have no place in judgment; but it no ways excludes grace and mercy. These things have been so often confuted that there is no occasion to consider them again.

LXXII. It is a new opinion, and an extraordinary postulatum, to say, that the works of those who are to be justified, and according to which they shall be judged, will be " perfect, yea most perfect, that nothing may derogate from the righteousness of the judgment of that day." It is a certain truth, that the *persons* then to be justified, will be perfect: 1st. *In Christ*, on account of his most perfect righteousness imputed to them, Col. ii. 10. 2dly. *In themselves*, being then perfectly sanctified : For they who died before that time are called *just men made perfect*, Heb. xii. 23.; and they who shall at that day be alive *shall be changed*, 1 Cor. xv. 51, 52. and doubtless obtain perfect holiness by that change which the others obtained at death. But that the works which they performed in this life, can then be said to be most perfect, is neither consonant with scripture nor reason.

LXXIII. The scripture declares, that the works which were done by believers in this life, were not without blemish ; because they who performed them had the old man still remaining, who mixed and tainted them with some corruption of his own, Rom. vii. 22, 23, 24. Gal. v. 15.: This is without dispute. But the scripture no where says, that these works shall appear otherwise at the last judgment, than they did in this life ; nay, it asserts the contrary, when it testifies, that every one shall be judged *according to that he hath done in his body*, 2 Cor. v. 10.; but it is certain that the things done in the body were imperfect. It is also contrary to reason, to say that actions which were imperfect while they were performing, and actually existing, should be declared to be perfect when they were no more ; and perfect not only in the estimation of God the Judge, but also by, I know not what, sanctification, really perfecting them when they had no further existence. No doubt *habits*, which are holy when first infused, are perfected by a further sanctification ; but that *actions* which were imperfect while they existed, should become perfect, after they have ceased to be, is inconceivable.

LXXIV. Seeing what we are taught in scripture concerning the perfection of believers by a progressive sanctification and the death of the body, regards their *persons*, about the perfection of which there is no dispute, it is erroneous to apply it to their antecedent works. That God refines those works like gold, purging away all their tin and dross, so as to be altogether pure in his eyes, is an unscriptural fancy. The passages, Isa. i. 25. Zech. xiii. 9. Mal. iii. 3. do not treat of *works* but of *persons*, nor speak of their absolute perfection, nor have a reference to the day of the last judgment, but relate to the condition of the present life, as will plainly appear to any who will peruse them; and can therefore with no probability be wrested to this sense.

LXXV. Indeed the good works of those who die in the Lord are said to follow them, Rev. xiv. 13. but they are such as they were performed here; and they follow, not in themselves, but in their fruits and effects; in so far as God, in regard of their good works, does good to the pious even after death. For this end it is not requisite that they be perfect; it is sufficient that they be performed in faith, and by the Spirit of Christ. I do not remember that the scripture says, that good works shall rise with them. They who speak thus, mean no more, at least they ought to mean no more by that phrase, but that in the resurrection of the just, the pious shall rejoice in the gratuitous reward of their holiness. It is said indeed that he, who hath begun a good work in believers, " will perform it until the day of Jesus Christ," Phil. i. 6. But by a good work is there meant the communication of the grace of Christ revealed in the gospel, as appears from ver. 5. which God perfects in certain degrees, till the finishing hand is put to it at the last day. There is nothing in that passage relating to the perfection of our actions, which are already over and gone.

LXXVI. In the last place, if good works are there to appear perfect, there can be no reason why they should not be meritorious. For that is certainly meritorious which satisfies every demand of the law; if merit is to be ascribed to such a work, which when a man does, he is to live therein, according to the law of the covenant of works. It is not required to meritorious works, in the sense now in debate, that they are not due and properly our own, that is, that they are done in our own strength without the grace of God. For the Papists themselves readily acknowledge, that there are no such meritorious works. But by those meritorious works, which are the present subject of dispute, are understood such actions, on performing which one has a right to life. But the only or at least the principal reason, why our works are not meritorious, is what the catechism assigns, because they * are imperfect and stained with sin.

LXXVII. Nor will the righteousness of the judgment of that day be in the least diminished, though the works of believers, by which they shall be judged, are imperfect. For, they will not be mentioned as the causes of their right to claim the reward, to which perfection is requisite; but as effects and signs of grace, and of union with Christ, and of a living faith, and of justification by faith, and of a right to life: for which their unfeigned sincerity is sufficient. We therefore conclude, that the justification in the next world is not to be so very much distinguished from the justification in this world.

LXXVIII. As this doctrine of free justification, on account of the righteousness of Christ, apprehended by faith alone, is founded on clear testimonies of scripture; so it proves itself to every pious conscience, by its most excellent uses and fruits.

LXXIX. 1st. It tends much to display the glory of God, whose most exalted perfections shine forth with an eminent lustre in this matter. It sets forth the infinite *goodness of God*, by which he was inclined to procure salvation freely for lost and miserable man, " to the praise of the glory of his grace," Eph. i. 6. It displays also the strictest justice, by which he would not forgive even the smallest offence, but on condition of the sufficient engagement, or full satisfaction of the Mediator, " that he might be just, and the justifier of him which believeth in Jesus," Rom. iii. 26. It shews further the unsearchable wisdom of the Deity, which found out a way, for the exercise of the most gracious act of mercy, without injury to his strictest justice and infallible truth, which threatened death to the sinner: justice demanded that the soul that sinned should die, Rom. i. 32. Truth had pronounced, " cursed is he that continueth not in all things," Deut. xxviii. 26. Goodness, in the mean time, was inclined to adjudge life

---

* Q. 62. Why cannot our good works be righteousness, or some part of righteousness before God?

A. Because that righteousness, which must stand before the judgment of God, must be in all points perfect and agreeable to the law of God. But our works, even the best of them, are imperfect in this life, and defiled with sin.

to some sinners, but by no other way than what became the majesty of the most holy God. Here wisdom interposed, saying, " I will fully satisfy my goodness, and say to mine elect, I, even I am he that blotteth out thy transgressions for mine own sake, Isa. xliii. 25. Nor shall you, my justice and my truth, have any cause of complaint, because full satisfaction shall be made to you by a mediator." Hence the incredible philanthropy of the Lord Jesus shineth forth, who, though Lord of all, was made subject to the law, not to the obedience of it only, but also to the curse ; " made sin for us, that we might be made the righteousness of God in him," 2 Cor. v. 21.

LXXX. Ought not the pious soul, who is deeply engaged in the devout meditation of these things, to break out into the praises of a justifying God, and sing with the church, Mic. vii. 17. " who is a God like unto thee, that pardoneth iniquity, and passeth by transgression !" " O ! the purity of that holiness, which chose rather to punish the sins of the elect in his only begotten Son, than suffer them to go unpunished ! O ! the abyss of his love to the world, for which he spared not his dearest Son, in order to spare sinners ! O ! the depth of the riches of unsearchable wisdom, by which he exercises mercy towards the penitent guilty, without any stain to the honour of the most impartial Judge ! O ! the treasures of love in Christ, whereby he became a curse for us, in order to deliver us therefrom." How becoming the justified soul, who is ready to dissolve in the sense of this love, with full exultation to sing a new song, a song of mutual return of love to a justifying God ?

LXXXI. 2dly. This doctrine is likewise calculated for the humility of the sinner, from whom it cuts off all boasting, that the glory may remain unstained to God alone. " What hast thou, O man, to boast of ? What, wherewith thou canst stand before the tribunal of God ? Good works ? But all thy righteousnesses are as filthy rags, Isa. lxiv. 6. If thou leanest on them, they are, Pope Adrian VI. himself being Judge, like the staff of a reed which shall break, and pierce thy leaning hand. Perhaps thou wilt boast of thy faith, as if by the excellency of that thou canst please God. But even that is like a shaken and shattered reed, to which thou canst not safely trust ; and whatever it be, it is the gift of God, Phil. i. 29. Thou hast received ; why dost thou glory as if thou hadst not received ? 1 Cor. iv. 7. Thou hast nothing of thine own to present to God. Indeed thou hast a great deal of thine own, but it is either sin, or at least what is stained with sin; for which if thou has deserved any thing, it is only hell, or that which is worse than hell, if any such thing can be. And canst thou, O most wretched creature, boast of any such vanity!" Rom. iii. 27.

LXXXII. 3dly. It conduces above all to the consolation of the afflicted soul, bewailing his sins with godly sorrow; whom we may address in this manner, from the very genius, or nature of this doctrine. "Indeed, thy sins are both more numerous and greater, than thou canst either conceive or express: but *behold the Lamb of God, which taketh away the sins of the world.* Every thing in thee is infected with much sin: but thanks be to God, the cause of thy justification is not to be sought for in thee: we are justified freely by his grace. Thou hast to do with a most righteous judge, who will not clear the guilty: but behold Jesus the Surety, who, by a full expiation, has brought it to pass, that he can justify the ungodly, without any violation of his justice. Having such a leader and guardian, approach without fear to this judge, being assured, that Jesus thy patron or powerful friend will so plead thy cause, that thou shalt not be cast. Canst thou not yet venture? What should hinder? Do thy sins, thy nakedness and thy pollution affright thee? But take shelter behind Christ, hide thyself in his wounds, wrap thyself in his death and blood, receive, with the hand of faith, the offered fine linen, the righteousness of the saints. Is thy faith itself so weak that thou art ashamed and grieved? But again thanks be to God, that thou art not to be justified for thy faith, or for any worthiness that is in it, but if it is true and sincere, however weak, it is the band of thy union and communion with Christ. And being united to him, present thyself to God without fear, undauntedly also before the devil, and all who take pleasure to accuse thee. Humbly confess whatever sin may be objected against thee: but add, that they shall no doubt triumph in the judgment when they shall make it appear, that the merits and satisfaction of Christ are not sufficient to atone for and remove them, or thou not suffered to plead those merits of Christ in judgment. I challenge the devil and all his accomplices: *Who shall lay any thing to the charge of God's elect? It is God that justifieth,* &c. Doest thou believe these things? Thou doest, but with faultering and hesitation. Fight manfully against all the temptations of unbelief, and even now, thou shalt receive that white stone, and new name written thereon, which none knoweth, but he who receiveth it; and the hidden manna, which having tasted, thou wilt enjoy thy life in patience, and death in desire." This is comfort indeed : they, who build not on these foundations, are certainly, like Job's friends, miserable comforters. It is memorable what the reverend Voetius, Disput. ii. p. 754. relates of John Frederic, duke of Saxony, who acquainted Luther that George, duke of Saxony, comforted his son John, in the agonies of death, with the righteousness of faith, desiring him to look to Christ alone, and disclaim his own merits and the invocation of saints. And when the wife of the aforesaid John (who was sister to Philip landgrave of Hesse) asked duke George, why these things were not thus publicly taught, made answer, *O daughter, such things are to be said to the dying only.* O the force of truth, breaking forth even from the breasts of those who are set against it.

LXXXIII. 4thly. This doctrine is exceedingly powerful to promote godliness. 1. Because it lays, as a foundation, a submissive humility of soul, presuming nothing of itself, without which there is no holiness that deserves the name. 2. Because we teach, that no faith justifies, but what is the fruitful parent of good works. And can any one really believe, that he, who is himself a most unworthy sinner, is, without any merit of his own, received into the favour of God, delivered from the expectation of hell, and favoured with the hope of a blessed eternity, and not, in every respect, and by all means be obedient to so benevolent a Lord? Can he believe, that God the Father spared not his own Son, that he might spare this slave : that God the Son bore so many things grievous to mention and hard to suffer, that he might procure pardon for the guilty, and a right to life : that God, the Holy Ghost, should enter his heart, as the messenger and earnest of so great a happiness, and love those so ardently, who had no love for him? Can he then provoke the Father by disobedience? Trample on the Son by his wickedness, and profane his blood? Can he grieve the Spirit the Comforter? Indeed, such a one knows not what faith is, who imagines, that it consists in a strong persuasion destitute of good works. 3dly. Because it teacheth a sublime pitch of holiness, by which a person, laying aside every mercenary affection, can love God and virtue for itself, direct every thing to the glory of God alone, and securely trust him with the free reward of his works. Here now we appeal to the conscience of our adversaries, which is the safer way, whether that which we point out to our people, or what they would have theirs to walk in? We both agree, that without good works none shall be saved. Now whether is it safer to say, Do good works, with a presumption of merit; or, do them with all diligence and energy of soul; because you cannot be saved without them: yet, having done all, own thyself to be an unprofitable servant, and look for heaven as a free gift. If works merit nothing, doubtless he offends God who boasts of his merits. But if they deserve any thing, yet I, though performing them diligently, dare not arrogate any thing to myself from merit: of what detriment, pray, will that humility be? We conclude, that a doctrine, whose advantages are so many, and so considerable, cannot but be true.

CHAP. IX.

Of Spiritual Peace.

I. Reconciliation stands in close connection with justification, the consummation of which is a spiritual, holy, and blessed *peace*: " therefore being justified by faith, we have peace with God, through our Lord Jesus Christ," Rom. v. 1.

II. This peace is " a mutual concord between God and the sinner, who is justified by faith ; so that the heart of God is carried out towards man, and in like manner, the heart of man towards God, by a delightful inclination of friendship." God thus addresses the church, when reconciled to him ; " thou shalt no more be termed forsaken, neither shall thy land be any more termed desolate : but thou shalt be called, Hephzi-bah (my delight), and thy land, Beulah (married): for the Lord delighteth in thee, and thy land shall be married," Isa. lxii. 4. And the church in her turn, replies, " I will love thee, O Lord, my strength," Psal. xviii. 1.

III. This blessed peace presupposes that unhappy and destructive war, which the inconsiderate sinner had raised between God and himself; concerning which the prophet says, " your iniquities have separated between you and your God, and your sins have hid his face from you," Isa. lix. 2. By sin man lost the favour and friendship of God, and incurred his righteous hatred and displeasure, which " is revealed from heaven against all ungodliness and unrighteousness of men," Rom. i. 18. and is threatened by the curse of the law, Deut. xxvii. 26. felt in the conscience, which trembles at every voice of God, Gen. iii. 8. and is the bitter source of all that anguish, which is the forerunner of eternal destruction. And on the other hand, man is carried out to a dreadful hatred of God, Rom. i. 30. After sin became his delight, he became an enemy to all holiness, and consequently a most bitter enemy to God, because he is the most unspotted holiness. Whatever wisdom he has, it is enmity against God, Rom. viii. 7. He hath joined himself to the devil, under whose banner he fights against God. " He stretcheth out his hand against God, and strengtheneth himself against the Almighty : he runneth upon him, even on his neck, upon the thick bosses of his bucklers," Job xv. 25, 26. If any thing is propounded to him out of the law of God, he the more boldly acts contrary to it, Rom. vii. 8. Whenever he feels the effects of divine indignation, he with the most reproachful words, reviles the most holy justice of God, Isa. viii. 21. And almost goes so far as to wish, that either there was no God, or that he did not punish sin. The first of these tends to destroy the existence of God ; the other his holiness, without which (horrid to think !) he would be a wicked spirit. But seeing God *is greater than man*, Job xxxiii. 12. this war cannot but prove fatal to man. " God is wise in heart, and mighty in strength ; who hath hardened himself against him, and hath prospered ?" Job ix. 4.

IV. In this very grievous war, all hopes of an uniting peace seem to be entirely cut off. For it cannot be devised, in what manner, either God can be reconciled to man, or man to God. The holiness of God does not suffer him to allow the sinner communion with himself, lest he should seem to be like him, Psal. l. 21. The justice of God demands punishment, Rom. i. 32. The truth of God threatens death, Gen. iii. 3. And it is on no account to be expected, that God would make a peace in favour of man who despises him, to the prejudice of any of his own perfections : for *he cannot deny himself*, 2 Tim. ii. 13. And man on his part is no less averse to peace, for though he will find nothing but ruin in this war, and all manner of good in this peace, yet he is so infatuated, so much an enemy to himself, that he madly hardens himself to his own destruction. Being subjected to the power of sin and Satan, he freely and fully serveth them. These blind the eyes of his understanding, " lest the light of the glorious gospel of Christ should shine unto them," 2 Cor. iv. 4. And so lead him captive at their will, that he neither can, nor dare think in what manner *he may recover himself out of the snare of the devil*, and be reconciled to God, 2 Tim. ii. 26.

V. But God, " whose understanding there is no searching out," Isa. xl. 28. was able to find out a method and way, whereby all these difficulties could be surmounted. For he hath a Son, who being given to be the mediator and surety, made satisfaction to his holiness, justice, and veracity, and thus on his part God is reconciled, 2 Cor. v. 19. Moreover that Son has a Spirit far more powerful than the infernal spirit, who by his turning and inclining efficacy, can expel the hatred of God out of our hearts, and shed abroad the love of God there. To whose guidance and influence, if man gives himself up, that blessed peace will be soon procured of which we are now to treat.

VI. Hence it appears, that the rise and beginning of this peace is from God; accordingly it is called *the peace of* God; and God himself *the God of peace*, Phil. iv. 7, 9. The Father hath established *the counsel of peace*, Zech. vi. 13. And therefore it is ascribed to him as the original of it, that " having made peace, he reconciled all things unto himself," Col. i. 20. The Son hath executed that counsel of peace, and by shedding his precious blood, removed all obstructions, and actually obtained for the elect the grace and favour of his Father, which was long before designed for them. He therefore calls this *his own* peace; and declares *that he gives it*, John xiv. 27. nay he is called *the Prince of peace*, Isa. xi. 5. and *king of peace*, prefigured by Melchizedek, Heb. vii. 2. and the *peace*, Mich. v. 5. and *our peace*, Eph. ii. 14. The Holy Spirit, the messenger of so great a happiness, like Noah's dove with an olive-branch, flies at the appointed moment of grace to the elect, and effectually offers and brings home to them the peace decreed by the Father, and purchased by Christ: Hence *peace* is said to be *by the Holy Ghost*, Rom. xiv. 17.

VII. The fountain of this peace, and the first cause of it, can be nothing but the infinite mercy and philanthropy of God: and this is the reason why the apostles in their epistles wishing *peace* to believers, usually set *grace* before it, as the spring of that peace. Which is the more evident, because as there was nothing in man, that could invite God to make peace with him, (for, when we were enemies, we were reconciled to God by the death of his Son, Rom. v. 10.) so in like manner, God, who is all sufficient to himself for all happiness, could gain nothing by this peace. The whole advantage thereof redounds to man: the glory of so great a work is due to God alone.

VIII. Man surely ought not to hear the least report of this peace, without being directly carried with the greatest vigour of soul, to obtain it for himself. And though he should be obliged to go to the utmost end of the earth, for instruc-

tion in the manner how to procure it, he should undertake
the journey with the utmost diligence and readiness.   But
behold the incredible benevolence of the Deity, who not only
in his word, sufficiently instructs men in the excellency of so
great a blessing, but also fully informs them in what manner
they may enjoy it; by putting the word of reconciliation
in the mouth of his servants, 2 Cor. v. 29.   " I create the
fruit of the lips, peace to him that is afar off and to him
that is near, saith the Lord," Isa. lvii. 19.   But this is not
all, for he also is the first who sends ambassadors to men
to offer peace.   Would it not have been inestimable grace if,
after many and solicitous entreaties, he had suffered himself
to be at length prevailed upon by us as Herod, who with
difficulty granted peace to the Tyrians after their most earnest requests? Acts xii. 20.   But he not only freely offers,
but also solicits and affectionately entreats and *beseeches* men
by his ambassadors, that they would not refuse to be reconciled to him, 2 Cor. v. 20.   And though his tremendous majesty
has been often scornfully despised, and though he has for a long
time addressed himself to their ears by his most alluring invitations, and all to no purpose, yet he does not desist, but again
and again presses, over and over urges that affair of peace, and
compels, with so much gentleness, the most obstinate to partake
of his friendship and love, Luke xiv. 23.   Such is the infinite
goodness of the Supreme Being!

IX. But he does not stop here, for as the word of grace,
though preached in the most pathetic manner, actually draws
none, without the secret operation of the Spirit of God, so
he graciously bestows that Spirit on man; who at length
opens the eyes of the understanding, that wretched men may
see, how bad their case is, while they continue in that dreadful hostility, and on the other hand, what superabundant happiness, the peace so often tendered, will bring along with it.
He tames the wild and savage hearts, and subdues them to
the obedience of God and of Christ; first he strikes them to
the heart with a view of their sins, and with some sense of
divine indignation; upon this he presents them with some
distant hope of obtaining peace; after this, he declares with
greater earnestness the loving kindness of God to the trembling soul; and then excites the greatest longings after the
enjoyment of it, and thus, by little and little, he disposes the inmost powers of the soul, to hate whatever is contrary to God, to
declare war against his enemies, submissively to entreat his
favour, cheerfully to accept of it when actually offered, and
give themselves up, without reserve, to be governed by the

Spirit who procures so great a happiness for them. Thus at
length the man is translated into such a state, that all enmity
being on both sides blotted out, God lays aside the remembrance of past offences, appears no more as an enemy to him,
but being reconciled, deals with him as a friend : the man likewise being grieved for having formerly offended God, now endeavours with all care to please him. And these are the beginnings of the spiritual peace with God.

X. But these are beginnings only : for, no sooner is the man
in covenant with God, but he becomes the confederate and the
friend of that great king, Jam. ii. 23. John xv. 14, 15. The
gates of the heavenly palace are set open to him, and free access
in the Spirit is granted him at all times, by night or by day.
He may behold the king of glory nigh at hand ; pour out all
the oppressing grievances of his soul into his bosom ; confidently make known his stammering requests for a fuller measure
of grace ; while God, instead of forbidding him, does even, by
his condescending goodness, give him encouragement to attempt
it, *Cantic.* i. 14. : he may often be earnest for the same
things, and with a friendly and agreeable importunity wrestle
with God, with reverence of his majesty be it spoken, who
condescends as it were, to solace himself with us, till we have
in a manner forced the blessings we stand in need of, out of
his hands. Moses is an example of this, Exod. xxxiii. 12. and
following verses.

XI. God also himself sometimes descends from heaven by
his grace, and graciously visits the soul whom he loves, and
who is filled with love for him, John xiv. 23. *speaks to his heart,*
Hos. ii. 14. displays the riches of his supereminent goodness,
and " what is the hope of his calling, and what the riches of
the glory of his inheritance in the saints," Eph. i. 18. He com-
forts him when dejected, and *wipes away his tears with his own
hand,* Rev. vii. 17. and puts them as a precious liquor *into his
bottle,* Ps. lvii. 8. " He gives beauty for ashes, the oil of joy
for mourning, the garment of praise for the spirit of heaviness,"
Isa. lxi. 3. " Kisses her with the kisses of his mouth," *Cantic.*
i. 2. and if, at any time, she is sick of love, " his left hand is
under her head, and his right hand doth embrace her," *Cantic.*
ii. 6. In fine, whatever good he is possessed of (and what is
there he is not ?) he liberally communicates all, in that time,
order, and degree, which his wisdom knows to be most expedient. And what will he not give, who gives himself, as *an exceeding great reward ?* Gen. xv. 1.

XII. Who can doubt, but they who taste this incredible
sweetness of divine love, do infinitely prefer the friendship of

God to all other things? Hence when they gratefully acknowledge the things they have been so graciously favoured with
beyond what they deserve, they carefully avoid every thing
unworthy of such friendship, and which mars such a propense
favour of the Deity by any coldness. Whereas they most
readily perform what they know to be acceptable to God; and
then at length it is, they seem to themselves to live, when in
the whole tenour of their lives they approve themselves to
God. And seeing they know that love deserves love, and that
true friendship consists in this, that friends choose and refuse
the same things, they stir up all their powers to make returns
of love, and submit their will to that of God, and give it up to
be swallowed up, as it were, in the divine will, and thus at
length, with the king of angels, they bear the sweet yoke of
love. " The love of God begets the love of the soul, and at-
tracts it to him. God loves, in order to be loved. When he
loves, he desires nothing more, than to be loved again, knowing those to be happy in love who love him. The soul that
loves, renounces all its affections, and minds nothing but love,
that it may give love for love. And when it has poured out
itself wholly in love, what is that to the constant flow of the
fountain? As Augustine piously speaks, Manual. c. 20.

XIII. During these transactions in the soul, and while the
daily contest of mutual friendship between it and God is renewed, it cannot but enjoy the most delightful *peace of conscience*. When it discovers the favourable sentence of God concerning the man, and intimates the same to him, and at the
same time bears testimony to his unfeigned piety towards God,
it spreads a surprising serenity and calm over the whole soul.
Consequently the peace of God necessarily brings with it peace
of conscience, and much confidence in God, Rom. xiv. 7. Eph.
iii. 12. The soul no where reposes itself more comfortably,
than in that bed of tranquillity, and in the bosom of Jesus, its
lovely spouse, singing at that time to its adversaries; " know
that the Lord hath set apart him that is godly for himself. I
will both lay me down in peace and sleep; for thou, Lord, only
makest me dwell in safety," Psal. iv. 3, 8. " I laid me down
and slept, I awaked for the Lord sustained me," Psal. iii. 5.

XIV. There is also *a friendship with all* the other *friends
of God*, not only *holy men*, who mutually help and comfort one
another by communion of prayers and other duties of brotherly
love, Psal. xvi. 3. and who without envy, mutually congratulate
each other on the gifts conferred on every one in particular, by
their common friend; but also with *the blessed angels*, who
were formerly enemies to man, when he was the enemy of God,

and kept our first parents from all access to paradise, Gen. iii.
24.; but now minister to man with the greatest complacency
and readiness, Heb. i. 14. " encamp round about him," Psal.
xxxiv. 9. " keep him in all his ways, bear him up in their hands,
lest he dash his foot against a stone," Psal. xci. 11, 12. till, at
the command of God, they convey the reconciled soul to the
blessed choir of the inhabitants of heaven.   And though at present they do not usually appear in a visible form, yet they familiarly surround and guard the friends of God, avert very many
evils, procure good, and acknowledge them for their fellow servants, Rev. xix. 10.   On this account the apostle testifies, that
believers, even in this world, *are come to myriads [an innumerable company] of angels*, Heb. xii. 22.   And can mortals have
any thing more glorious, than next to God, to be admitted into
the bonds of fellowship and friendship, with these most noble
spirits, whom the apostle, Col. i. 16. calls *thrones, dominions,
principalities, and powers.*

XV. I add, that peace being made with God, none of the
creatures can exercise any acts of hostility against believers,
to the prejudice of their salvation.   According to the promise, Job v. 23, 24. " thou shalt be in league with the stones
of the field: and the beasts of the field shall be at peace with
thee.   And thou shalt know that thy tabernacle shall be in
peace:" which is repeated Hos. ii. 18. " and in that day will
I make a covenant for them with the beasts of the field, and
with the fowls of heaven, and with the creeping things of the
ground."   The plain meaning of these passages seems to be
this: rocks and stones shall be soft to the friends of God, they
shall not hurt their feet: they shall not be molested by any
rocky dismal places, where either robbers usually lie in wait,
or in which the beasts of the field harboured.   For, God so
restrains them, that they are not able to hurt them: but are
compelled to submit and be subservient to them: the raven-
ous fowls themselves and poisonous reptiles, and they who
are emblematically represented by these, as well men as malignant spirits, shall have no power to do them harm, Psal.
xci. 13. Mark xvi. 18.   It is true, they cannot have any amicable peace with the enemies of God, the world, and the devil; and it is certain, that they are then most grievously
harassed by their persecutions, when they cultivate peace with
God: nevertheless, all the attempts of hell and the world
against them are in vain: " Behold, all they that were incens-
ed against thee, shall be ashamed and confounded; they shall
be as nothing, and they that strive with thee shall perish: thou shalt seek them, and shalt not find them, even them
that contended with thee: they that war against thee shall

be as nothing, and as a thing of nought," Isa. xiv. 11, 12. Add Isa. liv. 14—17.

XVI. And the efforts of their enemies are not only in vain, but without their knowledge, and against their will, they promote their salvation: and the devils are constrained to bring the friends of God nearer to heaven, from which they themselves shall be for ever banished. Thus the chief master of pride proved, by his buffetings, a teacher of humility to Paul, 2 Cor. xii. 7. So true it is, that all things work together for good to them that love God, Rom. viii. 28.

XVII. Abundance of all salutary good things flow from this peace which the Psalmist, Psal. cxliv. 13. describes to the life. And though it often happens, that the friends of God, as to the outward man, drag a life which scarce deserves that name, amidst poverty, contempt, and diseases; yet since the least good thing they enjoy in all these calamities, is bestowed upon them by the special love of God, is the most noble fruit of the cross of Christ, and gives them to taste the infinite goodness of the Deity. Therefore " that little that a righteous man hath, is better than the riches of many wicked," Psal. xxxvii. 16. For, he has it from, and with the favour of God, who is the inexhausted fountain of all desirable things. Nay, the very evils with which they are overwhelmed turn to their advantage, for they serve to humble them, to build them up in faith, patience, and self-denial, and wean them from the vanities of the world, and carry them towards heaven. Hence in their very adversities they find matter of joy and glorying, Rom. v. 3. Jam. i. 2.

XVIII. From what we have said, the excellency of this peace is easily concluded, which the apostle, Phil. iv. 7. describes, *as passing all understanding:* it is therefore worthy to be sought after with the utmost diligence; kept when obtained, and renewed when interrupted.

XIX. God, indeed, graciously tenders it in the word of the gospel: but not as if the sinner is to do nothing, before he enjoys the inward sense of it. For this purpose it is necessary, 1st. That he confess, that, on account of his very many and very heinous offences, he is altogether unworthy of the peace and friendship of God, and seriously grieve for them, Luke xv. 21. Psal. xxxii. 5, 6. Prov. xxviii. 13. 2dly. With sorrow observe and declare, that he can do nothing that is fit to appease the justly provoked Deity, Mic. vi. 6, 7. but put all his hopes in the blood of Christ alone, the application of which depends on the good pleasure of the Lord himself. 3dly. Give himself up humbly to God, thus thinking with

himself, " Since without peace with God there is nothing but
ruin, I will approach to the throne of grace, humbly begging
for pardon and mercy ; if he is pleased to reach out his golden
sceptre of grace to me, I will eternally praise him; but if in
anger he turns away his face, I will confess his justice and
proclaim it worthy of all praise, though it should be rigid
to my destruction; and say, I will die at his feet without
repining :" See Esther iv. 16.   This absolute resignation and
surrender, cannot but be acceptable to God, and salutary to
man.   That he add, to his devout prayers, reformation of life ;
sincerely keep his heart and actions from what he knows to
be contrary to God ; declare war against God's enemies ; will,
love, and do what becomes the friends of God.   In this way,
let him " draw nigh to God, and God will draw nigh to him,"
Jam. iv. 8.

XX. No less diligent care is necessary to preserve the
peace thus obtained, and daily to increase in intimacy with
the divine favour and friendship.   For this, there is required
1st. A daily exciting of his love to God by devout meditation, both on the divine perfections, on account of which
he is most highly amiable in himself, and on his infinite
love, wherewith he first loved us, and the inestimable benefits flowing from that infinite love.   For God cannot possibly suffer himself to be exceeded in love by
man, John xiv. 21. " he that loveth me, shall be loved of my
Father, and I will love him, and will manifest myself to him."
2dly. Frequent intercourse with God ; so that worldly cares
being for a little laid aside, and a pleasant retirement
sought out, you may by frequent and repeated exercises of
reading, meditation, and prayer, with a modest boldness, obtain familiarity with God, Job xxii. 21. " acquaint now thyself with him, and be at peace, thereby good shall come unto
thee."   It was a fine advice of Jerome to Eustachius, de custo-
dia virginitatis : " Let the privacy of thy chamber always
keep thee : let thy bridegroom always delight himself within
thee : when thou prayest thou speakest to thy bridegroom,
when thou readest, he speaketh to thee : let foolish virgins
wander abroad ; be thou within with thy bridegroom, because,
if thou shuttest thy door, and according to the precept of the
gospel, prayest to thy Father in secret, he will come, and
knock, and say, Behold, I stand at the door and knock." 3dly.
The practice of inoffensive and strict godliness, with an attentive watchfulness against " the sins that so easily beset us."
These things flow from the love of God, and without them
none can have familiar converse with him, John xiv. 23. " if
a man love me, he will keep my words, and my Father will

love him, and we will come unto him, and make our abode with him." The exercise of Christian virtues, or graces, is, that chain of the spouse, with which the heart of the Lord is ravished, Cant. iv. 9. " The work of righteousness shall be peace, and the effect of righteousness, quietness and assurance for ever," Isa. xxxii. 7. compare Isa. lxiv. 5. 4thly. Because in this imperfect state of our sanctification, it cannot altogether be avoided, but at times the godly may fall, and turn a little either to the right hand, or to the left: they are in that case, presently to rise from their fall, and return to their God, unless they would greatly impair their familiarity with him. When he calls us, " return, ye backsliding children, and I will heal your backslidings;" we are directly to answer, " behold, we come unto thee, for thou art the Lord our God," Jer. iii. 22. 5thly. It also contributes very much to preserve the sense of the divine friendship, if in all things you commit yourself to the conduct of his providence, always approving his will towards thee, to be just, holy, wise, and good ; and saying with Job xxxiv. 12. " yea surely, God will not do wickedly :" In whatever befalls thee, give him thanks; and denying all thy own desires, give up thy will to be swallowed up in his. " Be careful for nothing—and the peace of God, which passeth all understanding, shall keep your hearts and minds through Christ Jesus," Phil. iv. 6, 7.

XXI. Although it is not possible, that any who is admitted into peace and friendship with God, should altogether fall from it, (for the covenant of divine peace, which stands firmer than the mountains and hills, shall never be removed, Isa. liv. 10.) yet the sense and relish thereof are often interrupted. For, 1st, God doth not always shew his pleasant countenance to his friends; sometimes *he hides himself*, Isa. viii. 17. *standeth afar off*, Psal. x. 1. admits them not into familiarity with him, nor fills them with the abundance of his consolations; he hears not when they call, Psal. xxii. 2, 3. as if he regarded them not. 2dly. Nay, he thrusts them from him with a kind of contempt, as if a father had disdainfully spit in the face of his daughter, Num. xii. 14. and is angry against their prayer, Psal. lxxx. 4. 3dly. He terrifies them with many sorrows; not only by hiding his face, without which there is no joy, Psal. xxx. 7. but " by his fierce anger going over them," Psal. lxxxviii. 16, 17, 18. Isa. lvii. 17. 4thly. He seems to deal with them as an adversary, and holdeth them for his enemies, and pursues them, though become like the dry stubble, " writes bitter things against them, putteth their feet in the stocks, and setteth a print upon the heels of their

feet," Job xiii. 24, 26, 27. 5thly. Gives them up sometimes
to be vexed and buffeted by the devil, Job ii. 6. After that
the light of the divine countenance is set, immediately the
beasts of the forest come forth against the soul, " the young
lions roaring after their prey," Psal. cxiv. 20, 21.

XXII. The reasons of this conduct of God towards his
friends are various: some respect God; others the friends of
God. God thus deals with his people, 1st. In order to shew
that he is the Sovereign Lord, and most free dispenser of his
own grace, Mat. xx. 15. Thus himself owns that he afflicted
Job ii. 3. without cause. Not that Job had done nothing to
deserve these, or even greater afflictions; but that God had
found nothing in him, for which to treat him with greater severity than his other friends. This was an act of mere sovereignty,
" that the works of God should be made manifest in him," as
is said in a similar case, John ix. 3. 2dly. Likewise, to shew
the difference between heaven and earth. For here he will
have all things subject to various vicissitudes, and accustom
his people to the alternate changes of a rough winter and an
agreeable spring; because in heaven they are to exult in a constant uninterrupted joy in his friendship and love, Rev. vii.
17. 3dly. That he may the more endear unto them the sweetness of his grace, which, when tasted at intervals, especially
after a draught of a cup of bitterness, must be most delicious to
the pious soul. 4thly. That he may give a demonstration of
the exceeding greatness of his power and goodness, when he
preserves the soul in its spiritual life, though oppressed with
so many sorrows, restores him to his former vigour, makes him
triumph over Satan, and gives him the more abundant comfort, the more distant he was from all the sense of his favour.
" This is to shew wonders to the dead," Psal. lxxxviii. 10. and
to revive the wounded spirit, which Solomon, Prov. xviii. 14.
declares, exceeds any created power.

XXIII. The reasons with respect to the friends of God, are
two fold; for either they regard *the time past,* or *the future.*
As to the time past, God usually restrains the beams of his favour, 1st. When his friends have been guilty of some grievous sin: for, in that case, his holiness is concerned, that they
feel the rod of his paternal displeasure, and not be suffered
to have then familiarity with him, Psal. li. 9, 11, 12. " If
they be bound in fetters, and be holden in cords of affliction:
then he sheweth them their work," Job xxxvi. 8, 9. and
really, as it were calls out to them; " know therefore and see
that it is an evil thing, and bitter, that thou hast forsaken
the Lord thy God," Jer. ii. 19. " When they rebelled and

vexed his holy Spirit, therefore he was turned to be their enemy," Isa. lxiii. 10. 2dly. When abusing the goodness of God, they worship his majesty with less reverence and begin to flag in the exercise of devotion. 3dly. When carnal confidence, and vain glorying have seized upon them, Psal. xxx. 6, 7. " and in my prosperity I said, I shall never be moved: thou didst hide thy face, and I was troubled." 4thly. When the offer of divine grace is unworthily entertained through a kind of indolence and drowsiness, Song v. 3, 4, 5.

XXIV. The following reasons refer to the time to come. 1st. That God may try and exercise their faith, 1 Pet. i. 6, 7. which ought to be in exercise, even when nothing is to be seen; and their love, by which they are bound to love God for himself, though they are not sensible, that they themselves are loved: and the sincerity of their worship, which is not to proceed from a mere relish of the reward, but from an acknowledgment of the divine dignity or authority; and the constancy of their religion, by which they must keep close to God, even when he appears as a stranger to them. 2dly. That he may stir them up to the practice of prayer, in which Heman was fervent at such a time, Psal. lxxxviii. 1. " O Lord God of my salvation, I have cried day and night before thee;" see also verses 9 and 13. 3dly. That he may instruct and bring his people to true wisdom: for this distress gives excellent understanding; " tribulation worketh patience, and patience experience," Rom. v. 3. 4. Heman was early introduced into this school, and such hard exercises were put upon him, that he was almost distracted: yet at length he made so great a proficiency, as to be reckoned among the wisest in his day, 1 Kings iv. 31. 4thly. That they may, for the future, more carefully preserve the divine favour when they have once recovered it. When the spouse at last found her beloved, who had withdrawn himself, " she held him, *kept him fast*, and would not let him go, until she had brought him into her mother's house, into the chamber of her that conceived her," Cant. iii. 4.

XXV. But what course is the soul now to take, in order to renew the interrupted friendship of God? For we are not to think, that God will be angry with his people for ever. " I will not contend for ever, neither will I be always wroth: for the spirit should fail before me, and the souls which I have made," says the Lord, Isa. lvii. 16. see Isa. liv. 8. And 1st. We are, in order to this, carefully to enquire into the cause of this estrangement, that it may be removed: for

generally we have provoked God, to deal thus with us, either
by some sin, or by our carelessness, Lament. iii. 40. " let us
search and try our ways, and turn again to the Lord."   And
should it be, that a person cannot find out the cause of that
estrangement (which is rarely the case with the serious and
careful enquirer), he is then to consult the word of God,
and by repeated prayer, say, " do not condemn me : shew me
wherefore thou contendest with me," Job x. 2. 2dly. He is
to renew his faith and repentance ; promise God as by a
solemn oath, that he will, for the future, improve his grace
to better purpose, and keep it with greater care, if he may
again enjoy it.   Nay he is to protest, and that sincerely, that
he will serve God, because God is worthy to be served, and
because it is his glory to serve him though he should never
again, which God forbid, taste the sweetness of divine favour.
Nothing can be done by man, more acceptable to God. 3dly.
He is to be instant in continual prayer, pleading with the
greatest earnestness possible, that he may not be cast away
from his presence, but that he would have mercy upon him,
according to his loving kindness, and restore again the joy of
his salvation, Psal. li. 1, 11, 12.   The Holy Spirit himself has
dictated forms of prayer, Psal. lxxxviii. and cii. 4thly. He is
patiently to wait for the hour, in which God may be pleased
to receive him into favour, not omitting his duty to God
in the mean time, Lament. iii. 26. " it is good, that a man
should both hope and quietly wait for the salvation of the
Lord."

XXVI. To him who acts in this manner, will come, at
length will come, the blessed day, when God will change the
bitter water of tears into the most delightful wine of consolation ; receive and entertain his friend with the greater familiarity, the longer and the more mournfully he had been deprived of the delightful sense of his love, and abundantly repay all
with interest.   Believers have generally experienced this : whose
triumphant songs we remember to have read and heard, no less
than their mournful complaints.   And it scarce ever happens
otherwise : but should there be no appearance of being restored
on earth, to the sweet sense of divine love, all however is re-
served to be fully bestowed upon them in heaven.   The abundance of which, the former dry and parched state will render,
beyond what can be either expressed or conceived, extremely
sweet and delightful.

XXVII. From what has been said it is evident, this spiritual peace differs very much from *carnal security*.   For, 1st.
The latter arises from mere ignorance of one's own state, into

which he never made any serious enquiry, or in forming a judgment about it, he deceived himself by false reasoning. But the former rests upon a sure foundation, and is preceded by sorrow for sin, a sense of misery, a hunger and thirst after grace, diligent self-examination, and a sense of his union with Christ. 2dly. The latter makes a man well pleased with, and to have an inward joy on account of that imaginary good, though in other respects he neglects God; whereas the former ravishes the soul with admiration of the divine goodness, and makes him confess himself unworthy of so great an honour and favour. 3dly. By the latter men are swallowed up in pleasure, are dull and heavy in that which is good, and unhappily give themselves up to an irregular life, thinking " they shall have peace though they walk in the imagination of their heart," Deut. xxix. 19. But the former keeps the heart in safety, Phil. iv. 7. that they may be in the fear of God continually; and this is what neither can be obtained, nor preserved without a strict exercise of godliness. 4thly. Though the latter falsely imagines, that he is the object of God's love, yet he himself is destitute of all love to God. But the former consists in mutual friendship. The same Abraham, who Jam. ii. 23. is called the *friend*, is Isa. xli. 8. called *the lover* of God.

XXVIII. As spiritual peace is the consequence of justification, it was a blessing of the Old, as well as it is of the New Testament, as we shall shew in its proper place, and consequently the ancient fathers were also partakers of it; who by an unfeigned faith, believed that they were reconciled to God, on account of the Surety, the Messiah, that the enmity caused by sin was removed; they had a most delightful and experimental sense of this, and often gloried in the Lord. We indeed cannot deny, that peace was eminently promised to the New Testament-church, Psal. lxxii. 3. Isa. ix. 5, 6. Hag. ii. 10. Zech. ix. 10. But we are not to understand this of peace and friendship with God absolutely, which is a benefit of the covenant of grace, and not of the New Testament alone: But, 1st. Of the more abundant sense of the divine favour, with respect to believers in general. 2dly. Of the agreement between the believing Israelites with the Gentiles, " having abolished in his flesh the enmity, even the law of commandments contained in ordinances," Eph. ii. 15. 3dly. Of the peace of God granted likewise to the Gentiles. This is expressly mentioned Zech. ix. 10.

CHAP. X.

Of Adoption.

I. WHOM God has admitted into a state of peace and friendship with himself, *he has* also *adopted* for his sons; that they
may enjoy the benefits both of grace and glory, not only by
the favour of friendship, but also by a right of inheritance.
There is no friendship more familiar than that between a father
and his children. Or rather that natural affection between
these exceeds in familiarity and sweetness, every thing that can
be signified by the name of friendship. There is not any one
word, any one similitude, borrowed from human affairs, that
can sufficiently express or represent this most happy band of
love; which can hardly be explained by a great number of
metaphors heaped together. To express tranquillity of conscience, the scripture calls it *peace:* to shew us the pleasantness of
familiarity, it calls it *friendship:* and when it illustrates a right
to the inheritance, it speaks of *adoption;* which is to be the
subject of this chapter.

II. We assert that believers are the sons of God. The apostle John proclaims it, saying, " behold what manner of love the
Father hath bestowed upon us, that we should be called the sons
of God: beloved, now are we the sons of God," 1 John iii.
1, 2. This is God's covenant with them: " and I will be a
Father unto you, and ye shall be my sons and daughters, saith
the Lord Almighty," 2 Cor. vi. 18.

III. But they are not so, only on this account, that God, as
creator, gave them being and life, Mal. ii. 10. and as *preserver*,
supports and provides them with all necessaries, Acts xvii. 25, 28.

IV. Neither are they called the sons of God, on account of
any *external prerogative* only; whether *political*, as magistrates are called *the children of the Most High*, Psal. lxxxii. 6.
or *ecclesiastical*, in respect of an external federal communion;
according to which some are called *the sons of God*, Gen. vi. 7,
and *the children of the kingdom*, Mat. viii. 12.; in this sense
also the Lord commanded Pharaoh to be told concerning Israel,
Israel is my son, even my first born, Exod. iv. 22. For this
regarded that *national covenant* which God entered into with the
children of Israel, according to which he preserved them above
all other nations, and heaped many blessings upon them, both
of a corporal and spiritual kind, which he did not vouchsafe to
other people, Deut. vii. 6. He called them his sons, because
he managed their concerns with as much solicitous care as any

father could possibly do those of his own children, Deut. xxxii. 10, 11.: Nay, he called them his *first born, not only because* he loved them far better than other people, beyond the measure of common providence, *shewing his word unto Jacob, his statutes and his judgments unto Israel,* Psal. cxlvii. 19. as the first born had a double portion in the paternal inheritance, Deut. xxi. 17.; *but also because* he had apointed them to have a kind of dominion over other people, *let people serve thee, and nations bow down to thee, be Lord over thy brethren,* &c. Gen. xxvii. 29. Though these words were indeed spoken to Jacob, yet they were to be chiefly verified in his posterity: of which we have illustrious evidences in David's time, 2 Sam. viii.

V. But however excellent these things were, yet they are very far below that dignity for which believers are called the sons of God: for most of those, who were called by the name of *Israel* and the *first born,* were such, with whom, *God was not well pleased,* and never were promoted to the inheritance of the land of Canaan, much less the heavenly inheritance, but *were overthrown in the wilderness,* 1 Cor. x. 5. That very people to whom Moses said, " is not Jehovah thy Father, hath he not magnified [established] thee?" are in the same breath called *a foolish people and unwise,* Deut. xxxii. 6. Nay, they are of " the children of the kingdom, who shall be cast out into utter darkness," Mat. viii. 12. For that national covenant, without any thing else, did not bestow saving grace, nor a right to possess the heavenly inheritance.

VI. *The elect and believers* are therefore in a far more eminent sense, *the sons of God:* wherein John observed a love never enough to be commended, 1 John iii. 1. Angels indeed, have the glorious appellation of sons of God, Job xxxviii. 7. with which the Lord honours them, not only because he formed them, but also because he imprinted upon them the image and resemblance of his own holiness, Job iv. 18. and because, as children of the family, they familiarly converse with God in his house, which is heaven, Job i. 6.: in fine, because something of the dignity and authority of God is vouchsafed unto them, as we have just said that magistrates are also called *the children of the Most High.* These are *thrones, dominions, principalities, powers,* Col. i. 16.: nay they are also called *Gods,* Psal. xcvii. 7. compared with Heb. i. 6.

VII. In almost the same sense, Adam seems also to be called *the son of God,* Luke iii. 38. for seeing that name which has the article אֵת set before it, denotes father in all the foregoing verses, as *the Syriac* in place of אֵת always puts בֵּן ; no reason can be assigned why here, altering the phrase, we should translate with Beza, *who was of God;* in which he has followed the Syriac, who translated it *who is of God.* For no doubt can be made, that Adam may be fitly called the son of God, the reasons of which Philo elegantly explains in the passage adduced by the illustrious Grotius on Luke iii. 38.; in the manner Josephus has also written, that men *were born of God himself:* namely, 1. God created Adam. 2. In his own image. 3. Eminently loved him. 4. Gave him dominion over the creatures. For these reasons he is deservedly called the son of God, though God had not yet declared him heir of his peculiar blessings. Nor does he seem without reason, to mention Adam as the son of God. For, this tends, as Grotius has learnedly observed, to raise our mind, by this scale, to the belief of the birth of Christ. For he, who from the earth, without a father, could produce man, was able in like manner to make Christ to be born of a virgin without a father.

VIII. But Adam did not long maintain that dignity, on account of which he was called the son of Gnd; for neglecting holiness, and losing that excellency in which he was created, and suffering himself to be overcome by the devil, he became *the servant* of Satan by whom he was foiled, 2 Pet. ii. 19.; and at the same time, *a child of wrath,* Eph. ii. 3. together with all his posterity. But what the elect have lost in Adam, they recover in Christ; namely, the same, nay a far more excellent degree, or rank among the children. For let the disparity between Christ and believers be ever so great, *yet he is not ashamed to call them brethren,* Heb. ii. 11.

IX. But the elect obtain this degree of children of God several ways. *First,* They become the sons of God by a new and spiritual generation, descending from above: John speaks of this chap. i. 12, 13. " But as many as received him, to them gave he power to become the sons of God, even to them that believe on his name; which were born, not of blood, nor of the will of the flesh, nor of the will of man, but of God." This illustrious passage, which is variously explained by interpreters, requires some particular consideration.

X. The apostle describes this generation, or birth, whereby the elect become the sons of God, both *negatively* and *positively:* he denies it to be *of blood,* that is, natural or ordinary, like that, whereby the children come to be partakers of flesh and blood, Heb. ii. 14. and which is judged to be of blood: neither is it *of the will of the flesh,* that is, from any carnal desire of having children by any means; hence it is, that one, by giving too much indulgence to the corrupt reasoning of the flesh, makes use of means for that end, which God never prescribed:

something like this we may observe in Sarah, when from a desire of having children she gave Hagar to Abraham : nor in fine
is it *of the will of man*, who, for certain reasons of his own,
loves one above others, and so appoints him to the principal
part of the inheritance : just as this was the will of Isaac with
respect to Esau.   Nothing human can give being to this spiritual generation, which is only of God, who decreed it from eternity, and actually regenerates at the appointed time.

XI. To those, who are thus born of God, he *gave power to
become the sons of God*. Εξυςία here denotes *right* and *power*,
Rev. xxii. 14. *that they may have* εξυσία *right to the tree of life*.
But it may seem strange, how they who are born of God, may
have a right to become the sons of God ; seeing, by their very
nativity from God, they are already become his children.   To
remove this difficulty, three things chiefly have been observed by
very learned men : 1st. As γενεςθαι, *to become*, is the second Aor-
ist, it may fitly be taken for the preterperfect ; to this effect,
he gave them that power, that right, that dignity, that they
might become the sons of God, and enjoy the privileges which
are suitable to that condition.   2dly. Γινεςθαι τοιϋτον denotes in
scripture phrase, *to be such a one*, or *to behave*, as becomes
such a one.   Thus it is used, Mat. v. 45. οπως γενηςθε υιοι τυ πατρος
υμω, *that ye may be the children of your Father*, that you
may behave yourselves, as becomes the children of God, see
1 Thess. ii. 7, 10.   3dly. It might also be referred to that perfect filial state, which shall be conjoined with *the redemption
of our body*, and which the apostle, Rom. viii. 23. enjoins
us to *wait for :* and so the meaning may be, that God has
granted those who are born of him, a right to the heavenly inheritance, and that unparalleled honour, by which, both in soul
and body, they shall rejoice, as children of the family, in the
palace of their Father : in such a manner, that it shall not be
in the power of any creature to strip, diminish, or cut them off
from that dignity.   The reader may choose which expositions
he has a mind.   We are not a little pleased with the last ; but
wherein this new birth consists, we have explained at large,
Chap. VI. of this book.

XII. And this is the first foundation of that glorious state.
Secondly, We become the children of God by *marriage* with the
Lord Jesus ; for when we become his spouse, then we pass with
him into his Father's family, and the Father calls us by the endearing name of *daughter*, Psal. xlv. 10.: and the Lord Jesus
calls her also his *sister*, whom he names his *spouse*, Cantic. v. 1,
2.   God had provided by his law, that if " a man betroth his
maid-servant unto his son, he shall deal with her after the manner

of daughters," Exod. xxi. 9.: in the same manner, he is pleased to deal with elect souls. By nature, they were as maid-servants to sin and Satan; lay exposed in the open field, and were a loth-ing to all. However, he graciously offers them a marriage with his only begotten Son: they, by faith accept the proposal, almost in the same manner that Abigail did, when she was invited to marry David, 1 Sam. xxv. 41. And thus, by the same act, by which they become "the spouse of Christ, *they also become* the daughters of the living God," 2 Cor. vi. 18.

XIII. *Thirdly*, By adoption, which is "an economical act of God, whereby they who are regenerated after his image, and be-trothed by faith to his only begotten Son, are received into his family, and obtain the right and privileges of children, and the in-heritance itself, by an immutable testament. They are of the household of God," Eph. ii. 19.; *if children then heirs*, Rom. viii. 17.; for the communication of the image of God alone does not give a right to the heavenly inheritance. This appears with respect to Adam in his state of innocence, who, indeed, was in the way of acquiring a right; but had not yet obtained it. The alone foundation of that right is the perfect and constant obedi-ence, either of man himself, or of his Surety. Christ therefore having appeared for us, fulfilled all righteousness, and *was ap-pointed heir of all things*, Heb. i. 2. The elect being regener-ated receive, and claim to themselves, by faith, Christ and all his benefits, even his perfect righteousness: and being thus adopted by the Father, and become the brethren of Christ, *they are heirs of God, and joint heirs with Christ*, Rom. viii. 17. And in this sense principally we think John speaks, " to them which are born of God, he gave power to become the sons of God," as explained above, § XI.

XIV. For the better understanding what has been said, we are now to observe, that the Spirit of God, in order to explain these mysteries, uses metaphors, borrowed from human things. But these metaphors are to be so adjusted, as one may not destroy but rather supply the defects of the other. It would seem, in other respects absurd, that the soul, which *is born* of God, *should be adopted* for a daughter, and *joined in marriage* to the only begotten *Son* of God. Yet the scripture has wisely ordered matters, when it declares all these things concerning believers. In order to express the original of spiritual life, and of the image of God in man, it says, that he was *born* of God: to set forth our most delightful union with Christ, which is full of mutual affection, it calls it *marriage:* and to shew the ground and firm-ness of our inheritance, it declares that we are *adopted* in Christ.

And it is on account of each of these things, that we may be called the children of God.

XV. And this *adoption* is a most precious blessing of the covenant of grace. But it was very different, according to the different economies, or dispensations of that covenant. It is however, not to be doubted, that believers, at all times, were the children of God. Elihu, who was not of the people of Israel, called God *his Father*, * Job xxxiv. 36. To understand this in that diminutive sense, in which the heathen called Jupiter the father of gods and men, is not suitable to the illustrious faith and piety of a man who was commended by God himself. A celebrated expositor has said well on this place: " God is called Father, as Mal. i. 6. a ' son honoureth his father, and a servant his master: if then I be a Father, where is mine honour?' And Isa. lxiv. 8. ' but now, O Lord, thou art our Father.' By this appellation he sets forth the affection of God in this respect, namely, his paternal care; his own affection in requesting his brotherly love; the end of the trial, and a filial reverence and confidence."

XVI. All we have thus far said of the grounds of this glorious state, is even applicable to the Old Testament believers. They had likewise a new life by *regeneration,* and were created again after the image of God: they were, in like manner, *betrothed* to Christ, Hos. ii. 19, 20. " their maker was their husband," Isa. liv. 5. And ver. 1. the church of the Old Testament is expressly said to be *married:* nor were they without their " adoption; who are Israelites, to whom pertaineth the adoption," Rom. ix. 4. And to conclude, *were heirs of all,* Gal. iv. 1. heirs of *the grace* of God in *this* life, Psal. xvi. 5. and of *the glory* of God in the life *eternal,* Psal. xvii. 15.

XVII. Though the condition of believers under the Old Testament was very illustrious, if compared with that of unbelievers, who continue children of wrath, and heirs of the treasures of divine indignation; yet all that splendor, comparatively speaking, was eclipsed to an almost incredible degree, before the august majesty of believers under the New Testament, as the light of the stars before that of the sun: as will appear by comparing them together.

XVIII. Believers under the Old Testament were indeed sons; but sons who were subject to their Father, and to the severity and discipline of tutors, who bound heavy burdens, and grie-

---

* In our version it is *my desire is that Job may be tried:* but our marginal reading is, *my father, let Job be tried;* for some observe, that the same Hebrew word signifies both *my desire* and *my father.*

vous to be born, and laid them on their shoulders; nevertheless, their Father said with respect to these tutors; " all whatsoever they bid you observe, that observe and do, Mat. xxiii. 3, 4. Namely, as long as they commanded nothing that was contrary to, or inconsistent with the will of the Father. They were obliged to be subject to the weak and beggarly elements of the world, and like children, to be engaged all the day in the trifling ceremonies of the Mosaic institution, which were, in a manner, the play-things of the church. They were taught like infants, without being left to their own choice, not knowing how to conduct themselves, or what was fit for them, *touch not, taste not*, Col. ii. 21.

XIX. Besides, they were not admitted to that familiarity with their Father, as to penetrate into the mysteries of his will. " The mighty God did then hide himself," Isa. xlv. 15. their tutors indeed, at times acquainted them with some things relating to God's purpose of grace, but that only rarely, and in mysterious expressions, and under enigmatical or parabolical representations. And though many prophets and righteous men desired to see and hear many things, yet they were not gratified, Mat. xiii. 17.

XX. None of them was allowed to approach the Holy of holies, which was, as it were, the secret place of their Father: nay, they had not access to the temple itself, which was the Father's house, but by means of the altar, sacrifices, and priests, without which, if they took upon them to approach to God, instead of a blessing, which they sought after, they incurred their Father's displeasure. Neither was it lawful for them to omit the constant morning and evening sacrifice, Exod. xxvi. 28, 42.

XXI. Their inheritance was the land of Canaan, a pledge indeed of the heavenly inheritance, but somewhat obscure, and such, as they were commanded to be, in some measure, subjected to, and which the godly themselves, were sometimes obliged to be destitute of, when forced into banishment. However they were to have such a tender regard to this land, that when banished from their dear country, they were in their prayers to turn their faces thitherward, nor were they to pay their vows to heaven, without directing their eyes to that country, 1 Kings viii. 48. Dan. vi. 11. In all this, there was a notable subjection to this pledge.

XXII. The case of believers under the New Testament is quite different. For after our elder brother, having taken upon him human nature, had visited this lower world, and freely undergone a state of various servitude for us, he brought us into true liberty, John viii. 36. removed the tutors, blotted out the hand-writing of ordinances, which was contrary to us, declared us to be dead with himself, set free from the elements of the world, so as they never after should have any dominion over us, Col. ii. 16, 20. He would no longer have us subject to these minute observances, but called us to a reasonable service, Rom. xii. 1. and having broken and removed that troublesome yoke, which was laid on the jaws of the ancients, Hos. xi. 4. laid his own upon us, which is easy and light, Mat. xi. 30.

XXIII. He introduced us into the Father's secret counsels, and sucking the breasts of our mother, taught us the things he so much desired the spouse should be taught, Cant. viii. 2. declared to us what he had seen in the bosom of the Father, nay, and even the Father himself, John i. 18. and in himself presented the Father to our view, so that we have no longer any occasion to say, *shew us the Father*, John xiv. 9. He brought along with him those times of which Jeremiah prophesied, chap. xxxi. 34. He abundantly poured out upon us " the unction from the Holy One which teacheth all things," 1 John ii. 20, 27. In a word, he does not now account us as servants ; " for the servant knoweth not what his Lord doeth ; but he hath called us friends : for all things that he hath heard of his Father, he hath made known unto us," John xv. 15.

XXIV. He hath also obtained for us a free access to the Father, " having consecrated for us a new and living way, in which we may walk in full assurance of faith," Heb. x. 20, 22. By his death the vail of the inmost sanctuary was rent, and all believers are made a royal priesthood, 1 Pet. ii. 9. none is excluded the holy of holies ; and though the Father still sits on a throne of majesty, yet it is at the same time a throne of grace, to which we are invited to approach with boldness, Heb. iv. 6. without sacrifice, without priests, trusting only on the alone offering of Jesus our High Priest, " whereby he hath for ever perfected them that are sanctified," Heb. x. 14. and this is " that better hope, by the which we draw nigh unto God," Heb. vii. 19.

XXV. Nor hath he burdened us with any subjection to a typical inheritance ; but hath called us directly to an inheritance of spiritual and heavenly good things, and " appointed unto us a kingdom, as his Father hath appointed unto him." Luke xxii. 29. There is now no corner of the earth, which we should desire, as more holy and more acceptable to God, than another ; for, " the earth is the Lord's, and the fulness thereof,"

Psal. xxiv. 1. Nor does he disdain an altar in the midst of Egypt, Isa. xix. 19. And thus " he hath made *us* partakers of a better covenant, which was established upon better promises," Heb. viii. 6.

XXVI. On account of those excellent prerogatives, believers under the New Testament are eminently and emphatically called *the sons of God*, 1 John iii. 2. *beloved, now are we the sons of God*, namely, by a much better right and title than before. To this the apostle has undoubtedly an eye, Gal. iv. 4, 5, 6, 7. *but when the fulness of the time was come;* namely, *that appointed time*, (till which the children were to be under tutors, ver. 2.) *God sent forth his Son to redeem them that were under the law*, setting them free from the infantile use of ceremonies, *and that we might receive the adoption*, not only that adoption whereby we are distinguished from the children of the devil and of wrath, but also that whereby we excel infants, not much differing from servants: " wherefore thou art no more a servant, *as formerly*, but a son." That this is Paul's meaning, the whole connection of the discourse and the scope of the writer evince. For the whole tends to shew, that believers under the New Testament are set free from, nor ought they any longer to be oppressed with, the yoke of the old servitude, which the false judaizing teachers, with the utmost endeavours, struggled to lay on their necks.

XXVII. Certainly the condition of the sons of God is most excellent. If David put such a value on being called the son-in-law of such a king as Saul, 1 Sam. xviii. 23. how highly should we esteem it to be called the sons of the living God? 1st. How unparalleled is that *royalty*, by which we derive the origin of our pedigree, not from any earthly prince or monarch, but from the king of heaven? 2dly. What can be more glorious than that *divine nature*, we obtain by a new generation? 2 Pet. i. 4. God himself glories in his sons, as his peculiar property : nay, calls them *the first fruits of his increase*, Jer. ii. 3. who may be to him *in praise, and in name, and in honour*, Deut. xxvi. 19. Almost as parents who glory before others in those of their children, who are remarkable for their beauty. 3dly. What even can be more desirable than that *marriage*-relation to the only begotten Son of God, than which thought itself can conceive nothing more honourable, more advantageous, and in a word, more glorious? He is *white and ruddy, the chiefest* (standard-bearer) *among ten thousand*, Cant. v. 10. When David, though not yet come to the crown, sent his men to Abigail, to procure her in marriage, that prudent widow " bowed herself on her face to the earth, and said, behold, let thine hand-maid be a servant to wash the feet of the servants of my Lord," 1 Sam. xxv. 41. And what may our soul say, whenever it reflects that, having broke off the former marriage with Nabal, which was not a state of marriage, but of adultery, it is joined to the heavenly David in a marriage covenant that cannot be broken ? 4thly. and lastly, Nothing can be more excellent than that *inheritance*, which in right of adoption, the sons of God obtain, and which is bequeathed to them by an irrevocable testament.

XXVIII. It will not be unprofitable to insist a little on this point, and having opened the *testament* of our Father, to enquire *what* and *how considerable the goods*, and under what *stipulations* he bequeathed them to us. By the *testament* we mean, " the last and immutable will of God, recorded in the writings of the holy scripture, and ratified by the death and blood of Jesus, whereby he hath declared his chosen and believing people to be his heirs of the whole inheritance." I say the testament is *the will* of God, or *that counsel of his will*, Eph. i. 11. by which he has appointed both the heirs and the inheritance, and of which our Saviour was speaking, Luke xii. 32. ευδοκησεν ο πατηρ, *it is your Father's good pleasure to give you the kingdom :* I add, *it is the last and irrevocable will* of the Father ; for as this is required to a valid testament, Gal. iii. 15. so it is not deficient in this respect : " wherein God willing more abundantly to shew unto the heirs of promise the immutability of his counsel, confirmed it by an oath : that by two immutable things, in which it was impossible for God to lie, we might have a strong consolation," Heb. vi. 17, 18. By this his will, he appointed or settled both *the inheritance as well of grace as of glory*, of which we shall speak just now ; and also *the heirs*, not indefinitely, whosoever believes ; but by name, this and the other persons, *whose names are written in heaven*, Luke x. 20. and *graven upon the palms of God's hands*, Isa. xlix. 16. This his will he has expressed in the sacred *writings of both instruments*, which for that reason, are also called a *testament*, 2 Cor. iii. 14. In fine, that nothing might be wanting, the whole is confirmed and *sealed by the blood and death of the Lord Jesus Christ*, Heb. ix. 16, 17. In order to understand this, we must observe, that God the Father did, by testament, give and bequeath that honour to his Son Jesus Christ, to be the head of the elect in glory, and have a right to bestow upon them all his goods. Psal. ii. 8. Jesus again, does by the power made over to him by the

Father, dispose by testament of his goods to be communicated to the elect: " and I διατιδεμαι appoint by testament unto you a kingdom, as my Father hath διεδετο appointed by testament unto me," Luke xxii. 29. So that this making of the testament is, indeed, originally from the Father, yet immediately from Christ the mediator : who died, not to vacate or annul, by his death, the inheritance ; for, *he is alive for evermore*, Rev. i. 18. but to seal the promises, and acquire for his people a right to the inheritance. Hence the blood which he shed, is called *the blood of the testament*, Zech. ix. 11. Mat. xxiv. 28.

XXIX. The goods or blessings bequeathed by this testament, are of all others the most excellent ; as became, 1st. The riches and liberal bounty of our heavenly Father, from whom we may expect so extraordinary goods or blessings, which neither eye hath seen nor ear heard, nor hath entered into the heart of man to conceive any like them, 1 Cor. ii. 9. Concerning this the Psalmist deservedly sings, O how great is thy goodness which thou hast laid up for them that fear thee ; which thou hast wrought for them that trust in thee before the sons of men ! Psal. xxxi. 19. 2dly. The glory of our elder brother, whose *joint-heirs* we are, Rom. viii. 17. and who glories in his heritage, Psal. xvi. 6. 3dly. As became that dignity, to which God hath raised us, having adopted us for his sons ! for to them he gives *great and precious promises*, 2 Pet. i. 4. Did we minutely prosecute these points, we should write a large volume; at present we will reduce the whole to three principal heads.

XXX. *The first is the possession of the whole world :* for it was promised to Abraham and his seed that they should be *heirs of the world*, Rom. iv. 13. On which place let us hear the commentary of Ludovicus de Dieu : " as sin, by separating us from God, and subjecting us to his curse, banished and disinherited us, so that we have no spiritual right or dominion, as became sons of God, over the meanest creature ; so on the other hand, when God becomes our God, and we his blessed people, we are restored as sons, to the right and dominion of all our paternal inheritance ; and seeing there is nothing besides God and the world, we are made heirs of the world, both the earthly, the heavenly, the present, and the world to come." When God introduced Adam into the habitable earth, he constituted him Lord of the world, and gave him a right and claim to use the rest of the creatures for his own advantage, Gen. i. 28. But Adam, by his sin, lost that right ; so that neither himself, nor any

of his posterity, while in a state of sin, have any true and
spiritual right which can stand in the court of heaven, to
touch any creature. But Christ has made a new purchase of
it for himself and his brethren, Psal. viii. 6. Whence 1 Cor.
iii. 21. *all things are yours:* and among these all things, *the
world* is mentioned ver. 22. and whatever is in it, *things
present and things to come.* For, adds the apostle, ver. 23.
ye are Christ's.

XXXI. Now this possession of the world consists in these
following things: 1st. That every son of God does possess
so much of the good things of this world, as the wisdom of his
heavenly Father has ordained, to be so sufficient for the support
of his animal life, that his spiritual may suffer no detriment,
and that he truly possess it in such a manner, as in the use
and enjoyment thereof, he may taste the love of his Father,
bestowing that upon him, as an earnest of a far better good, and
of his elder brother who became poor, that his people might
be rich, 2 Cor. viii. 9. This love of God the Father, and of
Christ, when added to the least crumb of bread, or drop of
cold water, makes these preferable, in the highest degree, to all
the most exquisite dainties of the rich of this world: " a little that a righteous man hath, is better than the riches of many
wicked," Psal. xxxvii. 16. 2dly. That all the creatures ought
to serve them as steps, by which to ascend to the Creator. For
in all of them they view, as in a bright mirror, his adorable
perfections, Psal. civ. 24. and in that meditation they exult,
Psal. xcii. 4, 5. Above all, they perceive in them the love
of God towards them. When they view the sun, the moon,
the stars, they rejoice that their Father has lighted up so many
tapers for them, at which they may work, what becomes the
sons of God : nor do they less admire this, than if every one
had his own sun or his own moon, shining upon him. Neither do they exceed the bounds of decency, Psal. viii. 3, 4. when
they think, that the world remains in its present state on
their account, and that the wicked are indebted to them for
this : for *the holy seed is the substance* (support) of the world,
Isa. vi. 13. 3dly. That all the creatures, and the whole government of God about them, *may work together for their
good*, Rom. viii. 28. This is so extensive, that both angels
and devils are obliged to this service : as to angels, are they not
" ministering spirits, sent forth to minister for them who
shall be heirs of salvation ;" Heb. i. 14. Psal. xxxiv. 7. and
Psal. xci. 11. And with respect to that infernal spirit, the
teacher of arrogance; was he not constrained, by his buffetings, in spite of himself, and acting from a different view, to

teach Paul humility ? 2 Cor. xii. 7. 4thly. If this world, which is subjected to vanity because of sin, shall not suffice them ; from its ashes, when perished, God is to form another ; to make " a new heaven and a new *earth*, wherein dwelleth righteousness," 2 Pet. iii. 13. , There is none of these things, which may not be included in that general promise of the inheritance of the world.

XXXII. The *second* good thing in this testament is " a spiritual *kingdom ;* I appoint unto you a kingdom," Luke xxii. 29. To which, even the most despicable of the children of God in other respects, even man-servants and maid-servants, are called ; " hath not God chosen the poor of this world, rich in faith, and heirs of the kingdom, which he hath promised to them that love him ?" Jam. ii. 5. To this belong (1.) The excellency of the sons of God, whereby they surpass all other men, Prov. xii. 26. (2.) Victory over sin, and the unruly lusts of the flesh, to which kings themselves and the most dreaded tyrants are subject and inslaved, Rom. vi. 14, 18. (3.) The bruising of Satan under their feet, Rom. xvi. 20. (4.) Triumph over a whole conquered world, for notwithstanding its rage, they shall be for ever saved, 1 John v. 4, 5. (5.) Inestimable riches of spiritual gifts, Psal. xlv. 9. even in the midst of poverty, Rev. ii. 9. (6.) Holy peace of soul and·joy in the Holy Ghost, Rom. xiv. 17. All these begin here in grace, and shall be consummated hereafter in glory.

XXXIII. The third benefit is GOD himself, Rom. viii. 17. *Heirs of God :* here is a mutual inheritance ; believers are God's portion, and God is their portion, for these are made reciprocal, Jer. x. 16. " the portion of Jacob is the former of all things, and Israel is the rod *(tribe)* of his inheritance." In this possession of God, his children find, (1.) Protection against every evil, Psal. xci. 2. " I will say of the Lord, he is my refuge and my fortress. *Why ?* He is my God, in whom I will trust." See Psal. xxvii. 1, 2. Isa. xliii. 2, 3. (2.) Communication of every good, Psal. xxxvi. 7. For *first*, all that infinity of perfections, which are in God himself, will appear glorious and admirable in the children of God, and be enjoyed by them to complete their consummate happiness. And what can the soul desire beyond that infinity ? Psal. lxxiii. 25. *Secondly*, What will not God give those, to whom he gives himself ? 1 Cor. iii. 22, 23.

XXXIV. There are no proper *stipulations* in this testament, if considered in its whole extent, together with all its promises ; for it consists of absolute and mere promises, which depend on no condition, to be performed in our own strength. Yet divine providence hath so disposed every particular in it,

as to have a certain and wise order among themselves, and the *
practice of the former benefits, which are promised, is to pave
the way for the possession of further blessings. We have at
large treated of this, chap. i. § X. seq. of this book. To which
I now add the words of Ames in his *Coronis ad Collectionem
Hagicusem*, Art. V. chap. ii. " The whole of the disposition
hath the nature of a testament, as considered simply, either in
the whole or its parts; but if the benefits bequeathed are compared together, then one bears to the other the relation, as it
were, of a condition."

XXXV. In the same books therefore, in which the testament
is contained, God commanded, that whoever would take comfort from the promised inheritance, should, 1st. Love, search into,
meditate upon, and keep in his heart the writings exhibiting the
testament, as no contemptible part of his inheritance, Deut. xxxii.
4; nay, *esteem them beyond his necessary food*, Job xxiii. 12.
Deut. vi. 6. 2dly. Highly value, as it deserves, the promised
inheritance. (1.) That he hunger and thirst after it, and be satisfied with nothing short of it, Mat. v. 6. (2.) Reckon all
other things, in comparison thereof, as loss and dung, Phil. iii.
8. Most readily part with every thing, in order to procure this
pearl of inestimable value, Mat. xiii. 46. (3.) Glorify God
for the greatness of his love, Ps. xxxi. 19. (4.) Diligently
keep what he has received, Rev. ii. 25. and iii. 11. 3dly.
So walk, as becometh his condition, and the expectation of so
great an inheritance, 1 Thess. ii. 12. 1 John iii. 3. 4thly. Be
ready to impart to his brethren, what he has received from his
Father, both in temporals and spirituals, Rom. xii. 13. 1 Thess.
ii. 8. And endeavour, that others also may be brought to enter
on the same inheritance with himself, Acts xxvi. 29. For none
suffers any loss for the numbers that partake with him: that
he has rather an additional pleasure, his joy being greatly
heightened from the abundance of love.

CHAP. XI.

Of the Spirit of Adoption.

I. HAVING thus explained the nature of Adoption, as far as
our design required, we are now carefully to enquire, what
the Spirit of Adoption is? and this is " the Holy Spirit, operating those things in the elect, which are suitable to, and becoming the sons of God, who love God, and are beloved by him.

---

* Faith, repentance, and the like, are blessings promised in this testament, and
the practice or exercise of these makes way for the possession of the eternal kingdom.

II. *This Spirit* differs from *the spirit of bondage* in this, that the spirit of bondage represents God as an austere master, and a tremendous judge ; hence it is, that they, who are actuated by this spirit, in so far as they act thereby, perform the commands of their master from dread and terror. But the Spirit of adoption discovers God to the believing soul, as a kind and indulgent Father; and by giving him assurance of the love of God, and sweetly cherishing the hope of the future inheritance, makes him, with alacrity and generous emotions of a filial reverence, willingly obey God, as an affectionate parent.

III. Moreover, seeing *all believers* were *sons of God* in every period of time, we may with propriety assert, that the Spirit of adoption was granted to them all in their measure and degree. For certainly what Paul says, Gal. iv. 6. " because ye are sons, God hath sent forth the Spirit of his Son into your hearts," and Rom. viii. 9. " if any man have not the Spirit of Christ, he is none of his," is true of all periods. All who are regenerated, are born of the Spirit, John iii. 5, 6, 8. From the Spirit proceedeth faith, Gal. v. 22. by which they obtained a right to become the sons of God. And if they had any degree of love, righteousness, peace, holiness and the like, without which true faith cannot subsist, they could have them from no other but the Spirit. And as the Spirit they had, was doubtless, such as became their state ; and they themselves were the adopted sons of God ; why then should we not call it the Spirit of adoption ?

IV. We more than once read in the Old Testament of that Spirit, as bestowed on believers at that time : such was that generous spirit in Caleb, which made him *follow God fully*, Numb. xiv. 24. Such that, concerning whom Nehemiah said, ch. ix. 20. " thou gavest also thy good Spirit to instruct them ;" which we are to understand of the elect among the Israelites, in that perverse generation. Such was that, which David prayed might be given him, Psal. cxliii. 10. " thy Spirit is good, lead me into the land of uprightness," and Psal. li. 10, 11, 12. " renew a right Spirit within me; take not thy Holy Spirit from me ; uphold me with thy free Spirit." In short, as God said to Israel of old, " surely they are my people, children that will not lie ;" so also " he put his holy Spirit within them," Isa. lxiii. 8, 11.

V. Moreover, the operations of this Spirit may be considered either *absolutely* in themselves, or in *relation* to the distinct economies of the several periods. What the Spirit of adoption operates *indiscriminately* in the sons of God, are principally these things. As God has, ever since the very first sin of our first parents, proposed his gracious covenant, the summary whereof was in all ages, handed down by the instruction of the patriarchs; it was a part of the office of the Spirit of adoption, to stir up and lead, by the hand, the minds of believers to the knowledge, meditation and apprehending of that saving grace; to intimate to the soul the things externally handed down by the tradition of the oracles, vouchsafed to the patriarchs and prophets, and thus impart some relish of divine love, first more sparingly, afterwards more abundantly. By this means, that horrow or dread is banished, which the thunders of the law, a consciousness of guilt, and the just apprehension of divine vengeance had begot in the soul.

VI. While the Spirit does this, he, by the same work, inflames the hearts of the children of God, with returns of love; whereby they yield obedience to God, not any longer from a fear of punishment, but from a pure and sincere affection, and a generous reverence for their most beloved Father, and that with willingness, and alacrity, as becomes children of such an extraction; with a denial of their own will, and a diligent care to do nothing, unworthy of that glorious condition.

VII. Besides this, the Spirit likewise presents to their view the promised inheritance, and confirms them in the expectation of it, by the word and sacraments, whose moral efficacy, as it is called, he accompanies with a supernatural, internal and operative virtue; and gives them the enjoyment of it in hope: nay, sometimes he raises them on high, so that, by removing the vail, and drawing up the curtain, he in some measure, gives them a view of those good things, which are laid up for them in the heavenly country, whereby, with gladness and exultation they " rejoice in hope of the glory of God," Rom. v. 2.

VIII. These three things are the natural consequences of adoption. 1st. A persuasion of the greatest love of the adopter. 2dly. An obedience of love agreeable to the laws of the family into which he is received, and to the nature and will of the new parent. 3dly. An expectation of the inheritance. The Spirit therefore, who produces these things in the elect, is justly called the Spirit of adoption.

IX. The ancient believers had all these things; though God in his wisdom appointed degrees and limits, as the times required. Their soul exulted in the Lord, Psal. iv. 7. they delighted themselves in the faith, hope, sense and relish of divine love, Psal. xxxi. 7. Psal. li. 14. Psal. xxxvi. 7, 8, 9. Psal. lxiii. 5. [*Heb.* the familiar converse] " the secret of God was in or upon their tabernacles," Job xxix. 4. They also loved God as their Father, Psal. lxxxi. 1. Psal. cxvi. 1. and from love yielded

obedience to him, Psal cxix. 10. with readiness and delight in
his commandments, Psal. cxix. 9, 11, 14, 16. They comforted themselves in adversity with the unfailing expectation of a
blessed inheritance, Psal. xvii. 25. Which, though at a distance,
yet God presented to their view, and gave them initial preliba-
tions of, Psal. xxxi. 19. As all these things follow upon adoption, and ought to be ascribed to the Spirit, they make it evident,
that the Spirit of adoption is by no means to be reckoned a peculiar benefit of the New Testament, as if the Old Testament believers were destitute of it. Paul himself expressly asserts, that
the same Spirit of faith, by which we speak (which certainly, is
the Spirit of adoption) was also in the fathers, 2 Cor. iv. 13.

X. However, it is not to be denied, that those operations
of this free and noble Spirit, were of old, more rare and sparing than afterwards, and mixed with much terror. The legal
economy was then in its vigour; as the covenant of grace
was revealed more obscurely, and in much enigmatical darkness, so likewise it was not intimated to the conscience with
such evidence of demonstration: a hand-writing, in the mean
time, was also required to be renewed by the blood of daily
sacrifices, as by so many subscriptions; a thirst after better promises was raised, though not yet to be quenched: by these
means, those noble operations of the Spirit were so clouded
in most, that in comparison of the joyful abundance under the
New Testament, the Spirit is said, John vii. 39. not to have
been under the Old. This is not to be understood in such a
restricted sense, as to make us imagine, that the extraordinary
gifts of the Spirit, poured out on the day of Pentecost, are
here only intended. For, something is promised, which is
common to all believers in Christ, and which is said not to
have been before Christ was glorified. But what is that?
It is the full and illustrious exhibition of the Spirit, which
Christ deferred, till he took solemn possession of his kingdom,
and which appeared in those visible gifts, as in so many mirrors,
which is also to be extended to the gracious fruits of adoption:
as Calvin has well observed on this place.

XI. And indeed, we often find in scripture, that the Holy
Spirit is so promised to the New Testament, as if there was
no such thing under the Old, Isa. xxxv. 6, 7. and xliv. 3.
Ezek. xxxiv. 26, 27. Joel ii. 28. Zech. xiv. 8. compared with
Ezek. xlvii. 1.—All which things belong to the times of the
Messiah's kingdom now manifested in the world. To this also we are to refer, what John the Baptist said of Christ, Mat.
iii. 11. that he would baptize the children of Abraham with
the Holy Ghost and with fire. For seeing the Baptist speaks

this not to the apostles, but to the Jews that flocked to hear him; that miraculous effusion of the gifts of the Holy Spirit on the apostles, which our Lord himself calls a baptism, seems not to be denoted only, but also that sanctifying grace of the Spirit, which had, and exerted a fiery efficacy on the hearts of believers, by penetrating, illuminating, setting on fire, purging, separating * the dross from the pure gold, or the precious from the evil, and by elevating and transforming the object enflamed into its own nature; and with this passage it seems we should by all means compare what is said, Isa. iv. 4. " when the Lord shall have washed away the filth of the daughters of Zion, and shall have purged the blood of Jerusalem from the midst thereof, by the Spirit of judgment and by the Spirit of burning." Moreover, that extraordinary work, which was wrought in the apostles, contained the first fruits and earnest of the fulfilment of the general promises concerning the Spirit, as appears from the application of the prophecy of Joel, and Peter's explication of it, Acts ii. 28, 39. Chrysostom therefore observes well, Homil. xi. that John, by this expression, signified *the abundance, the vehemence, and the irresistibleness of grace.*

XII. As these things were promised, so they were also fulfilled under the New Testament. For the Spirit of God then produced a clearer manifestation of the covenant of grace, a higher sense of divine love, a more delightful freedom of the kingdom of God, a more confident boldness, more abundant consolations, a stronger assurance, more spiritual holiness, and who can pretend to recite all? This will appear if we make a just comparison of heroes with heroes, and of more ordinary believers with others of the same kind; according to the prophecy of Zech. xii. 8. See Tit. iii. 5, 6.

XIII. Mean while, we are to observe, that in the beginning of the New Testament, God distributed much more plentifully to believers, than frequently afterwards. Certainly, nothing can be spoken with greater pomp of language than what Paul often declared concerning himself, and other believers in his day. For, as to consolation and tranquillity of soul, what can be more excellent than what he assured the Philippians, even peace which passeth all understanding, Phil. iv. 7. Agreeable to this is what Peter writes; that they who love Christ and believe in him, rejoice with joy unspeakable and

---

* I confess this does not come up to the full force of the author's words, which are *seperando heterogenea ab homogeneis,* though they express his general meaning.

glorious, full of glory, 1 Pet. i. 8. And what John also says, that perfect love, such as is produced by the gospel, casteth out all fear, 1 John iv. 18. And really it seems evident, that in a peace so noble and serene, in a joy almost so incredible, there can be no room for any unruly passion, fear or trembling.

XIV. And then the apostle gives such excellent encomiums of their holiness, as may be judged very far to transcend the measure of our days: when he thus declares concerning himself, that he was crucified with Christ, that he did no longer live, but Christ lived in him, as if his spirit and life, like that of an inferior order, were swallowed up in the more illustrious Spirit and life of Christ, as the sun in the heavens extinguishes the light of the stars; and all the life, he lived, flowed from no other principle, but the faith and love of the Son of God, Gal. ii. 20. Nay he openly declares his contempt of all the things which other men so highly value, and that he prizes Christ alone, and that forgetting the things which are behind he presses forwards with a large pace, and a most speedy course to perfection, Phil. iii. 7, 8, 14. Who of us will deny, that he does not come far short of these high attainments?

XV. The apostle every where openly professed an incredible hope and assurance of the future inheritance: and he undoubtedly describes his assurance, towards the close of the eighth chapter to the Romans, in such magnificent language, that nothing more emphatically strong can be conceived. Let that animated gloriation in the Lord be attentively read, and we shall see, that it sets forth, in an extraordinary pomp of words, the immense abundance of the Spirit inhabiting his noble breast, and the sparkling flames of the love of God kindled in his heart. He also clearly displays his hope, 2 Cor. v. 1, 2. 2 Tim. iv. 8. Phil. i. 23. whereby he was so far from fearing death, at the mention of which most people are ready to tremble for fear, that on the contrary, he embraced it with open arms, and longed to be dissolved, that he might have the more full enjoyment of Christ.

XVI. Indeed if any one shall compare these magnificent expressions, with what is observed among believers at this day, he will be obliged to own, that they come far short of that eminence and excellence; they are so mean, poor and fading in comparison of these unparalleled expressions, which with astonishment we admire in the apostle. But doubtless the Spirit bloweth when, how, and where he listeth : it does not become us to set bounds to him. In the beginning of the gospel

God shewed what he can do, and what on the other hand he will do, when he shall restore life, as it were, from the dead, Rom. xi. 15. *arise, arise, thou charming friendly sun!*

XVII. To this Spirit the apostle principally ascribes two effects, Rom. viii. 15, 16. the former of which is, the making us cry, Abba, Father; the latter, that together with our spirit, itself beareth witness, that we are the children of God: and as these two things contain the highest consolation, it will not be improper to explain them with all the accuracy we are able.

XVIII. The Holy Spirit is never idle; where he is, there the heart *brings forth a good speech*, Psal. xlv. 1. The Spirit is that mystical new wine, which *makes the virgins cheerful*, (eloquent) Zech. ix. 17. *and causeth the lips of those* that *are asleep to speak*, Cant. vii. 9. They who have the Spirit of faith, *as they believe so they speak*, 2 Cor. iv. 13.

XIX. Nor do they only speak, muttering like the ventriloquists, who speak from the belly, or like those who scarce speak out what they have conceived in their mind, fear having restrained their faultering tongue; but they confidently cry out with a loud voice. Nor is it in vain, that the apostle both here and Gal. iv. 6. uses the term *crying*. It denotes that boldness, freedom, and courage, with which we are commanded to approach the throne of grace, Heb. iv. 16. and present our requests there.

XX. But what does he principally teach us to cry? Abba, Father. Servants and hand-maids of old, were not suffered to call their masters by the name of Father, as the very learned *Selden, de Successionibus*, c. 4. has shewn from the law of the Hebrews. But the servants and hand-maids of God, both under the Old and New Testament, are allowed this privilege, as was shewn above from Isa. lxiii. 26. Job xxxiv. 36. To which I now add, Isa. xliv. 8. and Jer. iii. 4. When Christ commanded his disciples to pray, *Our Father, which art in heaven*, he used an expression well known to, and very common among the Jews. Thus Maimonides in Tephilloth—*Our Father, who art in heaven, so deal with us, as thou hast promised by the prophets.*

XXI. And the doubling of words, Abba, Father, both here and in the epistle to the Galatians, is very emphatical. The former being of Hebrew, and the latter of a Greek original. Did not the apostle by this intend to teach us, that under the influence of the Spirit, God was now to be called Father, by believers of whatever nation, or in whatever language? For the reason of this repetition, seems here to be different from that

in Mark, chap. xiv. 36. where we have a summary of Christ's
prayers, and the latter may be imagined to be added by Mark,
as an explanation of the former. For, Christ spoke not in Greek,
as Paul wrote in that language. The observation of the celebrated Lightfoot, on Mark xiv. 36. is worth mentioning; that
though אבי *Abbi* may, indeed, denote, not only a natural, but
also a civil father, as an elder, a lord, or master, a teacher, a
magistrate : yet אבא *Abba*, only a natural, or adopting father.
For the proof of this he gives us a great number of examples.
Thus therefore, Christ calls God, *Abba*, in the strongest sense !
and believers also according to their condition.

XXII. Unless we rather say, that this repetition of the word
is an evidence that the appellation was pleasant and familiar.
For ἄππα, *Appa*, which differs not much from *Abba*, was not
in that sense unknown even to the Greeks. Thus Callimachus,
in his hymn to Diana, brings her in as a little girl playing in
the bosom and arms of her father Jupiter, and calling him in
a familiar and enticing manner *Appa*. Hence also *Abare*,
which in *Ausonius* stands for ἀδελφίζειν, and signifies *to address
one in a kind manner, as one brother does another*. See what
Ludov. Capellus has learnedly collected to this purpose in his
Spicilegium on Mark xiv. 36.

XXIII. Nor does this appellation consist in bare words, as
if we flattered God only with our lips : but if we are really
partakers of adoption, it shews that there is faith, and the full
assurance of it, in the heart, and by making a profession of it,
we honour God, and celebrate the glory of his grace, whereby
he hath raised us, the most unworthy of mortals to such a high
pitch of honour. We also profess, that we pray in faith, and
expect from him, what children ought to expect from a most
indulgent father. And at the same time by calling him Father, we bind ourselves to an obedience, a reverence and a love
becoming such a Father. And therefore when the apostle says,
that by the Spirit we cry Abba Father, he thereby teacheth us
that this Spirit is the author of faith, holiness, confession, piety
and sincere obedience.

XXIV. But let us now consider the other effect of the Spirit,
which according to the apostle, consists in this that he " beareth witness with our spirit, that we are the children of God."
Here we have two witnesses, agreeing in one testimony : the
one of a lower rank, *our spirit* ; the other of the highest, *the
Spirit of Adoption*, who is the Spirit of the Son of God, Gal.
iv. 6. Both may be well qualified for this, but each in his own
measure, degree and order.

XXV. By *our spirit* is understood, the mind and conscience

of every believer, whereby he may be conscious of what passes in his own heart. In this sense the apostle said, " what man knoweth the things of a man, save the spirit of man which is in him?" 1 Cor. ii. 11. It is otherwise called " the heart of man, condemning or acquitting him," 1 John iii. 20, 21. or ὁυνειδησις συμμαρτυρȣσα ," conscience joining to bear witness, and thoughts the mean while accusing, or else excusing one another," Rom. ii. 15.

XXVI. The testimony of our spirit consists in an exact representation of our state by certain marks, and a full assurance of faith, which is followed by a most quiet tranquillity of soul, and a joy unspeakable. For as the spirit which beareth witness, and the man to whom he does so, are in effect all one, no other testimony needs here be thought of, than the composure of the soul which, by infallible marks, is conscious of its own happiness. Accordingly our apostle, when he would tell us, that he was fully persuaded, that he spoke in sincerity, affirms, that his *conscience bears him witness,* Rom. ix. 1. whose witness can be no other than a representation of the truth plainly perceived by it.

XXVII. It is indeed very requisite, that this testimony, which is given of an affair of the greatest moment, be solid and well grounded. We are therefore above all, to attend to two things. 1st. It is necessary, that our spirit be very exactly instructed from the word of God about the marks by which a child of God may be known and distinguished. The word of God alone is the silver seven times purified and refined. By this rule we are both to think and speak of the things that relate to salvation : all the dictates of our spirit are to be tried by it ; neither must we admit any thing, as worthy of credit, in the matters of salvation which does not in the exactest manner agree therewith. Then, a most careful self-examination should be added, whether we have the marks which God has given of his children in the scripture.

XXVIII. The marks of the children of God are of two kinds. 1st. A certain good habit or disposition of soul, with a consistent tenour of a pious life : then, peculiar acts of God towards his beloved people, which he vouchsafes only to those whom he loves as a Father.

XXIX. The marks of the former kind are such as these : 1st. The impression and expression of the divine image, with a holy conformity to our Father and elder brother. For what is more natural, than for a son to resemble his Father, and one brother be like another? As therefore the natural Son of God is " the brightness of the Father's glory," Heb. i. 3. it is fit also, that we in our order and measure, be so too. As corrupt Adam " begat a son in his own likeness, after his image," Gen. v. 3. so likewise when God begets children, he forms them in his own likeness, in *righteousness and true holiness*, Eph. iv. 24. And indeed, this likeness of God, is gradually perfected by familiar intercourse with him ; till, having obtained that adoption of which the apostle speaks, Rom. viii. 23. we are become perfectly like him, 1 John iii. 2.

XXX. 2dly. A new life that is worthy of God and the effect of the Spirit of adoption, who is *the Spirit of life*, Rom. viii. 2. As is the spirit of the creatures, so is their life. The natural man has not a more noble spirit, nor a more excellent principle of life than his soul : consequently he only lives an animal life. But as the children of God are endowed with that *free Spirit*, Psal. li. 12. who is the Spirit of Christ, Gal. iv. 6. so in their measure they live, as Christ formerly lived, imitating his example and pattern to the utmost of their power ; that what Christ declared in the highest degree of himself, may in some measure be applied to them, " the Son can do nothing of himself, but what he seeth the Father do : for what things soever he doeth, these also doth the Son likewise," John v. 19. Paul's exhortation is excellent, Eph. v. 1. " be ye followers of God as dear children."

XXXI. 3dly. A true and sincere love of God. Even nature teacheth this. For what genuine son does not love his father ? This law is not only written, but born with us. And this love arises, partly from the consideration of the most amiable perfections of God, which his children are admitted to contemplate in a familiar way, *seeing the king in his beauty*, Isa. xxxiii. 17. Psal. lxiii. 2. Partly from the rays of the divine love reflected upon them, whereby they cannot but be inflamed, 1 John iv. 19. They never attentively reflect on this love, but they look upon the whole capacity of their soul, as insufficient to make due returns of love.

XXXII. 4thly. A filial fear and obedience, Mal. i. 6. 1 Pet. i. 17. flowing from the foresaid love, which forbids them to do any thing that may displease God, and cannot bear to see his honour impaired by any other, Psal. xlii. 3, 10. On the contrary, it makes the person cheerful and ready in all the duties of religion, John xiv. 21. does not suffer him to be at rest, if haply by any ill advised conduct he should provoke God, and be deprived of the sight of his blessed and gracious face as formerly. In fine, this constrains him to fall down in profound reverence, at the feet of his Father, and with sorrow and tears, plead for the pardon of his offences, and promise a more careful observance for the future, Luke vii. 38.

XXXIII. 5thly. Unfeigned brotherly love, which he entertains for all those in whom he observes the image of God, and a participation of the same grace with himself. As that natural affection of Joseph, for his brother Benjamin, discovered itself by the most evident tokens, Gen. xlv. 14, 15. so likewise while other marks are often indiscernible, this brotherly love gives to the doubting soul an evidence of its state, 1 John iii. 14. For the love of the brethren cannot be separated from the love of God. Whoever loves the original, will also love the copy: whoever loves God, will also love him who belongs to God, and in whom he observes the virtues of God, and whom he believes to be loved by God, 1 John. iv. 20. Our spirit ought to be well assured of these things, before it can testify any thing about our state; and likewise to know, that all these things are to be found with the sons of God, and with them only as the effects of the regenerating Spirit.

XXXIV. But besides, there are some special acts of divine love which God vouchsafes only to his own children. *The Lord,* indeed, *is good to all: and his tender mercies are over all his works,* Psal. cxlv. 9. But he reserves a certain peculiar and unparalleled goodness for his elect; of which the Psalmist says, Psal. xxiii. 1. *Truly God is good to Israel, even to such as are of a clean heart.* Hence it is, that, while they are sometimes ravished on high by his Spirit, he surrounds them with the beams of his supercelestial light, gives them a view of his face shining with the brightest love, kisses them with the kisses of his mouth, admits them to the most endearing, mutual intercourse of mystical love with himself, and, while he plentifully sheds abroad his love in their hearts, he gives them to drink of rivers of honey and butter, and that often in the greatest drought of the parched soul, when expecting no such thing. There are many more mysteries in this secret intercourse with our heavenly Father, which believers sometimes see, taste and feel, and which no pen of the learned can represent, as they deserve. And it is not fit, that the spirit of man should be unacquainted with these things since it is admitted as a witness of his state; for, though this is not the lot of all the children of God, nor the case at all times, nor indeed frequently : yet they, whose lot it has at any time been, are certainly children of God.

XXXV. After our spirit is well instructed about all these things, it is further necessary it make a strict scrutiny concerning itself, and, as under the eye of an omniscient God, diligently search every particular without dissimulation or disguise;

to see whether these things, which we said, were the marks or characteristics of the children of God, are to be found in us: as also whether, at any time, we have experienced, in prayer, or other exercises of devotion, the peculiar favour of the most gracious God, exciting, inflaming, comforting, and carrying heavenwards our otherwise dull and drowsy hearts. For when our spirit discovers these things by evident indications, then it confidently testifies that we are the children of God, represents that truth to our minds, and gives us to know it, and enable us to say, *this I know, for God is for me*, Psal. lvi. 9.

XXXVI. These things, indeed, tend greatly to the consolation of God's children: but when, both by scripture and experience, they know, that their heart is deceitful, and that they are assured by the wisest of kings, that *he that trusteth in his own heart is a fool*, Prov. xxviii. 26.; and as they would not wish to be deceived in nothing less than in this, which of all others is of the greatest moment; then at length they entirely acquiesce, when to *the testimony of their own spirit* is superadded *that of the Spirit of God*. This is what David wrestled for by earnest prayer with God, Psal. xxxv. 3. *say unto my soul, thou art my salvation*.

XXXVII. That testimony is given principally in this manner: *first*, the Spirit of God makes those holy habits, which, we said, were the distinguishing marks of the children of God, and which at times are often involved in much darkness and covered with much rubbish and filth, to shine with clearness in their soul, and, as it were, readily present themselves to the contemplation of the mind, when examining itself. And then excites our spirit, otherwise ready to faint, to the diligent observation of the things in our mind, both transacted in and by it, enlightens the eyes of the understanding with supernatural light, to prevent our being deceived by what is specious rather than solid, or our overlooking those things, on the observation of which our consolation depends. There is *moreover* a certain internal impulse, which no human language can explain, immediately assuring God's beloved people of their adoption, no less than if they were carried up to the third heavens, and had heard it audibly from God's own mouth; as the apostles formerly heard in the holy mount *a voice from the excellent glory*, 2 Pet. i. 17. *Lastly*, seeing no testimony is stronger than that which is proved by facts, the Spirit of God does not leave himself *without witness* in that respect; for he excites generous motions and the sweetest raptures in believers, and delights them with consolations so ravishing and ecstatical, and even exceeding all thought, that they cannot consider them, in any other light, but as so many testimonies of their adoption.

XXXVIII. Nor is there any reason to apprehend, the children of God will, in this case, suffer themselves to be imposed upon, or admit, for a testimony of the Holy Spirit, what is a lie and mere illusion of the deceiving spirit.   For, in this voice of the Spirit of God, there is so much clearness, majesty and efficacy, whereby it penetrates, with an irresistible power, into the bottom and inmost recess of the heart, that they, who have been accustomed to that voice, can easily distinguish it from all others. *The world, certainly, cannot receive this Spirit, seeth him not, neither knoweth him,* John xiv. 17. : but *Christ's sheep know the voice of their shepherd,* John x. 4.   And when it sounds, not so much in their ears as in their hearts, they joyfully exclaim, *this is the voice of my beloved, behold! he cometh,* Cant. ii. 8.   As formerly in extraordinary appearances, God gave such clear indications of his majesty to the prophets, as to leave no room for doubt ; so in like manner, the Spirit, the Comforter, irradiates the minds of the elect with such beams of light, that they can easily distinguish him from the spirit of darkness.   But, as the proper sound of any voice cannot be distinguished but by the hearing of it ; so these things are only to be learned by experience.

XXXIX. But the Spirit of God does not usually comfort the elect with such glad tidings, unless their hearts are first broken by a long continued acknowledgment of their sins, and a deep sense of their misery, Isa. lxi. 1, 3. and lvii. 15, 18. Generally a boisterous wind goes before the rending of mountains, and breaking in pieces the rocks before the Lord, and an earthquake and a fire, before the still small voice is heard. 1 Kings xix. 23.   This balm is poured only into the broken heart, Psal. li. 8.

XL. And the souls of the elect are never refreshed with the sweet consolation of the Spirit, but they are at the same time, inflamed with the love of God, and excited to the vigorous exercise of strict religion.   The same Spirit, who is the Comforter, is also, by the same act, the Sanctifier, Psal. li. 12, 13.   Nor can it be otherwise.   When the soul is assured by the Spirit himself of the infinite love of God towards him, he bursts out into a flame of mutual love, breaking out into the warmest thanksgivings ; saying, " Lord, hast thou honoured me, in a manner so extraordinary and undeserved, that thou takest me for thy son ! Hast thou thyself declared this so familiarly unto me, by shedding abroad thy love in my heart by the Holy Spirit, which thou hast given me ! and shall I not love, worship, honour and obey thee to the utmost of my power! O! that I was emptied of every thing else, that I might be filled with thy love!" and this is an undoubted token of the Holy Spirit, when the man, who rejoices in soul, is, at the same time, become more ardent in love to God, and more cheerful in his worship. The spirit of the flesh and of hell, with its deceitful allurements, intends every thing else besides this.

XLI. We have indeed delivered these things, in a very imperfect manner, on this mystical subject, which is the marrow of internal Christianity; which, that the Holy Spirit himself may inwardly teach * those who are consecrated to God, and exhibit to their eyes, ears, and taste, we ardently pray. So be it, Lord Jesus! AMEN.

---

* The author's words are, *Naziræos suos doceat*, teach his Nazarites, but as that sounds harsh in English, I therefore have expressed his meaning by a paraphrase.

END OF THE FIRST VOLUME.